This new book covers a comprehensive, in depth and example
theoretical and empirical foundations of Labour Economics. It
balance between "classical" models and new research fronti
matter. Scholars and students interested in the changing shape
especially in the UK context, will find this extremely valuable.

Dr Randolph Bruno, *University College London, UK*

This book offers a fresh, in-depth and extremely well-resourced coverage of labour
economics concepts, with numerous applications relevant to the undergraduate and
postgraduate student, as well as to researchers in the field. The comprehensive
treatment of the relevant theory is supported by numerical analysis (algebra) inserts,
while case studies are presented alongside an eclectic mix of relevant empirical
articles. It is, thus, a must-have and must-read book for labour economists, in view
of the high level of useful information presented within a modern and inspiring
structure that delivers both quantitative and qualitative detail, as well as an
interesting and useful balance between theory and its wide applications.

Dr Alina Ileana Petrescu, *University of Central Lancashire, UK*

A truly comprehensive and contemporary textbook on Labour Economics
incorporating theory as well as relevant and interesting examples and case studies.
Its particular strength is that it incorporates several models, based on a rich survey
of research literature, to explain a concept. This will enable students to get a clear
understanding about the complexity of the functioning of labour markets and related
issues.

Dr Amita Dharmadhikary-Yadwadkar, *University of Pune, India*

Sloane, Latreille and O'Leary have produced an excellent book which takes readers
to the frontier of contemporary labour economics research. The book blends the
latest theoretical developments, including search theory and asymmetric
information, with up-to-date empirical facts and current policy debates. I highly
recommend *Modern Labour Economics* to advanced undergraduate and post-
graduate students, and to all researchers grappling with contemporary labour market
issues.

Professor Garry Barrett, *The University of Sydney, Australia*

Modern Labour Economics

Labour economics as a discipline has changed dramatically in recent years. Gone are the days of a "job for life". These days, firms and employees are part of a less regulated, more fluid and more international labour market. Knowledge, training, human resource development and human capital are all major factors on the contemporary scene.

This new textbook is the first properly international textbook to reflect these swingeing changes. Its key areas of concentration include:

- the increasing importance of human capital including education and occupational choice;
- the major subdivision of personnel economics including economic inactivity and absenteeism;
- comparative cross-country studies and the impact of globalisation and migration on national labour markets;
- equal opportunities and issues of discrimination on the basis of race, gender and disability; and
- conflict at work, including both strikes and, uniquely, individual disputes.

Other issues explored include the supply and demand of labour, wages, the current role of trade unions, bargaining and conflict, and working time. The book is written in a clear, accessible way with some mathematical exposition, reflecting the text's grounding in current microeconomic theory. The book also contains case studies designed to illuminate theoretical concepts and exercises and discussion questions to test the students' understanding of the various concepts outlined in the text.

Peter Sloane is Emeritus Professor of Economics at Swansea University, UK, where he was the Director of the Welsh Economy Labour Market Evaluation and Research Centre. He is also Adjunct Professor at the National Institute of Labour Studies, Flinders University, Australia. Inter alia he is author of *Labour Economics*, *Employment Equity and Affirmative Action: An International Comparison* and *The Economics of Sport*.

Paul Latreille is Professor of Management at the University of Sheffield, UK. He is an expert on workplace conflict and its resolution, including Employment Tribunals and mediation, vocational training, disability and inactivity.

Nigel O'Leary is a Reader at Swansea University and an Associate Professor at the National Institute of Labour Studies, Flinders University, Australia. He has published extensively in international journals in the areas of the economics of discrimination, educational economics, trade unions and labour market attachment.

Modern Labour Economics

Peter Sloane, Paul Latreille and
Nigel O'Leary

LONDON AND NEW YORK

First published 2013
by Routledge
2 Park Square, Milton Park, Abingdon, Oxon OX14 4RN

Simultaneously published in the USA and Canada
by Routledge
711 Third Avenue, New York, NY 10017

Routledge is an imprint of the Taylor & Francis Group, an informa business

British Library Cataloguing in Publication Data
A catalogue record for this book is available from the British Library

Library of Congress Cataloging in Publication Data
Sloane, Peter.
 Modern labour economics/Peter Sloane, Paul L. Latreille and Nigel O'Leary.
 pages cm
 1. Labor economics. I. Latreille, Paul L. II. O'Leary, Nigel C. III. Title. IV. Title: Modern labor economics.
 HD4901.S556 2013
 331–dc23
 2012030480

ISBN: 978-0-415-46980-7 (hbk)
ISBN: 978-0-415-46981-4 (pbk)
ISBN: 978-0-203-06930-1 (ebk)

Typeset in Times NR and Frutiger
by Wearset Ltd, Boldon, Tyne and Wear

Printed and bound in Great Britain by
TJ International Ltd, Padstow, Cornwall

Contents

Figures

Figures

Tables

Preface

One stimulus for writing this book was the knowledge that the main existing texts used in the UK in particular were becoming somewhat dated. Thus, two widely used texts, R.F. Elliott's *Labor Economics: A Comparative Text* and D. Bosworth, P. Dawkins and T. Stromback's *The Economics of the Labour Market*, were published in 1991 and 1996 respectively. Mention should also be made of Stephen Smith's *Labour Economics*, second edition, 2003, also published by Routledge. This is pitched at a somewhat lower level and does not include as broad a range of issues and has little material relating to the twenty-first century. We are also aware that much has changed in labour economics in recent years. For one, there has been a growing recognition that labour markets are imperfect, as illustrated by the dynamic monopsony model and an increased stress on information asymmetries. Job–search models have grown in influence as recognised by the award of the Nobel Prize in Economics to three of its main proponents in 2010. In many countries, unions have declined in terms of membership and influence, and collective bargaining has declined relative to individual bargaining. Strike action is increasingly a strategy of last rather than first resort. The wage distribution has widened in Anglo-Saxon countries in particular as a result of skill-biased technological change. The labour force has become more skilled with increasing numbers of graduates. The use of incentive payments for senior managers has become particularly contentious, prompting the UK Coalition Government to propose reforms at the time of writing of this preface.

We have tried to reflect these changes in the text and there are in particular sections on job satisfaction, absenteeism, international migration, shift-working, labour shortages, over- and under-education, tournament theory, individual conflict resolution, the labour-managed firm and the wage curve, which tend to receive no, or cursory, treatment elsewhere. The boundaries between labour economics and related fields such as personnel economics, the economics of education, population economics and part of health economics have become blurred, as the problem of an ageing workforce has become more prominent.

The book is targeted at undergraduates, who are most likely studying Labour Economics in their final or penultimate year as an optional course, though we hope it will also be useful to post-graduate students, and for this reason we have included extensive bibliographies. We assume prior knowledge of basic microeconomics and macroeconomics. We include the results of empirical work, requiring some knowledge of econometrics, which we assume the students will be studying elsewhere in their course. We highlight key concepts when first introduced in each chapter and give brief descriptions of them. Each chapter contains sections on learning outcomes, an introduction, boxes giving examples of particular applications, a summary, key concepts, examination questions, further reading and detailed references.

The book is supported by a companion website: www.routledge.com/cw/sloane. Here you will find multiple choice questions, specimen answers to end of chapter questions, downloadable tables and figures from the book, and a compilation of useful weblinks to data, policy and research.

P. J. Sloane, P. L. Latreille and N. C. O'Leary
July 2012

Acknowledgements

The authors and publisher would like to acknowledge and thank the reviewers who provided valuable feedback throughout the writing process. They are:

Professor Tim Barmby, University of Aberdeen, UK

Professor Garry Barrett, University of Sydney, Australia

Dr Roberto Bonilla, Newcastle University, UK

Dr Sarah Bridges, University of Nottingham, UK

Dr Michael Brookes, Middlesex University, UK

Professor Sarah Brown, University of Sheffield, UK

Dr Randolph Bruno, University College London, UK

Dr Amita Dharmadhikary-Yadwadkar, University of Pune, India

Dr Benoit Pierre Freyens, University of Canberra, Australia

Professor Robert McNabb, Cardiff University, UK

Arlene Ozanne, University of Otago, New Zealand

Dr Alina Ileana Petrescu, University of Central Lancashire, UK

Dr Martin Robson, Durham University, UK

Professor Michael Svarer, Aarhus University, Denmark

Ken Yamada, Singapore Management University, Singapore

Chapter 1

Labour force participation

> ## Learning outcomes
>
> At the end of this chapter, readers should have an understanding that:
>
> - Occupational choice is influenced by family background, education and relative earnings;
> - There is a difference between private and social rates of return;
> - Labour force participation (or activity rates), part-time working and self-employment vary considerably across countries, as well as by gender and age;
> - The discouraged worker and additional worker hypotheses operate in different ways over the business cycle;
> - There are explanations for why participation rates of women should have risen, while at the same time those of men were falling;
> - The choice of voluntary or mandatory retirement can be explained in economic terms.

Introduction

Individuals spend a considerable part of their lives in gainful employment, so that the decision when to work, how much to work and in which occupations to specialise are among the most important decisions in an individual's life. The first decision is whether to leave school as soon as possible after the end of compulsory schooling or to delay entry in order to acquire additional qualifications. This investment incurs extra costs as well as the opportunity cost of foregone earnings. To some extent, the additional investment may lock the individual into a limited number of occupational groups, so that the provision of information on rates of return and the nature of employment in particular occupations becomes crucial and may require considerable occupational guidance. Some individuals may be influenced by family and friends, though little detailed information is available on this. Outcomes may also be determined by the relative size of the cohort entering the labour market and the degree of tightness or slackness existing in the labour market when entry is made.

On entering the labour market, the individual has to choose an employer or perhaps become self-employed, though for many the latter follows a period of employment in which specific knowledge is gained about the nature of particular activities. The intensity of work may vary through the use of overtime, whether paid or unpaid, or by part-time work rather than full-time work. A small number of individuals may hold multiple jobs. For married women, in particular, there may be a number of episodes of entry to and exit from the labour market in order to produce and raise children, though parental care arrangements may enable men also to participate in some of these activities. Labour supply choices may, therefore, be family rather than individually based.

When to leave the labour market through retirement is another key decision and may be determined, in part, by the health and life expectancy of the worker, as well as by economic variables such as expected income in retirement. In part, retirement may be an employer decision based on the productivity and costs of employing older workers. Retirement may be compulsory or voluntary. As populations age, this may also impose burdens on the State, which may lead to the extension of the working life through increases in the retirement age.

The aim of this chapter is to examine each of these three questions – entry into the labour market, intensity of participation within it and exit from it as sequential decisions. On the first question, we focus on rates of return to education and the impact of family background and inter-generational transmission mechanisms, which may imply that some siblings follow parental occupations. Key aspects of the second question include the role of gender and ethnicity in determining occupational choices, the nature of the employment contract, and additional and discouraged worker effects over the cycle. On the third question, we focus on the problems of an ageing workforce and the determinants of optimal retirement decisions. We return to some of these issues in Chapters 2, 3 and 11.

1.1 Entry into the labour market – education and occupational choice

For most workers, prospects in the labour market are already fairly well determined by the time initial entry into that market is made. Though it is fair to say that the occupational hierarchy is not entirely rigid as far as individuals are concerned, with a fair degree of movement in both upward and downward directions, nonetheless, the best predictor of the occupational position of a man aged 60 is his occupational position when he first enters the labour force (see Nickell 1982). In this respect, the key decision is how much to invest in human capital and what form this investment should take.

We would expect entry into particular occupations to be influenced by relative earnings, especially where information on the nature of employment is limited. There is abundant evidence on returns to education for particular groups, occupations and countries. Psacharopoulos (1985), for example, surveys studies relating to no fewer than 61 countries at different points in time. These point to a declining rate of return over time by country controlling both for level of education and per capita income. Thus, the returns for each level of education are highest in African and lowest in the more advanced industrial countries. This means that there is a danger that new entrants may overestimate the returns available to them if they simply assume the future will replicate the past.

We must, however, distinguish between **private and social rates of return**. The former can be defined as the added value of the gains due to education as a percentage of the costs to the individual of acquiring that level of education, made up of foregone earnings and the individual's contribution to tuition and maintenance costs. The social rate of return takes into account not only the private costs to the individual, but also that share of costs borne by the rest of society through taxation, which is designed to ensure that more individuals are able to participate. This takes into account external benefits of education such as improved health, reduced crime and a higher rate of economic growth. Generally, private returns exceed social, because of the presence of state subsidies and the fact that it is difficult to include measures accounting for all the social benefits. We cannot necessarily conclude, therefore, that education is necessarily more beneficial to the individual than to society as a whole.[1]

Despite tendencies to declining rates of return, *ceteris paribus*, average returns in general have been fairly stable over time. This is explained by the fact that the growth in demand for educated manpower has kept pace with a substantial increase in supply both for developing and developed countries.

A detailed analysis of both private and social rates of return to education at the upper-secondary school and tertiary levels in various OECD countries has been carried out by Blöndal *et al.* (2002). They note that net benefits are strongly influenced by policy-related factors such as study length, tuition-fee subsidies and student support grants, so there is little reason to expect internal rates of return to be similar across countries given differences in policies in relation to such issues. Thus, foregone earnings will be influenced by course duration, which is much longer in some countries than others. Private tuition costs tend to be low in most European countries because of public subsidies. Similarly, financial support to students in the form of grants and favourable loan support is more generous in some countries than it is in others.

The net gains to individuals, i.e. the comprehensive **internal rate of return** summarised in Table 1.1 for ten OECD countries for post-compulsory education ranges between 9 and 19 per cent, with the UK and US having higher rates than elsewhere. In some cases, adjusting for taxes, unemployment risk, tuition fees and student support increases the internal rate of return because public benefits outweigh taxes, but in the UK, for instance, the difference between the narrow and comprehensive rates is much smaller than in some other countries.

Because of the difficulties in estimating comprehensive social rates of return, Blöndal *et al.* limit themselves to the narrow definition which does not incorporate externalities or non-economic benefits (such as effects on crime and health) and assume that any wage gains from education represent associated productivity gains (Table 1.2).

Reflecting the fact that social costs exceed private costs of education, because of educational subsidies, social internal rates of return are generally much lower than private ones. Nevertheless, social rates of return are typically well above 5 per cent measured in real terms for both upper-secondary and tertiary education. This

Private rate of return to education

The added value of an increase in earnings due to education as a percentage of the cost of acquiring that education in terms of foregone earnings and the individual's contribution to tuition fees and maintenance costs.

Social rate of return to education

This also takes into account the share of education costs borne by society through increased taxation and, where calculable, education externalities such as improved health, reduced crime and a higher rate of economic growth.

Internal rate of return

The discount rate at which the net present value of an investment is zero. This tells us whether a prospective investment is viable, as when the internal rate of return is higher than the rate of interest at which an individual can borrow.

Table 1.1 Private internal rates of return to education in the OECD, 1999–2000(%)

	Men				Women			
	Upper secondary		*Tertiary*		*Upper secondary*		*Tertiary*	
	Narrow	*Comprehensive*	*Narrow*	*Comprehensive*	*Narrow*	*Comprehensive*	*Narrow*	*Comprehensive*
Canada	11.9	13.6	8.4	8.7	10.8	12.7	10.6	9.9
Denmark	11.3	11.3	7.9	11.5	8.3	10.5	6.0	11.1
France	7.5	13.5	13.3	14.3	10.5	17.9	12.1	15.8
Germany	10.0	10.8	7.1	9.1	6.1	7.0	7.0	8.4
Italy	9.5	11.2	8.0	7.5	7.9	8.4	9.4	10.8
Japan	4.4	6.8	8.0	7.9	6.6	9.4	8.0	7.2
Netherlands	6.9	7.9	11.7	12.1	7.9	8.4	9.4	12.5
Sweden	3.9	6.4	9.4	11.4	–	–	7.4	10.8
UK	12.4	15.1	18.1	18.5	–	–	16.4	16.1
US	14.4	16.4	18.9	14.9	10.6	11.8	18.8	14.7
Unweighted Average	9.2	11.3	11.4	11.6				

Source: Adapted from Blöndal *et al.* (2002).

Notes: Narrow rate is based on pre-tax earnings and the length of studies

Comprehensive rate adjusts for the impact of taxes, unemployment rate, tuition fees and public student support where relevant.

For the UK data on earnings of women up to age 30 with lower-secondary education were not available. For Sweden earnings differentials for women between upper and lower secondary levels are not large enough to allow a positive rate of return to be made.

Table 1.2 Narrow estimates of social rates of return to education in the OECD, 1999–2000(%)

	Upper Secondary		Tertiary	
	Men	Women	Men	Women
Canada	–	–	6.8	7.9
Denmark	9.3	8.7	6.3	4.3
France	9.6	10.6	13.2	13.1
Germany	10.2	6.0	6.5	6.9
Italy	8.4	–	9.7	–
Japan	5.0	6.4	6.7	5.7
Netherlands	6.2	7.8	10.0	6.3
Sweden	5.2	–	7.5	5.7
UK	12.9	–	15.2	13.6
US	13.2	9.6	13.7	12.3

Source: Adapted from Blöndal *et al.* (2002).

Note: – Reliable data lacking.

suggests that public investment in education, particularly in the UK and US, is worthwhile, especially given positive externalities in relation to economic growth and social cohesion. Indeed, the presence of supernormal returns might indicate that there is a disequilibrium in educational provision or a situation of temporary excess demand, with the expectation that in due course returns to education would decline to match those of other productive assets. However, an alternative possibility is that returns to marginal students are much lower than the returns to average students, so that the market is, in fact, in equilibrium.

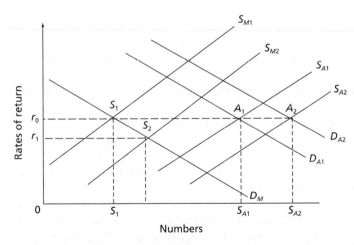

Figure 1.1 Educational expansion, average and marginal students and rates of return.

Suppose A represents an average student and M a marginal student with supply curves given by Sa and Sm respectively and demand curves given by D_A and D_M respectively. Assume the rates of return are initially the same for each group at r_0 because the supply of marginal students is restricted. Now suppose demand for average students increases to D_{A2}. If supply increases in line with demand to S_{A2}, the rate of return to the average student will remain the same. However, if there is no extra demand for marginal students, but the supply of marginal students expands to S_{M2}, the rate of return to the marginal student will fall to r_1. If this return equals that available on alternative investments the market can be said to be in equilibrium.

It should be noted, however, that there is heterogeneity in the returns to tertiary education according to the type of course followed, the institution attended and the quality of the individual's academic performance (see Case Study 1.1).

While in the past the great majority of those reaching the minimum school-leaving age entered the labour market directly, some receiving on-the-job training or entering an apprenticeship, greater numbers are now choosing to continue their education and thus to delay entry into the labour market. As far as the UK is concerned, well over half of 16 year olds now choose to remain in education beyond the compulsory school-leaving age. It is important, therefore, to understand what determines the decision to continue education beyond the minimum school-leaving age. For the US, Willis and Rosen (1979) attempted to determine the extent to which alternative earnings prospects, as distinct from family background and financial constraints, influence the decision to stay on in education.

Using a 1968–71 survey of Second World War veterans, they found, consistent with the **theory of comparative advantage**, that this decision is, indeed, influenced by expected gains in lifetime earnings. The tendency to respond to economic incentives appears, in fact, to be particularly marked in relation to professional occupations. Freeman (1971), for example, found an extremely close relationship between changes in college engineering enrolments and changes in engineering starting salaries. The market for engineers could be accurately described by means of a **cobweb model** with stable, highly damped fluctuations. This arises because it takes four years for a newly enrolled engineer to graduate and the supply of new graduates depends on salaries about four years earlier.

In Figure 1.2, S_0 represents the number of engineers currently graduating, with demand at D_1, so that the market is in equilibrium with the wage W_0. Now assume demand increases from D_1 to D_2. As the supply cannot be increased for four years, the wage rises from W_0 to W_1 and this will encourage more students to enrol on engineering courses as shown by the long run supply curve S_L. This, in turn, leads to overshooting when the extra numbers given by S_1 appear on the labour market, thereby reducing the wage below W_1. There follows a period of undershooting as given by S_3, but eventually supply and demand converge at E. Thus, the cobweb model suggests that recurrent shortage and surplus situations are likely to arise particularly in professional labour markets as a result of such cyclical fluctuations.

For Britain, Pissarides (1981, 1982) found that both expected relative earnings and aggregate per capita incomes play a part in the decision to stay on in the period up to the late 1970s. More recently, Whitfield and Wilson (1988) using more sophisticated co-integration techniques have related this rate of staying on to four variables – the rate of return to higher education; a measure of the changing class structure; the adult unemployment rate; and the scale of government youth training and employment schemes. Their model is quite successful in explaining trends in

Theory of comparative advantage

The idea that economic agents are most efficiently employed on activities in which they perform relatively better than in others.

Cobweb model

A simple dynamic model of cyclical demand and supply in which there is a time lag between the responses of individuals to, say, a change in wages, which, in turn, is a consequence of the time taken to acquire qualifications.

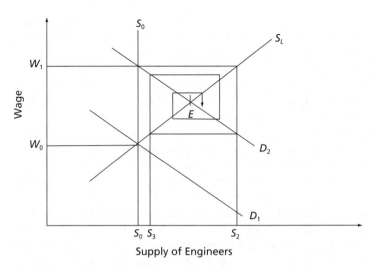

Figure 1.2 The cobweb model (the supply of and demand for engineers).

education staying-on rates, with the class variable being a major factor, having an elasticity of 6.0 compared to only 0.6 for rates of return.[2]

The relationship between education and family background may be related to both supply and demand factors (Figure 1.3). On the supply side, the propensity of parents to invest in the education of their children may be income-related because of imperfections in the capital market, which make the marginal costs (MC) of education greater for children of poor parents. On the demand side, children of such parents may be favoured because of information advantages (which increase the number of potential jobs to which they can apply through social networks), nepotism (which means that a sibling is more likely to be hired in a family firm) or because they are on average more able. Hence, we would expect children of rich

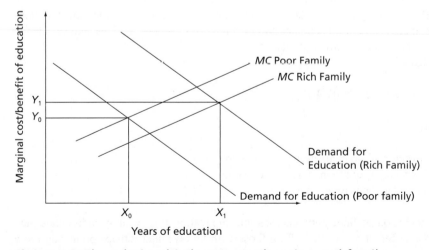

Figure 1.3 The relationship between education and family background.

parents to receive more education (X_1) than those of poor parents (X_0), though rates of return may not differ very much. Thus, in Figure 1.3, those from rich families have more education than those from poor families, X_1 compared to X_0, and the marginal returns are slightly higher at Y_1 compared to Y_0.

Drawing from both UK and US empirical work, Siebert (1989) suggests that a child with a father in the bottom quintile of the earnings distribution will earn about 30 per cent less than a child with the same endowments, but whose father has average earnings. If imperfections in the capital market could be removed, so that everyone faces the same marginal costs of education, he finds that **regression to the mean** (which measures the extent to which the children of rich parents tend to be less rich than their parents and, conversely, the children of poor parents better off than their parents) would be twice as fast as it actually is. Further evidence of the inter-generational transmission of inequality is contained in the Atkinson, Maynard and Trinder (1983) study of the working-class population of York conducted in 1975–8. Their regression analysis suggests that the coefficient relating the earnings of fathers and sons (adjusted for age) is of the order of 0.4 to 0.5. Accounting for factors such as length of education, type of school, education qualifications and migration still leaves a coefficient of 0.25, suggesting a large remaining association with family background.[3] In a further paper, Micklewright (1989) examines a sub-sample of children born in 1958 from the National Child Development Study (NCDS) to explain what distinguishes those choosing to acquire no further schooling beyond the minimum leaving age from others. The results of his analysis indicate the importance of family background variables (such as whether either parent stayed on beyond the minimum leaving age, their occupation and the number of children in the family). The effect of either parent staying on alone reduces the child's probability of leaving by some 20 per cent. Between one-half and two-thirds of the family background effect remains when controls for the child's academic ability and type of school are introduced.

This relationship between family background and length of education feeds directly into occupational choice. The **economic theory of occupational choice** assumes that an individual will select the occupation that maximises his or her utility function within the constraints of the market and ability. Following Freeman (1971), we may assume that the individual calculates the expected lifetime income in relevant occupations, makes a comparison of the utilities of wage income, non-wage income and non-pecuniary attractiveness of those occupations, and selects the career that offers the greatest total utility.

That is

$$\text{Max } M(X_i, W_i, Y_f) \tag{1.1}$$

where

X_i = a vector of job characteristics in occupation i.
W_i = expected lifetime income in occupation i.
Y_f = non-wage family income.

The inclusion of family income has the implication that wealthy individuals may choose different occupations from those with less wealth, perhaps preferring more aesthetic and prestigious jobs to those offering high pay and few non-pecuniary advantages. In general, it is not feasible to choose a combination of occupations

Regression to the mean

The idea that extremes in a distribution will, over time, tend to move towards the mean of that distribution. Thus, children of high-earning parents will tend to earn less and children of low-earning parents more than their parents.

Economic theory of occupational choice

This is based on the proposition that an individual will select that occupation which maximises his or her utility subject to constraints such as ability and the market situation. This would involve comparisons of lifetime incomes in alternative occupations and their relative attractiveness in terms of working conditions.

because of the length of training required and the finite span of working lives. Further, there is a close relation between career selection and the allocation of time to work. Hence, equation (1.1)) may be adapted as follows:

$$\text{Max } U(\lambda X_i, W_i, (1 - \lambda)L + \lambda X_i, N_i) \tag{1.2}$$

subject to the single occupation constraint $X_i = 1, 0$, and the maximum time constraint $0 \leq \lambda \leq 1$

where
λ = fraction of time devoted to work
L = utility of leisure
N_i = non-pecuniary utility of work.

Thus, hours devoted to work as given by λ will vary according to the relative pleasantness or otherwise of work as given by N.

A variant of such a model has been tested for Britain by Robertson and Symons (1988) using the NCDS. Ability is measured by maths and reading scores in NCDS tests and tastes for occupations are proxied by father's occupation, with future earnings discounted at 10 per cent. They find in line with earlier studies a strong tendency for individuals to remain in the same occupational class as their parents (which they term **dynastic hysteresis**)[4] and for the children of parents in higher occupational classes to score better on the ability measure. However, the R^2s on their regressions are quite low, so that there is a substantial unexplained component. Although social class is clearly important, it does not explain everything, but the general conclusion from the above studies stands, namely that occupational choice seems to accord fairly well with the predictions of economic theory.

Institutional economists have, however, criticised the theory of occupational choice and the prediction that there will be a tendency towards equality of net advantages in the long run on a number of grounds.[5] It is alleged, for instance, that relative wages are not a major factor in choice of jobs, that the desire for security leads to a preference for current jobs over better-paid alternatives and that workers do not rationally weigh up alternatives, but base decisions on habit. It should be noted that the standard theory does not imply that the wage is the only determinant of occupational choice. For instance, some jobs are riskier than others and risk-averse individuals may shun risky jobs even if they pay more. While it may be true that some workers do not consider the full range of jobs available to them, the above studies suggest that there are sufficient numbers in the labour market prepared to try to maximise net advantages to make the theory a reasonable predictor of equilibrium outcomes.

Dynastic hysteresis

The tendency of children to choose the same occupation as their parents.

Case Study 1.1

Does it pay to take a degree?

In Britain, there was a substantial increase in the number of individuals taking a degree compared to those having the entry qualifications for higher education but choosing to enter the labour market after obtaining Advanced level GCE qualifications. The increment to earnings for men ranged from over £27,000 for certain arts disciplines to over £222,000 in mathematics and computing. For women, the range was from £113,000 in arts to £244,000 in education. Thus, the choice of degree programme can make a dramatic difference to expected lifetime earnings. This makes no allowance for externalities such as the consumption benefits of higher education, increased employability or positive effects on health. The higher returns to women reflect the lower earnings of women choosing not to enter university and seem to have elicited an appropriate response, as women now constitute well over half of those entering higher education.

	Males				Females			
	ΔEarnings	R-0	R-1000	R-3000	ΔEarnings	R-0	R-1000	R-3000
All degrees	141,539	10.1	9.0	7.3	157,982	15.0	13.0	10.3
Medical related (a)	175,108	12.8	11.4	9.3	208,021	22.0	18.5	14.4
Sciences	142,079	10.2	9.1	7.4	151,521	14.7	12.7	10.0
Maths and computing	222,419	17.3	15.1	12.2	227,939	24.8	20.6	15.9
Engineering and technology	196,293	14.9	13.1	10.7	165,329	16.6	14.3	11.3
Architecture and related	88,877	5.5	4.8	3.6	196,838	20.0	17.0	13.4
Social sciences	145,820	10.3	9.2	7.5	152,158	14.6	12.7	10.0
Business and finance	155,431	11.1	9.9	8.0	169,322	16.7	14.3	11.3
Arts	22,458	−2.0	−2.3	−3.0	113,185	10.2	8.9	7.0
Education	151,583	11.0	9.8	8.0	244,740	27.7	22.7	17.4
Combined	128,821	9.1	8.1	6.6	131,347	12.2	10.6	8.4

Source: O'Leary and Sloane.

Notes: Figures are for January 2002, and refer to earnings net of taxes; rates of return are calculated for a typical three-year degree course for residents of England and Wales only; rates of return are calculated for a married individual working full-time and living in the south-east of England (outside London) in 2002; discount rate assumed of 4%; foregone (net) earnings of graduates are calculated at £31,643/£34,821 (women/men); graduates assumed to be in continuous employment from ages 21 to 59/64 (women/men); A-level holders assumed to be in continuous employment from ages 18 to 59/64 (women/men); (a) excludes medicine and dentistry; R-x refers to the rate of return when annual tuition fees are £x.

Nigel C. O'Leary and Peter J. Sloane, "The Return to a University Education in Great Britain", *National Institute Economic Review*, No. 193, July 2005, pp. 75–89.

As a footnote, Yu Zhu of the University of Kent has updated figures up to 2006, which show that economics graduates have the highest earnings premium over those with at least two A levels among all graduates at 42% for men and 68% for women respectively. Thus, studying for an economics degree is a sound proposition (see www.kent.ac.uk/economics/news/archive/earnings.html).

1.2 Labour force participation between entry into the labour market and retirement

The **labour force participation rate**, or activity rate – the two terms can be used interchangeably – refers to the section of the population that is in work or seeking work. Those in employment, together with the unemployed, make up the labour force. Some studies place the emphasis on activity and others on its mirror image – inactivity. Care needs to be taken in making comparisons as sometimes the activity rate is expressed as a proportion of the working-age population and in other cases as a proportion of those aged 16 and over. The latter avoids the problem of changing retirement ages and includes those who are still in work though over retirement age. Comparisons also need to take into account the fact that hours of work may vary across groups and, in particular, the proportion working part-time may vary. There are also important differences between employees and the self-employed. For these and other reasons, there is a wide variation in the activity and inactivity rates among countries. Thus, in 2002, the inactivity rate in Poland was 32 per cent compared to only 20 per cent in Sweden.

Weir (2003) notes that comparisons between countries may be problematic because of differences in the economic climate, social and cultural norms, legislation, benefit systems, demography and variations in higher-education participation rates. The inactive population includes students, those who have retired, women looking after children and those with short- or long-term illnesses or disability. The inactive population has traditionally been distinguished from the unemployed population because it consists of those who have not been actively seeking work in the previous few weeks, but it has increasingly been recognised that some of those who are inactive could be encouraged to enter the labour force, given appropriate incentives to work or disincentives to continue in inactivity. Thus, in the UK, the Department of Work and Pensions reported in 2002 that 4 million of the 7.7 million inactive people were in receipt of state benefits, such as incapacity benefits, disability allowances and income support, and therefore potentially susceptible to changes in the benefit regime.

A jobless individual's decision whether to be inactive, unemployed or search for a job will also be influenced by the potential wage. Thus, Bicakova (2005) observes that both in the UK and the US the inactivity rate for low-skilled men exceeds the percentage of unemployed, whereas in France the reverse is the case. In the UK and

Labour force participation rate

The percentage of the working-age population (or sometimes those above school-leaving age) that is in employment or seeking work.

the US, wages are flexible, so that, as a consequence of **skill-biased technological change**, the wages of the low skilled are pushed down, thus widening the wage distribution. This encourages the low skilled in these two countries to leave the labour force, whereas, in France, which has a higher national minimum wage than the other two countries, low-skilled workers remain active.

The Labour European Council of March 2000 set targets for employment of 67.0 per cent in 2003 and 70.0 per cent for 2010 in terms of the overall employment rate, while the corresponding figures for women were set at 57.0 per cent and 60.0 per cent respectively. In the case of older workers aged 55–64, a target of 50.0 per cent was set for 2010. The labour force participation rate for the working-age population in the Euro area rose from below 65.0 per cent in the early 1980s to 70.9 per cent by 2007, while the equivalent female rate increased by more than 15.0 per cent, reaching 63.3 per cent in 2007 (compared to 78.6 per cent for males at this date), thereby surpassing the Lisbon targets. The gap between the labour input levels narrowed significantly between the Euro area and the US. Balleer *et al.* (2009) suggest that, while there is considerable individual country heterogeneity, changes or differences in labour taxes, union density, unemployment benefits and the average number of children per household all play a part in improving labour force participation. However, demographic factors will become less favourable as the population ages, increasing the importance of positive participation trends within age and gender cohorts.

In considering the above improvements in activity rates, the increase in the share of part-time employment needs to be borne in mind. According to *Employment in Europe 2009*, in the EU 27 part-time employment as a percentage of total employment rose from 28.7 per cent in 1998 to 31.1 per cent in 2008, but there is substantial variation in this figure across countries, ranging in 2008 from 2.7 per cent in Bulgaria to 75.3 per cent in the Netherlands. Within these figures, part-time work by women predominates. Jaumotte (2003) suggests there are three motives for firms to hire part-time workers. First, the **optimal staffing model** implies that part-time jobs enable firms to better match labour to changes in workload (e.g. parts of the service sector where demand peaks at certain times of the day). Second, the **secondary labour market model** implies that firms create part-time posts in order to obtain cheaper and/or more flexible labour. For example, this may make it easier to cover for workers who are sick or who are unable to work on specific projects. In addition, part-time contracts may enable employers to avoid certain costs, such as pensions, which have to be provided for full-time employees. Third, the **responsive firm model** implies that firms create part-time jobs because their labour requirements would otherwise remain unmet, as more people are available to work part-time than full-time.

On the supply side, the **gender role model** predominates, which suggests that married women with young children and lower education qualifications (or wealthy women who can afford not to work) will prefer part-time over full-time work. Jaumotte notes that there is a pay penalty for part-time work in English-speaking countries such as Canada, the US and the UK, but a pay premium for such work applies in countries such as Germany, Austria and the Southern European countries. Marginalisation can be measured by the difficulty of moving from part-time to full-time work and a weak attachment to the labour market. Evidence for this is found by Reilly and Bothfeld (2002), who note that in both the UK and Germany only a small number of part-time women are able to use part-time work as a stepping stone back into full-time work and a substantial percentage, especially in the case of workers with more than one child, drop out of employment altogether. Connelly and Gregory (2008), using British data, also find that one-quarter of women moving from a full-time to a part-time job experience downgrading in terms of the utilisation of skills. Paull (2008) uses British Household Panel Survey (BHPS) data to show that a substantial movement into part-time work for women occurs with the birth of a first child and this continues steadily for ten years. The gender gap in hours diminishes subsequently but still persists even after children have grown up. In contrast, births have little effect on the working hours of men.

Not all workers, however, are employees. Some work on their own account, usually without any employees. **Self-employment** in the EU 27 declined from 14.0 per cent in 1998 to 11.9 per cent in 2008 (*Employment in Europe 2009*). Again, there is considerable variation in incidence across countries ranging from around 3 per cent in Denmark and Sweden as a percentage of total employment to around 30 per cent in France, Greece and Romania. The incidence of self-employment is much higher for men than women. Thus, for Britain, Sloane *et al.* (2005) report a self-employment rate of 17.3 per cent for men and 7.3 per cent for women. Further, they show that the degree of gender segregation across self-employed occupations is higher than is the case for employees. One reason for these findings is that men are less risk averse than women as illustrated by a number of studies. Thus, Ekelund *et al.* (2005), using psychometric data on a large cohort of Finns, find that lower **risk aversion** makes men significantly more likely to become self-employed than women. In contrast, ethnic minorities are over-represented in self-employment. Clark and Drinkwater (2000) suggest that this may be a rational response to labour market obstacles, such as employer discrimination facing ethnic minorities, which reduce the opportunity cost of this form of employment. The existence of ethnic enclaves with shared language and tradition may also encourage self-employment. Blanchflower (2000) notes that survey evidence suggests that many individuals who are currently employees would prefer to be self-employed, but restrictions on the supply side, such as lack of capital, prevent this from happening. Thus, Blanchflower and Oswald (1998) find that the probability of self-employment depends positively on whether the individual has ever received a gift or inheritance. There may also be cyclical influences, with movements into self-employment being correlated with increases in unemployment (Blanchflower and Oswald 1990). Care needs to be taken, however, in making international comparisons, as in some countries individuals who report themselves as being self-employed may be unpaid family workers in the agricultural sector.

As noted above, one of the most striking features of the labour market in many countries over recent years are the divergent pattern of male and female labour force participation, which are summarised by Pencavel (1986) as follows, in relation to male employees:

> For a century or so, at least in North America and Western Europe, a declining fraction of a man's lifetime has been spent at market work. This decline has been manifested in a number of ways; more years have been spent at school and the age of entry into full-time market employment has advanced; workers have been wholly or partly retiring from the labour force at younger ages; fewer hours have been worked per day and per week; and there have been more holidays and longer vacations.

Gender role model

The supposition that married women with young children and lower educational qualifications will prefer part-time over full-time work.

Self-employment

Working on one's own account as a proprietor of an unincorporated business, either with or without employees.

Risk aversion

A preference for work that involves fewer risks, whether in terms of accidents, employment volatility or other factors.

Income and substitution effects

The income effect measures the change in spending power resulting from a change in the real wage with all product prices remaining constant, while the substitution effect measures the extent to which work is substituted for leisure or vice versa with a change in the real wage.

Discouraged worker hypothesis

This suggests that, when economic activity declines, some workers who lose their jobs (particularly married women) will leave the labour force rather than search for another job, so that the size of the labour force declines.

Additional worker hypothesis

This suggests that, when economic activity declines, some secondary workers (such as married women) will enter the labour force in order to offset reductions in family income resulting from lost earnings of primary workers who have either lost their jobs or are on short-time working arrangements.

In contrast, the labour force participation rate of women has increased in the vast majority of countries over the twentieth century and particularly since the 1960s.[6] Thus, in the US, female civilian participation increased from 23.3 per cent in 1920 to 50.5 per cent in 1980, and, in Britain, the corresponding figures were 32.3 per cent in 1921 and 45.6 per cent in 1981. However, within these totals, the participation rate of married women has increased (in Britain, for example, from 8.79 per cent in 1921 to 47.2 per cent in 1981), while the participation of single women has decreased in line with that of men. Can economic theory explain these trends, or at least some of them? Much of the theoretical and empirical work has been influenced by Mincer's 1962 study, which emphasises the need to analyse labour force participation decisions in a family as opposed to an individual context. In this respect, one must consider a three-way allocation of time between market work, household production and leisure. In principle, changes in the wage rate for any family member could influence the time allocation of any other family member, depending upon the relative productivities and wage rates of the various individuals in market and household production and the possibilities of substitution among them. However, taking the wife as an example, we can write labour force participation of a married woman P_m as:

$$P_m = a + b_1 Y + b_2 W + e \tag{1.3}$$

where
Y = family income
W = wife's potential market earnings
e = a set of conditioning variables including education, family size and location.

In considering reactions to changes in family income as a result of changes in real wages we must distinguish between **income and substitution effects**. Assuming an increase in wages, the income effect measures the increase in spending power resulting from a change in the real wage with all product prices assumed to be constant, while the substitution effect measures the extent to which work, which is now more attractive, is substituted for leisure. The income effect is captured by a rightward shift in the budget line, which indicates the financial resources available to the family, while the substitution effect is captured by the movement along a given indifference curve, which represents different combinations of income and leisure providing the same level of satisfaction. (For a more detailed diagrammatic exposition, see Chapter 3.)

Returning to equation (1.3) when permanent family income rises, for example, through an increase in the husband's wage, the wife will be less inclined to participate in market work. Thus, b_1 is a measure of the income effect, which is generally expected to be negative. In contrast, an increase in the wife's potential wage will serve as an inducement to enter the labour force participation over the business cycle as indicated by b_2.

There are two competing hypotheses in relation to participation decisions over the business cycle. According to the **discouraged worker hypothesis**, when the level of economic activity declines, some workers (particularly married women) will lose their jobs and leave the labour force rather than search for another job. In contrast, according to the **additional worker hypothesis**, labour force participation may actually increase as economic activity declines, provided sufficient numbers of secondary workers (e.g. married women) enter the labour force in order to offset reduced family incomes consequent upon lost earnings (via reductions in overtime earnings or loss of job by the husband). Mincer's equation can be modified to take account of the above by introducing two new variables – y_t (which measures the short-run deviation of family income from the norm or full employment level) and w_t (which measures the short-run deviation of earnings from normal earnings).

$$P_m = a + b_1 Y + b_2 W + C_1 y_t + C_2 w_t + e \qquad (1.4)$$

Hence, in this equation, C_1 will represent the additional worker effect and C_2 the discouraged worker effect. As few data-sets contain direct measures of these short-run deviations, it is common to substitute unemployment (U) as a proxy on the assumption that this variable will be negatively related to y_t and w_t. Thus,

$$P_m = a + b_1 Y + b_2 W + b_3 U + e \qquad (1.5)$$

Mincer used this single equation model to analyse variations in the labour force participation rate of married women in 57 Standard Metropolitan Statistical Areas in the Northern Areas in the Northern States of the US in the 1980s. In line with a priori expectations, he finds that wives' wages have a strong positive effect and husbands' incomes a weaker but negative effect on participation. These two variables alone are sufficient to explain half of the observed variation in participation.

Other studies have extended the above model in various ways. Bowen and Finegan (1969), for example, consider not only various labour market indicators but also the effects of personal and household characteristics, estimating the following equation:

$$P_m = a + b_1 A + b_2 C + b_3 S + b_4 H + b_5 CH + b_6 OFI + b_7 LH + b_8 WF$$
$$+ b_9 U + b_{10} DF + b_{11} SF + e \qquad (1.6)$$

The first three explanatory variables A (= age), C (= colour) and S (= level of education) relate to personal characteristics of the woman herself; the middle group – H (= size of mortgage), CH (= number of children), OFI (= other family income) and LH (= labour force status of husband) – relate to characteristics of the household; and the final group – WF (= level of female earnings), U (= overall unemployment rate), DF (= demand for female labour) and SF (= supply of labour) – relate to the characteristics of the labour market.[7] Cain and Dooley (1976) attempted to improve the specification of the model by using a three equation system in which wives' labour force participation, fertility and wage are all endogenous. Their results for 1970 are in line with those of Mincer. However, Fields (1976), also using data relating to 1970, finds weaker effects, which suggest the possibility that the work-role orientations of women may be changing over time – their labour force attachment having features which approximate more closely to that of primary than secondary workers. Clark and Summers (1981, 1982) also find that female labour force participation is not very sensitive to cyclical factors. In part, this may be explained by the fact that their study controls for possible serial correlation, whereas Mincer's does not, and, in part, by the fact that this result is caused largely by the behaviour of women aged 45 or over – the participation of teenage and prime-age women remaining sensitive to cyclical variation.

The cross-section results suggest that increases in family income should reduce labour force participation. How then can we explain the substantial increase in participation of married women over a period when family incomes have increased appreciably in real terms? In a time series analysis covering the period 1948–78, O'Neill (1981) finds that women's earnings have the expected positive effect and men's earnings the expected negative effect. The continued growth of female participation in the most recent decade is to be explained by the fact that the slowdown in the growth of women's real earnings was exceeded by an even greater slowdown in the real incomes of husbands, together with a sharp increase in the divorce rate.[8]

The dramatic change in the labour force participation rate for British women is revealed by the data contained in Table 1.3 over the period when such changes were particularly marked (for more recent changes, refer to Table 1.4).

Between 1911 and 1986, the participation rate for married women increased from 9.6 per cent to 53.0 per cent, the relative stability of the overall participation rate owing much to the decline in the male rate from 90.5 per cent in 1931 to 73.4 per cent in 1986. In the late 1970s, there were a number of attempts to explain these tendencies. Using 1971 Census data, Greenhalgh (1977) and McNabb (1977) both find that the substitution effect of changes in the wife's own wage exceeds the income effect of family income.

This result was confirmed by Lightman and O'Cleireacain (1978) using DHSS data on average annual earnings. However, unlike McNabb who found a much stronger discouraged worker effect, they find that the additional and discouraged worker effects cancel each other out. Using the 1974 General Household Survey, Layard *et al.* (1980) find that the probability of participating responds positively to the wife's own wage with an elasticity of 0.5 and negatively to the husband's wage with an elasticity of 0.3. Thus, the estimated income effect is very low and both elasticities are about half those found in the US, suggesting a smaller responsiveness to monetary incentives in Britain. Time series analyses have been carried out by Berg and Dalton (1977) and Owen and Joshi (1987). The former finds that women are responsive to both unemployment and real wage effects over the period 1947–73. The latter, examining the period 1951–81, finds in line with the more

Table 1.3 Participation rates in the UK, 1911–86 (as a percentage of all aged 16 and over)

	Males	All females	Married females	Other females	Total males and females
1911	87.2	32.2	9.6	N.A.	56.7
1921	87.1	32.3	8.7	53.8	58.1
1931	90.5	34.2	10.0	60.2	60.7
1951	87.6	34.7	21.7	55.0	59.6
1961	86.0	37.4	29.7	50.6	60.5
1971	82.5	43.0	42.3	44.4	61.3
1981	76.5	47.6	49.5	43.6	61.4
1986	73.4	49.2	53.0	44.2	60.8

Source: Employment Gazette – various issues.

Table 1.4 Activity rates in the UK, 1990–2020

	All people aged 16 and over	All people aged 16–59 or 64	All people aged 16–64	Men aged 16 and over	Men aged 16–64	Women aged 16 and over	Women aged 16–59	Women aged 16–64
1990	64.5	80.7	78.3	75.9	88.7	54.0	72.0	68.0
1995	62.4	78.2	76.1	72.2	85.0	53.3	70.9	67.3
2000	63.1	78.9	76.8	71.5	84.6	55.2	72.9	69.2
2005	63.1	78.5	76.6	70.5	83.4	56.1	73.4	69.6
2010	62.8	79.0	76.7	69.6	83.2	56.3	74.4	70.4
2015	62.3	79.5	77.7	68.3	83.4	56.6	75.3	72.0
2020	61.7	79.8	78.1	67.0	83.2	56.6	76.1	73.1

Source: Labour Market Trends, January 2006, p. 21.

recent US findings that the discouraged worker effect in the recession is not very large.

The above analyses have concentrated on female participation and particularly that of married females. What of male labour force participation? There is almost continuous labour force participation for men when they have completed their education, but the younger and older age groups do appear to be sensitive both to wages and to incomes. For the US, Bowen and Finegan find a strong positive correlation between participation and education for men in general. Further, a white man is about 2 per cent more likely to be a member of the labour force than a black man, and a prime-age married man is 8 per cent more likely to be in the labour force than a man with a different marital status. Greater non-wage income is also associated with lower participation. For Britain, Greenhalgh (1979) has examined male participation using 1971 Census data and confirms, as in the US, that implied elasticities for wages and income are rather small, though in general the variations that do occur are largely explained by variables as outlined in the theory of labour supply.

More recently, attention has focused on the problems of ageing workforces in Europe and elsewhere. By 2020, the proportion of the labour force in the UK that lies below the age of 50 will fall to 69 per cent compared to 75 per cent in 2005. As shown in Table 1.4, overall activity rates will decline somewhat, but less so for those below current retirement age. This conceals, however, a tendency for male activity rates to decline further and for female activity rates to continue their rise.

Over this period, the gap between male and female activity rates will narrow further. In 2007, the UK government announced that the state retirement age would rise to 66 in 2024, 67 in 2034 and 68 in 2044, with the gender gap in retirement ages gradually disappearing, so this would add to the diminishing gender activity gap. Retirement issues are discussed further in section 1.3.

1.3 The retirement decision

As noted in *Employment in Europe 2007*, one of the most notable features in European labour markets in recent years has been a substantial increase in the employment of older people, reversing an earlier trend for it to decline. Since 2000, the employment rate for people aged 55–64 has risen by seven percentage points in the EU 25, compared to a rise of 2.3 percentage points for the working-age population as a whole. This is important since population ageing is seen as one of the most important labour market challenges facing the EU. The 2001 Stockholm European Council set a target that by 2010 at least 50 per cent of the EU population aged 55–64 should be in employment, while the 2002 Barcelona European Council concluded that "a progressive increase of about 5 years in the effective average age at which people stop working in the EU should be sought by 2010".

Exit from the labour market may take several forms; it may imply total withdrawal from the labour market or a more gradual process in which hours and earnings are diminished for a number of years before complete retirement; and the age at which it occurs may be mandatory. However, one of the more noticeable features in the labour market until comparatively recently has been the tendency towards earlier retirement, particularly for male employees. It is tempting to attribute this to an income effect, as increasing real incomes may be expected to lead to a tendency to increase leisure at the expense of reduced working lifetimes. Yet the international

Table 1.5 Labour force participation – workers aged 65 and over, selected countries

Country	1956	1975	2004/5
Belgium	13.8	6.3	3.0
Denmark	20.0	19.9	14.0
France	20.7	7.1	3.0
Germany	16.5	10.0	6.0
Italy	15.6	7.1	7.0
Netherlands	13.1	6.8	10.0
Sweden	20.5	10.9	15.0
UK	16.2	10.7	15.0
US	23.7	14.6	N.A.

Source: 1956 and 1975 (Lazear 1986). 2004/5 figures are employment rates for persons aged 65–69, European Commission, *Europe's Demographic Future*, Luxembourg, 2007.

evidence contained in Table 1.5 is not entirely consistent with this proposition. Though the tendency for the labour force participation rates of the over-65s to decline is common to all these countries up to 1975, the absolute levels (and the rates of decline) do not seem to be consistently smaller (greater) for countries with lower (higher) standards of living. It is possible, of course, that disaggregated data would show a correspondence between standard of living and retirement for individuals, and Table 1.5 does not include data for workers younger than 65. In the Netherlands, Sweden and the UK, the tendency for participation to decline has been reversed for those aged 65–9 according to the latest figures for 2004/5.

It is necessary to consider the optimal age for retirement in a life-cycle context. Following Mitchell and Fields (1982), we may suppose that an individual with T years of life remaining aims to maximise lifetime utility, which is a function of consumption and leisure. Consumption will be constrained by lifetime earnings capacity and pension income in particular. Thus, we assume that the lifetime labour supply path (H) is a function of the lifetime earnings stream (E), pension income (P) and a vector of other relevant explanatory variables (X). Hence,

$$H = H(E, P, X) \tag{1.7}$$

Income is positively related to earnings until age of retirement R, $(E_1, E_2, \ldots, E_R)$, and to pension income subsequent to retirement ($P_{R+1}, P_{R+2}, \ldots, P_T$). Hence,

$$Y = Y(E_1, E_2, \ldots, E_R; P_{R+1}, P_{R+2}, \ldots, P_T) \tag{1.8}$$

Pension income will be determined by years of service, wage in the highest n years preceding retirement, contributions to a pension fund, or some combination of these, which we designate as Y_W. Thus,

$$P_T = P_T(R, Y_W) \tag{1.9}$$

Let Y_W be a non-decreasing function of lifetime labour supply, H. Then,

$$Y_W = Y_W(H) \tag{1.10}$$

Finally, hours of work and leisure use up total annual hours

$$H + L = c \tag{1.11}$$

where c is a constant.

Collapsing equations (1.6) to (1.9) into a single equation, we obtain

$$U = U\{C[E_1, E_2, \ldots, E_R; P_{R+1}(Y_W(L), R), \ldots, P_T(Y_W(L), R)]H\} \tag{1.12}$$

This life-cycle theory specifies that labour supply and retirement status in any period will be determined by earnings from work and pension income in *all* periods. Hence, empirical studies which are limited to current values of these variables are likely to suffer from omitted variable bias and measurement error.[9] Other relevant explanatory variables (X) include the net wage stream in the next best alternative job, social security benefits and contributions, and pension contributions. Yet no empirical studies to date appear to have included all these variables.

Mandatory retirement

A legal requirement for workers to retire at a certain age when state pensions become payable. Its incidence has been reduced or the provisions weakened with the advent of age-discrimination legislation.

However, not all workers can choose when to retire. In the UK, **mandatory retirement** has traditionally applied to many men aged 65 and women aged 60 (though the latter case has been modified by equal opportunities legislation). In the US, mandatory retirement applied to 35 per cent of the labour force prior to the Age Discrimination in Employment Act (ADEA), which raised the retirement age to 70.[10] If retirement is mandatory, and also mandatory at a common age, this must reduce the ability of workers to maximise their utility given heterogeneous income-earning opportunities, pension rights and tastes. However, there is reason to believe that the proportion of workers so affected may be relatively small. Parnes and Nestel (1981), using longitudinal data, were able to classify a sample of 1,600 US retirees in the 1970s into three categories – those whose retirement is purely voluntary; those who have retired through ill health; and those who have retired because of mandatory schemes. Of this sample, 51 per cent fall into the first category, 46 per cent the second and only 3 per cent into the third. Thus, retirement due to ill health is much more important than involuntary retirement through mandatory schemes. The latter is, however, influenced by retirement prior to mandatory age as well as by those who have no desire to work beyond that age.[11]

This raises the question: why should there be mandatory retirement in the first place? Lazear (1979) explains the phenomenon in terms of age–earnings profiles, which will influence both the workers' choice of hours worked, including retirement date, and worker productivity in those cases where effort can be controlled by the worker. From the employer's perspective, the problem is that adjusting the age–earnings profile in such a way that it induces a sufficient input of effort from the worker also tends to distort hours of work and the retirement date that the worker would willingly choose.

Let us assume in Figure 1.4 that the worker's effort over the working lifetime is represented by MVP_t and the reservation wage by $\overline{W}_t$. The age at which these two schedules intersect, t^*, defines the date of efficient retirement and is the one that the worker would willingly choose if free to do so, assuming he was paid according to

MVP_t. There are, however, an infinite number of possible wage paths. One possibility is W_t, which attempts to increase worker attachment by paying him less than MVP up to t_1 and more than MVP thereafter. If we assume that W_t provides the same net present value from t_0 to R as earnings stream MVP_t, the worker will be indifferent between these two alternatives. W_t, however, will require mandatory retirement because the worker's preference at R would be to continue in employment as $W_t > \overline{W}_t$, his reservation wage.

The assumption made is that working at maximum effort decreases the probability of job termination. It is important to recognise, however, that effort is not independent of the choice between W_t and MVP_t. Assume the worker chooses to reduce his effort to MVP' given wage stream MVP_t. If he is fired as a consequence, he will suffer a loss equal to MVP_t, but a gain of $\overline{W}_t$ taken as time spent in leisure. Certainly, there is no incentive to work at maximum efficiency MVP_t. If, in contrast, the worker is paid W_t, job termination will mean a loss equal to W_t and a gain of only $\overline{W}_t$. The difference $W_t - \overline{W}_t$ acts as an inducement to work at a higher level of effort. Thus, mandatory retirement can be seen to be a consequence of the employer's attempt to choose a wage profile which maximises effort. As a corollary here would be an incentive for the firm to default by sacking the worker at t_1 were it not for the fact that this would make it difficult to hire workers at $W_{(t)} < MVP_{(t)}$ early in the working career. It will, however, provide firms with an inducement to buy out workers through favourable early-retirement schemes, which are much in evidence. This situation can also provide a justification for pensions based on highest pay achieved, which may help to maintain effort throughout the working life.

It should also be recognised that the retirement process is far more complex than a simple choice between work and no work. A significant number of workers choose to spend the latter part of their working life in an intermediate state of partial retirement. This may be simply reduced hours or responsibilities in existing employment, a change of employer or a transfer into self-employment. Honig and Hanoch (1985), using a sample of 3,550 white males drawn from the US Retirement History Survey 1969–73, find that 19.7 per cent of the sample are partially

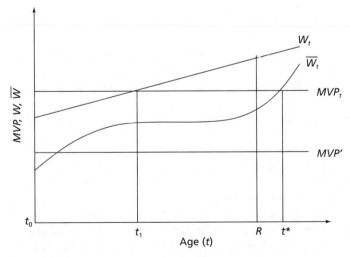

Figure 1.4 Pay back-loading and retirement.

retired. Health, pensions coverage, expected social security income, non-wage income, self-employment and labour force experience are all found to be relevant to the choice of retirement state.[12]

These variables have also been found to be significant in empirical studies of complete retirement decisions. Thus, Quinn (1977), using a data-set containing 4,354 US men aged 58–63, finds that a health-limitation dummy is the single most significant regressor, though eligibility for social security and for a private pension are also significant. Zabalza *et al.* (1980) also find for the UK that poor health is a very important determinant of the retirement decision. Further, women appear to be more responsive than men to economic incentives, a result confirmed by another UK study (Warburton 1987). Though the theoretical prediction is ambiguous, studies by Burkhauser (1979) and Gordon and Blinder (1980) find that the higher the net present value of earnings, the lower the probability of retirement. Education has been found to have a negative and significant effect and being married a positive and significant effect on continuance of employment.[13] There is also substantial evidence that **state dependence**, which measures the extent to which being in a particular state increases the probability of being in that state in future periods regardless of personal characteristics, has a major impact on the retirement decision. However, none of these studies has taken account of all these variables and they employ revenue streams as opposed to current values, so we must treat these results with a degree of caution.

State dependence

A causal link exists between previous labour market experience and future labour market outcomes, independently of personal characteristics.

Summary

- Individuals will make occupational choices which at least in part reflect relative lifetime earnings and these may vary substantially across occupations. While, in general, rates of return compare reasonably favourably with those obtainable from other forms of investment, access to them may be influenced by family background. However, governments may be prepared to subsidise this process because of equity considerations and because of positive externalities from education.
- Labour force participation rates are higher for men than for women and vary considerably across countries. A distinction is normally made between unemployment and inactivity since those who are unemployed are part of the workforce, but those who are inactive are not. Yet this distinction becomes blurred when in-work and out-of-work benefits are taken into account. Part-time employment, largely a female preserve, also varies considerably across countries, being influenced both by supply- and demand-side forces. Self-employment, which also varies substantially across countries, is influenced by gender differences in attitudes towards risk and the availability of funds.
- There are cyclical influences on labour force participation with the additional worker and discouraged worker effects being competing hypotheses, but the latter seems to predominate, so that participation is procyclical. These effects emphasise the family nature of participation decisions.
- Ageing populations in much of the world suggest that it may be necessary to extend the working lifetimes of many individuals in order to provide adequate incomes in retirement and reduce the dependency burden on the State. This

raises the question of the optimal retirement age and whether retirement should be voluntary or mandatory. This must be considered in a life-cycle framework, which takes into account income in all time periods. Lazear's model, based on pay back-loading, which drives a wedge between the wage and the marginal product, suggests that there may be tensions between the interests of employers and of workers.

Questions

1 Lifetime earnings vary considerably across professional occupations. What are the implications for investments in higher education by the individual and the State?

2 "Equity considerations suggest that it may be necessary for the State to subsidise education." Discuss.

3 Why should labour force participation, part-time work and self-employment vary so much across countries?

4 Explain the additional worker and discouraged worker hypotheses in relation to labour force participation rates. Which is likely to predominate and why?

5 What are the labour market implications of an ageing labour force at the level of the firm and of the economy?

6 What are the arguments for and against the imposition of mandatory retirement? Is this likely to be optimal from the point of view of the worker or of the employer?

Notes

1 There is evidence that rates of return in the competitive (private) sector exceed those in the non-competitive (public) sector. Returns by gender suggest that, particularly in developing countries, the rate of return to women is actually higher than that for men, despite the absolutely lower levels of pay for women throughout the occupational spectrum.

2 While Whitfield and Wilson (1988) find that increasing unemployment discourages entry into the labour market, Micklewright, Pearson and Smith (1988) find the reverse. This may be attributable to the fact that the former but not the latter include a Youth Training Scheme variable which has a strong negative effect on the decision to continue in education.

3 The investigators also found in relation to the two major employers in York – British Rail and confectionery – that there is a definite tendency for sons to follow fathers. In the former case, it appears that fathers place the sons' names on the waiting list for apprenticeships.

4 This should not, however, be exaggerated. No fewer than 47.8 per cent of children have the same occupational rank as their father, 24.9 per cent are one rank greater, and 5.5 per cent two ranks greater, while 17.6 per cent are one rank fewer and 4.1 per cent two ranks fewer.

5 For a further discussion of these criticisms of the theory, see the interchange between Rottenberg (1956) and Lampman (1956).

6 Killingsworth and Heckman (1986) point out that these trends pose an interesting question. Has the secular decline in female weekly working hours been sufficiently great to offset the secular increase in female labour force participation and reduce the total number of market hours worked by women? In fact, it appears that, even with the hours reduction, female labour inputs have increased in net terms.

7 The average participation rate of married women conceals three major work patterns during the child-bearing years. Some women do not return to work until the completion of family formation; some work at least part of the time between the first and last birth; others never return. In both Britain and the US, there is a marked trend to an earlier return to work and this has contributed to increased female labour force participation of married women. This tendency is itself related to earnings potential. For a fuller discussion, see Dex and Shaw (1986).

8 It might be expected that the secular increase in female participation would lead to an increase in the average years of work experience of women in employment. Goldin (1989) finds, however, that, in the US, average experience increased from 9.1 to only 10.5 years over the 1930–50 period as increased participation brought in women with little prior work experience.

9 In fact, as Beenstock (1987) points out, there is an inevitable trade-off between financial security (or lifetime earnings capacity and pension income) and the amount of time enjoyed in retirement.

10 In 1988, mandatory retirement was abolished completely. In the UK, the Employment Equality (Age) Regulations 2006 set a default retirement age of 65. This means that employers can retire employees or set retirement ages in their organisation at or above 65. Retirements below the default retirement age need to satisfy the test of objective justification. Fixed retirement ages are not necessary and employees have the right to request to continue working beyond their retirement age, while employers have a duty to give consideration to such requests. Recently, the UK government has announced future increases in the age at which individuals will qualify for state pensions.

11 Parsons (1981) notes that, in the US, the secular decline in participation of middle-aged men has been much more pronounced among blacks than among whites. Thus, between 1948 and 1976, for those aged between 55 and 64, the participation rate of the former fell by 23 percentage points, compared to 14 per cent for the latter. He suggests that a plausible explanation for this phenomenon is found in the increased availability and generosity of transfer payments. These will be particularly attractive to those in less skilled occupations, where blacks are disproportionately represented.

12 Honig (1985) finds that partial retirement is also important for women and, as for men, seems to be related to structural shifts in the labour supply function. Unlike the case of men, however, partial retirement does not involve reductions in earnings and weeks of work, merely in hours.

13 Filer and Petri (1988) note that, to the extent that jobs involve different working conditions and worker productivities and tolerances alter evenly with age, the expected retirement age will differ from job to job. Their regression results

indicate that more onerous jobs for older workers tend to be associated with earlier retirement and to provide pension plans with greater than normal early benefits. Thus, the causal relationship between pensions and retirement age may be the opposite of the one normally postulated.

References

Atkinson A.B., Maynard A.K. and Trinder C.G., *Parents and Children: Incomes in Two Generations*, Heinemann, London, 1983.

Balleer A., Gomez-Salvador R. and Turunen J., "Labour Force Participation in the Euro Area: A Cohort Based Analysis", European Central Bank Working Paper Series No. 1049, May 2009.

Beenstock M. and Associates, *Work, Welfare and Taxation: A Study of Labour Supply Incentives in the UK*, Allen and Unwin, London, 1987.

Berg S.V. and Dalton T.R., "United Kingdom Labour Force Activity Rates; Employment and Real Wages", *Applied Economics*, 9, 1977, pp. 265–70.

Bicakova A., "Unemployment versus Inactivity: An Analysis of the Earnings and Labor Force Status of Prime Age Men in France, the UK, and the US at the Turn of the Century", Department of Economics, Johns Hopkins University, Baltimore, US, 11 March 2005.

Blanchflower D.G., "Self Employment in OECD Countries", *Labour Economics*, 7(5), September 2000, pp. 471–505.

Blanchflower D.G. and Oswald A.J., "What Makes an Entrepreneur?", *Journal of Labor Economics*, 16(1), January 1998, pp. 26–60.

Blanchflower D.G. and Oswald A.J., "Self Employment in the Enterprise Culture", in Jowell R. and Witherspoon S., editors, *British Social Attitudes: The 1990 Report*, Gower Press, Aldershot, UK, 1990.

Blöndal S., Field S. and Girouard N., "Investment in Human Capital through Post-compulsory Education and Training: Selected Efficiency and Equity Aspects", OECD Economics Department Working Paper No. 333, July 2002.

Bowen W.G. and Finegan T.A., *The Economics of Labor Force Participation*, Princeton University Press, New Jersey, 1969.

Burkhauser R., "The Pension Acceptance Decision of Older Workers", *Journal of Human Resources*, 14, 1979, pp. 63–75.

Cain G.G. and Dooley M.D., "Estimation of a Model of Labour Supply, Fertility and Wages of Married Women", *Journal of Political Economy*, 84, August 1976, pp. S-179–99.

Clark K. and Drinkwater S., "Pushed Out or Pulled In? Self Employment among Ethnic Minorities in England and Wales", *Labour Economics*, 7(5), September 2000, pp. 603–28.

Clark K.B. and Summers L.H., "Demographic Influences in Cyclical Employment Variation", *Journal of Human Resources*, 16, 1981, pp. 61–79.

Clark K.B. and Summers L.H., "Labour Force Participation: Timing and Persistence", *Review of Economic Studies*, 49, Supplement, 1982, pp. 825–44.

Connelly S. and Gregory M., "Moving Down: Part-time Work and Occupational Change in Britain", *Economic Journal*, 118(526), February 2008, pp. F52–F76.

Dex S. and Shaw L.B., *British and American Women at Work*, Macmillan Press, Basingstoke, Hants, 1986.

Ekelund J., Johannson F., Jarvelin M.R. and Lichtermann D., "Self Employment and Risk Aversion: Evidence from Psychological Test Data", *Labour Economics*, 12(5), October 2005, pp. 649–59.

European Commission, *Europe's Demographic Future*, Luxembourg, 2007.

Fields J., "A Comparison of Inter-city Differences in the Labor Force Participation Rates of Married Women in 1970 with 1940, 1950, and 1960", *Journal of Human Resources*, 11, Fall, 1976, pp. 568–77.

Filer R.K. and Petri P.A., "A Job Characteristics Theory of Retirement", *The Review of Economics and Statistics*, LXX(1), February 1988.

Freeman R.B., *The Market for College Trained Manpower: A Study in the Economics of Career Choice*, Harvard University Press, Cambridge, Mass., 1971.

Goldin C., "Life Cycle Labor-Force Participation of Married Women: Historical Evidence and Implications", *Journal of Labor Economics*, 7(1), January 1989, pp. 20–47.

Gordon R. and Blinder A., "Market Wages, Reservation Wages and Retirement Decisions", *Journal of Public Economics*, 14, 1980, pp. 277–308.

Greenhalgh C., "A Labour Supply Function for Married Women in Great Britain", *Economica*, 44(175), August 1977, pp. 249–65.

Greenhalgh C., "Male Labour Force Participation in Great Britain", *Scottish Journal of Political Economy*, 26(3), 1979, pp. 275–86.

Honig M., "Partial Retirement Among Women", *Journal of Human Resources*, XX(4), Fall, 1985, pp. 613–21.

Honig M. and Hanoch G., "Partial Retirement as a Separate Mode of Retirement Behaviour", *Journal of Human Resources*, XX(1), Winter, 1985, pp. 21–46.

Jaumotte F., "Female Labour Force Participation: Past Trends and Main Determinants in OECD Countries", OECD Economic Department Working Paper No. 376, 2003.

Killingsworth M.R. and Heckman J.J., "Female Labor Supply: A Survey", in Ashenfelter O. and Layard R., editors, *Handbook of Labor Economics*, 1, 1986, North Holland Amsterdam, pp. 103–204.

Lampman R., "On Choice in Labor Markets: A Comment", *Industrial and Labor Relations Review*, 9(4), July 1956, pp. 629–36.

Layard R., Barton M. and Zabalza A., "Married Women's Participation and Hours", *Economica*, 47(185), 1980, pp. 51–72.

Lazear E.P., "Why is there Mandatory Retirement?", *Journal of Political Economy*, 87, 1979, pp. 1261–84.

Lazear E.P., "Retirement from the Labor Force", in Ashenfelter O. and Layar R., editors, *Handbook of Labor Economics*, 1, North Holland, Amsterdam, 1986, pp. 305–55.

Lightman E.S. and O'Cleireacain C.C., "Activity Rates of Married Women in England and Wales – 1971", *Applied Economics*, 10, 1978, pp. 271–7.

McNabb R., "The Labour Force Participation of Married Women", *Manchester School*, 45(3), September 1977, pp. 221–35.

Micklewright J., "Choice at Sixteen", *Economica*, 56(221), February 1989, pp. 25–39.

Micklewright J., Pearson M. and Smith S., "Unemployment and Early School Leaving", *Institute for Fiscal Studies*, Working Paper No. 9, 1988.

Mincer J., "Labor Force Participation of Married Women", in Lewis G., editor, *Aspects of Labor Economics*, NBER, Princeton, 1962, pp. 63–97.

Mitchell O.S. and Fields G.S., "The Effects of Pensions and Earnings on Retirement: A Review Essay", in Ehrenberg R.G., editor, *Research in Labor Economics*, 5, JAI Press Inc, Greenwich, Connecticut, 1982, pp. 115–55.

Nickell S., "The Determinants of Occupational Success in Britain", *Review of Economic Studies*, XLIX, 1982, pp. 43–53.

O'Leary N.C. and Sloane P.J., "The Return to a University Education in Great Britain", *National Institute Economic Review*, 193(1), July 2005, pp. 75–89.

O'Neill J.A., "A Time-Series Analysis of Women's Labor Force Participation", *AEA Papers and Proceedings*, 71(2), May 1981, pp. 76–80.

Owen S.J. and Joshi H.E., "Does Elastic Retract?: The Effects of Recession on Women's Labour Force Participation", *British Journal of Industrial Relations*, XXV(1), March 1987, pp. 125–84.

Parnes H.S. and Nestel G., "The Retirement Experience", in Parnes H.S., editor, *Work and Retirement: A Longitudinal Study of Men*, MIT Press, Cambridge, Mass., 1981, pp. 155–97.

Parsons D.O., "Black White Differences in the Labour Force Participation of Older Males", in Parnes H.S., editor, *Work and Retirement: A Longitudinal Study of Men*, MIT Press, Cambridge, Mass., 1981, pp. 132–54.

Paull G., "Children and Women's Hours of Work", *Economic Journal*, 118(526), February 2008, pp. F8–F27.

Pencavel J., "Labor Supply of Men: A Survey", in Ashenfelter O. and Layard R., editors, *Handbook of Labor Economics*, 1, North Holland, Amsterdam, 1986, pp. 3–102.

Pissarides C.A., "Staying on at School in England and Wales", *Economica*, 48, 1981, pp. 345–63.

Pissarides C.A., "From School to University: The Demand for Compulsory Education in Britain", *The Economic Journal*, 92, September 1982, pp. 654–67.

Psacharopoulos G., "Returns to Education: A Further International Update and Implications", *Journal of Human Resources*, XX(4), 1985, pp. 583–604.

Quinn J.F., "Micro-economic Determinants of Early Retirement – A Cross-Sectoral View of White Married Men", *Journal of Human Resources*, 12, 1977, pp. 329–41.

Reilly J. and Bothfeld S., "What Happens after Working Part-time? Integration, Maintenance or Exclusionary Transition in Britain and West Germany", *Cambridge Journal of Economics*, 26(4), July 2002, pp. 409–39.

Robertson D. and Symons J., "The Occupational Choice of British Children", *Centre for Labour Economics*, LSE, Discussion Paper 325, September 1988.

Rottenberg S., "On Choice in Labor Markets", *Industrial and Labor Relations Review*, 9(2), January 1956, pp. 183–99.

Siebert W.S., "Inequality of Opportunity: An Analysis based on the Micro-economics of the Family", in Drago R. and Perlman R., editors, *Micro-economic Issues in Labour Economics: New Approaches*, Harvester-Wheatsheaf, Herts, 1989, pp. 177–97.

Sloane P.J., Grazier S. and Jones R.J., "Preferences, Gender Segregation and Affirmative Action", IZA Discussion Paper 1881, December 2005.

Warburton P., "Labour Supply Incentives for the Retired", in Beenstock M. and Associates, *Work, Welfare and Taxation: A Study of Labour Supply Incentives in the UK*, Allen and Unwin, London, 1987, pp. 185–234.

Weir G., "Economic Inactivity in Selected Countries", *Labour Market Trends*, June 2003, pp. 299–309.

Whitfield K. and Wilson R.A., "Staying on in Full-time Education: A Time Series Analysis", *University of Warwick Institute for Employment Research*, October 1988.

Willis R.J. and Rosen S., "Education and Self Selection", *Journal of Political Economy*, 87(5), part 2, October 1979, pp. S7–S36.

Zabalza A., Pissarides C. and Barton M., "Social Security and the Choice between Full-time Work, Part-time Work and Retirement", *Journal of Public Economics*, 14, 1980, pp. 245–76.

Further reading

Ashenfelter O. and Layard R., editors, *Handbook of Labor Economics*, volume I, North Holland, 1986, has a section on labour supply, which includes chapters by J. Pencavel on the labour supply of men, M.R. Killingsworth and J.J. Heckman on female labour supply, M. Montgomery and J. Trussell on marital status and child rearing and E.P. Lazear on retirement.

The Economic Journal, volume 118 (526), 2008, contains a feature on women's part-time work, which includes articles on the gender pay gap, the growing polarisation of part-time jobs in low-wage occupations, the downgrading experienced by women returning to the labour market and the effect of children on women's hours of work.

The European Commission publishes each year *Employment in Europe*, which contains detailed information on European labour markets, as well as special features on specific aspects. Thus, the 2007 edition contains a chapter on active ageing and labour market trends for older workers, including the demographic context, recent employment trends, factors affecting older workers' labour market experience and policy issues arising.

Chapter 2

The labour supply curve

Learning outcomes

At the end of this chapter, readers should have an understanding of:

- The multi-dimensional nature of labour supply;
- The distinction between income and substitution effects and how a backward-sloping labour supply curve is possible;
- How family income, taxes and overtime result in non-linearities in the labour supply function;
- The effect of the standard work-week on supply choices of individual workers;
- Why employers might prefer to have lower standard wage rates and higher overtime wage premium payments;
- What determines the incidence of part-time work, overtime working, absence rates and double-jobbing.

Introduction

We have already examined the decision whether or not to be a member of the labour force in Chapter 1, which focused on labour force participation, while the investment decision over whether to increase the qualifications and skills possessed by the individual is considered in Chapter 3. In this chapter, we focus more on the supply of hours and the constraints facing workers in optimising their combination of earnings and hours in particular jobs.

Labour supply is complicated by the fact that it is multi-dimensional. Effective supply may be varied by changes in the number of workers, changes in the number of hours worked by a given labour force, and changes in the intensity of work, which may be influenced, among other things, by the input of effort from the worker. Thus, not only are workers themselves heterogeneous, but also units of labour input offered by the same workers may vary over time as the nature of work or incentives alter, or through physiological factors such as settling in or fatigue.

The theory of labour force participation has dealt with the binary choice of whether to work in the labour market or not, so that here we are predominantly concerned with the intensity with which workers offer their services in terms of duration, the level of commitment being the concern of Chapter 10.

The standard model of labour supply assumes that the individual is faced with a choice between leisure and goods, with income and substitution effects pulling in opposite directions, so that, as the wage increases, we would expect work to be substituted for leisure, but the extra income may enable the individual to consume more leisure, resulting in a **backward-bending supply of labour curve**. When due allowance is made for other family income, progressive income taxes and overtime premium payments for work beyond the hours agreed for a standard work-week, non-linearities may occur in the budget constraint.

The level of sophistication in estimating labour supply functions has increased over time. "First-generation" studies in the 1960s and 1970s were based on a simple methodology, which neglected some important measurement issues, sample selection and questions of functional form. "Second-generation" studies attempted to deal with some of these issues and incorporate taxes and other factors. A third group of dynamic models focused on life-cycle effects. Finally, there has been a focus on collective behaviour in the household, which allows for specific preferences among the different members.

We then move on to consider the effects of hours constraints resulting from the use of standard work-weeks. This allows a distinction to be made between income and leisure preferences with preferences for overtime or moonlighting and part-time work or absenteeism respectively. Some workers may be described as under-employed and others as over-employed given their tastes for work and the opportunity set facing them.

2.1 The supply of hours

Backward-bending supply of labour curve

A situation in which a worker reacts to an increase in real wages by reducing his or her hours of work in order to consume more leisure.

Neo-classical model of labour supply

This is based on the proposition that individuals maximise their utility in making choices between income and leisure.

The standard **neo-classical model of labour supply** (or what Killingsworth, 1983, refers to as first-generation models) assumes that the individual is faced with a simple choice between leisure and goods:

$$U = U(G, L) \tag{2.1}$$

Income consists of income from work and other family income Y_F. Hence, the budget constraint may be written as:

$$P_G G = WH + Y_F \tag{2.2}$$

where
P_G = average product price
G = amount of goods consumed
W = the wage rate
H = the input of hours of work.

Hours of work are limited by a time constraint T. Hence,

$$T = H + L \tag{2.3}$$

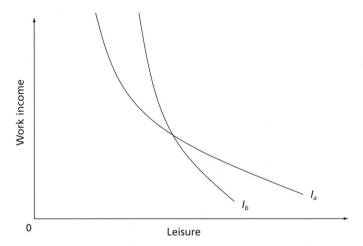

Figure 2.1 The individual's indifference map.

If leisure is a normal good, the **income and substitution effects** on leisure will pull in opposite directions with the possibility of a backward-bending labour supply curve. This will be determined by the shape of the individual's indifference map. Thus, where family size is large, the marginal utility of income is likely to be high and the trade-off between income and leisure relatively flat as I_a in Figure 2.1, whereas, where a high premium is put on leisure (e.g. by older workers), the trade-off will be steeper (I_b).[1]

The **budget constraint** is determined by the exogenously given wage and other family income (Y_F). Let us assume initially that other family income is zero and that successively higher wage rates are offered to the individual. We can then trace out the equilibrium choice of hours for the individual at the point of tangency between the wage line and the indifference curve of the individual. How will a worker react to an increase in wages? An employer may hope that such an increase will result in a rise in the labour input. However, this will depend on the relative size of income and substitution effects. We illustrate this graphically in Figures 2.2 and 2.3. The effect of a wage increase is to increase the opportunity cost of not working, so that leisure is now relatively more expensive. We might expect hours of work to increase (enabling more goods to be consumed) and leisure time consequently to decrease. The substitution effect, shown as a movement along a given indifference curve, makes this explicit. Any movement of the budget constraint to the right, will allow both income and leisure to increase. At the same time, the increase in real income would be expected to increase the demand for both goods and leisure, if the latter is a normal good. This income effect is shown as a rightward shift in the budget line, enabling both income and leisure to increase.

Thus, in Figure 2.2, assume the wage rises, so that the budget line swivels out from H_0W_1 to H_0W_2. The original number of hours worked will be determined by the point at which the indifference curve is tangential to the budget line at A, with H_0H hours being worked. With the increase in wages, a new equilibrium is attained at C, where indifference curve I_2 is tangential to the new budget line H_0W_2. We can now isolate the income and substitution effects, following Hicks (1932), by shifting the budget line leftwards parallel to H_0W_2, so that the individual is just able to

Income and substitution effects

The income effect measures the change in spending power resulting from a change in the real wage with all product prices remaining constant, while the substitution effect measures the extent to which work is substituted for leisure or vice versa with a change in the real wage.

Budget constraint

A downward-sloping straight line indicating, in the case used here, the maximum amount of income or leisure that can be obtained if all inputs are devoted to one or the other, and combinations of each in intermediate cases.

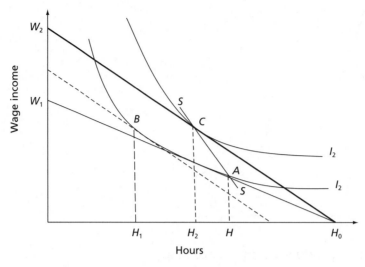

Figure 2.2 Income and substitution effects.

achieve the same level of satisfaction as before at B.[2] The movement along I_1 from A to B is the substitution effect, which results in an increase in hours of HH_1. The income effect is equal to BC, representing an increase in hours from H_1 to H_2. In this example, the size of the substitution effect is greater than the size of the income effect, so that both hours of work and wage income increase. SS is the supply curve of labour and is upward sloping when we measure hours of work from left to right (rather than from right to left as in Figure 2.2).

Another possibility, depending on the shape of the indifference curves, is that the size of the income effect outweighs that of the substitution effect as in Figure 2.3. In this case, we move from A to C when real income rises. The size of the substitution effect AB is less than that of the income effect BC, so that hours of work

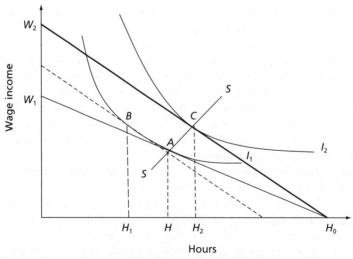

Figure 2.3 Backward-bending labour supply curve.

are reduced from H to H_2 and SS represents a backward-bending supply of labour curve. That is, if an employer were to increase the wage in the hope of achieving a greater labour input, he would be frustrated.

Figure 2.4 illustrates the concept of the backward-bending labour supply curve over the long run. In this figure, OW_1, OW_2, OW_3 and so on represent increasing levels of total wage income over a given period, say a week. Since hours of work are measured from right to left on the horizontal axis, each budget line represents a particular wage rate. At the wage rate given by AW_1, we have a corner solution as indifference curve I is tangential to AW_1 at A, and so no work will be undertaken. At the wage rate given by AW_2, AH_1 hours of work are performed. A further increase in wages has little influence on hours offered as BC is nearly vertical. As wages rise to a level given by AW_4, hours increase from AH_1 to AH_2, but a further increase in wages to a level given by AW_5 leads to a reduction in hours (DE) with AH hours worked. Here the negative income effect more than offsets the compensated positive substitution effect. The labour supply curve S_L, as in the figure, may well have positive and negative slopes at different levels of real income. See, for example, Dessing (2002), who refers to this possibility in relation to developing economies, and Barzel and McDonald (1973), who suggest that backward-bending supply curves are accepted as common by most economists.

In reality, the trade-off between income and hours worked is more complex than suggested by the Figure 2.4.[3] One example is the fact that sleep is treated as a fixed number of hours, while, in practice, it may be influenced by economic variables as in Case Study 2.1.

We must allow for the presence not only of other family income, but also of progressive income taxation and overtime premium payments. This may give rise to **non-linearities** in the budget constraint. There may be restrictions on hours that make such points of tangency between wage rates and indifference curves unattainable. This is likely where individual worker tastes for hours are heterogeneous and a standard work-week is agreed between employers and trade unions.[4] In Figure

Non-linearities

There may be kinks in the budget constraint as a result of the presence of income tax and other family income, which change the slope of the budget line and rule out the assumption of linearity.

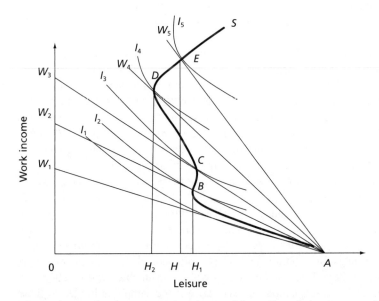

Figure 2.4 The long-run backward-bending labour supply curve.

Sleep and the supply of labour

People spend more time sleeping than they do at work or any other single activity, yet economists have neglected the possibility that time spent sleeping may be a choice variable. In fact, most studies of labour supply assume that a representative consumer has a fixed amount of time to allocate between work and leisure and ignore the possibility that time allocated to sleeping may be responsive to economic incentives.

Biddle and Hamermesh (1990) make use of data on time diaries in 12 countries obtained by Szalai (1972), which show a wide variation in the time devoted to sleep by particular individuals. Further, each hour of additional work reduces sleep by 13 minutes and results in a 47-minute decline in non-market time awake. The sleep/market-work elasticity is –0.14 and the non-market time awake/market-work elasticity is –0.36. There is also medical evidence that more time spent sleeping can improve productivity at work. In this case, in equilibrium the ratio of the marginal utilities of consumption of goods and sleep must equal the ratio of their respective prices. The price of a consumption good will reflect the cost of the goods required to produce it and the price of the time needed for production. The price of a unit of sleep is the wage rate minus any addition to labour income resulting from the positive effect of sleep on productivity. The impact of sleep on the wage rate makes the wage endogenous in the labour supply function.

Biddle J.E. and Hamermesh D.S., "Sleep and the Allocation of Time", *Journal of Political Economy*, 98(5), 1990, pp. 922–43.
Szalai A., editor, *The Use of Time: Daily Activities of Urban and Suburban Population in Twelve Countries*, Mouton, The Hague, 1972.

2.5, we assume AY measures other family income, WY gives the standard wage rate and AH_0 represents the standard work-week. The presence of other family income will influence the amount an individual is able to consume and, consequently, the choice of working hours, but is not itself influenced by hours of work. It is positive at zero hours of work. Now let AT represent the tax threshold, that is the level of income at which the worker begins to pay income tax, and assume other family income rises to AB. The effect of the tax will be to reduce the slope of the net wage from the point at which it bites, from, say, BC to CD. At H_0 hours, the worker becomes eligible for overtime premium payments, which are also subject to tax, but still increase the slope of the budget line to DE. The worker optimises at AH^* hours, working H_0H^* hours of overtime. Thus, the budget constraint is given by $BCDE$.

There have been numerous attempts to estimate labour supply functions, but early or "first-generation" studies in the 1960s and early 1970s, as outlined above, used a relatively simple methodology, which gave rise to problems of measurement, sample selection and functional form (Killingsworth 1983 and Heckman 1993). Problems of measurement arise because of the general use of average earnings rather than marginal wage rates. The two may differ appreciably where there are warm-up or fatigue effects, so that earnings for an additional hour of work depend on the number of hours already worked. Ordinary least squares (OLS) will be unsuitable for estimation purposes in this case. Sample selection bias will arise if the sample is limited to those with positive hours of work. Because of the absence of negative values, the estimated

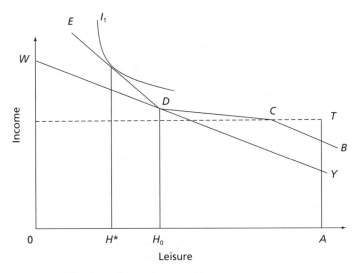

Figure 2.5 Non-linearities in the budget constraint.

regression line will lie above the true line and have a flatter slope, providing biased and inconsistent estimates. For these reasons, estimates from first-generation studies should be treated with a fair degree of caution. If we take them at their face value, the US estimates seem to suggest that male labour supply is much more sensitive to wage changes than is that of females. The former appears to be generally backward sloping, while the female schedule is strongly positively sloped. For Britain, Brown (1981) suggests an elasticity of –0.1 in line with US studies.

Second-generation studies are generally based on explicitly specified utility functions subject to explicitly specified budget constraints, which deal with sample selection bias and incorporate taxes and other factors. According to Killingsworth, the results in general tend to confirm the belief that male labour supply is considerably less sensitive to wage rates and property income than is female labour supply. They imply a **gross wage elasticity** for men ranging between –0.20 and +0.14, while the corresponding figure for women generally ranges from 0.60 upwards. There is also a suggestion from **labour segmentation theory** that there will be different supply responses in relation to wage changes in the primary and secondary segments of the labour market (Baffoe-Bonnie 1989).

Dynamic labour supply models incorporating life-cycle effects constitute a third group. These take account of the fact that individuals will take into consideration life-cycle effects in determining labour supply decisions. Weiss (1972) suggests that the behaviour of labour supply over time is influenced by three forces – an efficiency factor inducing individuals to work more in periods when real wages are higher; an interest rate factor inducing individuals to work more early in their working lives and less later on, since earnings can be invested at compound interest; and a time preference factor which induces workers to offer less work early and more work later on in their working lives because of a preference for consuming leisure now rather than in the future. These models usually assume the intertemporal separability utility function – that is, that marginal utility of consumption and leisure at a particular point in time is independent of the amounts consumed at all other times – and an interior solution – that is, that labour supply is positive at

Gross wage elasticity

A measure of the response of labour supply to a change in the wage rate (i.e. $[dH/dw]/[w/H]$, where w equals the wage and H equals hours of work).

Labour segmentation theory

This is based on the concept of non-competing groups or institutional constraints in the labour market that reduce the ability of workers to move between different segments of the market.

all ages. These do not alter the general finding that wage rates do influence labour supply, but more so for women than for men, and reinforce the importance of unobservables such as tastes and non-pecuniary aspects of work.

More recently, the unitary approach to decision-making in the household has been criticised on the grounds that a household consisting of several adults will not necessarily behave in the same way as a single rational maximising agent. Chiappori (1988 and 1992) developed models based on collective behaviour, but allowing for specific preferences and decisions on the part of individuals. Thus, the assumption of income pooling under which the source of the income is irrelevant to household behaviour is rejected. Compensated substitution effects between male and female leisure are found to be asymmetric and there may well be much inequality as a consequence. Blundell *et al.* (2007) consider four regimes under which one or the other partner works, both work or neither works. One finding is that, when male earnings increase, but the husband is not at work, there is a tendency for the wife to increase her working time, which is suggestive of an increase of resources in favour of the husband. Bargaining power is strongly influenced by wages, such that the husband retains a larger share of his wage when he is working for consumption purposes, and a lower proportion of unearned income and when he does not work at all.[5]

2.2 The effects of hours constraints

The above indicates that individual tastes for various combinations of work and leisure are likely to differ according to particular preferences, size of income, family circumstances and other factors. However, efficiency may well imply the grouping of workers into particular units of working time, such that marginal adjustments between work and leisure are not possible for many individuals. There are, however, some exceptions to this – see Case Study 2.2. An employer may specify uniform hours for all employees instead of offering a choice for two reasons. First, to the extent that workers are complementary to each other, non-uniformity of hours will lower productivity. Second, the costs of measuring contributions to output and relating this to pay may be substantially greater than the cost for uniform hours. Notwithstanding this, collective bargaining removes the freedom of the individual worker to select his or her own hours by the imposition of a common rule. The collective agreement is not a contract concerning an hour's pay for an hour's work, but a daily, weekly or monthly payment for the corresponding amount of work, according to the minimum length of notice specified in the contract of employment.

The existence of the standard work-week gives a meaning to the concept of part-time work and overtime by imposing a restriction on the minimum number of hours an employee may customarily offer and a premium rate on any offer to hours above the standard by the employer. Moses (1962) classified workers into two categories – income preferrers and leisure preferrers – and defined them in terms of a labour offer curve, which traced out a series of equilibrium points in relation to wage rates and hours. A leisure preferrer is an individual whose wage offer curve turns back before reaching the standard number of hours and is given by *OC* in Figure 2.6. This indicates that he or she would be better off with part-time work. If this is not possible and alternative work is not available, the result is likely to be increased

Case Study 2.2

The labour supply of taxi-drivers

The standard labour supply models implicitly assume that employers are free to set their own hours in response to changes in wages or at least are able to find a job that has an optimal wage/hours combination from their own perspective. However, as we have seen already in this chapter, such an assumption is often at variance with the facts. Thus, labour economists have sought to investigate situations in which workers have some control over the hours that they work. One example is the case of taxi-drivers (or cab-drivers as they are referred to in the US). In New York, for example, it is common for drivers to lease their cabs for pre-specified periods for a fixed fee with responsibility for fuel and some maintenance remaining with them. They retain 100 per cent of the fare income after meeting their fixed costs. They are free to choose how many hours they work each day.

One study by Camerer *et al.* (1997) found a substantial *negative* elasticity of labour supply, which they attributed to drivers having a target income and which was at variance with the standard neo-classical labour supply model. Another US economist, Farber (2005), was puzzled by this result, which implied that drivers would quit early when it was easier to make money and work longer hours when it was harder to do so. After talking to a number of cab-drivers about their behaviour and finding that the hourly wage fluctuated substantially over the day, implying that the instrumental variable approach adopted by Camerer *et al.* may be biased, Farber estimated a model of the decision to stop work or continue driving at the conclusion of each fare. Using new data, his results showed that the primary determinant of the decision to stop work was the cumulative hours already worked on each day and there were no substantial income effects. Thus, the labour supply behaviour of the cab-drivers was consistent with the standard neo-classical model.

Camerer C., Babcock L., Lowenstein G. and Thaler R., "Labour Supply of New York City Cab Drivers: One Day at a Time", *Quarterly Journal of Economics*, 112, 1997, pp. 407–41.
Farber H., "Is Tomorrow Another Day? The Labor Supply of New York Cab Drivers", *Journal of Political Economy*, 113(1), 2005, pp. 46–82.

absenteeism. At the wage rate OW_1 the individual cannot be in equilibrium at the standard hours S and will operate on a lower indifference curve I_0 compared with the preferred level of hours, H. An improvement in welfare can only come about through some combination of an increase in wage rates and reduction in standard hours, but the former cannot result in the attainment of equilibrium.

There is, however, one means of ensuring that there are at least some satisfied leisure preferrers. For there must be some overtime rate (AB) in Figure 2.6, which will make the individual as well-off as the preferred position without overtime (e.g. at OH hours) by restoring him or her to indifference curve I_1 operative at the lower level of hours.

An income preferrer can be defined as an individual whose wage-offer curve cuts the vertical standard hours line. In Figure 2.7 with wages given by OW_1 the individual cannot be in equilibrium at S hours and can only be made better off by some combination of increase in the wage rate or increase in standard hours. As in the case of disappointed leisure preferrers, thwarted income preferrers may demand

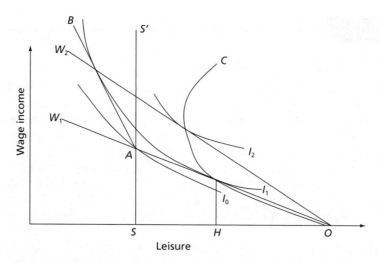

Figure 2.6 Standard hours, overtime and leisure preferrers.

wage increases to offset the fact that they are unable to obtain as much income as they would like. However, any demand for an increase in the number of standard hours is likely to be resisted by leisure preferrers and possibly by income preferrers working at overtime rates. Again, the appropriate overtime rate (AB) will convert a disappointed income preferrer into a satisfied one. In fact, it must make the individual better off than at standard hours.

If income preferrers cannot obtain work at overtime rates, they may seek additional employment elsewhere (i.e. double-jobbing or moonlighting may result). Further, an income preferrer may be prepared to accept secondary employment at a wage lower than that obtained in his or her primary job. If, on the other hand, wages are higher in the secondary job, why would a worker not transfer permanently to that job? Various factors may prevent this, such as differential non-pecuniary advantages between jobs, lack of stability of employment in the secondary job, fringe benefits, accumulated seniority and the possibility of tax evasion if two jobs

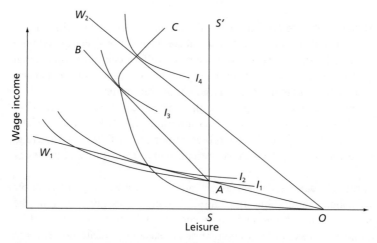

Figure 2.7 Standard hours, overtime and income preferrers.

are currently held. Moonlighting will be particularly feasible where shift systems in the primary job release workers at hours that coincide with labour peak demands in other sectors, or where non-work hours are less convenient for preferred leisure pursuits. Both the four-day week and, perhaps to a lesser extent, flexible working hours, which have become more common, will increase the possibilities of double-jobbing, as will reductions in the standard work-week.

One corollary of this analysis is that high rates of overtime do not necessarily indicate a low preference for leisure, and that most groups of workers can benefit in some way from the provision of overtime opportunities (providing the premium rate is sufficiently attractive). One puzzle, however, is why the employer should choose to pay or the employee prefer an overtime premium rate for additional hours as opposed to a straight increase in the hourly wage rate for all hours worked. As indicated in Figure 2.8, a uniform rate seems preferable to the employee as it brings him or her on to a higher indifference curve. However, he or she will work fewer hours than in the case of premium rate (since, in the latter case, the income effect is likely to be dominated by the substitution effect) and may conceivably work fewer hours than previously. In the figure, this is, indeed, the case. With the premium rate AB, the employer will offer OH hours but, with the uniform rate OW_2, he will only wish to offer OH_1 hours, which is fewer than standard hours.

Using a static model, it can be demonstrated that a straight wage as opposed to a lower basic wage plus a higher overtime premium designed to provide the worker with a given amount of utility will minimise the wage bill of the employer. Thus, overtime would appear to be inefficient for this reason. However, from the employer's point of view, another reason for preferring the premium rate is that this gives greater flexibility to the wage bill. With a uniform rate, the wage bill will be higher whenever standard hours are worked, while, from the employee's point of view, a premium rate may be seen as more equitable as recompense for inconvenient hours and cumulative fatigue.

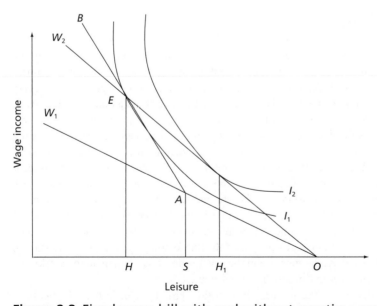

Figure 2.8 Fixed wage bill with and without overtime premia.

One attempt to test the proposition that the labour market consists in part of under- and over-employed workers because of hours constraints was made by Altonji and Paxson (1988).[6] They start from the proposition that the partial effect of a positive change in hours on the wage increment necessary to induce a quit will be larger for those workers who are currently over-employed in their initial job and smaller for those who are under-employed in their initial job. Using a sample of male heads of household from the US Panel Study of Income Dynamics covering the period 1968–83, they focus on the real wages and hours of those who quit their jobs over this period. This particular survey has the advantage of containing questions on the respondent's level of satisfaction with the duration of working hours (i.e. whether they would prefer to work fewer or more hours than they currently do if they were free to do so). The results of the OLS regressions are consistent with the notion that job changes are motivated by the desire to change hours in so far as under-employed quitters experienced greater changes in hours than those initially expressing satisfaction with their working hours. Further, individuals with perceived initial hours constraints experience greater wage changes than individuals initially satisfied with their hours. Thus, the results are consistent with the theory that workers trade off wage gains against desirable working hours when changing jobs. An extension of this approach is a study by Bender and Skatun (2009), who use data from the US National Longitudinal Survey of Youth on desired wages, hours and occupations to estimate an unconstrained labour supply curve. This is the basis for an estimate of the implied deadweight loss arising from hours constraints. This turns out on average to be up to 6 per cent, though losses are higher for some workers.

2.3 Patterns of hours, part-time work, overtime, absence and double-jobbing

2.3.1 Part-time work

As we have seen in Chapter 1, the growth of part-time employment has been without doubt one of the most significant events in the labour market in recent years, an increase in its proportion of total employment occurring in most European countries from the early 1970s. Indeed, in the UK, the proportion is now higher than in every industrialised country (other than Denmark) representing about a quarter of the workforce. Yet, in 1961, only 10 per cent of workers were part-time. In the UK, part-time employment is defined as voluntary work of 30 hours or less per week excluding meal-breaks and overtime, whereas, in the US, the definition is work for less than 35 hours, which makes true comparisons difficult. In the US, only the percentage of teenagers who work part-time, according to this definition, has increased since 1980, though the increase was more general before that date. Another important difference between European and US experience is that in the former the growth in part-time employment occurred at a time when full-time employment tended to decline, whereas in the latter both part-time and full-time employment showed substantial increases. Consequently, the increase in the proportion of part-timers in the workforce has been much stronger in Europe than it has in the US.

As already discussed, the increase in part-time employment in the UK has been marked among married women with children, who comprise the bulk of the part-time labour force. It also appears that part-time jobs are highly concentrated within a few low-status, low-paid occupational categories (Elias and Main 1982). Using data from the 1975/6 National Training Survey, Stewart and Greenhalgh (1984) were able to demonstrate further that, for women in the 45–54 age group, the proportion in non-manual occupations was 25 per cent for those with an uninterrupted work history and only 13 per cent for those with two or more breaks. Conversely, there were only 11 per cent of women with continuous work histories in personal service occupation compared to 29 per cent for women with two or more breaks in service. Continuous workers are of two main types – childless women and women who work continuously over the phase of family formation – and each of these groups are disproportionately located in full-time jobs (Dex 1984). The large majority of women, however, return to work after one or more breaks in employment, and here again there appears to be a difference between UK and US experience. Although, in both cases, the period spent out of work is diminishing, the duration of this non-work period is much greater for British than for American women. Dex and Shaw (1986) attribute part of the explanation for this to the tax concessions available in the US for expenditure on childcare. Using longitudinal data from the 1980 Women and Employment Survey, Joshi (1984) and Dex (1984) are able to show that a common pattern for women is an interruption of work associated with childbearing, a return to part-time work and subsequently to full-time work. Compared to uninterrupted careers, there is a loss of pay and occupational status at least while the children are young.[7] Additionally, Elias (1988) has shown that there is only a limited amount of occupational recovery following a period of downward mobility. It appears from Perry's (1988a) regression analysis based on the Women and Employment Survey that part-time employment following re-entry into the labour market is the single most important factor in explaining downward occupational mobility for women. Further, in line with human capital theory, more-qualified women are less likely to experience downward occupational mobility, as are those with more labour market experience, while delayed re-entry increases its likelihood. Again contrasting with British experience, Blank (1989), using the Panel Study of Income Dynamics 1976–84, shows that, for US women, part-time work is not frequently used as a transition between non-work and full-time work.

Implicit in much of the above analysis is the notion that part-time work is undervalued relative to full-time work. Main (1988), again using data from the 1980 Women and Employment Survey, has tested the proposition that part-time women are paid less than full-time women using a human capital model and correcting for sample selectivity bias. Full-time employees appear to have an overall wage advantage of 15 per cent of which 8 per cent can be attributed to lower pay for given characteristics. However, this finding may be spurious as the hourly earnings data on which the analysis is based contain an overtime component. Since part-time workers are generally not entitled to overtime payments until they have worked standard full-time hours, which will be rare, this biases the result in favour of finding discrimination against part-time workers.[8] It should also be recognised that many women may have a preference for part-time work and may be prepared to accept lower pay to obtain it. In the WES Survey, 83 per cent of women said they were happy with their hours, 6 per cent had a preference for shorter hours and only 11 per cent desired more hours. This accords with findings elsewhere in Europe. Thus, according to the 1984 European Labour Force Survey, only 7 per cent of part-timers in Germany and 9 per cent in France, compared to 13 per cent in Britain, were working part-time because they could not find a full-time job. Hence, the majority of part-time work seems to be voluntary.[9]

This leads on naturally to the question of whether the growth of part-time working is predominantly supply-side or demand-side led. Explanations have tended to focus more on the supply side, given the changing composition of the labour force and the fact that married women with children, young persons and older workers may all have a preference for part-time work. Additionally, the slope of the budget line, determined by gross earnings, various kinks or non-convexities caused by the structure of taxes, benefits and national insurance contributions will influence part-time labour supply (Disney and Szyszczak, 1984). More recently, however, the emphasis has shifted towards the demand side and the recognition that the ratio of part-time to full-time employment will be a function of the two types of labour and the size of quasi-fixed costs of labour. For the US, Montgomery (1988a and 1988b), noting that nearly 50 per cent of US firms have both full-time and part-time workers, has attempted to explain the intensity of use of part-time labour using the results of a 1980 survey of 5,000 private establishments. In the first paper, he utilises a two-equation system to predict both relative hours and the proportion of part-timers in the labour force. In line with the theoretical expectations, the ratio of part-time to full-time hours is higher the greater the cost of hiring and training new workers, the larger the size of establishment (given larger establishments have greater quasi-fixed costs from higher supervision and administration) and the higher the relative wage for part-timers. In the second paper, using the same data-set, he finds that high quasi-fixed costs and high costs of recruiting and training are significant impediments to whether part-timers are employed in an establishment.

However, these studies suffer from a lack of data on the supply side and from the fact that, in the absence of direct information on wages, reliance has to be placed on the ratio of part-time to full-time pay of high-school graduates in each geographical location. Both these difficulties are absent from the study of inter-industry determinants of part-time employment based on the 1984 Current Population Survey carried out by Ehrenberg *et al.* (1988). On the demand side, they postulate that the ratio of part-time to full-time employees (E_P/E_F) will be a function of the relative costs of the two groups and the industry's production technology, the latter being proxied by the share of the workforce in each of seven main occupational groups (Y). Hence,

$$\left(\frac{E_P}{E_F}\right) = D(R\bar{W}, R\bar{P}, Y) \tag{2.4}$$

where
$R\bar{W}$ = the part-time employee/full-time employee wage
$R\bar{H}$ = employer-financed part of health insurance
$R\bar{P}$ = private pension coverage

The supply side will also be influenced by these three variables above, though with opposite signs and by the characteristics of the workforce (Z). Hence,

$$\left(\frac{E_P}{E_F}\right) = S(R\dot{W}, R\dot{H}, R\dot{P}, Z) \tag{2.5}$$

In the demand equation the relative wage variable performs as anticipated and industries with a large percentage of manual workers are found to employ fewer part-timers. The private pension plan variable is, however, perverse. The authors explain this result in terms of savings on training and turnover costs consequent upon increased tenure, but it is not clear why this should favour part-timers relative to full-timers. In the supply equation, the wage differential is significant and the pension variable insignificant. In addition, the larger the number of children per worker and the larger the percentage of workers who are students, the greater the probability of part-time employment.

For the UK, Disney and Szyszczak (1984) attempt to test a model taking into account part-time employees, employer's national insurance contributions, the desired level of output and an adjustment parameter. The results for the relative wage variable are not entirely satisfactory as these appeared to be picking up supply responses (the sign being opposite to that expected). However, the employer's national insurance contribution rate appears to have a significant and negative effect on part-time female employment. Blanchflower and Corry (1987) use probit equations to explain the probability of an establishment being part-time, using data from the 1984 Workplace Industrial Relations Survey. Among the main results, part-time using establishments (PTUEs) are disproportionately represented in the non-manufacturing sector and probability of part-time employment increases with establishment size up to 1,440 and then decreases. However, the Survey does not contain any data on relative costs. Nor is information available on whether part-timers perform similar tasks to full-timers. Perry (1988b) is able to examine the supply of female part-time labour in a life-cycle context using WES. He distinguishes three aspects – the proportion of time spent in employment as opposed to non-work; the proportion spent in part-time employment; and the proportion spent in full-time employment. It appears that a woman's decision to work part-time is quite distinct from the decision to work full-time. In the part-time model, the age variable has a positive effect on the proportion of time spent working, but with a smaller coefficient than in the full-time model, and a similar result is found in respect to earnings potential. Unlike the part-time model case, all the children variables have a significant effect in deterring employment and qualifications in increasing it in the full-time model. Thus, in order to understand fully the nature of female labour supply, we must distinguish part-time from full-time employment.

2.3.2 Absenteeism

In surveying work on the economics of absence, Brown and Sessions (1996) suggest the fact that economists have tended to ignore the economics of absence is surprising, given the fact that the number of working days lost from it is comparable to those lost from unemployment and vastly greater than those lost as a result of strike activity. Absence may occur through valid (i.e. sickness) or invalid (i.e. shirking) reasons. As Barmby *et al.* (2002) note, workers who have access to compensation payments (sick pay) are more likely not only to absent themselves than those who do not have access, but also to take longer time off when absent.

We can illustrate this in Figure 2.9 (taken from Brown and Sessions 1996). First, assume all individuals receive sick pay at a rate $S < W$, where W represents the average wage, for each hour of absence. Let h^c represent contractual hours, h_1 "utility-maximising" hours, given the budget constraint drawn from T to E^C. The introduction of $S < W$ will cause the budget constraint to swivel at E^C to become $E^C E^3$, causing the individual to optimise at E_3 on indifference curve I_3. The introduction of sick pay has

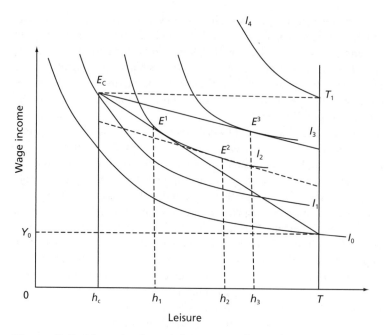

Figure 2.9 Absenteeism, labour supply and sick pay.

caused absence to increase from h_1 to h_3 hours of leisure. This is a result of both a substitution effect ($E^1 - E^2$) and an income effect ($E^2 - E^3$). If a sick-pay scheme provides full compensation (i.e. $S = W$), the budget constraint would become horizontal and we would end up at T_1 on indifference curve I_4, with no work being performed.

However, while such schemes do exist, the evidence is that workers do still turn up for work. Brown (1994) explains this in terms of Akerlof's (1982) gift–exchange model, in which workers offer a gift of not taking all their sick leave in return for the employer providing them with favourable treatment in the future, perhaps in relation to promotion. This is a form of the efficiency wage model. It should be noted that absenteeism is not necessarily inefficient as the worker is signalling to the employer that the existing employment contract is inefficient. If a firm attempts to reduce absence through monitoring and fines, this will involve costs, so that the optimal degree of voluntary absence is not zero.

Few empirical studies, however, examine such aspects of absenteeism. Barmby *et al.* (2002) examine absence in nine European countries, with sickness absence varying from 1.8 per cent in Luxembourg to 6.3 per cent in Sweden (which has a generous system for sick pay). In most cases, absence is higher for women than for men and rises with age, tenure and usual hours. Their multivariate analysis suggests that age and marital status can account for the entire difference in absence rates between men and women. Married women are responsible for the higher absence rates for women. People with longer tenure have higher absence rates, even when age is controlled for, suggesting that tenure increases job security and encourages workers to stay off work longer. Further support for this is found in a Swedish study by Arai and Thoursie (2005). They note that workers on temporary contracts have lower job security than those on permanent contracts as they have a higher risk of lay-offs. Thus, there is a greater incentive for job attendance on the part of temporary staff. Absence is found to be procyclical and the correlation between such rates and the proportion of temporary staff is negative, supporting the job security hypothesis.

Where part-time employment opportunities are limited and workers are leisure preferrers, theory suggests that absenteeism is likely to ensue. Early attempts to test this hypothesis were made for the US by Allen (1981) and for Australia by Kenyon and Dawkins (1989). Allen derives the following absence probability function from a standard utility-maximising framework incorporating budget and time constraints:

$$a = a(W, R, t^c, D, F) \tag{2.6}$$

with expected signs (?) (+) (?) (−) (−)

where
a = absence
W = wage rate
R = non-labour income
t^c = consumption time
D = lump sum penalty for absence (equivalent to reduced promotion opportunities)
F = scheduling flexibility permitted by one's employer

Using the 1972–3 Quality of Employment Survey, the results strongly support the belief that financial incentives and work-scheduling arrangements have an important effect on the work-attendance decisions of workers. In relation to the former, however, the elasticity of the absence rate with respect to the marginal wage is low (between −0.35 and −0.48), which means that it is prohibitively expensive to raise pay as a means of reducing absenteeism. In relation to the latter, what is important is flexibility in scheduling other activities during normal working hours (i.e. flexible working hours schemes, either formal or informal) rather than the number of contractual hours. Absence rates are found to be about 50 per cent higher among employees who work the same hours each day, 20 per cent higher among those working the standard workweek, and 25–30 per cent lower among those who receive some paid time off. Kenyon and Dawkins use a similar model, though without a flexibility variable, and come to very similar conclusions in relation to Australian time-series data, namely, variables that change the shape and/or shift the budget constraint facing workers influence absenteeism. Thus, while absence may indicate low worker morale (or poor industrial relations), the economic approach has much to offer in explaining its incidence.

2.3.3 Overtime working

Income preferrers will, as far as they are able, seek out employers who are prepared to offer overtime (consideration of the employer's demand for overtime is postponed until Chapter 5). Britain is very prone to overtime working by international standards. Thus, Bosworth and Dawkins (1981) show that, over the period 1952–79, the proportion of operatives working overtime rose from 22 per cent to 35 per cent and the average number of overtime hours worked by this group remained in the range 7.3 hours to 8.6 hours after 1950, being always in excess of 8 hours since 1964. This high level of overtime working continued in the 1980s despite rising unemployment. Supply-based models have suggested that overtime is used to offset low basic pay, and Hughes and Leslie (1975) find a significant and negative relationship between the growth in overtime and pay. Further actual hours of work fall less than proportionately to cuts in the normal work-week. There is also evidence of a ratchet effect, so that, when demand diminishes from its peak, workers resist, as far as they are able, a reduction in overtime working (Hart 1974), though it is also true that there is some variation in the extent of overtime working over the cycle. Hubler (1989) has estimated an overtime function using German individual micro-data and correcting for selectivity bias. His probit results point to a negative relationship between both wage levels and standard hours with overtime working. Further older workers and women are less likely to work overtime than younger workers and men. The latter could be a consequence of a greater willingness to work overtime by men than women or of the greater availability of it in their case.

2.3.4 Double-jobbing

Where overtime working is not available, workers may have recourse to moonlighting, double-jobbing or multiple job-holding (according to the terminology used). This may be defined as a situation in which an employee works for more than one employer or is partially self-employed. The number of workers subject to such arrangements is difficult to estimate, not least for reasons relating to the problem of tax evasion. Consequently, available data can only indicate a lower threshold. Official estimates in the UK range from over 3 per cent of all employees (derived from the General Household Survey) to over 7 per cent (Family Expenditure Survey); similar estimates are found in the US and even higher figures are evident in Scandinavia. Evidence from various countries shows that multiple job-holding, like overtime in the UK, has tended to increase when normal hours are reduced as some workers express a preference for income over leisure. There are several motives for double-jobbing. Smith Conway and Kimmel (1998) suggest that constraints on hours of work are one of them, but job heterogeneity is another. A second job may offer training, professional contacts or other desirable characteristics. A third is what Paxson and Sicherman (1996) refer to as the "**portfolio model**", in which workers choose packages of jobs in order to optimise over the mean variance of income. By ignoring this form of behaviour, researchers may be eliminating the most significant avenue for short-term labour-supply adjustments and bias wage elasticities downwards. For the US, Shishko and Rostker (1976) attempted to estimate the moonlighting supply curve using data from the Income Dynamics Panel (PSID), which revealed that about 18 per cent of those surveyed had second jobs, a rather larger figure than would be expected in the general population.[10] The following equation was estimated with the moonlighting wage (W_M) derived from a separate equation to predict W_M for the whole population:

$$L_M = \alpha_0 + \alpha_1 W_M + \alpha_2 W_0 + \alpha_3 L_0 + \alpha_4 I_0 + \alpha_5 A_0 \qquad (2.7)$$

+ descriptive statistics + error term

where
L_M = hours of secondary employment
W_0 = primary wage rate
L_0 = primary hours of work
I_0 = an interaction term involving W_M, W_0 and L_0
A_0 = non-labour income

Portfolio model

The idea that workers will choose a package of jobs in order to optimise with respect to the mean variance of income over different jobs.

The results reveal that the supply of moonlighting labour increases with the moonlighting wage (W_M) and decreases with primary job earnings ($W_0 L_0$). Further, family size (which proxies consumption) is significant and positively related to moonlighting hours. Finally, consistent with the life-cycle consumption hypothesis, age shows a significant negative relationship to moonlighting hours.[11]

In general, the characteristics of those seeking a second job appear to be very similar to those who seek extra income from overtime or shift-work (i.e. married men with families and financial commitments). This may explain the high percentage of non-manual workers who take second jobs, as their opportunities for shift-work and overtime may be severely constrained.

Summary

- Income and substitution effects will determine how many hours of work an individual would choose if able to do so, given the level of wages. One possibility, if a negative income effect more than offsets the positive substitution effect as wages rise, is that the labour supply curve becomes backward bending.
- As a result of the presence of the standard work-week, other family income, progressive income taxation and overtime premium payments, the budget constraint may be non-linear.
- Models of labour supply have become more sophisticated over time as they have attempted to deal with measurement issues, sample selection, different functional forms, life-cycle effects and collective family decision-making with different individual preferences.
- Given hours constraints, we can classify workers for when the standard work-week does not match their tastes for work as either income or leisure preferrers. The former are likely to demand overtime working or to seek a second job, while the latter may request part-time work, absent themselves from work more than other workers or seek pay increases, including the possibility that they will work overtime, so that the additional pay compensates for their leisure preferences.
- Employers may prefer a standard work-week augmented by overtime premium payments, as this enables them to obtain more hours from their existing workforce for the same level of weekly pay.
- Women may be leisure preferrers in the sense that part-time work better enables them to match work with family commitments, even though such work may be relatively low paid. However, the demand for part-time work by employers may also be an important factor in the growth of part-time work.
- Financial incentives and work schedules have an important effect on the work-attendance decisions of workers, on the extent of overtime working and on double-jobbing.

Questions

1 Using income and substitution effects, show the conditions under which a labour supply curve can be backward bending.
2 Why are standard work-weeks the norm rather than the exception?
3 Distinguish between income and leisure preferrers and discuss circumstances under which their utility from work might be increased.
4 Why has part-time work increased?
5 Are absence and overtime working opposite sides of the same coin?
6 Why might double-jobbing occur, is it likely to increase over time and what are the implications for estimates of supply elasticities?

Notes

1 The labour supply curve of the individual will itself be influenced by the labour supply of other family members. Different models make different assumptions in this regard. The male-chauvinist model assumes that the husband decides on his labour input without regard to his wife's labour supply decisions, whereas the wife views his earnings as one category of property income. The family–utility–family budget constraint model assumes that the members of the family attempt to maximise family utility consumption and the leisure time of each individual family member. The individual utility–family budget constraint model associated with Leuthold (1968) assumes, in contrast, that each individual family member attempts to maximise his or her own individual utility, which is a function of family consumption, but the individual's own leisure time. In the first and third of these models, it is possible for the labour supply decisions of individual family members to be inconsistent with each other. For a fuller discussion, see Killingsworth (1983) and the discussion in section 2.1.

2 An alternative approach was suggested by Slutsky, who moves the individual back to the position where he has the same income as before, such that he could purchase the original bundle of goods and leisure. The main features of the two approaches are, however, comparable.

3 Brown (1981) points out, for example, that where incentive payment systems apply individuals will simultaneously determine both the number of hours they are prepared to work and the input of effort, which in turn will influence the observed wage rate. Thus, we might expect better results for empirical tests which are based on workers paid according to time rates.

4 This may give rise to an identification problem. To the extent that the employer rather than the employee fixes the length of work-week, the regressions will measure the demand for labour rather than the supply of labour. This problem will be reduced to the extent that different employers offer different hours–wages packages.

5 Donni (2007) criticises the assumption in the above that men work full-time or not at all, whereas, in practice, the dispersion in hours worked by men is small.

6 An earlier study is Moffitt (1982). He estimates a Tobit model using data derived from various negative income tax experiments in the US to take

account of the fact that employers in general do not offer jobs with low hours of work. He found, at the mean of the independent variables, that desired labour supply averaged 21 hours per week, while the employers wished to offer 39 hours – a strikingly large difference.

7   Joshi's own regression analysis suggests that childbearing reduces subsequent labour market participation by about seven years and subsequent earned income by about one-half.

8   The same criticism can be levelled at the similar results obtained by Ermisch and Wright (1988) for the UK and Ehrenberg *et al.* (1988) for the US. The latter find an 18 per cent differential in favour of full-time employees. Part-time employees also have a lower probability of being covered by a health insurance plan.

9   Involuntary part-time employment should be taken here to result from a shortage of full-time jobs. Leppel and Heller Clain (1988) use the term involuntary part-time employment to refer to cases where part-time work occurs for economic reasons (or what in Britain is referred to as short-time working). This affects a much smaller proportion of the workforce than are engaged in voluntary part-time work. They find the incidence of involuntary part-time employment increased substantially in the US over the period 1967–84, much of which is explained by downturns in the business cycle and the expansion of the service sector.

10 This is explained by the fact that, over larger time periods, more individuals will take up second jobs. Thus, Paxson and Sicherman (1996) also using the PSID indicate that in any one year roughly 20 per cent of working males and 12 per cent of working females hold a second job. Furthermore, different people have second jobs in different years, so that more than 50 per cent of continuous working males hold a second job sometime during their working lives.

11 Renna (2006) using data from nine OECD countries, estimates the marginal effects which suggest that work-sharing as under the Aubry law in France which reduced the standard work-week from 39 to 35 hours would increase double-jobbing by 1.2 percentage points, while an increase in the overtime premium from 0.25 to 0.50 would increase double-jobbing by 0.9 percentage points as a consequence of the reduced demand for overtime on the part of employers.

References

Akerlof G., "Labor Contracts as Partial Gift-Exchange", *Quarterly Journal of Economics*, 97, 1982, pp. 543–49.

Allen S.G., "An Empirical Model of Work Attendance", *Review of Economics and Statistics*, LXIII, 1981, pp. 77–87.

Altonji J.G. and Paxson C.H., "Labor Supply Preferences, Hours Constraints and Hours-Wage Trade-offs", *Journal of Labor Economics*, 6(2), 1988, pp. 254–76.

Arai M. and Thoursie P.S., "Incentives and Selection in Cyclical Absenteeism", *Labour Economics*, 12(2), 2005, pp. 269–88.

Baffoe-Bonnie J., "Family Labour Supply and Labour Market Segmentation", *Applied Economics*, 21(1), 1989, pp. 69–83.

Barmby T.A., Ercolani M.G. and Treble J.G., "Sickness Absence: An International Comparison", *Economic Journal*, 112(480), 2002, F315–331.

Barzel Y. and McDonald R.J., "Assets, Subsistence and the Supply Curve of Labor", *American Economic Review*, 63(4), 1973, pp. 621–33.

Bender K.A. and Skatun J.D., "Constrained by Hours and Restricted in Wages: The Quality of Matches in the Labour Market", *Economic Inquiry*, 47(3), 2009, S12–S29.

Blanchflower D. and Corry B., "Part-time Employment in Britain: An Analysis Using Establishment Data", *Department of Employment Research Paper*, No. 57, 1987.

Blank R.M., "The Role of Part-time Work in Women's Labor Market Choices Over Time", *American Economic Review, Papers and Proceedings*, 79(2), 1989, pp. 295–9.

Blundell R., Chiappori P.-A., Magnac T. and Meghir C., "Collective Labour Supply: Heterogeneity and Non-Participation", *Review of Economic Studies*, 74(2), 2007, pp. 417–45.

Bosworth D.L. and Dawkins P.J., *Work Patterns: An Economic Analysis*, Gower, Aldershot, 1981.

Brown C.V. (editor), *Taxation and Labour Supply*, Allen & Unwin, London, 1981.

Brown S., "Dynamic Implications of Absence Behaviour", *Applied Economics*, 26, 1994, pp. 1163–75.

Brown S. and Sessions J., "The Economics of Absence: Theory and Evidence", *Journal of Economic Surveys*, 10(1), 1996, pp. 23–34.

Chiappori P.A., "Rational Household Labour Supply", *Econometrica*, 56, 1988, pp. 63–90.

Chiappori P.A., "Collective Labour Supply and Welfare", *Journal of Political Economy*, 100(3), 1992, pp. 437–67.

Dessing M., "Labor Supply, the Family and Poverty; the S Shaped Labor Supply Curve", *Journal of Economic Behavior and Organization*, 49(4), 2002, pp. 433–58.

Dex S., "Women's Work Histories: An Analysis of the Women and Employment Survey", *Department of Employment Research Paper*, No. 46, 1984.

Dex S. and Shaw L.B., *British and American Women at Work*, Macmillan, Hants, 1986.

Disney R. and Szyszczak E., "Protective Legislation and Part-time Employment in Britain", *British Journal of Industrial Relations*, XXII(1), 1984, pp. 78–100.

Donni O., "Collective Female Labour Supply: Theory and Application", *Economic Journal*, 117(516), 2007, pp. 94–119.

Ehrenberg R.G., Rosenberg P. and Li J., "Part-time Employment in the United States", in Hart R.A., editor, *Employment, Unemployment, and Labor Utilization*, Unwin Hyman, Boston, 1988.

Elias P., "Family Formation, Occupational Mobility and Part-time Work", in Hunt A., editor, *Women and Paid Work: Issues of Equality*, The MacMillan Press, Hants, 1988.

Elias P. and Main B.G.M., *Women's Working Lives: Evidence from the National Training Survey*, Institute for Employment Research, University of Warwick, Coventry, 1982.

Ermisch J.F. and Wright R.E., "Differential Returns to Human Capital in Full-time and Part-time Employment: The Case of British Women", *Birkbeck College Discussion Paper in Economics*, 88(14), 1988.

Hart R.A., "The Relationship between Overtime Working and Wage Inflation", *Bulletin of Economic Research*, 1974.

Heckman J.J., "What has been Learned about Labour Supply in the Past Twenty Years?", *American Economic Review, Papers and Proceedings*, 83(2), 1993, pp. 116–21.

Hicks J.R., *The Theory of Wages*, Macmillan, London, 1932.

Hubler O., "Industrial Overtime Functions with Double Correction for Selectivity Bias", *Economics Letters*, 29, 1989, pp. 87–90.

Hughes B. and Leslie D., "Hours of Work in British Manufacturing Industries", *Scottish Journal of Political Economy*, November 1975.

Joshi H., "Women's Participation in Part-time Work: Further Analysis of the Women and Employment Survey", *Department of Employment Research Paper*, No. 45, July 1984.

Kenyon P. and Dawkins P., "A Time Series Analysis of Labour Absence in Australia", *Review of Economics and Statistics*, LXXI(2), 1989, pp. 232–9.

Killingsworth M.R., *Labour Supply*, Cambridge University Press, Cambridge, 1983.

Leppel K. and Heller Clain S., "The Growth in Involuntary Part-time Employment of Men and Women", *Applied Economics*, 20(9), 1988, pp. 1155–67.

Leuthold J.H., "An Empirical Study of Formula Income Transfers and the Work Decision of the Poor", *Journal of Human Resources*, 3, 1968, pp. 312–23.

Main B.G.M., "Hourly Earnings of Female Part-time Versus Full-time Employees", *Manchester School*, vol. LVI(4), 1988, pp. 331–44.

Moffitt R., "The Tobit Model, Hours of Work and Institutional Constraints", *Review of Economics and Statistics*, 64, 1982, pp. 510–15.

Montgomery M., "On the Determinants of Employer Demand for Part-time Workers", *Review of Economics and Statistics*, vol. LXX(1), 1988a, pp. 112–17.

Montgomery M., "Hours of Part-time and Full-time Workers in the Same Firm", *Industrial Relations*, 27(3), Fall 1988b, pp. 394–406.

Moses L.M., "Income, Leisure and Wage Pressure", *Economic Journal*, 72, 1962, pp. 320–34.

Paxson C.H. and Sicherman N., "The Dynamics of Dual-Job Holding and Job Mobility", *Journal of Labor Economics*, 14(3), 1996, pp. 357–93.

Perry S., "Downward Occupational Mobility and Part-time Women Workers", *Applied Economics*, 20, 1988a, pp. 485–95.

Perry S., "The Supply of Female Part-time Labour over the Life Cycle", *Applied Economics*, 20, 1988b, pp. 1579–87.

Renna F., "Moonlighting and Overtime: A Cross-country Analysis", *Journal of Labor Research*, XXVII(4), Fall, 2006, pp. 575–91.

Shishko R. and Rostker B., "The Economics of Multiple Job Holding", *American Economic Review*, 66(3), 1976, pp. 298–308.

Smith Conway K. and Kimmel J., "Male Labor Supply Estimates and the Decision to Moonlight", *Labour Economics*, 5(2), 1998, pp. 135–66.

Stewart M. and Greenhalgh C., "Work History Patterns and Occupational Attainment of Women", *Economic Journal*, 94(375), 1984, pp. 493–519.

Weiss Y., "On the Optimal Pattern of Labour Supply", *Economic Journal*, 82, 1972, pp. 1293–315.

Further reading

R. Blundell and T. McCurdy, "Labour Supply: A Review of Alternative Approaches", *Handbook of Labor Economics*, 3, Elsevier, 1999, pp. 1559–645, surveys existing approaches to modelling labour supply and identifies some important gaps in the literature. It also examines recent policy reforms.

M. Killingworth, *Labour Supply*, Cambridge University Press, 1983, contains a good discussion of the strengths and weaknesses of the earlier literature on labour supply.

F. Contensou and R. Vranceanu, *Working Time: Theory and Policy Implications*, Edward Elgar, 2000, focuses on working time theory at a relatively advanced level.

Chapter 3

Investment in human capital

Learning outcomes

At the end of this chapter, readers should have a detailed knowledge of:

- The Mincer human capital model and some of the problems in using it;
- Reasons why the acquisition of human capital tends to occur early in the working life;
- The nature of screening or credentialism versus signalling and self-selection;
- The distinction between general and specific training and the role of asymmetric information in determining who pays for training;
- Reasons why some workers are more likely than others to receive training;
- Why government training schemes might be inefficient.

Introduction

It is difficult to overestimate the contribution of the human capital revolution of the 1960s and 1970s to the development of labour economics. Prior to that period, the institutional approach was dominant with little distinction made between labour economics and industrial relations. There were few empirical studies using econometric techniques. Subsequently, however, and largely driven by the human capital revolution, this changed and labour economics became a leader in many of the theoretical and empirical advances in economics as a whole.

We have already seen in Chapter 2 some evidence of this in estimates of the private and social rates of return to education in different countries. In this chapter, we first set out formally the Mincer human capital model based on years of education and the quadratic of experience. The model is also applied, later in the chapter, to the training decision, with consideration given to the distinction between general and specific training and who pays for it, a matter on which there is considerable debate.

Next, we turn to the empirical analysis where there are a number of important issues. First, are years of education or qualifications more appropriate for estimating the return to education? The **sheepskin model** suggests that returns are significantly higher in years in which qualifications are normally attained and the returns may not be linear as education increases, pointing in favour of using qualifications in empirical studies as opposed to years of education. Second, problems of ability bias have to be dealt with, such as by studying twins in the absence of direct data on ability. Third, the interpretation of the relationship between earnings and job tenure or seniority may not be straightforward. Fourth, **endogeneity** may be present if, not only does more education increase earnings, but also higher earnings induce individuals to consume more education. There are also questions relating to the influence of family, school and community background and the role of demand-side influences, such as earnings being affected by firm size and industry composition.

This leads naturally on to the **job-screening hypothesis** developed by Michael Spence and others, which challenges the assumption of the human capital model that education raises productivity, as opposed to merely identifying more productive individuals. That is, does education merely signal to employers the underlying employability of the individual? Differentiating between these two competing hypotheses is difficult and those empirical studies that have attempted to do so produce conflicting results.

The final section focuses on training issues. Here, governments often intervene on the grounds that otherwise there may be an under-provision of training through various forms of **market failure**. There are also equity considerations in relation to the probability of certain groups differentiated by age, gender and race receiving training. Training provision may also be influenced by size of firm, the presence of unions, wage compression, degree of competition and agglomeration effects.

3.1 The human capital model

Though human capital theory has antecedents that go back as far as Sir William Petty,[1] it is Becker's (1964, 1975) and Mincer's (1974) contributions to the theory, in particular, that have led to the mushrooming literature applying the theory to a considerable range of empirical data. We can define human capital as the individual worker's productive skills and knowledge as reflected in his or her marginal productivity. The extent of human capital can be increased through investment in education and training. Indeed, since additional education involves opportunity costs in the form of foregone earnings and the direct costs of tuition, the worker must be compensated in the form of higher lifetime earnings if there is to be long-run equilibrium in the labour market.

The value of a wage received many years into the future is not the same as the value of a wage received today, which could be put to use to earn a rate of interest. Thus, we must discount future earnings using an appropriate discount rate, which we will designate as r. Following Mincer, assume that n represents the length of the working life, E_s the annual earnings for an individual's lifetime earnings at the start of the working life (V_s) as given by

Sheepskin model

Returns to higher education by years of education are split into qualifying years and years in which qualifications are awarded, with the expectation that returns will be higher in qualification years, thus giving rise to non-linearities in returns.

Endogeneity

A situation in which an independent variable may not only influence the value of the dependent variable, but also itself be determined, at least partly, by the dependent variable.

Job-screening hypothesis

The idea that education does not in itself raise productivity, but is simply used by employers as a means of identifying innately more productive individuals.

Market failure

Outcomes which do not maximise market efficiency as a result of market imperfections such as asymmetric information (see below) or negative externalities.

$$V_s = E_s \sum_{t=1}^{n} \left(\frac{1}{1+r} \right)^t \qquad (3.1)$$

from which is derived

$$\ln E_s = \ln E_o + r_s \qquad (3.2)$$

Equation (3.2) states that percentage increases in earnings are strictly proportional to the absolute difference in time spent in education with r here representing the rate of return. Further, after entering the labour force in year j, the worker will invest additional resources (C_j) in on-the-job training such that

$$\Delta E_j = r_j C_j \qquad (3.3)$$

These investments will be concentrated at the start of the working life, since the later in the working life an investment is made, the shorter the payback period. Hence, education, normally a full-time activity, precedes on-the-job training, largely a part-time activity, and the latter will diminish rapidly with age. As Polachek (1995) points out, there are several implicit assumptions in this model. Specifically, human capital is assumed to be homogeneous: individuals are assumed identical with regard to time preferences, discount rates and other aspects; individuals know with certainty the length of their working lifetime and are assumed to work throughout it; finally, individuals are assumed to be risk neutral, so that stochastic factors play no part in decision-making. The timing and investment aspects of human capital are central to the **Ben-Porath model** (1967, 1970). Assume that the individual's length of life, T, is known with certainty, there is a given interest rate, r, and services of human capital obtain a return, w. Now define Kt to be the individual's homogeneous stock of human capital. Then earnings capacity, $Y(t)$, can be written as

$$Y(t) = wK(t) \qquad (3.4)$$

This stock of human capital can only be augmented by foregoing some income which could be derived from the existing stock of human capital and using it to purchase D inputs for use in producing additional units of human capital at the rate Q. This is summarised in the production function

$$Qt = [s(t)K(t), D(t)] \qquad (3.5)$$

Where s is the fraction of time devoted to human capital production on the assumption that time is allocated just between work and investment in education and training (i.e. leisure is ignored).

Now let the cost-minimising factor combination for producing a unit of human capital be (wsK', D'). Assuming K is large enough for $s < 1$. Then unit costs will be given by

$$I' = wsK' + PdD' \qquad (3.6)$$

I' is composed of a foregone earnings component (wsK') and a direct cost element (PdD'), where Pd is the unit price of the composite produced input. From this,

Ben-Porath model

A model based on the proposition that human capital can only be augmented by foregoing income derived from the existing stock of human capital and which predicts that net earnings will rise at a diminishing rate with age.

Ben-Porath derives the implied pattern of the change in earnings over the lifetime. Net earnings rise (at a diminishing rate) with age

$$E(t) = Y(t) - I(t) = wK(t) - I(t) \qquad (3.7)$$

$$dE(t) = wQ(t) - dI(t) > 0$$

due both to the increase in the stock of human capital and the decline in the rate of investment with age. If human capital depreciates, the earnings profile will eventually turn down towards the end of life (a fuller exposition of the model is contained in Polachek and Siebert 1993).

Overtaking year

This is the year in which earnings for those who deferred entry into the labour market in order to obtain additional qualifications overtake the earnings of those who entered the labour market at the time the other group deferred entry.

An important concept in the Mincer approach is that of the **overtaking year**. Suppose (Figure 3.1) that the population consists of two groups – those entering the labour market after sixth-year college and university graduates. The latter incur direct costs (e.g. tuition costs) of *ABCD* and opportunity costs (foregone earnings) of *ABFO* and are compensated by increased earnings after the overtaking year (0). Then the population's earnings distribution would be relatively wide for the young, decline to zero at year 0 and widen substantially thereafter. (Note this figure is not drawn to scale.)

On the basis of US data, Mincer finds that the overtaking year for a cohort of male employees is eight years after school-leaving age. This is the most appropriate point to measure the effect of education on earnings as the return to previous education is just about equal to the cost of current investment. At this point, differences in education can explain one-third of the inequality in annual earnings.

3.2 Empirical analysis

Mincer human capital earnings function

In the simplest version, the log of earnings is regressed against years of education and the quadratic of experience.

The standard **Mincer human capital earnings function** takes the form

$$\log E_t = a + \alpha_1 S + \alpha_2 X_t + \alpha_3 X^2 + \varepsilon_1 \qquad (3.8)$$

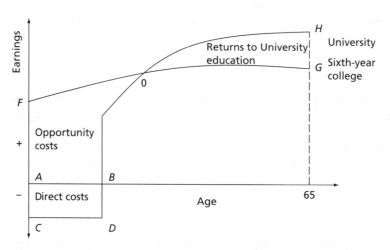

Figure 3.1 The overtaking year and returns to education.

where

E_t = earnings at time t

s = years of schooling

X = years of experience

a = intercept term

α = coefficients of the variables

ε = stochastic error

In some cases, qualification dummies are substituted for years of schooling or some qualitative measure of education is included. Mincer (1993) suggests that the average rate of return to schooling as measured by α_1 varies between 7 and 11 per cent on various bodies of data, the rate of return to post-school investments is about 13 per cent and the two variables (schooling and work experience) account for a third of the variance in wage rates. Willis (1986) suggests "as an empirical tool, the Mincer earnings function has been one of the great success stories of modern labour economics" and goes on to speculate why this should be so.

Interpretation of these results has, however, given rise to considerable controversy. Years of schooling seems a rather crude proxy for the quality of education, as Mincer himself recognised (1993: 88). In the US, there are practical reasons for using years of education, as this has been the form in which schooling is measured in the major data-sets there. The imposition of a linear specification is, however, highly questionable. In the European context, there is less need to utilise it and, in practice, most studies there use educational qualifications that allow for a non-linear relationship. Heckman *et al.* (2003) note:

> Assuming stationarity of the economic environment, the analyst can use the Mincer model to identify both skill prices and the rate of return to investment. This happy coincidence only occurs under special conditions, which were approximately valid in the 1960 census data used by Mincer (1974). Unfortunately, these conditions have been at odds with the data ever since. As a result the widely used Mincer model applied to more recent data sets does not provide valid estimates of returns to schooling.

In general, Heckman *et al.* find that imposing **linearity** in schooling leads to upward-biased estimates to grades that do not produce a degree in the US and downward-biased estimates for degree-completion years in line with the predictions of the sheepskin model (discussed below). Walker and Zhu (2001) test the linearity restriction, using the UK Labour Force Survey, with dummies for long degree programmes, gap years and early achievement, and find that this restriction is soundly rejected by the data for women and marginally so by the data for men. This also points to the need to undertake separate estimation for men and women. Studies using the so-called sheepskin model include both years of education and qualification dummies (see, for instance, Belman and Heywood 1991 and 1997; Hungerford and Solon 1987; Jaeger and Page 1996; and Park 1999). These studies generally find that returns to education are significantly higher in years in which qualifications are normally attained, consistent with the view that part of the return is due to **signalling** or **credentialism**. However, even in the presence of sheepskin effects, there are a number of possible interpretations of this outcome in addition to the screening hypothesis (discussed below), which suggests that education is simply

Linearity

In the case here, the assumption that earnings rise in proportion to the number of years in education.

Signalling

The use of educational qualifications by those seeking work to indicate their employability to employers. A rational employee will select signals that maximise the difference between offered wages and signalling costs.

Credentialism

The use of educational qualifications by employers to attract the best employees for particular occupations.

used as a filter to identify high-capacity individuals. On similar lines, Chiswick (2003) argues that drop-outs may be inefficient learners who realise that staying on in the education system will do little to improve their employability. Similarly, graduates may be overwhelmingly efficient learners who complete their studies precisely because they believe extra education will raise their productivity and earnings. In order to obtain unbiased estimates, direct information is required on both years of education and diploma attainment, since some individuals may fail to obtain the qualifications for which they are enrolled and others may take either shorter or longer periods of time than the norm to obtain a particular qualification. Not all data-sets provide such information, but in one of the few studies able to divide actual years of education into different components, Groot and Oosterbeek (1994), using Dutch data, are able to identify effective years, repeated years, inefficient routeing years and drop-out years. This classification proves to be substantially superior to the more usual classification of actual and effective years of schooling.

Institutional quality may be measured in a number of ways – school expenditure per student, pupil–teacher ratios, teachers' salary levels or school ratings. Johnson and Stafford (1973) find that a 10 per cent increase in school expenditure per student leads to a 2 per cent increase in the annual rate of return to schooling. Large quality effects are also reported by Taubman and Wales (1973) and Card and Krueger (1992) among others. However, these studies tend to use quality averages based on locality rather than the particular school attended and many are limited to spending per pupil data. Betts (1995) uses National Survey of Youth data, which enable him to identify actual school attended and three measures of school quality – the pupil–teacher ratio, teachers' salaries and percentage of teachers with a higher degree. While the paper rejects the hypothesis that workers' earnings are independent of the particular high school attended, the various measures of teacher quality are not significant. He speculates that structural changes may have weakened the link between traditional measures of school quality and earnings. Studies of institutional quantity have also been conducted at tertiary level. Thus, Battu *et al.* (1999) find that those graduating from long-established British universities earn between 8 and 11 per cent more than those graduating from former polytechnics. Likewise, Chevalier and Conlon (2003) find that, after controlling for personal characteristics, those graduating from the more prestigious British Russell Group institutions earn up to 6 per cent more than those graduating from former polytechnics.

Another potential problem is that the estimated rate of return to education may be biased upwards if individual ability is unobserved and high-ability individuals have higher school attainment than low-ability individuals. This **ability bias** will cause us to overstate the extent to which an increase in education for a person with a given ability will increase earnings.

Ability bias

The belief that higher-ability students will have higher school attainment than low-ability students which would bias upwards the true rate of return to education.

Following Becker (1964, 1975) and Blackburn and Neumark (1995), suppose functions representing the marginal costs and benefits of education take the form

$$MC(P_i, S_i) = \exp(-P_i)S_i^x \tag{3.9}$$

$$MB(A_i, S_i) = \exp(kA_i)S_i^y$$

where P_i represents an individual's opportunity for investing in human capital, S_i is years of schooling, A_i is ability and x and y are parameters. Assuming that $x > 0$ and

$-1 < y < x$, the optimal amount of investment in education is given by

$$S_i^* = \exp\left[\frac{kA_i + P_i}{x - y}\right] \qquad (3.10)$$

which means that higher-ability individuals (or those with greater opportunities to invest in education) will receive more education. The wage equation is given by

$$\log E_i = -\log(1 + y) + (1 + y)\log(S_i^*) + kA_i \qquad (3.11)$$

thus, if ability is omitted from the estimating equation, this will lead to an upward bias in the estimated return to schooling.

Most data-sets do not contain information on ability, so that, in these cases, ability bias is a type of omitted variables bias. One exception is the British National Child Development Survey (NCDS), which analyses periodically a cohort of individuals born in 1958. The survey includes measures of both reading and mathematical ability (see Blundell *et al.* 2000, who find that both A level scores and ability tests at age 16 are both significant and reduce returns by over one-third for men, but by a much smaller amount for women). In the US, the problem of ability bias has generally been dealt with by including specific ability measures such as IQ or family background, by treating ability as fixed effect using panel data, by exploiting the differences between twins in levels of schooling and earnings on the grounds that this eliminates differences in innate ability or motivation, or by exploiting exogenous influences on the schooling decision such as season of birth. It is recognised that IQ or other scores may not necessarily measure the ability to earn, so that a range of approaches should be adopted (Zax and Rees 2002). An example using test scores is that of Blackburn and Neumark (1995), who utilise the Armed Services Vocational Aptitude Battery (ASVAB) tests of 1979 and 1980 on the National Longitudinal Survey Youth cohort. Their results contrast with some earlier ones in finding an upward bias of roughly 40 per cent when test scores are omitted. In order to deal with possible measurement error bias in the wage equation estimates, they then include family-background variables as potential determinants of ability, which results in an estimated schooling coefficient some 30 per cent lower than the OLS estimate including test scores or about half of the OLS estimate excluding test scores. However, it is also possible that schooling is endogenous and correcting for this raises the rate of return to schooling from 5.8 to 7.9 per cent. This does not negate their conclusion that omitting ability measures overstates the economic return to schooling.

An alternative approach to the problem is to use a sample of twins. If twins are identical and have been reared together, they possess the same family background. Differences in earnings between identical twins can then be attributed purely to differences in the education they have received. In an early study, Taubman (1976) concludes that genetic factors could account for 20–40 per cent of the variance in earnings and common family environment for a further 8–15 per cent. In contrast, Ashenfelter and Krueger (1994), using data on 149 pairs of identical twins who attended a twins festival in 1991, find that, when they correct for omitted ability variables and measurement error, ability and family background make little difference to the rate of return to schooling. This study suffers, however, from small sample size and the peculiar nature of the sample. Miller *et al.* (1995) rectify this defect by utilising data on 3,808 Australian twins, which provides large samples of both identical and non-identical twins. It is noteworthy that 56 per cent of identical twins and 38 per cent of non-identical twins report the same level of education, thus potentially frustrating the experiment. Using an OLS approach, they find that roughly one-third of the variance in earnings can be attributed to each of education, ability and family background. However, when they attempt to replicate the Ashenfelter and Krueger study by estimating both **fixed effects** and **selection effects** models and after correction for measurement error in self-reported schooling, ability and family background appear to have a much more modest role. In particular, the rate of return to education for identical twins rises from 2.5 per cent to between 5 and 8 per cent. It appears, therefore, that the conventional OLS estimate of rates for return to education may not be as seriously biased by the omission of ability and family background effects as had been believed earlier. In one UK study of twins (Bonjour *et al.* 2003), it is found that 55 per cent of the twin pairs have the same education years. The study is based on 6,600 individuals (3,300 same-sex female pairs), but only 214 identical twin pairs have complete wage and schooling information. They attempt to correct for ability bias by using a number of instruments (including smoking, which they ultimately reject as a valid instrument). They conclude that measurement error biases their estimates downwards and that the returns to education of 7.7 per cent are very similar to those obtained from OLS, suggesting that ability bias and measurement error cancel each other out.

There has also been considerable debate on another element of the Mincer human capital model, namely the relationship between earnings and job tenure or seniority. The basic hypothesis is that earnings are positively related to job tenure because productivity increases with tenure. However, various authors, such as Abraham and Farber (1987), Altonji and Shakotko (1987) and Hofler and Murphy (1992), have argued that the positive relationship between earnings and tenure is a consequence either of unobserved individual heterogeneity or imperfect job matching arising from the fact that the quality of the job or firm–employee match is higher for longer-tenure workers. This generates a spurious correlation and an upward bias in OLS estimates of cross-section earnings equations. In contrast, Brown (1989), Hersch and Reagan (1990) and Topel (1991), among others, have derived consistent estimates that provide strong support for the proportion that the relationship does reflect genuine productivity effects.

The problem may be illustrated as follows. Let us suppose

$$\ln E_{ijt} = T_{ijt}B_1 + X_{ijt}B_2 + \varepsilon_{ijt} \tag{3.12}$$

where
$\ln E_{ijt}$ = the log of earnings for individual i in occupation j at time t,
T = current job tenure
X = total labour market experience.

B_1 may be interpreted as a return to specific human capital and B_2 as a return to general human capital. Biases arise, however, in estimating these returns as a result of covariance between the regressors and the unobservables, ε_{ijt}, which may be decomposed as

$$\varepsilon_{ijt} = U_{ijt} + U_i + V_{ijt} \tag{3.13}$$

where

U_{ijt} = the stochastic component of earnings specific to the worker–firm pair
U_i = the person-specific effect (e.g. ability)
V_{ijt} = measurement errors and random shocks.

One particular form of bias arises from the fact that the most-able workers may be the most mobile individuals, since it is more than likely that they will receive the most favourable alternative job offers and have more to gain from job mobility. Such cases will be included in data-sets as workers with short job tenure, so that OLS will tend to underestimate the return to tenure. In particular, there may be a differential gender effect, since men are more likely to make advantageous job moves than women, who are often likely to be constrained by family circumstances.[2] Topel and Ward (1992) show that, in the first ten years in the US labour market, a typical male worker holds seven jobs and wage gains at job change account for at least one-third of early career wage growth. Further, Loprest (1992) shows that, for young workers in the first four years in the labour market, the average wage growth for men with job change is 8.7 per cent and for women only 4.1 per cent.[3] The appropriate strategy for dealing with the problem of such heterogeneity is to utilise **panel data**. Thus, Topel (1991) uses Panel Study of Income Dynamics data for 1968–83 to estimate the combined effect of tenure and experience, eliminating factors such as good matches and ability by relating changes in earnings to changes in tenure for those workers who did not change jobs. He finds that such within job wage growth is about 12 per cent in the first year of tenure for those without any experience, declining to 6.5 per cent in the first year of tenure for those who have ten years' experience. It appears, therefore, that, when appropriate adjustments are made for heterogeneity, seniority does have a substantial effect on earnings.

In addition to ability bias, there is a potential endogeneity problem. In the standard OLS treatment, the quantity of schooling is exogenous. However, if schooling results in higher earnings, these higher earnings may themselves result in an increase in the amount of education consumed and this is more likely the higher the ability of the individual (endogeneity bias). One way of dealing with this is to find real-world events that can assign individuals to randomly different treatments. This requires a suitable instrument for education that is uncorrelated with earnings. Thus, Harmon and Walker (1995) compare the earnings of those who left school at 16 when the school-leaving age was raised to 16 with those who left school at 15 just before the minimum school-leaving age in Britain was raised in 1973. One can then compare the effect of an extra year's schooling on those who would not have chosen it with the effect on those who would have chosen it. In a later paper using this same event, Chevalier et al. (2004) find strong support for the human capital explanation over the signalling hypothesis, which is explained below. An alternative approach is to group observations according to childhood smoking behaviour on the grounds that those who have chosen to smoke at an early age have a higher discount rate in terms of time preference than those who do not (Chevalier and Walker 2001). A schooling equation is then estimated and the predicted values from this are inserted into the earnings function in place of the actual schooling levels to produce unbiased estimates. The evidence is that such an **instrumental variable (IV)** approach produces much higher estimates of the rate of return than the standard OLS approach. However, if one believes that OLS imparts an upward bias

Panel data

Data obtained from the same sample of individuals usually on an annual basis. In a balanced panel, each person is interviewed in every year, while, in an unbalanced panel, some individuals do not appear in every year. Sample attrition over time may mean that it is necessary to add new individuals to the sample.

Instrumental variables

These allow consistent estimation when explanatory (independent) variables are correlated with the error terms of a regression relationship (as in the case of reverse causation).

61

through omitted ability, one would expect IV estimates to yield lower rates of return, not higher. The observed outcome could occur if lower-income families are credit constrained, so that, at the margin, returns to schooling are higher for this group, as they are investing a sub-optimal amount in their own education. In fact, in another study, Caneiro and Heckman (2002) find no evidence that this is the case in practice. Further, they argue that most of the instruments used in the literature are invalid, often being correlated with schooling and ability. This points to the need to treat IV estimates of the rate of return to education with a degree of caution.

It has increasingly been recognised that economic success depends on the context in which the individual is placed, including family, school and community background, as well as on the work effort expended. Using the British NCDS, Robertson and Symons (2003) find strong evidence for the importance of peer groups, parental social class and parental academic achievement on future earnings. In the US, Zimmerman (2003) uses data on roommates at Williams College and finds that there is a link between academic performance and SAT scores of roommates who are randomly assigned. In another study, Zax and Rees (2002) find that, when controls for family and high-school background are introduced into their model, the estimated effect of IQ on earnings is dramatically reduced, and the introduction of high-school class rank reduces it still further. Indeed, as 85 per cent of the variation in earnings at age 35 and 75 per cent of it at age 55 is independent of explanatory variables included at age 18, there is plenty of scope for individuals to overcome any deficiencies in their own endowments and environment. The importance of personality traits is also emphasised by Cawley et al. (2001). Excluding human capital measures, they find that cognitive ability can explain between 14 and 20 per cent of the variance in earnings, but, when controlling for human capital measures, this falls between 0.7 and 2.7 per cent. This difference is the result of personality and social skills, which are strongly associated with future educational attainment. The rate of return to ability also varies across different race and gender groups, with black females having the highest return, followed by Hispanic males. Unfortunately, there are no similar studies to these two US studies elsewhere. However, it does seem clear that social skills are very important in determining future employment and earnings opportunities. This may explain why parents are prepared to invest such large sums in the private education of their offspring. As Card (1999) observes, there is a long tradition of utilising family-background data such as fathers' and mothers' educational attainment to control for unobserved ability. There is, indeed, a high correlation between children's educational attainments and those of their parents. Data from the US General Social Survey suggest that each additional year of education of a parent raises completed years of education of a child by 0.4 years, and no less than 30 per cent of the variation in education is explained by parental education. Similar relationships have been found in the UK (see, for instance, Dearden et al. 1997). Recently, Cunha and Heckman (2007) and Heckman (2000, 2008) have emphasised the importance of early intervention (including pre-school years) if one is to raise the prospects of the underprivileged, as returns are higher the younger the person concerned and the more skilled are likely to accumulate further human capital. This is true for both cognitive and non-cognitive skills.

The Mincer human capital model in its simplest form is entirely supply-side driven, but there is substantial evidence that the level of earnings varies according to the location of employment.[4] Thus, Krueger and Summers (1986) find that inter-industry wage differentials across countries appear to follow a regular pattern, with manufacturing industries tending to pay about 20 per cent more than service industries for comparable workers. Similar regularities are found for gender, age group and occupation. Thurow (1975) even argues that the demand side of the market is the major determinant of relative earnings. His **job competition model** assumes that employers use personal characteristics including education as a criterion or screen for hiring workers, on the supposition that employing more educated workers will require a lower investment in training by the firm. In the extreme case, education simply serves to obtain a job and there is a zero return to surplus human capital, as all workers in a given job are paid the same wage. This model is consistent with the screening hypothesis, which is explained below. If it were true that the only purpose of education was to provide signals to potential employers about the employability of particular individuals, this would raise serious questions about the appropriateness or otherwise of public investment in education. However, formal tests tend to reject the hypothesis of a zero return to excess education and most tests of the human capital model include structural variables such as size of firm, as well as personal characteristics in the estimating equation.

> **Job competition model**
>
> This assumes that employers use personal characteristics, such as education, as a screen for hiring workers on the supposition that the more educated require a lower investment in training.

3.3 An alternative interpretation – the job-screening approach

The relationship between education and earnings does not necessarily imply that education itself raises innate productivity. It is possible that education merely identifies those individuals who are more productive in the market for other reasons, in a situation in which the employer has imperfect information about worker capabilities. Signalling, self-selection, screening and credentialism are all means by which workers may be assigned to jobs and which differ in their implications from the standard human capital model. Screening and credentialism refer to the demand side of the labour market or the behaviour of the employers, while signalling and self-selection refer to the supply side or the behaviour of potential or actual employees.

Spence (1973) was the first to note that, of those observable personal attributes that a job applicant presents, some, such as race or sex, are fixed, which he describes as indices, and others, such as education, are alterable, which he describes as signals. Since increasing a signal imposes costs, individuals are assumed to select signals in such a way that they maximise the difference between offered wages and signalling costs.

Spence describes the properties of informational equilibria as follows. Suppose an employer believes some level of education S^* will produce a situation in which productivity is one with a probability of one if $S < S^*$ and productivity two with a probability of one if $S \geq S^*$. Then the offered wage schedule as a function of the level of education will be as in Figure 3.2.

Let us suppose there are two distinct groups of potential employees (group 1 and group 2). Given the wage schedule in Figure 3.2, each group will select optimal levels of education. Those choosing $S < S^*$ will set $S = 0$, the lowest level of education, because education is costly and up to S^* there are no wage gains to any increase in S, given the employers' hypothesised beliefs. Similarly, those choosing

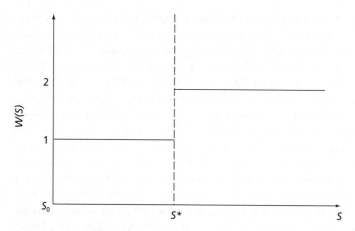

Figure 3.2 Signalling equilibria.

$S \geq S^*$ will, in fact, select $S = S^*$, since further increases in S will not produce any corresponding wage gains. Thus, everyone will select $S = 0$ or $S = S^*$ as illustrated in Figure 3.3, which incorporates signalling costs C.

Assuming $C_1 = S$ and $C_2 = S/2$, each group will select S to maximise the difference between the offered wage and the costs of education. Thus, group 1 will select S_0 and group 2 S^*.

Group 1 will select S_0 if $1 > 2 - S^*$

Group 2 will select S^* if $2 - S^*/2 > 1$

Putting these two conditions together the employer's initial beliefs will be confirmed, provided that the parameter S^* satisfies the inequality

$1 < S^* < 2$

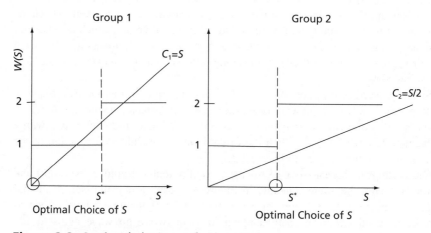

Figure 3.3 Optimal choices of education.

This implies there will be an infinite number of possible equilibrium values for S^*. In practice, however, educational qualifications tend to be obtained in discrete units, e.g. in the UK, General Certificate of Education, degree and so on, so that the number of possible equilibria may be limited.

In a related approach, examining job matching from the perspective of the employer, Salop and Salop (1976) define a screening device as essentially a rule of thumb that ranks applicants' prospective job performance on the basis of endowments of personal characteristics correlated with the parameter of interest. In addition to educational qualifications, this could be race, sex, appearance or past work experience. In general, screening devices will not sort perfectly, but there is a trade-off between the accuracy and cost of sorting. If, for example, firms know or believe that a significantly higher proportion of graduates have the necessary skills for a particular job than those with lower qualifications, educational qualifications may be used as a preliminary screen in order to save on hiring costs. The case for screening rests on market failure resulting from a lack of knowledge or the cost of obtaining it and is one reason why the social rate of return to education will differ from the private one.[5]

Another approach to gathering information is a self-selection device which can be defined as a pricing scheme that causes the applicant to reveal truthful information about him- or herself by his or her market behaviour (i.e. it is a solution to a particular principal–agent problem, as outlined in the introduction to Chapter 5). Thus, by appropriately structuring wage differentials in favour of those with educational qualifications, firms can ensure that only those with appropriate levels of intelligence pursue educational credentials and thus qualify for high-paying jobs. Or, in order to minimise turnover costs, earnings may be linked to tenure in order to encourage only low-turnover employees to apply.[6]

There have been a number of attempts to test whether various versions of the screening hypothesis can explain in part or in whole the relationship between earnings and education. Taubman and Wales (1973), for example, use a sample of air-force volunteers from NBER-Thorndike data in 1955 and 1969, which include a battery of intelligence tests, and find that certain types of mental ability and various personal characteristics are as important as education in determining earnings, the omission of such variables biasing the education coefficients by up to 38 per cent. They take their results, with important caveats, to support the view that education is used as a screening device. Another test is to assume that those who do not need to identify their productivity prior to employment (e.g. the self-employed) have less incentive to acquire education than others. Using such an approach, Wolpin (1977), with the data-set described above, but limiting the sample to those whose first and last reported jobs are self-employed and a similarly stable group of salaried workers, finds that there is little difference in the level of schooling between the two groups. This is not consistent with a predominantly screening interpretation. This result is also confirmed by Cohn *et al.* (1987), using the 1978 wave of the Panel Study of Income Dynamics. They also test alternative hypotheses. The first of these suggests that screening is more likely to be found in non-competitive sectors of the economy where bureaucratic procedures such as credentialism are more likely to flourish, as this is an environment in which productivity measurement is often problematic. However, according to their results, there appears to be no association between rates of return to education and the degree of competitiveness. They also distinguish between weak and strong forms of screening. The former postulates that employers use educational credentials to determine only starting salaries, with productivity influencing earnings in later years. The latter asserts that education only has informational value so that any earnings differentials by years of education must be attributed to screening. As information gradually accumulates about workers' abilities, under this scenario we would expect rates of return to education to gradually diminish. Thus, an appropriate test is whether mid- to early-career earnings ratios by educational qualifications diminish over time. In fact, in general, such ratios increase rather than decrease, with the exception of the government sector where they are constant. Finally, Groot and Oosterbeek (1994) note that two predictions of screening theory distinguish it from human capital theory, namely, first, that the more rapid the completion of a degree, the greater the degree of ability signalled and hence the higher the expected earnings; and, second, years spent in education without obtaining a degree should not result in higher earnings. In fact, their results show strong support for the human capital theory and refute the predictions of screening theory, since skipped years tend to reduce future earnings and repeated years have no effect upon them. Further, the positive return on drop-out years is consistent only with the human capital model. Chevalier *et al.* (2004), using British Labour Force Survey data pooled over the period 1993–2001, revisit a test used by Lang and Kropp (1986) which exploits differences in changes in education levels in response to a change in the minimum level of education, in their case across US States. Under signalling, if a low-productivity group were to raise its education because of some policy intervention, the more productive would also want to invest more in education to distinguish themselves from the less productive. Under the human capital approach, educating one group to a higher level has no effect on the decisions of others, so there should be no spillover effects. In England and Wales, there was an increase in the minimum school-leaving age (ROSLA) in 1973. Prior to ROSLA, close to 25 per cent of each cohort left at the minimum age of 15, while after the reform compliance was high, so that virtually everyone stayed on. Using Figure 3.3, suppose a minimum schooling level of S* is imposed, the lower-productivity workers in the left-hand figure will then be constrained to select S*, forcing employers to cut wages to reflect these workers' lower productivity, while the higher-productivity workers in the right-hand figure, faced with downward pressure on wages, will choose a higher level of education. Thus, under signalling, we expect all education levels to rise. However, Chevalier *et al.* (2004) find no ripple effects from ROSLA, supporting the human capital interpretation of the correlation between education and wages rather than the signalling interpretation. However, strong support for the signalling hypothesis is found for certain jobs, in which there is an excess of actual education over required education, by Chatterji *et al.* (2003). See Case Study 3.1.

Perhaps we should not be surprised by these conflicting results. Despite claims to the contrary, screening appears to be a highly costly means of selecting more-able candidates and, in many cases, particular qualifications are necessary to gain the expertise to perform the task at all, e.g. teaching, medicine, law and divinity. Signalling by employees may, however, occur under certain circumstances. Thus, some workers may offer more hours than required (unpaid overtime) in order to signal to employers their work commitment and to increase the probability of promotion (Anger 2008).[7]

Case Study 3.1

A test of the signalling hypothesis

Education increases wages in two ways: first, directly by increasing individual productivity and, second, indirectly through education being positively related to productive-employee attributes that cannot be directly observed by the firm (such as ability). The second aspect implies that education has a role as a signal of ability, but the problem is that this is not often easily observable. Despite the potential importance of each of these two roles, few earnings analyses make a distinction between the two because of the lack of availability of suitable data. This means that estimates of the return to education will be biased. In an ingenious attempt to overcome this problem, Chatterji *et al.* model the signal aspect of education as a form of over-education, assuming that firms optimally set education requirements in excess of what is truly necessary to perform the job from a purely efficiency viewpoint, with the signal depending on firm size and factors that determine the monitoring technology – a simple variant of the efficiency wage model.

The motivation for a firm to hire a worker whose education level is in excess of the technically required minimum arises from the possibility that such workers may require lower supervision and monitoring. Thus, firms may hire workers with higher educational qualifications than are strictly required to do the job in order to reduce monitoring costs, but workers will require a higher wage to compensate them for obtaining more education. This implies that such workers will be paid more than appropriately qualified workers, a common finding in the literature.

The authors use a UK data-set covering six local labour markets with diverse economic conditions in 1986 – The Social and Economic Life Initiative (SCELI). Workers were asked first "if they were applying today what qualifications if any would someone need to get the type of job you have now" and second "how necessary do you think it is to possess those qualifications to do your job competently". A positive answer to the first question and a negative answer to the second one is symptomatic of signalling. Further, responses to the second question were divided into a number of categories. If a particular level of education was said to be essential, the signal was classified as zero; if it was said to be fairly necessary, the signal was classified as a weak signal with a value of 1; if it was not really necessary, this was a strong signal equal to 2; and if it was totally unnecessary, it was classified as a pure signal equal to 4.

In an ordered probit equation using this classification to explain the incidence of over-education, dummy variables for supervision and clocking on were used to indicate high monitoring costs and both were found to be positive and significant, as was the size of firm variable, which was assumed to reflect the increased complexity of monitoring. A second stage earnings equation provided evidence that employers obtain a positive rate of return to the signal and consequently earnings equations that exclude the signal underestimate the coefficient on education. Women appear to rely on signals more than men.

M. Chatterji, Paul T. Seaman and Larry D. Singell, Jr., A Test of the Signalling Hypothesis, *Oxford Economic Papers*, SS, 2003, 191–215.

3.4 Training in theory and practice

From the perspective of the firm, profit maximisation implies that in equilibrium the discounted returns from training must equal discounted costs (or wages)

$$\sum_{t=1}^{n} \frac{MP_t}{(1+r)} = \sum_{t=1}^{n} \frac{W_t}{(1+r)} \tag{3.14}$$

Where MP_t = returns from training.

Following Becker (1975), let us assume that on-the-job training takes place only in the initial period, so that expenditures in the initial period equal wages plus the outlay on training. Then,

$$MP_0 + \sum_{t=1}^{n} \frac{MP_t}{(1+r)^t} = W_0 + K_0 + \sum_{t=1}^{n} \frac{W_t}{(1+r)^t} \tag{3.15}$$

where K equals the outlay on training.

Let us define

$$G = \sum_{t=1}^{n} \frac{MP_t - W_t}{(1+r)^t} \tag{3.16}$$

Then we rewrite equation (3.15) as

$$MP_0 + G = W_0 + K_0 \tag{3.17}$$

Now the true opportunity cost of training also includes foregone output, that is the difference between potential output (MP_0') and actual output (MP_0), while undergoing training. Let us now define C as the sum of opportunity costs and training outlays. Then equation (3.17) becomes

$$MP_0' + G = W_0 + C \tag{3.18}$$

Now G measures the return to the firm from providing training and the wage and marginal product of labour will only be equal provided $G = C$.

This leads on to the important distinction between **general training** and **specific training**. The former increases the marginal productivity of trained labour as much in other firms as it does in the firms in which the training takes place, while the latter has no productivity-enhancing effect that would be useful to firms other than the one offering the training. At the limit, firms will only provide general training if they do not have to bear the costs of it. Such costs would then be borne by the trainee in the form of lower wages. In the case of purely specific training, the firm would, however, have an incentive to bear the cost, as it could appropriate future returns. This has led to the suggestion that allegations of "poaching" of trained labour by firms that do not themselves undertake training are unfounded. By definition, specifically trained labour cannot be poached and firms do not pay for the costs of obtaining general skills.

In practice, however, training costs and benefits may be shared between firms and workers.[8] Becker himself noted that the standard model ignores the possibility

General training

Training that imparts skills that can be used elsewhere (i.e. other than in the firm in which it took place).

Specific training

Training that is useful only in the firm in which it took place, such as induction training.

of labour turnover. The departure of a specifically trained worker would be damaging to the firm because he or she could not be replaced by an equally profitable new recruit. Firms might allow for this by paying higher wages than such workers could obtain elsewhere. In turn, that would lead to an excess demand by workers for specific training, which would lead firms to transfer some of the costs of such training on to the trainees themselves. It would then follow that specifically trained workers would receive a higher wage than they could obtain elsewhere. Specifically trained employees would have less incentive to quit and employees would have a lower incentive to fire such workers than those with general skills or no skills, such that quit and lay-off rates would be inversely related to the degree of specific training.

In this situation, there would be a divergence between the wage and marginal product as indicated in Figure 3.4. Assume training lasts t_1 years and that MP_0 represents the marginal product during training, and MP_s the marginal product post-training, while W_c and MP_c represent the wage and marginal product respectively without specific training. If the firm pays the full costs of training and takes all the benefits (represented by W_c and MP_s), the worker has no strong incentive to remain with the firm. In contrast, if the worker pays the full costs of training and takes all the benefit (wage payments equal MP_0 during training and MP_s post-training), there is no strong incentive for the firm to retain the worker. An incentive compatible bargain might result, however, in a wage W_0 during training and W_s after training, so that both costs and benefits are shared.

The Becker argument that firms will be unwilling to finance *general* training has been challenged by a number of authors. See, for example, Balmaceda (2005) who shows that there are certain bargaining models that indicate that, if specific and general training are complements, the conventional findings relating to the sharing of costs and the returns to both specific and general training may be overturned. Here, we follow the approach of Katz and Ziderman (1990), who suggest that workers may possess the wrong type of general training, given non-negligible transactions costs and **information asymmetries** between training and recruiting firms. General training includes a number of components for more advanced training, skills that can be used in various tasks and ability to deal with new technology. Informational asymmetry will impose costs on the recruiting firm which will reduce

Information asymmetry

Knowledge that is not available to the same extent to all participants.

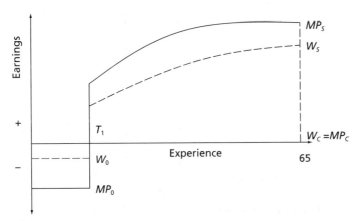

Figure 3.4 Sharing the costs of specific training.

the value of a worker trained elsewhere. The reduced inter-firm mobility of such workers may make firms willing to finance part or all of general training.

Katz and Ziderman explain this as follows. Because of information asymmetry, the value of a generally trained worker will be highest in the firm in which the training took place. If a worker were to move, therefore, there would be a loss of value (L) where $L = V_T - V_N$ and T refers to the training firm and N to the recruiting firm. Now let C represent the cost of general training. Then, if $C > L = V_T - V_N > 0$, the training firm will be prepared to pay up to $V_T + L - C$ towards the worker's general training with the worker being required to contribute the remaining costs $C - L$. The gain to the worker from mobility is $V_T - L$ and the loss on the prior investment $C - L$. In a competitive equilibrium, V_T would equal C, the net gains from moving would be zero and poaching would not be profitable.

In Figure 3.5, the divergence in worker value between training and non-training firms (i.e. $V_T - V_N$) is displayed vertically and information asymmetry (0 to 1) horizontally. The shaded area represents the extent of worker finance of general training, which diminishes as the difference between V_T and V_N increases.

A firm will bear the costs of training as long as there is information asymmetry. In the Becker case, OB' information is perfectly symmetrical and the worker pays all the costs. If, in contrast, $I > I'$ the value of a trained worker in the hiring firm will not exceed that of an untrained worker and the firm will be prepared to finance all the costs. At I^*, the worker will bear costs equal to I^*A and the firm costs equal to AB. Any increase in the symmetry of training information between training firms and other firms will increase the worker share of training investment costs.

Stevens (1994) suggests that there is a simple and plausible theoretical explanation for all these problems, namely that the general–specific training distinction does not cover all types of training. In particular, where firms possess some market power, they may be able to obtain a return on transferable skills because labour will not be freely mobile. This may also give rise to an under-investment in training.[9]

Training is usually distinguished from education through the fact that it commonly occurs after entry into the labour market has taken place on completion of

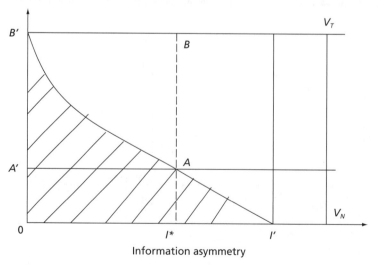

Figure 3.5 Sharing the costs of general training.

education. It must be recognised, however, that training can take many forms including induction training, on-the-job and off-the-job, formal and informal, training for young workers and (re-)training for adults. Its incidence can be measured through the proportion of workers trained by establishment, employer or industry and/or by the duration of training. This makes the assessment of its impact particularly problematical.

3.4.1 Government intervention

Traditionally, governments have intervened in the provision of training for industry. In the UK, for example, a number of studies have pointed to an apparent under-provision of training compared to other countries[10] and the government has adopted various policy measures to act as a stimulus.[11] At the level of the European Union, action with regard to vocational training and retraining has expanded over time.[12] This seems to indicate some form of market failure. Chapman (1993) suggests three main forms have been identified. First, individuals may be deterred from training because the capital market is imperfect, though this would seem to apply more strongly to education than to training. Second, employment contracts may prevent both employers and employees from achieving efficient outcomes, perhaps because wages are too rigid. Third, there may be a free-rider problem, as discussed earlier in this chapter. As Ziderman (1978) points out, whether insufficient quantities of trained manpower are a consequence of lack of worker demand for training or the offer of an insufficient supply of training places by industry, the answer does not necessarily imply that state provision of training places is appropriate. If the problem is basically one of inadequate demand for training by workers, the remedy would appear to lie in state subsidies to firms or workers, or possibly trainee loans. If the problem is, however, mainly one of lack of knowledge of the potential returns from training, dissemination of information on training opportunities would seem to be an appropriate response. In contrast, if the problem arises from an inadequate supply of training places offered by employers, legislative regulation or improved institutional arrangements seem to be implied. Other issues relate to the form that interventions into the market for training should take (see Case Study 3.2).

One reason why there might be an under-provision of training is that investment tends to fluctuate with the business cycle and, unlike investment in plant and machinery, trained workers cannot be kept in stock indefinitely. It might, therefore, be appropriate to make public provision for some speculative training capacity to soak up unemployed workers, so that skill bottlenecks are avoided in the upturn.

Basic questions to be answered are: what are the characteristics of workers who are most likely to obtain either on-the-job or off-the-job training and what are the wage effects stemming from such types of training? As noted above, there is, however, a measurement problem. As Brown (1990) notes, while formal training is relatively well defined and we should be able to determine how many hours workers have spent on it or how much investment employers have made on it, in the case of informal training, such estimates are much more elusive, as such training is produced jointly with the primary output of the trainer and trainee. While the problem of informal training appears to be intractable,[13] it seems that we may appropriately proxy specific training by **on-the-job training** (ONJT) and general training by **off-the-job training** (OFFJT). Lynch (1991) finds that, for the US, ONJT raises wages in the current job only and thus is highly specific, whereas OFFJT has little effect

On-the-job training

Training that does not require that the individual leaves the workplace, such as learning on the job, perhaps with the guidance of co-workers. This may be informal.

Off-the-job training

Training that requires that the individual leaves the workplace perhaps to participate in a college course. This may be formal.

Case Study 3.2

Should firms be made to pay for vocational training?

Policy makers in a number of countries have attempted to raise investment in vocational training by imposing a training levy as a percentage of the payroll on those firms that do not train themselves. Examples are the UK over the period 1964–82, France from 1971 and Australia over the period 1990–4. The economic rationale is that training can create external benefits to non-participants who can free ride on the training undertaken by other firms by poaching the trained labour. Traditionally, economists have rejected this argument on the grounds that workers will bear the training costs themselves where training is general, while specific training cannot be poached as it is only useful to the firms in which it takes place. Stevens (2001) asserts, however, that there are two conditions under which market failure is possible. First, as Becker (1964) points out, if there are credit constraints facing potential trainees, there may be under-investment in general training because human capital cannot normally be used as security on a loan. This may be a consequence of information asymmetries, and the associated moral hazard, that make it unfeasible to write complete loan contracts or insure against risk. Second, the market for skilled labour may be imperfect, so that the wage does not equal the marginal product of labour. This may occur because there are a limited number of employers for skilled labour of particular types or search frictions.

Stevens models the supply and demand in the training market, assuming imperfect labour and capital markets. She suggests that there is an important distinction between DEMAND-SIDE POLICIES (such as loans to trainees and training subsidies financed by a tax on wages), which affect the demand for training by workers only, and SUPPLY-SIDE POLICES (such as a profit tax or regulation), which affect only the amount of training supplied by firms. Paradoxically, she finds that training levy schemes are only effective on the demand side, which means they may resolve problems arising from capital market imperfections, while some economists suppose they will influence the supply side. If the problem is, however, perceived to be one of labour market imperfections, the appropriate policy would be a profit tax. Thus, contrary to appearances, training levy schemes, as traditionally used, do not "make firms pay". Rather, they affect the decisions of trainees rather than firms.

M. Stevens, Should Firms be Required to Pay for Vocational Training? *Economic Journal*, 111(473), July 2001, pp. 485–505.

on current earnings, but does raise earnings in subsequent jobs. Consistent with this, she also finds, using a hazard function approach, that ONJT has a negative effect on the probability of leaving an employer and OFFJT a positive effect.

3.4.2 Who receives job-related training?

One pan-European study (Arulampalam *et al.* 2004) used the first six waves of the European Community Household Panel 1994–1999 to examine the incidence of training in 10 European countries for individuals between the ages of 25 and 54. In this case, individuals were asked whether at any time in the previous year they had received vocational education or training, including any part-time or short courses. There are substantial differences in incidence across countries. In three countries

(Britain, Denmark and Finland), incidence is high (over one-third); in four (Austria, Belgium, France and Spain), it is medium at between 10 and 16 per cent; and in three (Ireland, Italy and the Netherlands), it is low at less than 10 per cent. Training is positively associated with public-sector employment, high educational attainment and a high relative position in the wage distribution. Thus, evidence suggests that there are strong complementarities between education and training.

Most earlier studies[14] have found differences among men and women in the probabilities of receiving training opportunities. Thus, in the US, Lynch finds that men are significantly more likely to receive ONJT than women and are significantly less likely to receive OFFJT, which may explain at least part of the gender wage gap. In the UK, Booth (1991), utilising the 1987 British Social Attitudes Survey, reports that, while the percentage of men receiving formal training is slightly larger than for women (44.7 per cent as opposed to 42.7 per cent), on average, the duration of training tends to be longer for women (15.0 as opposed to 11.4 days). This confirms earlier findings by Greenhalgh and Stewart (1987) and Green (1991), the latter finding, however, that the probability of training is one-third less for a typical 20 year old woman compared to a corresponding man and three-fifths less if married with a young child. One manifestation of discrimination is differential access to training opportunities, and both US (Brown 1990 and Lynch 1992) and UK (Booth 1991) empirical evidence supports the proposition that racial minorities, *ceteris paribus*, are likely to suffer a disadvantage in this respect. Indeed, Lynch suggests that "the characteristics that appear to influence the probability of receiving training are primarily race and gender". However, recent evidence suggests that women have now overtaken men in terms of training opportunities. Thus, Jones *et al.* (2009) find that, in the UK, women are more likely to receive training, regardless of type, than are men, reversing the earlier situation, and training incidence would be even higher were it not for the fact that many women work part-time. Furthermore, there is similar evidence for a number of other countries. Consideration of changes over the period 1995–2001 suggests that most of the change is not due to the changing occupational distribution of the labour force by gender, consistent with a shift in labour demand towards female rather than male employment.

Results show consistently that age has a depressing effect on the probability of training in line with expectations. Green (1993), for instance, shows that, for men, the likelihood of training declines sharply with age, while, for women, the decline is much more gradual; and Allen *et al.* (1991) show that the probability of application for retraining declines with age after 27 years. Formal schooling may be a signal that an individual has the ability to learn and hence increase the likelihood of training, and this has generally been found to be the case both for training and retraining, although Lynch (1992) finds, for the US, that the impact is smaller for ONJT than for OFFJT. Booth (1991) argues that unemployment experience may be either positively related to probability of training, because the loss of specific human capital makes retraining a more urgent requirement, or negatively related, if it acts as a (negative) signal about trainability. In fact, she finds that, for men, the negative effect dominates. In contrast, Allen *et al.* (1991) find that the probability of application for retraining is higher for those men in the sample for whom expected unemployment is greatest, namely for those leaving industries in long-term decline.

There is general agreement that employer size has an important influence on the extent of training, but less agreement on the exact form of this relationship. Brown (1989) argues that, at least for the US, the evidence suggests that, although larger employers provide more training, the very much smaller ones also tend do so.[15] Likewise, there is evidence that learning among new entrants into the labour force is disproportionately concentrated in small firms, which, on balance, tend to lose workers to larger firms. The most detailed examination of training and employer size is that of Holtman and Idson (1991), who hypothesise that larger firms would be more willing to invest in workers with characteristics associated with greater risk of investment loss. For an increase in plant size of 100 employées, the probability of ONJT increases by 3.2 percentage points. Further, the predictions across different types of worker are consistent with their risk model but not with competing models, such as those based on scale economies, physical or capital complementarities and monitoring problems. British studies confirm this positive relationship between training and firm size.

Mincer (1983) suggests that training will be lower in unionised firms because union seniority rules prevalent in the US discourage workers from investing in general training. These seniority rules may themselves be necessary in internal labour markets to encourage the co-operation of co-workers in the provision of training (Reagan 1992). We must also take into account union wage and **exit-voice effects**, which reduce turnover and the possibility that union training effects are themselves linked to size of firm.[16] Thus, Holtman and Idson (1991) find that there is a positive union effect, but one which declines with firm size. British evidence also supports a net positive effect of unions on training. Table 3.1 drawn from Shields (1998) summarises the British evidence.

Exit-voice effects

A dissatisfied worker may exit the job (quit). An alternative is to voice his or her complaints to the employer, perhaps via a trade union.

Table 3.1 The main findings from the British literature on the determinants of training

Variable type	Variable List	Effect on the probability of training	Level of agreement
Personal	Age	–	#
	Female	–	?
	Married	+	?
	Dependent child(ren)	–	?
Work-related	Qualifications	+	#
	New to job	+	#
	Trade union membership	+	#
	Part-time worker	–	#
Employer	Public sector	+	?
	High-technology industry	+	?
	Small employer	–	#
	High regional unemployment	–	?

Source: From Michael Shields, "Changes in the Determinants of Employer-funded Training for Full-time Employees in Britain, 1984–94", *Oxford Bulletin of Economics and Statistics*, 60(2), 1998, pp. 189–214. © John Wiley and Sons. Reprinted with the permission of the publisher.
Note: A "#" in the final column indicates a relationship which has a general consensus, while a "?" refers to relationships for which conflicting findings are observed.

The incentive to train will also be a function of the degree of competition in the labour market and the extent to which wages are compressed. Acemoglu and Pischke (1998) develop an imperfect competition model based on the notion that the degree of monopoly power of an employer in the local labour market will decline the greater the employees' probability of re-employment with other employers. The denser or more concentrated in terms of population the local labour market, the better the matching opportunities for potential employees and the higher the probability of re-employment either through workers changing jobs voluntarily or employers poaching workers from other firms. This will have the effect of making training more general and less profitable to the employer, thereby reducing the incentive to train. Such **agglomeration effects** have been found for Britain by Brunello and Gambarotto (2004), using the European Community Household Panel for 1997, and for Italy by Brunello and De Paola (2008). The results for Britain suggest that a 10 per cent increase in geographic density will reduce the probability of employer-provided training by 0.07 (more than 20 per cent of its average incidence). Related to these agglomeration effects is the notion that the employers' incentive to provide training will be greater the greater the **degree of wage compression** (i.e. the narrower the gap between the pay of skilled and unskilled workers). Almeida-Santos and Mumford (2004) find that higher levels of wage compression (whether measured in absolute or relative terms) are, indeed, positively related to the incidence of training.[17]

Agglomeration effects

The idea that labour market behaviour is influenced by the size of the local labour market or its density.

Degree of wage compression

A decline in the wage differential between skilled and unskilled labour.

3.4.3 Is training effective?

Whether the provision of training leads in due course to higher earnings is an important question in itself and also has implications for the propensity of individuals to offer themselves for training. For Europe, see Groot and Mekkelholt (1995) on the return to on-the-job training. For the US, Lynch (1992) finds that all types of training are associated with higher earnings, but that the effects are complex. Off-the-job training, in particular, is significantly related to wages. In the case of the UK, Booth (1991) finds that training has a large and significant effect on earnings (18.1 per cent for women and 11.2 per cent for men). However, she also finds that the positive effect on earnings decreases with days of training received.[18] The negative sign on training days seems contrary to the predictions of human capital theory, but is consistent with the view that less-able individuals require more training. Arulampalam and Booth (2001) estimate the impact of work-related training (measured as the number of training courses of at least three days' duration) on the wage growth of a cohort of young men drawn from the British NCDS over the decade 1981–91. After correcting for endogeneity, which arises when participation in a training programme is non-random, they find that training incidence has a significant positive impact on wage growth and those with higher levels of education are more likely not only to be trained, but also to experience substantially higher wage growth.

Tamkin *et al.* (2004) note that most training periods are short, much of it is driven by statutory requirements, such as health and safety rather than business needs, and only about half of it leads to formal qualifications. Therefore, it is doubtful if all training activities impact positively or equally on performance. However, they report that several studies at the level of the firm have shown that increased training activity, the *type* of training provided and its *depth* can all, in practice, positively influence performance. Jones *et al.* (2009), using WERS 2004, find that training of less than two days appears to have no beneficial effect on performance and that only when training covers a large proportion of the workforce does it appear to have beneficial effects on financial performance and productivity. Care needs to be taken, however, in measuring productivity. Dearden *et al.* (2006) point out the standard approach in the literature is to assume that wages equal marginal productivity and, therefore, suffice to capture the impact on productivity. That is, if wages increase after training, the assumption is that this is the case because workers are more productive as a consequence of the training. Dearden *et al.* are, however, able to measure the impact on productivity directly using a panel of British industries over the period 1983–96. They find that a 1 percentage point increase in training, using the LFS measure of incidence, is associated with an increase in value added per hour of almost 0.6 per cent, but an increase of wages of only 0.3 per cent, due to the monopoly power of the employer in the labour market. It appears, therefore, that part of the improvement in productivity is captured by the employer, so that using wages to measure productivity will tend to underestimate the size of the productivity gain. Finally, when they compare their industry and individual level wage regressions they find that longer lengths of time in training are associated with significantly higher wages, consistent with training externalities.

The importance of type of training was highlighted by Barrett and O'Connell (1998), who suggest that it is vocational training that has the greatest impact on wages and productivity when it is specific to the firm providing it. General training, on the other hand, tends to have less impact on individual firm performance. Depth of training has been examined by Cosh *et al.* (2003), who conclude that training is linked to improved business performance, at least over part of the periods they analyse. They also find a strong and significant effect of training on employment growth for small firms that are persistent trainers, but not for those that are ad hoc trainers. Finally, especially for larger firms, there seems to be an association between intensity of training and profitability.

Judging the effects of government-financed training schemes is rendered difficult by the bias resulting from non-random selection for training. Such bias can arise either because of self-selection by workers themselves or because of decisions made by training administrators. If no correction is made for this, relating training and earnings would imply an upward bias for the effect of training on earnings. There may also be sizeable displacement and substitution effects if graduates from these programmes simply force out other workers from the jobs they obtain. For the US, Ashenfelter (1978) finds positive training effects, but allowance has to be made for substantial foregone earnings in the training period. For the UK, Main and Shelly (1990) find that participation in the Youth Training Scheme (YTS) has a significant but small effect on the probability of obtaining a job, but no significant effect on earnings. O'Higgins (1994), using Youth Cohort Study data for England and Wales, finds, following the Main and Shelly approach, that the employment impact of YTS is between 3 and 8 percentage points, but, when he explicitly allows for the problem of sample selection bias in the determination of employment and the effects of **heteroskedasticity**, estimates range from 1 to 21 percentage points depending on the type of individual. However, one should also allow for employment effects varying over time. Dolton *et al.* (1994) apply survivor functions to the Youth Cohort Study data and find that YTS participation activity lowers the employment probability of men, though not of women, and the negative effect

Hetero-skedasticity

Ordinary least squares analysis is based on the assumption that the error term is normally distributed. A group of random variables is heteroskadastic if a sub-population of these have different variances than others, so that the standard errors are biased.

dominates for the whole sample. This is consistent with Dolton's earlier (1993) findings that employment and training programmes may have their greatest impacts and largest social returns for those who have the least previous labour market experience (for example, women), but, in general, there have been negligible wage effects and possibly negative employment effects for those experiencing government-sponsored youth training programmes. Andrews *et al.* (2002) investigate whether the popular view in the UK that the skills problem is due to a lack of demand for vocational education by young people is, in fact, correct. They find for a large sample of school-leavers in Lancashire that more express a preference for skilled occupations than actually enter them, primarily because of poor examination performance and the fact that training suppliers are unwilling to finance general training because of poaching, imperfect capital markets and imperfect information. In the light of the above, it is perhaps questionable whether the form of training provided is always optimal in meeting the requirements of the labour market.[19] The UK, in particular, has suffered from a rather piecemeal approach to training policy and a lack of continuity.

Summary

- The Mincer human capital model emphasises the importance of years of education and experience in determining lifetime earnings. The investment in human capital may take a number of years before positive returns are made as reflected in the overtaking year.
- The model also applies to the training decision. While early studies suggested that employers would only pay for specific training and the costs of general training would be borne by the employee, later studies suggest that, depending on the extent of labour turnover, transactions costs and information asymmetry, costs may be shared between employers and employees.
- The empirical implementation of the human capital model is not straightforward. The use of years of education (as opposed to qualifications obtained) has been questioned on the grounds that the relationship between earnings and education levels may be non-linear. Sheepskin models control both for years of education and qualifications. The quality of the institutions in which education takes place may also influence earnings as well as the ability of the individual (e.g. IQ). In the absence of such information, samples of twins have been used to unravel the separate effects of education and ability.
- The relationship between earnings and job tenure or seniority has also raised a number of issues such as whether this implies that productivity increases with tenure or is simply the result of unobserved heterogeneity or imperfect job matching in the case of short-tenure workers. Also, more-able workers may be more mobile, implying that many of them will be included in data-sets as short-tenure workers, thereby leading to underestimates of the return to tenure.
- The relationship between earnings and human capital may be endogenous if those with high earnings choose to consume more education, which is more likely if they are also high-ability individuals. To deal with this problem, one must find a suitable instrument for education which is uncorrelated with earnings. Such instruments have included changes in the minimum school-leaving age and childhood smoking behaviour, but whether these are valid instruments has been questioned.

- Family, school and community background may also affect economic outcomes, as well as personality traits and social skills. Children's educational attainments and those of their parents are highly correlated.
- The industry in which an individual is employed, as well as other demand-side factors, may also exert an independent influence on earnings.
- The job-screening hypothesis suggests that education has no direct effect on productivity, but simply identifies those who are more productive for other reasons. Thus, individuals can signal their employability to employers through acquiring more education. Spence hypothesises that individuals will select signals in such a way that they maximise the difference between offered wages and signalling costs. Employers may also use educational qualifications as a screen to save on hiring costs. Tests of the screening hypothesis have included comparisons between the self-employed and employed, since the former have less incentive to acquire qualifications; competitive versus non-competitive sectors, since the latter are more likely to adopt more bureaucratic procedures (credentialism); and groups who complete their education more slowly or quickly than others on the grounds that the human capital model suggests a greater return for those who take longer, unlike the screening hypothesis. However, the results of these tests are conflicting, with some support for both competing hypotheses.
- The analysis of training is also beset with problems relating to form (proportion trained or duration of training), types of training (on-the-job or off-the-job) or formal versus informal, which may go unrecorded.
- Governments have intervened in the training market because of feared under-provision related to the business cycle or perceived market failure due to poaching or wage rigidity.
- The incidence of training is not random and may be influenced by personal characteristics such as age, gender and race. On the demand side, size of employer, unionisation and the degree of competition have all been found to have significant effects on the amount of training.
- Nonetheless, training appears to yield positive returns to both employers and employees, although the fact that it has larger effects on productivity than it does on wages implies that employers receive an economic rent from the activity.

Questions

1 Assess the contribution of the human capital model in explaining why some people earn more than others.
2 To what extent can the distinction between general and specific training explain who pays for the training?
3 Explain the kind of problems that are likely to arise in making the human capital model operational in an empirical sense.
4 Explain what is meant by the screening hypothesis and evaluate the extent to which it poses a challenge to the human capital model.
5 What factors are likely to determine who receives training and where it is likely to take place?
6 Should governments intervene in the market for training and, if so, under which circumstances?

Notes

1 See Polachek (1995).

2 Sloane and Theodossiou (1993), using three-stage least squares for their British sample, obtain contrasting results for men and women, which are consistent with different lifetime labour force behaviour between the sexes. In particular, earnings have a significant effect on tenure only for women. Men gain from mobility, particularly in the early stages of their working lives, which tends to obscure any positive return to tenure. In contrast, for women and particularly those married women with constrained employment opportunities, it is more difficult to change employer, and the underlying relationship between tenure and earnings is therefore revealed.

3 One implication of the general human capital model is that, at the level of the individual, there should be a negative relationship between initial wage level and wage growth for inexperienced workers. Noting that previous attempts to test this may be influenced by a spurious correlation stemming from regression towards the mean, Neumark and Taubman (1995) find such a negative relationship, even after correcting for such negative biases and consistent with the general human capital model.

4 Mincer (1974) was well aware that demand factors needed to be taken into account. On page 137 he states, "The model of worker self-investment as the basic determinant of earnings might be criticised as giving undue weight to the supply of human capital while ignoring the demand side of the market. Certainly demand conditions in general, and employer investments in human capital of workers in particular, affect wage rates and time spent in employment, and thereby affect earnings. It should be clear, however, that the earnings function in the study is a reduced form equation, in which both demand conditions and supply responses determine the levels of investment in human capital, rate of return and time worked. The present approach is an initial and simple one, and greater methodological sophistication is clearly desirable. There is a need to relate employers' behaviour both as demanders of and investors in human capital to the observed distribution of earnings."

5 One implication of the screening hypothesis is that fluctuations in the demand for labour should lead to variations in hiring standards as well as variations in pay.

6 Salop and Salop (1976) point out that, in such a model, workers would pay their own training costs and receive the full value of their marginal product in earnings, so that, in contrast to the Becker prediction, workers would pay for the costs of specific training.

7 Using West German data over the period 1993–2004, Anger finds that for West German workers unpaid overtime is associated with an increase in earnings of 10–17 per cent, whereas for East German workers the signalling value of unpaid overtime is to lower monthly income by 22 per cent.

8 Hashimoto (1981) develops a transactions cost model to explain this. For a detailed exposition, see Chapman (1993).

9 Elias (1994), using data from a single British labour market, finds that, while for females there is a negative relationship between training and turnover, this is not the case for males. For the latter group, training does not appear to reduce turnover, which is consistent with US research.

10 Various studies have been conducted by the National Institute for Social and Economic Research. Thus, Prais and Wagner (1983) compare the training systems in five occupations in Britain and Germany, contrasting Germany's practice of testing acquired skills under examination conditions with the British practice of serving time as an apprentice. Daly *et al.* (1985) associate skill differences in matched German and British plants with the Germans' ability to deliver more complex or higher-quality products. Skills differences also prove to be relevant to the German plants' ability to utilise more sophisticated equipment and to repair it promptly following breakdowns. Thus, it seems probable that Britain suffers from low intensity of the vocational training that is provided and from the accumulation of low skill levels, from operatives through to managers, that limits the ability of British plants to employ sophisticated equipment and processes and to turn out complex products.

11 In Britain, a major policy initiative was the 1964 Industrial Training Act, which set up 27 Industrial Training Boards to implement training policies via a levy/grant system. All firms in a covered industry had to pay the levy (a payroll tax), but only those firms undertaking training to the satisfaction of their Board obtained a grant (subsidy). No distinction was made between general and specific skills, nor was allowance made for the possibility that in equilibrium it might be appropriate only for certain firms to undertake training because of economies of scale in its provision or comparative advantage. Eventually, this system was abandoned to be followed by a Training Opportunities Programme Scheme (TOPS) in 1972, a 1973 Employment and Training Act, a 1978 Youth Opportunities Programme and a 1983 Youth Training Scheme. In 1988, Employment Training for the adult unemployed was introduced and 1990 brought the formation of Training and Enterprise Councils (TECs) in England and Wales and Local Enterprise Councils (LECs) in Scotland.

12 Addison and Siebert (1994) point out that the European Union sees training programmes as an essential element in increasing competitiveness of the European economy and as a means of combating social exclusion. Much EU policy appears to be driven by apparent differences in the amount of training provided by the various member states.

13 Brown (1990) suggests that informal ONJT is at least as important as formal training.

14 Since most estimates are derived from reduced form equations rather than structural supply of and demand for training equations, we cannot say for sure whether such differences as have been found emanate primarily from the supply side or the demand side of the labour market.

15 Parsons (1990) suggests, however, that training in small firms may be concentrated on rudimentary job skills, while intensive job training is concentrated in large firms where internal financing is easier.

16 It may also be linked to public-sector employment. Booth argues that the private sector may train less than the public sector as it is more likely to be constrained by (short-run) profit considerations. She finds that men in the private sector are much less likely to obtain training.

17 They also find that training is positively associated with having a recognised vocational qualification and with current trade union membership. It is negatively related to being non-white, having shorter current job tenure and being part-time or on a fixed-term employment contract. See also Acemoglu and Pischke (1998) for the US and Booth and Bryan (2005) for Britain on the determinants of training.

18 This is inconsistent with human capital theory, but consistent with the hypothesis that less-able individuals require more training. There are, however, limitations to Booth's approach. First, earnings are bounded and limited to gross earnings, while the training question is limited to the previous two years, which allows little time for training to impact. Second, she does not deal with the problem of endogeneity because of problems of identification with her data (the self-selection of particular types of worker into training).

19 For a critical view of such training provision, see Shackleton (1992) and, for a more positive view, Layard *et al.* (1994).

References

Abraham K.G. and Farber H.S., "Job Duration, Seniority and Earnings", *American Economic Review*, 77, 1987, pp. 278–97.

Acemoglu D. and Pischke J.S., "Why Do Firms Train? Theory and Evidence", *Quarterly Journal of Economics*, 113(1), 1998, pp. 79–119.

Addison J.T. and Siebert W.S., "Vocational Training and the European Community", *Oxford Economic Papers*, 44, 1994, pp. 696–724.

Allen H.L., McCormick B. and O'Brien R.J., "Unemployment and the Demand for Retraining: An Econometric Analysis", *Economic Journal*, 101(405), 1991, pp. 190–201.

Almeida-Santos F. and Mumford K., "Employment Training and Wage Compression in Britain", IZA, Discussion Paper No. 1197, Bonn, 2004.

Altonji J.G. and Shakotko R.A., "Do Wages Rise with Job Seniority?" *Review of Economic Studies*, 69, 1987, pp. 437–59.

Andrews M.J., Bradley S. and Stott D., "Matching the Demand for and the Supply of Training in the School to Work Transition", *Economic Journal*, 112(478), March 2002, pp. C201–C219.

Anger S., "Overtime Work as a Signalling Device", *Scottish Journal of Political Economy*, 55(2), May 2008, pp. 167–89.

Arulampalam W. and Booth A., "Learning and Earning: Do Multiple Training Events Pay?", *Economica*, 68(271), 2001, pp. 279–400.

Arulampalam W., Booth A. and Bryan M., "Are there Asymmetries in the Effects of Training on the Conditional Male Wage Distribution?", IZA Discussion Paper No. 984, 2004.

Ashenfelter O., "Estimating the Effects of Training Programmes on Earnings", *Review of Economics and Statistics*, 50, 1978, pp. 47–57.

Ashenfelter O. and Krueger A., "Estimates of the Economic Return to Schooling from a New Sample of Twins", *American Economic Review*, 84(5), December 1994, pp. 1157–73.

Balmaceda F., "Firm Sponsored General Training", *Journal of Labor Economics*, 23(1), 2005, pp. 115–33.

Barrett A. and O'Connell P.J., "Does Training Generally Work? The Returns to In-Company Training", Centre for Economic Policy Research Paper No. 1879, London, 1998.

Battu H., Belfield C. and Sloane P.J., "Overeducation among Graduates: A Cohort View", *Education Economics*, 7(1), 1999, pp. 21–38.

Becker G.S., *Human Capital: A Theoretical and Empirical Analysis, with Special Reference to Education*, New York, London, NBER and Columbia University Press, 1st edition, 1964; 2nd edition, 1975.

Belman D. and Heywood J.S., "Sheepskin Effects in the Returns to Education, An Examination of Women and Minorities", *Review of Economics and Statistics*, 73, 1991, pp. 720–4.

Belman D. and Heywood J.S., "Sheepskin Effects by Cohorts: Implications of Job Matching in a Signalling Model", *Oxford Economic Papers*, 49, 1997, pp. 623–37.

Betts J.R., "Does Schooling Quality Matter? Evidence from the National Longitudinal Survey of Youth", *Review of Economics and Statistics*, LXXVII(2), May 1995, pp. 231–50.

Blackburn M.L. and Neumark D., "Are OLS Estimates of the Returns to Schooling Biased Downward?: Another Look", *Review of Economics and Statistics*, LXXVII(2), May 1995, pp. 217–30.

Blundell R., Dearden L., Goodman A. and Reed H., "The Returns to Higher Education in Britain: Evidence from a British Cohort", *Economic Journal*, 110(461), February 2000, pp. F82–F99.

Bonjour D., Cherkas L., Haskel J., Hawkes D. and Spector T., "Returns to Education: Evidence from UK Twins", *American Economic Review*, 93(5), December 2003, pp. 1799–812.

Booth A., "Job Related Formal Training: Who Receives it and What is it Worth?", *Oxford Bulletin of Economics and Statistics*, 53(3), 1991, pp. 281–94.

Booth A.L. and Bryan M.L., "Testing Some Predictions of Human Capital Theory: New Training Evidence from Britain", *Review of Economics and Statistics*, 87(2), May 2005, pp. 391–4.

Brown C., "Empirical Evidence on Private Training", in Bassi L.J. and Crawford D.L., editors, *Labor Economics and Public Policy, Research in Labor Economics*, Vol. 11, Greenwich, Connecticut, JAI Press, 1990, pp. 97–113.

Brown J.N., "Why do Wages Increase with Tenure? On-the-Job Training and Life Cycle Wage Growth Observed within Firms", *American Economic Review*, 79(5), December 1989, pp. 971–91.

Brunello G. and De Paola M., "Training and Economic Density: Some Evidence from Italian Provinces", *Labour Economics*, 15(1), 2008, pp. 118–40.

Brunello G. and Gambarotto F., "Agglomeration Effects on Employer-Provided Training: Evidence from the UK", IZA Discussion Paper No. 1055, Bonn, 2004.

Caneiro P. and Heckman J.J., "The Evidence on Credit Constraints in Post-Secondary Schooling", *Economic Journal*, 112(482), October 2002, pp. 705–34.

Card D., "The Causal Effect of Education on Earnings", in Ashenfelter O. and Card D., editors, *Handbook of Labor Economics*, vol. 3, Amsterdam, Elsevier Science, 1999, pp. 1801–63.

Card D. and Krueger A.B., "Does School Quality Matter? Returns to Education and the Characteristics of Public Schools in the United States", *Journal of Political Economy*, 100, February 1992, pp. 1–40.

Cawley J., Heckman J.J. and Vytlacil E., "Three Observations on Wages and Measured Cognitive Ability", *Labour Economics*, 8, September 2001, pp. 419–42.

Chapman P.G., *The Economics of Training*, New York, London, Harvester Wheatsheaf, 1993.

Chevalier A. and Conlon G., "Does it Pay to Attend a Prestigious University?", Centre for Economics of Education, LSE, London, March 2003.

Chevalier A., Harmon C., Walker I. and Zhu Y., "Does Education Raise Productivity or Just Reflect it", *Economic Journal*, 114(499), November 2004, pp. F499–F517.

Chevalier A., and Walker I., "The United Kingdom", in Harmon C., Walker I. and Westergaard-Nielsen N., editors, *Education and Earnings in Europe: A Cross Country Analysis of the Returns to Education*, Cheltenham, Edward Elgar, 2001, pp. 302–30.

Chiswick B.R., "Jacob Mincer, Experience and the Distribution of Earnings", IZA Discussion Paper No. 847, IZA, Bonn, August, 2003.

Cohn E., Kiker B.E. and Mendes de Olivera M., "Further Evidence on the Screening Hypothesis", *Economics Letters*, 25, 1987, pp. 289–94.

Cosh A., Hughes A., Bullock A. and Potton M., "The Relationships between Training and Business Performance", DfEE, Research Report 245, London, 2003.

Cunha F. and Heckman J.J., "The Technology of Skill Formation", *American Economic Review*, 97(2), May 2007, pp. 31–47.

Daly A., Hitchens D. and Wagner K., "Productivity, Machinery and Skills in a Sample of British and German Manufacturing Plants: Results of a Pilot Study", *National Institute Economic Review*, No. 111, February 1985.

Dearden L., Machin S. and Reed H., "Inter-generation Mobility in Britain", *Economic Journal*, 187, January 1997, pp. 47–66.

Dearden L., Reed H. and van Reenan J., "The Impact of Training on Productivity and Wages: Evidence from British Panel Data", *Oxford Bulletin of Economics and Statistics*, 68(4), 2006, pp. 397–421.

Dolton P., "The Economics of Youth Training in Britain", in Policy Forum, The Economics of Youth Training, *Economic Journal*, 103(420), September 1993, pp. 1261–78.

Dolton P., Makepeace G.H. and Treble J.G., "The Youth Training Scheme and the School to Work Transition", *Oxford Economic Papers*, 46(4), October 1994, pp. 629–57.

Elias P., "Job-related Training, Trade Union Membership and Labour Mobility", *Oxford Economic Papers*, 46(4), October 1994, pp. 563–78.

Green F., "Sex Discrimination in Job Related Training", *British Journal of Industrial Relations*, June 1991, pp. 295–304.

Green F., "The Determinants of Training of Male and Female Employees in the UK", *Oxford Bulletin of Economics and Statistics*, 55(1), February 1993, pp. 103–22.

Greenhalgh C. and Stewart M., "The Effects and Determinants of Training", *Oxford Bulletin of Economics and Statistics*, 49(2), 1987, pp. 171–89.

Groot W. and Mekkelholt E., "The Rate of Return to Investment in On-the-Job Training", *Applied Economics*, 27(2), February 1995, pp. 173–82.

Groot W. and Oosterbeek H., "Earnings Effects of Different Components of Schooling: Human Capital Versus Screening", *Review of Economics and Statistics*, 76(2), 1994, pp. 317–21.

Harmon C. and Walker I., "Estimates of the Economic Return to Schooling for the United Kingdom", *American Economic Review*, 85, 1995, pp. 1278–86.

Hashimoto M., "Firm-Specific Capital as a Shared Investment", *American Economic Review*, 71, 1981, pp. 475–82.

Heckman J.J., "Policies to Foster Human Capital", *Research in Economics*, 54, 2000, pp. 3–56.

Heckman J.J., "Schools, Skills and Synapses", *Economic Inquiry*, 46(3), 2008, pp. 289–324.

Heckman J.J., Lochner L.J. and Todd P.E., "Fifty Years of Mincer Earnings Equations", IZA Discussion Paper No. 775, May 2003.

Hersch J. and Reagan P., "Job Match, Tenure and Wages Paid by Firms", *Economic Inquiry*, 28, 1990, pp. 488–508.

Hofler R.A. and Murphy K., "Underpaid and Overworked: Measuring the Effect of Imperfect Information on Wages", *Economic Inquiry*, XXX, July 1992, pp. 511–29.

Holtman A.G. and Idson T.L., "Employer Size and On-the-Job Training Decisions", *Southern Economic Journal*, 58(2), October 1991, pp. 339–55.

Johnson G.E. and Stafford F.P., "Social Returns to Quantity and Quality of Schooling", *Journal of Human Resources*, 8(2), 1973, pp. 139–55.

Jones M.K., Latreille P.L. and Sloane P.J., "Crossing the Tracks? Trends in the Training of Male and Female Workers in Great Britain", *British Journal of Industrial Relations*, 46(2), June 2009, pp. 268–82.

Hungerford T. and Solon G., "Sheepskin Effects and the Returns to Education", *Review of Economics and Statistics*, 69, 1987, pp. 175–7.

Jaeger D.A. and Page M.A., "Degrees Matter: New Evidence in Sheepskin Effects in the Returns to Education", *Review of Economics and Statistics*, 78, 1996, pp. 733–40.

Katz E. and Ziderman A., "Investment in General Training: The Role of Information and Labour Mobility", *Economic Journal*, 100, December, 1990, pp. 1147–58.

Krueger A. and Summers L.H., "Reflections on the Inter-Industry Wage Structure", 1986, in Lang K. and Leonard J.S., editors, *Unemployment and the Structure of Labor Markets*, Basil Blackwell, New York, 1988, vol. 101, pp. 609–24.

Lang K. and Kropp D., "Human Capital versus Sorting: The Effects of Compulsory Attendance Laws", *Quarterly Journal of Economics*, 101, 1986, pp. 609–24.

Layard R., Mayhew K. and Owen G., *Britain's Training Deficit*, Aldershot, Avebury, 1994.

Loprest L.P., "Gender Difference in Wage Growth and Job Mobility", *American Economic Review, Papers and Proceedings*, 82(2), May 1992, pp. 526–32.

Lynch L.M., "The Role of Off-the-Job vs On-the-Job Training for the Mobility of Women Workers", *American Economic Review*, Papers and Proceedings, May 1991, pp. 151–5.

Lynch L.M., "Private Sector Training and the Earnings of Young Workers", *American Economic Review*, 82(1), March 1992, pp. 299–310.

Main B.G.M. and Shelly M.A., "The Effectiveness of YTS as a Manpower Policy", *Economica*, 57, 1990, pp. 495–514.

Miller P., Mulvey C. and Martin N., "What do Twins Studies Reveal about the Economic Returns to Education? A Comparison of Australian and US Findings", *American Economic Review*, 85(3), June 1995, pp. 586–99.

Mincer J., *Schooling, Experience and Earnings*, New York, NBER and Columbia University Press, 1974.

Mincer J., "Union Effects: Wages, Turnover and Job Training", in Reid J.D., editor, New Approaches to Labor Unions, *Research in Labor Economics*, Supplement 1, Greenwich, Connecticut, JAI Press, 1983, pp. 217–52.

Mincer J., *Studies in Human Capital: Collected Essays of Jacob Mincer*, Vol. 1, Aldershot, Edward Elgar, 1993.

Neumark D. and Taubman P., "Why do Wage Profiles Slope Upward? Tests of the Hierarchical Human Capital Model", *Journal of Labor Economics*, 13(4), October 1995, pp. 736–61.

O'Higgins N., "YTS, Employment and Sample Selection Bias", *Oxford Economic Papers*, 46(4), October 1994, pp. 605–28.

Park J.H., "Estimation of Sheepskin Effects Using the Old and New Measure of Educational Attainment in the Current Population Survey", *Economic Letters*, 62, 1999, pp. 237–40.

Parsons D.O., "The Firm's Decision to Train", in Bassi L.J. and Crawford D.L., editors, *Labor Economics and Public Policy, Research in Labor Economics*, Vol. 11, Greenwich, Connecticut, JAI Press, 1990, pp. 53–75.

Polachek S.W., "Earnings over the Life Cycle: What Do Human Capital Models Explain?", *Scottish Journal of Political Economy*, 42(3), August 1995, pp. 267–89.

Polachek S. W. and Siebert W. S., *The Economics of Earnings*, Cambridge, Cambridge University Press, 1993.

Prais S.J. and Wagner K., "Some Practical Aspects of Human Capital Investment: Training Standards in Five Occupations in Britain and Germany", *National Institute Economic Review*, No. 105, August 1983.

Reagan P., "On-the-Job Training, Lay-off by Inverse Seniority and the Incidence of Unemployment", *Journal of Economics and Business*, 44(4), November 1992, pp. 317–24.

Robertson D. and Symons J., "Do Peer Groups Matter? Peer Group versus Schooling Effects on Academic Attainment", *Economica*, 70, February 2003, pp. 31–53.

Salop J. and Salop S., "Self Selection and Turnover in the Labour Market", *Quarterly Journal of Economics*, 90, November 1976, pp. 619–27.

Shackleton J.R., *Training Too Much? A Sceptical Look at the Economics of Skill Provision in the UK*, Hobart Paper No. 118, London, Institute of Economic Affairs, 1992.

Shields M., "Changes in the Determinants of Employer-Funded Training for Full-time Employees in Britain, 1984–1994", *Oxford Bulletin of Economics and Statistics*, 60(2), 1998, pp. 189–214.

Sloane P.J. and Theodossiou I., "Gender and Job Tenure Effects on Earnings", *Oxford Bulletin of Economics and Statistics*, 55(4), November 1993, pp. 421–38.

Spence M., "Job Market Signalling", *Quarterly Journal of Economics*, 87, August 1973, pp. 355–79.

Stevens M., "A Theoretical Model of On-the-Job Training with Imperfect Information", *Oxford Economic Papers*, 46(4), October 1994, pp. 537–62.

Tamkin P., Giles L., Campbell M. and Hillage J., *Skills Pay: The Contribution of Skills to Business Success*, Skills for Business Research Reports, September 2004.

Taubman P., "The Determinants of Earnings: Genetics, Families, and Other Environments: A Study of White Male Twins", *American Economic Review*, 66(5), 1976, pp. 858–70.

Taubman P. and Wales T.J., "Higher Education, Mental Ability and Screening", *Journal of Political Economy*, 81, January/February 1973, pp. 28–55.

Thurow L.C., *Generating Inequality*, New York, Basic Books, 1975.

Topel R., "Specific Capital, Mobility and Wages: Wages Rise with Job Seniority", *Journal of Political Economy*, 99, 1991, pp. 145–76.

Topel R. and Ward M.P., "Job Mobility and the Careers of Young Men", *Quarterly Journal of Economics*, CVII(2), May 1992, pp. 439–80.

Walker I. and Zhu Y., "The Returns to Education; Evidence from the Labour Force Survey", Department of Education and Skills, Research Paper RR 313, November 2001.

Willis R., "Wage Determinants: A Survey and Reinterpretation of Human Capital Earnings Functions", in Ashenfelter O. and Layard R. editors, *Handbook of Labor Economics*, Vol. 1, Elsevier, BV, 1986, pp. 525–602.

Wolpin K.I., "Education and Screening", *American Economics Review*, 67(5), December 1977, pp. 949–58.

Zax J.S. and Rees D.I., "IQ, Academic Performance and Earnings", *Review of Economics and Statistics*, 84, November 2002, pp. 600–13.

Ziderman A., *Manpower Training: Theory and Policy*, London, Macmillan, 1978.

Zimmerman D.J., "Peer Effects in Academic Outcomes; Evidence from a National Experiment", *Review of Economics and Statistics*, 85(1), February 2003, pp. 9–23.

Further reading

The classic texts are Gary Becker, *Human Capital; A Theoretical and Empirical Analysis, with Special Reference to Education*, New York, National Bureau of Economic Research and Columbia University Press, 1st edition, 1964; 2nd edition, 1975, and Jacob Mincer, *Schooling, Experience and Earnings*, New York, National Bureau of Economic Research and Columbia University Press, 1974. Few books have had such an impact on labour economics in general.

Geraint Johnes and Jill Johnes, editors, *International Handbook of the Economics of Education*, Edward Elgar, Cheltenham, UK and Northampton, MA, USA, 2004, contains a number of useful contributions, particularly those by G. Psacharopoulos and H. Patrinos on human capital and rates of return, S. Brown and J. Sessions on signalling and screening, and P. Dolton on the economic assessment of training schemes.

A. Booth and D. Snower, editors, *Acquiring Skills*, Centre for Economic Policy Research and Cambridge, Cambridge University Press, 1996, contains a number of contributions focusing on market failures, their symptoms and appropriate policy responses.

E. Leuven, "The Economics of Private Sector Training: A Survey of the Literature", *Journal of Economic Surveys*, 19(1), 2005, pp. 91–111, summarises existing theoretical work in this area, focusing on investment efficiency, finance and turnover, with an emphasis on market imperfections.

Changing jobs
The economics of job search

Introduction

Chapter 1 examined labour force participation in terms of entry into the labour market, the overall activity rates when in the labour market and the retirement decision. In this chapter, we focus on the process of job changes. Many workers will have a number of jobs with different employers over their working lifetime, perhaps with intervening periods of unemployment.

We start by examining gross labour market flows, which can be examined from the perspective of an individual employer or from the perspective of the employee. Employer-to-employer flows are common and positively related to the business cycle, but whether the flows are voluntary or involuntary is important in determining whether a move is advantageous from the point of view of the individual.

Next, we consider the role of information as it is unlikely that workers are fully informed about levels of pay among different employers and they are likely to know even less about the nature of the workplace environment. **Asymmetric information models** can lead to very different predictions about whether or not mobility will take place depending on the gradients of the relevant curves.

In section 4.3, we look at the role of job satisfaction in influencing labour mobility. This is an area that economists have increasingly studied in recent years, as we expect that, if workers are dissatisfied, they will be more likely to move to another job in order to raise their job satisfaction, which can be regarded as a proxy for the utility of work. This prediction seems to hold in practice, as most workers report high levels of satisfaction in their existing jobs whether or not they have moved.

The theory of job search has also expanded considerably in recent years and gives rise to important questions such as the relative importance of **off-the-job search** and **on-the-job search**, the **optimal stopping rule** and the role of the **reservation wage**. In one sense, the whole of this chapter is relevant to job search, which is basically concerned with the implications of imperfect information on jobs and wages. Unemployed job seekers may devote more effort to looking for work than employed job seekers, but on-the-job search may result in a lower reservation wage because lower costs are involved in the search process. Perfect competition models are unable to deal with search theory because, in dealing with frictions, the latter drops the assumption of perfect knowledge.

Finally, we consider migration both within and across regions and countries. In the case of internal migration, the nature of the housing market is an important consideration, which in some circumstances may outweigh the significance of compensating wage differences. International migration has become increasingly significant with important political as well as economic considerations. Whether such migration has long-run economic benefits which outweigh economic costs is the focus of attention here.

4.1 Gross labour market flows

The amount of job change in the economy is substantial and strongly influenced by stages of the business cycle. This includes workers reallocating themselves among jobs and between employment and joblessness and events that alter the distribution of available jobs among establishments. The former may involve employment-to-employment movements for reasons of job advancement, improved job satisfaction in relation to the quality of worker–job matches and retirement. The latter may involve the growth and decline of markets, restructuring of firms and industries or changing patterns of domestic and foreign competition (see Haltiwanger *et al.* 1998).

Total worker turnover at time *t* will equal the number of accessions plus the number of separations that occur during the interval t-1 to t. Gross job reallocation

---

Asymmetric information models

In these models, it is assumed that some individuals or groups possess information that is not available to others.

Off-the-job search

A situation in which individuals have left their previous job and are searching for another job while unemployed or inactive.

On-the-job search

A situation in which workers search for another job while currently employed.

Optimal stopping rule

The point at which job search ceases because the expected marginal benefits from future job search equal the expected marginal costs of engaging further in such activities.

Reservation wage

The lowest wage that is acceptable to an individual, given his or her circumstances and the nature of the job.

equals the sum of employment gains (or job creation) and losses (or job destruction) across establishments during the interval from t-1 to t. It is estimated that roughly one worker in four experiences a change in employer or employment status each quarter. This implies that many workers experience repeated transitions or ones that are reversed during the year. These gross flows lie at the heart of the **Diamond–Mortensen–Pissarides search and matching framework** discussed below as there is heterogeneity among workers and labour market frictions that prevent instantaneous matching of new vacancies and unemployed workers, and result in unemployment and unfilled vacancies. According to Joseph *et al.* (2004), the job turnover rate in most OECD countries is between 15 and 25 per cent each year, which is roughly the same as in North America, with slightly positive net employment rates (the differences between job creation and job destruction) being associated with very large job reallocations.

Turnover consists of both job accessions and job separations. Turning to job separations, for the UK, Clancy (2009) shows that total separations were 5.8 million in 1998, but fell to 4.3 million by 2008. It is important, however, to distinguish between involuntary and voluntary turnover. See Jones and Martin (1986) for the UK. The former include dismissals, redundancies, terminations due to ill health, retirements and family or personal reasons. **Voluntary turnover** is more substantial than involuntary (3.1 million compared to 1.2 million in 2008). Overall separation rates are higher for women and young workers. However, these statistics obscure the fact that most employees do not move regularly among employers. Rather, voluntary turnover is concentrated among relatively few workers who move frequently. As Creedy and Disney (1981) note

> the data clearly show that previous experience is important: those who (are) prone to previous lengthy work interruptions are likely to experience the same in the future. Conversely, those with stable work histories, have a greater probability of remaining in full employment in the future.

There are substantial variations in the extent of turnover among industries. Jones (1985) shows that the incidence of redundancy is considerably lower in industries characterised by high voluntary turnover.

Gomez-Salvador *et al.* (2004) find that job reallocation is inversely correlated with capital intensity and that the number of jobs being created and destroyed is greater in services than in manufacturing. Job creation is also negatively associated with firm age and size. Institutional factors are also important. They find that the strictness of employment protection across 13 European countries has a negative effect on job creation, as does the generosity of unemployment benefits and the extent of wage bargaining co-ordination.

It is also important to note that **employment-to-employment job flows** are substantial. For the US, Fallick and Fleischman (2004) estimate that on average 2.6 per cent of employed persons change employers each month, a flow that is twice as large as that from employment to unemployment. On-the-job search, which is implied by this statistic, is an important element in hiring, as nearly two-fifths of new jobs started between 1994 and 2003 represented employer changes. These flows are also markedly procyclical. Similarly in the UK, Pissarides and Wadsworth (1988) suggest that about one-half of all new hirings are of workers who already have jobs.

Diamond–Mortensen–Pissarides search and matching framework

This is based on the proposition that heterogeneity among workers and labour market frictions prevent instantaneous matching of new vacancies and unemployed workers.

Voluntary turnover

Job quitting that results from the free choice of an individual worker and is not the result of dismissals, redundancies, ill health, retirement or other non-work-related reasons.

Employment-to-employment job flows

Changes of employer that occur without an intervening period of unemployment or inactivity.

In order for workers to move successfully between jobs, they need to be well informed about alternatives and we now turn to consideration of this aspect of mobility.

4.2 Information in the labour market

It is generally hypothesised that workers will move jobs in order to maximise net advantages, both pecuniary and non-pecuniary, but this requires information not only on the distribution of wage rates among employers and opportunities for over-time working, but also on the nature of the workplace environment and, as Stigler (1962) observes, it is highly unlikely that any worker can be fully informed about what conditions he or she might obtain from all potential employers. There is, in fact, a substantial dispersion of wage rates for supposedly homogeneous labour. Indeed, one study of over 1,000 related engineering establishments in 1972 (Mayhew 1977) found that not only was inter-plant dispersion for semi-skilled and unskilled males substantial, but so also was intra-plant dispersion. In such circum-stances, there must be considerable uncertainty about the probability of receiving particular wage offers.

Rees and Schultz (1970), in their study of the Chicago labour market, found that for blue-collar workers informal job sources of information were much more impor-tant than formal, and within this category employee referral was most significant.[1] From an applicant's point of view, this can provide information which is simply unavailable to the public or private employment service, such as the nature of working conditions or attitudes of supervisors. These imperfections in knowledge may extend to employers. Mackay et al. (1971) found in their studies of engineer-ing in Birmingham and the West of Scotland that employers in one plant often knew very little in detail of competitors' wage structures and made mistakes accordingly.

This raises the question of information asymmetry and whether it is employers or employees who are better informed. Stark (1991) notes that most relevant previ-ous research and particularly that relating to implicit labour contracts has tended to assume that employers are better informed than employees, but there may well be situations in which the reverse is true. Asymmetric information models are particu-larly relevant to international labour migration, but can be applied equally to other cases of labour mobility. Noting that the most natural application of the concept of informational asymmetry is where employers are uncertain about the productivity level of potential employees, Stark sets out to model the relationship between inter-national migration and asymmetric information when workers possess, at least ini-tially, more information than potential employers in the host country, which is assumed to be richer than the country of origin.

Following Stark's approach, let us assume that H represents a high-paying employer in the host country and P a low-paying employer in a relatively poor country of origin, that S represents a skill level between zero and one, with pay positively related to skill level, and that P workers have preference for employment in P because of non-pecuniary and/or locational advantages, so that a discount factor applies to employment in H from the perspective of the potential migrant, such that $kW_H(S) > W_P(S)$, where $0 < k < 1$. Further, assume that the skill of each potentially mobile worker is known in P, because P can observe performance, but is unknown in H, and that each worker is fully informed as to his or her true skill level. Then H will pay an identical wage to each recruit from P based on average skill or productivity.

Now consider the case where a worker with a particular skill level S is contemplating moving from country P to country H. The effect of asymmetric information on mobility then depends critically on the slopes of $kW_H(S)$ and $W_P(S)$. In Figure 4.1 these are positively sloped from left to right, indicating that higher skills attract higher wages. The slopes indicate the size of the wage premium for skilled over unskilled labour and it is possible that the gradient may be shallower or steeper in P compared to H. However, W_H lies above W at every point because productivity is higher in H than in P at all skill levels and workers are paid according to the value of their marginal products. Assuming again that $kW_H(S) - W_P(S) > 0$, then workers of all skill levels will move regardless of whether information is symmetric or asymmetric as shown in Figure 4.1.

The effect of asymmetric information is to lower the slope of the H wage schedule from $kW_H(S)$ to $k\overline{W}_H(S^*)$ starting from the vertical wage axis as indicated by the broken line. The assumption is that asymmetric information does not matter for a totally unskilled worker, but its importance increases with the level of skill. However, this does not affect the outcome as the effect of asymmetric information is not sufficient to force the operative wage schedule in H below that in P. As workers will be paid more in H than in P, all workers, regardless of skill level, would move from P to H under this scenario.

An alternative possibility is that $kW_H(S)$ lies everywhere above $W_p(S)$, but $k\overline{W}_H$ intersects the latter. In this case illustrated in Figure 4.2, migration will be limited to workers in the interval $[0, S_1]$. Thus, asymmetric information has the consequence of reducing both the amount of mobility and also the skill level of those who are mobile.

A third possibility (Figure 4.3) is that $kW_H(S)$ and $W_P(S)$ intersect. This could arise if the skill premium in P was greater than the skill premium in H. Again, the effect of asymmetric information is to reduce both the quantity and quality of migrant workers as mobility of $[S_2, S_1]$ skill levels is eliminated. Thus, the effect of asymmetric information, when it does have an impact, is always to reduce the

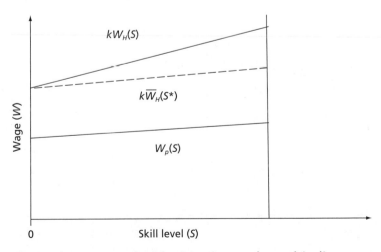

Figure 4.1 International migration and non-binding asymmetric information.

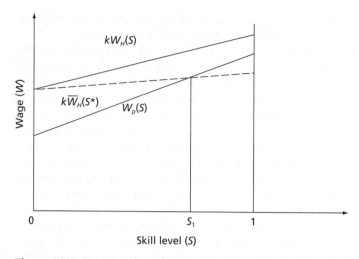

Figure 4.2 International migration and partially binding asymmetric information.

amount and quality of labour mobility.

The case where $kW_H(0) \leq W_P(0)$ is rather more complex. This implies that unskilled labour in P is paid more than unskilled labour in H, perhaps because the structure of the economy in P is favourable to unskilled labour and there are few jobs for skilled workers there. Then the use of the $k\overline{W}_H(S^*)$ curve is inappropriate because mobility in this case starts from $S = 1$ rather than $S = 0$. There are two possibilities. First, the lowest point on the $k\hat{W}_H(S^*)$ curve lies below the highest point of the $W_P(S)$ curve. Since the former curve represents the discounted wage each mobile worker would receive if everyone moved, the implication is that it will shift downwards until an equilibrium is reached where no mobility occurs. In the reverse

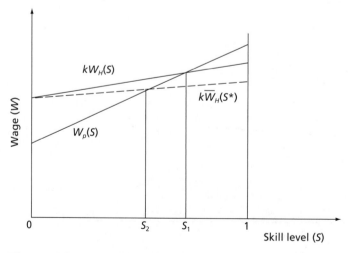

Figure 4.3 International migration and fully binding asymmetric information.

case, Stark shows that mobility will occur in the interval $[S_2, 1]$ and $k\hat{W}_H(S^*)$ will move upwards until equilibrium is reached with all skill levels mobile.

Thus, the conclusion of Stark's analysis is that the effect of asymmetric information on mobility patterns is asymmetric. That is, when the discounted wage differential at the lowest skill level is not positive, so that mobility is not desirable, the introduction of asymmetric information results in total mobility or zero mobility depending on the gradients of the relevant curves.

Lack of perfect information leads naturally on to the study of search behaviour. As Lippman and McCall (1979) note,

> The acquisition of information is exactly what search theory is all about. Any theory that ignores search by either assuming that firms and customers are perfectly informed or that the cost of information is zero labours under severe handicaps. Commonplace occurrences, like different prices for identical goods, advertising, queuing, and persistent positive levels of unemployed resources will be invisible in such a deterministic portrait of the economic landscape. Search theory provides a ready explanation of these events.

Whether traditional search theory is descriptive of the majority of job-seeking behaviour in the labour market is debatable, as we shall see. But before turning to this we first consider the role of job satisfaction in determining mobility. If a worker is dissatisfied with his or her current job, we would expect that this would increase the inclination to move and we consider below whether this is, indeed, the case.

4.3 Job satisfaction and labour mobility

While socio-psychologists have analysed job satisfaction in considerable detail, economists, at least until recently, have been reluctant to do so. Freeman (1978) suggested that this might reflect the professional suspicion of what is a subjective variable and, indeed, one that purports to measure individual utility. Yet studies of job satisfaction reveal consistent and robust relationships with various labour market variables such as labour market mobility.

Standard theory suggests that workers will attempt to maximise net advantages (both pecuniary and non-pecuniary) and, since in long-run equilibrium net advantages should be equalised, differences in job satisfaction among individual workers or work groups should reflect differences in tastes, lack of perfect mobility (Hamermesh 1977) or lack of information and the existence of market power, including the presence of unions (Borjas 1979).

There will be uncertainty about non-pecuniary characteristics of jobs prior to taking up a job, and we might assume that in a life-cycle context individuals will sample jobs until a satisfactory job match is found. Assuming competitive labour markets, perfect mobility and homogenous tastes, we may, following Hamermesh, define job satisfaction at time t during individual i's working life as

$$JS_i = \int_{QX}^{\sigma} u(w + dx)F_{ix}^t(w)dw - u(w_0 + d_0) \qquad (4.1)$$

where JS = job satisfaction, Q_X defines the lower limit of the distribution, F_{ix}^t, and sigma the upper, which is the probability distribution of wages foreseen in occupation x by the ith individual at time t, w the wage and dx equals the monetary value of non-pecuniary benefits. The equilibrium condition[2] ensures that there will be no substantive differences in job satisfaction across occupations at time t_0, but over time worker uncertainty about the wage σ_W decreases and job satisfaction provides an economic rent for workers who undertake the risk of entering an occupation with a specific training requirement. This leads to the prediction that job satisfaction will be greater for workers who are older or more experienced and in occupations which require more occupational-specific training. Characteristics that improve efficiency in job search should increase job satisfaction by ensuring better job matches, and Borjas suggests that education falls into this category. However, in practice, the relationship between job satisfaction and job tenure is less certain because in the cross-section we may observe individuals in both pre-and post-matching periods.

Job satisfaction should also be greater for those who are paid more for given characteristics, but the relationship between pay and job satisfaction is complex with the suggestion that both relative and absolute earnings are relevant. As Rees (1993) observes, "neo-classical wage theory is based on the premise that a worker's utility is based on his own wage and his own hours of work, without reference to the wages and hours of others" but "the wages of others are a powerful force in determining worker satisfaction such that utility goes down when the wages of others go up".

This idea has been formalised by Baxter (1973, 1993) as **relative deprivation** and applied to job satisfaction by both Hamermesh (1977) and Clark and Oswald (1996). The starting point of this approach is J.S. Adams' (1963) and (1965) **equity theory of exchange** which suggests that equity exists when there is a correspondence between the inputs and outputs of different individuals and groups.[3] Baxter suggests that worker a's pay goal can be expressed as

$$w_a = w_a^* = k\overline{W}_{rb} \tag{4.2}$$

where w_a equals the actual wage of individual a, w_a^* equals a's perception of his equitable wage and $k\overline{W}_{rb}$ equals the equitable wage expressed as a proportion of the reference group rb. Considerable effort will go into ensuring that one's relative position is maintained over time. Such a measure may be obtained as the deviation of actual from expected earnings, calculated as the residual from human capital earnings equations. However, as Hamermesh notes, there are two potential problems in doing so. First, part of the above residual may include unmeasured differences in ability, thereby biasing estimates in the job satisfaction regression towards zero. Second, there is a potential problem of **endogeneity**, since job satisfaction may not only be higher when pay is higher, but push up pay as more highly satisfied workers are likely to co-operate more with management. A third problem of this particular specification, noted by Clark and Oswald, is that the significance of the residual in the satisfaction equation might simply reflect **mis-specification**. In a recent paper, Clark *et al.* (2009), using the Danish sample of the European Community Household Panel Survey for the years 1994–2001, find that individual job satisfaction is actually higher where other workers in the same establishment are *better* paid. They attribute this to the fact that their reference group is co-workers and the higher pay of this group acts as a signal about potential earnings which outweighs any negative status effect.

Relative deprivation

The idea that worker well being is determined by the position of individuals relative to others in a comparator group, as opposed to absolute levels of welfare.

Equity theory of exchange

This is based on the idea that equity exists when there is a correspondence between the inputs of effort by various individuals and groups and the rewards from their outputs.

Endogeneity

A situation in which an independent variable may not only influence the value of the independent variable, but also itself be determined, at least partly, by the dependent variable.

Mis-specification

A situation in which an economic theory on which a model is based is incomplete, resulting in the estimated parameters being biased.

4.3.1 Estimation

Information on job satisfaction varies depending on the data-set between binary variables (satisfied/dissatisfied) and examples can be found of rating scales varying between one and five, one and seven or zero and ten. Rating scales can be linearised and estimated by OLS, although it may be better to regard such scales as ordinal. It is suggested that OLS in this case will provide biased estimates and the explanatory power of the OLS models is generally low (frequently below 5 or 6 per cent). It is also possible to rescale responses to produce a **z score**, measuring the number of standard deviations between a given response and the mean response. Binary variables overcome such problems and can be estimated by **maximum likelihood methods**, but at the expense of some loss of information. An ordered probability model (ordered probit) seems superior to either of the above, but it is difficult to apply where the number of categories is large. Few utilise a **simultaneous equations approach**, exceptions being Bender and Sloane (1998) and Borjas (1979). Where attempts are made to split the sample into men and women or unionists and non-unionists, the results may also be subject to sample selection bias, but only a few studies such as Meng (1990), Hampton and Heywood (1993), and Bender and Sloane (1998) attempt to deal with this problem. Finally, some data-sets contain information not only on overall satisfaction but also on various facets of it. This gives rise to the question of whether models focusing on relative deprivation should test for this phenomenon in relation to overall job satisfaction, satisfaction with pay or both elements.

4.3.2 Empirical studies

Studies may be divided into those that examine job satisfaction for the workforce as a whole – Hamermesh (1977), Freeman (1978) and Clark and Oswald (1996); those which focus on men and women separately – Clark (1997), Hampton and Heywood (1993), and Sloane and Williams (2000); those which compare the job satisfaction of trade union members relative to non-members – Borjas (1979), Miller (1990), Meng (1990), and Bender and Sloane (1998); and one which focuses on establishment size – Idson (1990).

Most studies estimate equations of the form

$$u_i - u(y, y^*, h, i, j) \qquad (4.3)$$

where u represents the utility of the ith individual obtained from work (i.e. job satisfaction), y is the wage and y^* is the comparison wage, h represents hours of work and i and j are vectors of individual and job-specific characteristics respectively. The empirical tests generally support the predictions of the model. Freeman is particularly concerned with the relationship between job satisfaction and quits, finding that most variables like age, wages and race had the expected oppositely signed coefficients on satisfaction compared to quits. He also finds that, while tenure is associated with much lower quit rates, it has hardly any effect on job satisfaction and, while trade union membership has a similar negative effect on quits and would be expected to raise job satisfaction, it too either has little effect on job satisfaction or actually lowers it. Clark and Oswald, using British data, find that, while job satisfaction is at best weakly correlated with absolute earnings, it is significantly

---

Z score

A statistical measure that quantifies the distance (measured in standard deviations) a data point is from the mean of a data-set.

Maximum likelihood methods

These select values of the model parameters that produce a distribution that gives the observed data the greatest probability of being correct.

Simultaneous equations approach

This is designed to deal with the problem that not all variables in a model may be exogenous by using instrumental variables and estimating the model in two stages.

related to their measure of comparison income. Further, they find a strong negative relationship between job satisfaction and educational attainment which they suggest is due to education raising aspiration targets.

Idson finds that, when there are no controls for attributes of the work environment, job satisfaction (net of wages and fringe benefits) is lower in larger establishments. However, when a vector of 31 work environment variables are added to the equations, satisfaction is significantly reduced, suggesting that the observed lower satisfaction in larger establishments may be largely attributed to greater rigidity in the structure of the working environment.

It is generally found that women express themselves as more satisfied at work than men.[4] Clark suggests that this may be explained by the fact that it is easier for women than for men to leave the labour force. However, it could be argued that it is easier for men to quit their current place of employment for another job if they are dissatisfied. Clark tests the hypothesis using wave one of the British Household Panel Survey, which contains information on seven aspects of job satisfaction as well as a seven-point scale for overall satisfaction. T statistics for differences in mean job satisfaction for men and women show that only in the case of two aspects (initiative and promotion opportunities) are women not significantly more satisfied than men. However, when regressions are run controlling for job and personal characteristics, work values and household structure, the female–male pay satisfaction differential becomes insignificant, but the statistically significant differential for overall satisfaction remains. It should be noted, however, that Clark, unlike Clark and Oswald, does not include a comparison income variable. Hampton and Heywood focus on a different issue: women's perceptions of underpayment in relation to actual gender wage discrimination by examining data on young male and female doctors contained in a 1987 American Medical Association Survey. Respondents were asked to say what they considered to be an adequate income for their stage of career. They estimate separate equations for men and women to explain both actual annual income and claimed adequate income. For men, it is found that adequate income is 25 per cent more than actual and for women 29 per cent more than actual. Their fundamental test is to estimate the determinants of female perceived underpayment (FPU_i) in a regression that controls for male estimated underpayment $M\hat{P}U$, speciality, personal characteristics and estimated discrimination ($\hat{D}$). Thus, we have

$$FPu_i = B_j X_{ij} + \alpha_1 M\hat{P}U_i + \alpha_2 \hat{D}_i + e_i \tag{4.4}$$

where X_{ij} represent personal characteristics.

If women accurately perceive discrimination, we would expect α_2 to be equal to or close to one, and, if men and women have similar beliefs about underpayment, that α_1 would be equal or close to one. This, in fact, turns out to be the case. They also suggest that this needs to be tested over a wider range of occupations.

Having considered the amount of mobility in the economy, the role of information and the determinants and consequences of job satisfaction, we are now in a better position to consider in more detail the theory of job search itself.

4.4 Job search

The **economic theory of job search** attempts to provide answers to a number of questions such as: how do prospective employees search for jobs (e.g. formal versus informal methods), what types of search provide the best pay-offs (e.g. the intensity of job search, choice of reservation wage), and what are the labour market implications of these methods of search for wage and occupational distributions (see Fearn 1981 and Jones 1989). Uncertainty is brought within the framework of analysis by assuming that workers sample wage offers from a distribution and accept only those which have an acceptable wage equal to or above the reservation wage, so that luck can explain part of the unexplained variance in standard wage regressions and some unemployment will be required to enable workers to find jobs (Kiefer and Neumann 1989). At the centre of the theory is the reservation wage. This represents the lowest wage that is acceptable to the worker, given his or her circumstances. This may alter with the length of time an individual has been searching for a job and may be higher for jobs requiring geographical relocation or higher commuting costs, given existing place of residence, or jobs which require a higher degree of responsibility. Assuming leisure is a normal good, an increase in non-wage income including higher unemployment benefits will lead to an increase in the reservation wage and reduce the probability of finding a job at an acceptable wage.

In Figure 4.4, we assume the distribution of wage offers by employers is known and represented by a normal distribution. However, the individual job seeker does not know which particular firms will offer a particular wage rate. Then the individual must choose how many searches to make within a given time period and accept the highest resulting wage offer, assuming this is above the reservation wage. As the number of firms sampled increases, the cost of search will rise and hence the expected return will alter and together these will determine the optimal sample size of searching.

In Figure 4.4, ww represents the number of firms offering particular levels of wages as given by a normal distribution ww with a mean of w_0. Assume that w_r is

Economic theory of job search

Models designed to analyse how individuals search for jobs, which types of search are likely to provide the best pay-offs and how these decisions affect wages and occupational distributions.

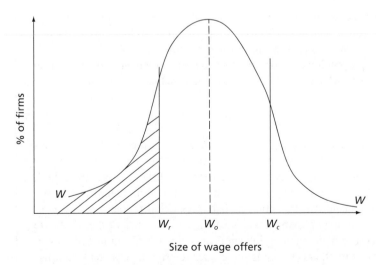

Figure 4.4 Wage offers and the reservation wage.

the reservation wage, then hours of work will be positive if $w > w_r$ as in the case of w_c. When then are job searches likely to be successful? Diamond (2011) suggests that

> a key short-cut which makes search analyses tractable is the matching function which gives the rate of meetings of workers and firms in the process of seeking employment as a function of the number of searching workers and job vacancies.

(see Case Study 4.1)

Mortensen (2011) notes that, for any individual, the probability that the next offer will be accepted is $1 - F(R)$, where R represents the worker's reservation wage and $F(w)$ is the cumulative wage offer distribution (such as ww as in Figure 4.4). By definition, R will equate the expected present value of the worker's future income stream, were he or she to accept a particular job offer, with the value of foregoing the employment opportunity by continuing to search for an alternative offer. It should be noted that the **matching function** is not the same as the **Beveridge Curve**, which is discussed in detail in Chapter 11. While the latter considers different combinations of unemployment and vacancies, the former relates the number of hires to the unemployment–vacancy ratio (see Shimer 2005; Pissarides 2011).

Case Study 4.1

The matching function

Movement in the labour market is not instantaneous. There are various functions not just limited to information imperfections, but also extending to heterogeneities among potential employees and employers. Petrongolo and Pissarides (2001) note that it was not until the late 1970s that the matching function, which lies at the heart of job-search theory, explicitly appeared in equilibrium models of the labour market, based on the work of Diamond, Mortensen and Pissarides, each of whom was to share the Nobel Prize for Economics in 2010.

The matching function concerns the means by which potential employees and potential employers come together to create productive matches. This is summarised in a well-behaved function which gives the number of jobs formed at any moment in time in terms of the number of people looking for jobs, the number of employers looking for workers and a small number of other relevant variables. Petrongolo and Pissarides provide the simplest form of the matching function as

$$M = m(U, V) \tag{1}$$

where M is the number of jobs formed during a given time period, U is the number of unemployed workers looking for jobs and V is the number of vacant jobs. This matching function is assumed to increase in both its arguments, to be concave and exhibit constant returns to scale. It is illustrated graphically by the Beveridge Curve, which is discussed in some detail in Chapter 11. If workers and jobs are heterogeneous, the transition probabilities will differ across the labour market, as will the mean durations of unemployment and vacancies. If only one worker is able to occupy each job and there is no co-ordination among job applicants, this will result in overcrowding in some jobs and no applications to others (which is sometimes referred to as a "balls in urns" problem). The dependence of mean transition rates on the number of workers and firms engaged in a search gives rise to possible externalities. The average time it takes for an employer to fill a vacant post depends on the behaviour of workers. The greater the number of workers searching for a job, the more the market is congested, which represents a negative externality from the perspective of the worker. Likewise, the probability of a worker finding a job depends on the behaviour of employers. The more employers there are searching the market for workers, the thicker the market, which is a positive externality from the perspective of workers, and this increases their probability of obtaining a job in a given time period.

Some of the above factors can be analysed, following Petrongolo and Pissarides, by adapting the simple matching function outlined above. Assume that an individual can choose intensity of search, with the number of units of search being the key parameter. If individual i supplies S_i units of search and individual j S_j units, then over a given period individual i will be S_i/S_j times more likely than individual j to find a job. Each individual will optimise his or her search intensity depending on search costs, the costs of being unemployed and the expected returns from employment.

The matching function will be given by

$$M = m(SU, V) \tag{2}$$

If we now assume there is a distribution of wage offers, an individual will choose a reservation wage and reject any wage offers below this reservation wage, drawn from a probability distribution $G(w)$. If this distribution is known to job seekers, the optimal policy of an individual is characterised by a reservation wage R_i, such that the job is accepted if $w \geq R_i$, and rejected otherwise. As a first approximation, we can define R as the average reservation wage and write the aggregate matching function as

$$M = [1 - G(R)]m(U, V) \tag{3}$$

This function implies that aggregate variables, such as demographic variables, unemployment insurance and housing transactions, should be introduced into the matching function as these are likely to have an effect on reservation wages and search intensity.

B. Petrongolo and C.A. Pissarides, "Looking into the Black Box: A Survey of the Matching Function", *Journal of Economic Literature*, 39(2), 2001, pp. 390–431.

A key question is whether a worker takes the first reasonable offer that is made or continues to search until some ideal offer is forthcoming. Under a **fixed sample size strategy** (see McKenna 1985), a worker will decide to sample a particular number of firms and accept the best wage to be found among them, while, under a **sequential search strategy**, the individual decides in each case whether to accept or reject an offer in favour of sampling an extra firm. Adopting the former assumption, Stigler (1962) suggests the optimal stopping rule would be to continue to search until the expected marginal benefits from further search equalled the expected marginal search costs. It is assumed that the worker knows the distribution of wage offers and search costs, so that the searcher is able to calculate the expected returns and costs for each possible number of searches n. The choice of sample size before search commences is then critical.[5]

Following McKenna (1990), let the distribution of wage offers equal $F(W)$ with a density function $F'(W)$. For a given sample size n, the searcher estimates the maximum *expected* wage offer $E[\max W|n]$. With constant unit search costs C, this is given by

$$R(n) = E[\max W|n] - Cn \tag{4.5}$$

Fixed sample size strategy

A situation in which an individual decides prior to undertaking a search of potential jobs to sample a particular number of firms and to accept the best offer received from them.

Sequential search strategy

A situation in which an individual decides in each case

whether to accept
or reject an offer
rather than
sampling an extra
firm.

Given the likely shape of the distribution of wage offers, the probable additional gain from job search will be subject to diminishing returns as in Figure 4.5.

Then an increase in the marginal search cost C reduces the amount of search from n_1^* to n_2^* and a reduction in wage offers from E[max $W/n]_1$ to [max $W|n]_2$ does likewise.

Under the sequential search model, the worker samples a wage offer in one period and decides whether to accept employment at that wage or reject it and sample another wage offer in the next period, and empirical evidence suggests this is more common than the above phenomenon. In most models, this decision is based on the reservation wage property. The reservation wage is chosen at the beginning of the period in order to maximise the expected returns from search. If the wage offer is equal to or greater than the reservation wage, the job is accepted; otherwise, it is rejected. Sample size or the number of wage offers received is random rather than predetermined as in the Stigler model. Assume a job is accepted that is expected to last m periods, then the return to search R is given by $(W|1 + i)^m$ where i equals the rate of interest. The reservation wage W^* must then satisfy the condition

$$R = \frac{W^*}{(1+i)^m}$$ (4.5)

That is, the reservation wage is that wage which makes acceptance of a job and its rejection equally attractive alternative as in Figure 4.6.

It can be demonstrated (see McKenna 1990) that the optimal reservation wage w^* is that which maximises:

$$R(w) = E(W \mid W) \geq w) - C / (\Pr(W \geq w))$$ (4.6)

where W equals wage offer and w the reservation wage. As Pissarides (1985) notes, two questions arise in relation to the reservation wage. First, is the reservation wage affected by changes in various parameters and, second, what is the dynamic path of the reservation wage during the search process? It appears that the reservation wage depends critically on the expected mean wage offer and the number of wage offers.

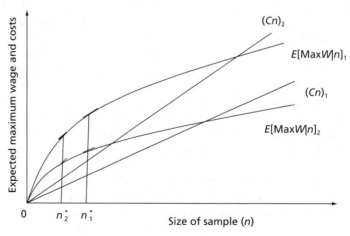

Figure 4.5 The gains from job search.

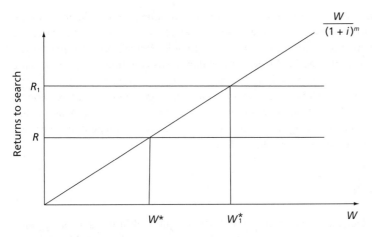

Figure 4.6 The optimal stopping rule.

Further, its optimal path will almost certainly decline as search continues through the existence of a finite number of opportunities for search, rising search costs and the deteriorating financial reserves of the individual searcher.

Failure to obtain a job through search will lead to unemployment and such failure may be related to the reservation wage. Thus, search theory can contribute to our understanding of unemployment. A reduction in the costs of search such as through the payment of unemployment benefit will tend to raise the reservation wage and increase the duration of the search.[6] In Figure 4.6, the reservation wage increases to w_1^* as the returns to search are raised from R to R_1 as a consequence of the reduced costs of search. Further, it is possible that the equilibrium level of unemployment may be inefficient in a search environment. Lockwood (1986) shows that, given skill differences in the workforce, the presence of highly skilled workers will lower the acceptance probabilities of low-skilled workers below the social optimum.

But is the assumption that there is an intervening period (of unemployment) between jobs generally valid? In practice, it seems unlikely that most people will leave jobs voluntarily before they have fixed themselves up with a new job.[7] Thus, as indicated earlier, on-the-job search may be a common phenomenon. Indeed, empirical evidence suggests that it may be much more common than off-the-job search.[8] Stein (1960) found, for the US in 1955, that 55 per cent of all job changes occurred without intervening unemployment, and Mortensen and Neumann (1989) found a figure of 60 per cent for male workers in Seattle and Denver. For the UK, see Hughes and McCormick (1985a). Yet, it has been argued that on-the-job search is itself inefficient, as unemployment enables workers to specialise in search and thus search more efficiently (Alchian 1970).[9] In their analysis of Denver and Seattle, Mortensen and Neumann (1989) found that about one-third of movers experienced a wage cut, and a smaller but still substantial number of those who moved directly from one job to another did so. However, job transitions with an intervening spell of unemployment or non-participation result in average wages that are about 5 or 6 per cent less than the wages of individuals moving directly to a new job.[10] Pissarides (1976) concludes, "It appears that the evidence contradicts the assumption of efficiency in information-gathering while unemployed, or at best it suggests that it is not correct in all cases".

However, an even more serious criticism of conventional search theory is that it is apparently rare for unemployed workers to reject job offers (for the UK, see Jackman 1985) and most jobs are filled by a single job offer (for the US, see Barron *et al.* 1985). This result may be due to the fact that the assumption that searchers are fully informed about the distribution of wage offers is erroneous.[11]

So far, we have neglected the fact that there is a geographical dimension to changing jobs, which might include preferences for living in some regions or countries rather than others, taking into account language, laws, climate and other features. This is the focus of sections 4.5 to 4.7.

4.5 Migration

Speculative migration

Migration in which the individual chooses to search in the region possessing the highest reservation wage net of distance costs.

The job-search decision is even more complex when job mobility is across regions[12] and, in this case, it is necessary to distinguish between **speculative migration** and **contracted migration**. In the former, the individual may choose to search in the region possessing the highest reservation wage net of distance costs and possibly choose the first offer in that region that exceeds the reservation wage. However, for the majority of the population, contracted migration is likely to be the norm and the relevant question then is: what determines the probability of receiving a job offer from a particular region and the likelihood of its acceptance? The housing market in both current and potential locations will be relevant to both cases.[13] The migration literature provides two distinctive approaches to the explanation of actual migration patterns – labour flow or gravity models and the human capital approach – and it is necessary to examine each in turn.

Contracted migration

Migration that results from already having received and accepted a job offer in a particular region other than his or her own.

As Shields and Shields (1989) note, migration can be viewed as a response to market disequilibrium. Where there are differences in real returns, factor mobility should reduce them until wage differences are explained by wage rigidities, differences in living costs, the costs of movement, imperfect information and barriers to migration. In its simplest form, movement (M) between regions i and j is given by

$$M_{ij} = B_{ij}(w_j - w_i) \qquad (4.7)$$

where B_{ij} = barriers to migration such as distance, imperfect information, etc.

Push and pull factors

Push factors are negative influences in the region of origin that induce movement, while pull factors are positive influences in the region of in-migration that have a similar effect.

In this model, both **pull and push factors** may operate and an important question is whether migration responds more to differences in wages or to differences in employment opportunities. In fact, both appear to be important. Housing tenure may also be critical, as expanded on below. Public-sector house tenants tend to be particularly constrained with respect to regional migration and the availability of housing is likely to be critical in terms of degree of in-migration.

Migration can also be viewed as an investment decision in which a worker compares the benefits of movement in the form of a higher real wage with the costs of movement, both direct in the form of monetary expenditure and indirect in the form of costs of adjustment. This will be given by

$$VM_{ij} = \sum_{t=1}^{n} \frac{(W_{jt} - W_{it})}{(1+r)^t} - \sum_{t=1}^{n} \frac{(C_{jt} - C_{it})}{(1+r)^t} - I_{ij} \qquad (4.8)$$

where

VM_{ij} = the net present value of migration between regions i and j
W = earnings in the two locations
n = time horizon
C = the cost of living
r = rate of discount
I = initial costs of migration.

It is likely that personal characteristics such as age, education, occupation, marital status, sex and family size will be important influences on the migration decision. Whether the individual is employed or unemployed is also likely to be an important factor.[14]

4.6 Theory and empirical evidence: internal migration

Do workers move jobs in accordance with the predictions of theory? Answers to this question in the UK are bedevilled by the fact that official statistics do not commonly distinguish between voluntary and involuntary turnover. Nonetheless, a number of investigators have used total separations data, arguing that this does not detract significantly from the results. Thus, Wickens (1978) suggested the following model:

$$q = f(V, C/W) \qquad (4.9)$$

where V = vacancies and C/W the costs of search.

The theory is tested by assuming that C is a decreasing function of the percentage of employees recruited in the previous period on the grounds that such recruits will have greater knowledge of the labour market and hence lower search costs. In the absence of quit data (q), Wickens substitutes the total separation rate and his two-stage least squares results provide support for the theory that workers are more likely to move when wages are lower in the current location. Likewise, Shorey (1980) finds that firms can influence quit decisions significantly by wage adjustments. In his model, a difference in wages of 10 index points means a difference in quits of 45 per 1,000 workers per annum. Other findings are that skilled workers are less likely to quit as are prime-age workers, those working on low female-intensive activities, on shifts and in rapidly expanding or large establishments. Local labour market conditions are also found directly and indirectly to affect quit rates. However, Shorey offers several caveats to these findings. The results may be affected by simultaneity or **multi-colinearity**; involuntary separations might vary systematically across industries; there are no data on applications and redundancy relationships in the latter respect. In a more recent paper, Boheim and Taylor analyse the internal migration patterns of men aged 21–59 using the British Household Panel Survey (BHPS) over the period 1991–2002. They limit the analyses to men, since many married women may be **tied movers** and, therefore, unable to optimise their own situation as opposed to the family as a whole. They find that there is a wage growth premium that is attached to migration and that is largest for continuously employed men who migrate for job-related reasons. Further, the wage

Multi-colinearity

This refers to the correlation, if any, which exists between the independent variables in a regression and which will make the application of least squares in the estimation of the parameters in an equation inadmissible.

Tied movers

Migrants whose location choices are limited by family considerations.

growth effect is substantial relative to non-migrants in relation to local authority district boundaries.

A major constraint on worker mobility particularly in Britain is, however, the nature of the housing market. A large number of studies suggest that the structure of housing tenure is an important determinant of, or deterrent to, mobility. If we compare home-owners and public tenants with private tenants, it is suggested that the former will have lower reservation wages in local areas compared to other regions and are consequently more likely to accept a local job and less likely to accept a job in distant locations. Thus, Hughes and McCormick (1981), using individual household data from the 1973 GHS, find that council-house tenancy significantly reduces the probability that a household will migrate from one region to another in a given time period, even when controlling for socio-economic characteristics. Expanding on this work, Hughes and McCormick (1985b) show that the much lower probability of actual mobility for council-house tenants is not due to lack of willingness to move, but to the fact that such tenure reduces the probability of successful search, while increasing its costs. In contrast, council-house tenure does not appear to reduce significantly local job mobility. Bover *et al.* (1989) note that, for owner-occupiers, the regional house price–earnings ratio may influence the ability to migrate, and find that relative house prices do, indeed, appear to dominate net migration between London and the rest of the South-East. They conclude that the absence of a substantial rented sector is a major explanation of the low rate of labour mobility in Britain, compared to, say, the US, and that this may be even more significant than the system of allocating council houses. More recently, Battu *et al.* (2008), using the BHPS over the period 1991–2003, show that home ownership is a constraint for the employed and public renting more of a constraint for the unemployed. Public renters who are unemployed are much less likely to enter a distant job than private renters.

The above studies put the primary focus on wage differences in inducing mobility, but the **theory of net advantages** suggests that, where jobs differ in attractiveness, there will be compensating wage differences and allowance must be made for this in assessing the impact of wage differences on actual mobility. Further, there are a number of difficulties attached to the testing of this hypothesis. Garen (1988),[15] for example, notes that workers with greater amounts of human capital and higher earnings potential will selects jobs with fewer disamenities, so that OLS estimates may be biased and this may account for the somewhat mixed results of US tests of the hypothesis. In the first British study of its kind, Marin and Psacharopoulos (1982) examined male employees in 1975 and found significant compensation for the fatal accident rate in the respondents' industry. McNabb (1989), using 1975 GHS data for male employees, likewise found that earnings compensated for unfavourable job characteristics with an earnings premium of 3.5 per cent per annum for inconvenient hours, 2.3 per cent for unfavourable working conditions and 2.0 per cent for lack of employment security. However, when the sample was split according to non-manual and manual employees, these premia were found to be restricted to the latter group. Elliott and Murphy (1986), using NES data, tested four broad categories of non-pecuniary advantages – the number and timing of hours worked, the intensity of work effort within these hours, the nature of the work environment and the extent of fringe benefits. They found general support for the hypothesis, apart from fringe benefits, in which case the sign was positive and significant. The weight of evidence does, therefore, seem consistent with the hypothesis that there are compensating wage differentials for jobs with unpleasant working conditions.

Theory of net advantages

This is based on the idea that wage differences will compensate for unattractive or attractive features of jobs, and allowance should be made for this in judging the impact of wage differences on actual mobility.

4.7 International migration

Migration from one country to another is a significant feature of the world economy with countries such as the US and Australia having grown rapidly as a result of in-migration over a long period of time and, more recently, through the formation and extension of the European Union, which provides for free mobility of labour within the Union.[16] Flows from one member state to another have become sizeable (see Table 4.1).

As Dustmann and Weiss (2007) note, there are distinctive types of migration with different implications. Motives for migration may be economic or non-economic, due to factors such as natural disasters or persecution (e.g. asylum seekers). Immigration may be temporary or permanent, or perhaps circulatory with frequent movement between host and source countries. Return migration, whereby migrants return voluntarily to their country of origin, is also common. The economic implications arising from each of these are quite distinctive. In analysing the economics of immigration, Borjas (1994) suggests there are three substantive questions. First, how do immigrants tend to perform in the host country's economy? Second, what impact do immigrants have on the employment opportunities of the indigenous population? Third, what sort of immigration policy is most beneficial to the host country?

4.7.1 How do immigrants perform in the host country?

Early work in North America by Chiswick (1978) and Carliner (1980) looked at how immigrant skills adapted to the host country's labour market and estimated a cross-section equation as

$$\log w_i = \alpha_1 X_i + \alpha_2 A_i + \alpha_2 I_i + \alpha_4 y_i + \varepsilon_1 \tag{4.10}$$

where w_i = the ith worker's wage rate, X_i is a vector of socio-economic characteristics such as education and region, A_i is the worker's age or potential labour market experience, I_i is a dummy variable for whether or not the individual is an immigrant, and y_i represents the number of years of residence in the host country. The coefficient α_3 gives the percentage wage differential, which is expected to be negative, and α_4 the rate at which the earnings of migrants rise relative to those of the indigenous workers, which is expected to be positive. A number of studies confirm that the effect of a year of education on earnings is higher for native-born than foreign-born employees. Chiswick (1978) found that native-born Americans received a return of 7.2 per cent for a year of education compared to 5.7 per cent for the foreign-born and similar findings have been reported for Canada (Baker and Benjamin 1994), Australia (Beggs and Chapman 1998), and the UK (Shields and Wheatley Price 1998), as well as in a number of other countries. According to Chiswick and Miller (2008), there are three possible explanations for the difference in rates of return between native Americans and immigrants. First, the migrants may be self-selected in a way that impacts more on the less well educated. Second, there may be a low degree of international skill transferability and, third, there may be discrimination, which increases with level of education. Chiswick and Miller (2009) elaborate further by suggesting that immigrants may lack information on the nature

Table 4.1 Inflow data based on residence permits or on other sources, selected OECD countries (thousands)

		1999	2000	2001	2002	2003	2004	2005	2006	2007	2008
AUS	Australia										
	Permanent inflows	98.3	107.1	127.9	119.1	123.4	146.4	161.7	176.2	189.5	203.9
	Temporary inflows	194.1	224.0	245.1	240.5	244.7	261.6	289.4	321.6	368.5	420.0
CAN	Canada										
	Permanent inflows	190.0	227.5	250.6	229.1	221.4	235.8	262.2	251.6	236.8	247.2
	Temporary inflows	223.0	254.2	268.5	247.9	228.3	228.2	229.6	250.1	279.9	313.8
FRA	France	82.8	91.9	106.9	124.2	136.4	141.6	135.9	135.1	128.9	136.0
GBR	United Kingdom	239.5	260.4	262.2	288.8	327.4	434.3	405.1	451.7	455.0	456.0
IRL	Ireland	22.2	27.8	32.7	39.9	42.4	41.8	66.1	88.9	89.5	67.6
ITA	Italy	268.0	271.5	232.8	388.1	–	319.3	206.8	181.5	252.4	–
KOR	Korea	–	185.4	172.5	170.9	178.3	188.8	266.3	314.7	317.6	311.7
MEX	Mexico	5.4	6.4	8.1	5.8	4.8	8.5	9.2	6.9	6.8	15.1
NZL	New Zealand	31.0	37.6	54.4	47.5	43.0	36.2	38.5	34.2	40.6	41.8
POL	Poland	17.3	15.9	21.5	30.2	30.3	36.9	38.5	34.2	40.6	41.8
PRT	Portugal	10.5	15.9	151.4	72.0	31.8	34.1	28.1	22.5	32.6	32.3
TUR	Turkey	154.3	162.3	154.9	151.8	147.2	148.0	169.7	191.0	174.9	175.0
USA	United States										
	Permanent inflows	644.8	841.0	1058.9	1059.4	703.5	957.9	1122.4	1266.3	1052.4	1107.1
	Temporary inflows	1106.6	1249.4	1375.1	1282.6	1233.4	1299.3	1323.5	1457.9	1606.9	1617.6
EU-25 (among above countries) + Norway and Switzerland		**1847.3**	**2107.0**	**2375.8**	**2576.4**	**2124.8**	**2791.8**	**2696.0**	**2880.7**	**3232.1**	**2664.3**
North America (permanent)		**834.7**	**1068.5**	**1309.5**	**1288.4**	**924.9**	**1193.7**	**1384.6**	**1517.9**	**1289.2**	**1354.4**

Source: Adapted from OECD International Migration Data, 2010.

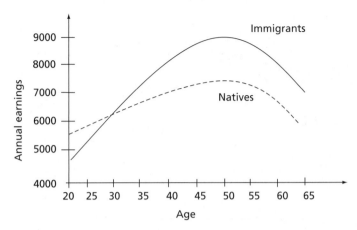

Figure 4.7 Age–earnings profiles of immigrants and native men in a cross-section.

of the host-country labour market, although this should diminish over time. Experience in country of origin may not transfer easily to the host country and, although education may be more easily transferrable, employers in the host country may be uncertain about the value of qualifications acquired abroad. These differences may be more marked where there is a large gap in terms of economic development between countries of origin and host countries.

According to Chiswick (1978), the differences summarised above should diminish as the migrants assimilate into the host country's customs and practices. Using the 1970 Census, he found that, at time of arrival, immigrants earned 17 per cent less than natives as shown in Figure 4.7, but, as a result of faster wage growth, migrants overtake natives within 15 years and earn about 11 per cent more than comparable native workers after 30 years. This is a consequence of greater investment in human capital by migrants compared to native workers and/or greater ability and motivation.

Borjas (1985) challenged these results by arguing that one cannot draw references about the evolution of earnings over time from a single cross-section. Suppose as in Figure 4.8 that we have three waves of immigrants, 1950, 1970 and 1990, as designated by P, Q and R respectively, with the 1970 wave having the same age-earnings profile as native-born Americans, the 1950 wave a higher profile, and the 1990 wave a lower profile. This is in line with evidence that more recent waves of migrants are relatively less skilled than earlier waves. Using a single cross-section would produce a profile such as CC, joining R^*, Q^* and P^* and indicating a more rapid increase in earnings for migrants when in reality there is no wage convergence.

4.7.2 Do immigrants have an adverse impact on native earnings and employment?

Borjas (1994) reports that studies of specific labour markets in the US confirm the finding that immigration appears to have little impact on local workers even when immigration flows are substantial. However, some allowance needs to be made for

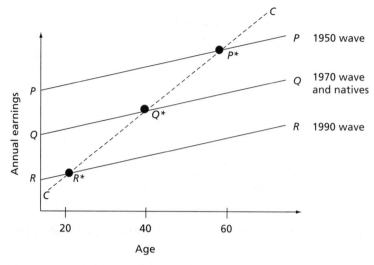

Figure 4.8 Cohort effects and immigrant age–earnings profiles.

the fact that some local workers may move out of locations in which immigration is large and, as Dustmann *et al.* (2005) point out, the construction of the counterfactual (i.e. what would have happened without the immigration) is not straightforward. Manacorda *et al.* (2006) find evidence that native-born and immigrants are imperfect substitutes – a 10 per cent rise in the share of immigrants in the local population increases the native–migrant male wage differential by just 2 per cent and this on its own could explain why there are few signs of a negative impact of immigrants on local workers. There is also some support for Borjas's suggestion that immigrants in a specific area may simply push local workers out of the locality, thereby defusing the local labour market effects. Thus, Hatton and Tani (2005) find that an increase of 100 in net immigration to a region from abroad generates a net out-migration to other regions of 35. As Dustmann *et al.* (2005) note, immigration inflows will change the skill composition of the host-country labour force if the skill composition of immigrants differs from that of the host country, so the restoration of equilibrium implies a need for short-run changes in both wages and employment for different levels of skill or even perhaps long-run changes in the economy's output mix. In the UK, the main impact has been to put labour market pressure on low-skilled rather than high-skilled workers, thereby tending to widen the skill wage distribution. As Card (2005) notes, there is little robust evidence that immigrants have harmed native employment opportunities. See also the evidence contained in Case Study 4.2.

4.7.3 What sort of immigration policy is appropriate?

The evidence in general suggests that immigration has a beneficial impact on the economy overall. But politicians tend to react negatively if the scale of immigration is regarded as too high. In Europe, it is only possible to control immigration from outside the EU. A number of countries, however, have guest-worker programmes, which enable them to obtain increases in their labour forces without incurring a

Case Study 4.2

Are migrants a threat to indigenous workers?

The opening up of the European Union to accession countries in the East from 2004 gave rise to substantial migration, particularly to the UK and Ireland, where the local economies were buoyant, and many of the migrants possessed English as a second language. It was estimated that the stock of migrants in the UK from the A 10 countries was 800,000 in 2007, with over half of them then coming from Poland. Gordon Brown, the Prime Minister at the time, used the expression "British jobs for British workers" in a speech and this was later used by trade union leaders to attack the use of foreign workers by an Italian company on a Teesside construction site, although the rules for free mobility of labour within the European Union meant that the foreign workers, being EU residents, were entitled to be employed in the UK. To what extent, then, do foreign migrants really represent a threat to indigenous workers?

Blanchflower and Shadforth (2009) note that natural population growth in the UK had been relatively low in comparison to the rest of Europe. Further, there was a favourable macroeconomic climate with low unemployment and a high GDP per capita which made migration to the UK attractive. Added to this, there was evidence that network effects were important, as measured by the coefficient of the stock of immigrants of one's own national background already resident in the country. Most of the migrants took up low-skilled jobs on a temporary basis, which were unattractive to local labour. Despite the fact that as many as 45 per cent of the immigrants possessed degrees, they were willing to accept such jobs at low rates of pay and, according to employers, were very productive with a good work ethic. Few of them failed to gain employment and the propensity to claim benefits was low. An earlier study by Dustmann and Fabbri (2005), using LFS data for the UK over the period 1983–2000, showed little evidence of any adverse outcomes for natives in terms of wages or employment and this was consistent with the findings of similar studies in the US and elsewhere.

Despite this, Blanchflower and Shadforth, using data from the European Working Conditions Survey, show that fear of unemployment was widespread and growing. Further, fear of unemployment, which does not appear to be associated with worker quality, lowers wages. Therefore, the influx of immigrants served to reduce wage pressure and allowed the economy to operate at high levels of demand without producing inflationary pressures. The fact that migrants used a substantial part of their income as remittances to their country of origin meant that their effect on aggregate demand was limited, so that they increased supply more than demand, thereby reducing the natural rate of unemployment. Regions with the biggest influx of labour from Eastern Europe tended to have the smallest increases in unemployment rates, consistent with migrants being attracted to regions where unemployment was lowest. There also appeared to be a negative relationship between changes in annual rates of wage inflation among the least skilled and the change in the share of migrants from the access countries. Thus, while it is possible that some low-skilled young workers may have found it more difficult to obtain jobs, overall negative effects appear to have been limited.

D.G. Blanchflower and C. Shadforth, "Fear, Unemployment and Migration", *Economic Journal*, 119(535), 2009, F136–F182.
C. Dustmann and F. Fabbri, "Immigrants in the British Labour Market", *Fiscal Studies*, 26(4), 2005, pp. 423–70.

permanent increase in their population, as the work permits are of fixed durations. There may also be restrictions on the employment of migrant workers to certain sectors or occupations through the adoption of points systems. As many migrants return home when economic conditions become unfavourable, this acts as a built-in stabiliser in terms of employment and unemployment. Borjas (2001) also shows, for the US, that new immigrants tend to cluster in States that offer the highest wages for the types of skills they have to offer and that wage convergence across regions is faster during high immigration periods.

There are, however, questions relating to the integration of migrants in society and the need to protect them from discrimination, which may include payment below the statutory minimum wage. The process of job search may be more difficult for migrants, and this is particularly so if they are members of ethnic minorities (see Frijters *et al.* 2005 and Battu *et al.* 2010). Certain immigrants may choose to reside in enclaves, which largely comprise members of their own ethnic group, while others assimilate with the indigenous population, and this may influence the extent to which immigrants are accepted into the community. Battu and Zenou (2010) refer to *"oppositional identities"* where those socially excluded from the majority group reject the majority culture. This itself may give rise to an employment penalty.

Demographic factors and ageing populations may lead to declines in the size of the national workforce in many advanced countries unless there is net in-migration, so migration policy is likely to remain high on the political agenda.

Summary

- The amount of job change in the labour market is substantial and influenced by stages of the business cycle. Whether these moves are advantageous will depend in part on whether they are voluntary or involuntary or directly from one employer to another or not.
- The advantage of a move will also depend on the extent of information the individual has about the distribution of earnings and the nature of the workplace environment. There is in practice likely to be a degree of information asymmetry and this will impact on the degree of labour mobility.
- Low levels of job satisfaction will be associated with high levels of voluntary job turnover and characteristics that improve efficiency in job search should increase job satisfaction. The level of job satisfaction is influenced by relative as well as absolute levels of pay. It is also influenced by gender, trade union membership and establishment size.
- The theory of job search assumes that movement in the labour market is not instantaneous and influenced by heterogeneity among both employees and employers. Different job-search strategies include finite sample size strategies and sequential search strategies, and both of these will be influenced by the individual's reservation wage. Job-to-job search also seems to be an important strategy, as this avoids intervening periods of unemployment.
- There are two distinctive approaches to the study of migration patterns – labour flow or gravity models and the human capital approach, but regardless of this the type of housing tenure turns out to be important in determining the extent of internal migration. There is some evidence consistent with the hypothesis

that there are compensating wage differentials for jobs with unpleasant working conditions.

- Broader issues are relevant to the question of international migration such as the degree to which skills are transferable across countries and the degree to which immigrants assimilate into the host-country labour market, which itself may depend on language skills. Evidence that immigration has negative effects on host-country workers is limited. In general, evidence suggests that immigration has a beneficial effect on the host-country economy.

Questions

1 Assess the role of information asymmetry in limiting the efficiency of the operation of labour markets. To what extent does this apply in the case of individuals and of employers?
2 What factors are important in determining the job satisfaction of workers and how does this influence the degree of labour mobility?
3 Explain the fixed sample size strategy and sequential models of job search. Why might this distinction be important in determining labour market outcomes?
4 Assess the role of housing markets in determining the degree of labour mobility across regions.
5 To what extent are there compensating wage differentials for unpleasant jobs?
6 Should immigration be controlled and, if so, under which circumstances?

Notes

1 The problem is perhaps even greater in relation to regional migration of labour. As Molho (1986) observes, in general, individuals lack information on all available opportunities, which is necessary in order to calculate the relevant knowledge benefits and costs and the acquisition of such information also has costs (see section 4.4).

2 The equilibrium condition is $\int_{QX}^{\sigma} u(w + dx) F_{ix}^0 (w) dw - U(w_0 + d_0)$. This assumes the same distribution applies to all future wages in x viewed at $t = 0$.

3 Let O_i and I_i be the weighted sums of outputs and inputs in activity i and a and b represent two groups between which comparisons are made. Then equity requires that

$$\frac{\Sigma Q_{ia}}{\Sigma I_{ia}} = \frac{\Sigma O_{ib}}{\Sigma I_{ib}}$$

The question then arises as to how far outputs and inputs correspond to marginal productivities and human capital endowments. As Main *et al.* (1993) point out, there are two conflicting explanations of the structure of pay. Tournament theory suggests that it is efficient to pay top executives more than the value of their marginal revenue product as an incentive to more junior staff to emulate them. But status-based models such as those of Frank (1984) and

Fershtman and Weiss (1993) suggest it is efficient to compress the wage structure as those in high-status positions will receive psychic income.

4 Dex reviewing the literature in this area suggests, "Just why large proportions of workers, and often women more than men, declare themselves satisfied with work and its aspects – is not clear. On the issue of gender differences in satisfaction, controlling for differences in occupations and work content between men and women often eliminates much of the apparent difference in satisfaction, although not all" (1988: 12). She goes on to suggest that, if circumstances altered such that men had equal responsibilities for childcare, remaining differences would disappear (p. 153).

5 Coles (1994) and Coles and Smith (1996) consider the implications of the assumption that job seekers have complete information about available job opportunities and apply simultaneously to all those they believe likely to be acceptable. Since all acceptable job matches will be filled, there will be no co-ordination failure as outlined in Case Study 4.1. Further, in the next job-search round, those not matched in the previous round will not return to the previous list of vacancies.

6 For a detailed discussion of the relationship between job search and unemployment benefit, see Shorey (1989).

7 Some papers have examined on-the-job search for Britain. Hughes and McCormick (1985), using 1973 and 1974 GHS data, find that workers who belonged to pension schemes were significantly less likely to search. Pissarides and Wadsworth (1988), using the 1984 Labour Force Survey, find that mean occupational wages are positively correlated with on-the-job search but the biggest influence is the nature of the job. Long-tenure employees are much less likely to be looking for an alternative job. See also Burgess (1989).

8 Using a 1982 Economist Intelligence Unit report, Jones (1989) finds that the mean total weekly hours of search is slightly under six, with women searching less than men. It seems feasible for employed persons to at least match this degree of job search.

9 It is known that the methods of job search are very different for unemployed workers as illustrated from the following table taken from Adnett (1989):

	Source from which employee heard about present job started in previous 12 months		Main method of unemployed seeking work	
	Men %	Women %	Men %	Women %
Job Centre, Careers Offices	20	19	42	31
Private Employment Agency	2	3	1	2
Advertisements	20	22	29	42
Direct Approach to Employers	31	31	11	8
Friends and Relatives	5	3	3	3

Sources: 1986 Labour Force Survey; 1984 GHS.

10 Petrongolo and Pissarides (2001) suggest that in principal there is no difficulty, however in introducing on-the-job search into the matching function. If this mainly affects the choice of search intensity and the reservation wage equation 4.3 would be appropriate under the reasonable assumption that job seekers will have a higher reservation wage than the unemployed.

11 A number of authors have argued that it is more realistic to assume that the searcher lacks knowledge of the true wage distribution and continually revises his or her estimate of the perceived wage distribution as he or she searches. Melnik and Saks (1977), for example, investigated the search behaviour of college graduates and found evidence for such behaviour.

12 Adnett (1989) notes that only 13 per cent of job moves in the UK are long distance (over 80 kilometres) and the majority of moves are not, in fact, job related. Indeed, only a minority of job-related moves involve a change of employer.

13 Hughes and McCormick (1987), for example, find that migration rates in the US were two or three times as great as in the UK and attribute this to the prevalence of public-sector housing in the UK. Migration rates are four times greater for owner-occupiers than for public-sector tenants (who make up 28 per cent of British households).

14 Shields and Shields (1989) point out that empirical tests of the model may be difficult because they are dependent on average regional employment and wage data, while migrants are atypical and so these data may not be relevant to them.

15 He finds that there is substantial heterogeneity in the returns to fatality and injury risk. This imparts bias to reported OLS results, implying a substantial underestimation of returns to job risk.

16 Emigration may also be a concern as well as immigration. The elite brain drain is one example. Hunter *et al.* (2009) find that less than one-half of elite scientists work in the country in which they were born and attribute this in part to the fact that the costs of migration in the modern world are relatively low.

References

Adams J.S., "Towards an Understanding of Equity", *Journal of Abnormal and Social Psychology*, 67(5), 1963, pp. 422–36.

Adams J.S., "Towards an Understanding of Equity", in Berkowitz L., editor, *Advances in Experimental Social Psychology*, volume 2, pp. 267–99, Academic Press, New York, 1965.

Adnett N., *Labour Market Policy*, Longman, London, 1989.

Alchian A.A., "Information Costs, Pricing and Resource Unemployment", in Phelps, E.S. *et al.*, editors, *Microeconomic Foundations of Employment and Inflation Theory*, Norton, 1970.

Baker M. and Benjamin D., "The Performance of Immigrants in the Canadian Labour Market", *Journal of Labor Economics*, 12(3), 1994, pp. 369–405.

Barron J., Bishop J. and Dunkelberg W., "Employer Search – the Interviewing and Hiring of New Employees", *Review of Economics and Statistics*, 67, 1985, pp. 43–57.

Battu H., Ma A. and Phimister E., "Housing Tenure, Job Mobility and Unemployment in the UK", *Economic Journal*, 118(527), 2008, pp. 311–28.

Battu H., Seaman P. and Zenou Y., "Job Contact Networks and the Ethnic Minorities", *Labour Economics*, 2010, doi:10.1016/j.labeco.2010.07.001.

Battu H. and Zenou Y., "Oppositional Identities and Employment for Ethnic Minorities: Evidence from England", *Economic Journal*, 120(542), 2010, pp. F52–F71.

Baxter J.L., "Inflation in the Context of Relative Deprivation and Social Justice", *Scottish Journal of Political Economy*, 20, 1973, pp. 263–82.

Baxter J.L., *Behavioural Foundations of Economics*, Macmillan, 1993.

Beggs J.J. and Chapman B.J., "Immigrant Wage Adjustment in Australia: Cross-Section and Time Series Estimation", *Economic Record*, 64(186), 1988, pp. 161–7.

Bender K.A. and Sloane P.J., "Job Satisfaction, Trade Unions and Exit-Voice Revisited", *Industrial and Labor Relations Review*, 51(2), 1998, pp. 222–40.

Blanchflower D.G. and Shadforth C., "Fear, Unemployment and Migration", *Economic Journal*, 119(535), 2009, pp. F136–F182.

Boheim R. and Taylor M.P., "From the Dark End of the Street to the Bright Side of the Road? The Wage Returns to Migration in Britain", *Labour Economics*, 14(1), 2007, pp. 99–118.

Borjas G.J., "Job Satisfaction, Wages and Unions", *Journal of Human Resources*, XIV(1), 1979, pp. 21–40.

Borjas G.J., "Assimilation, Changes in Cohort Quality and the Earnings of Immigrants", *Journal of Labor Economics*, 3(4), 1985, pp. 463–89.

Borjas G.J., "The Economics of Immigration", *Journal of Economic Literature*, 32(4), 1994, pp. 1667–717.

Borjas G.J., "Does Immigration Grease the Wheels of the Labour Market?", *Brookings Papers on Economic Activity*, No. 1, 2001, pp. 69–119.

Bover O., Muellbauer J. and Murphy A., "Housing, Wages and UK Labour Markets", in Wages and House Prices: A Symposium; *Oxford Bulletin of Economics and Statistics*, 51(2), 1989, pp. 97–136.

Burgess S.M., "Employment and Turnover in UK Manufacturing Industries, 1963–82", *Oxford Bulletin of Economics and Statistics*, 51(2), 1989, pp. 163–92.

Card D., "Is the New Immigration Really So Bad?", *Economic Journal*, 115(507), 2005, pp. F300–F323.

Carliner G., "Wages, Earnings and Hours of First, Second and Third Generation American Males", *Economic Inquiry*, 18(1), 1980, pp. 87–102.

Chiswick B.R., "The Effect of Americanisation on the Earnings of Foreign Born Men", *Journal of Political Economy*, 86(5), 1978, pp. 897–921.

Chiswick B.R. and Miller P.W., "Why is the Pay-off to Schooling Smaller for Immigrants?", *Labour Economics*, 15, 2008, pp. 1317–40.

Chiswick B.R. and Miller P.W., "The International Transferability of Immigrants' Human Capital", *Economics of Education Review*, 28, 2009, pp. 162–9.

Clancy G., "Labour Demand: The Need for Workers", *Economic and Labour Market Review*, 3(2), 2009, pp. 21–9.

Clark A.E., "Job Satisfaction and Gender: Why are Women so Happy at Work?", *Labour Economics*, 4, 1997, pp. 341–72.

Clark A.E., Kristensen N. and Westergaard-Nielsen N., "Job Satisfaction and Co-worker Wages: Status or Signal?", *Economic Journal*, 119(536), 2009, pp. 430–47.

Clark A.E. and Oswald A.J., "Satisfaction and Comparison Income", *Journal of Public Economics*, 61(3), 1996, pp. 359–81.

Coles M.G., "Understanding the Matching Function: The Role of Newspapers and Job Agencies", CEPR Discussion Paper No. 939, London, 1994.

Coles M.G. and Smith E., "Cross-section Estimation of the Matching Function: Evidence from England and Wales", *Economica*, 63(252), 1996, pp. 589–98.

Creedy J.A. and Disney R., "Changes in Labour Market Status in Great Britain", *Scottish Journal of Political Economy*, 28(1), 1981, pp. 76–85.

Dex S., *Women's Attitudes towards Work*, Macmillan Press, 1988.

Diamond P., "Unemployment, Vacancies and Wages", *American Economic Review*, 101(4), 2011, pp. 1045–72.

Dustmann C. and Fabbri F., "Immigrants in the British Labour Market", *Fiscal Studies*, 28(4), 2005, pp. 423–70.

Dustmann C. and Weiss Y., "Return Migration: Theory and Evidence for the UK", *British Journal of Industrial Relations*, 45(2), 2007, pp. 236–56.

Dustmann C., Fabbri F. and Preston I., "The Impact of Immigration on the British Labour Market", *Economic Journal*, 115(507), 2005, F324.

Elliott R. and Murphy P. "The Theory of Net Advantages", *Scottish Journal of Political Economy*, 33(1), 1986, pp. 46–57.

Fallick B. and Fleischman C.A., "Employer-to-Employer Flows in the US Labor Market: The Complete Picture of Gross Worker Flows", Finance and Discussion Series 2004–34, Board of Governors of the Federal Reserve System, 2004.

Fearn R. M., *Labor Economics: The Emerging Synthesis*, Winthrop Publishers, Cambridge, Mass., 1981.

Fershtman C. and Weiss Y., "Social Status, Culture and Economic Performance", *Economic Journal*, 103, 1993, pp. 946–59.

Frank R.H., "Are Workers Paid Their Marginal Products?", *American Economic Review*, 74(4), 1984, pp. 549–71.

Freeman R.B., "Job Satisfaction as an Economic Variable", *American Economic Review*, 68, 1978, pp. 135–41.

Frijters P., Shields M.A. and Price S.W., "Job Search Methods and Their Success: A Comparison of Immigrants and Natives in the UK", *Economic Journal*, 115(507), 2005, pp. F359–F376.

Garen J., "Compensating Wage Differentials and the Endogeneity of Job Riskiness", *Review of Economics and Statistics*, 1988, pp. 9–16.

Gomez-Salvador R., Messina J. and Vallanti G., "Gross Job Flows and Institutions in Europe", *Labour Economics*, 11(4), 2004, pp. 469–86.

Haltiwanger J., Manser M.E. and Topel R.H., *Labour Statistics Measurement Issues*, National Bureau of Economic Research, USA, 1998.

Hamermesh, D.S., "Economic Aspects of Job Satisfaction", in Ashenfelter O.E. and Oates W.E., editors, *Essays in Labor Market Analysis*, John Wiley, New York, 1977, pp. 53–72.

Hampton M.B. and Heywood J.S., "Do Workers Accurately Perceive Gender Wage Discrimination?", *Industrial and Labor Relations Review*, 47(1), 1993, pp. 36–49.

Hatton T.J. and Tani M., "Immigration and Inter-regional Mobility in the UK, 1982–2000", *Economic Journal*, 115(507), 2005, pp. F342–F358.

Hughes G.J. and McCormick B., "Do Council Housing Policies Reduce Migration Between Regions?", *Economic Journal*, 91, 1981, pp. 911–37.

Hughes G.J. and McCormick B., "An Empirical Analysis of On-the-Job Search and Job Mobility", *Manchester School*, 41(1), 1985a, pp. 76–95.

Hughes, G.J. and McCormick, B., "Migration Intentions in the UK: Which House-holds Want to Migrate and Which Succeed?", *Economic Journal*, 95, Supplement, 1985b, pp. 113–23.

Hughes G.J. and McCormick B., "Housing, Unemployment and Labour Market Flexibility in the UK", *European Economic Review*, 31, 1987, pp. 615–45.

Hunter R.S., Oswald A.J. and Charlton B.G., "The Elite Brain Drain", *Economic Journal*, 119(538), 2009, pp. F231–F251.

Idson T.L., "Establishment Size, Job Satisfaction and the Structure of Work", *Applied Economics*, 22, 1990, pp. 1007–29.

Jackman R., "Search Behaviour of the Unemployed Men in Britain and the United States", *Centre for Labour Economics LSE Working Paper* 550, 1985.

Jones D.R., "Redundancy, Natural Turnover and the Paradox of Structural Change", *Bulletin of Economic Research*, 37(1), 1985, pp. 41–54.

Jones D.R. and Martin R.L., "Voluntary and Involuntary Turnover in the Labour Force", *Scottish Journal of Political Economy*, 33(2), 1986, pp. 124–44.

Jones S.R.G., "Job Search Methods, Intensity and Effects", *Oxford Bulletin of Economics and Statistics*, 51(3), 1989, pp. 277–96.

Joseph G., Pierrard O. and Sneessens H.R., "Job Turnover, Unemployment and Labour Market Institutions", *Labour Economics*, 11(4), 2004, pp. 451–68.

Kiefer N.M. and Neumann G., *Search Models and Applied Labour Economics*, Cambridge University Press, 1989.

Lippman S.A. and McCall J.J., editors, *Studies in the Economics of Search*, Amsterdam, North Holland, 1979.

Lockwood B., "Transferable Skills, Job Matching and the Inefficiency of the 'Natural' rate of Unemployment", *Economic Journal*, 96(384), 1986, pp. 961–74.

Mackay D.I., Boddy D., Brack J., Diack J.A. and Jones N., *Labour Markets Under Different Employment Conditions*, London, Allen and Unwin, 1971.

Main B.G.M., O'Reilly, III, C.A. and Wade J., "Top Executive Pay: Tournament or Teamwork?", *Journal of Labor Economics*, 11(4), 1993, pp. 606–28.

Manacorda M., Manning A. and Wadsworth J., "The Impact of Immigration on the Structure of Male Wages: Theory and Evidence from Britain", IZA Discussion Paper No. 2352, Bonn, 2006.

Marin A. and Psacharopoulos G., "The Reward for Risk in the Labour Market; Evidence from the UK and a Reconciliation with Other Studies", *Journal of Political Economy*, 90(41), 1982, pp. 827–53.

Mayhew K., "Earnings Dispersion in Local Labour Markets: Implications for Search Behaviour", *Oxford Bulletin of Economics and Statistics*, 39(2), 1977, pp. 93–107.

McKenna C.J., *Uncertainty and the Labour Market, Recent Developments in Job Search Theory*, Brighton, Wheatsheaf, 1985.

McKenna C.J., "The Theory of Search in Labour Markets", in Sapsford D. and Tzannatos Z., editors, *Current Issues in Labour Economics*, Macmillan, Basingstoke, 1990, pp. 33–62.

McNabb R., "Compensating Wage Differentials, Some Evidence for Britain", *Oxford Economic Papers*, 41, 1989, pp. 327–38.

Melnik A. and Saks D.H., "Information and Adaptive Job Search Behaviour: An Empirical Analysis", in Ashenfelter O. and Oates W., editors, *Essays in Labor Market Analysis*, Halsted Press, New York, 1977.

Meng R., "The Relationship between Unions and Job Satisfaction", *Applied Economics*, 22, 1990, pp. 1635–48.

Miller P.W., "Trade Unions and Job Satisfaction", *Australian Economic Papers*, 29(55), 1990, pp. 226–48.

Molho I., "Theories of Migration: A Review", *Scottish Journal of Political Economy*, 33(4), 1986, pp. 396–419.

Mortensen D., "Markets with Frictions and the DMP Model", *American Economic Review*, 101(4), 2011, pp. 1073–91.

Mortensen D.T. and Neumann G.R., "Inter-firm Mobility and Earnings", in Kiefer N.M. and Neumann G., editors, *Search Models and Applied Labour Economics*, Cambridge, Cambridge University Press, 1989.

Petrongolo B. and Pissarides C.A., "Looking into the Black Box: A Survey of the Matching Functions", *Journal of Economic Literature*, 39(2), 2001, pp. 390–431.

Pissarides C.A., *Labour Market Adjustment: Microeconomic Foundations of Short-run Neoclassical and Keynesian Dynamics*, Cambridge, Cambridge University Press, 1976.

Pissarides C.A., "Job Search and the Functioning of Labour Markets", in Carline D. *et al.*, editors, *Labour Economics*, London, Longman, 1985.

Pissarides C.A., "Equilibrium in the Labor Market with Search Frictions", *American Economic Review*, 101(4), 2011, pp. 1092–105.

Pissarides C. and Wadsworth J., "On-the-job Search: Some Empirical Evidence", Centre for Labour Economics, *LSE Discussion Paper*, No. 317, July 1988.

Rees A. and Schultz G.P., *Workers and Wages in an Urban Labor Market*, University of Chicago Press, 1970.

Rees A., "The Role of Fairness in Wage Determination", *Journal of Labor Economics*, 11(1), Part 1, Essays in Jacob Mincer, 1993, pp. 243–52.

Shields G.H. and Shields M.P., "The Emergence of Migration Theory and a Suggested New Direction", *Journal of Economic Surveys*, 3(4), 1989, pp. 277–304.

Shields M.A. and Wheatley Price S., "The Earnings of Male Immigrants in England: Evidence from the Quarterly LFS", *Applied Economics*, 30, 1998, pp. 1157–68.

Shimer R., "The Cyclical Behavior of Equilibrium Unemployment and Vacancies", *American Economic Review*, 95(1), 2005, pp. 23–49.

Shorey J., "An Analysis of Quits Using Industry Turnover Data", *Economic Journal*, 90(360), 1980, pp. 821–37.

Shorey J., "The Consequences of Job Search Requirements on Unemployment Benefits", *Scottish Journal of Political Economy*, 26(1), 1989, pp. 36–58.

Sloane P.J. and Williams H., "Job Satisfaction, Comparison Income and Gender", *Labour*, 14(3), 2000, pp. 473–502.

Stark O., *The Migration of Labour*, Cambridge, Basil Blackwell, May 1991.

Stein R.L., "Unemployment and Job Mobility", *Monthly Labor Review*, 83, 1960, pp. 350–8.

Stigler G.J., "Information in the Labour Market", *Journal of Political Economy*, 70, Supplement, 1962, pp. 94–105.

Wickens M., "An Econometric Model of Labour Turnover in UK Manufacturing Industries, 1956–1981", *Review of Economic Studies*, 45(3), 1978, pp. 469–77.

Further reading

C.A. Pissarides, *Equilibrium Unemployment Theory*, 2nd edition, MIT Press, Cambridge, Mass., 2000, contains chapters on labour turnover and on-the-job search, search intensity and job advertising and stochastic job matching and the role of policy from a theoretical perspective.

Two feature sections of the *Economic Journal* focus on immigration. The first of these – "Labour Market Effects of Immigration", 115(507), 2005, F297–376 – includes discussions on the impact of immigration on the British labour market and job-search methods and their success among immigrants. The second is concerned with the integration of immigration and its consequences, including the economic situation of first- and second-generation immigrants and oppositional identities.

O.B. Bodvarsson and H. Van den Berg, *The Economics of Immigration: Theory and Policy*, Heidelberg and London, Springer, 2009, provides a comprehensive introduction to immigration economics from both a theoretical and empirical perspective and including source- and destination-country perspectives.

Chapter 5

The demand for labour

Introduction

Labour demand analyses the employment relationship from the perspective of the employer. In any industry, there will be a particular size distribution of employers, which itself will have a substantial impact on the employment relationship. Ronald Coase posed the question in 1937: why do firms exist? (This draws a strong distinction between the firm and the market.) In the firm, the main function of the entrepreneur is to co-ordinate factors of production, including labour, while, in the market, the "invisible hand" of market forces produces the same outcome. Why then do firms supplement the market in some cases, but not in others? The answer lies in the relative costs of using the market. Firms arise only when they represent the most efficient method of organising production. In other words, firms economise on

Transactions costs

The costs of using the market through buying in rather than producing in-house.

Internal governance

Management responsibilities arising from undertaking activities within a firm.

Bounded rationality

The idea, first proposed by H. A. Simon, that in decision-making rationality of individuals is limited by the information they possess, the cognitive limitations of their thinking power and the finite amount of time they have to make a decision.

Principal–agent theory

This examines the problem that arises from the fact that a principal (e.g. an employer) may not have full information about the circumstances and behaviour of an agent (e.g. an employee). How then can the principal get the agent to act in the principal's best interests?

transactions costs. Thus, in the absence of firms, each individual would have to negotiate a separate contract for each exchange transaction with every other individual whose co-operation is required.

These ideas were developed further by Williamson (1985), who suggested that there were three key factors that tended to lead to **internal governance** as opposed to market exchange. First, internal governance is more likely the greater the frequency of the relevant transaction because this enables the setup costs associated with internal governance to be spread over a greater quantity of output. Second, the existence of uncertainty makes internal governance more likely because this makes it more difficult to draw up market contracts especially given **bounded rationality** and the possibility of opportunistic behaviour. Third, the existence of transaction-specific assets such as physical capacity or human knowledge, which have low values in alternative uses, increase the likelihood of internal governance. All of these have implications for the presence or otherwise of vertical integration or the presence of multi-product firms or can explain the recent trend for multinational companies to locate call centres in low-wage countries.

A first cousin of the transaction costs approach is **principal–agent theory** which focuses on contracts as opposed to transactions. A principal–agent relationship exists when one party (the agent) agrees to act in the interests of the other party (the principal). Thus, we could regard the principal as the management of the company and its employees as the agent. The problem is how can the principal induce the agent to act in the principal's interests when the former does not have full information about the circumstances and behaviour of the agent? Two conditions must hold for agency relationships to pose problems. First, the agent's objectives must differ from those of the principal. Second, the principal must have access to less information than is available to the agent on facts such as real costs and market conditions and aspects of the agent's actual behaviour. This is a classic problem of asymmetric information in which a monitoring problem exists. What is the optimal incentive payment scheme in order to induce the agent (employee) to act in the best interests of the principal in a situation in which the agent has an incentive to misrepresent information in the message he or she sends to the principal? For instance, a low-productivity worker has an incentive to claim to be a high-productivity worker. The design of an appropriate contract will then have to take into account the problem of adverse selection by offering the agent an incentive to put in high effort by linking rewards to contract performance. Thus, payment by results can induce employees to work harder. Where output cannot easily be increased, however, time rates of pay may be used together with close supervision. Profit-sharing or share-ownership may also be used to stimulate effort. An optimal contract will provide the agent with an expected utility from adopting high effort which is just greater than the expected utility from adopting low effort. Such a contract will require the agent to accept a degree of risk. If the agent is more risk averse than the principal, this may lead to a sub-optimal degree of risk.

The issues above are a core component of managerial economics textbooks, and are not discussed further in this chapter, though they are important background influences on many of the issues discussed in this chapter, as well as, in particular, in Chapter 8, which focuses on collective bargaining, and Chapter 10, which focuses on wage incentives.

In this chapter, we first consider the nature of demand for labour under various market structures. This is outlined in a fairly basic manner to remind readers of what they may already have learned in introductory economics courses. Whether or not labour markets are competitive has been an area of considerable debate, but we spend some time on a predominantly supply-side issue, namely the notion of **dynamic monopsony**, which generalises the traditional monopsony model to cover a much wider range of possibilities and has a substantial impact on the relationship between the marginal revenue product and the wage. We highlight the **Marshallian rules of derived demand**. The departures from competitive labour markets imply that, though marginal productivity and wages are related, divergences from equality of the two may be common. This has a number of implications. For example, where one cannot easily measure productivity, as is sometimes the case in the public sector, wages are used as a proxy for productivity. Thus, the true level of productivity may be understated.

There follows a discussion on the choice of employing more workers or working the existing workforce more intensively through the use of overtime working. We also introduce the reader to the concept of capital utilisation, which allows that firms can also utilise the capital stock more or less intensively. Despite its significance, this is often neglected in labour economic textbooks. There follows a discussing of hiring costs and labour hoarding, drawing on Walter Oi's seminal work on **labour as a quasi-fixed factor**, which links into business-cycle effects on labour utilisation.

5.1 The marginal productivity principle

5.1.1 Competitive labour markets in the short term

Demand for labour is a derived demand depending on consumers' demand for particular products, which may be sold in competitive or monopolistic product markets. Similarly, labour markets may be competitive or monopolistic. In the short term, assume that there are just two factors of production, capital and labour with capital fixed and labour variable. In the short term, the law of diminishing returns will eventually set in as more labour is employed with a fixed amount of capital, although initially there may be increasing returns. Let the Total Physical Product (*TPP*) represent this output so that the production function is

$$TPP = F(K, L) \tag{5.1}$$

This can be represented as in Figure 5.1 (a) from which is derived the Average Physical Product (*APP*) or *TPP/q* and the Marginal Physical Product (*MPP*) or $\Delta TPP/\Delta q$.

In Figure 5.1 (a), *TPP* increases initially at an increasing rate, as there are too few workers to make optimum use of the equipment available (often referred to as under-manning), but eventually this situation changes as more workers are employed and *TPP* increases at a decreasing rate (and eventually leads to over-manning). The change is represented by the point of inflection, *a*, where the tangent to the curve which measures the *MPP* is steepest. Hence, *a* represents the highest point on the *MPP* curve in Figure 5.1 (b). The slope of a straight line from the origin to points on the *TPP* curve represents the *APP* and at *b* this becomes tangential to the curve and thus equals *MPP* or the point at which the *MPP* curve intersects the *APP* curve at its highest point in Figure 5.1 (b). At *c*, *TPP* reaches its

Dynamic monopsony

This is based on the notion that the supply of labour to the firm is not perfectly elastic because of various frictions such as ignorance, heterogeneous preferences and mobility costs.

Marshallian rules of derived demand

These state that the elasticity of derived demand (or relative bargaining power) is a function of the elasticity of product demand, the elasticity of substitution, the elasticity of the supply of capital and labour cost as a proportion of total cost.

Labour as a quasi-fixed factor

The idea, associated with Walter Oi, that, because of various fixed costs associated with the employment of labour, labour is not a truly variable factor of production in the short run.

(a)

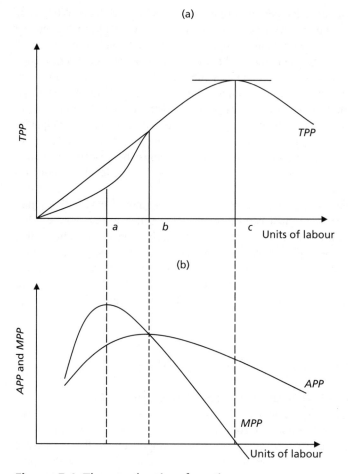

Figure 5.1 The production function.

highest point and the employment of extra workers will be counterproductive. Thus, in Figure 5.1 (b), the MPP curve intersects the x origin and becomes negative.

The profit-maximising level of employment is determined by product demand and the supply curve of labour. In a competitive product market, firms are sufficiently small that their output has a negligible impact on total output, so that the firm can sell as much as it wishes at the prevailing market price. Thus, $MPP_L \times P = MVP_L$, as shown in Figure 5.2. In imperfectly competitive product markets, firms are sufficiently large as a proportion of the total industry that price must be lowered in order to sell more output. Hence, Marginal Revenue Product (MRP) is the Marginal Revenue (MR) that the firm gains from employing an extra worker. Hence, $MRP_L = MPP_L \times MR$.

In a competitive labour market, the employer can obtain as much labour as is required at the prevailing wage rate, so that the labour supply curve is horizontal as $MC_L = W$ in Figure 5.2. In a competitive product market, demand is given by MVP_L and OQ_C is the profit-maximising level of employment where $MC_L = MVP_L$. To the left of this point, $MVP_L > MC_L$ and this represents foregone profit. Similarly, to the right of this point, $MC_L > MVP_L$ and this difference also represents foregone profits.

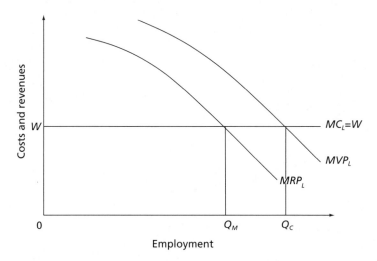

Figure 5.2 Product market competition and competitive labour
market.

In imperfect product markets, the profit-maximising level of employment occurs at
OQ_M where $MC_L = MPP_L$, the difference between OQ_C and OQ_M representing
monopoly restriction of output, but wages will be identical in each case. The competitive case may be approximated in agricultural and horticultural markets where
producers tend to be small on average and wages may be set by agricultural wage
boards or labour supply is flexible because of the presence of migrant workers.
Perfect wage equality requires, however, that workers have identical abilities, there
is perfect mobility of labour, all jobs are equally attractive, all employers and
workers have perfect knowledge of prevailing market conditions and wages are
determined entirely by supply and demand. If wages are raised for one reason or
another, such as an increase in the bite of a national minimum wage, there will be a
movement along a given MVP_L or MRP_L curve. In contrast, a change in productivity
or in demand conditions will result in a shift in the MVP_L or MRP_L curves.

5.1.2 Competitive labour markets in the long run

In the long run, all factors are variable and there arises the possibility of substituting factors for one another as relative factor prices change. According to the
proportionality rule

$$\frac{P_L}{MPP_L} = \frac{P_K}{MPP_K} = MC_X = P_X \tag{5.2}$$

This says that the optimal combination of factors is one in which the marginal

physical products are proportional to factor prices. If $\dfrac{P_L}{MPP_L} > \dfrac{P_K}{MPP_K}$, then it

would be possible to reduce costs by substituting capital for labour until equality
was achieved again, thereby ensuring technical or productive efficiency. This can
be shown graphically by isoquant and isocost curves, as in Figure 5.3.

Proportionality
rule

The optimal
combination of
factors of
production occurs
when marginal
physical products
are proportional to
factor prices.

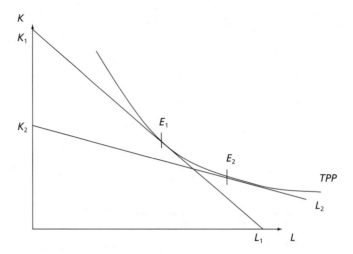

Figure 5.3 The proportionality rule.

TPP represents a particular level of output and K and L different combinations of capital and labour required to achieve it. K_1L_1 is a particular isocost curve and E_1 represents the least cost combination of capital and labour inputs designed to achieve the level of output represented by *TPP*. The shape of the isoquant illustrates a diminishing marginal rate of factor substitution. As one moves down the isoquant from left to right, total output will, by definition, remain the same. That is the loss in output due to less capital ($MPP_K \times \Delta K$) being used must be exactly offset by the gain in output due to more labour ($MPP_L \times \Delta L$) being used. Thus, $MPP_L \times \Delta L = MPP_K \times \Delta K$ and rearranging we have:

$$\frac{MPP_L}{MPP_K} = \frac{\Delta K}{\Delta L}(= MRS) \tag{5.3}$$

So the *MRS* (normally designated as σ) is equal to the inverse of the marginal physical product ratios of the two factors. If the relative prices of the two factors alter, the isocost line will swivel round, producing a new least cost combination. Thus, if the price of capital rises relative to the price of labour, the isocost curve will become shallower as represented by K_2L_2 and the least cost combination will shift from E_1 to E_2. At the extremes, factors may have to be used in fixed proportions, so that the isoquants are L shaped and $\sigma = 0$, or the isoquants may be linear so that the factors may be substituted without limit and $\sigma = \infty$. Over the longer period, it is possible to build more flexible plants, so that the inter-temporal elasticity of substitution is expected to have a higher value than the cross-section estimate at a particular point in time.

We may also estimate σ between capital and different types of labour. It has been suggested that capital and unskilled labour are more substitutable than capital and skilled labour (see Stevens and Behar 2009). This capital–skill complementarity argument can explain the rise in wage inequality observed in a number of countries, particularly the US and the UK, as the increased availability of capital has reduced the demand for unskilled labour, while increasing education encourages further investment in capital.

Over time, both inputs and outputs may alter. If there are increases in both capital and labour and relative factor prices remain the same the isocost curves will shift to the right parallel to themselves, and as greater levels of output can be achieved the isoquants will also shift to the right. There will be scale effects with constant, increasing or decreasing returns to scale showing the relationship between the percentage change in inputs and the percentage change in outputs.

The **scale effect** (sometimes referred to as the output effect) reflects the firm's decision to change the level of output and is illustrated by a movement from one isoquant to another, while abstracting from the change in relative factor prices. In contrast, the **substitution effect** abstracts from the change in output and captures only the firm's reaction to the change in relative prices. It is represented as a movement along a given isoquant, as in Figure 5.4.

In Figure 5.4, $I_1, I_2, \ldots, I_n$ represent isoquants with increasing levels of output. In the short run, the capital stock is fixed as indicated by K_0 or K_1, whereas the **expansion path** is long run and obtained by increasing units of both capital and labour. With capital fixed, output increases at a diminishing rate as units of labour are added (i.e. there are diminishing returns to labour as illustrated earlier in the TPP_L curve).

Consider now labour demand in the long run with several variable inputs. The firm's labour demand curve will no longer be represented by the MVP curve. This is because a change (e.g. a fall) in the price of labour will not merely imply an increase in the amount of labour associated with a given capital stock, but also lead to an increase in the amount of capital it is profitable to utilise. There is a scale effect with the greater factor inputs enabling a higher level of output to be achieved. The firm will choose a particular scale of plant in order to maximise profits on the basis of given factor prices. However, if the price of labour falls, it may be profit maximising to increase plant size. Under such circumstances, the size of the labour force will be increased because the capital–labour ratio moves in favour of labour and the amount of capital itself increases. This possibility is shown in Figure 5.5(a).

In Figure 5.5(a), the scale effect move from B to C (which represents the extent to which more capital and labour are now available after the reduced price of labour compared with the previous price ratio) outweighs the substitution effect move

Scale effect

The movement from one isoquant to another as a consequence of a change in relative factor prices, allowing more or less output to be produced.

Substitution effect

A movement along a given isoquant resulting from a change in factor prices in favour of that factor that is now relatively cheaper.

Expansion path

The locus of long-run equilibrium positions resulting from changes in factor inputs.

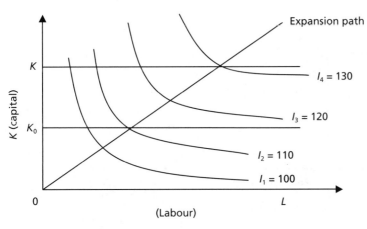

Figure 5.4 The scale effect.

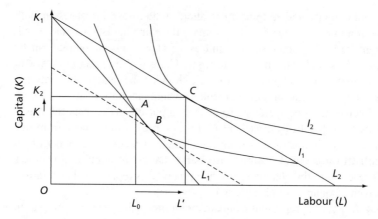

a

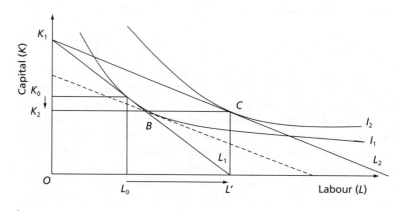

b

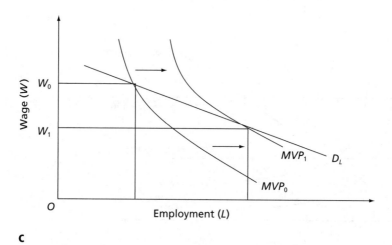

c

Figure 5.5 Labour demand with several variable inputs.

from A to B, which indicates the extent of the move along the original isoquant caused by the relative change in factor prices, so that more capital is used after the wage reduction. This is reflected in the rotation of the isocost line from K_1L_1 to K_2L_2. However, this is not the only possibility. In Figure 5.5(b), the scale effect is less than the substitution effect, so that less capital is used after the wage reduction than previously. It follows that, if the scale effect outweighs the substitution effect, so that more capital is used than previously, the long-run labour demand curve will be shallower than either of the underlying short-run curves as in Figure 5.5(c). If the scale effect is outweighed by the substitution effect, on the other hand, so that less capital is used than previously, the long-run demand curve will be steeper.

The effect of the lower wage is to shift the short-run MVP_0 curve to the right (to MVP_1), so that the demand for labour curve (D_L) is shallower (or more elastic) than the short-run MVP curves.

Similar considerations apply to the derivation of the market demand curve for labour. The industry demand curve is unlikely simply to be the sum of the individual firms' MVP curves. Product price and prices of factors of production other than labour are normally taken as given in deriving these curves. However, when all firms are contracting or expanding simultaneously as a consequence of external events, such assumptions are hardly tenable. If an industry is very small in the context of the whole economy, one might plausibly maintain the assumption of given factor prices. However, for the majority of cases, we would expect factor prices to increase with the expansion of an industry (i.e. there will be pecuniary external diseconomies). In any event, the price of an industry's output is bound to vary as its output changes. This is illustrated in Figure 5.6. Suppose the wage falls from w_0 to w_1. This, in turn, will result in an increase in labour usage throughout the industry, so that industry output increases and product price falls. This will shift each firm's MVP to the left.

Since ab represents the locus of all such points, we would expect the industry labour demand curve D_I to be less elastic than the individual firms' demand curves unless there are strong forces favouring technical external economies. Such forces might include information economies or improved transport infrastructure that are associated with larger industry size. These, however, only come about in the long term, so that it is reasonable to assume that the short-run industry demand for labour will be less elastic than the demand curves facing individual firms.

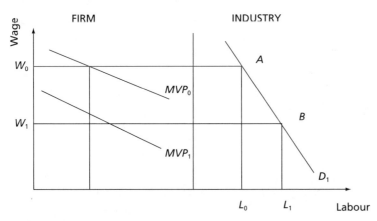

Figure 5.6 The market demand curve.

5.2 Marginal productivity and imperfectly competitive markets

The micro-level analysis above assumes that firms can obtain all the labour they require at the prevailing wage rate, but such an assumption has recently been called into question by Manning (2003), who suggests that this is equivalent to implying that a wage cut of a cent or a penny would cause all existing workers to leave their current employer immediately. The classic case of monopsony is a one-company town, but economists have argued that such examples must have receded in importance as transport improvements took place, which allowed workers to search for jobs over wider areas. It may apply to some extent to women who have more restricted job search because of family commitments, but we do not have precise information on such cases. Where monopsony is present, **monopsonistic exploitation** (the payment of a wage below the value of the *MRP*) will apply and an increase in wages need not lead to a decline in employment (Figure 5.7).

In Figure 5.7, the employer maximises profits by employing *OE** workers at a wage of *W** and *ab* is a measure of monopsonistic exploitation. Increasing wages up to *OW*₁ would lead to an increase in employment, but, once *OE*₁ level of employment is reached, the negative relationship between wages and employment is restored.

Manning's conception of monopsony is, however, different from the single-company town case, being based simply on the proposition that the supply of labour to the firm is not perfectly elastic. He assumes that there are frictions in the labour market caused by ignorance, heterogeneous preferences and mobility costs, so that employers have the power to set wages within certain limits. This means that there are economic rents, the existence of which makes the relationship between workers and employers one of **bilateral monopoly** (Figure 5.8) with an indeterminate outcome. This is illustrated more easily if one assumes that a trade union negotiates on behalf of the individual workers.

> **Monopsonistic exploitation**
>
> The payment of a wage less than the value of the marginal revenue product of labour as a consequence of an upward-sloping labour supply curve.
>
> **Bilateral monopoly**
>
> A situation in which both employer and employees (or their representatives) have a degree of monopoly bargaining power.

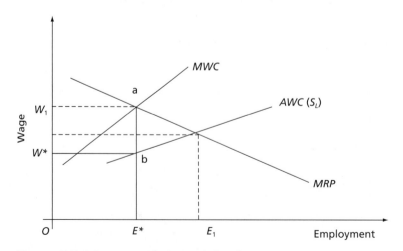

Figure 5.7 Monopsonistic exploitation.

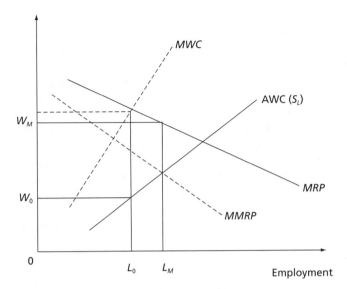

Figure 5.8 Bilateral monopoly.

The employer will attempt to maximise profits by employing OL_0 workers at a wage OW_0. A monopoly union will attempt to restrict sales of members' employment by equating the S_L curve to the curve marginal to the employer's demand curve, in order to maximise the economic rent, and so prefer employment to be higher at OL_M and the wage to be set at OW_M. The final outcome will depend on the relative bargaining power and skill of the protagonists.

Manning has a simple dynamic monopsony model which casts further light on these issues. First, assume that workers leave the firm at a rate Q that depends negatively on the wage rate, while the firm recruits workers at a rate R that depends positively on the wage rate. If the firm employed N_{t-1} workers in the previous period, where N represents the number of workers, at a wage rate of wt, its labour supply will be given by

$$N_t = [1 - Q(wt)]N_{t-1} + R(wt) \tag{5.4}$$

where $Q(w)$ is the separation rate and $R(w)$ the recruitment rate. In a steady state, total separations QN must equal recruits R, so that we have

$$N(w) = \frac{R(w)}{Q(w)} \tag{5.5}$$

giving us a positive long-run relationship between employment and the wage. In this case, the elasticity of the labour supply curve facing the firm can be written as

$$E_{Nw} = E_{Rw} - E_{Qw} \tag{5.6}$$

where E_{Rw} is the elasticity of the recruitment rate with respect to the wage and E_{Qw} is the elasticity of the separation rate with respect to the wage.

Manning also derives the result that the higher the fraction of recruits from non-employment, the more monopsonistic is the labour market. The empirical evidence from the US and the UK suggests that 45 to 55 per cent of all recruits were previously non-employed, a level which is likely to give employers considerable bargaining power. As far as the strategy for dealing with those already in employment is concerned, if it were possible to wage discriminate, it would seem optimal to adopt a strategy of offer-matching, whereby the employer offers the same wage as that offered by other firms competing for the worker's services when a worker receives an outside offer and this is not above his or her MP in the current firm. Likewise, the firm may offer to pay slightly more than the current wage to workers elsewhere, if this is consistent with their MP to the recruiting firm. However, such a strategy is uncommon, perhaps because it would give workers an incentive to increase their on-the-job search activities and consequently raise the quit rate. Further, it may be difficult to verify outside job offers. Implementing seniority-based wage systems may be a better option.

In 2010, the *Journal of Labor Economics* devoted an entire issue to labour market monopsony, including empirical studies on both static and dynamic versions. The editors (Ashenfelter *et al.*) report a remarkable common feature of all these studies, namely the high degree of monopsony power implied by the firm-level estimates of labour supply. Thus, this provides strong evidence that labour markets are far from competitive. Further corroboration comes from Australia. Using data from the Households Income and Labour Dynamics in Australia (HILDA) Survey, Booth and Katic (2011) report a wage elasticity of supply to a firm of around 0.71. This is close to the figure of 0.75 reported by Manning (2003) for the UK.

Another more longstanding approach to understanding relative bargaining power in the labour market comes from the application of the Marshallian rules of derived demand. Assuming two factors of production (capital and labour), these state that the elasticity of derived demand for either factor will be higher in absolute value (and bargaining power weaker).

1 the higher is the elasticity of demand for the output produced by the two factors
2 the higher is the elasticity of substitution between the two factors
3 the higher (lower) is the share of the factor in the cost of production, provided that the elasticity of product demand is higher (lower) than the elasticity of substitution
4 the higher is the elasticity of supply of other factors.

The third of these rules, often referred to as the importance of being unimportant, was revised as above by Hicks in 1932 (see Pierson 1988). Hicks' standard elasticity formula for the absolute elasticity of labour demand λ is

$$\lambda = \frac{\sigma(e+n) + eG(n-\sigma)}{e+n-G(n-\sigma)} \tag{5.7}$$

where

σ = elasticity of substitution between capital and labour

n = elasticity of product demand

e = elasticity of supply of capital

G = share of labour in total costs.

The four rules are established by the partial differentiation of (5.7), which requires that the RHS variables are exogenous. However, as pointed out by Maurice (1975) and Pemberton (1989), this is unlikely to be the case for G, as this is an outcome of the firm's maximising decisions about the appropriate levels for labour and capital. Equation (5.7) is, therefore, a special case, in which G is exogenously fixed as in the **Cobb–Douglas production function**.

A variety of approaches have been adopted to estimate the elasticity of demand for labour. Two distinct approaches are to hold output constant and estimate the own-wage elasticity, which captures only the substitution effect, or to allow for scale effects by holding constant price and quantities of other factors of production. Hamermesh (1993) surveyed a large number of such estimates and concluded that

> the absolute value of the constant-output elasticity of demand for homogeneous labour for a typical firm, and for the aggregate economy in the long run, is above zero and below one. Its value is probably bracketed by the interval 0.15–0.75, with 0.30 being a good "best guess".
>
> (1993: 135)

What of cases when output is allowed to vary? Here we expect higher estimates and this appears to be the case. For example, Symons and Layard (1984) obtained a very short-run labour demand elasticity of –0.1 and a medium-term one of –1.8. In addition, models involving several types of labour enable us to study the degree of substitutability between different types of labour and other factors of production. One such study, again using British data (Nissim 1984), found that the elasticity of demand for labour was lower the higher the level of skill, but there was considerable responsiveness in demand for all levels of skills to exogenous wage changes. Thus, a 10 per cent increase in nominal wage demand decreased the amount of skilled labour demanded by about 3.9 per cent on impact and 10.6 per cent by the time a new equilibrium was reached. A 5 per cent decrease in the wage rate of skilled to semi-skilled labour, through possibilities for substitution, would lead to a final 13 per cent increase in the relative employment of skilled labour. In some areas, it is easier to estimate marginal productivity than others. Thus, Frank (1984) made direct estimates of marginal productivity in a variety of enterprises for car salesmen paid on commission, estate agents paid likewise and professors in research universities judged on the basis of research budgets. In each case, the employees appeared to be paid less than the value of their marginal revenue products (see Case Study 5.1). Other examples can be found in sports where we can observe individual performance directly on the field of play (see e.g. Scully 1974).

Cobb–Douglas production function

A production function in which there are constant returns to scale, so that output increases in proportion to the increase in inputs.

Case Study 5.1

Are workers paid their marginal products?

The standard neoclassical model suggests that, in competitive labour markets, workers will be paid their marginal products. However, Cornell University economist Robert Frank observed that, in practice, pay schedules seemed to be much more egalitarian than productivity considerations would imply. While a number of factors could explain this, he suggests that the answer lies in status considerations. Workers are prepared to accept a relatively low wage if they are at the top of a particular occupational group, while those at the bottom require some compensation for their lower status. Thus, in Figure 5.1.1 we have three occupational groups AA_1, BB_1 and CC_1 with the straight lines denoting the relationship between marginal product and pay. They are relatively flat. If workers were paid according to their marginal products, the relationship would be shown by the 45° line drawn from the origin. AA_1 is a low-productivity occupation with only the highest performer having a productivity level equal to MP_0. CC_1 is a higher-productivity occupation with an average performer achieving a productivity level of MP_0, while BB_1 is a high-productivity occupation with the lowest performer achieving a productivity level of MP_0. In each case, the pay schedules are flat such that the lowest performers are paid more than productivity considerations would imply and the highest performers less. A_1X measures the underpayment of the highest performer in occupation AA_1 and BX measures the overpayment of the lowest performer in occupation BB_1.

Three examples in conformity with this in occupations in which the measurement of productivity is relatively straightforward are car salesman commissions, estate agent commissions and pay schedules for university professors in research-led institutions. In the case of car salesmen, the slope of the earnings functions in 13 dealerships in the US ranged from 0.165 to 0.30, well below 0.45. Sales commissions in four real estate agencies in New York were all well below the level at which they would equate to MP_0. Likewise, using data from Cornell and the University

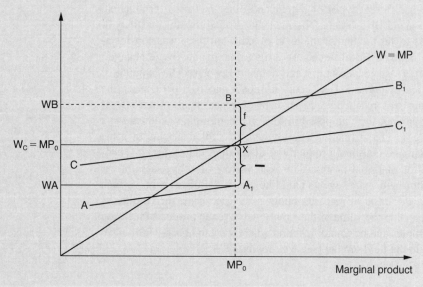

Figure 5.1.1 Marginal productivity and status.

of Michigan, he finds there are substantial differences in the value of research grants brought in by individual professors, but relatively small differences in annual salary levels between top and bottom performers.

Frank puts forward two propositions (see Figure 5.1.1):

Proposition 1

For cost-minimising firms in competitive labour markets, an employee's wage, W, will be related to his or her marginal product according to a wage schedule in which the slope dW/dMP takes a value significantly smaller than one.

Proposition 2

Other things being equal, as the tasks performed by one group involve more sustained and intense interaction and contact with co-workers, values taken by dW/dMP must be smaller and/or the variation in earnings across the group must fall.

It should be noted that these propositions seem far removed from those of tournament theory, which suggests that widening the earnings distribution in an internal labour market will act as an incentive to those in lower occupations to work harder in order to be promoted to higher-paying jobs. Thus, widening the gap in pay between the Chief Executive and the next highest-ranked individuals will induce greater effort in order to achieve Chief Executive status in due course. (See, for example, Eriksson 1999.) This suggests that different considerations may apply within occupations and across occupations.

R.H. Frank, "Are Workers Paid Their Marginal Products?", *American Economic Review*, 74(4), 1984, pp. 549–71.

5.3 The demand for workers or the demand for hours?

5.3.1 The standard work-week and overtime

Employers have choices not only about how many workers to employ but also on how many hours each worker should be utilised. That is why we must consider not only the extensive margin based on number of employees but also the intensive margin based on the intensity of hours per time period. As noted by Hamermesh (1993), the fact that there are substantial differences in weekly hours across industries suggests that there is considerable scope for substituting hours for workers either because of technological or cost differences among workers. Two key questions are: first, why do we have standard work-weeks and overtime paid at premium rates; and, second, what determines the optimal employee/hours mix?

Hart (2004) suggests the following reasons why employers might prefer a standard work-week – to minimise organisational costs, to maximise available trading hours across integrated sectors, to facilitate team working, because of the presence of line production and because of the need to deal with outside agencies. However, the standard work-week is often accompanied by substantial overtime working at premium wage rates. Thus, Hart finds that 1.25 applies in Japan, 1.3 in the UK and 1.5 in the US. Overtime working is not, however, randomly distributed. It is highly procyclical and affects some workers much more than others. Thus, in the UK, in the past overtime has averaged three or four hours a week, but only affects 50 to 60 per cent of non-managerial workers who may work on average up to five or six hours of overtime per week. For managerial employees, unpaid overtime is much more common than paid overtime and signals a worker's commitment to the job.

Apart from the reasons above, the use of a standard work-week and overtime paid at premium rates may be one means whereby the employer can elicit a greater input from the workforce (Figure 5.9). First, we make use of the indifference curve approach. Analogous to the isoquant analysis utilised earlier in this chapter, the indifference curve shows a particular level of satisfaction obtained from varying combinations of two goods, wage income and leisure, which can be substituted for one another by varying the number of hours worked.

A standard work-week set at OS hours is optimal for a representative worker with an indifference curve given by IC_1, but with workers with heterogeneous tastes this may not be the preferred work-week. Now suppose the wage rate is set at OW_0, with an overtime premium rate at W_0W_2. The representative worker will be just as well-off at OH^* hours as at the standard work-week, but the input of hours will be greater. Payment of a premium for overtime hours produces a large substitution effect relative to the income effect as it is confined to *marginal* daily hours. In terms of job generation, increasing the size of the overtime premium may be a more effective tool for creating jobs than cutting the length of the standard work-week (see Case Studies 5.2 and 5.3).

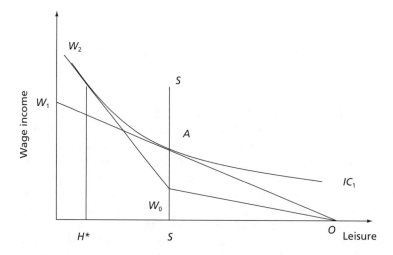

Figure 5.9 The demand for overtime.

5.3.2 Capital utilisation (shift-working)

Firms are able to vary, subject to agreement, not only the hours that their employees work, but also the hours over which capital is utilised. (This is not to be confused with **capacity utilisation**, which refers to the fact that firms may produce less than maximum output due to lack of demand in the recession.) This means that capital can be used for a period greater than the length of the standard work-

Capacity utilisation

The degree to which actual output is below maximum output at full capacity due to a shortfall in demand.

Case Study 5.2

Work-sharing: the case of the French 35-hour week

France has historically suffered from high levels of unemployment and various governments, seemingly driven by the lump of labour fallacy, have seen work-sharing as a means of sharing a given amount of labour demand among a larger number of workers.

In 1982, François Mitterrand's socialist government passed a law reducing the length of work-week from 40 to 39 hours. The overtime premium wage rate was also fixed at 1.25 times the regular rate and its maximum amount fixed at 30 hours per year in order to discourage its use, while the retirement age was reduced from 65 to 60. In analysing the effects of the hours reduction, Crépon and Kramarz (2002) find that subsequently the probability of making a transition from employment to unemployment rose by between 2.3 and 3.9 percentage points and the government sought to introduce incentives to employers to take on additional labour. Under the 1996 Loi Robien, firms that simultaneously reduced hours of work (by 10 per cent) and hired additional workers would benefit from a significant social charge benefit (amounting to some 30 to 40 per cent of the employers' contribution) for up to seven years. However, unemployment remained stubbornly high.

In 1998, when unemployment stood at 11.5 per cent, the government mandated a reduction in the work-week to 35 hours for firms employing more than 20 workers to be achieved by 2000, while the same was to apply to small firms by 2002. To ease the transition for small firms, the law reduced the size of their overtime wage premium and increased their annual limit on overtime hours relative to that for large firms, so that they would still be able to work 39 hours without a significant increase in costs. Overall, weekly wages were to remain roughly the same but with some compensation from more flexible accounting for overtime work by changing from a weekly to an annual basis. Crépon et al. (2005) use firm-level data to estimate the effect of the introduction of the 35-hour week on productivity, the cost of labour and employment, finding that total factor productivity fell by 3.7 per cent from 1997 to 2000 in firms that reduced the length of the work-week relative to those that did not. At the same time, employment increased by 9.9 per cent in making the change. However, they do not estimate net employment effects. Estevao and Sá (2006) use matched firm-level data and a difference in differences estimator for treatment (large firms) and control group (small firms) over the period 1993–2002 to estimate short-run effects of the new law. They find that a significant number of employees attempted to maintain their hours either by taking a second job or by moving to a small firm that did not face the same restrictions. The law increased dual job-holding by 3.3 percentage points, which is quite large in terms of the numbers holding dual jobs. Further, those who moved from large to small firms worked longer hours than those who stayed in large firms. They find employment in large firms remained largely unchanged. Finally, French workers did not become more satisfied with their hours of work relative to other European workers, suggesting no general preference for shorter hours.

Similar negative conclusions concerning work-sharing have been arrived at in Germany. In 1990, the trade union IB Metal negotiated a sector agreement with the employers to reduce hours of work to 35 without loss of pay. By early 1995, such framework agreements on work-sharing had been signed in 10 industrial sectors, covering 6.5 million workers. Using German Socio-Economic Panel data, Hunt (1998, 1999) concluded that the net effect of these agreements was to reduce employment overall over the period 1984–94.

Case Study 5.3

Mandatory overtime premium payments

For many years, the State of California required that most female employees be paid an overtime premium of time-and-a-half for hours worked beyond eight hours a day. In 1980, this daily overtime penalty was extended to men also, thus allowing one to estimate the effect of an exogenous increase in the relative price of overtime work on actual hours and thereby measure the elasticity of demand for hours of labour. There were also Federal laws relating to overtime premium payments, but these only required covered workers to be paid time-and-a-half for hours of work beyond 40 in a given week rather than a daily limit. The Californian requirement was repealed in 1998, bringing it into line with the Federal requirement.

Hamermesh and Trejo used the opportunity provided by the extension of the Californian mandatory requirement to men to compare California with States which had not regulated daily overtime, covering the periods both before and after the legal extension to men in California. Using a difference in difference estimator with women as the control group, they found that there was a substantial decline in the prevalence of daily overtime among men in California compared to men elsewhere. The implied price elasticity of demand for daily overtime hours was at least 0.5.

See D.S. Hamermesh and S.J. Trejo, "The Demand for Hours of Labor; Direct Evidence from California", *Review of Economics and Statistics*, vol. 82(1), February, 2000, pp. 38–47.

Capital utilisation

This measures the number of hours over which capital is used relative to the 168 hours implied by continuous operation.

week and workers can use the same capital stock at different times. Foss (1981) attempts to explain why, in the US, **capital utilisation** rose by 25 per cent (though hours of work declined from 50 hours to 40 hours). He concludes that the rise in manufacturing plant hours was explained in part by a rise in capital intensity and a related increase in continuous operations in industry through technical necessity. Plant hours were, however, short in single-plant firms, probably reflecting preferences by owners of small firms for leisure over income. The increased employment of women had also inhibited the use of shift-work, as they needed to reconcile work with family activities. On the other side, the overtime premium payment of time-and-a-half had contributed to a trend towards longer plant hours by making shift-working relatively cheaper compared to overtime working. For the UK, Bosworth (1994) reports that the incidence of shift-working among manual workers in manufacturing had risen from 12.5 per cent of such workers in 1954 to 25.5 per cent in 1987. These consisted of various types of shift-working patterns, including two-shift, three-shift, night-work and continental shifts (involving rotating the workers between different shifts on a regular basis). In the service sector also, shifts are required because consumer demand occurs out-with the normal working day hours. Examples include hospitals, transport and retail distribution, including, in the latter case, 24-hour opening times in the case of some supermarkets. The aversion of workers to work at unpopular times requires shift-work premium payments.

In the light of the incidence of shift-working, it is necessary to adapt the standard production function approach. A popular model is the Cobb–Douglas production function, which may be written as

$$Q_r = AL_t^\alpha K_t^{1-\alpha} \tag{5.8}$$

where Q = output, L = labour, K = capital, A is a given constant and α plus $1 - \alpha$ denotes constant returns to scale. Instead, we can write

$$Q_r = AN_t^{a1}H_t^{a2}K_t^{a3}U_t^{a4} \tag{5.9}$$

where N = number of workers, H = number of hours, K = capital stock and U = capital utilisation. In other words, firms can adjust the hours of capital as well as the hours of workers. The firm has two basic choices in determining the level of output: either to build a large plant and operate it with a single shift or to build a small plant and operate it with multiple shifts. However, Marris (1964) suggests that it would not pay to operate all plant continuously – there is an **optimal degree of idleness**. The prices of various factor services vary over time, so that a firm will often maximise profits by planning to produce its desired output with an "unnecessarily large" plant.

Winston (1974) suggests that optimal utilisation would be a function of four factors.

i   relative factor prices;
ii the amplitude of the input price rhythm (shift differentials and the price of electricity being important here);
iii the capital intensity of the productive process;
iv the elasticity of substitution between capital and labour (σ).

Combining (i) and (iv), it can be shown that the higher the rate of interest relative to the wage rate, the more profitable is shift-work, but where:

a $\sigma > 1$, the increase in the price of capital will cause the capital–labour ratio to fall as labour is substituted for capital. As it now pays to economise on labour, shift-working will decrease.

Optimal degree of idleness

The extent to which it pays not to engage in continuous operation because of the variation in the prices of various factors of production over time.

b $\sigma = 1$. As the capital–labour ratio remains constant, there will be no effect on shift-work.

c $\sigma < 1$. An increase in the rate of interest will lead to an increase in the measured capital–labour ratio; hence, shift-working will increase.

The empirical evidence suggests that (c) predominates.

Two other factors will determine the degree of capital utilisation. The first is the relative extent of depreciation of capital and the extent of capital obsolescence. The latter appears to be twice as important as the former, and the greater its extent, the more profitable is shift-work, as obsolescence is a function of time. The second factor is productivity. Medical evidence suggests that biologically it is detrimental to work at night, as body temperature and alertness fall. However, the empirical evidence in support of this is mixed, suggesting perhaps that those most able to adapt select themselves into work at uncongenial times.

Mayshar and Solon (1993) found that shift-working in the US was extremely procyclical. Using data on full-time production workers in various US cities, they discovered that the late-shift share of cyclical employment variation was about twice its share of the level of employment. When full-time employment declined during a recession, about one-half of the decline for manufacturing production workers and one-third for the whole economy-wide decline occurred on late shifts. Note, fewer workers are employed on late shifts because of the shift-work premium and these figures imply that the proportional decline in output is greater than that in employment in the recession. This explains the longstanding puzzle of procyclical productivity.

5.4 Hiring costs and labour hoarding

Before considering the optimal employee–hours mix, we must distinguish between fixed and variable costs. Fixed labour costs consist of once-over setup costs that an employer faces each time new labour is hired and recurrent fixed labour costs that continue as long as the worker remains in employment, but do not vary with the number of hours worked or with the intensity of work. Examples of non-recurring fixed costs are hiring and screening costs, induction and training costs, and potential firing costs. Recurrent fixed costs include employer contributions to national insurance and pensions, certain fringe benefits and holiday and scheme benefits. Together, these can amount to a substantial proportion of the wage bill, perhaps 25 per cent in the UK and US and much higher in some European countries. Walter Oi (1962) suggested that, because of these costs, the classical treatment of labour as a purely variable factor was erroneous and labour was really a quasi-fixed factor. The distinction between fixed and variable labour costs could explain many labour market phenomena such as labour hoarding, part-time employment and the impact of work-sharing and marginal employment subsidies. More particularly, it can explain the simultaneous presence of overtime and unemployed workers.

The theoretical explanation is as follows. Let us define the demand for labour (L) in terms of the number of workers (N) and the number of hours worked (H)

$$L = F(Q^*, K, T) \tag{5.10}$$

where
$Q*$ = expected sales
K = existing stock of capital
T = level of technology

the partial derivatives are

$$\frac{\partial L}{\partial Q*} > 0, \frac{\partial L}{\partial K} < 0, \frac{\partial L}{\partial T} < 0$$

$$L = g(N, H) \tag{5.11}$$

$$H = HS + HP \text{ (standard and premium hours)} \tag{5.12}$$

$$C = \left(HS_{ws} + HP_{wp} + F_1 + F_2(q) \right) N \tag{5.13}$$

where
C = costs
F_1 = recurring fixed employment costs
F_2 = once-over fixed costs
q = quit rate

$$nw = F_1 + F_2(q) \tag{5.14}$$

$$wp = \alpha ws, \ \alpha > 1 \tag{5.15}$$

$$N* = h_1(HS, \frac{nw}{ws}, L) \tag{5.16}$$

where
$N*$ = optimal combination of employees

$$H* = h_2(HS, \frac{nw}{ws}, L)$$

where
$H*$ = optimal combination of hours per worker

$$\frac{\partial N*}{\partial \left(\dfrac{nw}{ws} \right)} < 0 \quad , \quad \frac{\partial H*}{\partial \left(\dfrac{nw}{ws} \right)} > 0$$

Thus, an increase in the rates of non-wage to wage costs will be alleviated by employers utilising their existing labour force more intensively. Further, a reduction in the length of the normal work-week will increase the marginal cost of new employees, since a smaller proportion of the average work-week will be purchased at the standard wage rate. This will encourage firms further to increase overtime working rather than employ additional workers. Therefore, the presence of overtime working at the same time as the presence of unemployed workers can represent rational behaviour on the part of the employer.

Next, we examine employment dynamics over the business cycle. Walter Oi (1962) provided the rationale for the hoarding of labour over the business cycle by a profit-maximising/cost-minimising firm. If we assume that labour is a quasi-fixed factor, the decision by a firm to lay off workers during the downswing of a business cycle implies that the firm is writing off a previous investment in fixed costs. Clearly, the greater the degree of fixity of labour, the more reluctant it will be to do so. As Bowers and Deaton (1980) note, this does not necessarily imply that the firm is inefficient – it is not the same as over-manning or feather-bedding. It does, however, imply that labour is not fully utilised and that there are likely to be procyclical swings in labour productivity. This contrasts with the assumption of diminishing marginal returns, which suggests that, as full employment is attained, labour productivity is likely to be negatively related to output. During the early stages of a recession, employers will be reluctant to lay off workers until they are sure that the downturn is long-lived rather than the consequence of a very temporary decline in demand, so that there will be a lag in employment relative to changes in output. Likewise, during the early phases of a recovery, employers will be reluctant to take on extra workers until they are sure that the recovery is prolonged, or that again there is a lagged adjustment of employment relative to output. This may be reinforced by institutional factors such as contractual requirements that prevent firms from laying off workers at short notice, fixed labour–machine ratios or simply the need to maintain goodwill and avoid job insecurity. Whatever the reason two implications follow:

1 a given change in the output of a firm will be associated with a less than proportionate change in the employment of higher-fixity labour in the short run; and

2 the speed of adjustment of the firm's labour input towards the firm's long-run desired labour will be slower for higher-fixity labour.

Labour hoarding

The tendency to retain workers in a recession, despite the fact that output has declined.

As Clark (1973) notes, the extent of **labour hoarding** will be determined by the costs of adjustment. Suppose desired employment E^* fluctuates as in Figure 5.10 with firing costs (F) applying at t_0 and hiring costs (H) at t_1, assuming that t_0 and

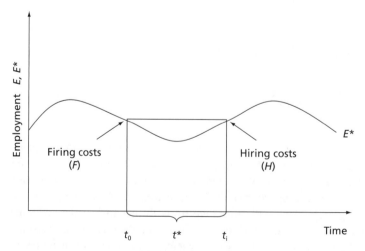

Figure 5.10 Labour hoarding.

t_1 are the points at which the respective decisions have to be made. As long as $w_t < H + F$, where w_t = the wages of workers retained over the period of the slump t^*, labour hoarding will be the least cost option. There will also be a hoarding maximum $t^* = (h + F)/w$, which is cost minimising.

Given this scenario, there are, however, two choices open to firms reacting to a downturn in demand – either to reduce the number of employees or to reduce the number of hours worked by each employee. Thus, the gap between actual output per worker and its potential level is reflected by two phenomena:

i a temporary cyclical shortening of the work-week, resulting in unpaid labour hoarding, the costs of which are borne by the employee; and

ii a temporary cyclical decline in output per man-hour, the costs of which are borne by the employer.

This is illustrated below.[1] First, the price of workers in terms of hours can be derived from the wage bill (B)

$$B = ntw \tag{5.17}$$

where
n = number of workers
t = average hours per worker
w = wage rate

It follows from (5.15) that the isocost curve is simply

$$n = \left(\frac{B}{w}\right) \cdot \frac{1}{t} \tag{5.18}$$

which is a rectangular hyperbola with $\left(\dfrac{B}{w}\right)$, the given constant. This is illustrated in Figure 5.11 where the broken hyperbolae (C^0, C^*) represent isocost curves, X^* is an isoquant representing maximum output, and X^0 represents output in the recession.

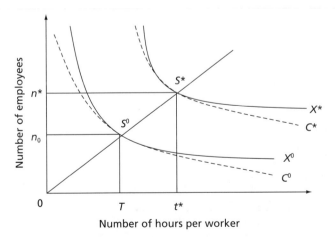

Figure 5.11 Employee or hours reductions in the recession.

X^0 can be achieved by reducing the number workers from $0n^*$ and the number of hours from $0t^*$ to $0t_0$.

We must also allow for overtime, which is paid at premium rates, the wage bill then becomes

$$B = n(t_a w_a + t_b w_b)$$ (5.19)

where
t_a = normal hours
w_a = the standard wage rate
t_b = overtime hours
w_b = the overtime wage rate

Once again, by solving for n, the price of workers can be expressed in terms of hours

$$n = \frac{B}{t_a w_a + t_b w_b}$$ (5.20)

This implies that the isocost curves will have a kink at the point at which overtime working begins with the expectations that the initial reactions of employers will be to cut hours by reducing overtime and only subsequently reduce employment levels. Employers may also be constrained from reducing the number of employees and the hours they work to the short-run optimal level as illustrated in Figure 5.12.

The shaded areas A, B and C, constitutes the **unemployment gap**, i.e. the difference between actual and maximum output. X^* represents peak output, X_0 desired output and X_1 potential output from the existing labour input. Alternatively, $n_1 t^*$ equals the supply of man-hours willingly offered by n_1 employed workers; $n_1 t_1$ equals the man-hours purchased by the employer when output is at X_0 and $n_0 t_0$ equals the optimal combination of workers and hours assuming that output were to remain permanently at X_0. It follows from these definitions that $n^* t^* - n_0 t_0$ is the unemployment gap, which can be sub-divided into $(n^* t^* - n_1 t^*)$ – the unemployed man-hours of dismissed workers – plus $(n_1 t^* - n_1 t_1)$ – the unemployed man-hours resulting from a shorter work-week than would be willingly offered by workers –

Unemployment gap

The difference between the number of workers and the number of hours utilised and what is implied by the current level of output (i.e. surplus workers and surplus hours)

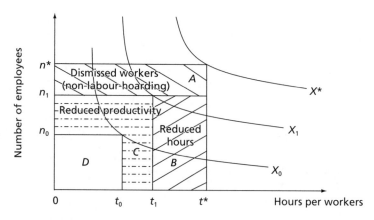

Figure 5.12 The unemployment gap.

plus $(n_1t_1 - n_0t_0)$ – the unemployed man-hours due to a temporary reduction in labour productivity below the full-employment level.

The actual measurement of labour hoarding is not straightforward, but a common approach is the **trends-through-peaks procedure** (TTP), which is based on the proposition that deviations in the output/employee ratio from linear segments fitted to the peaks in output/employee time series indicate the extent to which employed labour is not being fully utilised. Hart and Malley (1996) suggest that there is direct evidence from the US labour market that the TTP approach provides a reasonably accurate measure of actual firm behaviour. However, there are competing explanations for variations in labour productivity such as technology shocks, increasing returns to labour and cyclical change in work organisation and practices. Thus, Fay and Medoff (1985) suggest that firms may reallocate labour to other tasks, such as machine maintenance, during downtime in economic activity, and Aizcorbe (1992) notes, for example, that, in the US automobile industry, there is a correlation between labour specialisation and assembly-line speeds that influences the rate at which productivity grows. Nonetheless, labour hoarding remains the main explanation for procyclical movements in labour productivity.

Hart and Malley examine the extent of labour hoarding in four countries – Japan, Germany, UK and US, noting that lifetime employment has characterised the Japanese economy, where there are significantly higher firm-specific investments in human capital, which we would expect to be reflected in a greater degree of labour hoarding. This is borne out by the facts using a number of measures. Thus, the coefficient of excess labour, which measures the extent to which the number of excess workers is eliminated each quarter following a recession, is only 6 per cent in Japan compared to roughly a quarter in the other three countries. Similarly, the coefficient for the adjustment of hours to desired hours is higher in Germany (50 per cent per quarter) and lowest in Japan (15 per cent). An alternative approach is to carry out a simulation of the model they adopt in order to obtain estimates of excess hours for various time periods, and the results are shown in Table 5.1. For the whole period 1970–91, the average estimated excess hours per week are nearly twice as high in Japan as in Germany, which itself has a significantly higher figure than in the UK and US.

When the time periods are split to cover two separate recessions, namely 1970–80 and 1981–91, it can be seen that the differences narrow, which Hart and Malley suggest is consistent with the fact that the Japanese economy performs better relative to other countries in the later period.[2]

There is, however, evidence from many developed economies that firms are becoming more flexible both in terms of the external and internal margin, thereby

> **Trends-through-peaks procedure**
>
> This is a method of measuring the underutilisation of resources by fitting linear segments to the peaks in output/ employees time series over the cycle.

Table 5.1 Excess hours per week for selected time periods

	1970–91	1970–80	1981–91
Japan	4.69	6.22	3.35
Germany	2.84	2.62	2.47
UK	1.76	1.24	2.20
US	1.66	1.68	1.63

Source: Adapted from Hart and Malley (1996).

reducing the extent of labour hoarding. Thus, Haskel *et al.* (1997), examining data on 396 establishments in the 1990 UK Workplace Employment Relations Survey, find that 45 per cent of the sample had reduced over-manning or become more flexible in the use of labour over the previous three years. More-flexible firms are much more likely to respond to a demand shock by adjusting employment and hours of work than those which have not adopted such practices.

To conclude, how to adjust the number of employees and the hours they work is an important decision for employers as the business cycle begins to bite.

Summary

- Demand for labour is a derived demand, so that it is influenced by the degree of competition in the product market. In the short run production function capital is fixed and eventually there are diminishing returns to the employment of additional labour. In the long run, all factors are variable and there will be scale effects through the possibility of substituting capital for labour and vice versa, as indicated by the value of the elasticity of substitution. While in competitive product markets there will be equality between the marginal product and the wage, the slopes of industry demand curves will generally differ from those of firm demand curves.
- In imperfectly competitive labour markets, monopsonistic employers will offer wages less than the value of the MRP in order to maximise profits. Manning's concept of dynamic monopsony suggests that this situation may be the norm. This leads on to bilateral monopoly situations in which the outcomes may be indeterminate. The Marshallian rules can, however, help us to understand better the determinants of relative bargaining power.
- Employers must choose not only how many workers to employ, but also how intensively to utilise them. Given standard work-weeks, this normally implies overtime working, the combination of the two inducing a greater total labour input. However, it is also possible to increase the input by extending the hours over which capital is utilised by utilising various forms of shift-work. This does not necessarily imply continuous operation as there is an optimal degree of idleness depending on the relative costs of working at different times of the day and night.
- Walter Oi developed the notion that, rather than being a variable factor in the long run, labour was really a quasi-fixed factor and this can explain various labour market phenomena such as labour hoarding. That is, during recessionary periods, firms will be reluctant to lay off workers who have a greater degree of fixity of labour, so that there is lagged adjustment of employment relative to output. In addition to the dismissal of some workers, there will be some reduction in hours of work and in productivity.

Questions

1 Explain what is meant by the demand for labour being a derived demand? How is this influenced under different competitive conditions in product and factor markets?
2 What conditions must be fulfilled for workers to be paid a wage equal to their marginal products?
3 To what extent can the Marshallian rules of derived demand explain relative bargaining power b etween employers and trade unions?
4 Why should there be a standard work-week rather than a situation in which individual workers are free to choose their hours of work?
5 Why should overtime co-exist with unemployed workers?
6 Under what circumstances will it pay firms to hoard labour?

Notes

1 This analysis is drawn from Taylor (1970).
2 Hours rigidity is also reflected in a higher inventory-stock ratio in Japan than in the other three countries.

References

Aizcorbe A., "Pro-cyclical Labour Productivity, Increasing Returns to Labour and Labour Hoarding in US Auto Assembly Plant Employment", *Economic Journal*, 102, 1992, pp. 860–73.

Ashenfelter O., Farber H. and Ransom M., "Labor Market Monopsony; Introduction", *Journal of Labor Economics*, 28(2), 2010, pp. 203–10.

Booth A.L. and Katic P., "Estimating the Wage Elasticity of Labour Supply to a Firm: What Evidence is there for Monopsony?", *Economic Record*, 87(278), 2011, pp. 359–69.

Bosworth D., "Shift-work in the UK: Evidence from the LFS", *Applied Economics*, 26, 1994, pp. 617–26.

Bowers J. and Deaton D., "Employment Functions and the Measurement of Labour Hoarding", *The Manchester School*, 48, 1980, pp. 157–86.

Clark C.S., "Labour Hoarding in Durable Goods Industries", *American Economic Review*, 63(5), 1973, pp. 811–24.

Coase R., "The Nature of the Firm", *Economica*, 4, 1937, pp. 386–405.

Crépon B. and Kramarz F., "Employed 40 Hours or Not Employed 39 Hours: Lessons from the 1982 Mandatory Reduction of the Workweek", *Journal of Political Economy*, 110(6), 2002, pp. 1355–89.

Crépon B., Leclair M. and Roux S., "RTT, Productivité et Emploi: Nouvelles Estimations sur Données d'Entreprises", *Economie et Statistique*, INSEE, no. 376–77, June 2005, pp. 55–89.

Eriksson T., "Executive Compensation and Tournament Theory; Empirical Tests for Danish Data", *Journal of Labor Economics*, 17(2), 1999, pp. 262–80.

Estevao M. and Sá F., "Are the French Happy with the 35-Hour Workweek?", *IMF Working Paper* WP/06/251, November 2006.

Fay J. and Medoff J., "Labor and Output over the Business Cycle", *American Economic Review*, 75, 1985, pp. 638–55.

Foss M.F., "Long-Run Changes in the Workweek of Fixed Capital", *American Economic Review*, 71(2), 1981, pp. 58–63.

Frank R.H., "Are Workers Paid Their Marginal Products?", *American Economic Review*, 74(4), 1984, pp. 549–71.

Hamermesh D.S., *Labor Demand*, Princeton University Press, Princeton, New Jersey, 1993.

Hamermesh D.S. and Trejo S.J., "The Demand for Hours of Labor: Direct Evidence from California", *Review of Economics and Statistics*, LXXXII(1), 2000, pp. 38–47.

Hart R.A., *The Economics of Overtime Working*, Cambridge University Press, Cambridge, 2004.

Hart R.A. and Malley J.R., "Excess Labour and the Business Cycle: A Comparative Study of Japan, Germany, the United Kingdom and the United States", *Economica*, 63, 1996, pp. 325–42.

Haskel J., Kersley B. and Martin C., "Labour Market Flexibility and Employment Adjustment: Micro-evidence from UK Establishments", *Oxford Economic Papers*, 49, 1997, pp. 362–79.

Hunt J., "Hours Reductions as Work-sharing", *Brookings Papers on Economic Activity*, no. 1, 1998, pp. 339–81.

Hunt J., "Has Work-sharing Worked in Germany?", *Quarterly Journal of Economics*, 114(1), 1999, pp. 117–48.

Manning A., *Monopsony in Motion: Imperfect Competition in Labor Markets*, Princeton University Press, Princeton, New Jersey, 2003.

Marris R., *The Economics of Capital Utilisation: A Report on Multiple-shift Work*, Cambridge University Press, Cambridge, 1964.

Maurice S.C., "On the Importance of Being Unimportant: An Analysis of the Paradox in Marshall's Third Rule of Derived Demand", *Economica*, 42, 1975, pp. 385–93.

Mayshar J. and Solon G., "Shift-work and the Business Cycle", *American Economic Review*, 83(2), 1993, pp. 224–8.

Nissim J., "The Price Responsiveness of the Demand for Labour by Skill: British Mechanical Engineering, 1963–78", *Economic Journal*, 94(376), 1984, pp. 812–25.

Oi W., "Labor as a Quasi-Fixed Factor", *Journal of Political Economy*, 70, 1962, pp. 538–55.

Pemberton J., "Marshall's Rules for Derived Demand: A Critique and Generalisation", *Scottish Journal of Political Economy*, 36(4), 1989, 396–403.

Pierson J., "The Importance of Being Unimportant: Marshall's 3rd Rule of Derived Demand", *Scottish Journal of Political Economy*, 35(2), 1988, pp. 105–14.

Scully G.W., "Pay and Performance in Major League Baseball", *American Economic Review*, 64(60), 1974, pp. 915–30.

Stevens M. and Behar A., "The Allen/Uzawa Elasticity of Substitution under Non Constant Returns to Scale", University of Oxford, 27 August 2009.

Symons J. and Layard R., "Neoclassical Demand Functions for Six Major Economies", *Economic Journal*, 94(376), 1984, pp. 788–99.

Taylor J., "Hidden Unemployment, Hoarded Labour and the Phillips Curve", *Southern Economic Journal*, XXXVII(I), 1970, pp. 1–16.

Williamson O., *The Economic Institutions of Capitalism*, Free Press, New York, 1985.

Winston G.C., "The Theory of Capital Utilisation and Idleness", *Journal of Economic Literature*, 12(4), 1974, pp. 1301–20.

Further reading

For an extensive treatment of labour demand, see D.S. Hamermesh, *Labor Demand*, Princeton University Press, 1996. This covers both static and dynamic theories of labour demand and summarises much of the available empirical literature for a range of countries.

R.R. Betancourt and C.K. Clague, *Capital Utilisation: A Theoretical and Empirical Analysis*, Cambridge University Press, 2008, cover the theory and econometric tests of the theory using international data.

A. Manning, *Monopsony in Motion: Imperfect Competition in Labor Markets*, Princeton University Press, Princeton, New Jersey, 2003, is a powerful challenge to much of the earlier literature that suggested that monopsony was simply a special case.

Chapter 6

Extensions of labour demand
Mismatches in the labour market

Learning outcomes

At the end of this chapter, readers should understand that:

- It is not straightforward to determine what is a labour shortage or labour surplus;
- Non-price adjustments are the most common response by employers to labour shortages;
- Over-education and under-education are common phenomena with effects on wages, job satisfaction and mobility;
- Labour market discrimination may originate from employers, co-workers or consumers with distinctive consequences in terms of wages and segregation;
- There is an index number problem in estimating the degree of discrimination using the standard decomposition method;
- Different considerations apply to discrimination on account of gender, race, disability and age;
- Some discrimination may be statistical rather than taste-based.

Introduction

In Chapter 5, the assumption was made that the labour market was in or moving towards an equilibrium position in which labour supply equalled labour demand. In this chapter, we examine three situations in which there is a mismatch of one sort or another between labour supply and labour demand. These are: first, conditions of labour shortage or labour surplus; second, over- or under-education; and, third, labour market discrimination on the part of the employer. For the sake of completeness, we consider other forms of discrimination here, such as customer and co-worker discrimination whether on account of gender, race, disability, age or religion.

In each of these three cases, identifying the extent of the mismatch is not straightforward. Thus, employers may believe there is a labour shortage when the real problem is a failure to pay the market wage necessary to attract, retain and motivate sufficient labour of the right quality. Such a belief is more likely to be held in a monopsonistic labour market where raising the wage is necessary to expand the labour force. Perhaps this explains why non-wage adjustments are often the preferred response in dealing with labour shortages. Skill mismatch or over- and under-education may result from the nature of jobs changing over time or differences in worker abilities given their level of education. Some jobs may advertise only a minimum educational requirement, and other forms of human capital, such as experience, may be substituted for formal qualifications. The source of discrimination may be employers, employees or consumers, and this may affect different groups in different ways, which may not be easy to detect. In the case of age or disability, lower earnings may reflect lower productivity. The conventional residual method of estimating discrimination may be susceptible to omitted variable bias, if certain variables are not included in the estimating equation.

6.1 Labour shortages

As noted by Bosworth (1993), "skill shortages are notoriously difficult to define and measure", but, broadly speaking, a shortage indicates a disequilibrium situation in which the demand for labour is in excess of supply at the ruling market price or wage. Three possible indicators of this are:

- relatively high rates of return in particular occupations;
- a situation in which the number of available workers increases less rapidly than demand at salaries paid in the recent past; and
- a situation in which relative earnings increase, but not fast enough to catch up with increasing demand. Arrow and Capron (1959) refer to this as a **dynamic shortage**.

Dynamic shortages

Situations where relative earnings increase in shortage occupations, but not fast enough to eliminate the shortages.

However, a situation in which an employer is not willing to pay the going rate required to eliminate a shortage should not be regarded as representing a labour shortage.

Assume there is an increase in demand, from D_0 to D_1 in Figure 6.1. Even in a competitive market, the movement from one equilibrium, a, to another, b, will not be instantaneous, so that at the prevailing wage w_0 there will be shortage E_0E.

In the competitive case, Figure 6.1(a), the acid test is the relative wage. The shortage E_0E should lead to a wage adjustment w_0w_1, which will lead to more individuals offering themselves for work, while, at the same time, the higher costs will increase product price, so that the quantity demanded falls. In a monopsonistic market, as in Figure 6.1(b), a firm may believe that there is a shortage E_0E despite the fact that the market is in equilibrium. Here the problem is that labour supply is constrained.

In practice, there is evidence that wage changes are not the main method of adjustment in the case of labour shortages. For example, firms may invest more in the recruitment and training of new staff or improve conditions of work (see Thomas and Deaton, 1977).

The level of demand for labour itself may be conditioned by the nature of employment. Thus, in the public sector, in particular, formal "establishment" figures or norms may differ from working norms, which take into account financial

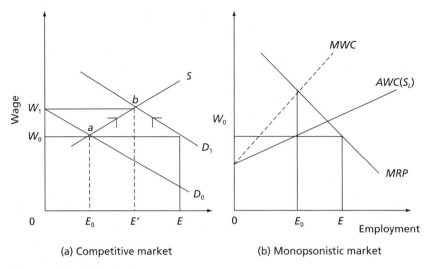

(a) Competitive market   (b) Monopsonistic market

Figure 6.1 Labour shortages.

or union constraints. Thus, in the teaching profession, the pupil–teacher ratio is in reality a political decision. It is necessary also to distinguish between stock and flow balances. A shortage could result from the desired stock being greater than the actual stock or from the desired flow being greater than the actual flow.

In Figure 6.2, taken from Thomas and Deaton, a distinction is made between actual and desired employment. In period t_0t_1, both stocks and flows are in balance, i.e. the actual level of employment E_i equals the desired level E_i^*. The stock balance is preserved because inflows and outflows of workers balance.

Now suppose at time period t_1 there is an increase in the desired stock of employees. A stock shortage as shown by the gap ab emerges, though there is a flow balance. At time period t_2, the firm raises pay in an attempt to reduce the outflow and increase the inflow of labour, so that, over the period t_2t_3, E_i is increasing and there is a net inflow. At time period t_3, stock and flow balance is again achieved, but in the interim an unintended failure to meet production targets results, which will require other forms of adjustment.

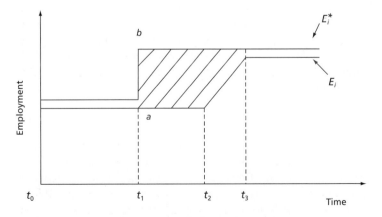

Figure 6.2 Actual and desired employment.

Lags in decision-making as in the case above were the focus of a classic paper by Arrow and Capron (1959). These lags result from the time taken to recognise there is a need to raise salaries, in obtaining approval for the increases and in putting the new policy into practice. Arrow and Capron call the rate at which price (the wage) rises relative to the excess of demand over supply the reaction speed. Then a given shortage will tend to disappear faster the greater the reaction speed and the greater the elasticity of demand.

$$\delta p / \delta t = k(D - S) \tag{6.1}$$

where k equals the reaction speed.

A dynamic shortage occurs when $\delta p / \delta t$ < market clearing $\delta p / \delta t$. The reaction speed will be influenced by institutional arrangements such as the presence of long-term contracts and partly by the rapidity with which information about salaries, vacancies and the availability of workers becomes generally available throughout the market. Arrow and Capron note certain features prevailing in the US engineering-scientist market at the time, which gave rise to dynamic shortages. There had been a rapid and steady increase in demand. The elasticity of supply was low because of the length of time required to produce and train graduates. The reaction speed was slow because of the prevalence of long-term contracts, the heterogeneity of the market, which slowed down the flow of information, and the dominance of a relatively small number of firms in research and development, which resulted in a lack of competition.

However, as stated above, there is a good deal of evidence that price adjustments are only part of the large range of possibilities and in certain cases **non-price adjustments** predominate. There appear to be four main methods for alleviating shortages:

Non-price adjustments

Shortages may be tackled by reducing output, introducing or extending overtime working, reducing the quit rate, lowering hiring standards or through adopting more vigorous hiring practices.

- a reduction in desired total man-hours (i.e. reduced output);
- an increase in average hours worked per employee (overtime);
- a reduced outflow of labour (e.g. through deferred rewards); and
- an increased inflow of labour (through more vigorous recruitment or reduced hiring standards).

The state of the product and labour markets will affect the relative costs of such alternatives and hence the choice of instruments. The higher the level of unemployment, the more elastic will be the labour supply function and the less costly the pay instrument. Thus, we expect the preference for non-wage adjustment to be greater when labour markets are tight. Stevens (2007) suggests that employment cycles will be asymmetric because of the effect of skill shortages on firms' hiring costs. Consider the following identity:

$$\Delta N \equiv E - S = E - (Q + L) \tag{6.2}$$

where ΔN = change in employment, E = engagements, S = separations, Q = quits and L = lay-offs. Quits may be costless to the firm, while lay-offs and hires incur costs. A positive quit rate means that firms have a costless mechanism for reducing employment in a downturn, whereas increasing employment in the upturn will incur extra costs. These costs are likely to be higher in a tight labour market. Stevens analyses an unbalanced firm data-set for the UK over the period 1982–94 and finds support for these propositions, though the effects are quantitatively small. However, this analysis ignores the births and deaths of firms which may add to the effect.

Another example of an empirical study of labour shortages in Britain is that of Haskel and Martin (1993). They relate skill shortages to **vacancy duration**. Thus, rather than regarding shortages as a binding labour supply constraint in a disequilibrium sense, they regard them as implying that firms must wait longer than normal or search more actively in order to hire workers. According to job-matching theory, vacancy duration will depend on three factors – the number of available job slots, the number of job seekers and the relative intensity of job search (see Chapter 4).

Assume we have a firm i operating in local labour market j, key internal factors determining vacancy duration will be relative wages, w_i/w_j, other job characteristics u_i and the determinants of the level of vacancies β_i. Key external factors will be the number of job seekers and search effectiveness. Define S' as the number of job seekers adjusted for search effectiveness and V' as the number of vacancies offered by other firms, again adjusted for search effectiveness. Then we have

$$\text{duration } i = f\left(\underset{-}{\frac{w_i}{w_j}}, \underset{-}{u_i}, \underset{+}{\beta_i}, \underset{-}{S'_j}, \underset{+}{V'_s}\right) \qquad (6.3)$$

where the signs represent the expected direction of the relationships.

Using such a model applied to the 1984 British Workplace Industrial Relations Survey (WIRS), Haskel and Martin (1993) find no evidence for firms setting higher wages to eliminate labour shortages, since w_i is insignificant. However, w_j is positively significant as higher wages attract more workers into the local labour market. As expected, increases in demand lead to increases in labour shortages, while shortages diminish when local unemployment is higher. Characteristics of the firm also matter, since establishments with unions and profit-related pay face fewer labour shortages. This is in line with Bosworth (1993), who finds that skill shortages are less apparent in establishments with a well-developed internal labour market.

6.2 Over- and under-education

It is now well established that many workers, including graduates, are employed in jobs for which their current qualifications are not a requirement, while others lack the qualifications that are required of current recruits in the jobs which they hold. This is, therefore, another form of mismatching, the implications of which are hotly debated. Further, the proportions over- or under-educated are sizeable. Thus, in the US, Duncan and Hoffman (1981), Sicherman (1991), Cohn and Kahn (1995) and Hersch (1991) report estimates of **over-education** among the whole workforce ranging up to 40 per cent. In Europe, Hartog and Oosterbeek (1988) report a figure of 16 per cent for the Netherlands, Alba-Ramirez (1993) 17 per cent for Spain, and Sloane et al. (1999) 31 per cent for six British local labour markets. These estimates are derived from data sets that contain an explicit question on the educational requirements of a job as well as the educational attainment of individuals. In other cases where data-sets lack an explicit question on over-education, researchers have constructed estimates on the basis of the distribution of qualifications across

Vacancy duration

The average length of time it takes to fill a vacancy.

Over-education

A situation in which the level of education of an individual is higher than the norm for the occupation in which he or she is currently employed.

Extensions of labour demand

individuals, with over-education defined as that level of education more than one standard deviation above the mean for a given occupation. Such estimates have been produced by Rumberger (1981), Verdugo and Verdugo (1989), Cohn and Kahn (1995) and Groot (1996). Since these are estimates of substantial over-education, they are invariably lower than estimates based on direct questions on over-education and should not be compared with them. Further, if the extent of over-education is much greater (or less) than **under-education**, estimates will be biased and it is more appropriate to base them on the mode rather than the mean in terms of the distribution of qualifications in particular occupations.

Apart from the above, another measurement issue relates to the use of **objective or subjective measures of over-education**. The former is based on finding the appropriate level of qualifications required to perform a particular job through the use of systematic job evaluation, but, although it is based on objective measurement, it may be subject to error if the nature of the job changes over time. An example of the latter is worker self-assessment based on questions on the level of education required to get, or to do, the job. If there is **credentialism**, firms may specify a higher level of education to obtain a job than is required to do it. Another form of mismatch may occur where an individual has the current level of education to perform a job, but one which is of the wrong kind (or what is referred to in the literature as **horizontal mismatch**).

The naïve Mincer human capital model implies that earnings are determined just by the personal characteristics of the individual, so that where an individual is employed is immaterial to the level of earnings. At the other extreme is the Thurow (1975) **job competition model**, which assumes that productivity resides in the job rather than the worker, with higher personal characteristics merely serving to push the individual towards the front of the job queue. Thus, in this case, all workers within a particular job should be paid the same regardless of their qualifications. In the Thurow model, it is the demand side which dominates so that

$$\log w_i = \alpha + \alpha_1 q^r + \varepsilon \tag{6.4}$$

where q^r equals the *minimum* qualifications required to get the job.

A more general model was put forward by Duncan and Hoffman (1981) who decompose educational qualifications into those required to do the job (q^r), those surplus to requirements (q^s) and those which are lower than currently required (q^u). Hence, in this case

$$\log w_i = \beta_0 + \beta_1 q^r + \beta_2 q^s + \beta_3 q^u + \varepsilon' \tag{6.5}$$

with q^r set as the default, so that the expected sign on q^s is positive and that on q^u negative. According to the naïve human capital model, $\beta_1 = \beta_2 = \beta_3$ and returns are not influenced by the circumstances of employment. In the case of the job competition model, in contrast, $\beta_2 = \beta_3 = 0$, as only required education determines pay in this case.

Between these two extreme cases sits the Sattinger (1993) **job assignment model**, which is based on the proposition that there is a possible allocation problem in assigning heterogeneous workers to jobs of varying complexities. Suppose S_i represents the extent to which a skill i is required by a particular employer and t_i the extent to which this is possessed by potential employees. Then, on the demand side of the labour market, employers will specify a frequency distribution $M(s_1, s_2, \ldots s_m)$ of the number of employees they require at various skill levels. Similarly, on the supply side of the labour market, potential employees will appear with a frequency distribution of skills $N(t_1, t_2, \ldots t_n)$. If

$$M(s_1, s_2, \ldots, s_m) \neq N(t_1, t_2, \ldots, t_n) \tag{6.6}$$

Over- or under-education will result and might well be a persistent problem if both distributions are subject to continuous change.

There are a number of possible explanations for the persistence of over- and under-education. First, over(under)-education may be a substitute for training and experience. Thus, Sloane *et al.* (1996), using 1986 Social and Economic Life Initiative (SCELI) data from six British local labour markets, examine whether those who possess more formal education than required in a particular job are simply compensating for a lack of other forms of human capital. They find that the over-educated have less experience and tenure than matched workers and that the over-educated tend to be in jobs in which it takes longer to become fully proficient in the job, while the reverse applies to under-educated workers. This is consistent with a situation in which employers hire individuals with more education than is strictly needed to do the job because such individuals learn faster and/or are more productive than workers matched in terms of their educational level. Thus, over-education may not necessarily be wasteful, though whether it is a least cost option remains to be determined.

A second question is: why do some individuals end up over-educated and not others? One UK study by Battu *et al.* (1999) uses a survey of a panel of graduates from a range of higher-education institutions who were interviewed one year, six years and, in the case of one cohort, eleven years after graduation. They find that both the quality and type of degree are significant in determining the subsequent probability of a satisfactory match between graduates and work. Students with lower degree classifications and who follow degree programmes not leading directly to professional jobs are significantly more likely to be in jobs for which degrees are not required. A further study by Chevalier and Lindley (2006) on a more recent cohort of UK graduates attempts to distinguish whether the over-education is genuine or not by examining the respondents' expressed level of satisfaction with the job match. They find that 65 per cent of graduates are well matched, 15 per cent genuinely over-educated and 20 per cent only apparently so. The genuinely over-educated are much less likely to utilise the skills they had acquired at university and are much more likely to experience periods of unemployment than the two other groups. This suggests, therefore, that at least some of the over-educated are of inferior quality to those with the same qualifications, but who are properly matched.

A third question is whether over-education results in an earnings penalty. An early US study by Sicherman (1991) suggests that there are two stylised facts relating to over- and under-educated workers. First, over-educated workers receive less than those with the same level of education but who are properly matched, but more than co-workers who have a lower, but appropriate, level of education. Second, under-educated workers receive higher earnings than those with the same level of education, but who are in an inferior job, but less than their work colleagues who have a higher, but appropriate, level of education. These stylised facts have been confirmed by a number of studies in various countries, though it is unclear how

Job competition model

This demand-side model, associated with Lester Thurow, assumes that productivity resides with the job rather than the worker and, therefore, education simply serves to move a job applicant closer to the front of a job queue.

Job assignment model

This model, associated with Michael Sattinger, is based on the proposition that there is an allocation problem in assigning heterogeneous workers to heterogeneous jobs, so that, unlike the job competition model, both supply and demand are important.

and/or why employers differentiate in terms of pay on these bases. Ability differences may be part of the explanation. Thus, Battu *et al.* (1999) find that over-education, degree quality, type of university and type of degree all significantly impact on earnings of graduates six years after graduation, while Chevalier and Lindley (2006) find that those who are genuinely over-educated earn 23 per cent less than matched graduates compared to only 7 per cent for the apparently over-educated. Including various measures of skill reduces but does not eliminate the penalty for over-education.

A fourth question is whether or not over-education is a temporary phenomenon. Sloane *et al.* (1999) find that the over-educated often move from one state of over-education to another or fail to hold on to jobs with higher educational requirements to which they have moved, while Battu *et al.* (1999) find that 30 per cent of graduates interviewed 11 years after graduation have never been in a job requiring graduate qualifications. The fact that some graduates move from matched to unmatched work suggests perhaps that the importance of qualifications diminishes with time spent in the labour market. Most of these studies do not examine, however, the degree of mismatch. The plight of a graduate in a job requiring just A levels should not be compared with that of a graduate in a job requiring no qualifications at all. Thus, a study by Felstead *et al.* (2002) finds that three-quarters of graduates feel their qualifications are either essential or fairly necessary to do the job, while only between 5 and 8 per cent think their qualifications are totally unnecessary to do the job.

What then have we learned from the over-education literature? First, in relation to the human capital model, it seems that where a worker is employed does matter and, in this respect, assignment-type models seem to outperform either the naïve human capital model with its stress on personal circumstances and the job competition model with its stress on demand-side features of the labour market. Second, education is just one form of human capital with many possibilities of substitution in one form or another. Third, interpreting labour market outcomes requires detailed knowledge of the abilities and skills of individual workers. Recent work by Mavromaras *et al.* (2010) using Australian panel data shows that it is a combination of educational and skill mismatch which is particularly damaging to workers in terms of job satisfaction. It appears that a substantial part of what is referred to in the literature as over-education simply reflects unobserved heterogeneity of abilities and skills within education levels and in no way represents a form of market failure.

6.3 Labour market discrimination[1]

Taste for discrimination

This model, associated with Gary Becker, assumes that certain groups have an aversion towards other groups and are prepared to pay a price to avoid contact with them.

A key issue is whether one can apply a common framework to analyse unequal treatment against members of minority groups based on race, gender, religion, age, disability or against immigrants. In the first serious work to examine the subject, Gary Becker, in the *Economics of Discriminations* (1957), argues that certain groups have a **taste for discrimination** based on an aversion to other groups, for which they are prepared to pay a price, as in the case of any other commodity. He introduces a gains from trade model, which suggests that the discriminator, as well as society as a whole, pays a price for discrimination in the form of reduced output, though in the context of racial discrimination white labour and black capitalists might gain. But the application of such a model to gender discrimination does not seem straightforward, since men and women frequently marry. Marriage causes intermittent labour force participation for most women and this may influence job choice. For other groups, such as older workers, the disabled and immigrants, there may be questions relating to productivity which drive employer decisions rather than any taste for discrimination per se.

Before a group can be subjected to discrimination, it must be clearly identifiable. Gender, colour, age and language clearly fall into that category as do certain forms of disability. Marital status or religion are less obvious characteristics to identify, though such information could be acquired by inserting appropriate questions in an application form. Immigrants, particularly those from ethnic minorities or lacking in indigenous language skills, are not only clearly identifiable, but they may also lack knowledge of the local labour market and its institutional or cultural norms. Thus, in this case also, it may be difficult to establish whether the inferior position of an immigrant is a consequence of discriminatory treatment or of inferior attributes related to productivity. Two contrasting features dominate the literature on the economies of immigration concerning mobility of immigrants, namely the **assimilation and enclave hypotheses**. The assimilation hypothesis implies that over time the earnings of immigrants, which start at a relatively low level, will tend to converge with those of comparably qualified indigenous workers, as they accumulate skills more appropriate to the host country. In addition, as they become more efficient at information gathering, they will tend to move into those jobs where they have a productivity advantage. The assimilation effect should also include improvements in host-country language proficiency. Language ability may also influence occupational choice, given that jobs are heterogeneous in their language requirements. For all these reasons, we should expect that first- and second-generation offspring of immigrants will be better assimilated than their parents (see, for instance, Borjas 1993, for the US; Sloane and Gazioglu 1996, for the UK; Rooth and Ekberg 2003, for Sweden' and Maani 1994, for Australia). The enclave hypothesis, in contrast, is based on the observation that immigrants tend to locate in areas where immigrants of their own country of origin have settled and this concentration may extend into the workplace. Thus, for example, De Freitas (1991) finds that over half of the Mexican immigrants into the United States work principally with members of their own ethnic group, often in relatively small establishments. One possibility is employment catering for customers who are predominantly from one's own ethnic group and who are likely to demand products of which the immigrant has particular knowledge, as in grocery stores or restaurants. For immigrants lacking fluency in the host-country language, such employment minimises language disadvantages. This also provides an explanation for Kossoudji's (1988) puzzling finding for the US that lack of English-language ability does not appear to lead to a loss of productivity. Together, the assimilation and enclave hypotheses may result in multiple equilibria with those immigrants possessing skills complementary to those of indigenous workers gaining greater benefits from assimilation and those lacking such skills obtaining most benefit from employment in enclaves where they have a greater comparative advantage.

For these and other reasons, it is not always appropriate to treat members of different ethnic minorities as a homogeneous group. Thus, in the US, Gwartney and Long (1978) examine the relative earnings of eight such groups and find wide differences in outcomes, with the Japanese and Chinese faring much better in the labour market and Mexicans worse than members of other ethnic minority groups.

Assimilation hypothesis

Over time, migrants will acquire labour market and social skills that help them to integrate into the indigenous population.

Enclave hypothesis

Immigrants tend to migrate to areas where their own country nationals are concentrated and host-country language and other skills are less important.

Likewise, in the UK, Leslie *et al.* (1998) find that the Chinese do relatively well, whereas Pakistanis and Bangladeshis do much worse in terms of both employment and earnings. They note that certain groups such as black Caribbeans have been in the UK over a long period, whereas others, notably Bangladeshis, are of relatively recent arrival. Thus, where data permit, it is better to analyse different ethnic groups separately in order to gauge accurately the extent of racial disadvantage.

Most analyses focus on employer discrimination, though it is far from certain that this dominates the other possible sources – employers or trade unions and customers. The Becker taste-based model assumes that employers are prepared to forfeit profits in order to hire members of minority groups even under competitive conditions or where the marginal value product of such workers exceeds the marginal costs of hiring them. The extent to which this happens is referred to as the **market discrimination coefficient** (*d*), which is measured by

Market discrimination coefficient

This measures the extent to which the majority wage rate exceeds that of the minority or the wage rate of the indigenous population exceeds that of immigrants.

$$d = \frac{w_{MAJ} - w_{MIN}}{w_{MIN}} \tag{6.7}$$

where w_{MAJ} is the equilibrium wage rate for members of the majority group and w_{MIN} the equilibrium wage for the minority group. Now assume

1 all firms have identical utility and production functions;
2 members of majority and minority groups are perfect substitutes for each other in terms of production;
3 labour supply is perfectly inelastic for each group;
4 capital is fixed, so that output is simply a function of employment, i.e. *f*(*MAJ* + *MIN*) where *f* is strictly concave and increasing;
5 employers maximise a utility function *U*(Π, *MAJ*, *MIN*) where *UMAJ* > 0 and *UMIN* < 0. In other words, employers derive positive utility from the employment of workers of the majority group and negative utility from the employment of members of the minority group.

Then (see Arrow 1972, 1973) profits for the firm are given by

$$f(MAJ + MIN) - W_{MAJ} MAJ - W_{MIN} MIN \tag{6.8}$$

Substitution into the utility function yields

$$U = U\left\{\left(f\left(MAJ + MIN\right) - W_{MAJ} MAJ - W_{MIN} MIN\right), MAJ, MIN\right\} \tag{6.9}$$

Maximisation with respect to *MAJ* and *MIN* respectively gives

$$U_\Pi(F' - W_{MAJ}) + U_{MAJ} = 0 \tag{6.10}$$

and

$$U_\Pi(F' - W_{MIN}) + U_{MIN} = 0$$

Hence,

$$U_\Pi(F' - W_{MAJ}) + U_{MAJ} = U_\Pi(F' - W_{MIN}) + U_{MIN} \tag{6.11}$$

and

$$F' = W_{MAJ} - \frac{U_{MAJ}}{U_\Pi} = W_{MIN} - \frac{U_{MIN}}{U_\Pi} \qquad (6.12)$$

Letting

$$-\frac{U_{MAJ}}{U_\Pi} = d_{MAJ} \text{ and } -\frac{U_{MIN}}{U_\Pi} = d_{MIN}, \quad F' = W_{MAJ} + d_{MAJ} = W_{MIN} + d_{MIN} \quad (6.13)$$

Under the assumption of discrimination against the minority group

$$d_{MIN} > 0, \; d_{MAJ} < 0$$

Hence,

$$W_{MAJ} > F' > W_{MIN} \qquad (6.14)$$

Though in this model wage rates are given from the firm's perspective, it treats the price of minority labour as the minority wage rate plus the discrimination coefficient (d). That is, the demand curve for minority labour must lie to the left of that for majority labour, the extent being determined by the discriminations coefficient (d) and with inelastic supply curves wage differences must result. If $W_{MAJ} = W_{MIN}$, by arbitrary assumption then, the forces which yield (6.14) will be reflected in hiring decisions with few, if any, members of the minority group being employed. In general, however, with **employer discrimination**, we expected to observe majority workers being paid more than minority workers. This is illustrated in Figure 6.3.

The indifference map (I_0, I_1, I_2) shows the employer's tastes for combinations of profits and majority group employment. Assume first that majority and minority employees are perfect substitutes and are paid equally. In this case, profits are given

Employer discrimination

Discriminatory employers will only employ minority workers if the latter are prepared to accept a lower wage than majority workers are paid, even though this reduces employer profits.

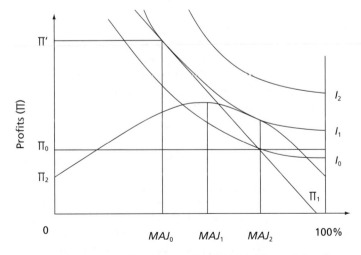

Figure 6.3 Employer discrimination.

by Π_0 and are horizontal as they are independent of the *MAX/MIN* ratio and a rational employer would only hire majority employees in order to attain the highest possible indifference curve. Now, if we allow $W_{MAJ} > W_{MIN}$, profits will be downward sloping as given, say, by Π_1 as %*MAJ* increases. Under this situation, $0MAJ$ majority workers would be employed, but $\Pi_0\Pi'$ profits would have been foregone, as it is cheaper to employ all *MIN* workers. A third possibility is that *MAJ* and *MIN* workers are imperfect substitutes (e.g. men have a comparative advantage in physically demanding jobs and women in jobs requiring manual dexterity). Then profits will be given by a function such as Π_2 with an optimal distribution of employees given by $0MAJ_1$. Here the employer will employ a greater proportion of *MAJ* workers $0MAJ_2$ than would maximise profits in order to reach the highest possible indifference curve I_1. The important point is that lower wages for the minority group is a mechanism for overcoming the employer's aversion to hiring minority workers. Therefore, wage discrimination is evidence of employer discrimination. Another implication is that there will be a relationship between employer discrimination and product market monopoly, since, in a competitive market, a failure to hire cheaper minority workers should drive the discriminatory employer out of business. However, attempts to test for this have proved somewhat inconclusive, which might suggest that other sources of discrimination are more important or that competitive forces are not powerful enough.

Employee discrimination

Majority employees demand a higher wage if they have to work with minority workers, which leads to segregation by occupation or firm.

A number of economists have argued that **employee discrimination** is more plausible than employer discrimination. Indeed, Becker himself came precisely to this conclusion in his Nobel lecture. It is employees who have direct contact with members of minority groups and who may attempt to deny access to jobs altogether or oppose being subject to orders from members of minority groups in managerial or supervisory positions. Alternatively, members of minority groups or immigrants, particularly where they are present in substantial numbers, may be seen as a threat to both job and income security. Hence, majority workers may be prepared to trade off short-run wage gains in order to exclude minority group members from employment in the belief that this will maximise wages in the long run. If we assume members of the two groups are perfect substitutes and wage rates are (initially) identical, employers will face increased wage bills if they attempt to integrate their workforce. Competitive forces should ensure that any such wage differences are removed as non-discriminatory employers will hire minority workers so long as they are cheaper to employ. Long-run equilibrium implies the presence of completely segregated firms or perhaps completed segregated occupations where the two groups are complements rather than substitutes in production.

This is illustrated in Figure 6.4 with the indifference map in this case representing the majority employee utility function with a trade-off between wages and the percentage of the workforce which is in the majority group.

If majority and minority employees are perfect substitutes with identical wage rates, employment of integrated workforces will raise the employer's costs, as with W_{MIN} employees would maximise utility with $MAJ = 100$ and integration to, say, $0MAJ_1$ would raise wages to $0W_1$. Thus, the prediction is that employee discrimination is consistent with group segregation at the firm level, though, as Arrow (1972) notes, costs of adjustment (e.g. hiring and firing costs) may inhibit firms from replacing black (female) employees by white (male) employees. A simple test of the model is that the more integrated the workforce in an industry or region, the greater the dispersion of majority incomes, and Chiswick (1973) finds some evidence of this.

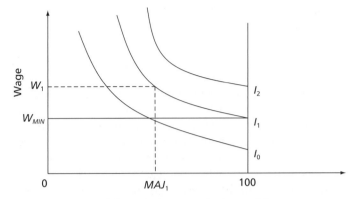

Percentage of the majority group in the workforce

Figure 6.4 Employee discrimination.

A third possible source of discrimination is **customer** or **consumer discrimination**, a situation in which prejudiced consumers refuse to purchase goods from members of minority groups unless such goods are sufficiently cheaper than those sold by members of the majority group to offset their taste for discrimination.

Cain (1988) argues that consumer discrimination is unlikely to play a major role because most goods are not produced with customer contact, but, as the majority of workers are now employed in services, this argument seems less than convincing. Further, customer discrimination actually lowers the productivity of those discriminated against and so is unlikely to be removed through competitive forces (see Nardinelli and Simon 1990). In such circumstances, we would expect that racial minority workers would specialise in the sale of goods where customer contact is minimised and thus avoid being paid a wage that is lower than that received by majority workers. Segregation by race or gender is the predicted outcome as in the case of employee discrimination. However, Kahn (1991) notes that the impact of anti-discrimination legislation is likely to be different under consumer discrimination than under the other two main sources of it. If a government imposes both equal pay and equal employment opportunities for minorities, the resulting allocation of resources would, given certain assumptions, be identical to the non-consumer discrimination case, thus eliminating this form of discrimination. Becker (1957) himself notes that, in a political democracy, we would expect the government to act on the basis of the median taste for discrimination among the electorate. As the ratio of the minority to total population rises, one might expect discrimination to diminish as there are more minority votes at stake. Yet, under such circumstances, the minority becomes more of a perceived threat to the majority in terms of competition for jobs. If, however, the issue of minority rights is critical to minority voters but marginal for majority voters, more votes are to be gained from implementing equal rights than are to be lost from frustrating them.

There is now a huge literature that has attempted to estimate the degree of discrimination against various minority groups, yet such estimates are far from straightforward. The standard approach is to estimate separate Mincer human capital models for each group, which allows membership of each group to influence the coefficients on personal characteristics. Earnings are decomposed into differences resulting from varying endowments and coefficients and the unexplained

Customer discrimination

Customers expect to pay a lower price for goods if they are to be served by members of the minority population.

differential is the constant term. Thus, taking as an example, men (M) and women (W), the crude mean wage differential can be decomposed as

$$\bar{W}_M - \bar{W}_F = (\alpha_M - \alpha_F) + (\bar{X}_M - \bar{X}_F)b_M + X_F(b_M - b_F) \tag{6.15}$$

Discrimination is then taken to be equal to the first and third terms on the RHS of the equation. Yet, the constant term might be considered to be a measure of our ignorance and, in some cases, differences in the constant term outweigh differences in the explanatory variables. It could reflect differences in tastes for particular kinds of work among majority and minority members (e.g. between men and women). The residual approach is, therefore, susceptible to omitted variable bias.

There is also an **index number problem**, which is illustrated in Figure 6.5. Assume we are examining gender discrimination. There are two choices. One could assume that men and women would be paid according to the male earnings function in the absence of discrimination or that they are both paid according to female function (see Oaxaca 1973). In the former case, estimated average female earnings ($\bar{F}_e$) are given by $\bar{F}_e = W_M(\bar{X}_F)$, where X_M represents the male earnings function and $\bar{X}_F$ is a vector of the mean personal characteristics of women. In this case, the difference in average male earnings ($\bar{M}$) and actual female earnings ($\bar{F}$) can be decomposed into $\bar{M} - \bar{F}_e$ or the difference in average earnings attributable to differences in average characteristics (E_1) and $\bar{F}_e - \bar{F}$ or the residual difference unaccounted for by characteristics. This represents a measure of discrimination consisting of differences in the intercept terms and differences in the slopes of the earnings functions. An alternative is to estimate average male earnings ($\bar{M}_e$) by $\bar{M}_e = W_F(\bar{X}_M)$. In this case, the difference between $\bar{M}$ and $\bar{F}$ is decomposed as $\bar{M}_e - \bar{F}$ or the difference in average earnings attributable to differences in average characteristics (E_2); and $\bar{M} - \bar{M}_e$ or the residual difference not accounted for by characteristics. Provided that the male earnings function lies above the female earnings function and has a steeper slope, the first approach will always give a smaller estimate of discrimination than the second approach (i.e. $cd > ab$).

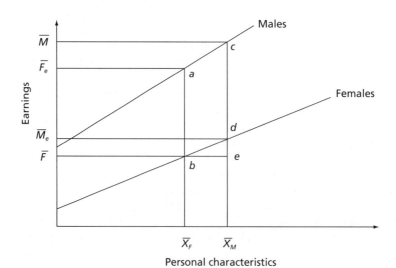

Figure 6.5 The index number problem in estimating discrimination.

where

$\bar{X}_F$ = average female characteristics
$\bar{X}_M$ = average male characteristics
$\bar{M}$ = average male earnings
$\bar{F}$ = average female earnings
$\bar{F}_e$ = average female earnings if paid according to the male earnings function
$\bar{M}_e$ = average male earnings if paid according to the female earnings function.

There are a number of possible solutions to the index number problem, but none of them is wholly satisfactory. Thus, some take the mean of the two results above (e.g. Reimers 1983), others use the shares of the two groups in the total population (e.g. Cotton 1988) and yet others a figure obtained from a pooled regression (e.g. Neumark 1988). However, assuming any discrimination can be removed, we do not know precisely how the labour market would adjust towards a new equilibrium.

One very extensive meta-analysis of gender wage differentials was carried out by Weichselbaumer and Winter-Ebmer (2007) covering 62 countries over 35 years ending in 1997. They suggest that the gender wage differential has dropped from about 65 per cent in the 1960s to 30 per cent in the 1990s and the decline mostly reflects more advantageous productivity characteristics of women including education and experience. For the United States, Blau and Kahn (1997) find a substantial decline in the unexplained part of the gender wage gap during the 1980s, though in the 1990s this improvement slowed down. However, whether remaining differences reflect discrimination remains contentious. Thus, Chevalier (2007) suggests that much of the unexplained residual is simply the result of **mis-specification**. Using a sample of recent UK graduates three years after graduation, he examines the use of choice variables such as subject of study, occupation, career expectations and aspirations. The evidence suggests that women are more altruistic and less career-orientated than men. On their own, career-break expectations can explain 10 per cent of the gender wage gap, which would remain unexplained without the inclusion of this variable.

Productivity considerations are particularly important in those studies that attempt to measure discrimination against older workers or the disabled. In the former case, older workers display a range of adverse labour market characteristics compared to younger workers including a higher propensity to long-term sickness, disability, low levels of educational attainment and possible skills obsolescence. To some extent, these may be compensated for by experience. In a life-cycle context, Lazear (1979) notes, as we have already seen in Chapter 1, that employers may attempt to adjust the age–earnings profile in order to increase effort by paying younger workers less than they are worth and older workers more than they are worth to increase worker attachment. Hutchens (1986) uses the presence of such back-loaded compensation together with the critical role of on-the-job training to explain why some firms employ older workers but do not hire them. In a 1988 paper, he finds that an index of hiring opportunity (namely the ratio of all hires aged over 55 to the fraction of employees aged over 55) is negatively related to tenure, pension provision and the presence of mandatory retirement. Daniel and Heywood (2007) and Adams and Heywood (2007) obtain similar results for Britain and Australia respectively.

Mis-specification

A situation in which an economic theory on which a model is based is incomplete, resulting in the estimated parameters being biased.

In the case of the disabled, not only is it difficult to determine relative productivities, but reporting of disabilities may itself be influenced by the presence of legislation if removal of the stigma encourages more to report its presence. Further, some who report a disability prior to the introduction of the legislation may not do so subsequently if improvements in the workplace mean that they are no longer limited in their work. Those who are out of employment may exaggerate the impact of disability to justify their employment status (justification bias). All these factors make it difficult to judge the impact of legislation such as the Americans with Disabilities Act, and more so since the impact is ambiguous depending on whether or not the legislation reduces the demand for disabled workers by raising the cost of employing them more than the increase in demand brought about by any reduction in discrimination. DeLeire (2001) attempts to estimate discrimination by distinguishing between the **work-limited and non-work-limited disabled**. Assuming that those who report no work limitations do not have lower productivity as a result of their disability relative to the non-disabled, one can interpret the unexplained residual in an Oaxaca-type decomposition as an estimate of discrimination in their case. Further, if the degree of discrimination is assumed to be the same for both groups of the disabled, the unexplained residual of the work-limited group of disabled may be considered an estimate of the lower productivity of this group. Using this procedure, DeLeire estimates that only 3.7 percentage points of the earnings gap in the US in 1984 is the result of discrimination and the amount of discrimination does not change significantly in the subsequent decade. Similar results are found using the same procedure for Britain by Jones *et al.* (2006).

Implicit in the above studies is the belief that employer discrimination is the driving force. Only one study has considered all three main types of discrimination – employer, employee and customer in a single wage model. Bodvarsson and Partridge (2001) consider the case of professional basketball in the US as it is relatively straightforward to measure productivity in this sport. They use a quadratic production function with diminishing returns to both white and non-white players. They assume that white fans are prejudiced against non-white players and non-white fans are prejudiced against white players (both cases of consumer discrimination). Employer discrimination is allowed for by assuming non-white players impose a cost on the owners, all of whom were white at the time. Finally, employee discrimination is captured by the premium in pay that a player requires for working with players of the opposite skin colour, this being a function of the team's racial mix. Their results suggest that equally productive black players earn between 9 and 19 per cent less than corresponding white players do. The team racial composition coefficient is positively and statistically significant in the case of whites, but not for non-whites, suggesting co-worker discrimination is present among white players. The manager–owner race coefficient is insignificant, suggesting an absence of employer discrimination.

Despite these caveats, we should not assume that labour market discrimination is unimportant. For example, in the case of racial pay differences, taste and productivity explanations may be less relevant. One possibility is **statistical discrimination**. As Phelps (1972) notes, an employer attempting to maximise profits will discriminate against non-whites or women if he or she believes them to be less qualified, reliable or productive than white males and if the cost of gaining information about the individual applicant is excessive. Suppose hiring decisions are based on some performance test, y, which measures imperfectly the true performance level, q, then

$$y = q + u \tag{6.16}$$

Work-limited disabled

Those disabled workers whose disability affects the kind and/or amount of work that they can do.

Non-work-limited disabled

Those disabled workers whose disability does not affect the kind or amount of work that they can do.

Statistical discrimination

Hiring decisions are based on the mean characteristics of a group to which an individual belongs, regardless of the fact that a particular applicant may not fit the stereotype.

> ## Case Study 6.1
>
> There is a widespread market for cards of sportsmen, just as there is for postage stamps or coins. Determinants of a card's price include the star quality of the player and the presence of racial discrimination. There is a national market in the US for such cards, which are collected by all age-groups and socio-demographic characteristics. In their study of the baseball-player-card market, Nardinelli and Simon (1990) find that prices range up to $6,000 for older cards with high scarcity value and that value is, indeed, determined by the quality of the career performance of the player, the age of the card and the number printed. The market for the cards of the average player set the minimum price for cards and on to this is added various performance characteristics. Different considerations apply to hitters and pitchers and race variables are added to each of their equations. Their results confirm the presence of customer discrimination. Among hitters, cards of non-whites sell for about 10 per cent less than those of whites of comparable ability, with the corresponding difference for pitchers being 13 per cent.
>
> C. Nardinelli and C. Simon, "Customer Racial Discrimination in the Market for Memorabilia: The Case of Baseball", *Quarterly Journal of Economics*, 105, 1990, pp. 575–96.

where u is a normally distributed error term and q is also assumed to be normally distributed and to have a constant variance. Statistical discrimination could then arise because of differences in the means of abilities across groups, differences in variance of abilities across groups or differences in the ability to predict accurately the true performance of groups from test scores. Assume white men have higher ability than the minority group. Then an employer is likely to hire a majority worker rather than a minority worker even though they have the same test scores as shown below

$$\hat{q} = (1 - \beta)\alpha + \beta y + u' \quad \text{where } 0 < \beta < 1 \tag{6.17}$$

and where
$\bar{q}$ = predicted value of q
α = mean performance level
β = regression coefficient measuring the reliability of the test.

Recognising that the residual approach has drawbacks, an alternative approach has been put forward as a means of capturing discrimination, namely **correspondence testing**. Riach and Rich (2002) note that carefully controlled field experiments to measure discrimination have been used over a period of forty years or so, in which matched pairs of bogus transactions are used to uncover racial, gender, disability and age discrimination in a number of countries. Rates of employment discrimination in excess of 25 per cent have been detected.[2] One method is to respond to job vacancies with written applications from presumed applicants who are well matched apart from, say, colour or gender and then observe the probability of being called for interview. If there are systematic differences in the probabilities, this is taken as evidence of discrimination, though, strictly speaking, it is more symptomatic of statistical discrimination than pure discrimination.

Correspondence testing

Matched pairs of fictitious job applicants, which differ only with respect to race or gender, are sent to employers and on the basis of the probability of being invited for interview discrimination is inferred.

Many countries have applied equal pay and equal opportunity legislation covering most forms of discrimination, but with varying degrees of effectiveness. This may include both financial penalties and affirmative action. We consider these further in Chapter 11.

Case Study 6.2

Occupational choice and male–female differences

In 2005, the President of Harvard University, Lawrence Summers, himself a distinguished economist and former US Treasury Secretary, gave a lecture in which he suggested that men were more naturally able than women at science and this explained why there were so few women scientists. This caused outrage and one female academic, who with others had walked out, said that had she not done so she would have fainted or thrown up.

Is there any evidence to support Summers' case? In 1990, Paglin and Rufolo noted that there was a long literature suggesting that occupational choice would be determined at least in part by comparative advantage. Their own results show that comparative advantage influences the choice of college major and that quantitative ability is one of the most important factors in this choice. They make use of two large-scale aptitude tests and classify undergraduate majors according to their quantitative and verbal scores based on these tests. Students self-select into those majors on the basis of their relative abilities. In the labour market, salaries are highly correlated with quantitative abilities, while there is no significant correlation with verbal abilities. They hypothesise that, if women differ from men in the kinds of educational capital they produce, this could account for part of the observed gender difference in earnings. In the aptitude tests, men have much higher relative frequencies than women in the top intervals for quantitative skills, though mean scores are close. However, the return for quantitative skills is slightly higher for women than for men. Thus, male–female earnings differences are due to differences in attribute levels rather than differences in rates of return. Females are predicted, in fact, to earn about 80 per cent of the male average salary, which closely matches the actual earnings ratio.

M. Paglin and A.M. Rufolo, "Heterogeneous Human Capital, Occupational Choice and Male–Female Earnings Differences", *Journal of Labor Economics*, vol. 8(1), part 1, January, 1990, pp. 123–44.

Summary

- A labour shortage indicates a disequilibrium state in which the demand for labour exceeds the supply at the ruling market wage. Actual employment will be below required employment. The Arrow–Capron model of a dynamic shortage results from lags in decision-making.

- Non-price adjustments are the most commonly used means of dealing with a labour shortage. Thus, firms may increase the use of overtime working or allow the duration of vacancies to rise.

- The matching of workers and jobs may be imperfect with some workers over-educated and others under-educated. There are a number of models that attempt to explain these forms of mismatch including the Duncan and Hoffman model, Thurow's job competition model and Sattinger's job assignment model. However, allowance should be made for the fact that education is only one form of human capital and other forms such as experience may be substitutable for it. Workers also differ in terms of ability.

- Over-education normally results in a pay penalty, but under-educated workers earn more than if they are properly matched. For some, but by no means all, workers, over-education may be a temporary phenomenon.

- A key consideration is whether one can apply a common framework to analyse discrimination against various gender, racial, age, disabled, religious or immigrant groups, but in some of these cases differential treatment may result from productivity differences or, in the case of immigrants, from a failure to assimilate fully with the indigenous population.

- Discrimination may originate from employers, employees or their representatives and from consumers, and outcomes may vary according to the originator. Thus, under certain assumptions, employer discrimination, unless prevented by legislation, may give rise to wage differences. Employee discrimination may result in segregation on the basis of firms or occupations. Consumer discrimination may lead to price differences, but, unlike in the case of employer discrimination, may not be weakened by product market competition.

- Many studies have attempted to estimate the level of discrimination using a residual approach in which earnings are decomposed into differences arising from varying endowments of human capital and in coefficients, or prices paid for a given endowment of human capital. This gives rise to an index number problem, depending on which group is used as the basis of comparison. The residual may be influenced by specification error, if, for instance, there are between-group taste differences.

Questions

1 Explain what is meant by a dynamic shortage of labour. Why is this likely to be common?

2 Why might the preferred response of an employer faced with a shortage of labour not be to increase wages, but instead to use non-price adjustments?

3 Explain the differences between the Duncan and Hoffman, Thurow and Sattinger models of labour market mismatch and assess the empirical evidence in favour of each.

4 Why might some workers be more prone to labour market mismatch than others? Does such mismatch necessarily indicate market failure?

5 Distinguish between employer, employee and customer discrimination and compare likely equilibrium outcomes under each case.

6 Explain what is meant by the residual approach to the measurement of discrimination and discuss the types of problem likely to be encountered in using it.

Notes

1 This section relies partly on Sloane (1985) and Sloane (2003).

2 Riach and Rich have also conducted field experiments in England, France and Spain in which pairs of (fictitious) men aged either 27 or 47 made unsolicited enquiries by e-mail about potential employment as waiters in a large number of hotels and restaurants. The attractiveness of the older applicants was enhanced by reference to their engagement in strenuous physical activities and their up-to-date knowledge of ICT. The detected level of net discrimination against older applicants (measured as the difference in favourable minus unfavourable responses) was extremely high.

References

Adams S.J. and Heywood J.S., "The Age of Hiring and Deferred Compensation: Evidence from Australia", *The Economic Record*, 83(261), 2007, pp. 174–90.

Alba-Ramirez A., "Mismatch in the Spanish Labour Market: Over-education?", *Journal of Human Resources*, 27(2), 1993, pp. 259–78.

Arrow K.J., "Some Mathematical Models of Race in the Labour Market", in Pascal AH, editor, *Racial Discrimination in Economic Life*, Lexington Books, D.C. Heath & Co., Lexington, Mass., 1972.

Arrow K.J., "The Theory of Discrimination", in Ashenfelter O. and Rees A., editors, *Discrimination in Labor Markets*, Princeton University Press, Princeton, New Jersey, 1973.

Arrow K.J. and Capron W.M., "Dynamic Shortages and Price Rises: The Engineer–Scientist Case", *Quarterly Journal of Economics*, 73, 1959, pp. 292–308.

Battu H., Belfield C.R. and Sloane P.J., "Over-education Among Graduates: A Cohort View", *Education Economics*, 7(1), 1999, pp. 21–38.

Becker G., *The Economics of Discrimination*, University of Chicago Press, Chicago, 1957.

Blau F.D. and Kahn L.M., "Swimming Upstream: Trends in Gender Wage Differentials in the 1980s", *Journal of Labor Economics*, 15(1), 1997, pp. 1–42.

Bodvarsson O.B. and Partridge M.D., "A Supply and Demand Model of Co-worker, Employer and Customer Discrimination", *Labour Economics*, 8(3), June 2001, pp. 389–416.

Borjas G.J., "The Inter-Generational Mobility of Immigrants", *Journal of Labor Economics*, 11, 1993, pp. 113–34.

Bosworth D., "Skill Shortages in Britain", *Scottish Journal of Political Economy*, 40(3), 1993, pp. 241–71.

Cain G.G. "The Economic Analysis of Labor Market Discrimination: A Survey", in Ashenfelter O and Layard PRG, editors, *Handbook of Labor Economics*, Elsevier, Amsterdam, 1988.

Chevalier A., "Education, Occupation and Career Expectations: Determinants of the Gender Pay Gap for UK Graduates", *Oxford Bulletin of Economics and Statistics*, 69(6), 2007, pp. 819–42.

Chevalier A. and Lindley J., "Over-education and the Skills of UK Graduates", *IZA Discussion Paper* no. 2442, Institute for the Study of Labor, Bonn, 2006.

Chiswick B.R., "Racial Discrimination and the Labor Market: A Test of Alternative Hypotheses", *Journal of Political Economy*, 61, 1973, pp. 1330–52.

Cohn E. and Kahn S., "The Wage Effects of Over-schooling Revisited", *Labor Economics*, 2, 1995, p. 67–76.

Cotton J., "On the Decomposition of Wage Differentials", *Review of Economics and Statistics*, 70, 1988, pp. 236–43.

Daniel K. and Heywood J.S., "The Determinants of Hiring Older Workers: UK Evidence", *Labour Economics*, 14(1), January 2007, pp. 35–52.

De Freitas G., *Inequality at Work: Hispanics in the US Labor Force*, Oxford University Press, New York, 1991.

DeLeire T., "Changes in Wage Discrimination Against People with Disabilities: 1984–93", *Journal of Human Resources*, 36, 2001, pp. 144–58.

Duncan G.J. and Hoffman S.D., "The Incidence and Wage Effects of Over-education in the US Graduate Labor Market", *Economics of Education Review*, 1, 1981, pp. 75–86.

Felstead A., Gallie D. and Green F., *Work Skills in Britain 1986–2001*, SKOPE, ESRC Centre on Skills, Knowledge and Organisational Performance, Universities of Oxford and Warwick, Oxford, 2002.

Groot W., "The Incidence of, and Returns to Over-education in the UK", *Applied Economics*, 28, 1996, pp. 1345–50.

Gwartney J.D. and Long J.E., "The Relative Earnings of Blacks and Other Minorities", *Industrial and Labor Relations Review*, 31, 1978, pp. 336–46.

Hartog J. and Oosterbeek H., "Education, Allocation and Earnings in the Netherlands: Overschooling?", *Economics of Education Review*, 7, 1988, pp. 185–94.

Haskel J. and Martin C., "The Causes of Skill Shortages in Britain", *Oxford Economic Papers*, 45, 1993, pp. 573–88.

Hersch J., "Education Match and Job Match", *Review of Economics and Statistics*, 73, 1991, pp. 140–4.

Hutchens R., "Delayed Payment Contracts and a Firm's Propensity to Hire Older Workers", *Journal of Labor Economics*, 4, 1986, pp. 439–57.

Hutchens R., "Do Job Opportunities Decline with Age?", *Industrial and Labor Relation Review*, 42, 1988, pp. 89–99.

Jones M.K., Latreille P.L. and Sloane P.J., "Disability, Gender and the British Labour Market", *Oxford Economic Papers*, 40(8), July 2006, pp. 823–45.

Kahn L.M., "Customer Discrimination and Affirmative Action", *Economic Inquiry*, 29(3), 1991, pp. 555–71.

Kossoudji S., "English Language Ability and the Labor Market Opportunities of Hispanic and East Asian Men", *Journal of Labor Economics*, 6, 1988, pp. 203–28.

Lazear E.P., "Why is there Mandatory Retirement?", *Journal of Political Economy*, 87, 1979, pp. 1261–84.

Leslie D., with Blackaby D., Clark K., Drinkwater S., Murphy P. and O'Leary N., *An Investigation of Racial Disadvantage*, Manchester University Press, Manchester, 1998.

Maani S.A., "Are Young First and Second Generation Immigrants at a Disadvantage in the Australian Labour Market?", *International Migration Review*, 28, 1994, pp. 865–81.

Mavromaras K., McGuinness S., O'Leary N., Sloane P. and Wei Z., "Job Mismatches and Labour Market Outcomes: Panel Evidence on Australian University Graduates", IZA Discussion Paper 5083, July 2010.

Nardinelli C. and Simon C., "Customer Racial Discrimination in the Market for Memorabilia: The Case of Baseball", *Quarterly Journal of Economics*, 105, 1990, pp. 575–96.

Neumark D., "Employer's Discriminatory Behavior and the Estimation of Wage Discrimination", *Journal of Human Resources*, 23, 1988, pp. 279–95.

Oaxaca R.L., "Sex Discrimination in Wages", in Ashenfelter O. and Rees A., editors, *Discrimination in Labor Markets*, Princeton University Press, Princeton, New Jersey, 1973.

Phelps E.S., "The Statistical Theory of Racism and Sexism", *American Economic Review*, 62, 1972, pp. 659–61.

Reimers C.W., "Labor Market Discrimination Against Hispanic and Black Men", *Review of Economics and Statistics*, 65, 1983, pp. 570–9.

Riach P. and Rich J., "Field Experiments of Discrimination in the Market Place", *Economic Journal*, 112(483), November 2002, pp. F480–F518.

Rooth D.O. and Ekberg J., "Unemployment and Earnings for Second Generation Immigrants in Sweden: Ethnic Background and Parent Composition", *Journal of Population Economics*, 16, 2003, pp. 787–814.

Rumberger R.W., *Over-education in the US Labor Market*, Praeger, New York, 1981.

Sattinger M., "Assignment Models of the Distribution of Earnings", *Journal of Economic Literature*, LXXXI, 1993, pp. 831–80.

Sicherman N., "Over-education in the Labor Market", *Journal of Labor Economics*, 9(2), 1991, pp. 101–22.

Sloane P.J., "Discrimination in the Labour Market", in Carline D. *et al.*, *Labour Economics*, Longman, Essex, 1985, pp. 78–158.

Sloane P.J., "Theories of Discrimination", in Jain H.C. *et al.*, *Employment Equity and Affirmative Action*, ME Sharpe, New York, 2003, pp. 56–69.

Sloane P.J., Battu H. and Seaman P., "Over-education and the Formal Education/Experience and Training Trade-off", *Applied Economics Letters*, 3, 1996, pp. 511–15.

Sloane P.J., Battu H. and Seaman P., "Over-education, Under-education and the British Labour Market", *Applied Economics*, 31, 1999, pp. 1437–53.

Sloane P.J. and Gazioglu S., "Immigration and Occupational Status: A Study of Bangladeshi and Turkish Fathers and Sons in the London Labour Market", *Labour Economics*, 3, 1996, pp. 399–424.

Stevens P.A., "Skills Shortages and Firms' Employment Behaviour", *Labour Economics*, 14(2), April 2007, pp. 231–50.

Thomas B. and Deaton D., *Labour Shortage and Economic Analysis*, Basil Blackwell, Oxford, 1977.

Thurow L., *Generating Inequality*, Basic Books, New York, 1975.

Verdugo R.R. and Verdugo N.T., "The Impact of Surplus Schooling on Earnings: Some Additional Findings", *Journal of Human Resources*, 24(4), 1989, pp. 629–43.

Weichselbaumer D. and Winter-Ebmer R., "The Effects of Competition and Equal Treatment Laws on Gender Wage Differentials", *Economic Policy*, April 2007, pp. 235–87.

Further reading

R.B. Thomas and D. Deaton, *Labour Shortage and Manpower Analysis*, Basil Blackwell, Oxford, 1977, though somewhat dated, is a comprehensive analysis of labour shortages, concerning both theoretical and empirical aspects from a UK perspective.

F. Buchel, A. de Grip and A. Mertens, editors, *Overeducation in Europe: Current issues in Theory and Policy*, Edward Elgar, Cheltenham, UK and Northampton, MA, USA, 2003, contains papers on a wide range of issues in a number of countries.

Gary Becker, *The Economics of Discrimination*, University of Chicago Press, Chicago, 1957, remains the classic text, which provided the foundations on which a vast literature has been constructed.

Chapter 7

Trade unions

Learning outcomes

At the end of this chapter, readers should understand:

- The determinants of union membership;
- How unions are able to influence wages and raise them above competitive levels;
- The efficiency implications for outcomes lying on or off the labour demand curve;
- The role that bargaining strength plays in determining negotiated outcomes;
- That empirical estimates of the union wage mark-up vary across worker groups and that such estimates are influenced by a range of econometric and data issues;
- That, aside from influencing wages, unions also affect performance in a number of other aspects.

Introduction

What do unions do? That is the question posed by a classic text by Freeman and Medoff (1984) and, in this chapter, we will analyse and discuss a number of the facets over which trade unions exert, or attempt to exert, some sort of control or influence. We begin with an overview of **union density** patterns and membership figures within industrialised economies from the 1970s onwards. The general pattern to emerge from this is that the institution of unionisation is in retreat, although there are substantial differences across OECD nations. We then move on to examine models of union behaviour, where there are clear efficiency differences between bargained wage and employment outcomes that lie either on or off a firm's labour demand curve. Next, an analysis of the extent to which unions are able to increase wages for their members, commonly referred to as the union wage effect or union mark-up, is given and an overview of the empirical evidence presented. Finally, we conclude with a discussion of the largely empirical literature on the

Union density

Calculated as the number of currently enrolled union members as a proportion of all those employees eligible to be members.

association between unionisation and aspects of efficiency, such as productivity, profitability and investment. Finally, note that, while unions are also associated with strike activity, a discussion of this issue and the process of conflict resolution is delayed until Chapter 8.

Case Study 7.1

A brief history of the union movement in Britain

The process of the Industrial Revolution between the late-eighteenth and mid-nineteenth centuries transformed Britain from a mainly agrarian society to one whose wealth was based upon industrial production, where the population was increasingly located within fast-growing towns. Coupled with the Napoleonic Wars with France (1793–1815) and huge rises in commodity prices, such events gave impetus to the formation of workplace combination and trade organisation. These were in spite of the infamous Combination Acts of 1799 and 1800, which made it illegal for workers to join together to collectively lobby employers over pay and conditions. Although the Combination Acts were repealed in 1824, to be replaced by the 1825 Combination Act which still limited union-ised activity, unions developed rapidly in the early nineteenth century, especially in the factory-based textile industry, within which female employment was prominent.

There were also attempts to form general unions of all workers regardless of trade, with one of the most prominent being the Grand National Consolidated Trades Union (GNCTU). In an attempt to smash the GNCTU in 1834, the government arrested six agricultural labourers from the village of Tolpuddle (Dorsetshire) and found them guilty in a show trial of administering illegal oaths. While the six "Tolpuddle Martyrs" were initially sentenced to transportation to Australia, a mass campaign pressured the government into commuting their sentences.

Following this temporary defeat of unionism in 1834, working-class activity concentrated upon other forms of mass campaign, and in particular Chartism. This was based upon the demands of a six-point charter for electoral reform and from this mass support came the first working-class political party, the National Charter Association, in 1840. Chartism was seen as a threat to the established order and lay behind the 1842 General Strike which followed the pro-posed cutting of wages in the cotton manufacturing industry. In April 1848, a mass Chartist dem-onstration on Kennington Common, London, was organised with the intention of presenting the third Chartist petition for electoral reform to Parliament. In the aftermath of this protest, the gov-ernment arrested a number of Chartist leaders, including William Cuffey, who was put on trial and convicted of planning an armed uprising. He was sentenced to transportation for life to the penal colony of Tasmania. Although not defeated, Chartism was never again the national mass movement that it once was.

With the construction of the railway network, stimulating growth in the coal, iron and engi-neering industries, came a new breed of industrialisation by the late 1840s and, coupled with cotton, these formed the mainstay of British industry and led to Britain having a virtual monop-oly over world trade. Workers in such industries benefitted from the booming conditions in the British economy and formed the basis of the revival in trade unionism that followed the demise of the Chartist movement. These "new model unions" were organised nationally and high mem-bership fees allowed them to employ full-time paid officials and offer improved friendly society benefits. Ideologies changed, and arbitration and negotiation became accepted practices and were much more common in resolving grievances over pay and conditions than strike action. The smaller craft unions, encompassing trades such as shoe-making and tailoring, also shared a similar ideology. Women, though, were excluded from most of these unions and attempts to organise the female workforce was often driven by the efforts of philanthropic women. A notable example of this was the Women's Protective and Provident League, formed in 1875 by Emma Paterson.

With the passing of the 1867 Reform Act that enfranchised the urban male working class in England and Wales, the working-class vote subsequently became important to all political parties. So much so that, within seven years of the 1867 Reform Act, two Royal Commissions had been established to look into trade unions. By the 1880s, therefore, a strong (albeit narrowly based) trade union movement had been created, and, up until the outbreak of the First World War, trade unions grew at a faster rate than at any other time in their history. Union activity spread to industries previously untouched by worker organisation, and, following a revival in socialist activity, a new mood of militancy was inspired. However, many of the gains of "new unionism" were reversed by the 1890s as employers began a counter-offensive. In particular, two legal rulings – the case of *Lyons vs Wilkins* in 1896 that set a precedent for outlawing even peaceful picketing, and the 1901 Taff Vale judgment that allowed an employer to sue for losses sustained during a strike – curtailed the mood of militancy that had come to dominate the union establishment. In a backlash to this, Syndicalists – a minority group within the labour movement who were hostile to the leadership of the political and industrial wings of the labour movement – engaged in a policy of direct action aimed at wrestling back some form of worker control in the face of the employers' offensive. They did this by utilising a strategy of mass strikes and rapid trade union recruitment.

Against the backdrop of all this, women continued to be under-represented within the union ranks up to the outbreak of the First World War. While the number of women in trade unions had increased by 1914, 90 per cent of all trade unionists were still male and over 90 per cent of female workers remained outside of union organisation.

The obvious divisions that had arisen within the labour movement were accentuated during the First World War and militancy continued to flourish. While the leaders of the labour movement became engaged within the State establishment in dealing with the war effort, the gulf between the leaders and the led widened. The election of shop stewards and the formation of shop stewards committees became commonplace and such infrastructures were to provide the *de facto* leadership of the rank and file union members.

With post-war industrial decline came large-scale unemployment in the industrial heartlands of the country and declining union membership from around six and a half million in 1920 to an inter-war low of three and a quarter million in 1933. However, the mood of militancy remained and culminated in the most powerful working-class display of strength ever seen, the General Strike of 1926. As well as being a period of economic readjustment, this was also a period of political realignment. The extension of universal suffrage to all adults over the age of 21 in 1928 heralded a new two-party political system where the Labour party replaced the Liberals as the main opposition to the Tory party. Indeed, two Labour governments were formed during the inter-war period in 1924 and 1929–31, albeit in minority administrations.

The third Labour government was formed between 1945 and 1951 and, reflecting the close links between the union movement and the Labour party, six of the twenty members of the first cabinet of Clement Atlee were union sponsored. The size of its election majority in 1945 also allowed it to set out a mandate that included addressing trade union law. In particular, the 1927 Trades Dispute and Trade Unions Act, introduced to outlaw secondary strike action after the General Strike of 1926, was repealed. A reduced Labour majority in the 1950 General Election meant that the decision was taken to hold a new election to give Labour a more workable majority.

This majority was not forthcoming and the next three elections from 1951 resulted in Conservative administrations. However, the three Conservative leaders (Churchill, Eden and Macmillan) over this period were all committed to maintaining the good relations with trade unions which had been fostered by the previous Labour government.

A notable feature of this time was the increased interest in trade unionism among white-collar workers in both public and private sectors. This extended the reach of trade unions out from their traditional strongholds among the ranks of manual workers and into occupations associated with specialist and professional workers.

The intervening period up until the post-1979 Thatcher years are seen as a time of consolidation and strengthening for the trade union movement in Britain. From the mid-1950s, though, industrial relations worsened, with Britain encountering balance of payments problems and experiencing slow growth and rising inflation. In light of increasing industrial conflict, the Labour government of 1964 appointed a Royal Commission on Trade Unions and Employers' Associations to oversee how industrial relations might be reformed. The Donovan Report, reporting to the Royal Commission, was published in 1968 and argued that the traditional system of industry-wide collective bargaining had been subsumed by a two-tier system: at the national level, a formal system with official institutions; and, at the enterprise level, an informal system. As established procedures at the establishment level were often lacking, industrial relations were characterised by a lack of order, unofficial disputes and wage demands that were unrelated to productivity. Over this period, closed-shop agreements also became more prevalent and the number of shop stewards increased and they became more important as a trend for individual plant-level or company-level bargaining developed. However, while formal workplace procedures had been tightened, there was no evidence of improving industrial relations as had been envisaged by the Donovan Report.

On the back of industrial and economic turmoil, a Thatcher-led Conservative administration swept into power in 1979 promising to roll back the power of the State by following a *laissez-faire* economic ethos, and trade union reform was at the heart of this. A series of acts were subsequently passed during the 1980s all aimed at regulating the influence that trade unions were able to exert over industrial relations. Major pieces of legislation were Employment Acts in 1980, 1982, 1986 and 1990 and the 1984 Trades Union Act, although this is far from an exhaustive list. The 1980 Employment Act limited secondary picketing, extended exemptions for the closed shop, provided public funds for secret balloting prior to strike action and regulated for the periodic election of union officials. The 1982 Employment Act narrowed the definition of a trade dispute to cover only disputes between workers and their own employer, allowed for those affected by unlawful industrial action to sue for damages, and outlawed the pre-entry closed shop. The 1984 Trade Union Act required secret ballots to be held every five years to elect union executives, a secret ballot every ten years for the political levy, and a secret ballot prior to any industrial action. Under the 1988 Employment Act, union members were given greater rights and support in taking action against their own unions, union disciplinary powers were reduced, and remaining statutory support for closed shops and their formation was removed. The 1990 Employment Act allowed firms to selectively dismiss workers engaged in unofficial disputes, all remaining secondary action was outlawed, and applicants who were refused a job on the basis of union membership status were entitled to legal compensation.

It is against such a backdrop that union membership in Britain has declined persistently since 1979. Collective bargaining is now much less likely to be on a multi-employer basis, which would have occurred predominantly at the industry level, with an increasing proportion of bargaining taking place at the organisation or company level.

7.1 Trade union membership

Basic to our understanding of union growth and behaviour is the question of why some workers choose to join trade unions and others do not (Farber and Saks 1980). In order to answer this, we need to distinguish between factors that affect the availability of unions and those that have an influence on the individual's decision to join. That is, an individual considering a new job may join a firm which is unionised or one which is non-unionised, and in the former case may choose whether to be a union member or to be a free rider (i.e. a worker covered by a collective agreement but not themselves a member of a union). In much of the empirical literature, such a distinction is absent, so that what is really being examined is the union status of jobs (Sinclair 1995).

What is striking is the wide variation in union membership across countries. While comparisons are rendered difficult because of differences among countries in relation to definitions of unions, data sources and coverage and in reporting techniques, these differences seem real enough.[1] Table 7.1 excludes the self-employed, retired and unemployed union members in order to ensure consistency. The density figures for Sweden, Denmark and Finland, in particular, are in sharp contrast to those in the US and France. Union membership increased in every country apart from France in the 1970s but has subsequently declined in a majority of countries through the 1980s and beyond. Indeed, it appears that, in general, it is in those countries that are more highly unionised that unions have been better able to preserve their position, both in terms of membership and density levels. In contrast, the fortunes of unions in countries that were already weakly unionised have deteriorated further.

More recently, a decline in unionism across Western Europe has been witnessed, being concentrated in the larger economies of Germany and the UK in particular. Indeed, focusing specifically upon the UK case, this has led some commentators to describe unions as "hollow shells" (see *inter alia* Millward *et al.* 2000) where the tendency has been for new establishments and new labour force entrants to be non-unionised (Willman *et al.* 2007). So marked has this trend been that Bryson and Gomez (2005) have noted a rising proportion of employees in the labour force who have never been a union member. While conveying a similar idea about the importance of new workplaces being born that are non-unionised, Blanchflower and Bryson (2008) also note that there has been a decline over time in the probability of **union recognition**. This was most prominent during the period 1980 98, although, since then (and up to 2004), there has been no clear trend in the likelihood of union workplace recognition in the UK.

Against such a backdrop, Bryson and Forth (2010) recount telling evidence for the UK as to a dramatic fall in the perception of the power wielded by unions in society. In the mid-1980s, the percentage of employees who thought that unions had too much power outnumbered those saying that they had too little by a factor of five to one. By 2007, the situation had been reversed, with those saying that unions had too little power outnumbering those who said that they had too much by a factor of two to one.

In one of the few studies to attempt to explain such international differences, Blanchflower and Freeman (1992) contrast changes in union density in countries with **centralised wage setting**, where they postulate union wage mark-ups (see section 7.3) will be relatively small, with decentralised wage-bargaining countries

Union recognition

The reverse state of affairs to derecognition, whereby a union is recognised at a workplace as having a formal bargaining role with employers.

Centralised wage setting

The situation where there is highly co-ordinated collective bargaining which is conducted at the national as opposed to local level.

Table 7.1 Trade union membership changes and density in the OECD, 1970–2008

| | Changes in Membership (%) | | | | Density (%) | | | | |
	1970–79	1980–89	1990–99	2000–08	1970	1980	1990	2000	2008
Australia	23.8	14.2	−29.4	−7.8	44.2	48.7	40.0	24.7	18.6
Austria	5.8	−4.8	−12.1	−14.7	62.8	56.7	46.9	36.6	28.9
Belgium	32.4	−4.5	3.5	16.0	42.1	54.1	53.9	49.5	51.9
Canada	53.6	16.1	−0.5	13.2	31.0	34.0	34.0	28.3	27.1
Denmark	43.3	9.1	3.6	−5.4	60.3	78.6	75.3	74.2	67.6
Finland	52.5	15.0	−2.4	−1.3	51.3	69.4	72.5	75.0	67.5
France	−1.7	−38.8	−11.1	1.5	21.7	18.3	10.3	8.1	7.7
Germany	16.3	−2.9	1.5	−18.4	32.0	34.9	31.2	24.6	19.1
Ireland	25.9	−12.5	11.0	8.5	50.6	54.3	48.5	38.4	32.3
Italy	50.5	−19.1	−11.8	10.9	37.0	49.6	38.8	34.8	33.4
Japan	6.1	−1.1	−3.6	−12.8	35.1	31.1	25.4	21.5	18.2
Korea	130.0	103.8	−21.5	9.1	12.6	14.7	17.2	11.4	10.3
Luxembourg	26.9	13.0	26.6	18.3	46.8	50.8	46.4	42.5	37.4
Netherlands	8.2	−14.0	17.7	−9.8	36.5	34.8	24.3	22.9	18.9
New Zealand	33.6	−9.1	−50.6	16.9	56.5	69.1	49.5	22.3	20.8
Norway	30.7	9.8	9.2	9.1	56.8	58.3	58.5	54.4	53.3
Sweden	27.8	10.5	−10.7	−5.3	67.7	78.0	80.0	79.1	68.3
Switzerland	11.7	−5.3	−10.7	−0.3	28.9	27.7	22.7	20.8	18.3
UK	16.8	−21.4	−21.8	−3.1	43.0	49.7	38.2	30.2	27.1
USA	3.5	−15.6	−1.6	−1.0	27.4	22.1	15.5	12.8	11.9

Source: OECD.

(such as the US) where union wage mark-ups are likely to be larger. Their results show that unions do better in countries with centralised as opposed to decentralised **collective-bargaining** systems.[2] Thus, in the US, the union wage mark-up is estimated to be 22 per cent, compared to 8 per cent for the other countries in the International Social Survey Programme (ISSP) data-set, and this gives management the incentive to oppose unions and can account for the decline in union membership.

Although not explaining differences in international rates of unionisation, Blanchflower (2007) looks at patterns of union membership across 38 countries (both inside and outside of the OECD) and finds clear evidence that the probability of being unionised follows an inverted U-shaped pattern with respect to individuals' age. Some evidence for strong cohort effects is found, but, even after controlling for these, the inverted U-shaped pattern remained across many countries with different density levels and trends and types of bargaining arrangements. However, the conclusion drawn is that because the age–membership profile is so widespread across such a diverse group of countries, its explanation is unlikely to be due to country-specific features.[3]

Rather than accounting for differences across countries, most econometric studies that have been conducted have focused on explaining changes in union membership or density within individual countries. The determinants fall into five categories: first, the macroeconomic climate as characterised in the business cycle; second, the composition of the workforce; third, the policy of the State in terms of the legal environment in which unions operate; fourth, the policies of employers; and, fifth, the policies of the trade unions themselves.

7.1.1 Macroeconomic climate

As Bain and Elsheikh (1976) note, business-cycle theories of growth go back to John R. Commons and the Wisconsin school in the early part of the twentieth century and were developed in particular by Davis (1941). An adequate theory of union growth must assess the extent to which fluctuations in the aggregate degree of unionisation are related to the business cycle and, in particular, to components such as the cost of living, unemployment and wages. The basic idea is that workers are encouraged to join unions by any acceleration in inflationary pressure, but the more that earnings rise faster than prices, the less likely are workers to join unions. Rising unemployment will have a negative effect on unions as employed members may choose to leave the union.

In a particularly influential paper, Ashenfelter and Pencavel (1969) estimate a model of union growth for the US, and similar models have been estimated by Sharpe (1971) for Australia and Bain and Elsheikh (1976) for Britain. The Ashenfelter and Pencavel estimating equation is given by:

$$\Delta T_t = \alpha_0 + \alpha_r \Delta P_t + \sum_{i=0}^{N} \alpha_{2i} \Delta E_{t-i}^* + \alpha_3 g(u_t^p, t-\theta) + \alpha_4 (T/E^*)_{t-1} + \alpha_5 G_t + \varepsilon_t$$

(7.1)

where ΔT is the annual percentage change in union membership; ΔP is the annual percentage change in consumer prices; ΔE^* is the annual percentage change in employment in unionised sectors; u_t^p is the level of unemployment in the previous

---

Collective bargaining

The process of negotiation over pay and conditions that occurs between groups of concerned parties and not between individuals.

trough of the business cycle; T/E^* is total union membership as a percentage of unionised employment; G is the percentage of Democrats in the US House of Representatives; and the α terms are the estimated regression coefficients.

This paper assumes that the stock of workers' discontent at any point in time is a function of the rate of unemployment in the preceding trough in the business cycle, which is in line with Davis (1941). Sharpe's model incorporates a dummy variable to capture the effect of compulsory arbitration in Australia in the early part of the twentieth century. Bain and Elsheikh posit a non-linear relationship between ΔT and ΔP. In general, these models appear to have relatively high explanatory power, with most of the estimated coefficients on the independent (i.e. explanatory) variables attaining significance at conventional levels. However, they have been criticised for failing to deal adequately with potential simultaneity between dependent and independent variables and for their failure to disaggregate across sectors of the economy.

Meanwhile, Carruth and Disney (1988) develop a model that is rather different from that of previous authors in attempting to separate out cycle and trend. This model can satisfactorily explain the two million decline in British trade union membership between 1979 and 1982 and they conclude that the economic environment prevailing at that time – a combination of persistent unemployment, steady real wage growth and a Conservative government – was particularly unfavourable to trade union membership growth. Metcalf (1991) points out, however, that the subsequent slowdown in real wage growth and rapid fall in unemployment should, according to their model, have led to an increase in union membership, which is not the case.

In a critique of previous studies, though, Disney (1990) argues that varying macroeconomic conditions are indeed the dominant factor behind British membership trends over the course of the 1980s and over the post-war period more generally, as opposed to other factors such as changing workforce composition or changing labour legislation. It is argued that previous business-cycle models failed to forecast the downturn in the 1980s because of model mis-specification, notably the failure to distinguish between union membership and **union coverage** as distinct phenomena.

7.1.2 Workforce composition

Econometric analyses in both the US and Britain suggest that union membership is also related to both personal and job characteristics. Thus, Bain and Elias (1985) characterise aspects influencing the probability of union membership as follows:

> The results suggest that an individual who is self employed, who works part time, who is a member of a white-collar occupation, or who possesses a degree or related professional qualification is generally less likely to be a union member, whereas a person who is male, who left school before the age of 16, who concurrently holds more than one job, who works in Wales or in the North of Britain, or who is employed in industries characterised by labour intensity or product market concentration is generally more likely to be a union member. The probability of being a union member also generally increases, but at a decreasing rate with size of establishment, work experience and level of earnings.[4]

Union coverage

The situation where unions are present at a place of work and the pay and conditions of workers here are influenced by the actions of the union, regardless of whether individual workers are members of that union or not.

In addition, it should be noted that unions are much stronger in the public sector, where two-thirds of employees are union members compared to less than one-third in the private sector.[5] Using shift-share analysis for the period 1983–9, Green (1992) finds that 30 per cent of the fall in union density can be accounted for by changes in composition of the labour force. Thus, it appears that trends in general are unfavourable to long-run union growth.

7.1.3 Government policy and legal environment

Governments can also influence the environment in which unions operate and thus make it easier or harder to recruit members. Thus, in Britain in the 1980s, the Thatcher government passed a series of legislative measures that, *inter alia*, restricted picketing and secondary boycotts, made it easier for employers to dismiss workers during an industrial dispute, narrowed the definition of a lawful industrial dispute, required secret ballots before industrial action and effectively prohibited the **closed shop**. Freeman and Pelletier (1990) attempt to attach quantitative estimates to the effects of changes in the legal environment affecting unions over the period 1945–86 on union density in the UK by constructing an index of favourableness to unionism of industrial-relations law in the UK and in Ireland, while controlling for cyclical changes and changes in the industrial composition of employment. In contrast to the above findings in relation to the effects of the business cycle and compositional effects, they conclude that "the vast bulk of the observed 1980s decline in union density in the UK is due to the changed union environment for industrial relations".[6]

7.1.4 Employer policy

However, it is also necessary to take into account the attitude and conduct of employers. In the US, Bognanno and Kleiner (1992) report that private-sector employers were increasingly able to affect new employment policies outside the normal collective-bargaining process and in many cases conducted anti-union campaigns. In countries such as Australia, Germany and Sweden, however, there is a much greater commitment to arbitration, pluralism and corporatism. In Britain, Gallie *et al.* (1994) suggest that the most important determinant of union membership is the extent to which employers are prepared to support trade union organisation. Disney *et al.* (1995) show that workplaces recognising unions for purposes of collective bargaining fell by almost 20 per cent between 1980 and 1990 and this is largely accounted for by a much lower rate of union recognition in new establishments. **Derecognition** is much rarer. Beaumont and Harris (1995), for instance, find that this involved less than 10 per cent of establishments over the period 1984–90. In attempting to explain the circumstances under which firms will recognise trade unions for purposes of collective bargaining, Disney *et al.* (1996) hypothesise that the level of expected **quasi-rents** relative to other establishments is likely to be an important determinant of union recognition success, regardless of whether this is contested by employers. They find in line with this hypothesis that recognition is a function of the establishment's environment when it was set up in relation to both product and labour market characteristics and variables representing the structure and control of the organisation of which the establishment is a part (such as foreign ownership). It is a moot point to what extent recognition has been influenced by the

Closed shop

The situation where employers agree to hire only union members and employees must remain union members in order to remain employed: in a pre-entry closed shop, the employee must join the union prior to gaining employment; in a post-entry closed shop, the employee must join a particular trade union within a specified period of time after taking up employment.

Derecognition

This refers to the situation where employers have ceased bargaining with a trade union, where once they would have bargained over pay and conditions.

Quasi-rents

The income earned from a sunk cost investment that is in excess of post-investment opportunity cost.

development of human resource management strategies and an increasingly flexible labour force.

7.1.5 Union policy

Some authors believe that the tactics and strategies of union organisations or their leaderships can influence the overall amount of union membership. Thus, Undy *et al.* (1981) argue that aggregate theories that discount such internal factors oversimplify the causes of union growth, and they reject Bain and Elsheikh's implication that unions are relatively powerless to affect aggregate growth through their own endeavours because the growth of one union may be at the expense of another, leaving the degree of aggregate unionisation unchanged. Metcalf (1991) notes that union leaders face a dilemma because, while recruitment drives can boost membership, they may also damage union finances, and he claims that this is one explanation for union merger activity. It does not, however, explain the wave pattern of union mergers, which is concentrated in the periods 1918–24, 1944–8 and 1966–79 (see Waddington 1988). Whether the union movement is unified or fractionalised may also be important, as in the former case unions may be more efficient in delivering services and employers may be more inclined to recognise the union.

In conclusion, it appears that unionisation is influenced by a range of factors including macroeconomic factors, public policy, employer attitudes, the sectoral and occupational composition of the labour force and internal union organisation. In many countries, trends appear unfavourable to trade union growth, though centralisation of collective bargaining in other countries has served to protect unions from membership erosion. We should also allow for the fact that unions may have effects beyond their own members as the numbers of free riders is substantial.

7.2 Trade union wage/employment behaviour

In surveying the literature on this topic, Hirsch and Addison (1986) came to the conclusion that "despite numerous attempts at modelling there is still no universally accepted model of union goals and behaviour". While it can be said that most of the theory that does exist is inspired by analogies with the theory of the firm (early examples being Dunlop 1944 and Berkowitz 1954) or of the household (Fellner 1949 and Cartter 1959 among early examples), a debate exists over the appropriate way to model union activity. The classic economic view of this is captured by the writing of Dunlop (1944), who argued that the economic theory of trade unions required that something was maximised or minimised. Even with this thought in mind, though, there has been little consensus over what this maximand (or minimand) should be, with the neutralisation of monopsony power, employment maximisation, wage bill maximisation, the maximisation of economic rent and utility maximisation *inter alia* proposed as objectives.

In contrast to the economic argument put forward by Dunlop, Ross (1948) argued that union policies are instead formulated on the basis of a politically driven decision-making process. In Ross's view, organisational survival is the central objective of the trade union leader who is concerned with re-election and must therefore balance pressure brought to bear both externally (from employers, other unions and the government) and internally (by disparate factions within the union).

Thus, while union behaviour is rational when viewed within a political framework, such behaviour would appear irrational when judged against orthodox economic analysis.

Such divergent views of union behaviour crystallised the so-called Dunlop–Ross controversy of the 1940s but, in essence, the difference in opinion between Ross and Dunlop can be reconciled by noting that the approaches differ only in regard to the relative weights attached to economic and political factors. While it is true that internal policy-making mechanisms are best understood within a framework that is wider than that suggested by conventional economic analysis, it is also true that union policies are in themselves expressed in terms of economic variables once these policies have been formulated. Thus, notwithstanding this tension between the political and economic being of trade unions, the focus in the following section will firmly be upon the economic rationale for union behaviour. This will begin with the monopoly union model as a starting point to frame much of the following discussion, although it should be recognised that few commentators hold this up as an observed statement of union behaviour. When market power is further extended to exist for both employers and unions, it turns out that the outcome of the bilateral union model is indeterminate. The right-to-manage model will then describe how outcomes along the labour demand curve are arrived at under the assumption that unions act as utility maximisers. Within such a framework, more recent formulations of union behaviour are also discussed where the unions and employers bargain over both the level of wages and of employment with the consequence that the outcome may not be on the demand curve, i.e. the efficient contract model.

7.2.1 The monopoly union model

The simplest way of thinking about how a union behaves is to view it as a monopoly seller of the labour services of its member to the employing firm. In such a way, it is reasonable to assume that the union will seek to equate the marginal revenue from the sale of members' services to their supply price. Such a situation is shown in Figure 7.1.

Consistent with the analysis of Chapter 5, the labour demand curve for a competitive firm will be traced out by the marginal revenue product of labour (which in itself is determined by the underlying short-run production function). On the assumption that diminishing marginal returns to labour eventually set in, this will dictate that the labour demand curve will slope downwards. This is labelled as Ld in Figure 7.1 and, using the analogy of the firm, this will represent the average revenue associated with the sale of members' services. The subsequent marginal revenue curve is therefore drawn as the more steeply sloping line labelled MR. The upward-sloping Ls curve is the supply curve for labour that the firm would face in the absence of the union.

Acting as the monopolistic seller of labour, the union will seek to supply $n1$ units of labour and demand a wage rate of $w1$. Such a wage–employment combination is consistent with the monopolistic maximising ideal of equating the supply price of labour with its marginal revenue. Compare this outcome, though, with that which would prevail in a perfectly competitive market with the same labour demand and supply curves but with no union intervention. The equating of labour demand and labour supply would imply a lower wage rate at wc but increased employment at nc. Hence, the monopoly union's ability to raise wages only comes at the expense of reduced employment of $nc - n1$ workers.

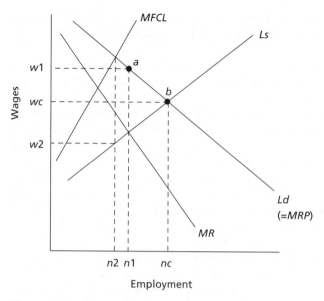

Figure 7.1 The monopoly union model.

While the monopoly union analogy is an appealing way to treat the union-maximising decision, the interpretation of the labour supply curve is problematic. The analogy of monopolistic behaviour would imply that the union is attempting to maximise the surplus of total wage income over individual supply prices for all of their members, but, unlike a monopolist, the union is not engaged in production and so incurs no production costs, as its role is merely that of an agent for members to facilitate the supply of their services. As therefore noted by Reder (1952), the union does not possess anything that can be interpreted as a cost function that would underpin the labour supply curve and, as such, the maximisation process that underpins the monopoly analogy would suggest quantities that would be unlikely to be of interest to the union. Furthermore, such an outcome would imply that jobs would need to be rationed in some way by the union to a level of $n1$. In this way, employed members would receive a wage of $w1$, which would be in excess of their supply price. However, there is an obvious divorce between wage gains and employment losses from such a union policy, with employed members gaining at the expense of the employment of others. In the absence of a union policy to redistribute gains from employed to unemployed members, it is unlikely that the political pressures within the union to balance enhanced employment opportunities from unemployed members with improved wages for employed members would lead to the maximising outcome predicted by the monopoly union model (Rees 1973).[7]

7.2.2 The bilateral monopoly model

Rather than market power being focused solely in the hands of the union, it is conceivable that the hiring firm will also be able to wield some form of monopsony power in the market for hiring labour. When we bring these two sides of monopoly power together, it formulates the bilateral monopoly for which the outcome of the collective-bargaining process between unions and employers is indeterminate. This situation is again illustrated with the aid of Figure 7.1.

As discussed previously, the monopoly union will want to restrict the sale of its members' services such that marginal revenue (MR) is equated with the supply price. This will dictate that $n1$ workers are employed at a unit wage rate of $w1$. On the other hand, the monopsonistic employer will wish to continue hiring workers up to the point where, at the margin, the additional cost of hiring an extra worker (i.e. the marginal factor cost of labour) is equal to the additional value of output produced by this worker (i.e. the marginal revenue product of labour). Given that the upward-sloping labour supply curve Ls represents the average factor cost of labour, the marginal factor cost of labour will be traced out by the more steeply sloping $MFCL$ curve. The labour demand curve has already been defined as describing the marginal revenue product of labour and so profit-maximising consideration will mean that $n2$ workers will be employed at a unit wage rate of $w2$. Thus, what we have under the bilateral monopoly formulation is a range of possible wage outcomes between $w1$ and $w2$ but not a unique prediction. Although it is usually argued that the precise value within this range will be determined by some process of collective bargaining between employer and union, the bilateral monopoly model does not in itself provide any theory as to how this bargaining will take place. Note also that the competitive wage that would be established at wc is still one of the possible wage outcomes that might arise out of such bargaining.

7.2.3 The right-to-manage model

In this model, the union and the firm are assumed to bargain over any surpluses available within the market to determine the wage rate, and once this has been established through the bargaining process the firm is free to choose the number of workers it wishes to employ. This will be done in reference to its labour demand curve.[8]

The union's preferences over wage rates and employment levels may be represented with a conventional set of indifference maps drawn for all possible combinations of the wage rate and employment level as shown in Figure 7.2. Intuitively, union utility will be increasing in both wages and employment, and so, along any given indifference curve, utility can only be maintained if increased employment is associated with lower wages and vice versa. Vertically higher indifference curves, representing superior wage–employment combinations, will therefore be associated with greater (ordinal) utility and following the maxim of utility maximisation unions will wish to be on their highest possible indifference curve.

However, the ability to attain higher indifference curves is subject to the constraint imposed by the firm's labour demand curve, i.e. the firm will only want to choose a wage–employment combination on the labour demand curve because this is consistent with its own maxim of profit maximisation. Moreover, each point on the labour demand curve will be associated with competitive profit maximisation and this will mean a position on the apex of any given iso-profit curve. Such a situation is depicted in Figure 7.3.

A selection of iso-profit lines are shown as $\pi0$, $\pi1$ and $\pi2$ and along which profits to the firm are constant. Points $A0$, $A1$ and $A2$ lie on the apexes of these iso-profit lines respectively and each of these points, consistent with the ideal of profit maximisation, will also lie on the labour demand curve (Ld). Note that the firm will

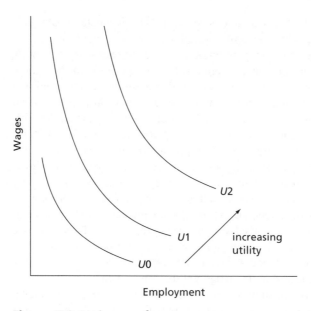

Figure 7.2 Union preferences over wages and employment.

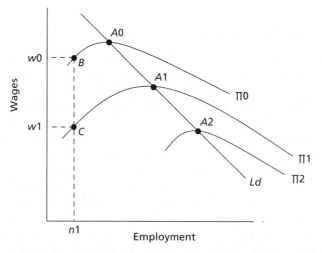

Figure 7.3 Iso-profit lines and the labour demand curve.

always choose a wage–employment outcome such as $A0$, $A1$ or $A2$. To see why, consider point B that lies on iso-profit line $\pi0$. Thus, employing $n1$ units of labour at a constant wage rate of $w1$ will yield a certain level of profit for the firm and this level of profit will be constant for all other wage–employment outcomes along $\pi0$. However, moving from point B to point C, which lies on the lower iso-profit line $\pi1$, will unequivocally increase profits; $n1$ workers are still employed but each of these workers will now receive a lower wage rate of $w1$ and hence lower iso-profit lines are associated with higher profits. Profit maximisation will therefore dictate that a firm will wish to be on the lowest possible iso-profit line. So, returning to point B, which does not lie on the apex of iso-profit line $\pi0$, this point cannot be consistent with the notion of profit maximisation, i.e. for a given wage rate of $w0$, the firm would never respond by choosing to employ $n1$ workers. If the firm chose to incrementally employ more workers than $n1$, it would move to the right of point B and this would now represent a wage–employment outcome that would lie on an iso-profit line below $\pi0$. As a result, profits would increase. Similar arguments would apply to all points on $\pi0$ other than the wage–employment combination at $A0$.

Bringing these two considerations of union utility maximisation and firm profit maximisation together yields the monopoly union outcome depicted in Figure 7.4. Subject to the constraint that the firm will choose a wage–employment outcome along the labour demand curve, the highest possible indifference curve that the union can attain is Ue, where the indifference curve and labour demand curve just touch, i.e. the indifference curve and labour demand curve are tangential at point E. This implies a utility-maximising wage rate of w^*, and, given this wage rate, the firm will choose to employ n^* workers.[9]

Note, though, that the outcome described above that lies upon the firm's labour demand curve implies an inefficient outcome. That is, it is possible to make a Pareto improvement by moving from point E to any wage–employment combination within (and bounded by) the shaded ellipse in Figure 7.4. Any movement to a point within this shaded area will mean that the union will be on a higher indifference curve (and subsequently better off) and simultaneously the firm will move to a lower iso-profit line (associated with increased profits). Hence, point E will be Pareto-dominated by any point within this Pareto-improving set, as we will be making at least one of the parties better off without making the other worse off. For that reason, it can be concluded that any bargained outcome that lies on the labour demand curve will be inefficient (in a Pareto sense), as all potentially mutually advantageous gains from bargaining have not been exploited.

Figure 7.4 The monopoly union outcome and Pareto inefficiency along the labour demand curve.

7.2.4 The efficient bargaining model

But what will it mean if the benefits from all mutually advantageous bargains have been exhausted and how will the outcome be characterised? As seen in section 7.2.3, central to trade union models specifying outcomes which lie on the labour demand curve is the assumption that the union unilaterally determines the wage and the employer is then free to adjust employment to achieve the profit-maximising level of employment (i.e. the right-to-manage model). However, if employees and unions bargain simultaneously over wages and employment (either explicitly or implicitly), so that firms are not left to adjust employment to ensure an outcome on the demand curve, it can be shown that outcomes on the demand curve are unlikely to be **Pareto optimal**.[10] Indeed, McDonald and Solow (1981) show that, for any given wage–employment combination on the demand curve, there will generally exist some combination off the curve with lower wages and higher employment that will be preferred both by the employer and the union. This is explained by the efficient bargaining model which is described in Figure 7.5.

In this model, the union and the firm determine both wages and employment simultaneously.[11] Figure 7.5 provides a more detailed focus upon the Pareto-improving set discussed in section 7.2.3 (and, in particular, identified in Figure 7.4), where any point that lies upon the labour demand curve, such as point E, will be Pareto inefficient. However, starting at point E, both parties will be better off with lower wages and higher employment. For example, at point A, the firm will be earning higher profits than at point E (because iso-profit line $\pi0$ is lower than iso-profit line πe), while the union will still be on indifference curve Ue and this will represent a Pareto improvement. Point A will also now represent a Pareto efficient point as there would be no way of making either of the parties better off without making the other worse off and is characterised by a tangency between the iso-profit line of the firm and the indifference curve of the union. If these curves were not tangential, it would mean that they would intersect one another and in doing so

Pareto optimal

An outcome is described as being Pareto optimal (or Pareto efficient) if it is not possible to make one party better off without making another party worse off. For a Pareto improvement to take place, at least one of the parties needs to be made better off without any of the other parties being made worse off.

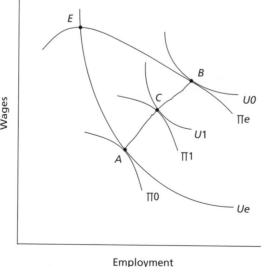

Figure 7.5 Efficient bargaining outcomes and the contract curve.

a Pareto-improving set would be created. Hence, a situation where iso-profit and indifference curves are not tangential cannot possibly be consistent with a Pareto optimal (or Pareto efficient) outcome. Only when they are tangential is there an efficient outcome. There will be a whole host of such points and, when these are connected, they will trace out the contract curve, the locus of all Pareto efficient points.

Thus, points B and C in Figure 7.5 will also lie on the contract curve, as each of these points is associated with a tangency between iso-profit lines and indifference curves. Unlike the scenario discussed at point A, though, the benefits associated with bargaining off the labour demand curve are not captured exclusively by the firm at these two points. At point B, while the firm remains on iso-profit line πe, the union has moved from indifference curve Ue to the higher curve $U0$. Therefore, the union has captured all bargaining gains in this movement from point E. In contrast, the Pareto efficient point C is associated with gains for both the firm (which moves from iso-profit line πe to iso-profit line $\pi 1$) and the union (which moves from indifference curve Ue to indifference curve $U1$) and, indeed, this will be the case for any point along the contract curve *between* points A and B.[12]

Case Study 7.2

The contract curve under various risk assumptions

Note that all points on the contract curve are associated with Pareto efficiency, which may be interpreted as implying that, subject to an arbitrarily fixed level of welfare of one party (let us say the union), the welfare of the other party (let us say the firm) is maximised. Using the same notation set out in the main text, this suggests that an efficient bargain over wages (w) and employment (n) solves:

$$\max_{w,n} pq(n) - wn \qquad (7.2.1)$$

subject to the constraint that

$$\frac{n}{t}(u(w) - u(b)) + u(b) = U* \qquad (7.2.2)$$

With n union workers out of a total workforce of t employed as an input into the production function $q(n)$, equation (7.2.1) represents the profit function of the firm, which it seeks to maximise subject to the consideration that the union makes an arbitrary (and fixed) level of expected utility $U*$. This latter consideration is given by equation (7.2.2), which states that the expected utility of the union equals the sum of indirect utility from the non-negotiated wage (b) plus the gain in indirect utility from the negotiated union wage multiplied by its likelihood of occurring (n/t).

Deriving and solving the Lagrangean for this constrained maximisation problem captured by equations (7.2.1) and (7.2.2) yields the following:

$$pq'(n) = w - \frac{u(w) - u(b)}{u'(w)} \qquad (7.2.3)$$

which will describe the contract curve. Furthermore, the slope of the contract curve may be found by totally differentiating equation (7.2.3) with respect to w and n. This will yield the following:

$$\frac{dw}{dn} = \frac{pq''(n)u'(w)^2}{u''(w)(u(w)-u(b))} \qquad (7.2.4)$$

A diminishing marginal revenue product of labour will lie behind the downward-sloping labour demand schedule faced by the competitive firm, and this in itself will be underpinned by diminishing marginal returns to labour and so $q''(n) < 0$. Thus, the numerator on the right-hand side of equation (7.2.4) will be negative and it is the sign taken by the denominator that will determine the sign of the slope of the contract curve. When the union, reflecting the preferences of its members, is **risk averse**, the indirect utility function with respect to wages will be concave and so $u''(w) < 0$. This will imply that the slope of the contract curve will be positive, i.e. upward sloping in wage–employment space as illustrated by line (III) in Figure 7.2.1. Intuitively, as wages increase above the competitive level the opportunity cost of becoming unemployed also increases and so the union insures its members against this risk by bargaining for increased employment (Booth 1995). Conversely, risk-loving behaviour would imply a convex indirect utility function with $u''(w) > 0$ and the contract curve would be negatively sloped. Meanwhile, risk neutrality ($u''(w) = 0$) would imply a vertical contract curve. These latter two scenarios are described by lines (I) and (II) respectively in Figure 7.2.1.

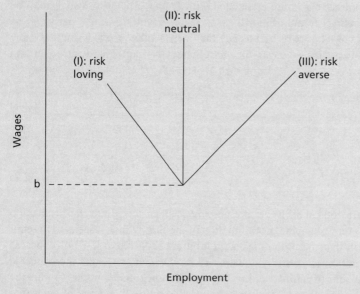

Figure 7.2.1 The contract curve under various risk assumptions.

By therefore moving to an employment contract within the Pareto-improving set of wages and employment combinations off the demand curve, either or both of the parties would be better off than if they remained on the labour demand curve. Thus, as Oswald (1982, 1985) points out, it is difficult to reconcile the efficient contract model with actual labour market behaviour. The prevalence of bargaining over wage implies that most employment contracts are likely to be inefficient with wages set too high and employment set too low.

Note, though, that all that has been identified is a range of possible bargained outcomes along the contract curve and not a *unique* outcome. Obviously, the exact outcome, and the relative benefits extracted from the bargaining process, will depend upon the relative bargaining strengths of unions and employers. Adopting a generalised Nash bargaining framework that allows for bargaining over wages and employment will therefore allow a single identifiable solution to be established. The Nash bargaining approach is an axiomatic approach which aims to find the weakest set of axioms under which a unique outcome can be identified. It is essentially static and focuses upon the outcome of bargaining and is a solution concept widely used in the literature. According to this approach, wages are determined by the maximisation of the product of each party's gains from reaching a bargain, weighted by their respective bargaining strengths.[13]

But what will be the gains from reaching a bargain for the respective parties? And what sanctions would one party have to induce the other party to enter into negotiations? While these might seem like two distinct questions, they are, in fact, inextricably linked as it is the threat of facing the costs imposed by the other party that induces firms and unions to bargain. This could be in the form of a strike by the union or a lockout by the firm. As such, then, it is the avoidance of these costs that determines the gains from entering into the bargaining process.

If we concern ourselves with the situation where the only factor input a firm uses is labour, the firm's production function may be denoted as $q(n)$, i.e. the maximum amount of output that can be produced with n workers. On the assumption of competitive (price-taking) behaviour that results in a market price of output of p, the value of output produced will equal $pq(n)$. Profits will equal such revenue less input costs, which are in themselves determined by the negotiated wage rate w that the firm needs to pay each of its n workers. The profit function is therefore given by:

$$pq(n) - wn \qquad\qquad (7.2)$$

and this profit function will represent the net gain to the firm from entering into a bargained solution with the union.

If we denote the non-union wage a worker can expect to receive as b (which we may think of as either the competitive wage offered in a non-unionised workplace or a form of unemployment insurance payment), the utility derived from such a non-negotiated outcome can be represented as $u(b)$. In the same way, the utility derived from the negotiated wage w can be represented as $u(w)$. In both instances, $u(\cdot)$ represents the underlying utility function of the union, which in itself is unimportant but it may be convenient at this juncture to think of the union's utility function as representing the preferences of a representative member. Thus, the expected utility of the union will be determined by the likelihood with which the representative member receives either the non-negotiated wage of b or the negotiated wage of w. If t denotes the total workforce and n denotes the number of union members

Risk averse

This situation occurs when there is a preference for work which involves fewer risks, whether in terms of accidents, employment volatility or other factors. **Risk-loving** behaviour implies that more risks are preferred, while **risk neutral** implies that the taking on of risk leaves an individual unaffected *ceteris paribus*.

who receive the negotiated wage w, the probability that a representative member will receive the union wage is therefore n/t. Similarly, the probability that they will receive the outside wage of b is $(1 - n/t)$. Thus, the expected net gain of the union is given by:

$$\left[\frac{n}{t}u(w)+\left(1-\frac{n}{t}\right)u(b)\right]-u(b) \tag{7.3a}$$

$$\frac{n}{t}\left[u(w)-u(b)\right] \tag{7.3b}$$

The term in square parentheses of equation (7.3a) describes the expected utility of the representative member/union and this is viewed with reference to the fall-back position where a lower wage of b can always be earned outside of the union. The net utility difference between these two positions is therefore the gain to the union from negotiations and can be simplified as shown in equation (7.3b).

Thus, the generalised Nash bargaining solution (B) can be represented as:

$$\max B = \left(\frac{n}{t}\left[u(w)-u(b)\right]\right)^{\beta} (pq(n)-wn)^{(1-\beta)} \tag{7.4}$$

where the first term in parentheses of equation (7.4) represents the previously derived bargaining gains for the union, the second term the bargaining gains for the firm, and β the bargaining strength of the union. The solution to this maximisation problem is characterised by the following two equations, which will represent the first-order conditions from the maximisation of equation (7.4) with respect to employment and wages respectively:

$$w = pq'(n)+\frac{u(w)-u(b)}{u'(w)} \tag{7.5a}$$

$$w = \frac{\beta pq(n)}{n}+(1-\beta)pq'(n) \tag{7.5b}$$

Equation (7.5a) will represent the contract curve already identified in Figure 7.5 and the unique outcome identified along this contract curve will be determined with reference to equation (7.5b), which we will refer to as the surplus sharing curve (SSC). Given that $pq(n)$ denotes the value of output produced, $pq(n)/n$ will describe the average value of output produced by each worker employed, i.e., the average revenue product of labour. Similarly, $pq'(n)$, the first derivative of $pq(n)$, will represent the marginal revenue product of labour. Thus, we may interpret the surplus sharing curve as the weighted average of the average revenue product of labour and the marginal revenue product of labour curves, where the weighting is given by the relative bargaining strength of the union (β) and the firm ($1 - \beta$). On the assumption that the labour demand curve (and hence the marginal revenue product of labour curve) is downward sloping, this will also imply that not only is the average revenue product of labour curve downward sloping but so too will the surplus sharing curve be negatively sloped in wage–employment space. This is illustrated in Figure 7.6.

When the union has no bargaining power (i.e. $\beta = 0$), the surplus sharing curve collapses to the marginal revenue product of labour curve. Note that, under this

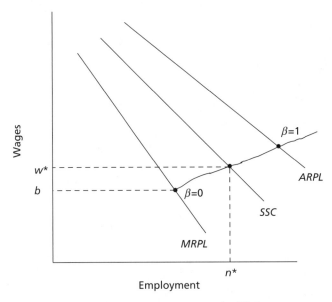

Figure 7.6 Bargaining power and efficient outcomes along the contract curve.

scenario, the first term in equation (7.5b) will equal zero. With no power to exert, the union is unable to raise member wages above those found in the non-union sector (b) and this level of wages will define the outcome on the contract curve. If, in contrast, the firm has no bargaining power (i.e. $\beta = 1$), then the second term in equation (7.5b) will equal zero and the surplus sharing curve will coincide with the average revenue product of labour curve. Anywhere between these two extremes, the surplus sharing curve will lie between the average and marginal revenue product curves and, in doing so, will intersect with the contract curve. Equations (7.5a) and (7.5b) tell us that this will describe the generalised Nash bargaining outcome and so the unique wage–employment combination identified on the locus of Pareto efficient points that is the contract curve will be w^*, n^* as indicated in Figure 7.6.

7.2.5 The competitive status seniority model

This being the case, why do employers and trade unions leave unexploited gains from trade? One possible explanation is that union indifference curves are flat, in which case efficient contracts could well lie on the labour demand curve. Let us assume that the union represents the median worker, that employment and lay-offs are determined strictly by seniority and that the median worker's utility, given employment, is a function only of his or her wage rate. Then the union's indifference curve, insofar as it represents the median worker, would become horizontal at levels of employment beyond that level that ensured the employment of the median worker. Such a situation is shown in Figure 7.7 by the representative indifference curves $Um0$, $Um1$ and $Um2$, which slope downwards up until employment level nm, the employment level at which the median worker is employed. Beyond nm, the median worker is unwilling to sacrifice wages for increased employment opportunities because he is already employed.

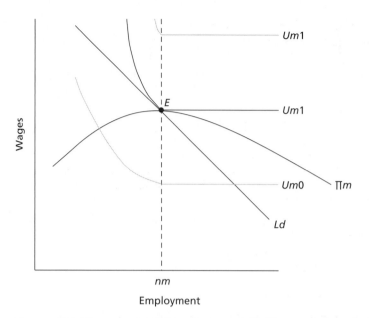

Figure 7.7 The competitive status seniority model and efficient outcomes on the labour demand curve.

Under such a scenario, the equilibrium outcome would occur at point E on the labour demand curve (Ld), where the union (median worker) is maximising utility on indifference curve $Um1$ subject to the constraint that profits of the employer are maximised on iso-profit line πm. Note, though, that at points such as E in Figure 7.7 the union's indifference curves are tangential to the employer's iso-profit lines. Hence there is no scope to make a Pareto improvement, which would only happen if indifference curve and iso-profit line intersected. All outcomes along the labour demand curve are therefore (Pareto) efficient.

The competitive status seniority model, as it has been called, has an uncomfortable implication as Lindblom (1949) and Turnbull (1988) have pointed out. Following the former, assume that wage policy is determined by majority vote, that every member votes exclusively for his or her own financial interest, that the position of the labour demand curve is known and that the order in which workers will be laid off, if circumstances require, is known. Then, the majority of members would always vote for that level of wages at which just less than half the members were unemployed. Over time, the union membership would dwindle and Turnbull notes that, under such circumstances, the firm would never be able to increase employment and the union would never be able to expand its membership. He points out, however, that, in practice, less than 20 per cent of members vote at branch meetings, and union leaderships may influence the membership. Further, "the seniority model not only ignores the behavioural consequences of altruism, but also involves an explicit form of egoism which is contrary to the avowed union objectives of egalitarianism, collectivism and solidarity".[14]

Additionally, we may also want to consider the extent to which last-in first-out is the norm in redundancy cases. Turnbull (1988) suggests that, even in the US, rigid seniority practices are not that common. In Britain, a major feature of redundancies in the last forty years or so has been the prevalence of voluntary severance schemes and, by definition, under such schemes the order of dismissals cannot be predicted. Hence, it is unlikely that flat indifference curves characterise the typical union.

7.2.6 Concluding comments

In conclusion, it must be stated that trade unions are complex organisations. Their behaviour will be conditioned both by the nature of the membership, whether homogeneous or heterogeneous, and the nature of the industrial environment in which they operate. Under conditions of bilateral monopoly, both wages and employment may be indeterminate. But the **Marshallian rules** will define the relative bargaining power of the two parties. Thus, the ideal conditions for a trade union to raise wages are:

- inelastic product demand, so that any wage increase raises unemployment by only a small amount;
- a low elasticity of substitution between capital and labour, so that it is difficult to substitute capital for workers;
- an inelastic supply of other factors of production, so that, as other factors are substituted for labour, their prices are forced up;
- labour cost is only a small proportion of total cost, so that the consequences of any wage increase on product price is limited.

Unions may attempt to create such favourable conditions in a number of ways. First, unions may attempt to reduce competition in the product market by unionising the whole industry. Second, governments may be persuaded to introduce import controls to reduce competition from abroad. Third, public ownership may be advocated, as this reduces competition in the product market. Fourth, by organising the entire industry occupational group, it may be possible to reduce the elasticity of substitution by eliminating non-union labour or imposing manning agreements that stipulate a fixed number of workers per machine. Finally, it may be possible to reduce the supply of substitute factors through occupational licensing. Thus, for example, the medical profession defines what kind of work nurses may undertake and the legal profession also defines what conveyancers may or may not do.

7.3 The union wage effect

If trade unions raise wages, by how much do they do so? This is the key question, but there is conflicting evidence in answering it, where empirical estimates of the size of the union wage effect will be influenced by data sets used, the time period analysed, the level of disaggregation and the methodology adopted.[15] Conceptually, there are at least five concepts relating to the effects of unions on wages:

i the absolute real wage effect considers the extent to which the wages of union members differ from those that would have existed in the absence of the trade union(s).[16] Ideally, this requires data on change of union status and is rarely used;

ii the effect of unions on the wage rates of union workers relative to non-union workers can be derived by comparing the earnings of two or more groups of

Marshallian rules

The necessary conditions for a stable equilibrium in a market.

workers who differ in the degree of unionisation. In considering this, we must allow for threat effects, since some employers may pay higher wages to keep out trade unions, and spillover effects, since some non-unionists may be paid the union wage rate as more workers are covered by collective agreements than are members of trade unions. Concentrating on the wage differentials of union members over non-union workers will not credit unions for either of these effects;[17]

iii as Freeman (1982) has observed, trade unions alter the distribution of wages and so affect income dispersion. First, by raising the wages of organised workers relative to others, unions will increase inequality when they organise higher-paid workers and reduce it when they organise the lower paid. In addition, simply by creating differentials between otherwise comparable workers, they increase inequality. However, by adopting common rule policies, they reduce inequality or wage dispersion in the unionised sector relative to the non-unionised sector;

iv the effect of unions on labour's share in national income will depend on the value of the elasticity of substitution between labour and capital (σ). If the effect of unions is to raise wages generally, labour's share will rise provided $\sigma < 1$ and fall if $\sigma > 1$. But to achieve a substantial effect on functional shares it is necessary that σ is substantially different from 1 and the effect of unions on wage rates is also substantial;

v the union effect on **efficiency wages** must be considered if we are to explain how unionised firms manage to stay in business. Freeman and Medoff (1984) argue that, while unions raise wages, there are also offsetting productivity effects. Unions may reduce **X-inefficiency** by lowering the quit rate, improving worker morale and keeping management on its toes. However, further consideration of these aspects is postponed until section 7.4.

Efficiency wages

A wage that is paid in excess of the market clearing wage in order to increase the efficiency or productivity of workers, or to elicit effort, or to reduce the likelihood of worker turnover.

X-inefficiency

This describes the situation in which management fails to minimise the costs of production and/or maximise output from a given set of inputs due to the absence of competitive pressures.

It is important to recognise that the non-union wage is not the same as the wage that would prevail in the absence of unions: the union/non-union wage differential will consist of both a positive wage premium that unions are able to exact from employers and any negative, depressive effects on the non-union wage that results. Rees (1963) showed that, under certain assumptions, the loss of real output caused by union wage effects was approximately half the product of the wage and employment effects.

The situation considered by Rees is described in Figure 7.8. On the assumption that there is a perfectly inelastic supply of labour curve and that homogeneous workers are employed in two sectors, U and N, the aggregate demand for labour across both sectors is described by the conventional downward-sloping curve Ldt. This aggregate curve is derived from the horizontal summation of the labour demand curves in sectors U and N, labelled Ldu and Ldn respectively. In the absence of unionisation, the competitive outcome is established at the intersection of the aggregate labour demand curve and the labour supply curve (Ls). This implies that a wage rate of wc will be paid to nu workers in sector U and to nn workers in sector N. Aggregate employment at this wage rate is then equal to $nu + nn$.

Now assume that sector U becomes unionised and through collective bargaining is able to raise the wages of its workers from wc to wu. This increase in the wage will lead to a contraction in the number of workers employed in this sector from nu

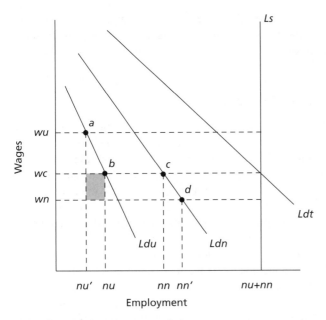

Figure 7.8 The Rees model.

to *nu'*. If these displaced workers transfer to the non-unionised sector *N*, employment will increase here up to *nn'*. The effect that these additional workers have upon wages in sector *N*, which are still competitively determined, is to bid them down from *wc* to *wn*.

Given that the competitive labour demand curve reflects the marginal productivity of workers, the area *abnunu'* under the labour demand curve for sector *U* will represent the value of output lost from employing fewer workers in this sector. In contrast, the additional workers employed in sector *N* will add *cdnn'nn* to economy output. However, the displacement of workers from sector *U* to sector *N* will mean that workers are now being employed in sector *N* where their productivity is reduced, i.e. the output that they would have produced in sector *U* is greater than the output that they produce in sector *N*. As a result, the unionisation of sector *U* will have led to a reduction in the total output of the economy equal to the net difference between areas *cdnn'nn* and *abnunu'* as approximated by the shaded rectangle in Figure 7.8. Thus, the union wage gain leads to a worse allocation of labour from the point of view of the economy, since a transfer of labour back to the union sector would increase total output. Were demand for labour to be inelastic in the union sector, perhaps because of union policies, and elastic in the non-union sector, workers in both sectors would gain in the sense that the wage bill would be higher in both sectors. In the converse case, workers would be worse off in this sense in both sectors.

On the assumption that the two labour demand curves are parallel, this area will equal:

$$\text{Loss} = 0.5(wn - wu)(nu - nn) \qquad (7.6)$$

and it was on the basis of this that Rees (1963) estimated the size of the welfare loss attributed to union wage effects in the US at a relatively small 0.14 per cent of GNP in 1957.[18] However, this makes no allowance for any unemployment effects of unions arising from wage rigidities or queuing by workers for union jobs. It is also conducted in a static framework which makes no allowance for union effects on productivity and profitability, and growth.

7.3.1 Measuring the union mark-up

The question of what should be measured in determining the union wage effect is not straightforward. Some studies focus on union membership and others on collective-bargaining coverage. The fact that there can be a substantial number of non-union members who are covered by a collective agreement means that the two measures may imply substantial differences in the size of the covered and uncovered areas of the labour market. In practice, the most appropriate comparison to make would be between union members who are covered by a collective agreement and non-union employees not subject to a union-negotiated collective agreement, but few data-sets contain sufficient information to enable these two groups to be empirically identified. It should also be noted that bargaining level matters. Local/national and establishment/firm level collective agreements (as well as the presence or otherwise of the closed shop or 100 per cent union organisation) can produce very different estimates of the size of the mark-up. In addition, there is the question of whether the analysis should examine wage rates net of or inclusive of overtime or other bonus payments. One study (Thomson *et al.* 1977) suggests that the whole of the union wage effect is confined to overtime premia, shift premia and bonus-related payments. There is also the issue of fringe benefits, but few data-sets contain information on these.

The union mark-up is traditionally measured by comparing the earnings of an average union member with those of an average non-union member. Thus, for individual i who is either a union member (denoted by the suffix u) or a non-member (denoted by the suffix n), wages may be represented as follows:

$$\ln W_{ui} = \beta_u X_{ui} + \varepsilon_{ui} \tag{7.7a}$$

$$\ln W_{ni} = \beta_n X_{ni} + \varepsilon_{ni} \tag{7.7b}$$

where W are wages, X is a column vector of regressors known to influence earnings and β is a conformable vector of coefficients describing the wage returns to the regressors X. Typically, this empirical estimation is conducted using a technique such as ordinary least squares (OLS). The error terms ε_{ui} and ε_{ni} are assumed to be normally distributed with zero means, constant variances and are serially uncorrelated.

The difference between mean values of $\ln W_u$ and $\ln W_n$ can be decomposed into differences in coefficients and differences in the average level of personal characteristics (contained within the vector X) of union and non-union members and from this a measure of the union wage mark-up can be identified as follows:

$$\ln \bar{W}_u - \ln \bar{W}_n = (\hat{\beta}_u - \hat{\beta}_n)\bar{X}_n + \hat{\beta}_u(\bar{X}_u - \bar{X}_n) \tag{7.8}$$

where the hats now signify that regression estimates are being used. From the formulation depicted in equation (7.8), the union mark-up is given by the second term on the right-hand side, namely $\hat{\beta}_u(\bar{X}_u - \bar{X}_n)$.[19] However, the formulation in equation (7.8) is not unique and gives rise to the familiar index number problem according to whether estimates are based on the mean characteristics of union or non-union workers (i.e. the loss of earnings which results from not being a union member or the gains to union members from being in the union).[20]

A number of econometric problems arise in this approach. First, union status is treated as exogenous and this leads to the possibility of **simultaneity bias**. That is, there is every reason to believe that union membership will at least be partly determined by the size of the union mark-up as workers will be attracted to joining a union if it can increase their wages relative to what they could get if they did not join. And naturally, as the wage mark-up increases, then so too does the incentive to join a union. As a result of this lack of independence between union membership and the union wage mark-up, OLS estimates of the wage mark-up will be inconsistent insofar as the disturbance (error) terms in the wage equations will be correlated with the decision to join a union.

Second, there may be immeasurable quality differences between union members and non-unionists arising from selective hiring or optimal job matching and this will lead to problems akin to **omitted variable bias**. For example, for any set of given (and observable characteristics) union workers may be more productive than their non-union counterparts. This may arise because of the queue of workers that exists to join the unionised workforce (who after all receive a premium on their earnings) and the desire by the firm to hire productive workers. If this supposition is true, there will subsequently be a positive correlation between union status and productivity. However, while factors such as an individual's level of education are easily observable, individual productivity is not and would typically be unaccounted for in empirical estimation of the union wage mark-up. As more productive workers would be expected to receive a higher wage anyway, estimates of the union mark-up may therefore be more to do with the effect of workforce composition rather than unionisation itself.

Third, the individual-level estimating equations fail to account for the extent of unionisation or bargaining coverage within industries. This is problematic as those industries with higher union density are more likely to be able to extract additional benefits for their members and those whose interests they represent due to a stronger bargaining position. Without such information on density patterns within jobs, there again exists the possibility of omitted variable bias in estimated mark-ups. Finally, it should also be noted that early studies of the union wage mark-up did not have information on the union status of individuals, but merely averages of wages and status by industry and occupation. This incomplete data method may give rise to the problem of **aggregation bias**, and Mulvey and Abowd (1980) suggest that this problem will bias estimates by as much as 50 per cent.

Returning to the simultaneity issue, following Lee (1978) and Duncan and Leigh (1985), the conventional way to deal with this problem is to estimate a three-equation system with a separate (**probit**) model to determine union status and separate wage equations for union and non-union members. Let us assume that union status is determined by the extent to which the union mark-up exceeds individual i's **reservation wage**, Wr_i, so that individual i is assumed to join the union if the following inequality holds:

$$\frac{W_{ui} - W_{ni}}{W_{ni}} > Wr_i \tag{7.9}$$

Simultaneity bias

A statistical bias that arises when one or more of the explanatory variables is jointly determined with the dependent variable.

Omitted variable bias

A statistical bias that occurs due to the omission of one or more important causal factors.

Aggregation bias

A statistical bias that results from the loss of detail that occurs when groups are aggregated together.

Probit

A form of regression model where the dependent variable can take only one of two values.

Reservation wage

The lowest wage that is acceptable to an individual given his or her circumstances and the nature of the job.

where the mark-up represented on the left-hand side of equation (7.9) will be approximated by $\ln \bar{W}_{ui} - \ln \bar{W}_{ni}$.[21] Assuming that Wr_i is a function of a vector of personal characteristics (X_i) and the costs of becoming a union member (C_i), the reservation wage can be written as:

$$Wr_i = a_1 X_i + a_2 C_i + \varepsilon_{1i} \qquad (7.10)$$

While direct information on C_i is generally unavailable, it can be assumed that costs are a function of personal characteristics (such as employment stability) and industry characteristics (such as industrial concentration and firm or establishment size). Hence, individual costs may be described as:

$$C_i = \beta_1 + \beta_2 X_i + \beta_3 Z_i + \varepsilon_{2i} \qquad (7.11)$$

where Z_i represents a vector of industry characteristics and both ε_1 and ε_2 are normally distributed idiosyncratic error terms with zero mean and constant variance reflecting unobserved random factors. Letting US_i refer to union status, such that it will take the value of 1 if individual i is a union member and zero otherwise, the following probit model can be specified:

$$US_i = \gamma_1 + \gamma_2 (\ln Wu_i - \ln Wn_i) + \gamma_3 X_i + \lambda_4 Z_i + \varepsilon_i \qquad (7.12)$$

Equation (7.12) will describe an individual's desire to join a union and this will be on the condition that the estimated right-hand side of the equation is greater than zero.[22] The model to be estimated will therefore involve the estimation of three equations simultaneously: equations (7.7a) and (7.7b) describing wages in the two sectors; and equation (7.12) describing sectoral attachment.

7.3.2 Estimates of the union mark-up

In examining the empirical work on the union mark-up, it is useful to distinguish four groups of studies: times series; aggregate cross-section: establishment-level cross-section; and individual-level cross section. Some of the earliest empirical work conducted on union/non-union earnings mark-ups used aggregate industry data, with estimated mark-ups differing wildly. More recently, empirical work has used micro-data to investigate the union issue, both at an establishment level and at an individual level. Estimates obtained from such sources have typically been smaller than those derived from aggregate sources, but have shown a wide diversity across individuals and sectors. General findings have been that wage mark-ups are greater for manual workers than for non-manual, and that union wage gaps are larger for women than they are for men.

Whereas some investigators have examined union *membership* wage differentials, others have used *coverage* (or an appropriate proxy) as their defining union condition. In countries such as the UK, for example, individual wages are more typically determined by a collective-bargaining agreement, regardless of whether or not a worker is a member of the negotiating union, and as such one might expect union coverage to be the important factor in determining union wage differentials. Where both types of information are available in a data-set, though, it is found that covered members get paid more than covered non-members, a feature reconcilable with union density patterns. For example, unions in firms with a high percentage of non-members may find it more difficult to engage in effective strike action because non-members are more likely to cross picket lines or ignore calls for strike action. Thus, in establishments with high density levels (or indeed closed shop situations), above-average mark-ups are likely to exist, which will be picked up as membership effects in individual-level studies that compare across establishments.

7.3.2.1 Time-series estimates

Time-series studies for the US collected together by Lewis (1986) reveal a mean mark-up over the period 1967–79 of 15 per cent. The wage gap increased during the 1970s, but fell at the end of the decade. Other studies suggest that the wage gap has been relatively stable since that period. For the UK, the only available series is that of Layard *et al.* (1978), since extended by Beenstock and Whitbread (1988) up to 1983. The mark-up for each year is derived from a cross-section regression over approximately 100 manufacturing industry groups for male manual workers whose earnings are explained by skill, age, location and coverage. The coefficient on coverage provides the union mark-up measure. This is ad hoc and produces mark-up estimates that are much higher than those derived from cross-section analysis – over 40 per cent by the 1980s. Their usefulness lies in observing *changes* over time. The differential appears to increase sharply when unemployment rises appreciably, supporting the view that unions are most effective in protecting workers from adversity. Beenstock and Whitbread find that the size of the mark-up is explained by the real benefit rate, the unemployment rate, union density and the party in government. We should, however, treat these time series studies with a degree of caution.

7.3.2.2 Aggregate cross-section estimates

The first attempt to measure the union wage mark-up for Britain using aggregate cross-section data was by Pencavel (1974), whose estimates refer to 1964. Using union membership data, he found that union members in industries that did not engage in a significant amount of plant bargaining did not enjoy any wage advantage over non-unionists. However, where plant bargaining was significant, the advantage was 14 per cent. Later studies using coverage data (e.g. Mulvey 1976; Mulvey and Foster 1976), confirmed the importance of local bargaining in raising the pay of union members over otherwise identical workers. Women, however, do appear to obtain a positive mark-up from national bargaining (Nickell 1977).[23]

7.3.2.3 Establishment-level cross-section estimates

Use of establishment-level cross-section data in Britain was assisted by the arrival of the Workplace Industrial Relations Survey (WIRS) of 2000 establishments in manufacturing and services, which has been conducted periodically since 1980 and enables a much more detailed examination of the wage mark-up to be made, including the effects of the closed shop. Blanchflower and Oswald (1988) suggest that, while the average mark-up using these data is 10 per cent, wages are raised principally by the closed shop and more precisely the pre-entry closed shop. This is confirmed by Stewart (1987), who finds it to be of prime importance for skilled and semi-skilled manual workers.[24] Blanchflower (1986) found that, while overall the mark-up was small, it was much larger in the public sector than in the private sector.

7.3.2.4 Individual-level cross-section estimates

An increasing number of studies have focused on individual-level cross-section data. Thus, Stewart (1983) studied a sample of male manual manufacturing workers in Britain and obtained a mark-up of 7.7 per cent. This differential varied significantly with personal characteristics (being higher for the more skilled) and particularly across regions (Wales having an estimated mark-up of 20 per cent). Across industries, the variation ranged from minus 5 per cent in Coal and Petroleum Products to 18 per cent in Shipbuilding. Shah (1984) analysed the 1968/69 Living Standards Survey of 1,000 manual males and obtained a mark-up of 10 per cent after allowance for job characteristics variables such as job severity, job security and fringe benefits, which reduced the mark-up by one-third and suggests that part of the union wage premium may be a compensating differential. Green (1988) utilised data from the 1983 General Household Survey (GHS) and found a mark-up of 12 per cent for manual workers and 4 per cent for non-manual workers (including women). The overall differential was only 5.2 per cent and varied inversely with size of establishment. However, the 1983 GHS included questions on both union coverage and union membership, thus allowing one to estimate the pure mark-up (i.e. covered members over non-covered non-members) and the size of any spillover effect. Making this distinction, Blackaby et al. (1991) find for manual males that the pure mark-up is 22 per cent and the spillover effect 10 per cent.

Similarly, O'Leary et al. (2004), using data from the UK Labour Force Survey (LFS), also draw a distinction between the wage effects of union coverage and union membership. Stratifying the analysis by gender and manual/non-manual status, estimated mark-ups are greater for manual workers than they are for non-manual workers, and are larger for female non-manuals than they are for male non-manuals. By extending the analysis away from the mean of the earnings distribution as is conventional to cover the whole of the earnings distribution, union benefits are seen to be greatest for male and female manual employees on the very lowest of wage scales and such benefits decline as we move to higher points of the earnings distribution. Even here, though, there are still substantial mark-ups to be found for manual workers. For male manual employees, the median total mark-up (encompassing both membership and coverage effects) is 9.3 per cent, although this ranges from a high of nearly 14 per cent to a low of just over 7 per cent over the entire hourly earnings distribution. The comparable median figure for manual females is 8.7 per cent. It is also found that membership imparts greater rewards for all non-manual workers than does coverage alone with the exception of some of the highest-earnings males, and this influence decreases (increases) for males (females) as hourly earnings increase. Meanwhile, both membership and coverage have a beneficial effect upon manual wages.

None of the above studies deals with problems of simultaneity and **sample selection bias** though. However, two papers using the 1986 Social and Economic Life Initiative (SCELI) data-set attempt to deal with some of these issues. First, Murphy et al. (1992) use a three-equation model, taking into account sample selectivity and find a wage mark-up of 6.9 per cent for manual men and 9.0 per cent for non-manual men, that is a lower mark-up for the latter, which contrasts with other studies. Second, Main and Reilly (1992) allow for the simultaneous determination of union and employment status where the latter is defined in terms of the full-time–part-time employment split for women and find a mark-up of 14.6 per cent for full-time women and 15.3 per cent for part-time women. Together, these results suggest

Sample selection bias

A statistical bias that occurs due to the non-random sampling of the population.

that the overall impact of unions is to partially close the gender wage differential.[25]

It should be noted that few investigators would doubt that union status is **endogenously determined** (i.e. that the decision to join a union is related to the earnings on offer in the unionised sector) and that, if this is uncorrected, it could lead to problems akin to an omitted variable bias. Indeed, this issue has received extensive treatment in the empirical US literature in particular, using either simultaneous equation estimation, **Heckman-type two-step estimation** procedures, **instrumental variable** methods, or **panel estimation**. However, major disagreement has surfaced about what has been learned from these attempts to deal with the endogeneity issue. In particular, Lewis (1986) is critical of attempts to deal with this problem and concludes, in a review of 28 simultaneous equation studies in the US, that "the difference between OLS wage gap estimates and their matching and supposedly unbiased SE [simultaneous equation] counterparts is so large that not even the sign of the omitted-variable or selectivity bias in the OLS figures is clear". By way of contrast, Robinson (1989) supports a more optimistic conclusion. His own review of large individual-level data-sets provides substantial evidence of a consistent rise in the union mark-up relative to OLS when the endogeneity of union status is addressed by instrumental variable or Heckman-type methods.

With regards to international comparisons, Blanchflower and Bryson (2003) provide a useful overview using data from the International Social Survey Programme (ISSP) over the period 1994–9. For both the US and the UK, unions are found to be able to raise wages substantially above the equivalent wage for non-unionists in spite of declining union representation in these countries. On average, the UK mark-up is estimated at 10 per cent, while that for the US is higher at 18 per cent. In a number of other countries (see Case Study 7.3), unions are also able to raise wages significantly, whereas in countries where union wage settlements often

Case Study 7.3

International estimates of the union wage mark-up

	Union coefficient		Union coefficient
Australia	0.118	Italy	−0.003
Austria	0.150	Japan	0.258
Brazil	0.337	Netherlands	−0.006
Canada	0.083	New Zealand	0.099
Chile	0.159	Norway	0.073
Cyprus	0.137	Portugal	0.179
Denmark	0.159	Spain	0.069
France	0.029	Sweden	−0.002
Germany	0.037		

Source: adapted from Blanchflower and Bryson (2003), Table 1.
Notes: Figures in bold signify statistically significant estimates at the 5% level or better; figures refer to log point estimates and not percentage wage effects.

Endogenously determined

This situation occurs when a regressor variable is not independent of the dependent variable in a regression model.

Heckman correction

A number of related statistical techniques (developed by James Heckman and including the **Heckman two-step**), which allow for the correction of sample selection bias.

Instrumental variable

An estimation technique that addresses the problem of endogenously determined regressors by using a non-endogenous proxy as an alternative regressor that is correlated with the known endogenous variable.

Panel estimation

An estimation technique that makes uses of repeated observations of the same individual and, in doing so, controls for unobservable differences between individuals.

spill over into the non-union sector (such as France, Germany, Italy, the Netherlands and Sweden), no significant union mark-up is found.

7.3.3 Union wage effects and the dispersion of earnings

Given the influence that trade unions exert over earnings, it is natural to assume that union activity will also affect the distribution, and hence dispersion, of earnings for members and non-members alike. However, it is not obvious a priori in which direction this will operate. Evidence for both the US and Britain suggests that trade unions reduce wage dispersion. In the former, Freeman (1980, 1982) and Hirsch (1982) find that US unions reduce wage dispersion. Meanwhile, in an examination of the link between the decline in unionisation and *trends* in male and female wage inequality in the US over the course of the 1970s through to the 1990s, Card (2001) highlights an important distinction between gender and sector of employment. Noting the rising level of wage inequality over this period, Card concludes that only around 15–20 per cent of the rise in overall male wage inequality can be explained by the decline in union membership among men. Given that there was a relatively stable fraction of female workers belonging to a union over the two decades under examination, unionisation shifts explain virtually none of the rise in overall wage inequality among female workers. In contrast, rising rates of unionisation were a significant force in limiting rising wage inequality in the public sector for both men and women. For men, 50–80 per cent of the slower growth in wage inequality in the public sector relative to the private sector was attributed to the differing trends in union membership between the sectors. For women, differences in unionisation explained 20–30 per cent of the difference in the growth of wage inequality between sectors.

For Britain, Blackaby *et al.* (1991) find that there is a much greater difference in the variance of earnings when covered unionists are compared with uncovered non-unionists, suggesting that unions exert a powerful influence on wage dispersion. Likewise, Murphy *et al.* (1992) find that unions have a significant effect in reducing the variance in earnings mainly because of differences in the variability of characteristics. Finally, Gosling and Machin (1995), using the 1990 WIRS, find that unions affect both across establishment and within establishment earnings dispersion and that declining unionisation has contributed to the rise in earnings inequality observed in the 1980s.

Focusing on the protection of low-paid workers, Dell'Aringa and Lucifora (1994) find a consistently similar result in the context of the Italian labour market. Using both industry- and establishment-level data, the conclusion drawn is that trade unions have shaped Italian pay policy through their pursuance of egalitarian objectives that have raised low wages and in doing so have been responsible for reducing wage differentials both among skill categories and across establishments.

7.4 Trade unions and efficiency

If unions raise wages, the issue arises of how unionised employers remain in business. Unions may, in fact, affect performance in a number of ways including not only productivity but also profitability, growth and employment.

7.4.1 Unions and productivity

The analysis of the effect of unions on productivity has been an area of contention.[26] The traditional view has been that unions lower productivity by reducing the freedom of management to manage in ways that will increase performance, by instituting and maintaining restrictive practices and make-work activities and by disrupting production through strikes and other forms of industrial action. In contrast, the collective-voice approach, adopted notably by the proponents of the Harvard School, implies that unions raise productivity by reducing labour turnover, raising employee morale, negotiating more efficient dispute-resolution mechanisms and by shocking management into greater efficiency.

An example of the latter approach is that of Brown and Medoff (1978) who, using 1972 cross-State establishment data for 20 two-digit US manufacturing industries, estimate the effect of trade unions on worker productivity. They begin with a modified **Cobb–Douglas production function** as follows:

$$Y = AK^{\alpha}(L_n + CL_u)^{1-\alpha} \tag{7.8}$$

where Y represents output, K is capital, L_n is non-union labour, L_u is union labour, α is the elasticity of output with respect to capital, A is the constant of proportionality and C reflects differences in productivity between the union and non-union sectors. As it is a Cobb–Douglas production function, C will denote the ratio of the marginal products of labour in the two sectors.

Brown and Medoff (1978) estimate equations for logarithmic value added/labour with labour unadjusted and adjusted for quality. In the former case, the coefficient on the fraction unionised variable is 0.24, implying that unionised establishments are 24 per cent more productive than non-unionised ones. When quality is controlled for, a difference of 22 per cent still remains. The unionised plants have substantively lower quit rates than the rest, but, when the quit rate was introduced as an independent variable, this only reduced the importance of the fraction unionised variable by about one-fifth. In fact, the union productivity effect and the union wage effect indicated by this study are of the same order of magnitude, which explains how unionised plants remain in business despite paying their workers more.

However, there is a flaw in this approach, as a number of economists have pointed out. If unions raise wages, then reduced employment must raise productivity as long as the demand curve for labour, reflecting the marginal revenue product of labour, is downward sloping. As Reynolds (1986) notes, "the union/non-union productivity differential is simply a classic distortion in the allocation of scarce labour and capital induced by monopoly prices, not something to applaud". He goes on to suggest that a more sensible question is whether unionisation fosters or inhibits productivity growth and technical change. The evidence is that, at least for the US, productivity growth is slower in industries where the proportion of union coverage is greater (see, for instance, Hirsch and Link 1984).

One way round the above problem is to measure output using a physical rather than value of output measure. Thus, Clark (1980) utilises a Cobb–Douglas production function approach along these lines to examine establishment data for the US cement industry. In the regression equations, there is little evidence of a significant negative impact of unions on productivity and the results in a sample restricted to new plants suggest the effect may be positive. Further, data on six establishments

Cobb–Douglas production function

A production function in which there are constant returns to scale, so that output increases in proportion to the increase in inputs.

that changed union status over the period 1953–76 support the conclusion that unionisation can lead to productivity gains in the order of 8–10 per cent. An alternative approach is to control for industry market structure to eliminate the monopoly union effect. Thus, Clark (1984) uses micro-data on over 900 US product line businesses and includes controls both for firm characteristics and market structure. In contrast to Brown and Medoff, he finds a significant negative effect of unions on productivity, though quantitatively small. Finally, Allen (1987) uses a translog cost function approach (which is just a generalisation of the Cobb–Douglas function) to analyse union and non-union building contracts in the commercial office sector, elementary and secondary schools, and hospitals and nursing homes. The results do not support a clear-cut cost (or efficiency) advantage in either the union or non-union sector. Thus, while union contractors had a cost advantage in large commercial office buildings, non-union contractors in school and hospital construction had lower costs at all output levels.

In the UK, attention has focused on whether or not unionised companies had faster or slower productivity growth than non-union ones and whether this had been influenced by the bargaining power of the unions, as reflected through changes in employment legislation and membership decline. In fact, there was a rapid increase in labour productivity in manufacturing during the 1980s. Nickell *et al.* (1992) find that unionised companies had slower productivity growth than did non-union ones from 1957 to 1978, but faster growth from 1979 to 1984. A similar conclusion, that unions appeared to close the productivity gap with the non-union sector in the 1980s, is arrived at by Bryson *et al.* (2005). Examining the later period 1984–9, Gregg *et al.* (1993) find evidence for a second productivity growth surge, with the improvement being more marked where unions were derecognised and where there was an increase in foreign competition. This is consistent with the reassertion of management's right to manage as union power has weakened. Also in line with this, Haskel (1991) finds that industries in which concentration declined had the highest productivity growth over the 1980s and concludes that an increasingly competitive product market had been at least part of the explanation for the increase in productivity growth over this period.

7.4.2 Unions and profitability

There is substantial evidence in both the US and Britain that trade unions reduce profitability.[27] Clark (1984), for example, finds in the former case that union businesses have a 12 per cent lower rate of return on capital and that, once additional controls for market structure and industry labour markets are added, the estimated effect rises to 19 per cent relative to the sample mean. Thus, owners of capital have rational grounds on which to oppose unionisation. The findings for Britain are equally robust. Machin and Stewart (1990), using 1980 and 1984 WIRS data, find that the presence of unions limits financial performance to a significant degree and there is an important interaction between market structure and union profit effects. Cable and Machin (1991) examined a sample of 52 engineering firms over the period 1978–82 and found that, when they normalised for the union wage effect, the negative union profitability effect vanished, which supports a pure redistributive hypothesis rather than an "efficiency" interpretation. Machin (1991), using a larger sample of US manufacturing firms pooled over 1984 and 1985, finds that, after controlling for both firm- and industry-specific effects, union recognition reduced the rate of return on sales by 24.5 per cent relative to the sample mean. When union recognition was interacted with market share, it appeared that operating in a firm with a higher market share was a prerequisite for unions being able to capture a significant share of economic rent.[28] Further, Machin *et al.* (1993) find that financial performance was inferior in plants where multiple unions were present and where they bargained separately.[29] In single-union plants or multiple-union plants with joint bargaining, the financial outcome was much the same as in non-union plants.

However, two later studies point to a change in the relationship between union presence and profitability. First, Machin and Stewart (1996), using 1984 and 1990 WIRS data, find that, in 1990, establishments with union recognition were 6 per cent less likely to report above-average financial performance and 2.5 per cent more likely to report below-average performance. The corresponding figures for 1984 were 12.6 per cent and 4.6 per cent respectively – substantially higher. However, in establishments with closed shop arrangements or where management recommended union membership, the 1990 figures were 12.6 per cent and 5.9 per cent respectively – a similar figure to 1984 and there was no effect in the remaining union establishments. Second, Menezes-Filho (1997), using an employer survey covering the same period of 1984–90, finds that a union profitability differential of minus 3 per cent in 1984 had been reversed to a differential of plus 15 per cent in 1990. However, an alternative estimation strategy by Menezes-Filho of taking first differences finds that firms that derecognised unions had faster productivity increases over the period than other firms. Further, a move to more fragmented bargaining arrangements also appeared to be associated with higher profitability.

7.4.3 Unions and investment

The potential impact of unions on investment and innovation is complex. Simons (1944) argued that returns on capital were vulnerable to capture by the union, which would realise that firms would continue to produce as long as they covered only their variable costs. Firms anticipating this would not invest. Similarly, inflexible working practices could reduce the rate of return on capital. On the other hand, higher wages will themselves encourage higher capital investment to reduce the dependence on expensive labour, and union "**voice effects**" could encourage workers to be more receptive to changes in work organisation. In view of these ambiguities, it is not surprising that empirical studies on this issue have been inconclusive. Thus, for the US, Clark (1984) finds that the union effect on the rate of growth relative to the market was small and insignificant once account was taken of market characteristics. For Britain, Machin and Wadhwani (1991), using WIRS data, find that there was no significant association between unionism and investment. However, when three variables – presence of organisational change, the presence of a joint consultative committee and higher wages – were excluded, there was a positive statistical association between unionism and investment. Likewise, Denny and Nickell (1992), also using WIRS data, find that, holding wages, product prices and productivity constant, the rate of investment was approximately 28 per cent lower in firms that recognised unions and that had an average union density for manual workers, relative to firms in which unions were not recognised. Taking account of the three variables above, the overall effect on investment was 16 per cent lower in competitive firms and 3 per cent lower in non-competitive firms.

Voice effects

The idea that an alternative to leaving is provided to workers if there is a divergence between desired and actual outcomes at the workplace. Thus, workers may engage in voice (as opposed to exit), discussing with employers the conditions that need changing.

Meanwhile, a cross-county comparison of results by Menezes-Filho and Van Reenen (2003) finds consistently strong and negative impacts of unions on research and development in North America. In contrast, European studies (mainly in the UK) do not generally uncover negative effects of unions on research and development. As for other aspects of innovations, such as technological diffusion, innovation and productivity growth, there is no reported consensus view as to the effects that unions have. While Menezes-Filho and Van Reenen surmise that such cross-country differences in the union impact on research and development could represent unsolved econometric issues, they conclude that institutional differences between nations in union attitudes and bargaining ability are likely to lie behind these findings.

7.4.4 Unions and employment

To the extent that unions raise wages, we would expect that employment would fall. However, once the size of the firm has adjusted to any wage shock, the effect of unions on employment is less clear-cut. In fact, there have been few attempts to test for the direct effects of unions on employment and unemployment. One of the few exceptions is Montgomery (1989), who finds for the US that union strength, as reflected both in union coverage and the size of the union wage differential, decreases employment and increases unemployment by a significant, but small, amount. Specifically, the probability of employment for an average worker is only 2 per cent less where union strength is highest than where it is least. Further, these effects are concentrated primarily among females and young male workers as opposed to prime-age males. Leonard (1992) uses data on Californian manufacturing plants to examine the relationship between unionism and employment growth, finding that employment growth is significantly slower, by approximately 2 to 4 percentage points per annum, in union than in non-union plants. A similar result is found for Britain – a 3-percentage points differential – by Blanchflower *et al.* (1991) using WIRS data. This latter result conflicts, however, with that of Machin and Wadhwani (1991) using the same data-set,[30] though there is partial support for the period 1979–84 using Exstat-Datastream data-sets. Machin and Wadhwani suggest that there is no systematic link between unions and employment growth.

7.4.5 Unions and utility

If we are to assess the full impact of trade unions, the fundamental question is whether trade unions raise the utility of their members. An increase in pay, for instance, may force employers to take countervailing action, such as reducing employment, imposing stricter standards of supervision or paying bonuses for improved performance. It is possible, therefore, that the benefits of higher pay negotiated by the union through collective bargaining may be negated by the harsher regime that follows as employers attempt to remain competitive. Utility can be proxied by job satisfaction and a number of studies have focused on differences in job satisfaction between union and non-union members. Surprisingly, the majority of such studies find that union members are less satisfied than their non-union members. The most popular explanation for this finding is the **exit-voice hypothesis**. Thus, Freeman and Medoff (1984) suggest that trade unions reduce turnover by creating desirable working conditions and by providing workers with a voice alternative to quitting their jobs. They explain the lower recorded job satisfaction of union members in terms of the distinction between "true" job satisfaction and "voiced" dissatisfaction. However, Bender and Sloane (1998) show that, at least for Britain, the inclusion of quality of industrial-relations variables in regression analysis often causes the net union effect to become insignificant, suggesting that the prime explanation for lower recorded job satisfaction among union members is a negative relationship between collective-bargaining and the industrial-relations climate.

Summary

- The determinants of union membership fall into five categories: the macroeconomic climate; workforce composition; state policy and the legal environment; employer policy; and policies of trade unions themselves.
- In many countries, trends appear unfavourable to trade union growth, though centralisation of collective bargaining in other countries has served to protect unions from membership erosion.
- The ability of unions to raise wages above competitive levels within the monopoly union model only comes at the expense of reduced employment.
- The outcome of the collective-bargaining process between unions and employers in the bilateral monopoly model is indeterminate.
- Any outcome described by the right-to-manage model will lie upon the firm's labour demand curve, and all such outcomes are Pareto inefficient.
- The efficient bargaining model will describe wage–employment outcomes between firms and unions where all mutually advantageous bargains have been exhausted.
- Some of the earliest empirical work estimating union wage mark-ups used aggregate industry data. More recent empirical work has used micro-data at both an establishment level and an individual level. General findings have been that wage mark-ups are larger for manual workers than for non-manuals, and larger for women than for men.
- The analysis of the effect of unions on productivity has been an area of contention. The traditional view has been that unions lower productivity by reducing the freedom of management to manage in ways that will increase performance. In contrast, the collective voice approach implies that unions raise productivity by reducing labour turnover and raising staff morale among other things.
- There is mixed evidence on the impact of unions on both profitability and investment.
- To the extent that unions raise wages, we would expect that employment would fall. However, empirical evidence shows that, once firm size has adjusted to any wage shock, the effect of unions on employment is less clear-cut.

Questions

1   What factors positively affect the decision to join a union? What factors reduce the likelihood of unionisation?
2   What does the "right-to-manage model" tell us about the wage–employment combination of a collectively negotiated (i.e. between employer and union) outcome?
3   In what regards may a wage–employment outcome on the labour demand curve be considered Pareto inefficient? What role does bargaining strength play in determining the final negotiated outcome?
4   To what extent are empirical estimates of the union wage mark-up affected by data source? In general, which worker groups have been found to have the largest estimated mark-ups?
5   How are unionised plants able to remain in business if they are paying wages that are higher than those found in non-unionised plants? What evidence is there to support such arguments?

Notes

1   There is the question of whether staff associations or employer-dominated bodies should be classified as trade unions or not. Further, some union members may be retired or unemployed and therefore not impact on the union's bargaining power relative to employers. Should the self-employed be included as potential members, or members of the armed forces, which in some countries are forbidden to engage in union activities?
2   Bean and Holden (1992) found for 16 OECD countries over the period 1980–5 that there was a positive and significant correlation between union density and the percentage of employees covered by national collective agreements. However, the size of the public sector was even more important.
3   A number of plausible explanations are suggested for this observed association between membership and age, although it is noted that the relative weights of each of these across countries is unclear: cohort effects; a life-cycle pattern; union members quitting their jobs from their late forties and moving to non-union jobs in other organisations; union members losing their jobs and becoming unemployed; union members quitting their jobs and being promoted to managerial jobs that are non-union; union members being disproportionately employed in older workplaces, many of which are in traditional industries that have been subject to increased competition; older union workers increasingly free-riding as they age; older and younger workers having less need for unions than prime-age workers; the most productive union members quitting because the seniority/wage compression rule reduces their potential earnings; and more highly unionised industries having a higher proportion of older workers because the benefits brought by unions reduce turnover.
4   Farber and Saks (1980) develop a model of vote determination in which individuals vote as if the effects of unionisation are to raise earnings and lower their dispersion. Thus, the perceived earnings advantage of unions will be

inversely related to the individual's position in the intra-firm earnings distribution. This is verified empirically.

5   Booth (1995) notes that, while in the US overall unionisation began to decline from 1983, public-sector union density actually increased from 13 per cent in 1956 to 37 per cent in 1991.

6   It could be argued, however, that the causation may be the reverse of that which Freeman and Pelletier assume. That is, declining union density may make the encounter of legislation unfavourable to unions much easier.

7   Note that the argument here implies that union members are not guaranteed employment and may still suffer from unemployment (or employment outside of the unionised sector). The line of reasoning is not meant to relate to the situation where higher union wages deny employment opportunities to new entrants who are not union members.

8   While it would be feasible to explicitly model the bargaining process within the right-to-manage model, a formal presentation of this issue is deferred until section 7.2.4. In the current section, the focus will be on describing how the right-to-manage model leads to an outcome along the labour demand schedule in readiness for a comparison with the (efficient) outcomes described in section 7.2.4.

9   The monopoly union outcome identified in Figure 7.1 is a special case of the utility-maximising outcome described in Figure 7.4. Indeed, it can be shown (see Booth 1995 – section 7.3) that wages will be set such that the proportional marginal benefit from a unit increase in wages to the union and the firm is equal to the proportional cost, but weighted by each party's relative bargaining strength. When the union holds all of the bargaining power, we have the monopoly union case (point a in Figure 7.1) and, when the union has no bargaining power, we have the perfectly competitive outcome (point b in Figure 7.1). When bargaining power is between these two extremes, the right-to-manage outcome will establish a wage of between w1 and wc as in Figure 7.1.

10 This idea can be traced back to Leontief (1946).

11 While such a model is extensively discussed in the literature for its efficiency properties, there is little supporting evidence to suggest that unions do indeed bargain over employment and wages jointly.

12 The contract curve depicted in Figure 7.5 is merely indicative of possible Pareto efficient outcomes. As it turns out, the contract curve identified would be consistent with risk aversion on the part of the bargaining union. This point is explained in Case Study 7.2, which is more technical in its approach and may be viewed as additional but not necessarily essential reading.

13 Nash (1950) argued that a bargaining solution can be expected to satisfy the following four axioms: Pareto optimality; symmetry; transformation invariance; independence of irrelevant alternatives. Nash proved that the only solution that satisfies these four axioms is the one at which the product of the players' utility increments (denoted F and G below) from the threat point is a maximum. Formally, the generalised Nash bargain over w and n is given by:

$$\max_{w,n} B = F^\beta G^{1-\beta} \tag{A7.1}$$

which will subsequently yield the following first order conditions:

$$B_w = \beta \frac{F_w}{F} + (1-\beta)\frac{G_w}{G} = 0 \tag{A7.2a}$$

$$B_n = \beta \frac{F_n}{F} + (1-\beta)\frac{G_n}{G} = 0 \tag{A7.2b}$$

14 An alternative way to represent this is following Carruth and Oswald (1987) who assume that members have priority over non-members in employment decisions and that unions are indifferent about increases in employment that accrue to non-members.

Thus, the general form of the utility function may be written as:

$$u = u(w, n) \tag{A7.3}$$

where $u(.)$ is the utility function of the individual member, w is the real wage and n is the level of employment. Taking account of the distinction between employment and members we may write:

$$u = nu(w) + (m - n)u(b) \tag{A7.4}$$

where m represents union membership and b is the alternative wage in the non-unionised sector or the unemployment benefit received by unemployed members. Where preferential treatment is given to union members the correct specification of (A7.4) is given by:

$$u = mu(w) + u(b) - u(w)\max(0, m - n) \tag{A7.5}$$

In this case, the indifference curves of the union become horizontal beyond the point at which all members are employed (i.e. where $n = m$).

Another way to look at this phenomenon is to treat members as insiders and non-members as outsiders where insider power is bolstered not only by union membership but also by hiring and firing costs, labour turnover costs and threats of non-co-operation (see Lindbeck and Snower 1988; Sanfey 1995).

15 A particularly useful illustration of this is given in Andrews *et al.* (1998).

16 It is possible for the absolute real wage effect to be negative in the long run. Imagine two sectors, one of which is unionised and the other which is not. Employers may respond to higher wages in the union sector by shifting to more capital-intensive methods of production. Rising costs in that sector may then lead to demand shifting relatively in favour of the non-union sector. In this case, the real wage of union members could fall.

17 Where monopsony prevails, the first task of the union is to raise the wage to the competitive level, which involves no cost in foregone employment. Hence, the expectation is that the impact effect of unions will be more marked than its subsequent effect. The wage effect will also vary with the state of the labour market, being small when the labour market is tight and large when the labour market is slack. In the former case, the quit–cost ratio is high relative to the strike–cost ratio when comparing the relative cost to the employer and worker and vice versa in the latter case.

18 This finding of minor losses attributed to resource misallocation in a partial equilibrium setting is also supported by the conclusions drawn from a general equilibrium setting by Johnson and Mieszkowski (1970).

19 While the mark-up identified in equation (7.8) will be in terms of log points, the percentage effect (%E) upon earnings will be given by:

$$\%E = (e^{-UC} - 1) \times 100$$

where UC is the log point estimate.

20 As such, the difference in mean earnings could also have been decomposed as the following:

$$\ln \bar{W}_u - \ln \bar{W}_n = \left(\hat{\beta}_u - \hat{\beta}_n \right) \bar{X}_u + \hat{\beta}_n \left(\bar{X}_u - \bar{X}_n \right)$$

where the union mark-up would now be represented by $\hat{\beta}_n(\bar{X}_u - \bar{X}_n)$. A fuller discussion of the index number problem is given in Chapter 6 in relation to discrimination.

21 Note that the wages of any individual will only ever be observed in one of the two states, that is either a union member or a non-member. Thus, $\ln W_{ui} - \ln W_{ni}$ requires the calculation of a counterfactual wage denoting what individual i could expect to earn if he or she was employed in the other union state.

22 The model in equation (7.12) ignores a potential problem with respect to the closed shop which implies a degree of involuntary union membership. However, recent legislative changes outlawing the closed shop should have reduced the size of this problem.

23 The year 1964 was a boom year and Pencavel obtains an overall wage mark-up of 8 per cent. The year 1973 was a slump year and produces mark-up estimates between 22 per cent and 26 per cent. This is consistent with unions being more successful in raising pay in periods of recession. Further support for this proposition is found by Demery and McNabb (1978), who include excess demand variables in their model.

24 Stewart finds that, for skilled workers with a pre-entry closed shop, the mark-up equals 7.5 per cent, otherwise it is zero. For semi-skilled workers, the mark-up varies with the size of establishment. In larger establishments with a pre-entry closed shop, the mark-up equals 12 per cent, otherwise it is zero. In smaller establishments, the mark-up equals 1.5 per cent and is not influenced by the type of bargaining arrangements. Only a minority of establishments pay more than they would if they were in the non-union sector.

25 An interesting question is the extent to which changes in the legislative framework and hence relative bargaining power in Britain have led to a decline in the union mark-up. Murphy et al. (1992) compare their results with those of Stewart (1983) for 1975 and find that for manual workers the mark-up has stood up quite well and for non-manual workers increased significantly. Meanwhile, Stewart (1995), using 1984 and 1990 WIRS data, finds that for skilled, semi-skilled and unskilled manual workers the mark-up declines in each case, but for all three groups the fall is not statistically significant.

26 Addison and Barnett (1982), for example, suggest that unionism is an exogenous variable which is jointly determined with productivity, which requires a

simultaneous equations approach. Further, Duncan and Stafford (1980) find that approximately 40 per cent of the quality-adjusted union–non-union wage differential for US manual workers may be explained by adverse working conditions and that differential productivity is not required to explain this difference.

27 The presence of a union may signal to the employer that industrial action will follow if an acceptable offer is not forthcoming in a reasonable period of time and thus is likely to erode profits.

28 The basic estimating equation is

$$\left(\frac{\pi}{s}\right) = \alpha + X'\beta + Z'\gamma + \varphi u + \varepsilon \tag{A7.6}$$

where π/s is a measure of profitability, X is a vector of firm level characteristics, Z is a vector of industry-level characteristics and φ is the union effect in the form of an intercept shift. However, one should parameterise φ as a function of some or all of the components of X and Y. Hence, we have

$$\left(\frac{\pi}{s}\right) = \alpha + \varphi_u u + \varphi_{MS}(u * MS) + w'\delta + \varepsilon \tag{A7.7}$$

where $w = [X, Z]$ represent other control variables from equation (A7.6), MS is market share and the union effect is $\varphi_u + \varphi_{MS}MS$.

29 Wages and the propensity to experience strikes in excess of one day were also higher in plants where multiple unions were present and the unions concerned bargained separately.

30 Blanchflower *et al.* suggest the differences occur because of Machin and Wadhwani's smaller sample size, which arises from their exclusion of variables with missing values.

References

Addison J.T. and Barnett A.H., "The Impact of Unions on Productivity", *British Journal of Industrial Relations*, 20(2), July 1982, pp. 145–62.

Allen S.G., "Can Union Labor Ever Cost Less?", *Quarterly Journal of Economics*, May 1987, pp. 347–73.

Andrews M.J., Stewart M.B., Swaffield J. and Upward R., "The Estimation of Union Wage Differentials and the Impact of Methodological Choices", *Labour Economics*, 5, 1998, pp. 449–74.

Ashenfelter O. and Pencavel J.H., "American Trade Union Growth 1990–1960", *Quarterly Journal of Economics*, 83, 1969, pp. 434–48.

Bain G.S. and Elias P., "Trade Union Membership in Great Britain: An Individual Level Analysis", *British Journal of Industrial Relations*, XXIII(1), March 1985, pp. 71–92.

Bain G.S. and Elsheikh F., *Union Growth and the Business Cycle: An Econometric Analysis*, Basil Blackwell, Oxford, 1976.

Bean R. and Holden K., "Cross National Differences in Trade Union Membership in OECD Countries, *Industrial Relations Journal*, 23, 1992, pp. 52–9.

Beenstock M. and Whitbread C., "Explaining Changes in the Union Mark-up for Male Manual Workers in Great Britain, 1953–1983", *British Journal of Industrial Relations*, XXVI(3), November 1988, pp. 327–338.

Beaumont P.B. and Harris R.I., "Union Derecognition and Declining Union Density in Britain", *Industrial and Labor Relations Review*, 48(3), April 1995, pp. 389–402.

Bender K. and Sloane P.J., "Job Satisfaction, Trade Unions and Exit-Voice Revisited", *Industrial and Labor Relations Review*, 51(2), January 1998, pp. 222–40.

Berkowitz M., "The Economics of Trade Union Organisation and Administration", *Industrial and Labour Relations Review*, 7(4), July 1954, pp. 575–92.

Blackaby D., Murphy P. and Sloane P., "Union Membership, Collective Bargaining Coverage and the Trade Union Mark-up for Britain", *Economics Letters*, 36, 1991, pp. 203–8.

Blanchflower D.G., "What Effect Do Unions Have on Relative Wages in Great Britain?", *British Journal of Industrial Relations*, 24(2), 1986, pp. 195–204.

Blanchflower D.G., "International Patterns of Union Membership", *British Journal of Industrial Relations*, 45(1), 2007, pp. 1–28.

Blanchflower D.G and Bryson A., "Changes Over Time in Union Relative Wage Effects in the UK and the US Revisited", chapter 7 in Addison J.T. and Schnabel C., editors, *International Handbook of Trade Unions*, Edward Elgar, Cheltenham, 2003.

Blanchflower D.G and Bryson A., *Union Decline in Britain*, IZA Discussion Paper No. 3436, April 2008.

Blanchflower D.G. and Freeman R.B., "Unionism in the United States and other Advanced OECD Countries", in Bognanno M.F. and Kleiner M.N., editors, *Labour Market Institutions and the Future Role of Unions*, Basil Blackwell, Oxford, 1992, pp. 56–79.

Blanchflower D.G. and Oswald A.J., "The Economics Effects of Trade Unions", *Economic Report*, 3(10), Employment Institute, 1988.

Blanchflower D.G., Millward N. and Oswald A.J., "Unionism and Employment Behaviour", *Economic Journal*, 101(407), July 1991, pp. 815–34.

Bognanno M.F. and Kleiner M.M., "Introduction", in Bognanno M.F. and Kleiner M.N., editors, *Labour Market Institutions and the Future Role of Unions*, Basil Blackwell, Oxford, 1992, pp. 1–12.

Booth A.L., *The Economics of the Trade Union*, Cambridge University Press, 1995.

Brown C. and Medoff J. "Trade Unions in the Productive Process", *Journal of Political Economy*, 86(3), July 1978, pp. 335–78.

Bryson A. and Forth J., *Trade Union Membership and Influence 1999–2009*, NIESR Discussion Paper No. 363, September 2010.

Bryson A., Forth J. and Kirby S., "High-Performance Practices, Trade Union Representation and Workplace Performance in Britain", *Scottish Journal of Political Economy*, 53, 2005, pp. 451–491.

Bryson A. and Gomez R., "Why have Workers Stopped Joining Unions? Accounting for the Rise in Never-Membership in Britain", *British Journal of Industrial Relations*, 43(1), 2005, pp. 66–92.

Cable J.R. and Machin S.J., "The Relationship between Union Wage and Profitability Effects", *Economics Letters*, 37, 1991, pp. 315–21.

Card D., "The Effect of Unions on Wage Equality in the US Labor Market", *Industrial and Labor Relations Review*, 54, 2001, pp. 296–315.

Cartter A.M., *Theory of Wages and Employment*, Irwin, Homewood, Illinois, 1959.

Carruth A.A and Disney R., "Where Have the Two Million Trade Union Members Gone?", *Economica*, 5(217), February 1988, pp. 1–19.

Carruth A.A. and Oswald A.J., "On Union Preferences and Labour Market Models: Insiders and Outsiders", *Economic Journal*, 97, 1987, pp. 431–45.

Clark K.B., "Unionisation and Productivity: Micro-econometric Evidence", *Quarterly Journal of Economics*, 95, December 1980, pp. 613–39.

Clark K.B., "Unionisation and Firm Performance: The Impact of Profits, Growth and Productivity", *American Economic Review*, 74, December 1984, pp. 893–919.

Davis M.B., "The Theory of Union Growth", *Quarterly Journal of Economics*, LV, August 1941, pp. 611–37.

Dell'Aringa C. and Lucifora C., "Wage Dispersion and Unionism: Do Unions Protect Low Pay?", *International Journal of Manpower*, 15(2), 1994, pp. 150–69.

Demery D. and McNabb R., "The Effects of Demand on the Union Relative Wage Effect in the UK", *British Journal of Industrial Relations*, XVI(3), November 1978, pp. 303–8.

Denny K. and Nickell S.J., "Unions and Investment on British Industry", *Economic Journal*, 102(413), July 1992, pp. 874–83.

Disney R., "Explanations of the Decline in Trade Union Density in Britain: An Appraisal", *British Journal of Industrial Relations*, 28(2), 1990, pp. 165–77.

Disney R., Gosling A. and Machin S., "British Unions in Decline: Determinants of the 1980s Fall in Union Recognition", *Industrial and Labor Relations Review*, 48(3), April 1995, pp. 403–19.

Disney R., Gosling A. and Machin S., "What Has Happened to Union Recognition in Britain?", *Economica*, 63, 1996, pp. 1–18.

Duncan G.J. and Stafford F.P., "Do Union Members Receive Compensating Differentials?", *American Economic Review*, 70, June 1980, pp. 35–71.

Duncan G.M. and Leigh D.E., "The Endogeneity of Union Status: An Empirical Test", *Journal of Labor Economics*, 3(3), 1985, pp. 385–402.

Dunlop J.T., *Wage Determination Under Trade Unions*, Macmillan, New York, 1944.

Farber H.S. and Saks D.H., "Why Workers Want Unions: The Role of Relative Wages and Job Characteristics", *Journal of Political Economy*, 88, 1980, pp. 349–69.

Fellner W.F., *Competition Among the Few*, Knopf, New York, 1949.

Freeman R.B., "Unions and the Dispersion of Wages", *Industrial and Labor Relations Review*, 34(1), 1980, p. 3–23.

Freeman R.B., "Union Wage Practices and Wage Dispersion within Establishments", *Industrial and Labor Relations Review*, 36(1), 1982, pp. 3–21.

Freeman R.B. and Medoff J., *What Do Unions Do?*, Basic Books, New York, 1984.

Freeman R. and Pelletier J., "The Impact of Industrial Relations Legislation on British Union Density", *British Journal of Industrial Relations*, 28(2), 1990, pp. 141–64.

Gallie D., Penn R. and Rose M., editors, *Trade Unions in Recession*, Oxford University Press, Oxford, 1994.

Gosling A. and Machin S., "Trade Unions and the Dispersion of Earnings in British Establishments, 1980–1990", *Oxford Bulletin of Economics and Statistics*, 57, 1995, pp. 167–84.

Green F., "The Trade Union Wage Gap in Britain: Some Estimates", *Economics Letters*, 27, 1988, pp. 183–7.

Green F., "Recent Trends in British Trade Union Density: How Much of a Compositional Effect?", *British Journal of Industrial Relations*, 30(3), September 1992, pp. 445–55.

Gregg P., Machin S. and Metcalf D., "Signals and Cycles? Productivity Growth and Changes in Union Status in British Companies, 1984–89", *Economic Journal*, 103(419), July 1993, pp. 894–907.

Haskel J., "Imperfect Competition Work Practices and Productivity Growth", *Oxford Bulletin of Economics and Statistics*, 53(3), 1991, pp. 265–79.

Hirsch B.T., "The Inter-Industry Structure of Unionism, Earnings and Earnings Dispersion", *Industrial and Labor Relations Review*, 34(1), 1982, pp. 22–39.

Hirsch B.T. and Addison J.T., *The Economic Analysis of Unions: New Approaches and Evidence*, Allen & Unwin, London, 1986.

Hirsch B. and Link A.N., "Unions, Productivity and Productivity Growth", *Journal of Labor Research*, 5(1), 1984, pp. 29–37.

Johnson H.G. and Mieszkowski P., "The Effects of Unionisation on the Distribution of Income: A General Equilibrium Approach", *Quarterly Journal of Economics*, 84(4), 1970, pp. 539–61.

Layard R., Metcalf D. and Nickell S., "The Effect of Collective Bargaining on Relative and Absolute Wages", *British Journal of Industrial Relations*, 16(3), 1978, pp. 287–303.

Lee L.-F., "Unionism and Wage Rates: A Simultaneous Equations Model with Qualitative and Limited Dependent Variables", *International Economic Review*, 19(2), June 1978, pp. 415–33.

Leonard J.S., "Unions and Employment Growth", *Industrial Relations*, 31(1), 1992, pp. 80–94.

Leontief W., "The Pure Theory of the Guaranteed Annual Wage Contract", *Journal of Political Economy*, 54(1), 1946, pp. 76–9.

Lewis H.G., *Union Relative Wage Effects: A Survey*, University of Chicago Press, 1986.

Lindbeck A. and Snower D.J., *The Insider–Outsider Theory of Employment and Unemployment*, MIT Press, Cambridge, Mass., 1988.

Lindblom C.E., *Unions and Capitalism*, Yale University Press, 1949.

McDonald I.M. and Solow R.M., "Wage Bargaining and Employment", *American Economic Review*, 71, 1981, pp. 896–908.

Main B.G.M. and Reilly B., "Women and the Union Wage Gap", *Economic Journal*, 102(416), January 1992, pp. 59–66.

Machin S.J., "Unions and the Capture of Economics Rents", *International Journal of Industrial Organisation*, 9, 1991, pp. 261–74.

Machin S.J. and Stewart M.B., "Unions and the Financial Performance of British Private Sector Establishments", *Journal of Applied Econometrics*, 5, 1990, pp. 327–50.

Machin S.J. and Stewart M.B., "Trade Unions and Financial Performance", *Oxford Economic Papers*, 48, 1996, pp. 213–41.

Machin S.J., Stewart M.B. and Van Reenen J., "The Economic Effects of Multiple Unionism: Evidence from the 1984 Workplace Industrial Survey", *Scandinavian Journal of Economics*, 95, 1993, pp. 279–96.

Machin S.J. and Wadhwani S., "The Effects of Unions on Investment and Innovation: Evidence from WIRS", *Economic Journal*, 101(405), March 1991, pp. 324–30.

Menezes-Filho N.A., "Unions and Profitability over the 1980s: Some Evidence on Union-Firm Bargaining in the UK", *Economic Journal*, 107(442), May 1997, pp. 651–70.

Menezes-Filho N.A. and Van Reenen J., "Unions and Innovation: A Survey of the Theory and Empirical Evidence", chapter 9 in Addison J.T. and Schnabel C., editors, *International Handbook of Trade Unions*, Edward Elgar, Cheltenham, 2003.

Metcalf D., "British Unions: Dissolution or Resurgence?", *Oxford Review of Economic Policy*, 7(1), Spring 1991, pp. 18–32.

Millward N., Bryson A. and Forth J., *All Change at Work? British Employment Relations 1980–1998, Portrayed by the Workplace Industrial Relations Survey Series*, Routledge, London, 2000.

Montgomery E., "Employment and Unemployment Effects of Unions", *Journal of Labor Economics*, 7, 1989, pp. 170–90.

Mulvey C., "Collective Agreements and Relative Earnings in UK Manufacturing in 1973", *Economica*, 43, November 1976, pp. 419–27.

Mulvey C. and Abowd J.M., "Estimating the Union/Non-Union Wage Differential: A Statistical Issue", *Economica*, 47, February 1980, pp. 73–9.

Mulvey C. and Foster J.I., "Occupational Earnings in the UK and the Effects of Collective Agreements", *Manchester School*, 44, September 1976, pp. 258–75.

Murphy P.D., Sloane P.J. and Blackaby D.H., "The Effects of Trade Unions on the Distribution of Earnings: A Sample Selectivity Approach", *Oxford Bulletin of Economics and Statistics*, 54(4), November 1992, pp. 517–42.

Nash J.F., "The Bargaining Problem", *Econometrica*, 18(2), 1950, pp. 155–62.

Nickell S.J., "Trade Union and the Position of Women in the Industrial Wage Structure", *British Journal of Industrial Relations*, XV(2), July 1977, pp. 192–250.

Nickell S.J., Wadhwani S. and Wall M., "Productivity Growth and UK Companies, 1975–86", *European Economic Review*, 36, 1992, pp. 1055–85.

O'Leary N.C., Murphy P.D. and Blackaby D.H., "Quantile Regression Estimates of the Union Wage Effect for Great Britain", *The Manchester School*, 72, 2004, pp. 497–514.

Oswald A.J., "The Microeconomic Theory of the Trade Union", *Economic Journal*, 92(367), 1982, pp. 576–95.

Oswald A.J., "The Economic Theory of Trade Unions: An Introductory Survey", *Scandinavian Journal of Economics*, 87(2), 1985, pp. 160–193.

Pencavel J.H., "Relative Wages and Trade Unions in the United Kingdom", *Economica*, 1(162), May 1974, pp. 194–210.

Reder M., "The Theory of Union Wage Policy", *Review of Economics and Statistics*, 34(1), 1952, pp. 34–55.

Rees A., "The Effects of Unions on Resource Allocation", *Journal of Law and Economics*, 6, 1963, pp. 69–78.

Rees A., *The Economics of Work and Pay*, Harper & Row, New York, 1973.

Reynolds M.O., "Trade Unions in the Production Process Reconsidered", *Journal of Political Economy*, 94(2), 1986, pp. 443–7.

Robinson C., "The Joint Determination of Union Status and Union Wage Effects: Some Tests of Alternative Models", *Journal of Political Economy*, 97, 1989, pp. 639–67.

Ross A.M., *Trade Union Wage Policy*, University of California Press, Berkeley, 1948.

Sanfey P.J., "Insiders and Outsiders in Union Models", *Journal of Economic Survey*, 9(3), September, 1995, pp. 255–84.

Shah A., "Job Attributes and the Size of the Union/Non-Union Wage Differential", *Economica*, 51, 1984, pp. 437–46.

Sharpe I.G., "The Growth of Australian Trade Unions: 1907–1969", *Journal of Industrial Relations*, XIII, June 1971, pp. 138–54.

Simons H.C., "Some Reflections on Syndicalism", *Journal of Political Economy*, 52(1), 1944, pp. 1–25.

Sinclair D.M., "The Importance of Sex for the Propensity to Unionise", *British Journal of Industrial Relations*, 33(2), June 1995, pp. 173–190.

Stewart M.B., "Relative Earnings and Individual Union Membership in the UK", *Economica*, 50, 1983, pp. 111–23.

Stewart M.B., "Collective Bargaining Arrangements, Closed Shops and Relative Pay", *Economic Journal*, 97, 1987, pp. 140–54.

Stewart M.B., "Union Wage Differentials in an Era of Declining Unionisation", *Oxford Bulletin of Economics and Statistics*, 57(2), 1995, pp. 143–66.

Thomson A.J., Mulvey C. and Farbman M., "Bargaining Structure and Relative Earnings in Britain", *British Journal of Industrial Relations*, XV(2), July 1977, pp. 176–91.

Turnbull P.J., "Industrial Relations and the Seniority Model of Union Behaviour", *Oxford Bulletin of Economics and Statistics*, 50(1), 1988, pp. 53–70.

Undy R., Ellis V., McCarthy W.E.J. and Halmos A.M., *Change in Trade Unions: The Development of UK Unions since the 1960s*, Hutchinson Radius, London, 1981.

Waddington J., "Trade Union Mergers: A Study of Trade Union Structural Dynamics", *British Journal of Industrial Relations*, 26(3), November 1988, pp. 409–30.

Willman P., Bryson A. and Gomez R., "The Long Goodbye: New Establishments and the Fall of Union Voice in Britain", *International Journal of Human Resource Management*, 18(7), 2007, pp. 1318–34.

Further reading

Freeman and Medoff (1984) is a classic text in the literature, while Booth (1995) not only provides a more contemporary discussion of the issues but also summarises extremely well the empirical literature on union wage effects (chapter 6). The article by Oswald (1985) provides a well-written and informative overview of the development of models of trade union determination. The article by Andrews *et al.* (1998), while not unique, is a good example of how empirical estimates of wage mark-ups are generated and how they differ over different groups of workers in the UK. This article also highlights how empirically estimated mark-ups are influenced by methodological issues.

Chapter 8

Bargaining and conflict

Learning outcomes

At the end of this chapter, readers should understand:

- How conflict at work may manifest in strikes (in the case of collective conflict between employers and workers) and complaints to labour courts (individual conflict between employers and employees);
- The dimensions of strike activity and the ways in which the pattern of disputes has changed over time in Britain and elsewhere;
- Theoretical models explaining why strikes might occur even though appearing irrational to the extent the same outcome might have been negotiated without the parties incurring the costs involved (the "Hicks paradox"); and, at an individual level, why union members might choose to participate in strikes despite the presence of a potential free-rider problem;
- The factors found to be associated with strike activity in empirical studies, together with some evidence on the associated costs in terms of lost output;
- The basic functioning of the Employment Tribunal (ET) system in Britain as a means for dealing with individual problems at work, the nature of disputes these bodies address and the outcomes that occur;
- How most claims to ETs are resolved without the need for a hearing, and the factors that might promote early settlement of claims, together with some early evidence on same;
- Current policy debates concerning ETs and their operation.

Introduction

Collective bargaining

The process of negotiation over pay and conditions that occurs between groups of concerned parties and not between individuals.

Chapter 7 dealt with the issue of **collective bargaining** between an employer and a trade union. The analysis there focused on the equilibria that might emerge from negotiations under alternative assumptions about the nature of bargaining and the (number and type of) matters under consideration, but did not address the question of what happens in the event of negotiation breakdown. In this chapter, we examine conflict at work, beginning with the collective-bargaining context and focusing on disputes in the form of strikes – that is, the temporary withdrawal of labour – as the result of bargaining impasse. Strikes impose costs on both sides in negotiations – to the employer in terms of lost output, and to workers in foregone pay – and it is these costs that, ultimately, elicit concessions by one or both parties and eventually lead to settlement.

A key issue in the literature concerns the observation that, to the extent the same outcome, absent a strike and its associated costs, would have been preferred by both sides, strikes are Pareto sub-optimal and, indeed, appear irrational (the so-called "Hicks paradox"). For this reason, we reflect the emphasis of much of the literature that seeks to explore why they occur, given this apparent paradox. In so doing, we will also examine their duration and the nature and size of the economic costs they entail, most notably in relation to lost output. From the workers' perspective, we will also consider individual incentives to participate in a strike given the presence of a potential **free-rider** problem, whereby non-strikers benefit from any increases in pay negotiated on their behalf by the union but without bearing the associated loss of earnings.

Free rider

An individual who exhibits the tendency to shirk or take it easy when success is dependent on the performance of a group rather than an individual.

However, as we will see, while strikes are often high profile and continue to attract considerable attention in the news (see for example Case Study 8.1), strike activity is, in fact, at historically low levels in most Western economies. In contrast, the UK individual conflict at work – as manifested by claims to **Employment Tribunals** (ETs) – is more prevalent and, arguably, a more important contemporary form of conflict. It is certainly a form of dispute that has grown significantly in recent years. We therefore describe the nature of such individual manifestations of workplace conflict and the role of the Employment Tribunal system as a mechanism for adjudicating rights-based disputes between employees (or potential employees) and their employers. Comparing ETs with civil litigation, we also explore reasons why most claims are, in fact, settled prior to a tribunal hearing. Finally, we briefly consider current policy debates in relation to ETs.

Employment Tribunals

Judicial bodies akin to labour courts, with responsibility for hearing claims made against employers in relation to disputes concerning employment rights.

8.1 Patterns of industrial conflict

The withdrawal of labour services by union members – strikes – is perhaps the most obvious manifestation of industrial conflict, at least in the public psyche, and typically occurs when attempts by unions and employers to negotiate changes in wages and other terms and conditions fail.[1] As with unemployment, where both numbers and duration are important (in that setting, feeding into the analysis of stocks and flows), there are a number of dimensions of strike activity. The most obvious is the number of **stoppages** (incidence/frequency), but numbers of workers involved and duration are also clearly important, especially if, as is typically the case, one wishes to obtain a measure of the *impact* of industrial stoppages. In this regard, the most commonly used indicator is working days lost, either in absolute terms or, for comparison over time and among countries, expressed as a rate per thousand employees.

Stoppages

Instances of cessation of work by union members as part of industrial action.

Case Study 8.1

British Airways: A bumpy ride

Between 2009 and 2011, British Airways (BA) and Unite, the union representing BA cabin staff, engaged in a lengthy and often acrimonious dispute over staffing, pay and benefits. Some 22 days of strikes took place, leading to disruption for passengers, lost earnings for those involved in the strike and an estimated bill for BA of £150 million.

The dispute was prompted by cost-cutting plans involving reductions in cabin-crew staffing levels, changes to working conditions and a two-year pay freeze aimed at securing annual savings of £140 million.

Changes were imposed in November 2009 after talks reached an impasse, despite Acas' intervention, leading the union to ballot members on strike action. A feature of the dispute was the extent to which it was played out in the courts, with BA seeking to secure injunctions declaring this and indeed two subsequent ballots illegal on technical grounds, and Unite successfully appealing one such decision. Matters were complicated too by BA's decision to withdraw travel perks from striking staff, itself the subject of a legal challenge by Unite, while some were the subject of disciplinary action including suspensions and the sack. Famously, in May 2010, protestors managed to invade Acas' Head Office and break up talks taking place there.

Following changes in the leadership at both BA and Unite, the dispute formally concluded in June 2011 with a ballot in favour of a negotiated settlement. This saw some of the changes to working arrangements confirmed, alongside a two-year 7.5 per cent pay deal, the reinstatement of travel perks and Acas arbitration to consider the cases of sacked workers.

BA dispute timeline

2009

6 October: The airline announces plans to cut 1,700 cabin-crew jobs and freeze pay. Union officials accuse the company of "holding a gun"' to the heads of staff and warn they are prepared to fight the proposals.

26 October: A ballot for industrial action is announced among almost 14,000 workers.

16 November: Thousands of cabin crew start voting, with more than 12,000 ballot papers issued.

14 December: A 12-day strike from 22 December to 2 January is announced for cabin crew after a 9–1 vote in favour of industrial action. BA says the strikes are "completely unjustified".

17 December: The High Court rules the strike cannot go ahead. BA wins its legal challenge after claiming that Unite had balloted hundreds of members who had subsequently left the company. Unite says a reballot will be held.

2010

15 March: Cabin crew vote in favour of industrial action. BA says it plans to keep 60 per cent of its customers flying if cabin crew go ahead with the first strike.

19 March: Talks between BA and Unite collapse. BA boss Willie Walsh confirms that any worker who joins the strike will lose their travel perks, including flights at vastly reduced cost.

20 March: At the stroke of midnight, BA cabin crew walk out, commencing three-day action.

24 March: BA tells striking cabin crew they will lose their travel perks. Unite vows to fight the action.

10 May: Following further strikes and Unite's rejection of a BA offer, the union announces plans for 20 days of action, the first to take place from 18 to 22 May inclusive.

14 May: BA announces it is to take legal action in a bid to prevent the strikes. Meanwhile, it is announced that conciliation service Acas has asked both BA and Unite to attend fresh peace talks.

17 May: Less than 24 hours before new action is due to start, BA wins an 11th-hour injunction banning strike action.

20 May: Unite wins an appeal against the BA injunction and announces strikes are back on and will commence on 24 May.

21 May: BA posts annual losses of £531 million.

22 May: Talks at averting the strikes end in disarray after demonstrators storm Acas' Head Office where they are taking place. Mr Walsh has to be escorted from the building by police.

24 May: Strike action begins, with members of Unite launching a five-day walkout.

2 June: Union leaders claim the strikes have cost the airline £112 million and it could lose £1.4 billion as passengers switch to other carriers.

8 June: Striking BA cabin crew stage their 21st day of industrial action.

24 June: BA launches a recruitment drive for new cabin crew under plans to cut costs.

25 June: BA makes a new offer to Unite in a fresh attempt to end the dispute.

27 June: Unite is set to postpone a new BA strike ballot so it can consider a fresh offer from the airline.

7 July: BA cabin crew to start voting on a new offer aimed at averting fresh strikes.

20 July: BA cabin crew reject the airline's final offer to end the dispute by 3,419 votes to 1,686.

26 July: The dispute takes a fresh twist when Unite announces it is taking legal action over the removal of travel concessions from cabin crew who have been on strike.

30 July: BA says it has made a pre-tax loss of £164 million for the three months to 30 June.

31 July: More than 80 cabin crew have been suspended and 13 sacked because of incidents related to the dispute, it emerges.

9 August: BA expresses "delight" after its Heathrow customer service staff vote overwhelmingly to accept new working practices.

19 August: The dispute is set to return to the courts with fresh legal action by the union.

23 November: Union leaders express anger at the suspension of a cabin-crew member after she collected contributions for colleagues facing disciplinary action.

24 November: Len McCluskey, newly appointed general secretary of Unite, attacks the "culture of fear" at British Airways.

2011

10 January: Almost three out of four members of BA cabin crew have witnessed or been victims of bullying, Unite says.

21 January: Cabin crew vote in favour of fresh strikes.

8 February: Unite to hold a fresh strike ballot following a "legal blitz" from the airline, the union says.

22 February: A fresh ballot will be held next month, it is announced.

28 March: Cabin crew vote by more than 8–1 to stage fresh strikes.

14 April: BA and Unite agree a 28-day extension before any further strike action is called.

12 May: The dispute is on the verge of being resolved following a breakthrough in crucial talks aimed at ending the long-running row.

12 May: BA and union leaders agree deal to settle dispute.

22 June: Unite members vote to accept deal.

Source: Timeline adapted from www.telegraph.co.uk/travel/travelnews/8508691/BA-dispute-a-timeline-travel-chaos.html

Working days lost (*WDL*) is calculated as:

$$WDL = S \times \bar{M}_s \times \bar{D}_s \qquad (8.1)$$

where S denotes the number of stoppages, $\bar{M}_s$ the average number of employees on strike in each case and $\bar{D}_s$ the average strike length (days). The rate per thousand employees is obtained as:

$$WDL(rate) = \frac{s \times \bar{M}_s \times \bar{D}_s}{\left(\dfrac{E}{1000}\right)} \qquad (8.2)$$

where E is total, economy-wide employment.

In Britain, industrial conflict of an organised form has been present since the eighteenth century, although it is only really since 1850 that unionisation ceased to be confined to "the few and to the skilled" (Laybourn 1992: 9), and, along with it, more regularised manifestations of collective conflict (see Case Study 7.1 for a brief historical overview of the union movement in Britain). Over the intervening period, as industrialisation proceeded and union membership strength grew, challenging the power of the employers, so the number of working days lost to strikes became correspondingly larger. The number of working days lost peaked in 1926, the year of the General Strike, with 160 million days lost.[2] Subsequently, the figures fell back, before rising again in the late 1960s and into the 1970s, when, despite the much lower numbers of days lost compared with the earlier period – some 200 million days over the two decades combined (Hicks and Allen 1999: 25) – Britain was widely perceived as being peculiarly strike-prone. Indeed, in some quarters, strikes became regarded as "the British disease", responsible in large part for its declining industrial fortunes (Knight 1989; Hart 2009).[3] During the Thatcher era in the 1980s, however, the number of strikes fell dramatically, reflecting an economic, political and legal environment that had moved firmly against unions, and strikes in particular. In terms of the legal changes concerning strikes, the gradualist programme of reforms included, among others, restrictions on picketing, the outlawing of "secondary action" (i.e. sympathetic activity by persons or groups not directly involved in a dispute), a reduction in union immunity from prosecution by employers for damages arising from disputes, and the requirement for **secret ballots** ahead of industrial action[4] (see Shackleton 1998, for an extended discussion of the reforms and their impact).[5]

Perhaps not surprisingly in light of the above, strike activity in the UK has fallen substantially over time, at least as measured by numbers of stoppages and working days lost. Figure 8.1, taken from Dix *et al.* (2009), plots three measures of strike activity over almost a 50-year period from 1960 onwards. As is evident, there has been a substantial change in both the level and pattern of strike activity over this period, with the most pronounced change being in relation to the number of stoppages, which have fallen from a peak of around 4,000 in 1970 to fewer than 500 a year in the last decade or so. The pattern also reveals changes in the number of workers involved, which have fluctuated significantly from year to year, but with particularly pronounced peaks in recent years. The number of working days lost per thousand employees also displays significant year-on-year variation. The three peaks in this series correspond to the miners' strike against the Edward Heath

Secret ballots

A ballot in which the individual's vote is anonymous. In relation to strikes, this can be contrasted with "shows of hands", in which the raising of hands to express a view at a public meeting can be observed by those present.

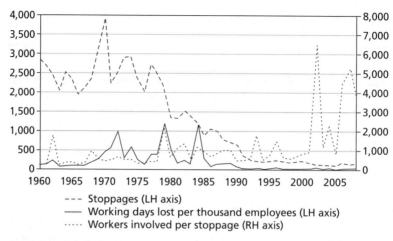

Source: Dix et al. (2009)

Figure 8.1 Strikes in the UK, 1960–2008.

government in 1972, the so-called "Winter of Discontent" in 1978–9 during the last months of the Callaghan administration, and the miners' strike of 1984–5 under the Thatcher government. As these data reveal, therefore, particular stoppages or related stoppages can have a profound effect on the statistics and, for this reason, strikes continue to attract prominent media coverage and political attention.

To give some idea of current strike levels in the UK relative to international comparators, and acknowledging differences in strike measurement accounting practices that exist among countries,[6] Table 8.1 shows the number of industrial disputes and working days lost both in aggregate and expressed as a rate per thousand employees for a selection of EU countries averaged over the period 2005–9. As can be seen, there is substantial variation. Poland, for example, has the highest number of recorded stoppages, but a low rate of working days lost per thousand workers, suggesting strikes are typically small and/or short in duration. France, on the other hand, has fewer stoppages but the highest number of total working days lost, although the rate of working days lost per thousand employees is actually lower than in Denmark, which tops the table on this measure. At the other extreme, conspicuously, Austria reported no (official) strikes over the period 2005–9, a phenomenon that also extends further back in time reflecting the operation of its economic and social partnership arrangements. Indeed, the first major strikes in 25 years took place in the metalworking industry as recently as October 2011, when 100,000 workers from around 200 firms went on strike for 2 days (Eurofound 2012).

Nor is the pattern of falling numbers of strikes and days lost described above confined to the UK.[7] Comparing the data in Table 8.1 with earlier figures reported in Brown and Wadhwani (1990) reveals that strikes have declined in significance in most of the countries for which comparisons can be undertaken (see Hale 2008a). For example, Finland's working days lost per thousand employees fell from 300 in 1978–82 to 73 in 2005–9; for Ireland, the figures are 800 and 39; for Spain, 1,110 and 60; while, for Italy, they have declined from 1,160 to just 35. Godard (2011) – aggregating across a selective set of countries (the UK, US, Canada, Germany, Netherlands, Belgium, Sweden, Australia and New Zealand), using data from van der Velden et al. (2007) and Hale (2008b), and acknowledging that "strike statistics

Table 8.1 Industrial disputes in selected European countries, 2005–9

Country	Average annual no. of industrial disputes	Average annual no. of working days lost	Average annual rate per 1,000 employees
Austria	0[a]	0[a]	0.0[a]
Belgium	n/a	287,511	78.8[a]
Denmark	483	422,580	159.4
Estonia	n/a	62	0.1
Finland	163	190,171	72.9
France	736[c]	1,657,000[b]	132.0[b]
Germany	n/a	216,355[a]	6.2[a]
Hungary	43	16,024	5.8
Ireland	13	74,788	38.5
Italy	632[a]	590,225	34.8
Latvia	4[a]	813[a]	0.8[a]
Lithuania	69	10,499	8.1[a]
Luxembourg	n/a	11,927[b]	4.1[b]
Netherlands	25	41,820	5.7
Norway	6	44,892	20.4
Poland	2,924	76,713	6.5
Portugal	136[b]	33,806[b]	11.3[b]
Romania	99	28,989[a]	6.0[a]
Slovakia	1	3928	2.0
Slovenia	7[b]	13,597[b]	16.9[b]
Spain	802	1,133,722	60.4
Sweden	9	24,323	6.2
UK	140	678,000	23.8

Source: Adapted from Eurofound (2010); UK figures for 2009 updated from Hale (2010).

Notes: Basis of statistics varies – see Eurofound (2010) for details. [a]denotes average for 2005–8; [b]average for 2005–7; [c] 2005 only.

are notoriously flawed" – shows that average days lost to strikes per thousand workers have fallen by around 90 per cent since 1970.

In relation to the issues giving rise to strikes, the data in Figure 8.2 show that pay represented the principal cause of the majority of strikes in the UK during most of the decade to 2009, with the exceptions of 2001 and 2009. As Hale (2010: 55) notes, variations from year to year may arise from one or two very large disputes, making comparisons over time difficult. Nonetheless, most disputes clearly have pay as an – if not *the* – issue under negotiation, suggesting that the focus on bargaining in relation to wages has some empirical validity. Strikingly (no pun intended!), the unusually high percentage of stoppages in relation to redundancy in 2009 clearly reflects the impact of recession and the subsequent austerity programme.

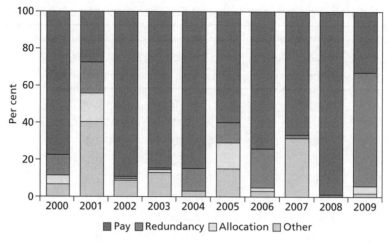

Source: Hale (2010), table 5.

Figure 8.2 Working days lost by principal cause of dispute in the UK, 2009.

One further interesting feature of the official data is that the number of stoppages in the public and private sectors is approximately equal (see Hale 2010, table 8b). However, the number of working days lost in the former is substantially higher and, as Dix *et al.* (2009) show using the WERS data, the *incidence* of both strike and non-strike action are far higher in the public sector. This may partly explain the regional dimension that appears to be exhibited in the working days lost rate data; although there is again variation from year to year: as Figure 8.3 reveals, working days lost per 1,000 employees tend to be higher (darker shading) in the northern regions (including Wales and Northern Ireland). Historical patterns of industrial location, and corresponding cultural legacies around trade unions are also likely to be a part of this story of course.

The UK data also reveal that strikes are typically small and of short duration: of the 98 stoppages recorded in the official data in 2009, almost half (49 per cent) were

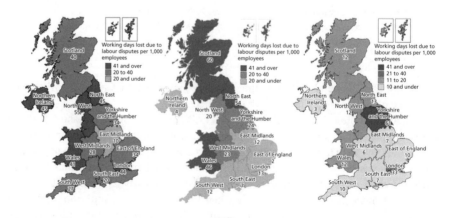

Source: Adapted from Hale (2008b, 2009, 2010).

Figure 8.3 Strike frequency by region, 2007–9.

of a single day's duration and involved 6,500 workers. In contrast, just 3.1 per cent of strikes lasted for more than 50 days (Hale 2010). However, the latter accounted for more than three-quarters (77.5 per cent) of total working days lost, reflecting 3 large disputes involving more than 175,000 workers. In general, however, the pattern appears to be towards the increasing and strategic use of shorter rather than indefinite stoppages, with such measures used as attempts to persuade management back to the bargaining table.[8] Of course, while such tactics potentially involve lower costs for both sides, enhancing their ability to sustain a dispute over a longer period, they also impose less pressure to settle, even though the amounts involved in lost output and pay can still be significant. For example, during the acrimonious dispute between British Airways (BA) and its cabin staff represented by the Unite union, which primarily centred around reductions in staffing levels on flights and ran for more than 18 months, the costs to BA of 22 days of short-term strikes was estimated to be approximately £150 million in terms of lost business (see Case Study 8.1).

8.2 Models of strike incidence

While individual strikes continue to attract attention and emotive language by parties and politicians, as the above illustrates, they are much less common now than historically, and involve far fewer working days lost. It is perhaps largely for this reason that research interest in strikes, with a few exceptions, largely fell into abeyance from the early to mid-1990s. Nonetheless, they remain part of the labour market landscape and, thus, the fundamental question in the literature on strikes concerning why they occur at all, given the potentially avoidable costs for both sides, remains.

As Hirsch and Addison (1986) note, there are a number of competing explanations for the existence of strikes in the face of the Hicks paradox.[9] Most economists begin from the basic notion of the bargaining problem as one involving **bilateral monopoly**, with its corresponding indeterminacy. Sapsford and Tzannatos (1993) note that overcoming this indeterminacy is achieved in the right-to-manage model of Chapter 7 by assuming that, whatever wage emerges from bargaining, the employer unilaterally chooses the level of employment. The monopoly union model is thus a special case in which the union sets the wage to maximise its utility subject to the constraint that the final outcome will be on the employer's labour demand curve. As we saw in Chapter 7, the efficient bargains approach, in contrast, potentially gives rise to an infinite number of possible solutions, with no explanation of which will occur and how the eventual outcome will be reached.

8.2.1 The Zeuthen–Harsanyi model

Microeconomists have suggested various models to solve bargaining problems of the type represented by unions and employers. Among the best known is that proposed by Zeuthen (1930). This was subsequently reformulated by Harsanyi (1956), who also demonstrated the outcome is the same as the more general solution by Nash (1950, 1953) arrived at using an axiomatic approach – that is, by specifying a set of criteria that a solution should satisfy (e.g. **Pareto optimality**).

Although Nash's approach is regarded as more "rigorous" (Farber 1986: 1055), Zeuthen's model is contextualised explicitly in the context of union–employer bargaining,

Bilateral monopoly

A situation in which both employer and employees (or their representatives) have a degree of monopoly bargaining power.

Pareto optimal

An outcome is described as being Pareto optimal (or Pareto efficient) if it is not possible to make one party better off without making another party worse off. For a **Pareto improvement** to take place, at least one of the parties needs to be made better off without any of the other parties being made worse off. A **Pareto sub-optimal** outcome is one where it is possible to improve outcomes for one or more parties without adversely affecting others (which is said to be **Pareto superior**).

so we will outline it here. The model is sequential in nature and focuses on the (relative) willingness of the bargainers to risk conflict by rejecting the current offer made by the other party in holding out for their own. Harsanyi's reformulation, which essentially translates Zeuthen's seminal contribution into utility terms, can be represented diagrammatically as shown in Figure 8.4 (following Bishop 1964).

Two bargainers – a union and an employer – face a static utility frontier, representing the gains for each side from settlement, with the origin denoting the outcome in the event of continued disagreement. The bargainers are initially likely to adopt extreme positions, as indicated in Figure 8.4 by points A (the demand made by the union) and B (the offer made by the employer), since bargaining will typically involve some element of "bluffing" (Hamermesh 1973), partly in recognition of the likelihood that concessions will need to be made subsequently.

A process of bargaining then ensues, with each party assumed to compare the utility associated with the certainty of accepting the offer made by the other, and the expected utility of turning it down and risking disagreement (conflict) in order to try to secure a more favourable offer subsequently. For example, if the union (denoted E) gains utility from an offer by the employer (F) of u_{EF}, while the utility from its own offer is u_{EE} if accepted by the employer and 0 if it is rejected, then the union will hold out for its own offer if: $u_{EF} \leq (1 - c_E)u_{EE}$, where c_E is the probability the union attaches to the probability of disagreement (i.e. that its offer will be rejected).[10] Similarly, the employer will hold out if $u_{FE} \geq (1 - c_F)u_{FF}$, where u_{FE} denotes the employer's utility from an offer made by the union, u_{FF} the utility from its own offer if acceded to by the union, and c_F its perception of the probability of disagreement. Rearranging each inequality thus gives the maximum probability that each side will risk in holding out for their own preferred outcome as

$$c_E \leq \frac{u_{EE} - u_{EF}}{u_{EE}} \text{ and } c_F \leq \frac{u_{FF} - u_{EF}}{u_{FF}} .$$

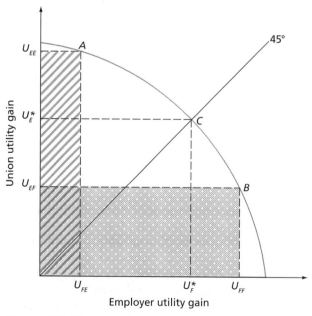

Figure 8.4 The Zeuthen–Harsanyi bargaining model.

Zeuthen assumes the party with the lower value of c ("risk-willingness") will make some form of concession. The union will do so if $c_E \leq c_F$, which will be the case if, on substitution and rearrangement, $u_{EE}u_{FE} \leq u_{EF}u_{FF}$. The left-hand side of this inequality is the utility product shown in Figure 8.4 as the hatched area, while the right-hand side is the dotted area. The situation in Figure 8.4 thus satisfies the criterion for the union to concede. The effect of this concession will be to raise the utility product $u_{EE}u_{FE}$ until it is large enough to reverse the inequality and elicit a corresponding concession by the employer, whose turn it now becomes to do so. Concessions by the employer will, in a similar way, increase the utility product $u_{EF}u_{FF}$ that it proposes. Successive concessions thus raise the overall size of the utility gains (the bargaining process is a **positive-sum game**), with the final outcome being where this product is maximised – point C in Figure 8.4 – which coincides with equal sharing of the utility gains (i.e. $u_F^* = u_E^*$).

Positive-sum game

A situation in which there is a mutuality of interests in securing particular choices by the parties in that the combined pay-offs are higher and thus all can be made better off.

While the Zeuthen–Harsanyi approach has a number of merits, not least the explicit recognition of concessions, which seems a feature of observed union–employer bargaining, it has also been criticised. Among other issues singled out for criticism are the ad hoc nature of the criterion determining which party concedes (Farber 1986) and how much (Bishop 1964); the lack of attention to the formation of subjective probabilities (Bishop 1964; Sapsford and Tzannatos 1993); and the failure of the parties to learn, either that the other party does not fully concede in successive rounds, despite this forming the basis of the above calculations (Saraydar 1965), or that the outcome might, in fact, be predicted and arrived at "without any play-acting" (Bishop 1964: 412).[11] In addition, in Zeuthen's model, one side or other concedes at each stage, and thus the model actually says little about strikes and other forms of industrial conflict that impose costs other than the failure to realise (utility) gains and, hence, may facilitate reconciliation of the demands of the two sides.

8.2.2 The Hicks model

Arguably the best known of all models of strike incidence, Hicks' (1932) model is represented in Figure 8.5. In this model, the employer's willingness to make

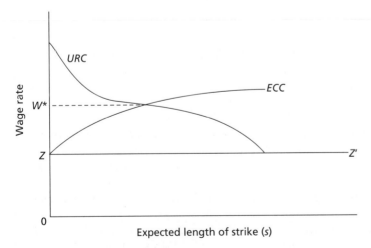

Figure 8.5 The Hicks model.

concessions in wage bargaining is positively related to *expected* strike duration(s), while the union's resistance to making concessions is inversely related to expected strike length.

The Employer Concession Curve (denoted ECC) in Figure 8.5 represents the locus of points at which the employer assesses the expected costs of a stoppage of a particular length are equal to the expected costs of concession in the form of higher wages, both appropriately discounted. In other words, it shows the *maximum* wage the employer would be willing to pay in order to avoid a strike of a particular duration. In the absence of a strike, this corresponds to 0Z, which might be thought of as the competitive wage.

Case Study 8.2

Who "wins" in bargaining?

Criticisms of the Zeuthen–Harsanyi approach notwithstanding, Hamermesh (1973) identified that the solution proposed in this model (which, as noted above, is identical to that proposed by Nash, albeit via a different logic) is explicit: namely, that the outcome involves the parties "splitting the difference". This outcome can thus potentially be tested with appropriate data to assess whether parties do indeed arrive at such an outcome, or whether one side instead "wins".

However, doing so is far from straightforward. This is because, as Hamermesh describes (1973: 1147), the theoretical model is specified in utility terms, while one argument in parties' utility functions – wages – is not. Moreover, departures from the predictions of the model may arise from differences in the amount of bluffing by each side. Thus, he argues, one must assume the two sides have identical, linear utility functions specified in terms of wages only, while, if they bluff, they do so symmetrically. As such, the model jointly tests these assumptions as well as the underlying theory.

Using data on initial demands, offers and settlements for 43 US public-sector negotiations between 1968 and 1970, Hamermesh reports average wage increases of 12 per cent, located roughly one-quarter of the distance between the average of employers' initial offers (mean of 8 per cent) and unions' initial demands (23 per cent). To test the model he calculates:

$$Z = \left[\dot{W}_D - \dot{W}_S \right] - \left[\dot{W}_S - \dot{W}_E \right]$$

where $\dot{W}$ denotes a percentage wage change, and the subscripts D, E and S correspond to the union's initial demand, the employer's initial offer and the final settlement respectively. A t-statistic of 3.83 indicates the mean of Z (7.23) is significantly different from zero, and thus is closer to the employer's starting offer.

While Hamermesh stresses the difficulties of testing the underlying theory, the implication is that unions secure less than half the difference between their initial demands and the employers' initial offers. This is a finding confirmed in subsequent work by Bowlby and Schriver (1978) using data on 252 bargains between unions and a single employer – the Tennessee Valley Authority – over a 16-year period. These authors report a lower average for each of demands, offers and settlements (11 per cent, 3 per cent and 6 per cent respectively), and also for Z (1.79), but the last remains significantly different from zero ($t = 8.56$). They also find Z varies among both years and unions.

As to the causes of the observed asymmetry, Bowlby and Schriver ascribe this to "differential bluffing" by the two sides, and, in particular, to greater bluffing on the part of unions which is argued to result from pressure on union leaders to maintain their credibility with rank and file union members (see section 8.2.3). They thus share Hamermesh's less than sanguine view concerning the validity of testing the "splitting the difference" hypothesis.

D.S. Hamermesh, "Who 'Wins' in Wage Bargaining?", *Industrial and Labor Relations Review*, 26(4), 1973, pp. 1146–9.
R. Bowlby and W. Schriver, "Bluffing and the Split the Difference Theory of Wage Bargaining", *Industrial and Labor Relations Review*, 31(2), 1978, pp. 161–71.

The ECC in Figure 8.5 is drawn as upward sloping, reflecting that, as expected, strike duration and hence costs increase, so the employer is prepared to concede higher wages in order to avoid those costs. However, its slope becomes progressively shallower, reflecting the existence of some upper bound on the wages the employer will agree to regardless of strike length, when it will instead prefer to shut down rather than accede to union demands.

Analogously, the Union Resistance Curve (URC) shows "the length of time [union members] would be willing to stand out rather than allow their remuneration to fall below the corresponding wage" (Hicks 1963: 142). This curve is assumed to be negatively sloped, since workers will contemplate longer stoppages with the greater associated "temporary privations" (p. 142) in the form of lost earnings in order to avoid accepting lower wages. Eventually, as shown in Figure 8.5, the *URC* cuts *ZZ'*, which thus shows the maximum expected strike length that will be countenanced; if a strike is expected to last beyond that point, the loss of earnings involved in striking become so great that workers will instead prefer simply to accept the competitive wage 0Z.

Hicks argues that, if both parties are equally well informed about the concession and resistance curves, and can thus identify the (unique) point at which they intersect, then they will agree to the wage *W** without a strike, thereby avoiding the costs that would otherwise be suffered by each side. According to Hicks, therefore, rational, fully informed agents will never engage in strikes since it is always possible to do better by negotiating.[12]

As Hirsch and Addison (1986: 81) describe, it is possible to (further) illustrate the **Pareto superiority** of the no-strike outcome diagrammatically as in Figure 8.6 by "restating the Hicks model along the lines suggested by Comay and Subotnik (1977)". The union's indifference curves (denoted I_U) are upward sloping, reflecting the trade-off between higher wages and the costs associated with greater expected strike length. For a strike of any given length, utility will be greater for higher wage rates, so indifference curves to the north-east in Figure 8.6 correspond to higher union utility. The employer's **iso-profit contours** are represented by π_F, which are downward sloping since the greater costs associated with a longer strike are offset by lower wages. Contours closer to the origin are associated with higher profits. In this framework, bargainers can improve on any point that is not on the vertical axis – i.e. that involves some non-zero strike length – which points must be Pareto inferior. For example, starting from point *B*, the union is at least as well-off at any point to the left along I_U^2, and better off at any point above that indifference curve. The employer, on the other hand, is as well off at any point to the left of *B* along π_F^2 as it is at *B*, and better off for any points below that iso-profit contour. Thus, there is a

Iso-profit contours

Combinations of variables (e.g. strike length and negotiated wage rate) such that the level of profits does not change.

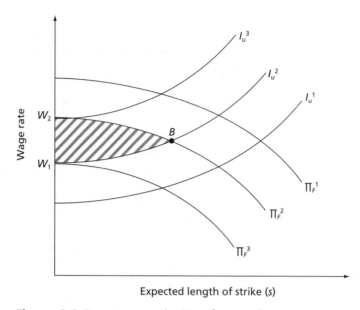

Figure 8.6 Pareto superiority of no-strike outcome.

range of outcomes shown by the hatched area in Figure 8.6 that are preferred by one or both sides to B, and any wage between W_1 and W_2 is thus a Pareto improvement.

This naturally raises the question as to why strikes occur. For Hicks, they were the result of incomplete or **asymmetric information**, and thus the result of misjudgements about the position and shape of the other party's concession curve. Thus, although recognising that it may sometimes be necessary/worthwhile for union leaders to call strikes in order to establish/maintain the credibility of the threat (since "weapons grow rusty if unused" (p. 146)), Hicks argued that "the majority of actual strikes are doubtless the result of faulty negotiation" (p. 146), and, as such, are accidents.

Hicks' insight concerning the role of errors has subsequently been extended and developed in a number of ways. For example, Mauro (1982) revised Hicks' model to place imperfect information centre stage, arguing that strikes are more likely where information is costly for the bargaining parties to acquire. Miscalculations about the shape and location of the concession curves may thus occur to the extent bargainers use the same variables in deriving both their own schedule and, mistakenly, in anticipating the other party's. Mauro uses the example of prices: the employer's concession curve might depend on the *product* price operating through labour demand, while the union's resistance curve might depend, via the real wage and labour supply, on *consumer* prices.

Figure 8.7 illustrates the potential effect of such differences. *ECC* and *URC* represent the true curves from Figure 8.5, while ECC_U is the employer's concession curve as perceived by the union, and URC_F is the union's resistance curve as perceived by the employer. As can be seen, each side holds optimistic views about the location of the other's curve, such that the union anticipates the outcome as W_U, while the employer expects W_F. Mauro thus concludes that strikes are more likely the greater the size of the disparity in expected wages.[13]

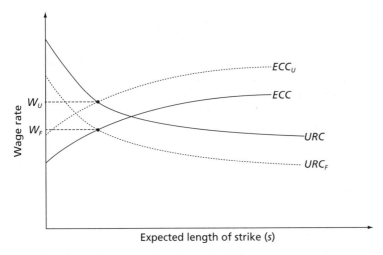

Figure 8.7 Mauro's extension to Hicks.

Siebert and Addison (1981) also focus on imperfect information in determining strike incidence, which they liken to traffic accidents: while individual accidents are unforeseen, the probability with which they occur on average is, and depends on choices made by drivers balancing the costs of time savings against the chances of an accident. In the strike context, Siebert and Addison argue that negotiators will therefore choose a negotiating period "and with it an associated wage increase and strike probability, so as to maximise income net of negotiating costs and expected strike losses" (1981: 392). In this framework, the optimum (finite) negotiating period will occur where the marginal costs and benefits for each party of extra information and the negotiating costs associated with obtaining this are equated. To the extent each side will be performing the same calculations, they may differ in their desired negotiating periods. Siebert and Addison assume such differences are reconciled by concessions on the part of the party gaining the most from negotiation, since this may ultimately make both sides better off.

Their model predicts that strikes are less likely when communication is easier (for example, in smaller firms, in contrast to the political models (see below)), where there is less to communicate (for example, during recessions when there may be limited scope for wage increases) and/or the bargaining environment and, hence, power of the parties are stable, and where the joint strike costs are highest (since the potential losses encourage the parties to negotiate for longer). As Hirsch and Addison (1986) note, the experience of the bargaining parties also matters, with more experienced pairs likely to be less prone to error, but being more likely to make mistakes in novel situations when bargainers have to operate largely *de novo*.[14]

The issue of joint strike costs is also considered by Reder and Neumann (1980).[15] In their model, however, rather than a longer negotiating period, such costs encourage the development of "bargaining protocols" or conventions governing behaviour in negotiations. These might include when and where the negotiations are to take place (including, for example, how close to contract expiry they are to commence), the persons to be involved on each side, provisions for third-party intervention in the event of impasse (for example, arbitration, conciliation or mediation, functions fulfilled in the UK by Acas – see Case Study 8.3), etc. Protocol specification is, however, costly, so Reder and Neumann argue bargaining pairs will choose the protocol that "balance[s] the cost reduction from reduced strike activity against the increased cost of specifying a more detailed protocol" (1980: 871). Thus, increasing joint strike costs reduces the probability of strikes by encouraging the development of more complex protocols among experienced bargaining pairs. As such, protocols might be described as constituting a choreographing of the negotiation "dance".[16]

The above models, which essentially fall within the class described as "Pareto optimal accident models" by Hirsch and Addison (1986), thus lead to the conclusion that strikes are more likely where negotiation costs, protocol costs and information costs are high relative to the (joint) costs of strikes. As they note (p. 86), these are testable hypotheses.

8.2.3 The Ashenfelter–Johnson "political" model

Possibly the most influential theoretical model of strikes among economists, however, is that of Ashenfelter and Johnson (1969). Drawing on early insights from Ross (1948), their model is "political" in the sense that it incorporates three parties to the negotiating process: management, union leaders and the rank and file union members they represent. The model involves a **principal–agent** relationship, with leaders and members possibly having different interests. Union leaders' objectives, for example, are argued to include the union's survival and growth as well as their own political survival. While these may largely coincide with the interests of members, they need not always do so. For example, rank and file members may be more extreme in their wage demands than their leaders. The latter, having superior information, may recognise that such demands are unattainable and, if unable to persuade members to accept a lower increase, may have to incur a strike rather than risk being seen to capitulate with management, even though this may not be in members' interests. Because strikes are costly to members, their aspirations moderate over time until they are low enough that leaders can settle without appearing to have "sold out". For Ashenfelter and Johnson, therefore, "the basic function of the strikes is as an equilibrating mechanism to square up the union membership's wage expectations with what the firm may be prepared to pay" (1969: 39).

More formally, Ashenfelter and Johnson define $y_A \equiv \dfrac{\Delta W}{\bar{W}}$ as the proportional wage increase acceptable to the rank and file, where ΔW is the absolute wage increase and $\bar{W}$ the existing wage. They assume this depends on strike length according to:

$$y_A = y^* + (y_0 - y^*)e^{-\tau S} \tag{8.3}$$

where y^* is the lower bound on acceptable wages, regardless of strike length (S), y_0 the wage increase acceptable at the start of negotiations (i.e. with no strike), and τ is the rate of decay of the acceptable wage increase as the strike proceeds. This is represented as the union concession schedule in Figure 8.8.

In this framework, union leaders pursue their own objectives subject to meeting the level of benefits acceptable to their members encapsulated in the concession schedule. The firm is assumed to know the parameters in this schedule, and attempts to maximise the present value of its current and future profits, choosing between

---

Principal–agent (theory)

This examines the problem that arises from the fact that a principal (say, an employer) may not have full information about the circumstances and behaviour of an agent (say, an employee). How then can the principal get the agent to act in the principal's best interests?

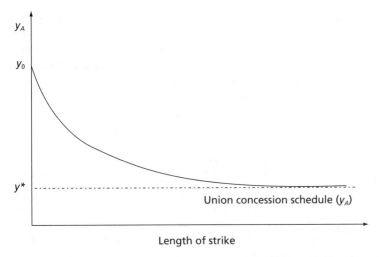

Figure 8.8 Ashenfelter and Johnson's model – the union concession curve.

paying a higher wage by agreeing to the union's last demand, or refusing this demand and accepting a strike in order to secure a lower settlement.[17]

The outcome which results can be shown diagrammatically[18] using the apparatus subsequently developed by Farber (1978) and reproduced in Figure 8.9. Thus, the firm's iso-profit contours are represented by the curves labelled π, with contours closer to the origin corresponding to higher profits (smaller wage rises and shorter strikes). The firm maximises profits subject to the union's concession schedule. In the left-hand panel, this occurs at the point of tangency A, which involves the firm "taking" a positive strike length s_0 and a wage rate y_s. In contrast, no strike will take place in the situation shown in the right-hand panel, since the firm's offer is better than or equal to the union's lowest acceptable wage increase (so equilibrium is at B).

As you may have noticed, the Ashenfelter–Johnson model, despite its widespread influence, and in many ways intuitively appealing predictions, has the less

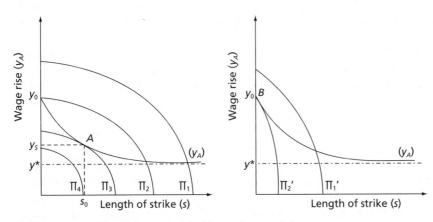

Figure 8.9 Ashenfelter and Johnson's model – outcomes.

attractive properties that (i) strikes are in some sense seen as "caused" by the union alone; (ii) the union leadership is essentially passive and "allows" the membership to go on strike (something that may even raise their political capital); and (iii) the asymmetry of treatment between a maximising employer with perfect knowledge and a non-maximising union with ignorant members. That said, there are also models extant in which the union maximises subject to an employer concession curve, for example, Siebert *et al.* (1985), as well as more fully two-sided models such as proposed by Rabinovitch and Swary (1976). In relation to the second criticism, Swint and Nelson (1978, 1980) develop a model in which the union leaders' interests are explicitly modelled and differ from those of their members.

Arguably the crucial feature in the Ashenfelter and Johnson model is the emphasis placed on the role of asymmetric information, which, as Hirsch and Addison note, means unequal access to the same information rather than the use of different information per Mauro. A number of subsequent papers have focused on this aspect, including contributions by Crampton (1984), Hayes (1984), Tracy (1987) and Card (1988). As Sapsford describes,

> Although precise details vary from one model to another, the basic idea is that one bargainer (typically the employer) possesses a larger information set than the other, and that the bargaining process serves as a learning mechanism, in which the less well-informed party infers information regarding the other's position by observing his or her behaviour during the negotiations.[19]
>
> (1990: 143)

In Hayes (1984), for example, a firm faced by a downward-sloping demand curve has more information about the state of the product market (and thus profitability) than the union. In the absence of any incentive for the firm to disclose the true state, the union offers a schedule of (declining) wages based on its expectation of the labour demand curve, so as to maximise its expected utility subject to the firm's maximising response. As Hayes argues (1984: 64), "the union is in effect offering wage/strike combinations ... [where s]trikes are used to achieve incentive compatibility" in the sense that the firm chooses the wage which reflects the outcome the union desires given that particular state. Strikes thus fulfil the function of providing information about the true state of nature.

Tracy (1987) instead assumes the asymmetry concerns the rents or size of the cake available to be divided between the parties. These rents include both **quasi-rents** arising from the specificity in the match and rents accruing from monopoly power in the product market. The firm is again assumed to be the fully informed party. Bargaining proceeds at each round with the union making a wage demand to maximise its expected return based on the information available, and which the firm either accepts or rejects. If the initial demand is rejected, a strike ensues. At each round, the union updates its information about the true size of the rents in light of the firm's acceptance or otherwise of the demand until settlement is reached. Again, therefore, the union learns from inferences drawn from the firm's responses.

Quasi-rents

The income earned from a sunk cost investment that is in excess of post-investment opportunity cost.

Although other models exist (see, for example, Booth and Cressy 1990), the above serves to illustrate the basic idea, which is that one party (the union) acts as leader, while the other (the employer) acts as follower. However, while containing useful insights, as in Ashenfelter and Johnson, the issue of asymmetry typically remains (see Kennan 1986; McConnell, 1990).

8.2.4 Individual strike rationality and the free-rider problem

Whereas the above considers the issue of strike rationality for the union as an entity, a further critical issue is why *individuals* might choose to take part in a strike when the benefits accrue both to all those covered by the collective bargain, (often) regardless of membership and individual adherence to a strike call. In other words, why individuals might choose not to free ride in the sense they could benefit from the gains from strikes without bearing any of the costs (of foregone income). This is an issue addressed by Naylor (1989), who brings together economics and sociology via a social custom model of strikes with its origins in the seminal contribution of Akerlof (1980) (in a similar spirit, see Booth's (1985) model of union membership).

Naylor assumes that an individual union member's utility function depends on five arguments:

$$u = u(M, R, s, b, \varepsilon) \tag{8.4}$$

where M is money income, R is reputation, s is a binary variable taking the value 1 if the individual adheres to the strike call and 0 if not, b is a binary variable taking the value 1 if the individual believes in the social custom and 0 if not, and ε denotes personal tastes. The population consists of some proportion μ of believers and, since $0 \leq \mu \leq 1$, a proportion $1 - \mu$ non-believers, these proportions being determined by external factors and fixed in the short run. Similarly, the proportion of strikers is λ, with $1 - \lambda$ non-strikers. The former is assumed to fall in the following period if $\lambda < \mu$, and to rise if the reverse holds.

Reputation depends on strike adherence (s), the proportion of believers and individual tastes, so that $R = R(s, \mu, \varepsilon)$, with the last of these distributed uniformly between ε_0 and ε_1, and high values characterising believers.

Using this model, Naylor proceeds to demonstrate a set of conditions under which even non-believers, rationally, will choose to strike. For example, he specifies the utility function as:

$$u = w(1 - s) + ds + \varepsilon \mu \bar{r} s - (1 - s)b\bar{c} - (1 - s)(1 - b)\bar{g} \tag{8.5}$$

where d is strike pay (from the union or government), $\bar{r}$ the coefficient on μ, $\bar{c}$ the loss of utility suffered by believers from disobeying the custom (not striking) and $\bar{g}$ the (smaller) corresponding loss of utility for non-believers.[20] Individuals are assumed to be utility maximisers, and so will strike if the utility from doing so is at least as great as that from not striking. From the above, a believer's utility if they strike ($b = 1$, $s = 1$) will be $u_i^s = d + \varepsilon_i \mu \bar{r}$. For a non-striking believer ($b = 1$, $s = 0$), it will be $u_i^{ns} = w - \bar{c}$. Thus, a believer will strike if $u_i^s \geq u_i^{ns}$, i.e. if $d + \varepsilon_i \mu \bar{r} \geq w - \bar{c}$. So the condition for a believer to strike is:

$$\varepsilon_i \geq \frac{w - \bar{c} - d}{\mu \bar{r}} \tag{8.6a}$$

For a non-believer, $b = 0$, and the corresponding condition as:

$$\varepsilon_i \geq \frac{w - \bar{g} - d}{\mu \bar{r}} \tag{8.6b}$$

As Naylor describes, the model can be depicted graphically, as in Figure 8.10. The line connecting $(\varepsilon_0, 1)$ and $(\varepsilon_1, 0)$ maps the proportion of believers (μ) against ε. At point k, for example, $\mu = 1$, and the entire population believes. The two curved lines in Figure 8.10 then show, for any value of μ, the critical value of ε, above which believers (shown as the lower of the two curves) and non-believers (the higher of the two curves) will strike. Thus, at point k, where everyone is a believer and will strike in response to a call, so the proportion of strikers, $\lambda = \mu = 1$. This is clearly an equilibrium, with "reputation effects and the disutility that would stem from disobedience offset[ting] the pecuniary incentive not to strike" (1989: 778). For points such as h, $\mu < 1$. For believers, $\varepsilon_h > \dfrac{w - \bar{c} - d}{\mu_h \bar{r}}$, the value which would induce

obedience, so all strike. Non-believers, on the other hand, would need a value of $\varepsilon > \varepsilon_h$ to induce compliance (read across at μ_h to the curve for non-believers to obtain $\dfrac{w - \bar{g} - d}{\mu_h \bar{r}}$). Thus, no non-believers will strike. This is an equilibrium since $\lambda = \mu$,

with no believers free riding, and all non-believers doing so.

Beyond point m, however, for example at n, the situation changes. There, all believers still have values of ε that exceed the level required for them to strike, so all will do so. But for non-believers, the critical value of ε is now $\dfrac{w - \bar{g} - d}{\mu_n \bar{r}}$, and, as can be seen, some proportion of non-believers, represented by the distance δ have values of ε that exceed this, and would thus be induced to strike. Thus, $\lambda > \mu$,

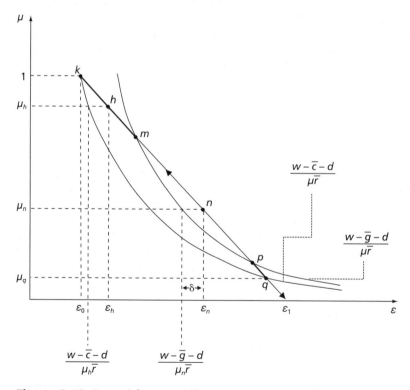

Figure 8.10 Free riders and the incentive to strike.

and in Naylor's model the latter will rise subsequently as shown by the directional arrow on the line segment *mn*. A similar logic can be applied to show that points between *p* and *q* are also equilibria, whereas points to the right of *q* will lead to movements towards ε_1. Thus, as Naylor describes, there are multiple equilibria in the ranges *km* and *pq* (shown by the heavier lines in Figure 8.10), and also where $\mu = 0$.

While highly stylised, this model illustrates that, because of social customs and the associated disutility effects of flouting a strike call, individually rational non-believers may still strike. As Naylor also argues, the model can also be used to explain phenomena such as union leaders emphasising the legitimacy of strikes and exaggerating the level of support/adherence. It also provides interesting insights into the need for union leaders, strategically, to time pre-strike ballots carefully.

Finally, a recent contribution by Olofsgård (2012) focuses on the issue of pre-strike ballots directly.[21] Union leaders are, as in Ashenfelter and Johnson's model, assumed to be better informed than the rank and file, but are also assumed by Olofsgård to be more militant than their members. Given the requirement for ballots ahead of industrial action, leaders will divulge information strategically so as to persuade union members to require higher wages. Crucially, union members may gain from electing leaders who are more militant than themselves (confirming earlier work by, *inter alia*, Jones 1989), since these may act to signal credible commitment to a particular information set (degree of ignorance) by the rank and file, which increases their bargaining power. In practice, however, turnouts in such ballots are frequently low, so that union leaders will emphasise the proportion of those voting who voted to strike, while the employer will stress the low turnout, thereby questioning the mandate.[22]

8.3 Empirical evidence on strikes

8.3.1 Determinants of strike activity

Given the number and variety of competing models of strike activity described above, ultimately it is necessary to attempt to discriminate among these empirically. This is, however, far from straightforward. In particular, testing is difficult due to the fact that suitable empirical proxies for many of the theoretical constructs (e.g. relative bargaining strength, concession rates, costs, etc.) are unobservable, while even more factual items, such as full sequences of offers/counter-offers from which one might draw inferences about parties' positions, are rarely observed, and, as Hamermesh (1973) and Bowlby and Schriver (1978) in Case Study 8.2 conclude, identification and other problems remain. As Hirsch and Addison (1986: 95) observe, studies also tend to confuse bargaining power and strike propensity.

In addition to conceptual problems, there is also the issue of how strikes themselves should be measured. As we have seen, they possess a number of dimensions – incidence/frequency, numbers involved, duration, days lost – potentially requiring different approaches and with different predictions.

In practice, much of the empirical literature has followed Ashenfelter and Johnson and focused on examining the relationship between strikes and the economic cycle. This is because, in implementing their model econometrically, Ashenfelter and Johnson utilise the unemployment rate and previous wage changes as proxies for y_0. Such relationships are, however, based on only loose theoretical underpinnings, in essence, the idea that, for example, union bargaining power falls and the costs of a strike to the union rise with unemployment. Ashenfelter and Johnson (1969) themselves find support for their own model using US data over the period 1952–67, with strikes found to be negatively related to unemployment, but positively related to past wage changes and also profits. While initially successful, and despite forming the basis of a number of studies and derivatives across various countries (e.g. Phipps 1977, for Australia; Walsh 1975 and Abbott 1984, for Canada; Turkington 1975 and Hazledine *et al.* 1977, for New Zealand; Reilly 1996, for Ireland; and Pencavel 1970; Shorey 1977; Davies 1979, for Britain), the model has been the subject of numerous criticisms, some of which were described above. Later studies such as Farber (1978), however, find effects that are weak and also that the model does not perform well against later data (Moore and Pearce 1982). This is perhaps not unsurprising and may be the consequence, as some have suggested, of flawed econometric technique and model (mis-)specifications (Shalev 1980; Abbott 1984).

Nonetheless, despite some exceptions (e.g. Farber 1978; Ingram *et al.* 1993; Nicolitsas 2000), the finding of a negative relationship between strike incidence and unemployment is something of an empirical regularity, replicated in many of the studies (see the survey by Paldam and Pedersen, 1982). It also appears to extend to more recent contributions such as Vroman (1989), Card (1990) and McConnell (1990), while Dickerson (1994) shows a strong procyclical relationship between the timing of cycles in production and strikes.

The importance of the measure of strikes used is illustrated by the fact that, in contrast to frequency, strike duration appears to be countercyclical, with a negative relationship between duration observed in most studies (e.g. Kennan 1985; Harrison and Stewart 1989; see also Kennan 1980). This is consistent with a joint-cost interpretation, which underpins several of these models (see also Tracy 1986). More recently, Devereux and Hart (2011) report evidence from the British engineering industry from 1920 to 1970. They consider the issues under negotiation, looking at pay and non-pay strikes, and durations are countercyclical for both, although only the latter is robust to controlling for union and firm **fixed effects**. In contrast, and reflecting the above discussion, the evidence suggests strike incidence is only weakly procyclical.

In relation to studies of the accident theories and their extensions, the limited evidence is broadly supportive. This class of models predicts strikes should be negatively related to the (joint) costs to both parties, a feature confirmed by Reder and Neumann (1980), Neumann (1980) and Mauro (1982).

In addition, there have been attempts to test asymmetric (private) information models. Examples include Tracy (1986) and McConnell (1989), although it is fair to conclude that support for these models is at best limited.

In relation to other factors that might affect strike incidence, various studies point to strikes being more likely in larger workplaces, aside from any recognition effects, reflecting the potential for communication breakdowns, more bureaucratic management and lower worker commitment. For the UK, for example, Marginson (1984), Blanchflower and Cubbin (1986), Booth and Cressy (1990) and Ingram *et al.* (1993) all confirm substantially higher incidence in larger plants, something that also appears to extend to strike duration. Marginson (1984), for example, finds the impact of both plant size and company size to be greater for strikes lasting for one day or more. Geroski *et al.* (1982) and Geroski and Knight (1983) also point to an

Fixed effects

Such models assist in controlling for unobserved individual heterogeneity in panel data when such heterogeneity is constant over time and correlated with the independent variables.

important role for market structure, suggesting that frequency is lower but duration longer in highly concentrated industries.

8.3.2 The costs of strikes

In section 7.4, we considered various dimensions of performance on which unions might impact. Here we focus more narrowly on the costs of unions arising from strike activity, and specifically in relation to output.[23] Such costs arise because, as the data in Figure 8.1 show, strikes involve lost working days. In the aggregate, however, the total loss of time (and hence output) to strikes is, in fact, very small, despite what at first sight might appear large numbers of days lost. For example, in the UK in 2008, some 759,000 days were lost to strikes, while the corresponding figure was slightly more than a million in 2007. That may appear a lot, but, to put it in context, and using a similar calculation to McConnell *et al.* (2006) for the US, even during the 1979 "Winter of Discontent", the number of days lost in the UK amounted to just 1.25 days per worker per year or, assuming an 8-hour day, the equivalent of 12 minutes per worker per week. The corresponding figure for 2008 was 0.25 minutes or just 15 seconds.[24] This is not, of course, to deny that the costs of strikes for particular firms and sectors are not substantial, and, indeed, this is part of the reason the tactic (or at least its threat) is deployed, but, at an economy-wide level, the costs are perhaps overstated.

Moreover, the local costs in terms of lost output may be lower than a crude measure of working days lost might initially suggest. For example, if **union density** is less than 100 per cent, firms may be able to continue production using non-striking employees and/or they may bring in external replacements (see Bastos *et al.* 2010 and the references there). Unless the good or service is highly perishable, they may also be able to continue supplying customers by running down inventories. All of these serve to reduce the effect (and potentially effectiveness) of strikes as a weapon. Moreover, some output may be caught up on resumption of production, and as such the net effects, at least directly on the firms immediately affected, are likely to be small. Indeed, it is possible productivity may even be boosted to the extent strikes are cathartic, enabling workers to "let off steam" (see Knight 1989).

Consideration of the output effects of strikes, however, also requires an assessment of any "spillover" effects, for example, to firms elsewhere in the **vertical chain** such as the firm's suppliers or downstream purchasers of the firm's output. Even here, however, matters are complicated by considerations such as downstream firms switching to alternative suppliers, whose output may increase to accommodate the extra demand. At the aggregate level, therefore, the picture is far from clear.

In relation to direct effects, empirical studies typically report only modest effects. For example, Knight (1989), using British industry-level data from 1968, estimates output per worker based on a Cobb–Douglas production function using:

$$\frac{\ln Q}{L} = \ln A + \frac{\alpha \ln K}{L} + (\beta + \alpha - 1)\ln L + \sigma' \mathbf{S} + e \qquad (8.7)$$

where A is a constant, Q is output, K is capital, L is labour, e is an error term and $\mathbf{S}$ is a vector of alternative strike dimensions. These include frequency (number of stoppages per person hour), working days lost and median duration, with both linear

> **Union density**
>
> Calculated as the number of currently enrolled union members as a proportion of all those employees eligible to be members.

> **Vertical chain**
>
> The sequence of stages in a production process from raw materials to finished product.

General-to-
specific approach

An econometric
methodology in
which a general
model is
sequentially
simplified by
eliminating the
least significant
variables until
further restrictions
are rejected by
significance tests.

and quadratic terms in each entered. After testing down the estimated model using a **general-to-specific approach**, Knight reports significant effects for only frequency and duration. The latter is found to reduce productivity (but at a diminishing rate) in almost all industries, in accordance with popular views. However, more frequent strikes are actually found to raise productivity. Consistent with earlier US findings by Neumann and Reder (1984), the combined effect is reported as being negative in 11 of the 52 industries studied, but is only small in magnitude (0.61 per cent). Knight argues this damage occurs primarily because these are industries where the ability to run down inventories is more limited. However, he finds strikes, in fact, impact positively in the majority of industries, albeit the effects are likewise numerically small (1.46 per cent).

More recently, Dickerson *et al.* (1997) adopt a frontier production function approach[25] using **panel data** for the period 1970–9, again at the industry level and based on a Cobb–Douglas specification with $Q = A \left[L \left(1 - \frac{S}{L} \right)^{\gamma} \right] K^{\beta}$. They estimate a fixed effects model with

Panel data

Data obtained from
the same sample of
individuals usually
on an annual basis.
In a balanced panel,
each person is
interviewed in
every year, while, in
an unbalanced
panel, some
individuals do not
appear in every
year. Sample
attrition over time
may mean that it is
necessary to add
new individuals to
the sample.

$$\ln Q_{it} = \delta_i + \alpha \ln L_{it} + \beta \ln K_{it} - \alpha \gamma \left(\frac{S}{L} \right) + v_{it} \qquad (8.8)$$

where i and t index industries and time respectively. This permits examination of two possible routes by which strikes may affect productivity. The first, direct route is measured via γ, while the second, indirect route, which might come about due to the insidious effects of strikes on the industrial-relations climate even when output is not disrupted, is captured by the industry-specific effects δ_i. Dickerson *et al.*, in fact, estimate a separate parameter for each i and t, allowing relative efficiency to vary over time. In a second stage, the contribution of strikes via this channel can then be examined by regressing these parameters on various characteristics, including strike frequency.

Their estimates show strike frequency has little direct effect on output, with the estimated coefficient being negatively signed, but insignificantly different from zero, even when added as a lag. This result is essentially confirmed when account is taken of strike duration and size, with only strikes of less than a day having a significant effect. Weighted least squares estimation of the δ parameters at the second stage also reveals little effect of strike frequency on technical efficiency.

As noted above, however, strikes may have spillover effects to other industries/firms. Dickerson *et al.* test for this by including a variable measuring the number of strikes in the same two-digit industry to which a particular three-digit industry belongs, but find little evidence for such effects. In contrast, McHugh (1991) considers the effect of strikes in industries with forward linkages and backward linkages, i.e. of strikes in supplying and purchasing industries using information on input–output structure. Using data from 1967 to 1981, he finds only modest evidence for the impact of own strikes, but statistically significant negative effects on labour productivity in linked industries.

Of course, as McHugh notes, this abstracts from within industry effects, with struck firms possibly losing goodwill and sales to non-struck competitors. This issue is examined by De Fusco and Fuess (1991). Using stock-market data for the period 1968–86, they find the stock-market values of airline carriers who were the subject of strikes were adversely affected, while those of non-struck firms were enhanced. As they note, however, these effects may arise because of the impossibility of using inventories in this context (a consideration relevant, of course, in the context of the BA dispute in Case Study 8.1).

8.4 Individual workplace conflict

8.4.1 Institutional background and the Employment Tribunal system

As discussed above, the level of strike activity has diminished substantially over time, a phenomenon evidenced across numerous countries. In Britain, this decline has been largely mirrored by a growing number of complaints in relation to (individual) employment rights, with such rights and unresolved conflict between employer and employee arising from them dealt with through the Employment Tribunal (ET) system – essentially a form of labour court.[26] As shown in Figure 8.11, the growth in the number of claims has been dramatic.

The recent origins of ETs lie in the Industrial Training Boards established in 1964 to consider exemptions to the training levy imposed on firms at that time. Their first "party vs. party" type of case (jurisdiction) was in relation to redundancy payments, followed by unfair dismissal (see Corby and Latreille 2012, for a short history). Since that time, the range of issues dealt with by tribunals has expanded substantially, and there are now around 80 jurisdictions, including, *inter alia*, unlawful deductions from wages, holiday entitlements and pay, equal pay, breach of contract, as well as discrimination on the grounds of sex, race, age, disability, sexual orientation and religion or belief. Part of the growth in tribunal claims is attributable to the wider range of legal grounds for complaint (Latreille *et al.* 2007), but other factors such as a growth in litigiousness and the displacement of collective to individual forms of grievance may also play a role. Indeed, some have argued that "Some unions … actively encourage individuals whose cases form part of what is, in effect, a class action against employers. The aim is to achieve through employment tribunals what can no longer be achieved through strikes" Shackleton (2002: 47). While this last view has been challenged given the different issues strikes and tribunals typically address (for example, Dix *et al.* 2009), it is difficult

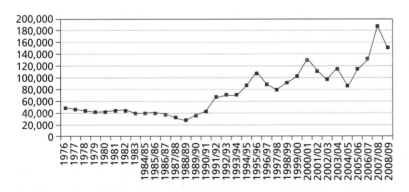

Source: ETS internal statistical information, 1976–97/8; ETS Annual Reports thereafter.

Figure 8.11 Claims to Employment Tribunals.

not to view the two as unrelated, even if only to the extent that they reflect the same underlying changes to the labour market and legislative environment.

The process of bringing a claim to an ET is summarised in Figure 8.12. It is initiated by the individual who considers their employment rights have been infringed submitting an ET1 form to the Tribunals Service setting out the nature and circumstances of the complaint. If the claim is accepted, the employer is then asked to complete a "notice of appearance" or ET3 form within 21 days. At this point, the claim will be referred to Acas, which has a statutory duty to attempt conciliation, i.e. to support the parties in attempting to resolve the dispute without the need for a full merits hearing (see Case Study 8.3). Depending on circumstances, one or more "interlocutory processes" may take place, for example, pre-hearing reviews or preliminary hearings to determine certain (often technical) issues, such as whether the individual is an employee. Where it is considered that the case or its defence is "misconceived" (i.e. has no reasonable chance of success), warnings are sometimes issued that, should the claim proceed and not be upheld, costs may be awarded.[27]

As Figure 8.12 shows, ETs can be resolved in a number of ways. For example, the parties may agree to some form of mutually acceptable settlement, the nature of which will depend on the type of claim but will often involve some form of financial compensation. Such settlements may be reached with the help of Acas (so-called COT3 settlements), or privately. The claimant may also withdraw their case without any concession on the part of the employer. Claims may also be dismissed by the tribunal without a hearing on what will often be technical reasons, such as being outside the permitted time limits (usually three months from the event giving rise to the claim).

If not otherwise resolved, the claim will be heard at a full merits hearing, which, as the name tribunal might suggest, typically involves a panel of three persons: an Employment Judge and two lay members, one chosen from each of two lists intended to be representative of employers and employees.[28] The tribunal will consider the evidence, including any provided by witnesses, before reaching a decision on the merits of the claim ("liability") and, if upheld, any remedy. The latter will typically involve compensation (see below).

In principle, individuals may bring complaints against their employer on the basis of more than one jurisdiction. The Tribunals Service refers to each type of complaint as a jurisdictional claim, and on average in 2010–11 each claim submitted to the employment tribunal contained 1.75 jurisdictional claims (see Table 8.2). As we have seen previously, the number of claims has risen dramatically over time, this being particularly true in the latter part of the period covered (see Figure 8.11), with 2009–10 establishing the record for the number of claims accepted at 236,100 claims and 392,800 jurisdictional claims.

As Figure 8.11 shows, the total number of claims shows significant variation from year to year, although the bulk of this is accounted for by so-called "multiples", that is, claims brought by more than one individual (akin to a class action). These typically relate to Working Time Directive or equal pay cases where a number of significant and large-scale claims have been brought in recent years.

The jurisdictional mix of claims accepted provides some clues to the nature of rights-based conflict at the workplace, and also to the factors driving the increase in numbers. For example, whereas unfair dismissal has historically been the single largest jurisdictional claim, in 2009–10 and 2010–11, the largest jurisdictional claim related to the Working Time Directive, with some 114,100 claims. Other than

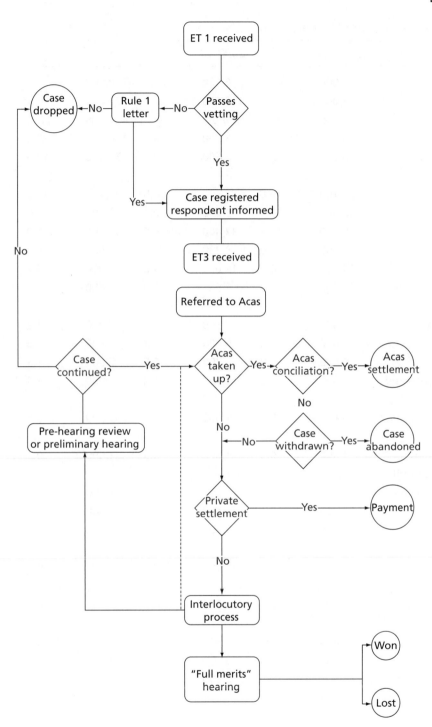

Source: Peters M. *et al.* (2010).

Figure 8.12 ET claim process.

Table 8.2 Claims accepted by Employment Tribunals

	2008–09		2009–10		2010–11	
Total claims accepted	151,000		236,100		218,100	
Total claims disposed	92,000		112,400		122,800	
Jurisdictions	*Number*	*%*	*Number*	*%*	*Number*	*%*
Working Time Directive	24,000	9.0	95,200	24.2	114,100	29.8
Unauthorised deductions (formerly Wages Act)	33,800	12.7	75,500	19.2	71,300	18.6
Unfair dismissal	52,700	19.8	57,400	14.6	47,900	12.5
Breach of contract	32,800	12.3	42,400	10.8	34,600	9.0
Equal pay	45,700	17.1	37,400	9.5	34,600	9.0
Sex discrimination	18,600	7.0	18,200	4.6	18,300	4.8
Redundancy pay	10,800	4.1	19,000	4.8	16,000	4.2
Redundancy – failure to inform and consult	11,400	4.3	7,500	1.9	7,400	1.9
Disability discrimination	6,600	2.5	7,500	1.9	7,200	1.9
Age discrimination	3,800	1.4	5,200	1.3	6,800	1.8
Race discrimination	5,000	1.9	5,700	1.5	5,000	1.3
Written statement of terms and conditions	3,900	1.5	4,700	1.2	4,000	1.0
Suffer a detriment/unfair dismissal – pregnancy	1,800	0.7	1,900	0.5	1,900	0.5
Transfer of an undertaking – failure to inform and consult	1,300	0.5	1,800	0.5	1,900	0.5
Part-Time Workers Regulations	660	0.2	530	0.1	1,600	0.4
Written pay statement	1,100	0.4	1,400	0.4	1,300	0.3
Written statement of reasons for dismissal	1,100	0.4	1,100	0.3	930	0.2
Discrimination on grounds of religion or belief	830	0.3	1,000	0.3	880	0.2
Discrimination on grounds of sexual orientation	600	0.2	710	0.2	640	0.2
National minimum wage	600	0.2	500	0.1	520	0.1
Others	9,300	3.5	8,100	2.1	5,500	1.4
Total of jurisdictional claims	266,500		392,800		382,400	
Average number of jurisdictions per claim	1.76		1.66		1.75	

Source: Adapted from Ministry of Justice (2011).

Note: Jurisdictions refer to the type(s) of complaint within each claim.

Table 8.3 Claims disposed of by Employment Tribunals

Jurisdictions	Number	Withdrawn %	Acas-conciliated settlement %	Struck out not at hearing %	Dismissed at preliminary hearing %	Successful at hearing %	Unsuccessful at hearing %	Default judgment %
Unfair dismissal	49,600	24.8	41.3	10.9	2.8	8.5	9.7	2.4
Wages Act	38,200	33.0	27.2	8.9	1.8	14.1	5.5	9.4
Breach of contract	31,800	23.0	32.4	8.5	2.4	17.0	7.2	10.1
Redundancy pay	14,100	26.2	18.4	9.9	1.4	22.7	4.8	15.6
Sex discrimination	15,600	48.7	27.6	16.0	1.3	1.9	3.8	0.6
Race discrimination	4,900	28.6	34.7	10.2	5.3	3.1	16.3	1.0
Disability discrimination	6,800	30.9	45.6	7.5	2.9	2.8	9.4	0.7
Religious belief discrimination	850	29.4	34.1	10.9	6.2	3.2	14.1	1.4
Sexual orientation discrimination	660	31.8	40.9	10.6	3.3	3.3	9.4	1.4
Age discrimination	3,700	40.5	35.1	9.5	3.2	2.4	8.6	0.6
Working time	24,100	26.1	29.5	7.9	2.2	18.3	5.8	10.8
Equal pay	25,600	59.8	11.7	20.7	0.1	1.1	6.6	0.0
National minimum wage	600	20.0	33.3	6.2	1.8	12.5	21.7	5.0
Others	27,400	28.1	23.0	5.1	1.9	16.1	20.8	5.1
All	244,000	32.1	29.3	10.5	2.0	11.5	8.7	5.9

Source: Adapted from Ministry of Justice (2011).

that, substantial numbers of claims are brought in relation to unauthorised deductions from wages, unfair dismissal and equal pay. Much smaller numbers are typically brought in relation to the various discrimination strands.

In relation to outcomes, Tribunals Service statistics also reveal some interesting features (Table 8.3). First, of the 244,000 claims disposed during 2010–11, around a third (32 per cent) were recorded as withdrawn, with a further 29 per cent as Acas-conciliated settlements. The figures for withdrawals do, however, need to be interpreted with caution, since they include both genuine withdrawals and private settlements; survey data suggest that, in 2008, more than half these "withdrawals" were, in fact, private settlements. Some 10 per cent of all claims in 2010–11 were struck out without a hearing, with 2 per cent dismissed at a preliminary hearing and a further 6 per cent issued a default judgment. Thus, of the claims brought, just 21 per cent were decided at a full merits hearing, with 12 per cent of the total number of claims brought resulting in a successful outcome for the claimant and the remaining 9 per cent being unsuccessful. Thus, of those claims decided at a hearing, the success rate across all jurisdictions is approximately 57 per cent. Focusing on success rates at hearings, again variation is evident. In the working time jurisdiction, for example, some three-quarters of cases heard are upheld, whereas the proportion of successful unfair dismissal cases is somewhat below half. For discrimination claims, however, success rates are even lower, falling to a third or less, and fewer than one in five for race and religion or belief discrimination claims.

Statistics for the compensation awarded are presented in Table 8.4, which shows the amounts involved are typically modest, with the exception of a small number of large awards (compensation is capped in unfair dismissal claims but not discrimination, so the maximum awards in Table 8.4 for the former jurisdiction indicate it was combined with another type of claim). Unfair dismissal claimants, for example, received median awards of just over £4,500 in 2010–11 (or around 11 weeks' pay for the average full-time worker on adult rates using ONS data). Even for jurisdictions where the upper limit is uncapped, however, the average amounts are not large.

Table 8.4 Compensation awarded by Employment Tribunals, 2010–11

	Maximum	Mean	Median
Unfair dismissal	£181,754	£8,924	£4,591
Race discrimination	£62,530	£12,108	£6,277
Sex discrimination	£289,167	£13,911	£6,078
Disability discrimination	£181,083	£14,137	£6,142
Religious belief discrimination	£20,221	£8,515	£6,892
Sexual orientation discrimination	£47,633	£11,671	£5,500
Age discrimination	£144,100	£30,289	£12,697

Source: Adapted from Ministry of Justice (2011).

Notes: Amounts are total compensation for claims involving the specified jurisdiction; claims may involve more than one jurisdiction.

8.4.2 Models of settlement

As should be evident from the account above, although not identical, the procedural framework for ETs possesses important similarities with civil litigation, where a plaintiff (claimant) brings a claim or claims against a defendant (respondent/ employer) alleging a grievance/wrongdoing by the latter.

As we have seen, most ET cases are resolved prior to a hearing, a feature shared with civil litigation, albeit settlement rates are higher (around 95 per cent) for the latter (Main and Park 2003: 177). In that context, there are now numerous studies exploring the determinants of pre-trial negotiation and resolution; so-called "bargaining in the shadow of the law" (Mnookin and Kornhauser 1979), some of which has begun to find its way into the literature considering ETs. A clear and succinct introduction to the main ideas is provided by Miceli (2004), while Hay and Spier (1998) offer a more comprehensive, but equally accessible survey of this work which is drawn on and contextualised for the ET setting in Latreille (2007).

The theoretical underpinning of this literature derives from the early contributions of Landes (1971), Gould (1973) and Posner (1973), with the explanatory workhorse being the notion of the "contract zone" (Farber and Katz 1979). This is a range of settlements that both parties to a dispute would prefer rather than allowing a third party to determine the outcome. The existence of this set of preferred outcomes essentially derives from the fact that the prosecution and defence of cases is costly: settlement permits savings on these costs and so generates a potential surplus to be distributed between the parties.

The question addressed in much of the theoretical literature is therefore why, given the potential existence of this bargaining range, a proportion of cases nonetheless fail to settle and hence result in a court (here, tribunal) hearing. In this respect, the literature is akin to that on strikes, in that a potentially preferred outcome fails to emerge. As Hay and Spier (1998: 442) describe, there are four major explanations for this failure to settle in the literature: divergent expectations concerning the trial outcome; failure to agree on a settlement point; the impact of (legal) representation; and "self-serving" biases (see below).

The first of these arises from expectational differences between the parties, and, in particular, over-optimistic expectations about the chances of success or the size of the award (something that Acas conciliators attempt to remedy). This can potentially shrink or even eliminate the contract zone and, hence, the chances of settlement. The contract zone may also be absent if the point at issue is non-divisible, for example, the desire to be reinstated in an unfair dismissal claim, and will be further affected by the costs and degree of risk aversion of the two parties (Cooter and Rubinfeld 1989). As should be evident, all else being equal, the greater the (court) costs incurred by each party, or the more risk averse is each side (the more attractive the certainty of settlement), the wider the bargaining range will be.

According to the civil-litigation literature, divergent expectations themselves may arise via one of two routes (Miceli 2004; Farmer and Tiefenthaler 2001): through overestimates of the chances of success ("optimism models"), or from asymmetric information concerning, for example, liability or damages. Without going into details, it is worth noting that these bear similarities to the literature on strikes, with the latter class of models reaching differing outcomes depending on which party is informed and makes the offer (see Hay and Spier 1998, for more details).

The second explanation for the failure to settle concerns the possibility that, even where a contract zone exists, the parties may not be able to agree on a division of the potential surplus (Cooter *et al.* 1982). Aspirations rates of time preference clearly matter here, with parties possibly declining offers if they believe improved offers will be forthcoming subsequently (Korobkin 2002). Parties may also decline offers that, while being within the bargaining range, are close to their reservation point and thus violate some concept of "fairness" (ibid.).

A further possible explanation concerns the impact that (in this literature, legal) representation may exert on the decisions of the parties. The direction of this influence is, however, ambiguous, a priori. On the one hand, representatives possess greater experience and legal/procedural knowledge that may reduce (even if not eliminate) error/optimism. Contingent-fee lawyers may also wish to settle quickly so as to minimise effort and cost and allow them to move to the next case (see Rickman 1999), even though this may not be in their client's best interests (an example of a principal–agent problem). Conversely, hourly paid lawyers have precisely the opposite incentive.

Finally, there is evidence from various settings that parties tend to process and interpret identical pieces of information selectively in ways that favour their perspective, a phenomenon known as "self-serving" bias (Loewenstein *et al.* 1993; Mnookin 1993; see Babcock and Loewenstein 1997, for a comprehensive review). Thus, **self-serving bias** arises when (optimistic) predictions vary from the same "facts", although concepts of fairness are also likely to reflect the perspective of the party (Babcock and Loewenstein 1997). They may, in addition, recall the same set of events very differently, something that is likely to further impede settlement (Latreille 2007).

As may be evident, these models, in some sense, assume a departure from pure rationality in that "the self-serving bias hurts both parties economically" (Babcock and Loewenstein 1997: 116). A more extreme departure would appear to apply in models such as those involving "spite", in which "players may receive utility or disutility from the final position of the other party" (Farmer and Tiefenthaler 2001: 164), or, as Latreille (2007) suggests in the ET context, issues of "principle". As we will see in section 8.4.3, a small number of papers consider issues relating to settlement, but the literature remains underdeveloped, and constrained by the availability of data.

Self-serving bias

A cognitive bias in which individuals interpret information in ways favourable to themselves, for example, relative contributions to a team task, or the evidence supporting their perspective in a dispute.

8.4.3 Empirical studies of tribunals

In the context of ET disputes, there is now a small literature, building on the early work of Dickens *et al.* 1984, 1985), that considers quantitative evidence on ETs and their operation. This literature explores a range of issues including the number/incidence of claims (Burgess *et al.* 2001; Brown *et al.* 1997; Knight and Latreille 2000a); pre-hearing resolution and settlement (Knight and Latreille 2000b; Latreille 2007; Saridakis *et al.* 2008); outcomes at hearings (Knight and Latreille 2001; Saridakis *et al.* 2008), including awards (Knight and Latreille 2001); and the role of representation (Latreille *et al.* 2005; Urwin *et al.*, forthcoming). Researchers have also examined views towards Acas (Latreille *et al.* 2007), the impact of cases on employers (Earnshaw *et al.*, 1998, 2000) and claimants' post-claim experiences (Drinkwater *et al.* 2011). Most recently, Corby and Latreille (2012) examine the views of judges and lay members, coincidentally at a time when proposals for further reductions in the latter's role was being proposed.

Case Study 8.3

Acas – settling workplace disputes since 1974[29]

The Advisory, Conciliation and Arbitration Service (Acas) in the UK has its origins in the Conciliation Act 1896, when the government set up a voluntary arbitration and conciliation service. Name changes followed in 1960 (to the Industrial Relations Service) and again in 1972 (to the Conciliation and Advisory Service), with Acas established in its current guise in 1974, when it was named the Conciliation and Arbitration Service and separated from government control. The "Advisory" part of the title was added in 1975, and in 1976 it became a statutory body under the provisions of the Employment Protection Act 1975. This enshrined the principle of Acas independence, although it remains largely funded by central government (currently the Department for Business, Innovation and Skills (BIS)). Its governance is provided by an independent Chair and a tripartite Council of 11 additional members including business experts, trade union representatives and independent members (e.g. academics).

In terms of its statutory remit, Acas' legislative terms of reference is "to promote the improvement of industrial relations". From 1975 until the late 1990s, Acas was largely a dispute-resolution organisation. Today, however, reflecting its mission statement "to improve organisations and working life through better employment relations", Acas' work focuses on four main areas: preventing and resolving disputes between employers and their workers; settling complaints about employee rights; providing information, advice and training; and encouraging people to work together more effectively.

In the dispute-resolution context, there are three main strands to Acas' work[30]: collective conciliation; individual conciliation; and pre-claim conciliation. The first of these involves a statutory power to assist employers and (typically) unions "Where a trade dispute exists … with a view to bringing about a settlement" (Trade Unions and Labour Relations (Consolidation) Act 1992, s.210(1)). Currently, around 1,000 disputes per year are dealt with, including high-profile disputes such as the BA/Unite dispute in Case Study 8.1. Tactics employed include trying to improve the environment within which dialogue can take place, bringing an independent view of parties' positions, generating new ideas and a means by which options can be explored indirectly through a third party without the protagonists appearing weak, and forcing consideration of the possible ramifications of continued disagreement. They appear to work. In 2010–11, 91 per cent of collective conciliation cases were settled or the parties resumed negotiations (compared with an 80 per cent performance target), with other benefits identified including faster resolution, improved morale, improved practices and better communication. Interestingly, the same legislation (s. 210(3)) states that "In exercising its functions … Acas shall encourage the parties … to use … agreed procedures for negotiation or the settlement of disputes"; in other words, to adopt bargaining protocols.

The second strand concerns individual conciliation, where Acas has a legal duty to promote settlement of claims referred to it involving claims to the Employment Tribunal. In 2010–11, more than 74,000 net cases were received for individual conciliation, with 78 per cent of the potential hearing days that might otherwise have been involved in these cases saved (on the basis of settlement or withdrawal of the claim). As Dix (2000) describes, drawing on a framework by Kressel and Pruitt (1985, 1989), the key roles played by Acas conciliation officers are "reflexive" – that is, building trust, rapport and establishing impartiality; "informative" – overcoming information deficits about legal positions and asymmetries between the parties (cf. strike models such as Tracy 1987, cited previously); and "substantive" – facilitating convergence of positions, for example, by encouraging parties to consider the strengths and weaknesses of their case, how it might be seen by the tribunal, etc. These roles have been explored empirically among a sample of representatives, such as lawyers and union officials, who are typically repeat users of the system. The evidence suggests Acas is largely successful in securing trust and being perceived as impartial, and is seen as an important factor in reaching settlement/bringing the parties closer together by more than half those surveyed (see Latreille *et al.* 2007).

The final (current) major dispute-resolution element of Acas' work is pre-claim conciliation, which involves attempting to resolve potential claims prior to their being lodged. Such potential claims are identified via the Acas Helpline, with the number of referrals rising since the scheme's full introduction in 2009–10, following a pilot, from 9,758 in the first year to 21,516 from April 2011 to February 2012.

The evidence suggests that, in 2009–10 and 2010–11, tribunal proceedings were avoided in around 70 per cent of such cases. Benefits to the parties from such early resolution include lower amounts of time and cost compared with a claim and hearing (for example, the average PCC case cost £475 for the employer, compared with £5,685 for an ET claim). Cases settled at PCC are also confidential, thus avoiding adverse publicity, and more flexible solutions that might not be deliverable under the legal constraints of an Employment Tribunal are also possible.

Perhaps because of Acas' success across a range of dispute-resolution areas (see Meadows 2007, for an evaluation of Acas' contributions in this area and more broadly, including advice, training and mediation), the government has recently announced that, from April 2014, "early conciliation" will be introduced for all potential, individual Employment Tribunal claims. Under these provisions, claimants will need to notify Acas before bringing a claim with a "conciliation pause" of one calendar month to allow conciliation to take place, the aim being to reduce the number of claims needing to be dealt with by Employment Tribunals.

For further details of Acas and its work, visit its web site at: www.acas.org.uk.

Acas, *Advisory, Conciliation and Arbitration Service (Acas) Annual Report and Accounts 2010/11*, The Stationery Office, London, 2011.
P.L. Latreille, J.A. Latreille and K.G. Knight, "Employment Tribunals and Acas: Evidence from a Survey of Representatives", *Industrial Relations Journal*, 38(2), 2007, pp. 136–54.
P. Meadows, *A Review of the Economic Impact of Employment Relations Services Delivered by Acas*, National Institute for Economic and Social Research, London, 2007.
B. Towers and W. Brown, editors, *Employment Relations in Britain: 25 Years of the Advisory, Conciliation and Arbitration Service* (which contains the chapter referred to above by Dix G., "Operating with Style: The Work of the ACAS Conciliator in Individual Employment Disputes").

The studies by Burgess *et al.* and Brown *et al.* are interesting in that they use time series data to consider the role of cyclical and other factors as drivers of the number of claims. This is important from a policy perspective in a climate in which government is keen to reduce the numbers of claims made (witness the Acas early conciliation scheme in Case Study 8.3) and the impact on the public purse. This is undoubtedly part of the rationale for the proposed introduction of fees for bringing/hearing claims recently put to consultation. Burgess *et al.* consider a range of jurisdictional types, finding that, as might be expected, different factors influence each. For example, unfair dismissal is found to be driven by observed (aggregate) past success rates (as a proxy for expected value of a case) and by the proportion of employees in small firms, the latter reflecting the more informal arrangements in such workplaces and, hence, the greater reliance on legislative redress (see Saridakis *et al.* 2008). The former is also important for Wages Act (now unlawful deductions) claims and redundancy payments. Unemployment, however, as a proxy for the cycle, turns out not to be significant. In contrast, Brown *et al.* (1997), focusing only on unfair dismissal, find cyclical proxies such as unemployment and vacancies to be more important than legislative changes (e.g. to the qualifying period).

In relation to settlement, Knight and Latreille (2000a) use data from the 1992 Survey of Industrial Tribunal Applications[31] to explore the *stage* of resolution (which includes both settlement and withdrawal of claims), relating this in a loose fashion to the concepts of error and the contract zone/bargaining range. Their results suggest that resolution at "conciliation" (immediately following receipt of the (now) ET3) is largely determined by applicant characteristics and jurisdiction, while at the "pre-tribunal" stage (any subsequent period prior to a full hearing), employer and case characteristics appear more important. While not a formal test, variables likely to be associated with error and "intent" (i.e. the costs of agreeing and disagreeing prior to a hearing) are found to operate consistently with such an interpretation.

Subsequently, Latreille (2007) has examined factors associated with offers of settlement by employers and acceptance of offers by claimants using the 2003 Survey of Employment Tribunal Applications. While subject to data limitations, the findings suggest offers are less likely the more optimistic the employer is about the chances of success, while the more optimistic claimants are about the size of any ET award compared with the offer, the less likely it is to be accepted. Both are consistent with the above discussion, suggesting that optimism shrinks the contract zone (for a formal attempt to estimate which, using Australian data, see Freyens 2011). Strikingly, Acas involvement increases both the chances of an offer and (conditional) acceptance.

Studies of hearing outcomes are also small in number. Knight and Latreille (2001) find gender to be a significant determinant in relation to liability in unfair dismissal claims using 1992 data, a finding they attribute to strength of case (for which there is no direct proxy, although controls are included for receiving a written statement of terms and conditions, a graduated series of warnings and for the presence and use of formal disciplinary/grievance processes). For remedy, they find tribunals are, on average, largely mechanistic, relating to characteristics that reflect the financial damage suffered by the dismissed individual, even though there is discretion for them to reduce the scale of an award to the extent the employee contributed to their dismissal. In contrast, Saridakis *et al.* (2008), using data from the 2003 Survey of Employment Tribunal Applications, suggest no significant gender differences across a broader range of jurisdictions. They do, however, report several important variations by employer size. In particular, they find small employers are more likely to be the subject of claims, to experience different types of claims and also to lose at a hearing than are larger organisations. The last is attributed to the smaller employer's more informal approach to personnel issues. Representation is also important, although – as Urwin *et al.* (forthcoming) indicate, reporting that unrepresented claimants have higher success rates at hearings – not always in the direction one might expect. Relevant to the above theoretical discussion, however, they find settlement is more likely where both sides are legally represented, although such cases are of longer duration.

Summary

- Strikes have been an important historical feature of the labour market reflecting a threat that unions may deploy in relation to bargaining over pay and other terms and conditions.
- There are several dimensions to strikes: frequency, size and days lost.
- Historically, the incidence of strikes and action short of a strike are at low levels across a range of countries, and there is evidence that the character of strikes has altered over time too towards shorter, intermittent stoppages.
- A key issue in relation to strikes concerns their rationality, given the costs to both sides (those imposed on the employer constituting part of the effectiveness of the weapon), something referred to as the Hicks paradox.
- A number of competing models of strikes exist, including those of Zeuthen–Harsanyi and Nash; Hicks; and Ashenfelter and Johnson. The last two have been particularly influential, giving rise to classes of models in which strikes emerge as "accidents" or from asymmetric information. Protocols are likely to emerge as a means of reducing the joint costs of strikes.
- Empirical evidence on the determinants of strikes points to their being broadly procyclical in terms of frequency, while their duration appears to be counter-cyclical.
- In Britain, much workplace conflict is now of an individual form, manifesting in complaints to Employment Tribunals – a form of labour court – with the number of applications having risen dramatically over time.
- Analysis of this feature of the labour market, and in particular the pre-hearing settlement of claims, can, in principle, be analysed using similar approaches to those deployed in the civil litigation literature.

Questions

1 Examine the view that strikes are accidents and, thus, part and parcel of the collective-bargaining process.
2 How might the requirement for pre-strike ballots affect the credibility of union bargainers to pursue their members' interests? Do low turnouts matter?
3 Discuss how the predictions of the Ashenfelter and Johnson model differ if one assumes that the union maximises its utility subject to the constraint of an employer concession curve (Siebert *et al.* 1985).
4 To what extent does the evidence suggest that changes in the pattern of workplace conflict over the last 30 years represent a fundamental shift in the nature of disputes at work?
5 Visit the European Industrial Relations Observatory web site and the country profiles (www.eurofound.europa.eu/eiro/country_index.htm) and compare the UK with one or more countries of your choice in terms of their industrial-relations actors, arrangements and outcomes. Who are the key players? How frequent are strikes and other forms of industrial action, and in what sectors? How many workers are involved and days lost? What are the main issues involved? What arrangements (if any) exist for resolving disputes (e.g. conciliation, arbitration)?

6   What measures might a government introduce to reduce the burden of Employ-
    ment Tribunals on (i) employers and (ii) the State? How do your suggestions
    compare with those introduced/being proposed in recent years?

Notes

1   In the UK, in the 1960s in particular, many strikes were small, short and "unof-
    ficial" – so-called "wildcat" strikes – called by shop stewards (local union
    organisers) in response to specific, local issues such as the disciplining of an
    employee. Many such strikes were not captured in the official statistics, which
    exclude those lasting less than a day (see note 2).

2   As Hicks and Allen (1999: 25) note, 90 per cent of the days lost during that
    year were, in fact, accounted for by strikes in coal mining.

3   As Shackleton notes (1998: 602), drawing on Brown and Wadhwani (1990),
    while working days lost in Britain were above the OECD average, Spain and
    Italy actually had much higher numbers of working days lost per thousand
    workers (approximately double) in the late 1970s.

4   An interesting and successful tactic by employers in recent years has been to
    challenge the validity of ballots through the courts, for example, the BA dispute
    above, as well as in a number of rail disputes. A recent Court of Appeal deci-
    sion (*RMT* v *Serco*) appears, however, to have made such challenges more dif-
    ficult.

5   The paper by Brown and Wadhwani (1990), cited in Shackleton is also worth
    reading.

6   The UK data, for example, include all strikes lasting at least 1 day where 10 or
    more workers are involved, or where 100 working days are lost, but exclude
    those "not directly linked to employment terms and conditions" (Eurofound
    2010: 6). For a comparison of coverage and methodology, see the Technical
    Note in Hale (2008a: 38–9).

7   In the UK context, it is possible that the change reflects factors associated with
    the decline in unionisation such as age of workplace (Machin 2000) or the rise
    of Human Resource Management (HRM), although the latter is not found to be
    of import in that context by Machin and Wood (2004).

8   Interestingly, however, there seems little evidence of the displacement of
    strikes into other, less costly forms of collective action such as go-slows,
    working to rule (strict adherence to contractual requirements), overtime bans/
    restrictions, etc. (see Dix *et al.* 2009 for snapshots of the changing patterns
    using the periodic Workplace Employment Relations Survey (WERS) series
    from 1980 to 2004). Further, Drinkwater and Ingram (2005) show that strikes,
    overtime bans, go slows and other forms of collective action are highly corre-
    lated over the period 1979–2000, and as such appear to be complements rather
    than substitutes.

9   These authors usefully group models into four categories: Pareto optimal acci-
    dent models in which agents are rational but may make errors/misjudgements;
    interactive bargaining models in which the two sides behave strategically to
    manipulate the other; "political" models in which the interests of, and the

information available to, union leaders and their members may differ; and sociological-institutional-political models emphasising the role of social customs and norms. We consider the first three of these – see Hirsch and Addison (1986: 93–5) for a review of the sociological models. In relation to sociology, however, we will consider Naylor's socio-economic model of individual strike participation, which examines the issue of the *individual* rationality of striking in the face of a potential free-rider problem.

10 The expected value of disagreement is $c_1 \times 0 = 0$, and is omitted.

11 The Nash version has also been criticised. For example, Farber (1986: 1056) argues that "the Nash model and most other axiomatic models are normative rather than prescriptive. They prescribe what an outcome *ought* to look like, and they are best considered prescriptions for arbitrators rather than a description of the likely outcomes of collective bargaining".

12 As Sapsford and Tzannatos (1993: 316) note, "there exists something of a confusion in the literature as to whether or not Hicks's theory is determinate", and thus predicts the wage rate shown above by the intersection of the ECC and URC curves, or instead whether this represents "the highest wage which skilful negotiation can extract from the employer" (Hicks 1963: 144). As these authors explain, the latter emerges from a second, asymmetric version of the model in which the union no longer possesses perfect information (see Sapsford and Tzannatos 1993 and the references there).

13 As Mauro shows, this conclusion holds if only one side holds misperceptions, and applies also where the intercepts are correctly calculated but the other side's rate of concession is overestimated (increasing the slope of the perceptions curves). Conversely, Mauro also notes that, if this rate is underestimated, strikes will be less likely.

14 Montgomery and Benedict (1989) use data for teacher negotiations in Pennsylvania public schools during the period 1978–84, finding that senior negotiator experience significantly reduces the frequency of strikes.

15 See also Kennan (1980).

16 Peter Harwood, the Chief Conciliator for Acas, talks about "rhythm and choreography" of disputes.

17 As Ashenfelter and Johnson note, the contract is assumed to last indefinitely, but is negotiated only once.

18 The firm's profits, assuming the firm produces a fixed amount sold for a constant price (P) in each period and assuming the firm is unable to pass on higher wage costs in the form of higher prices, are given by $\pi = \alpha P - \beta W - H$, where H is fixed costs. The firm's intertemporal maximisation problem, assuming discount rate r, is therefore to maximise the following, noting that $W = \overline{W}(1 + y_A)$:

$$V = \int_s^\infty \left[\left[\alpha P - \beta \overline{W}(1 + y^* + (y_0 - y^*)e^{(-\tau S)} \right] e^{(-rT)} dt - \int_0^\infty \left[He^{(-rtdt)} \right] \right]$$

(A8.1)

On integration, this gives the firm's problem as maximising:

$$V = [\alpha P - \beta \overline{W}(1 + y^* + (y_0 - y^*)e^{(-\tau S)}] \frac{e^{-rs}}{r} - \frac{H}{r}$$

(A8.2)

For a strike to take place, Ashenfelter and Johnson show that the following must hold:

$$y_0 > \frac{\alpha P - \beta \overline{W}\left(1 - \dfrac{\tau}{r} y*\right)}{\beta \overline{W}\left(1 + \dfrac{\tau}{r}\right)}$$
(8.7)

and, thus, strikes are argued to be more likely the greater are y_0 (the higher the union's initial acceptable wage) and τ (the concession rate, suggesting the union gives in more rapidly), and less likely for higher values of P, α/β (average product per worker), r and $y*$.

19 An alternative evolutionary framework proposed by Varoufakis (1996) regards the indeterminacy of bargaining as natural, and in which strikes help form the bargainers' "dispositions" rather than simply revealing them.

20 The above simplifies Naylor's original exposition slightly by assuming the coefficient on the reputational term is 1.

21 See also Manning (1993).

22 A study by the Forskningscenter for Arbejdsmarkeds- og Organisationsstudier (FAOS) reported at eironline (www.eurofound.europa.eu/eiro/2004/09/inbrief/dk0409102n.htm) found the main reasons for not voting among Danish union members were forgetting to return the ballot paper (30 per cent), lack of interest (27 per cent) and feeling that their vote made no difference to the outcome (12 per cent).

23 Addison and Teixeira (2006) consider the effect of strikes on unemployment (proxying industrial-relations climate and macroeconomic performance respectively). For a survey of the impact of collective bargaining more generally on macroeconomic performance, see Aidt and Tzannatos (2008).

24 McConnell et al. (2006) estimate the average loss for the US is around four hours per worker per year, or five minutes per worker per week.

25 More recently still, Rodríguez-Álvarez et al. (2007) have suggested an alternative approach based on input distance functions in which the cost of strikes is estimated as the shadow price of an undesirable input. They report costs of around 1.6 per cent of industry output value for the Spanish mining sector over the period 1974–97.

26 Historically, they were conceived of and referred to as the "industrial jury", except that the lay members arrive at their decision with the judge (see Corby and Latreille 2012).

27 Costs may also be awarded if the behaviour of the parties or any representatives is unreasonable. At the time of publication, the amount of costs is usually limited to £20,000, an amount that has recently been doubled. As this might imply, each side normally bears their own costs so that ETs normally correspond to what is termed the American fee-shifting regime. Where costs are awarded, it therefore flips to the English system where the loser pays both his or her own costs and those of the winning party. As might be expected, which regime pertains is likely to have a significant impact on the probability of pre-trial settlement, the exact effect depending on other assumptions within the

model (see Hay and Spier 1998 and Main and Park 2000 for a fuller discussion). In the ET context, whether costs will be awarded introduces a further uncertainty into the model beyond whether the claim will be upheld or not.

28 In a growing number of jurisdictions, however, judges may exercise the discretion to sit alone, a provision extended to unfair dismissal cases from April 2012 (see Corby and Latreille 2012).

29 This material draws in part on a talk by Peter Harwood, Acas Chief Conciliator, at Cardiff University, March 2012. Note that the Acas information relates only to the UK – other countries have developed other arrangements for resolution of disputes – see question 5.

30 A small number of cases (approximately 40 each year) are also dealt with via collective arbitration. This differs from conciliation in that the parties give up their control of the dispute, agreeing instead to be bound by the terms of the arbitrator's decision.

31 The survey's title reflects the earlier nomenclature for ETs.

References

Abbott M.G., "Specification Tests of Quarterly Econometric Models of Strike Frequency in Canada", in Ehrenberg R.G., editor, *Research in Labor Economics*, Greenwich, Conn., JAI Press Inc, 1984.

Acas, *Advisory, Conciliation and Arbitration Service (Acas) Annual Report and Accounts 2010/11*, The Stationery Office, London, 2011.

Addison J.T. and Teixeira P., "Does the Quality of Industrial Relations Matter for the Macro Economy? A Cross-Country Analysis Using Strikes Data", IZA Discussion Paper 1968, 2006.

Aidt T.S. and Tzannatos Z., "Trade Unions, Collective Bargaining and Macroeconomic Performance: A Review", *Industrial Relations Journal*, 39(4), 2008, pp. 258–95.

Akerlof G.A., "A Theory of Social Custom, of Which Unemployment May be One Consequence", *Quarterly Journal of Economics*, 94(4), 1980, pp. 749–75.

Ashenfelter O.C. and Johnson G.E., "Bargaining Theory, Trade Unions, and Industrial Strike Activity", *American Economic Review*, 59, 1969, pp. 35–49.

Babcock L. and Loewenstein G., "Exploring Bargaining Impasse: the Role of Self-serving Biases", *Journal of Economic Perspectives*, 11(1), 1997, pp. 109–26.

Bastos P., Kreickemeier U. and Wright P.W., "Open-shop Unions and Product Market Competition", *Canadian Journal of Economics*, 43(2), 2010, pp. 640–62.

Bishop R.L., "A Zeuthen–Hicks Theory of Bargaining", *Econometrica*, 32(3), 1964, pp. 410–17.

Blanchflower D. and Cubbin J., "Strike Propensities at the British Workplace", *Oxford Bulletin of Economics and Statistics*, 48(1), 1986, pp. 19–39.

Booth A.L., "The Free Rider Problem and a Social Custom Model of Trade Union Membership", Quarterly Journal of Economics, 100(1), 1985, pp. 253–61.

Booth A.L., *The Economics of Trade Unions*, Cambridge University Press, Cambridge, 1995.

Booth A. and Cressy R., "Strikes with Asymmetric Information: Theory and Evidence", *Oxford Bulletin of Economics and Statistics*, 52(3), 1990, pp. 269–91.

Bowlby R. and Schriver W., "Bluffing and the Split the Difference Theory of Wage Bargaining", *Industrial and Labor Relations Review*, 31(2), 1978, pp. 161–71.

Brown W. and Wadhwani S., "The Economic Effects of Industrial Relations Legislation Since 1979", *National Institute Economic Review*, 131(1), 1990, pp. 57–70.

Brown S., Frick B. and Sessions J., "Unemployment, Vacancies and Unjust Dismissals: The Cyclical Demand for Individual Grievance Procedures in Germany and Great Britain", *Labour: Review of Labour Economics and Industrial Relations*, 11(2), 1997, pp. 329–49.

Burgess S., Propper C. and Wilson C., "Explaining the Growth in the Number of Applications to Industrial Tribunals, 1972–1997", Department of Trade and Industry Employment Relations Research Series No. 10, 2001.

Card, D., "Strikes and Wages: A Test of a Signalling Model", NBER Working Paper No. 2550, 1988.

Card, D., "Strikes and Wages: A Test of the Asymmetric Information Model", *Quarterly Journal of Economics*, 105(3), 1990, pp. 625–59.

Comay Y. and Subotnik A., "A Reinterpretation of Hicks' Bargaining Model", in Ashenfelter, O. and Oates, W.E., editors, *Essays in Labor Market Analysis*, New York, John Wiley, 1977.

Cooter R.D. and Rubinfeld D.L., "Economic Analysis of Legal Disputes and their Resolution", *Journal of Economic Literature*, 27, 1989, pp. 1067–97.

Cooter R., Marks S. and Mnookin R., "Bargaining in the Shadow of the Law: A Testable Model of Strategic Behavior", *Journal of Legal Studies*, 11, 1982, pp. 225–51.

Corby S. and Latreille P., "Tripartite Adjudication – An Endangered Species", *Industrial Relations Journal*, 43(2), 2012, pp. 130–43.

Crampton P.C., "Bargaining with Incomplete Information: An Infinite-Horizon Model with Two Sided Uncertainty", *Review of Economic Studies*, 51, 1984, pp. 579–3.

Devereux P.J. and Hart R.A., "A Good Time to Stay Out? Strikes and the Business Cycle", *British Journal of Industrial Relations*, 49(S1), 2011, pp s70–s92.

Davies R.J., "Economic Activity, Incomes Policy and Strikes – A Quantitative Analysis", *British Journal of Industrial Relations*, 17(2), 1979, pp. 205–23.

De Fusco R.A. and Fuess S.M. Jr., "The Effects of Airline Strikes on Struck and Nonstruck Carriers", *Industrial and Labor Relations Review*, 44(2), 1991, pp. 324–33.

Dickens L., Hart M., Jones M. and Weekes B., "The British Experience Under a Statute Prohibiting Unfair Dismissal", *Industrial and Labor Relations Review*, 37(4), 1984, pp. 497–514.

Dickens L., Jones M., Weekes B. and Hart M., *Dismissed: A Study of Unfair Dismissal and the Industrial Tribunal System*, Blackwell, Oxford, 1985.

Dickerson A.P., "The Cyclicality of British Strike Frequency", *Oxford Bulletin of Economics and Statistics*, 56(3), 1994, pp. 285–303.

Dickerson A.P., Geroski P.A. and Knight K.G., "Productivity, Efficiency and Strike Activity", *International Review of Applied Economics*, 11(1), 1997, pp. 119–34.

Dix G., "Operating with Style: The Work of the ACAS Conciliator in Individual Employment Disputes", in Towers and Brown W., editors., *Employment Relations in Britain: 25 Years of the Advisory, Conciliation and Arbitration Service*, Blackwell, Oxford, 2000.

Dix G., Sisson K. and Forth J., "Conflict at Work: The Changing Pattern of Disputes", in Brown W., Bryson A., Forth J. and Whitfield K., editors, *The Evolution of the Modern Workplace*, Cambridge University Press, Cambridge, 2009.

Drinkwater S. and Ingram P., "Have Industrial Relations in the UK Really Improved?", *Labour*, 19(3), 2005, pp. 373–98.

Drinkwater S., Latreille P.L. and Knight K.G., "The Post-Application Labour Market Consequences of Employment Tribunal Claims", *Human Resource Management Journal*, 21(2), 2011, pp. 171–89.

Earnshaw J., Goodman J., Harrison R. and Marchington M., "Industrial Tribunals, Workplace Disciplinary Procedures and Employment Practices", Department of Trade and Industry Employment Relations Research Series, No. 2, 1998.

Earnshaw J., Marchington M. and Goodman J., "Unfair to Whom? Discipline and Dismissal in Small Establishments", *Industrial Relations Journal*, 31(1), 2000, pp. 62–73.

Eurofound, *Developments in Industrial Action 2005–2009*, European Foundation for the Improvement of Living and Working Conditions, Dublin, 2010.

Eurofound, "First Strikes in 25 Years Mark Start of Pay Round", 2012, www.eurofound.europa.eu/eiro/2011/12/articles/at1112011i.htm, last accessed 25/04/2012.

Farber H., "Bargaining Theory, Wage Outcomes, and the Occurrence of Strikes", *American Economic Review*, 68(3), 1978, pp. 262–71.

Farber H., "The Analysis of Union Behavior", in Ashenfelter O. and Layard, R., editors, *Handbook of Labor Economics, Volume II*, Elsevier, Amsterdam, Oxford, 1986.

Farber H. and Katz H., "Interest Arbitration, Outcomes, and the Incentive to Bargain", *Industrial and Labor Relations Review*, 33(1), 1979, pp. 55–63.

Farmer A. and Tiefenthaler J., "Conflict in Divorce Disputes: The Determinants of Pretrial Settlement", *International Review of Law and Economics*, 21, 2001, pp. 157–80.

Freyens B.P., "Dismissal Disputes and the Incentives to Bargain: Estimates of the Contract Zone", *Industrial and Labor Relations Review*, 64(3), 2011, pp. 576–98.

Geroski P.A. and Knight K.G., "Wages, Strikes and Market Structure: Some Further Evidence", *Oxford Economic Papers*, 35(1), 1983, pp. 146–52.

Geroski P.A., Hamlin A.P. and Knight K.G., "Wages, Strikes and Market Structure", *Oxford Economic Papers*, 34(2), 1982, pp. 276–91.

Godard J., "What Has Happened to Strikes?", *British Journal of Industrial Relations*, 49(2), 2011, pp. 282–305.

Gould J., "The Economics of Legal Conflicts", *Journal of Legal Studies*, 2, 1973, pp. 279–300.

Hale D., "International Comparisons of Labour Disputes in 2006", *Economic and Labour Market Review*, 2(4), 2008a, pp. 32–41.

Hale D., "Labour Disputes in 2007", *Economic and Labour Market Review*, 2(6), 2008b, pp. 18–29.

Hale D., "Labour Disputes in 2009", *Economic and Labour Market Review*, 3(6), 2009, pp. 26–38.

Hale D., "Labour Disputes in 2009", *Economic and Labour Market Review*, 4(6), 2010, pp. 47–59.

Hamermesh D.S., "Who 'Wins' in Wage Bargaining?", *Industrial and Labor Relations Review*, 26(4), 1973, pp. 1146–9.

Harrison A. and Stewart M., "Cyclical Fluctuations in Strike Durations", *American Economic Review*, 79, 1989, pp. 827–41.

Harsanyi J.C., "Approaches to the Bargaining Problem Before and After the Theory of Games: A Critical Discussion of Zeuthen's, Hicks', and Nash's Theories", *Econometrica*, 24, 1956, pp. 144–57.

Hart R.A., "Workers Made Idle by Company Strikes and the 'British Disease'", Stirling Economics Discussion Paper 2009–14, 2009.

Hay B. and Spier K.E., "Settlement of Litigation", in Newman P., editor, *The New Palgrave Dictionary of Economics and the Law*, Macmillan, Basingstoke, 1998.

Hayes B., "Unions and Strikes with Asymmetric Information", Journal of Labor Economics, 2(1), 1984, pp. 57–83.

Hazledine T., Holden K. and Howells J.M., "Strike Incidence and Economic Activity: Some Further Evidence", *New Zealand Economic Papers*, 11(1), 1977, pp. 92–105.

Hicks J.R., *The Theory of Wages*, Macmillan, London, 1963.

Hicks J. and Allen G., "A Century of Change: Trends in UK Statistics Since 1900", House of Commons Research Paper 99/111, 1999.

Hirsch B.T. and Addison J.T., *The Economic Analysis of Unions: New Approaches and Evidence*, Allen & Unwin, London, 1986.

Ingram P., Metcalf D. and Wadsworth J., "Strike Incidence in British Manufacturing in the 1980s", *Industrial and Labor Relations Review*, 46(4), 1993, pp. 704–17.

Jones S.R.G., "The Role of Negotiators in Union-Firm Bargaining", *Canadian Journal of Economics*, 22(3), 1989, pp. 630–42.

Kennan J., "Pareto Optimality and the Economics of Strike Duration", *Journal of Labor Research*, 1(1), 1980, pp. 77–94.

Kennan J., "The Duration of Contract Strikes in U.S. Manufacturing", *Journal of Econometrics*, 28, 1985, pp. 5–28.

Kennan J., "The Economics of Strikes", chapter 19, in Ashenfelter O. and Layard R., editors, *Handbook of Labor Economics Volume 2*, North-Holland, Amsterdam/London, 1986.

Knight K.G., "Labour Productivity and Industrial Relations in British Production Industries: Some Quantitative Evidence", *British Journal of Industrial Relations*, 27(3), 1989, pp. 281–94.

Knight K.G. and Latreille P.L., "Discipline, Dismissals and Complaints to Employment Tribunals", *British Journal of Industrial Relations*, 38(4), 2000a, pp. 533–55.

Knight K.G. and Latreille P.L., "How Far Do Cases Go? Resolution in Industrial Tribunal Applications", *The Manchester School*, 68(6), 2000b, pp. 723–44.

Knight K.G. and Latreille P.L., "Gender Effects in British Unfair Dismissal Tribunal Hearings", *Industrial and Labor Relations Review*, 54(4), 2001, pp. 816–34.

Korobkin R., "Aspirations and Settlement", *University of California, Los Angeles School of Law Research Paper*, No. 02–09, 2002.

Kressel K. and Pruitt D., "The Mediation of Social Conflict", *Journal of Social Issues*, 41(2), 1985, pp. 1–10.

Kressel K. and Pruitt D., "Conclusion: A Research Perspective on the Mediation of Social Conflict", in Kressel K., Pruitt D. and Associates, *Mediation Research*, Jossey Bass, San Francisco, 1989.

Landes W.M., "An Economic Analysis of the Courts", *Journal of Law and Economics*, 14, 1971, pp. 61–107.

Latreille P.L., "The Settlement of Employment Tribunal Cases: Evidence from SETA 2003", Department for Business, Enterprise and Regulatory Reform Employment Relations Research Series, No. 61, 2007.

Latreille P.L., Latreille J.A. and Knight K.G., "Making a Difference? Legal Representation in Employment Tribunal Cases: Evidence from a Survey of Representatives", *Industrial Law Journal*, 34(4), 2005, pp. 308–30.

Latreille P.L., Latreille J.A. and Knight K.G., "Employment Tribunals and Acas: Evidence from a Survey of Representatives", *Industrial Relations Journal*, 38(2), 2007, pp. 136–54.

Laybourn K., *A History of British Trade Unionism c. 1770–1990*, Alan Sutton, Stroud, 1992.

Loewenstein G., Issacharoff S., Camerer C. and Babcock L., "Self-serving Assessments of Fairness and Pre-trial Bargaining", *Journal of Legal Studies*, 100, 1993, pp. 426–41.

McConnell S., "Strikes, Wages, and Private Information", *American Economic Review*, 79(4), 1989, pp. 801–15.

McConnell S., "Cyclical Fluctuations in Strike Activity", *Industrial and Labor Relations Review*, 44(1), 1990, pp. 130–43.

McConnell C.R., Brue S.L. and Macpherson D.A., *Contemporary Labor Economics*, McGraw-Hill, New York, 2006.

Machin S.J., "Union Decline in Britain", *British Journal of Industrial Relations*, 38(4), 2000, pp. 631–45.

Machin S. and Wood S., "Looking for HRM/union Substitution: Evidence from British Workplaces," Centre of Economics Performance (CEP), London School of Economics and Political Science, Working Paper No. 0605, 2004, http://cep.lse.ac.uk/pubs/download/dp0605.pdf.

McHugh R., "Productivity Effects of Strikes in Struck and Nonstruck Industries", *Industrial and Labor Relations Review*, 44(4), 1991, pp. 722–32.

Main B.G.M. and Park A., "The British and American Rules: An Experimental Examination of Pre-trial Bargaining in the Shadow of the Law", *Scottish Journal of Political Economy*, 47, 2000, pp. 37–60.

Main B.G.M. and Park A., "An Experiment with Two-Way Offers into Court: Restoring the Balance in Pre-trial Negotiation", *Journal of Economic Studies*, 30, 2003, pp. 125–43.

Manning A., "Pre-Strike Ballots and Wage-Employment Bargaining", *Oxford Economic Papers*, 45(3), 1993, pp. 422–39.

Marginson P., "The Distinctive Effects of Plant and Company Size on Workplace Industrial Relations", *British Journal of Industrial Relations*, 22, 1984, pp. 1–14.

Mauro M.J., "Strikes as a Result of Imperfect Information", *Industrial and Labor Relations Review*, 35(4), 1982, pp. 522–38.

Meadows P. *A Review of the Economic Impact of Employment Relations Services Delivered by Acas*, NIESR, London, 2007.

Miceli T.J., *The Economic Approach to Law*, Stanford University Press, Stanford, CA, 2004.

Ministry of Justice, *Employment Tribunals and EAT Statistics, 2010–11, 1 April 2010 to 31 March 2011*, Ministry of Justice, London, 2011.

Mnookin R.H., "Why Negotiations Fail: An Exploration of Barriers to the Resolution of Conflict", *Ohio State Journal on Dispute Resolution*, 8, 1993, pp. 235–49.

Mnookin R.H. and Kornhauser L., "Bargaining in the Shadow of the Law: The Case of Divorce", *Yale Law Journal*, 88, 1979, pp. 950–7.

Montgomery E. and Benedict M.E., "The Impact of Bargainer Experience on Teacher Strikes", *Industrial and Labor Relations Review*, 42(3), 1989, pp. 380–92.

Moore W.J. and Pearce D.K., "A Comparative Analysis of Strike Models During Periods of Rapid Inflation: 1967–1977", *Journal of Labor Research*, 3(1), 1982, pp. 39–53.

Nash J.F., "The Bargaining Problem", *Econometrica*, 18(2), 1950, pp. 155–62.

Nash J.F., "Two-Person Co-operative Games", *Econometrica*, 21(1), 1953, pp. 128–40.

Naylor R.A., "Strikes, Free Riders and Social Customs", *Quarterly Journal of Economics*, 104(4), 1989, pp. 771–85.

Neumann G.R., "The Predictability of Strikes: Evidence from the Stock Market", *Industrial and Labor Relations Review*, 33(4), 1980, pp. 525–35.

Neumann G.R. and Reder M.W., "Output and Strike Activity in U.S. Manufacturing: How Large are the Losses?", *Industrial and Labor Relations Review*, 37(2), 1984, pp. 197–211.

Nicolitsas D., "Accounting for Strikes: Evidence from UK Manufacturing in the 1980s", *Labour*, 14(3), 2000, pp. 417–40.

Olofsgård A., "Union Leaders as Experts: Wage Bargaining and Strikes with Union-Wide Ballot Requirements", *Scandinavian Journal of Economics*, 114(1), 2012, pp. 200–27.

Paldam M. and Pedersen P.J., "The Macroeconomic Strike Model: A Study of Seventeen Countries, 1948–1975", *Industrial and Labor Relations Review*, 35(4), 1982, pp. 504–21.

Pencavel J.H., "An Investigation into Industrial Strike Activity in Britain", *Economica*, 37(147), 1970, pp. 239–56.

Peters M., Seeds K., Harding C. and Garnett E, "Findings from the Survey of Employment Tribunal Applications 2008", Department for Business, Innovation and Skills Employment Relations Research Series No. 107, 2010.

Phipps A.J., "Strike Activity and Inflation in Australia", *Economic Record*, 53, 1977, pp. 297–319.

Posner R.A., "An Economic Approach to Legal Procedure and Judicial Administration", *Journal of Legal Studies*, 2, 1973, pp. 399–458.

Rabinovitch R. and Swary I., "On the Theory of Bargaining, Strikes, and Wage Determination under Uncertainty", *Canadian Journal of Economics*, 9(4), 1976, pp. 668–84.

Reder M.W. and Neumann G.R., "Conflict and Contract: The Case of Strikes", *Journal of Political Economy*, 88(5), 1980, pp. 867–86.

Reilly B., "Strike Incidence and the Business Cycle in Ireland", *Applied Economics*, 28(6), 1996, pp. 765–71.

Rickman N., "Contingent Fees and Litigation Settlement", *International Review of Law and Economics*, 19, 1999, pp. 295–317.

Rodríguez-Álvarez A., del Rosal I. and Baños-Pino J., "The Cost of Strikes in the Spanish Mining Sector: Modelling an Undesirable Input with a Distance Function", *Journal of Productivity Analysis*, 27(1), 2007, pp. 73–83.

Ross A.M., *Trade Union Wage Policy*, University of California Press, Berkeley and Los Angeles, 1948.

Sapsford D., "Strikes: Models and Evidence", in Sapsford D. and Tzannatos Z., editors, *Current Issues in Labour Economics*, Macmillan, Basingstoke, 1990.

Sapsford D. and Tzannatos Z., *The Economics of the Labour Market*, Macmillan, Basingstoke, 1993.

Saraydar E., "Zeuthen's Theory of Bargaining: A Note", Econometrica, 33(4), 1965, pp. 802–13.

Saridakis G., Sen Gupta S., Edwards P. and Storey D.J., "The Impact of Enterprise Size on Employment Tribunal Incidence and Outcomes: Evidence from Britain", *British Journal of Industrial Relations*, 46(3), 2008, pp. 469–99.

Shackleton J.R., "Industrial Relations Reform in Britain Since 1979", *Journal of Labor Research*, 19(3), 1998, pp. 581–605.

Shackleton J.R., *Employment Tribunals: Their Growth and the Case for Radical Reform*, Institute for Employment Affairs, London, 2002.

Shalev M., "Trade Unionism and Economic Analysis: The Case of Industrial Conflict", *Journal of Labor Research*, 1, 1980, pp. 133–73.

Shorey J., "Time Series Analysis of Strike Frequency", *British Journal of Industrial Relations*, 15, 1977, pp. 63–75.

Siebert W.S. and Addison J.T., "Are Strikes Accidental?", *Economic Journal*, 91(362), 1981, pp. 389–404.

Siebert W.S., Bertrand P.V. and Addison J.T., "The Political Model of Strikes: A New Twist", *Southern Economic Journal*, 52(1), 1985, pp. 23–33.

Swint J.M. and Nelson W.B., "The Influence of Negotiators' Self-interest on the Duration of Strikes", *Industrial and Labor Relations Review*, 32(1), 1978, pp. 56–66.

Swint J.M. and Nelson W.B., "Self-motivated Bargaining and Rational Strikes: A Multiparty Model and its Implications for Industrial Strike Activity", *Southern Economic Journal*, 47(2), 1980, pp. 317–31.

Towers B. and Brown W., editors, *Employment Relations in Britain: 25 years of the Advisory, Conciliation and Arbitration Service*, Oxford, Blackwell, 2000.

Tracy J.S., "An Investigation into the Determinants of U.S. Strike Activity", *American Economic Review*, 76(3), 1986, pp. 423–36.

Tracy J.S., "An Empirical Test of an Asymmetric Information Model of Strikes", *Journal of Labor Economics*, 5(2), 1987, pp. 149–73.

Turkington D.J., "Strike Incidence and Economic Activity in New Zealand", *New Zealand Economic Papers*, 9, 1975, pp. 87–106.

Urwin P., Buscha F. and Latreille P., "Representation in UK Employment Tribunals: Analysis of the 2003 and 2008 Surveys of Employment Tribunal Applications (SETA)", *British Journal of Industrial Relations*, forthcoming.

van der Velden S., Dribbusch H., Lyddon D. and Vandaele K., editors, *Strikes Around the World, 1968–2005*, Aksant Academic Publishing, Amsterdam, 2007.

Varoufakis Y., "Bargaining and Strikes: Towards an Evolutionary Framework", *Labour Economics*, 3(4), 1996, pp. 385–98.

Vroman S.B., "A Longitudinal Analysis of Strike Activity in U.S. Manufacturing: 1957–1984", *American Economic Review*, 79(4), 1989, pp. 816–26.

Walsh W.D., "Economic Conditions and Strike Activity in Canada", *Industrial Relations*, 14, 1975, pp. 45–54.

Zeuthen F., *Problems of Monopoly and Economic Warfare*, Routledge, London, 1930.

Further reading

Kennan (1986) is arguably the classic survey of the strikes literature, although the text by Hirsch and Addison (1986) provides an extremely clear, readable and detailed overview. Booth (1995, section 5.6) contains a more succinct and up-to-date treatment of some of these issues. The literature on Employment Tribunals/labour courts is newer, at least for economists, although there are some interesting recent additions, for example Freyens' (2011) empirical examination of the contract zone and the paper by Saridakis *et al.* (2008) which explores a range of ET issues using the Survey of Employment Tribunal Applications 2003 data, focusing on small firms.

Selected web links

Acas: www.acas.org.uk

Ministry of Justice: www.justice.gov.uk (see especially www.justice.gov.uk/tribunals/employment and www.justice.gov.uk/tribunals/employment-appeals)

Department for Business, Innovation and Skills: www.bis.gov.uk/

Chapter 9

The structure of labour markets

Learning outcomes

At the end of this chapter, readers should understand:

- How the migration of workers across sectors or markets is crucial to the equalisation of wage rates within a neo-classical framework;
- That labour markets can segment and that the nature of jobs performed within the primary sector, and the characteristics of the workers who perform such jobs, are inherently different to those jobs within the secondary sector and the traits of the workers who perform them;
- That it may be appropriate to further divide jobs in the primary sector into upper- and lower-tier classifications, with pay and career-advancement opportunities differing between tiers;
- That a number of possible explanations for the emergence of segmented labour markets have been suggested, with cost minimisation and the institutional nature of corporations as central themes to many of these;
- That empirical validation of dual and segmented labour markets is influenced significantly by the techniques employed and by how market segments are classified;
- How Bulow and Summers (1986) show that the desire to reduce shirking can lead firms to pay an efficiency wage in the primary sector that is higher than the alternative available within the secondary sector;
- That, although the restriction of worker mobility between primary and secondary sectors is central to the existence of segmented labour markets, the empirical evidence in support of this claim is inconclusive.

Introduction

What is the structure of the labour market? Can it be viewed as a single, competitively operating entity or is it comprised of distinct and independently operating segments? Questions over this distinction have long fuelled debate and have led to the emergence of a substantial literature on segmented labour markets, in contrast to the **neo-classical** view at the heart of human capital theory. The maintained hypothesis of work in the neo-classical tradition is that the labour market is composed of one segment, while segmentationists argue it is more than one, with dualism being a special case. Thus, the distinguishing feature of such views is the existence of labour market segmentation, which Ryan (1981) defines as "the failure of the labour market to treat its participants even-handedly, in that it accords significantly different opportunities to otherwise comparable people".

Crucial to the existence of market segmentation is the restriction of mobility between sectors, which is the way in which different wage-determining processes will arise. Proponents of human capital theory have typically argued that there is sufficient mobility between labour markets to eliminate any qualitative differences between markets in the wage-determination process, at least between similarly characterised workers. Great importance has been placed upon theoretical models of utility maximisation and is typified empirically by the estimation of the wage-determination process of incomes or wages for all workers of a particular gender, race or age cohort regardless of sector of employment. In contrast, proponents of segmentation theory have emphasised the existence of barriers to mobility in the labour market and argue that mobility constraints allow for the emergence and persistence of different mechanisms for wage determination within particular segments of the labour market.

In this chapter, a neo-classical standpoint will be taken initially and will form the basis of discussion. Reasons for market segmentation will then be forwarded, in the context of both dual labour markets and the literature on more general segmented labour markets, before a theoretical treatment of the topic is given that provides a reasoning behind the existence of differentiated labour markets that differentially reward equally productive workers. The chapter then concludes with a review of the most relevant empirical studies that have tested for the existence of labour market segmentation, with a common theme in much of this literature being the validation of human capital theory or segmented labour market theory as the determinant of worker incomes. Within this section, a number of seminal empirical papers are described in detail in a series of Methodological Example boxes but understanding of the technical issues contained within these is not a pre-requisite for understanding the remaining material. These example Boxes are designed as additional reading to give further insights into how Empirical econometrics is used to validate economic theory. Finally, empirical evidence as relating to the issue of inter-segment mobility is also reviewed in this section.

9.1 Neo-classical approach

The most basic neo-classical model of the labour market suggests that wages should be equal for equally equipped workers, based upon the three underlying assumptions of perfectly competitive markets, of profit (and utility) maximisation and of worker homogeneity. Within this context, consider the following simplified setup,

Neo-classical economics

A school of economic thought that followed from the classical approach that focuses upon resource allocation as mediated through the theory of rational choice, be that utility maximisation by consumers or profit maximisation by firms.

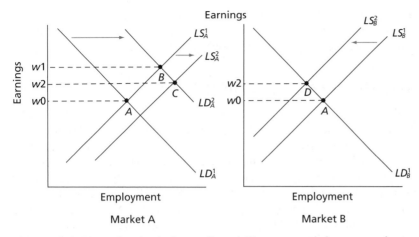

Figure 9.1 Neo-classical view of mobility across labour markets.

where the starting point for discussion is a very simple competitive model of earnings determination, a neo-classical approach where market forces ensure that there is a competitive equilibrium in local pay.[1]

Assume there are two local labour markets, A and B, each with their own labour demand and labour supply curves which independently establish the wages of workers (see Figure 9.1). The initial starting point in both markets is at equilibrium point A, where a common wage rate of $w0$ is established. Now assume that Market A faces a positive demand shock, perhaps caused by an increase in the demand for the output produced within this Market, and this results in a rightward shift in the demand for labour curve from LD_A^1 to LD_A^2. When this happens, the new labour market equilibrium in Market A now occurs at point B, with the wage rate increasing from $w0$ to $w1$.

Wages in Market A, however, are now above those found in Market B and this situation stimulates a (migratory) flow of workers away from Market B and towards Market A. That is, workers realise that, by offering their services in Market A, they will receive a higher remuneration than if they remained in Market B. Thus, this incentive to move results in a simultaneous leftward shift in the labour supply curve in Market B (as for any given wage rate fewer workers wish to work) and a rightward shift in the labour supply curve in Market A (as for any given wage rate more workers will now wish to work). This will cause a relative increase in the wage rate in Market B and a relative reduction in wages in Market A, and such movements will continue until the wages offered in both Markets have been equalised. Only then will there be no further incentive for workers to move between Markets. This will be characterised by the labour supply curve LS_A^2 in Market A and the labour supply curve LS_B^2 in Market B.

In Figure 9.1, the new equilibrium positions will occur at point C in Market A and at point D in Market B, where the wage rate is now $w2$ in both Markets. It should also be noted that, compared to the initial equilibrium point A in both Markets, employment patterns have been affected by the demand shock to Market A. This means that Market A now employs more workers than it did prior to the demand shock and Market B now employs fewer.

So, in a neo-classical model of wage determination, it is not possible for wage differentials to exist between Markets, for, as soon as they develop, workers migrate to the higher-wage Market in such numbers that any difference in wage rewards across Markets is bid away. In such a way, any differences in the rates of return to human capital characteristics would be erased by inter-segment migration.

9.2 The theory of equalising differences

Up until this juncture, a job (within a certain Market) has been deemed to be more attractive, and thus to stimulate a migratory move, if it offers a higher money wage. This is an incomplete picture and, more realistically, it is possible to categorise differences between jobs over a fuller range of inherent characteristics and properties, where negative (non-pecuniary) job traits require a monetary compensation or positive traits are a compensation for lower money wages. Such a line of argument pointing towards the existence of compensating differences in monetary rewards can be traced back to Adam Smith's *The Wealth of Nations* and is what is commonly referred to as the theory of equalising differences. According to Smith, wages were related to:

Employment agreeability – more amenable working conditions will lead to workers accepting a lower wage as their pecuniary reward is being compensated for by non-pecuniary rewards. Likewise, unpleasant, anti-social or dangerous work will require a higher compensating wage.

Ease of learning – jobs that take longer to learn or require skills that are difficult to learn will offer a higher wage. Thus, the opportunity cost associated with training or the additional effort required to acquire skills will be compensated for in the form of higher earnings.

Employment consistency – workers who face partial employment contracts, such as seasonal agricultural workers, need to be paid more to compensate for times of unemployment.[2]

Degree of responsibility – workers who assume positions of responsibility will be compensated for the risk associated with this in the form of higher wages.

Likelihood of success – employment where there is a high chance of success will be paid less than those jobs where there is a risk of failure.

Thus, taken together, it is these components that describe the monetary and non-monetary advantages of any job, and it is these that should be equalised across Markets and not necessarily money wages.

As noted by Rosen though within the context of regional labour markets, "the theory [equalising differences] must be considered as one of longer run tendencies and of equilibrium behavior in the steady state of a more complex dynamic process" (1986: 643). So, in the long run, net rewards will be equalised as labour markets attain their equilibrium positions, but, in the short run, labour markets will be in dis-equilibrium as they are continually in the process of moving towards equilibrium without ever actually arriving there. Thus, labour market differences under such a line of reasoning will reflect dynamic wage differentials – temporary differences that will tend towards eventual disappearance.

9.3 Dual and segmented labour markets

The dual labour market is a specific instance of the more general concept of segmented labour markets and the segmentation literature attributes the creation of these to secular trends in the economy and changes in the structure and organisation of firms, and the consequences that these developments have on the division of labour and politics at the workplace. The seminal work was conducted by Doeringer and Piore (1971) who themselves used the terminology of the "internal labour market" to describe the human-resource practices employed by firms within distinctly separate labour markets. Indeed, there are many overlapping issues between what has evolved into two strands within the recent economic literature: one that unpicks the "black box" of the internal operation of firms and is collectively referred to as the theory of internal labour markets; and the other strand that deals with segmented labour markets that implicitly borrows from the internal labour market literature.

In this section, we trace the history and development of the literature on labour market segmentation and provide a formal theoretical model where the payment of an **efficiency wage** aimed at deterring workers from shirking naturally leads to the formation of dual labour markets. The section concludes with a discussion and evaluation of the empirical evidence supporting the segmentation hypothesis.[3]

Efficiency wage

A wage that is paid in excess of the competitively determined market clearing level in order to increase productivity or efficiency.

9.3.1 Dual and segmented labour markets – an overview

In longer perspective, the notion of segmented labour markets can be traced back to the writings of Cairnes (1874), Mill (1909) and latterly Pigou (1945). Cairnes and Mill argued in favour of institutional rules substituting for market processes and for the existence of non-competing groups within the labour market. As Cairnes wrote, "[T]he average workman, from whatever rank he be taken, finds his power of competition limited for practical purposes to a certain range of occupations ... We are thus compelled to recognise the existence of non-competing industrial groups". Likewise, Mill argued that employment in the least agreeable jobs "devolves on the most helpless and degraded, on those who from squalid poverty, or from want of skill and education, are rejected from all employments". Mill further stated that "the more revolting the occupation, the more certain it is to receive the minimum of remuneration ... [and that] the inequalities of wages are generally in an opposite direction to the equitable principle of compensation". Thus, the existence of non-competing groups will mean equality in rates of return to different forms of human capital will not be brought about through competition as suggested by neo-classical theory.

Indeed, Pigou, a **classical** economist himself, acknowledged that labour markets would often fail to clear, as suggested by the classical model of competition, because of institutional features such as trade unionism. He also noted that labour markets were segmented due to restricted intra- and inter-industry movement and, while competition could compete away differentials within "centres of production", labour was not perfectly mobile among these centres as workers "are tied to the several centres as the result, maybe, of historical accident".

In what follows, we will trace out the evolution of the segmentation literature that built upon the views of Cairnes, Mill and Pigou. Beginning with the American Institutionalist School of the 1940s and 1950s that pre-dated the work of Doeringer and Piore (1971) and Piore (1975) on the formulation of dual and segmented labour markets, the radical theory of segmentation, job competition models and career labour markets have all been developed and forwarded as reasons for the need for, and subsequent emergence of, internal labour markets at the heart of the segmentation hypothesis.

Classical economics

Regarded as the first modern school of economic thought from the eighteenth and nineteenth centuries and is synonymous with the followers of David Ricardo and Ricardian economics.

9.3.2 An overview of internal labour markets

According to this view of labour markets, there is an important distinction between structured and unstructured labour markets. Within unstructured markets, there is no close attachment between workers and firms and they most closely resemble the workings of a competitive market. Labour is free to come and go as it seeks out the best alternative available to it. In contrast, in structured labour markets, there is a strong attachment between workers and employers, resulting from perhaps shared investments in education and training. These structured labour markets have two components, namely the internal and external market. The external market, or port of entry, is the conduit through which a firm recruits new workers, and, as such, the wages that a firm offers at this port of entry are likely to be sensitive to external competitive pressures. Wages and promotion within the internal market, in comparison, are governed by well-established rules, which, because of tradition, unionisation or managerial prerogatives, are not subject to the usual forces of demand and supply. Given that entry is restricted to the port of entry, and because wages are set within the internal labour market without reference to external conditions, the wage rate that workers receive within the internal labour market is typically higher than that which they could reasonably expect to receive outside the firm.

There is an extensive literature describing the functioning of such internal labour markets (see Lazear and Oyer 2012, for a review). Much of the earlier literature provided a theory that either modelled a fundamental feature of internal labour market operation or else provided an explanation for empirical observations. In the former category, Becker (1962, 1964) set the foundations for work on human capital; Holmstrom (1979, 1982) and Shavell (1979) for **agency theory**; and Rosen (1982) for worker allocation within employment hierarchies. Within the latter category, important contributions were made by Lazear (1979) on the issue of mandatory retirement; by Lazear and Rosen (1981) on **tournament theory**; and by Waldman (1984) on **promotion signalling**.

As the literature has matured, the focus has taken a more observational stance in that it has tried to explain observed phenomena. So, of the appropriately postulated theories, which fit best with the real world practices? There is an extensive literature in this area, beyond what can be discussed in this current section, but interested readers should consult Waldman (2012) for an extensive and informative review.

9.3.3 Dual and segmented labour markets

The foundations of segmented labour markets were laid by the American Institutionalist School, which argued that labour markets were affected by the complexity of modern economies and institutional establishments such as trade unions and large bureaucratic corporations. Key advocates of this approach were Kerr (1954) and Dunlop (1957), who emphasised the distinction between the internal and external aspects of an institution as a result of well-established sets of rules that defined an administrative internal labour market. Such arguments supporting the existence of internal labour markets were built upon by segmentation theorists and formed the basis of the dual and segmented labour market literature that was to develop from the 1970s onwards. In particular, Doeringer and Piore (1971) emphasised the idea of duality within labour markets to address a range of policy concerns of the 1960s, such as structural unemployment, racial discrimination and technological change. Central to this concept of duality was the existence of an internal labour market as an administrative unit, where rewards to labour were not governed by external reference to competitive forces but rather by a set of administrative rules and procedures. Outside of this internal labour market, an external market existed where pricing, allocation and training decisions were all controlled by the conventional competitive view of economic theory. As Doeringer and Piore noted, however, there was not perfect labour mobility across internal and external markets even if they were interconnected. Thus, movement to and from the internal labour market was at certain job classifications which constituted ports of entry and exit.

Doeringer and Piore outlined two factors that lead to the emergence of an internal labour market. The first was a desire to reduce costs that arise from labour turnover that will exist when companies require specific skills and give specialised training. Thus, the more specialised and demanding the skill-set required by employers, the more they need to spend recruiting and screening applicants and the more they incur in training costs. The second factor was customary law, where past precedent establishes codes of conduct and **implicit contracts** encourage and facilitate positive industrial relations, which in turn leads to employment stability. Indeed, this is the defining feature of internal labour markets, where clear career paths, rewards and sanctions are all designed to engender loyalty. This, in turn, reduces labour turnover among those staff who have been provided with company-specific training and skills.[4]

> **Implicit contracts**
>
> An employment agreement between employer and employee that sets out remuneration under different future circumstances.

Having formalised the existence and characterisation of internal labour markets, Doeringer and Piore extended their analysis to provide a link between their own work and the puzzling persistence of urban poverty in the US for disadvantaged groups in spite of targeted training for such groups. The theory they posited was that the labour market split over time into separate "primary" and "secondary" sectors. According to Doeringer and Piore, the primary sector comprised a series of internal labour markets, where institutional rules, possibly set by the actions of trade unions, and informal rules determine internal hiring practices, wages and promotion that do not accord with the ideals of profit-maximisation. As a result, there is limited employee mobility and external wage pressure, and any wage differentials that arise between primary and secondary sectors cannot be competed away. Thus, jobs in the primary sector will exhibit such traits as high wages, good promotion opportunities, amenable working conditions and stability in employment. In contrast, secondary-sector employment will be outside of internal labour markets, or in poorly developed internal labour markets, where jobs will tend to have low pay, low career-advancement opportunities and poor working conditions and be associated with high labour turnover.

Furthermore, just as it is possible to draw a distinction between the attributes of primary and secondary jobs, then so too is there a clear demarcation between the attributes of employees themselves. This led Doeringer and Piore to state that secondary-sector workers "exhibit greater turnover, higher rates of lateness and absenteeism, more insubordination, and engage more freely in petty theft and pilferage" than those in the primary sector. Indeed, reflecting the roots of the dual labour market theory upon which their own analysis was built, they concluded that "[d]isadvantaged workers are confined to the secondary market by residence, inadequate skills, poor work histories and discrimination".

Piore (1975) further developed the reasoning for the existence of the primary sector and explained its organisation as a response to the desire to protect firms and workers from uncertainty, although still recognising the importance of cost minimisation as a driver of market structure. Dual labour markets are a response to the industrial structure of the economy, where firms facing stable demand for their output will tend to create primary employment conditions. This arises due to the skill specificity of labour which necessitates the need to invest in specialised training to complement modern capital-intensive technologies and such sunk cost investments can only be contemplated by firms experiencing stable product demand. In contrast, variable product demand will be associated with labour-intensive production that avoids the need for the sunk cost investments of capital expenditure and specialised training.

Piore also suggests that a strict dichotomy of the labour market may not be appropriate and that the primary sector can be further divided into an upper and lower tier, which in themselves define and perpetuate socio-economic divisions within society. Within the upper tier of the primary sector are the high-status and high-paying professional and managerial jobs with good advancement opportunities, but also the high mobility and turnover patterns more typically associated with the secondary sector. In the lower tier of the primary sector, jobs are relatively lower paying and have less career-advancement opportunities and more rigid administrative rules. Such tiers, therefore, create an environment within which social mobility is reduced and resonates with the earlier rationale for duality and the implied discrimination towards disadvantaged groups. As Piore states,

> The points along a mobility chain may be termed stations: they generally include not only jobs but also other points of economic and social significance. Thus people in a given job will tend to be drawn from a limited range of schools, neighborhoods, and types of family backgrounds; and conversely, people leaving the same school or neighborhoods will tend to move into one of a limited set of employment situations.

(1975: 128)

9.3.4 Radical theory of segmentation

While recognising that institutional change and internal behavioural rules are important in explaining the existence of segmented labour markets, the radical theory of segmentation also emphasised the importance of institutional features and social relationships governing production. This embodied aspects such as sanctions, incentives and the assignment of responsibilities as a means of exercising power. According to Edwards *et al.* (1975), it was the emergence of giant corporate enterprises whose focus was the creation and exploitation of monopolistic control as opposed to short-run profit maximisation that led to labour market segmentation. As such, these enterprises strove to exert greater control over factors perceived as being vital for their continued existence, with influence over the supply of labour (through vertical integration) and internal relations assuming particular importance. One avenue through which the latter operated was through increased hierarchical control over the working masses, whereby subjective supervision was replaced by impersonal and institutionalised regulation. The effect of such internal reorganisation within these large corporations, which exhibited both stable production and stable sales, was to establish internal labour markets where employment stability was created through the creation of career ladders and rewards to firm tenure. Outside of these large (core monopoly) corporations, product demand was less stable and workers experienced higher turnover rates with lower wages, leading to a stratification of the working class between primary markets (where firms are organised bureaucratically) and secondary markets (where the organisation is along the lines of a simpler hierarchy).

9.3.5 Job competition model

The job competition model of Thurow (1970) places emphasis on on-the-job training and is embedded within neo-classical profit maximisation by firms whereby the emergence of internal (segmented) labour markets is a response by firms to minimise training costs. Under such a scenario, it is the quality of job that determines wages as opposed to the quality of the individual worker. Workers will be ranked according to the ease with which they can be given training, which in itself is related to a worker's background characteristics such as education and ability, and in such a way job queues are formed, which determine access to further job opportunities and subsequently higher wages. It should be noted, though, that the availability of training spaces, at the level of both the firm and the economy, is determined by technical progress and that the ability of the labour market to clear will be influenced by the on-the-job training process. This implies that Thurow's job competition model is dependent on the elimination of wage and employment competition between workers, as these provide a disincentive to invest in on-the-job training. Consequently, the emergence of internal labour markets, generating the required security over earnings and employment necessary to incentivise the investment decision, was a response emanating from firms' desire to minimise training costs.

9.3.6 Career labour markets

Okun's analysis of the labour market (Okun 1981) extends Thurow's job competition model by also incorporating the desire to reduce staff turnover as a means of cost minimisation. This involves the creation of career labour markets by which firms establish formal rules for hiring, remuneration, promotion, monitoring and discipline, with such hierarchical structures within institutions being isolated from the external labour market. As in the previously discussed internal labour market literature, ports of entry between external and career labour markets are limited, and on-the-job training is important in developing the skills utilised within the internal market. As a result, employees with a desire to pursue internally described career paths are protected from external competition and assured of continued employment at the hiring stage. Investments in training and reward systems are then used to motivate workers and induce loyalty, while at the same time enhancing productivity. With regard to employers, the outcome of such arrangements is to amortise the costs of hiring and training employees.

In these ways, career labour markets are similar to internal labour markets where partnerships are formed between firms and employees, and these long-term relationships spread the cost of recruiting and training for both employers and employees but at the expense of labour mobility. This rigidity within career labour markets in terms of employment and wages is best described by the workings of what Okun described as the "invisible handshake". Building upon the risk-sharing properties theory of implicit contracts suggested by Baily (1974) and Azariadis (1975), the idea is that workers, being risk averse, dislike wage fluctuations and are insured against this by the constant wage offered in the career labour market, which is insulated from the external labour market, which in itself is affected by the business cycle. Employers, meanwhile, also benefit from offering a lower constant wage under the implicit contract than would be expected if wages varied over the course of the business cycle.[5]

9.4 Dual and segmented labour markets – a theoretical treatment

Bulow and Summers (1986) developed a theoretical model of dualism in the labour market based on the implications of the payment of efficiency wages.[6] Building upon the work of Shapiro and Stiglitz (1984), who modelled involuntary unemployment, Bulow and Summers formulated a framework where the payment of high wages in the primary sector was used as a tool to prevent workers from shirking. In what follows, a detailed account of the Bulow and Summers model is set out but crucial to understanding this model is not how equation (9.5) that follows is derived but rather that equation (9.5) describes what will later be referred to as the 'non-shirking condition'. Appreciation of this will then only be required to interpret the future presentation of Figure 9.2 and what comes thereafter.

In the spirit of Bulow and Summers, assume there are N identical and infinitely lived agents who supply one unit of labour to produce $\bar{w}$ units of output. The economy is composed of two sectors, primary and secondary, and the instantaneous utility function of agents is related, in part, to the amount of output produced within each sector that they consume. In supplying their labour, agents also have the incentive to shirk because, in doing so, they receive an instantaneous gain in utility of α. However, reflecting the menial and repetitive nature of secondary-sector employment, workers here are able to be monitored perfectly and so have no possibility of shirking. In contrast, the detection of shirking in the primary sector is difficult and this is the key aspect of the model, in that firms in the primary sector need to incentivise workers, in the form of the wages that they offer, not to shirk.

From this, agents will aim to maximise lifetime welfare which is given by:

$$U = \int_0^\infty U(x_1, x_2 + \alpha s)e^{-rt}\, dt \qquad (9.1)$$

where x_1 and x_2 are the outputs consumed from production in sector 1 (primary) and sector 2 (secondary) respectively at time t, r is the discount rate and s is a 0/1 indicator of shirking activity.[7,8] Bulow and Summers further assumed that preferences are homothetic and that there are constant returns to labour.

Firms will choose to employ E_1 workers in the primary sector and E_2 workers in the secondary sector, such that the total workforce (N) equals $E_1 + E_2$. With equally productive workers who will produce their marginal product regardless of the sector in which they are employed being allocated across both sectors, the output produced in the primary sector will equal $\bar{w}E_1$ units and that in the secondary sector $\bar{w}E_2$ units.

For convenience, the price of secondary-sector output (*p. 2*) is normalised to unity, whereas the price for primary-sector output (*p. 1*) can be represented as the following using the homotheticity of the utility function and the production assumptions noted previously:

$$p_1 = f\left(\frac{x_1}{x_2}\right) = f\left(\frac{E_1}{E_2}\right) = f\left(\frac{E_1}{N - E_1}\right)_1 = g(E_1) \qquad (9.2)$$

Thus, given that output increases with employment and that price will be negatively related to output, the function g will be decreasing in E_1 i.e. $g' < 0$.[9]

With regard to the wages paid to workers, competition will ensure that wages in the secondary sector (w_2) will equal marginal product, such that $w_2 = \bar{w}$. In order to elicit effort from primary-sector workers, though, firms will need to pay an efficiency wage in excess of $\bar{w}$ because crucial to employment in the primary sector is the idea that the monitoring of workers is imprecise. In such a way, not only may shirking go undetected (a false negative outcome) but also workers who are not shirking may be accused of this (a false positive outcome). Under either scenario, being accused of shirking will result in a worker being fired.

It follows then that if d_1 represents the likelihood that a non-shirking worker is (incorrectly) labelled as a shirker and d_2 the likelihood of a shirking worker being identified, the probability increase of not being labelled a shirker over increment of time t for those who do not shirk is given by $(d_2 - d_1)\mathrm{d}t$. Denoting the present value of lifetime utility by PV_1 and PV_2 for workers in the primary and secondary sector respectively, this will mean that workers will therefore choose to shirk at any given point in time if the following condition is satisfied:

$$a > (d_2 - d_1)(PV_1 - PV_2) \tag{9.3}$$

i.e. the expected increment in utility offered through employment in the primary sector is less than the utility gained from shirking.

In addition to separations caused through the identification (either correctly or incorrectly) of shirking, there is also an exogenous separation rate (denoted as q) between workers and firms unrelated to the detection of shirking. Such separations may occur because of a desire on the part of workers to relocate, or withdraw from the labour force, or because of separations instigated by employers and driven by changes in product demand.

Intuitively, the difference in the present value of lifetime utility between a primary- and secondary-sector job will be related to the incremental wage from being in a primary-sector job ($w_1 - \bar{w}$) adjusted by the discount rate, the likelihood that a worker in the primary sector will drop into the secondary sector ($d_1 + q$), and the likelihood that a worker in the secondary sector will find employment in the primary sector ($E_1(d_1 + q)/(N - E_1)$). Thus,

$$PV_1 - PV_2 = \frac{w_1 - \bar{w}}{r + d_1 + q + \dfrac{E_1(d_1 + q)}{(N - E_1)}} \tag{9.4}$$

Solving equations (9.3) and (9.4) therefore yields the non-shirking condition on primary sector wages:

$$w_1 - \bar{w} = \frac{ar}{d_2 - d_1} + \frac{a(d_1 + q)N}{(d_2 - d_1)(N - E_1)} \tag{9.5}$$

The left-hand side of equation (9.5) will represent the premium that primary-sector firms need to pay workers to induce them not to shirk and we can see clearly that the greater the number of primary sector jobs *ceteris paribus*, the higher the wage rate that must be paid to primary-sector workers.[10] Intuitively, this is needed to

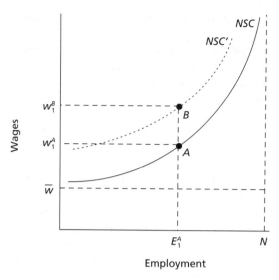

Figure 9.2 The non-shirking condition boundary.

maintain the opportunity cost of losing a primary-sector job as re-employment within this sector is more likely the greater the number of jobs available in the sector. As a result, the non-shirking condition may be represented graphically as in Figure 9.2.

With E_1^A jobs available within the primary sector (and by definition $(N - E_1^A)$ jobs available within the secondary sector) and a wage of $\bar{w}$ offered within the secondary sector, primary-sector firms will need to pay a wage of w_1^A to induce workers not to shirk. Any remuneration less than this and utility-maximising workers would find it optimal to shirk. Any increase in primary-sector jobs above the level of E_1^A would require a primary-sector wage greater than w_1^A to maintain non-shirking behaviour and vice versa. As a result, the boundary between shirking and non-shirking behaviour will be traced out by the upward-sloping NSC curve as shown in Figure 9.2.

Should the underlying parameters of the NSC curve change then this will impact upon the position of the curve. Such movements can be reasoned both intuitively and in reference to the non-shirking condition set out in equation (9.5). In Figure 9.2, all of the following illustrations will have the effect of moving the boundary between shirking and non-shirking behaviour upwards, such that, with E_1^A primary-sector jobs available, an increased primary sector wage of w_1^B would now be required to remove the incentive to shirk. First, as the utility from shirking (a) increases, primary-sector firms will find that they need to pay workers more. Second, as the probability of detecting shirking (d_2) declines, higher wages are needed to counter-balance the reduced likelihood of dismissal. Third, as the rate of turnover of non-shirkers ($d_1 + q$) increases, a higher wage is needed to maintain the value of a primary-sector job if future separation is more likely. Lastly, as the discount rate (r) increases, higher wages in the present will need to be offered, as the lower future income streams that would accompany secondary-sector employment are disliked less intensively. All such scenarios would be consistent with an upwards movement of the non-shirking condition boundary from NSC to (the dotted) NSC' line in Figure 9.2.

To characterise equilibrium in the product market, we recognise that workers in the primary sector (as they are in the secondary sector) are paid their marginal (revenue) product. Thus,

$$w_1 = p_1 \bar{w} = \bar{w} f\left(\frac{E_1}{E_2}\right) = \bar{w} g(E_1) \tag{9.6}$$

On the assumption that $p_1 > p_2$, this will mean that wages in the primary sector (w_1) will be greater than those in the secondary sector (which equal $\bar{w}$). As $g(E_1)$ is a decreasing function in E_1 (as noted in equation (9.2)), product market equilibrium will therefore mean that wages in the primary sector will also be a decreasing function with respect to primary-sector employment (E_1). Overall equilibrium will then be determined by the intersection of the product market equilibrium (PME) curve and the non-shirking condition (NSC) curve as shown in Figure 9.3.

An equilibrium will be established at point E, where E_1 workers are employed in the primary sector and E_2 workers are employed in the secondary sector. Note that this equilibrium will mean that primary-sector wages (w_1^E) exceed those in the secondary sector ($\bar{w}$) for equally productive workers. Even though workers in the secondary sector will be envious of these higher wages conferred by primary-sector employment, it would nonetheless be impossible for them to bid for primary-sector jobs by being willing to accept a lower wage. As highlighted previously, if they worked for a lower wage, they would have an incentive to shirk and so firms in the primary sector will not offer them employment at a lower wage. Thus, the desire to induce worker effort from primary-sector firms will lead them to pay an efficiency wage in excess of the wage found in the secondary sector.

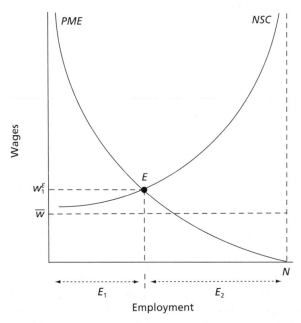

Figure 9.3 Determination of equilibrium across sectors.

9.4.1 Dual and segmented labour markets – the evidence

Consistent with the characteristics of primary and non-primary markets highlighted previously, the empirical identification of labour market segmentation has been based on the identification of: a low-skill sector(s) with no return to schooling/ experience/tenure and no on-the-job training; and non-economic barriers between sectors preventing mobility. An enduring problem in segmented labour market studies, though, is the difficulty of demarcating labour segments. A number of the earlier empirical studies used a priori methods to distinguish sectors, typically along the lines of occupational or industrial classifications. However, the assumption that all members of an occupation or industry are in the same sector is questionable. For example, there is little doubt that we would not want to classify managers and skilled workers as being in primary-sector jobs, even if the industries within which they worked employed a substantial number of secondary-sector workers. It is, therefore, possible that inconsistent results that have been found within the literature arise out of the inaccurate classification of sectors.

To this end, empirical techniques that do not rely upon a priori classification of sectors have been employed: factor analysis, cluster analysis and switching regression techniques all allow for labour market segments to be identified within data without any need for prior assumptions of where these segments might lie. The use of such techniques will be discussed in what follows and detailed case studies presented that will highlight how empirical econometrics is used to provide support or otherwise for postulated relationships arising from economic theory.

The final part of this section looks at empirical evidence for the second aspect of segmented labour market identification, namely the existence of non-economic barriers to worker mobility between sectors. In themselves, differentiated segments do not necessarily support the theory of segmented labour markets and there is no reason why segmentation along the lines of gender, age cohort or region should not arise within the neo-classical view if workers are not seen as perfect substitutes and if there are economic barriers to entry between markets – for example, migration costs that may inhibit the regional migration of workers. Thus, any proposal for the existence of segmentation within the labour market must necessarily be evidenced by the identification of non-economic barriers to worker mobility.

9.4.2 Human capital models with predetermined segmentation

Proponents of segmented labour market theory would postulate that the distinction between primary-sector and secondary-sector jobs would suggest that different mechanisms determine wages and employment within sectors. In particular, we would expect to see primary-sector wages determined along the lines predicted by human capital theory, with identifiable returns to human capital investment, while the returns to such characteristics would be minimal in the secondary sector. Indeed, it is likely that the wage profile in such segments would be completely flat. It is along these lines that empirical researchers have attempted to identify the existence of segmented labour markets by constructing classic human capital earnings functions and testing for differences in human capital returns within a predetermined number of segments. Such studies have been distinguished by those where a priori segmentation is defined by industrial characteristics and those where it is defined with respect to occupational characteristics, and if the hypothesis of segmentation is to be accepted human capital controls in regression wage equations will perform less well in the secondary sector.

Testing for segmentation along the lines of industrial structure, driven by differences in the demand for employee services, has emphasised the importance of aspects such as technology, industrial concentration, capital intensity, organisational structure, employment stability and unionisation. When looking to identify simple dual labour markets, the likes of McNabb (1987) found that human capital controls were important wage determinants in both low-wage (secondary) and high-wage (primary) sectors. The conclusion to be drawn from such empirical studies is that there is little evidence to support the notion of (dual) segmentation of labour markets. Meanwhile, Osberg *et al.* (1987) found that some form of labour market segmentation did exist, although they stressed that the low-wage and high-wage sectors were in themselves merely aggregates of a number of quite dissimilar sectors. This would go a long way to explaining the lack of evidence that is available to support the labour market duality hypothesis, not only in regard to industrial segmentation but also more generally within the empirical literature.

Defining segmentation in terms of occupations may be seen as having an advantage over industrial segmentation, as the segmentation process may, in reality, operate via employers segmenting their own workforces and it has little to do with the quality of jobs in core and peripheral industrial sectors. However, the results from such empirical studies tend to be either inconclusive or inconsistent. On the one hand, the work of Osterman (1975) – see Methodological Example Box 9.1 – suggests that occupational segregation may exist as evidence is found for wage differentials across labour segments of comparable quality in the US. Likewise, Neumann and Ziderman (1986) supported the idea of labour market duality in their Israeli study. In contrast, a similar methodological approach from McNabb and Psacharopoulos (1981) found no evidence for dual labour markets in the UK, confirming the earlier findings of Psacharopoulos (1978).[11]

Methodological Example Box 9.1

P. Osterman, "An Empirical Study of Labour Market Segmentation", *Industrial and Labor Relations Review*, 28(4), 1975, pp. 508–23.

The focus of this paper was to test the hypothesis that the US labour market can be segmented along the lines of three distinct sectors as suggested by Piore (1975): a secondary sector; a lower-tier primary sector; and an upper-tier primary sector. This was done using a sample of individuals from the 1967 Survey of Economic Opportunity that was restricted to black or white urban males with no reported health problems who were head of households and had been in the labour force at some time during the year.

Individuals were then assigned to one of the three segments on the basis of their occupation defined at the five-digit census level on the basis of a subjective classification system. Those occupations characterised by low wages and employment instability, for example, were classified within the secondary sector, while within the primary sector occupations were assigned to upper and lower tiers on the basis of the degree of worker autonomy and personal participation enjoyed within that occupation. As might have been expected, secondary-sector workers were characterised as poorer and less well educated and there was a higher proportion of non-white workers in the secondary sector than in others. Within the upper tier of the primary sector, this pattern was reversed.

The segmentation hypothesis and the underlying structure of the sectors imply that the determinants of earnings would differ across the three segments. Given the lack of structure within secondary markets and associated lack of skills in its workforce, seniority and education would be unlikely to play an important role in earnings determination. The inherent structure of the lower-tier primary sector would mean that the wage-setting process would be affected by firm and industry-level characteristics in addition to individual skills and attributes. Meanwhile, the informality of the upper tier would also be expected to be associated with substantial returns to education and experience. Subsequently, both personal and structural controls were used to model individual earnings in the three sectors in the following way:

$$\ln E = \beta_0 + \beta_1 A + \beta_2 A^2 + \beta_3 Ed + \beta_4 R + \beta_5 U + \beta_6 H + \sum_{I=7}^{20} \beta_I I + \varepsilon \tag{9.1.1}$$

where
E = annual earnings
A = age
Ed = years of schooling
R = race (1 if white, 0 if black)
U = weeks unemployed in previous year
H = hours worked in previous week
I = series of 1/0 dummy variables denoting industry of work

All three equations were estimated using ordinary least squares and yielded the following regression results shown in Table 9.1.1.

Results indicated that the wage-setting process differed significantly across sectors. In the secondary sector, earnings were influenced by only the number of hours worked and spells of unemployment, while work experience (proxied by age) and education had no significant effect.

Table 9.1.1 OLS regression results by sector

	Secondary	Primary – lower tier	Primary – upper tier
A (age)	0.00056 (0.03357)	0.06644[a,b] (0.00527)	0.10324[a,b] (0.02043)
A² (age squared)	0.00005[b] (0.00040)	−0.00069[a,b] (0.00006)	−0.00098[a] (0.00023)
Ed (schooling)	0.01433[b] (0.02175)	0.06170[a,b] (0.00283)	0.09553[a,b] (0.01057)
R (race)	0.11972 (0.13388)	0.22655[a] (0.03188)	0.31418 (0.22098)
U (unemployed weeks)	−0.05284[a,b] (0.01320)	−0.02705[a,b] (0.00205)	−0.01340 (0.03188)
H (hours worked)	0.01284[a,b] (0.00725)	0.00718[a,b] (0.00084)	−0.00696[a,b] (0.00266)
Constant	7.96659	6.22407	5.35066
R²	0.208	0.246	0.484
Sample size	234	4130	242

Notes: [a] denotes regression coefficient is significant at 0.05 level; [b] denotes that regression coefficient is significantly different from comparable coefficients in other sectors at 0.05 level; adapted from Table 1 in Osterman (1975).

Similarly, race also had no significant effect, supporting the notion that employers view workers as interchangeable and that identifiable differences in worker quality are unimportant in determining pay levels. In the primary sectors, both lower and upper tiers, there was evidence for the wage-setting process being more systematic with nearly all control variables being statistically significant. Moreover, the magnitude of the human capital controls (experience and schooling) was higher in the upper tier than the lower, implying that the human capital model better explains the wage-setting practices in this sector.

The conclusion drawn from these results was strong support for the dual labour market hypothesis. As predicted, the human capital model held up well for upper-tier workers in the primary sector but had little role to play for workers in the secondary labour market.

Technical Box 9.1

Methodological Flaw of Human Capital Models – Truncation Bias

As noted by Cain (1976), a fundamental problem arises within human capital models when testing for industrial or occupational segmentation when the criteria used to delineate segments is earnings. Such a methodological artefact is commonly referred to as truncation bias and its impact is shown in Figure 9.1.1.

Assume for simplicity that years of education is the only human capital variable that affects earnings, and that a fitted wage equation between observed earnings and education years for the entire population produces the regression Line 1 in Figure 9.1.1. The slope of this regression line

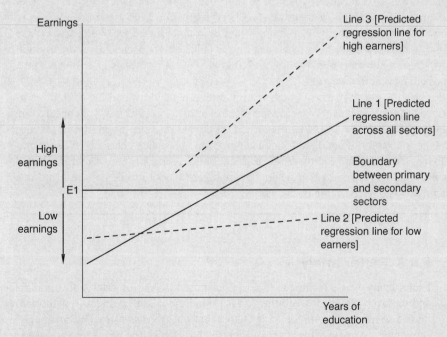

Figure 9.1.1 Truncation bias

will determine the relationship between years of education and earnings, with the slope reflecting the marginal increase in earnings following an additional year of education, which within a Mincerian earnings equation will reflect the return to education. The steeper the slope, the greater the returns to education and vice versa. Under the hypothesis of labour market duality, the "good" jobs in the primary sector are those with high earnings (an earnings level $E1$ or above) and those "bad" jobs in the secondary sector have low earnings below the level of $E1$.

While there will be workers across the entire educational spectrum in both sectors, with highly educated individuals having earnings below $E1$ and those with much lower levels of education having earnings above $E1$, it is only those highly educated workers of low ability (which is unobserved in the human capital wage equation) who will be observed in low-paying jobs and it is only those lowly educated workers of high ability who will be observed in high-paying jobs. After all, if we took a highly educated worker with high ability as an example, we would not expect to observe him in a "bad" job but rather in a high-paying "good" job. Hence, it is only low human capital accumulation and low ability combined that result in secondary-sector employment. What this will mean is that, when the focus is restricted to high earners, the sample of workers will be affected in two ways: first, the innate ability of workers with lower educational attainment will be from the higher reaches of the ability distribution (1); secondly, there is likely to be a censoring of the distribution of workers, with those of low educational attainment absent (2). Thus, an estimated regression between earnings and observed years of education will predict a steeper regression Line 3 in Figure 9.1.1 as the higher (unobserved) ability of workers would manifest itself as a higher return to years of education (1) and the censored observations will not be included within the regression calculation (2).

Conversely, the sample in low-paid employment will be disproportionately comprised of those with below-average ability and will be truncated at the far right-hand side of the figure, i.e. those with higher levels of education will not be observed in the secondary sector. The net outcome of these two effects will be a shallower predicted regression Line 2 as shown in Figure 9.1.1, which would imply a lower return to human capital in constructed wage equations. As a result, the a priori assignment of sectors when testing for industrial or occupational duality will naturally lead to a bias in human capital returns, and to lower education effects on earnings in the lower segment of the market in particular.

Note, though, that it is not only a strict demarcation between sectors along the lines of earnings that introduces truncation bias. So, while the likes of Harrison (1972), who delineated on ghetto residency, and McNabb (1987), who delineated on the basis of the proportion of females employed within an industry, did not directly focus upon earnings, such studies are still susceptible to truncation bias. In both cited examples, the criteria for assigning jobs into sectors is related to earnings levels, with ghetto residents and female employees tending to be paid less and this would subsequently lead to a truncation of the earnings distribution.

9.4.3 Factor analysis

Factor analysis is a technique that has been used to test for strict industrial dualism and removes the need to arbitrarily assign individuals to segments. Factor analysis finds a small number of common factors that linearly reconstruct as accurately and economically as possible a set of identified variables (or characteristics) and it is useful for identifying underlying patterns within data. Those characteristics most important in describing the underlying complex relationships will load more highly into the constructed factors, and, under the scenario of an identifiable core and peripheral industrial distinction, characteristics such as those related to the use of technology and capital intensity, i.e. those features highlighted within the dual labour market literature, will feature prominently. Factors scores calculated for individual industries are then used to determine whether the grouping of industries, driven by their underlying characteristics, is consistent with the idea of industrial duality. A prominent example of such a methodological approach is Oster (1979) – see Methodological Example Box 9.2 – who found evidence of a separation between core and peripheral industries. Although adopting a different perspective on what characterises core and peripheral sectors, Edwards (1975) also found evidence for industrial duality. Focusing on the idea that there are lower rates of separation and unemployment in large capital-intensive industries, considerable evidence was found for greater employment stability in core industries, consistent with the dual labour market hypothesis. By way of contrast, Sloane *et al.* (1993), having identified four important factors relating to human capital, job stability, workforce composition and industry effects, could find little evidence in support of labour market segmentation in Britain.

Methodological Example Box 9.2

G. Oster, "A Factor Analysis Test of the Theory of the Dual Economy", *Review of Economics and Statistics*, 61(1), 1979, pp. 33–9.

The focus of this work was to test for the existence of industrial dualism in the American economy. Supporters of such a hypothesis speculated that there existed a core industrial sector characterised by powerful, concentrated, unionised and capital-intensive industries that were technically progressive, and a peripheral core made up of industries that did not exhibit such traits. The investigation was carried out within the context of a factor analytic model that allows a small number of categories (or factors) to be identified from an underlying characteristic set, with the basic factor analytic model being of the following form:

$$x_i = a_{i1}F_1 + a_{i2}F_2 + \ldots + a_{ik}F_k + e_i \quad i = 1, \ldots, n \tag{9.2.1}$$

where each of the constructed x_i variables is made from a linear combination of $k + 1$ independent factors (that are common to all of the x_i variables) and a single unique factor. Each of the a_{ij} elements are termed loadings and will indicate the correlation between the ith variate and the jth common factor and subsequently the square of each a_{ij} will represent the proportion of the total unit variance in any x_i that is explained by the jth common factor, net of the contribution of all other common factors.

This investigation was implemented over 83 industries (classified on the basis of 3-digit 1960 Census classifications) in agriculture, communications and utilities, construction, manufacturing, mining and transportation. For these industries, 25 industrial characteristics capturing patterns of structural variation, both central to and outside of descriptions of core and periphery industries, were loaded into the factor analysis framework. If a core–periphery industrial demarcation existed, then a factor should emerge that loaded significantly on dimensions highlighted within the industrial duality literature such as concentration and capital intensity.

Initial factor loadings were identified by the technique of principal factors and the first three principal factors were retained. To aid the interpretability of these factors, they were orthogonally transformed using established criteria and the resulting factor loadings suggested three identifiable categories. The first factor (labelled *a tentative dual economy factor*) loaded significantly (and with expected signs) on variables reflecting industrial size and concentration and also loaded significantly and positively with regards to industry unionisation, the level of depreciable assets per production worker, and on the median years of male schooling. Although not suggested within the dual economy literature, the ratios of government purchases and government purchases plus exports to total industry receipts also loaded significantly, which were also deemed to be reasonable aspects of industrial variation along core–periphery lines.

The second factor (labelled *a sex factor*) appeared to reflect industry stratification associated with the gender composition of industrial workforces. In particular, there were positive loadings on the proportion of females within the workforce and there was a significant association between high female employment, labour-intensive technologies and low rates of employment growth. The third factor (labelled *a race factor*) appeared to define industrial stratification associated with the racial composition of male employment. In particular, there were strong links between high black male employment and industries characterised by relatively high unemployment and lay-off rates, a high incidence of seasonal or part-time employment, low profit rates, relatively stagnant productivity and a high proportion of unskilled labour.

Given the loading of those variables in the first factor that reflect the aspects separating core and peripheral industries, the factor score distribution across industries was examined for more concerted evidence of structural dualism using the method of moments. On the assumption that the probability density function of the observed sample data is of the form:

$$z_1 n(\mu_1, \sigma_1^2) + z_2 n(\mu_2, \sigma_2^2) \qquad (9.2.2)$$

where $z_1 + z_2 = 1$, the implication is that the observed probability distribution is a weighted sum of two underlying normal distributions with means of μ and variances of σ^2. Method of moments estimation allows the unknown parameters of μ_1, μ_2, σ_1^2, σ_2^2 and z_1 to be expressed as functions of the known population parameters and subsequently solved to yield sample moment estimators. The resulting mixture of estimated normal probability density functions was then tested for goodness of fit on the basis of a χ^2 test. An estimated test statistic of 17.43 suggested that the hypothesis that the industries in the sample were drawn from a mixture of two normal distributions could not be rejected. Thus, on the basis of the estimated component distributions within the sample and the identified factor that reflected the hypothesised core–periphery distinction, the notion of industrial duality was accepted and 55 industries were subsequently identified as peripheral and 28 as core.

9.4.4 Cluster analysis

Cluster analysis again solves the problem of a priori segmentation and is the name given to techniques that seek to uncover groups or clusters within data. The most commonly used class of clustering techniques contains methods that lead to hierarchical classifications of observations, starting at the stage where each observation is regarded as forming its own unique cluster and finishing at the stage where all observations are in a single group. Central to these approaches is the need to measure the "distance" between observations, which, in turn, defines their similarity or dissimilarity.

In terms of the empirical literature, results have been mixed. Flatau and Lewis (1993), for example, suggested that occupations naturally cluster into secondary, intermediate and primary sectors in Australia, with tiers also present within the primary sector. In the US, meanwhile, Anderson *et al.* (1987) and Boston (1990) came to differing conclusions. While Anderson *et al.* found no evidence for segmented labour markets, Boston – see Methodological Example Box 9.3 – identified a clustering of occupations into primary and secondary sectors, split along the lines of gender and race. In Britain, the results of Sloane *et al.* (1993) have been less conclusive. While the clustering analysis did reveal two distinct sectors, the characteristics of these sectors were not consistent with recognised views of segmented and internal labour markets.

Methodological Example Box 9.3

T. Boston, "Segmented Labour Markets: New Evidence from a Study of Four Race–Gender Groups", *Industrial and Labor Relations Review*, 44(1), 1990, pp. 99–115.

This study analysed the existence of a dual labour market distinction between primary and secondary sectors in the US using individual-level data from the 1983 Current Population Survey (CPS). To control for potential heterogeneity effects, segments were disaggregated along the lines of gender and race, allowing within-group differences to be examined in addition to between group differences.

The driving distinction between sectors was noted as the primary sector being characterised by a positive wage premium, as identified by an unexplained differential in earnings between sectors, even though the general economy has both involuntary unemployment and overly qualified workers confined to low-wage secondary-sector jobs. Recognising that the primary sector demands general and specific labour as opposed to the low or unskilled labour of the secondary sector that involves menial and repetitive tasks performed by interchangeable workers, the study partitioned markets in accordance with the general or specific skills needed to perform tasks in the primary sector. The dual partition of the labour market was derived from responses to a supplemental questionnaire entitled "Occupational Mobility, Training, and Job Tenure" in the January 1983 CPS asking survey respondents whether specific skills or prior training were necessary for their present (or previous) job. This provided an approximation of primary and secondary occupations. Such an adopted methodology was emphasised as being more desirable because sectoral boundaries were derived objectively from responses to questions detailing job prerequisites and not in a predetermined a priori fashion.

After controlling for variations in key attributes and adjusting for stochastic biases, the extent to which market segments exhibited unexplained earnings differentials, occupational mobility barriers and other characteristics was determined. To avoid the problem (also stochastic) of the censoring and truncation of segments, mean scores for the training and prior skills question were used to partition between primary and secondary segments. On the basis of a yes/no response to the question "Did you need specific skills or training to obtain your current (last) job?", the mean proportion of affirmative responses in 44 2-digit occupations was calculated. Cluster analysis, the name given to techniques that seek to uncover groups or clusters within data, was then employed on these means to group the data into natural clusters. With the calculated percentages describing the initial clusters, these were then grouped with the nearest cluster to form a new cluster. The proximity between new clusters was then recalculated and the grouping process continued until only two clusters remained. The mean scores for jobs requiring specific skills or prior training for the two identified occupational clusters were 74.28 per cent and 25.19 per cent, assumed to denote primary-sector and secondary-sector occupations respectively.

The highest concentration in primary-sector occupations was found for white women at 67.6 per cent, followed by white men (63.5 per cent), black women (52.7 per cent) and then black men (41.2 per cent). While the high representation for women at first seemed counter-intuitive, it was noted that women were concentrated in technical sales and administrative support occupations that in general require specific skills or training. Meanwhile, the ratio of secondary-sector earnings to primary-sector earnings were 0.70 for black men, 0.58 for white men, 0.53 for white women and 0.52 for black women.

Subsequently, the following earnings equation was estimated using ordinary least squares separately for primary and secondary sectors for each of the four gender–race groups.

$$\ln E = \beta_0 + \beta_1 A + \beta_2 A^2 + \beta_3 Ed + \beta_4 H + \beta_5 Ten + \beta_6 Exp +$$

$$\sum_{1=7}^{9} \beta_i R + \sum_{1=10}^{12} \beta_i M + \sum_{1=13}^{14} \beta_i C + \sum_{1=15}^{18} \beta_i Train + \sum_{1=19}^{20} \beta_i MH + \tag{9.3.1}$$

$$\sum_{1=21}^{23} \beta_i FH + \sum_{1=24}^{26} \beta_i EC + \sum_{1=27}^{35} \beta_i I + \varepsilon$$

where
E = weekly earnings
A = age
Ed = highest educational grade achieved
H = hours worked per week
Ten = tenure with current employer (years)
Exp = years in current occupation
R = series of 1/0 dummy variables denoting region
M = series of 1/0 dummy variables denoting marital status
C = series of 1/0 dummy variables denoting central city status
Train = series of 1/0 dummy variables denoting the extent of training to improve skills
MH = series of 1/0 dummy variables denoting male household head status
FH = series of 1/0 dummy variables denoting female household head status
EC = series of 1/0 dummy variables denoting employment class
I = series of 1/0 dummy variables denoting industry

Supporting evidence to confirm the existence of segmented labour markets was based upon the premise that earnings in the secondary sector should not be related to productivity, while those in the primary sector would be. The figures in Table 9.3.1 contain the relevant results.

All variables in the equations were significant at the 0.01 level or better, and a Chow test of the difference in coefficients between primary and secondary sectors was also significant at the 0.01 level. The estimated coefficients revealed that, in general, additional years of education generated higher returns for primary-sector workers than for secondary-sector workers. This was true for all groups except for black women. While segmented labour market theory postulates that experience and tenure will have a negligible influence over earnings in the secondary, results

Table 9.3.1 Selected OLS regression results by sector, gender and race

	White men		Black men		White women		Black women	
	Primary	*Secondary*	*Primary*	*Secondary*	*Primary*	*Secondary*	*Primary*	*Secondary*
Education	0.060[a]	0.032[a]	0.048[a]	0.016[a]	0.052[a]	0.003[a]	0.081[a]	0.073[a]
Age	0.065[a]	0.075[a]	0.057[a]	0.009[a]	0.036[a]	0.038[a]	0.005[a]	0.009[a]
Age squared	−0.001[a]	−0.001[a]	−0.001[a]	0.000[a]	0.000[a]	0.000[a]	0.000[a]	0.000[a]
Hours	0.009[a]	0.023[a]	0.012[a]	0.038[a]	0.028[a]	0.036[a]	0.003[a]	0.044[a]
Tenure	0.007[a]	0.010[a]	0.005[a]	0.008[a]	0.011[a]	0.008[a]	0.015[a]	0.007[a]
Experience	0.002[a]	0.001[a]	0.006[a]	0.000[a]	0.008[a]	−0.004[a]	−0.001[a]	−0.011[a]
Training								
• formal within job	0.069[a]	0.188[a]	0.047[a]	−0.147[a]	0.118[a]	0.192[a]	0.016[a]	0.354[a]
• school	0.037[a]	0.147[a]	0.115[a]	−0.251[a]	0.086[a]	−0.006[a]	−0.038[a]	0.356[a]
• other	0.057[a]	0.065[a]	0.197[a]	−0.462[a]	0.069[a]	0.330[a]	−0.066[a]	−0.314[a]
• none	−0.026[a]	0.015[a]	−0.155[a]	−0.242[a]	−0.024[a]	−0.144[a]	−0.174[a]	0.064[a]
Constant	3.203[a]	2.662[a]	3.288[a]	3.659[a]	2.974[a]	3.141[a]	3.759[a]	2.571[a]
Adj.R^2	0.403	0.596	0.465	0.708	0.468	0.634	0.516	0.742

Notes: [a] denotes regression coefficient is significant at the 0.01 level; results adapted from tables 4a/4b in Boston (1990).

were mixed. For women, the estimated returns on these variables were consistent with such expectations, as they were on the experience variables across all four gender–race groups. However, the effect of tenure was greater in the secondary sector than it was in the primary sector for black and white men, counter to expectations. Furthermore, the notion that formal on-the-job training and school training are expected to be unimportant considerations for secondary-sector workers was only supported for black men.

In summary, the group for which the greatest support of the segmented labour market hypothesis was found was black men, for whom the noted reversal of the importance of job tenure between primary and secondary was the only finding out of line with expectations. Meanwhile, least support was found in the case of white men, for whom job tenure and a number of aspects of training went against the hypothesised expectation. This, in itself, should not be taken as evidence against the existence of occupational segmentation, though, as segmented labour market theory would also argue that segmentation would have the least effect upon this group of workers and overall it was concluded that the results supported the existence of segmented labour markets.

To explain the differences in earnings across sectors for each of the groups, total differences were decomposed into two distinct components: the first, the part of the difference in (the log of) mean earnings between the primary and secondary sectors, which was explained by differences in average endowments of job-related characteristics; and the second component represented that part which was unexplained, i.e. related to the way in which characteristics were rewarded differently across sectors. Results showed that sizeable unexplained earnings differentials existed between sectors and, while the unadjusted ratio of secondary- to primary-sector earnings across all groups was 58 per cent, the adjusted ratio was 85 per cent. This figure suggested that the maximum proportion of the observed earnings differential between sectors that may be attributed to segmented labour markets was 15 per cent. This ranged from 11 per cent for black women to 18 per cent for white women, clearly demonstrating that there was a wage premium to primary-sector employment.

Investigating the existence of occupational barriers, the age-cohort profile of secondary-sector workers was identified as being consistent with the segmented labour market hypothesis. In particular, a high percentage of young workers, i.e. aged between 16 and 24 started their careers in the secondary sector. Subsequently, constructed logit equations, modelling the propensity for inter-sector mobility for all workers, estimated the probability of moving from the secondary sector to the primary sector to be 56.7 per cent for white women, 48.9 per cent for white men, 29.3 per cent for black women and 24.9 per cent for black men.

In conclusion, the earnings regressions for the separate race–gender groups generally supported the notion of segmented labour market theory, although earnings regressions for white men conformed the least well, and the hypothesis that primary-sector workers received a wage premium could not be rejected. Further, an examination of worker mobility between primary and secondary sectors revealed the existence of significant barriers to worker mobility and low levels of worker movement. Taken together, such findings were taken as being supportive of the theory of segmented labour markets.

9.4.5 Switching regressions

Switching regressions allow observations to be more flexibly assigned to labour market segments, as the requirement that all workers in an identified industry or occupation are in the same segment of the labour market is not imposed. As such, switching regression models assume that parameter estimates within wage equations are not only unknown but also random. The break between sectors is also treated as a random point and is determined through an iterative process rather than being imposed upon the data. Thus, such techniques allow the likelihood of an individual worker being attached to a sector to be inferred from their personal attributes and the distribution of wages and was the methodological approach adopted by Dickens and Lang (1985) – see Methodological Example Box 9.4. Their study found strong evidence for the existence of more than one labour market segment and of no returns to education and experience in the secondary sector, all consistent with the dual labour market hypothesis. Subsequent refinements and further investigation by the same authors left the underlying tenor of these results unchanged, although Dickens and Lang (1988) did conclude that the labour market may not necessarily consist of exactly two segments, but that the principle of labour market segmentation is clearly evident.

Methodological Example Box 9.4

W. Dickens and K. Lang, "A Test of Dual Labor Market Theory", *American Economic Review*, 75(4), 1985, pp. 792–805.

This paper provided a test of dual labour market theory by identifying whether there existed a distinct low-wage labour market in which there were no returns to schooling and workers did not receive on-the-job-training, and whether there were non-economic barriers that prevented some workers in this secondary sector obtaining better jobs in the primary sector. While it was noted that there are significant differences in views of the secondary labour market, potentially conclusive tests had not been specified for either the dual labour market typology or non-economic barriers to primary-sector employment. This paper proposed strong tests for both hypotheses using data drawn from two sources. The first was the 1980 Panel Survey of Income Dynamics (PSID) and restricted to male head of households in non-government jobs who worked for more than 1,000 hours in the previous year for whom data on education and marital status were available. This was termed the *full* sample which comprised 2,812 individual observations. An alternative sample (of 1,696 individual observations), termed the *restricted* sample, comprised only members of the Survey Research Center sample.

Among the research questions asked was: did two wage equations fit the data significantly better than one, and did the subsequently best-fitting equations conform with the predictions of the dual labour market hypothesis? If the proposed research questions were correct, one wage equation should have been upward sloping in schooling and experience, while the other equation should have been flat to human capital variables.

A switching model with unknown regimes was used for the estimation. This involved specifying two wage equations and a third equation that predicted sectoral attachment, with all three equations being estimated simultaneously. Thus, consider the following system of equations specified for individual workers in the primary and secondary sectors, denoted by the subscripts

p and s respectively:

$$\ln(W_p) = \beta_p X + \delta_p Y + \varepsilon_p \qquad (9.4.1)$$

$$\ln(W_s) = \beta_s X + \delta_s Y + \varepsilon_s \qquad (9.4.2)$$

$$y^* = \Gamma X + \varepsilon_w \qquad (9.4.3)$$

where W denotes log hourly wages, X is a vector of personal characteristics, Y is years of job experience, the β, δ and Γ denote conformable vectors of estimated regression parameters, y^* is a latent variable measuring tendency to be in the primary sector, and the ε are normally distributed error terms. However, y^* is not observed, but, if $y^* > 0$, an individual's wages will be determined by equation (9.4.1), otherwise they will be determined by equation (9.4.2). Furthermore, since the single-equation model (where there is no distinction between primary and secondary sectors) is nested within the switching model, the hypothesis that the two-wage equation model fits significantly better than the single-equation model could be tested using a likelihood ratio test.

While the existence of two sectors with inherently different wage-setting mechanisms is a fundamental requirement for the dual labour market theory, this is not in itself incompatible with human capital theory. Thus, such a finding may be entirely consistent with individuals choosing employment in that sector that maximises the expected present value of their lifetime utility. However, the rationing of primary-sector jobs, the second principle of dual market theory, is less compatible with human capital theory. Thus, even though individuals would want to choose their most-preferred sector, some workers would prefer to work in the primary sector but are unable to gain employment there. Although the general phenomenon of rationing is believed to be associated with periods of recession, only women and ethnic minorities are likely to experience rationing during other times.

To test for the existence of non-economic barriers to employment in the primary sector, a mechanism for allocating workers between sectors in the absence of rationing was formulated. To do this, it was assumed that experience gained in one sector had a greater wage return in that sector than it did in the other sector, and that workers behaved so as to maximise utility over the course of their lifetime. If preferences over non-pecuniary job aspects were constant over a lifetime, workers would choose employment in one sector at the beginning of their career and remain there for their entire working life.

It would be expected that workers choose the sector that yields the highest lifetime earnings if non-pecuniary attributes were similar across primary and secondary sectors, but a commonly accepted feature of primary-sector jobs is that they are characterised by superior non-pecuniary attributes. In contrast, starting wages may be higher in the secondary sector than in the primary sector, the pace of work may be slower, and secondary-sector employers may be less concerned with absenteeism and lateness.

Assume that workers will choose to work in the primary sector if the log of the net present value (NPV) of their income stream in the primary sector exceeds that available from the secondary sector by more than C (the cumulative inverse of the compensating wage differential for secondary-sector employment). By denoting primary-sector employment with the subscript p and that in the secondary sector with the subscript s as before, the probability (P) of primary sector employment may be formally written as:

$$P = prob\{\ln(NPV_p) - \ln(NPV_s) > C\} \qquad (9.4.4)$$

Net present value in primary and secondary sectors are derived from the previously specified wage equations (9.4.1) and (9.4.2). Under the assumption that a working life can be approximated by infinity, equations (9.4.1), (9.4.2) and (9.4.4) can be combined and reformulated as:

$$P = prob\{(\beta_p - \beta_s)X + \varepsilon_p - \varepsilon_s + C' > 0\} \tag{9.4.5}$$

where

$$C' = \ln((d - \delta_s)/(d - \delta_p)) - C \tag{9.4.6}$$

and d is the discount rate. Assuming that preferences over the non-pecuniary aspects of employment and discount rates do not vary with observable characteristics, C' may be formulated as being equal to a constant (C'') plus a normally distributed error term (ε_w). The hypothesis that workers choose their sector of employment such that they utility maximise can then be tested by estimating the following sectoral attachment equation:

$$P = prob\{(\beta_p - \beta_s + \beta_w)X + \varepsilon_p - \varepsilon_s + C'' + \varepsilon_w > 0\} \tag{9.4.7}$$

and investigating whether the return to observed personal characteristics equals $\beta_p - \beta_s$ (or, in other words, that $\beta_w = 0$). Acceptance of this hypothesis that $\beta_w = 0$ will imply that individuals are not constrained in their ability to utility maximise and are therefore choosing the sector of employment that maximises the net present value of lifetime earnings. Although it may not be reasonable to assume that preferences for non-pecuniary aspects of employment are unrelated to personal characteristics, at least some of the elements of the coefficient vector β_w may be expected to equal zero for those elements of X that are not related to tastes.

Results estimated using ordinary least squares estimation and the switching regression framework are shown in Table 9.4.1.

Results from the two samples were similar and the estimates from the OLS equations were similar to those found in other research. While the primary wage equation in the switching model was similar to the OLS equation, that of the secondary sector contrasted sharply. None of the coefficients was statistically significant and the hypothesis that the secondary-sector wage equation was completely flat could not be rejected. However, a likelihood ratio test easily rejected the single labour market model and the two-sector split between primary and secondary sectors fitted the data considerably better than a single equation. According to the estimates from this model, about 12 per cent of working male heads of household were employed in the secondary sector. The distinction between primary- and secondary-sector workers was further examined by calculating predicted probabilities of being in the primary sector. The distribution was distinctly bimodal, with one clustering of observations occurring over the 0–10 per cent probability range. This was taken as evidence of the model being able to successfully identify a distinct secondary sector.

Since a number of the parameters within the switching model were estimated imprecisely, a restricted model was also estimated that constrained the wage equation in the secondary sector to be flat, and education and marital status controls were removed from the switching equation. This restricted model, nevertheless, exhibited the same pattern across the parameter estimates as the unrestricted model. It was, therefore, concluded that the single labour market model was rejected and the predictions of dual labour market theory – that there are no returns to education or experience in the secondary sector – could not be rejected.

Table 9.4.1 OLS and switching regression results

	Restricted sample				Full sample			
	OLS	Primary	Secondary	Switch	OLS	Primary	Secondary	Switch
Metropolitan area (SMSA)	0.197	0.112	0.197	0.361	0.194	0.078	0.073	0.526
	(0.025)	(0.060)	(1.280)	(0.158)	(0.020)	(0.036)	(0.452)	(0.144)
Never married	-0.305	-0.261	-0.244	-0.157	-0.265	-0.286	-0.268	0.238
	(0.044)	(0.055)	(0.580)	(0.354)	(0.031)	(0.047)	(0.263)	(0.338)
Schooling	0.059	0.067	-0.003	0.020	0.063	0.069	0.006	0.037
	(0.005)	(0.005)	(0.072)	(0.031)	(0.004)	(0.005)	(0.034)	(0.024)
White	0.134	0.008	-0.192	0.796	0.180	0.006	-0.139	0.885
	(0.040)	(0.166)	(2.730)	(0.328)	(0.020)	(0.059)	(0.781)	(0.190)
Experience	0.010	0.013	0.001		0.010	0.014	0.000	
	(0.001)	(0.001)	(0.002)		(0.001)	(0.001)	(0.002)	
Constant	0.874	0.996	1.320	-0.006	0.760	0.982	1.270	-0.389
	(0.075)	(0.297)	(3.330)	(0.574)	(0.051)	(0.108)	(0.636)	(0.379)
Covariance with switching error		0.068	-0.009			0.155	-0.019	
		(0.389)	(4.420)			(0.084)	(1.180)	

Notes: Standard errors in parentheses; results adapted from table 1 in Dickens and Lang (1985).

A more crucial aspect of dual labour market theory is the assumption that primary-sector jobs are rationed. To test this assertion, constraints were imposed upon the switching equation using the full sample and likelihood ratio tests performed. If workers were unconstrained in their choice of sector of employment and their preferences for the non-pecuniary aspects of employment were unrelated to their personal characteristics, the estimated coefficients on these variables in the switching equation would be expected to be equal to the difference between the coefficients in the two wage equations. Surmising that such an invariance of preferences was unlikely to hold for those within and outside of a metropolitan area, the authors tested the restriction on equation (9.4.7) that $\beta w = 0$ for the variables never married, schooling and white. The hypothesis, consistent with workers having a free choice over which sector to work in, was rejected. On the basis that married workers would have a greater desire for the stability of employment offered within the primary sector, the hypothesis that coefficients on the schooling and white variables were zero was also tested and rejected. This led the authors to conclude that there were three potential explanations for their findings: first, that educated workers preferred secondary-sector employment more than their less-educated counterparts did; second, that blacks were less averse to secondary-sector jobs than were whites; and, third, in the absence of evidence for the previous two explanations, that blacks faced non-economic barriers to employment in the primary sector. Citing existing evidence against the first two posits, it was concluded that the latter was the most plausible explanation.

The conclusion drawn from these results was two-fold: namely, that there are two distinct sectors of the labour market, which have their own wage-setting mechanisms; and that there is a queue for primary-sector jobs, in that, rather than allocating jobs randomly, primary-sector employers discriminated against non-whites. These two aspects are the central tenets of dual labour market theory. In particular, the authors stressed that their conclusions were drawn from an approach that allowed the distribution of wages and worker characteristics to determine sectoral attachment, and, in doing so, avoided the problems of arbitrariness and sample selection bias that complicated the interpretation of earlier research.

9.4.6 Mobility

The second crucial strand of evidence necessary to validate segmented labour market theory is whether there is a rationing of better jobs. Indeed, as Dickens and Lang note: "If an individual can move out of the secondary sector in order to obtain returns on experience and education, the existence of a sector in which there are no returns is inconsequential" (1985: 793). Hence, a rationing of jobs in the primary sector is crucial.

Such a proposition, that the low-paid are confined to the secondary sector, represents a fundamental criticism of human capital theory because it implies that labour markets do not clear. Although several authors have investigated the issue of inter-sector mobility, the evidence presented does not provide a consensus view on the existence of labour market segmentation. On the one hand, we have evidence from Psacharopoulos (1978), who analyses both intra-generational socio-economic mobility and inter-generational mobility using constructed occupational scales for male employees in the UK. He found evidence for workers initially taking up less desirable jobs upon entering the workforce but then moving on to better jobs, and for upward mobility in occupational transmission between generations. From these findings, it was concluded that no support can be found to support the hypothesis that the labour market is segmented. Meanwhile, for the US, Leigh (1976) demonstrated not only substantial but also comparable earnings growth for black and white male workers over the course of the 1960s. Similarly, while Schiller (1977) found extensive upward mobility in the bottom of the US income distribution during the period 1957 to 1971, this was ascribed solely to discrimination and both authors argued that their findings refute dual labour market theory.

On the other hand, other authors have identified restricted worker mobility. Mayhew and Rosewell (1979) constructed a mobility matrix of a maximum of four possible jobs for male workers in the UK and assigned workers to upper primary, lower primary and secondary sectors on the basis of occupational classification. While some evidence was found for upward and downward mobility, there was also substantial evidence of immobility between sectors as the majority of workers remained in their initial sector. However, human capital variables were found to be important determinants of both initial sectoral placement and upward mobility between sectors and led to the conclusion that the UK labour market is not affected by the sort of immobility as predicted by segmentation theory. In a similar vein, Carnoy and Rumberger (1980) found that minority workers were more likely to begin their careers in the secondary sector, and, having started there, were less likely to leave this sector than were whites. Such differential mobility is taken as support for dual labour market theory. Similarly, Boston (1990) – see Methodological Example Box 9.3 – when examining worker mobility between primary and secondary sectors in a sample split by gender and race, identified the existence of significant barriers to worker mobility and low levels of worker movement, which were taken as supporting the notion of segmented labour markets.[11]

In contrast to the above studies, Dickens and Lang (1985) – see Methodological Example Box 9.4 – and Dickens and Lang (1992) examined not whether there is a lack of mobility between sectors but crucially whether there is a rationing of primary-sector jobs. That is, some workers would prefer to work in the primary sector but are unable to gain employment because of non-economic barriers. Using a switching regression framework, their evidence suggested primary-sector employers discriminated against blacks rather than allocating jobs randomly. On the basis of this, and without considering the relationship between discrimination and segmentation, they concluded that their results were consistent with the notion of dual labour markets.

9.5 Conclusions

Under the assumptions of perfect competition, perfect wage knowledge and perfect worker mobility, the neo-classical tradition would infer that equally qualified workers would receive equal returns to their accumulated human capital. That is, the labour market should operate as if it is a single homogeneous entity. Segmented market theorists, in contrast, have maintained that jobs can be roughly divided into two groups: those in the secondary sector with low wages, bad working conditions, unstable employment and little opportunity for advancement; and those in the primary sector with relatively high wages, good working conditions and opportunities for advancement into higher-paying jobs. As such, Piore summarises the difference between the two segments well:

The primary market offers jobs which possess several of the following traits: high wages, good working conditions, employment stability and job security, equity and due process in the administration of work rules, and chances for advancement. The … secondary market has jobs which, relative to those in the primary sector, are decidedly less attractive. They tend to involve low wages, poor working conditions, considerable variability in employment, harsh and often arbitrary discipline, little opportunity to advance.

(1975: 72)

However, while there is a consensus over what distinguishes primary-sector jobs from those outside, the empirical identification and validation of such sectors is less clear. It should be remembered, though, that a number of empirical studies, particularly those using a priori classification systems, tested only for the existence of two distinct sectors. While a number of such empirical studies failed to establish evidence for strict duality, this does not in itself mean that there is no evidence for labour market segmentation more generally. Indeed, Althauser and Kalleberg (1981) insisted that it was the inadequate specification of boundaries between sectors that undermined the corroboration of segmented labour market theory and impaired its early development.

In contrast, a series of studies by Dickens and Lang that have used more sophisticated econometric techniques, that, in particular, do not rely on the predetermined (and often arbitrary) demarcation of sectors, provides more concerted evidence for the existence of segmented labour markets with non-economic barriers inhibiting worker mobility.

Summary

- The most basic neo-classical model of the labour market suggests that wages should be equal for equally equipped workers. In a neo-classical model of wage determination, it is not possible for wage differentials to exist between markets, for, as soon as they develop, workers migrate to the higher wage market in such numbers that any difference in wage rewards across markets is bid away. In such a way, any differences in the rates of return to human capital characteristics would be erased by inter-segment migration.
- It is possible to categorise differences between jobs over a fuller range of characteristics and properties rather than just wages, where negative (non-pecuniary) job traits require a monetary compensation or positive traits are a compensation for lower money wages. This is what is commonly referred to as the theory of equalising differences. Taken together, it is the whole raft of monetary and non-monetary components that describe the advantages of any job, and it is these that should be equalised across markets and not necessarily money wages.
- The idea of duality within labour markets was emphasised to address a range of policy concerns of the 1960s such as structural unemployment, racial discrimination and technological change. It was posited that the labour market split over time into separate "primary" and "secondary" sectors. The primary sector comprised a series of internal labour markets, where institutional rules determine internal hiring practices, wages and promotion that do not accord with the

ideals of profit-maximisation and there is limited employee mobility. Jobs in the primary sector will exhibit such traits as high wages, good promotion opportunities and stability in employment. Secondary-sector employment will be outside of internal labour markets and jobs will tend to have low pay and low career-advancement opportunities, and be associated with high labour turnover.

- A strict dichotomy of the labour market may not be appropriate and the primary sector can be further divided into an upper and lower tier. Within the upper tier of the primary sector are the high-status and high-paying professional and managerial jobs with good advancement opportunities, while in the lower tier of the primary sector jobs are relatively lower paying and have less career-advancement opportunities.

- The job competition model of Thurow places emphasis on on-the-job training, whereby the emergence of segmented labour markets is a response by firms to minimise training costs. Okun's analysis of the labour market extends Thurow's job competition model by also incorporating the desire to reduce staff turnover as a means of cost minimisation.

- The empirical identification of labour market segmentation has been based on the identification of a low-skill sector with no return to schooling/experience/tenure and no on-the-job training, and on the identification of non-economic barriers between sectors preventing mobility.

- Although several authors have investigated the issue of inter-sector mobility, the evidence presented does not provide a consensus view on the existence of labour market segmentation.

Questions

1   How does the theory of equalising differences extend the orthodox neo-classical view of inter-segment worker remuneration?

2   Outline the views of Doeringer and Piore (1971) with regards to the emergence of segmented labour markets. What features define and distinguish these sectors?

3   In what ways do the models of Thurow (1970) and Okun (1981) differ from the view presented by Doeringer and Piore (1971) and in what ways do they differ from one another?

4   Describe how the Bulow and Summers (1986) model accounts for a higher wage being paid to workers in primary-sector jobs in comparison to equally productive workers in the secondary sector.

5   Explain how truncation bias influences empirical human capital studies that aim to test for industrial or occupational segmentation.

Notes

1   Further underlying such a theory (underpinned by the notion of perfect competition) are the assumptions of perfect wage knowledge, zero adjustment costs and perfect labour mobility.

2 It should be noted, contrary to Smith's assertion, that agricultural workers are, in fact, among the lowest paid in most developing countries.

3 The treatment of segmented labour markets in this chapter is exclusively from a microeconomic perspective. While the discussion encompasses considerations such as poverty and discrimination as factors leading to the formation of segmented labour markets, it does not examine the macroeconomic implications of labour market segmentation. Far less has been written on this latter issue, although the work of Saint-Paul (1996) is an excellent example of what is available.

4 Reflecting the development of the literature, the discussion in this chapter relates to advanced industrialised economies. Within the context of developing economies, though, the segmentation of labour markets is invariably drawn along the lines of *formal* versus *informal* sectors, although this distinction in itself is just a banner of convenience and could be substituted for modern/industrial/urban/good versus traditional/agricultural/rural/bad. However, even this simple demarcation hides a multitude of different practices. In Brazil, for example, the formal sector comprises those workers holding labour cards entitling them to employment protection and various benefits, while the informal sector consists of those who do not. In Latin America and the Caribbean, the informal sector is defined as the sum of non-professional self-employed, domestic workers, unpaid workers and those employed in small enterprises. In other contexts, the formal sector is distinguished according to whether the firm is registered with the government and pays taxes. In others, the informal economy is equated with drugs, prostitution and other illegal activities. An overview of such alternatives is provided by Jhabvala *et al.* (2003).

5 The theory of implicit contracts assumes that workers are risk averse and dislike fluctuations in wage rates and would instead prefer a constant known wage. However, employers would prefer a wage rate that moved with the business cycle and subsequently changes in demand. To compensate (risk-neutral) employers for offering a stable wage rate, the fixed wage offered under the system of implicit contracts would be lower than the average wage rate under a regime where the wage was variable. The difference between the two wage rates is the entrepreneurial return for the insuring of a constant wage rate.

6 Efficiency wage theory seeks to provide an explanation for wages that are above equilibrium levels and was first proposed during the 1950s to account for observed payment patterns in developing countries. The conclusion drawn was that equilibrium wages were not always sufficiently high to cover the basic health needs of workers and so, by paying higher wages, firms would increase the health, and by extension the productivity, of their employees. In terms of developed countries, the theory has developed as a consequence of *inter alia* employers seeking to discourage shirking, reduce workforce turnover and attract better-quality workers.

7 With a utility function of $U = U(x_1, x_2 + \alpha s)$, equation (9.1) presents the conventional way in which such a function would be summed over an infinite horizon while applying a fixed discount rate of r per period. Note also that Bulow and Summers set up the utility function in their model such that, starting at time t, the utility series discounted at time v is summed over the remaining time horizon to infinity. The integral presented in equation (9.1) serves the same purpose but is notationally simpler.

8 Bulow and Summers specified the utility function in this way purely on the grounds of tractability, as it allows the maximisation decision to be based upon the consumption of only two goods and removes the need to explicitly model the production input decision.

9 On the assumption of homothetic preferences, a consumer's utility maximisation occurs along a ray from the origin and therefore equalisation of the marginal rate of substitution and relative prices will always occur at a point on this ray. Hence, for any relative set of prices, utility maximisation will ensure that goods are consumed in the same proportion along this ray with a constant marginal rate of substitution. With the price of sector 2 output normalised to unity, this allows us to say that p_1 (as the numerator of relative prices) will be related to a fixed ratio of x_1 and x_2. This is the first part of equation (9.2). The assumption of constant returns to labour allows us to further state that the ratio between labour inputs E_1 and E_2 will likewise be maintained and be inviolable to output levels. This allows us to specify that the output ratio will be a function of the ratio of inputs in equation (9.2).

10 Note that as E_1 increases $(N - E_1)$ gets smaller and so the second term in equation (9.5) will also increase.

11 Avoiding the problems associated with truncation bias – see Technical Box 9.1 – Psacharopoulos (1978), McNabb and Psacharopoulos (1981) and Neumann and Ziderman (1986) used the Hope–Goldthorpe occupational rating scale to determine sectoral attachment.

12 There is also evidence to suggest significant worker mobility within developing economies. As noted by an Inter-American Development Bank report (IADB 2003): "According to [the dualistic view of labour markets], the formal and informal economies operated in segmented labor markets and there is limited mobility between the two. Nothing could be further from the truth ... In a given six-month period, about 16 percent of workers in Mexico and 11 percent of workers in Argentina move either in or out of an informal job".

References

Althauser R. and Kalleberg A., "Firms, Occupations, and the Structure of Labor Markets: A Conceptual Analysis", in Berg I., editor, *Sociological Perspectives on Labor Markets*, Academic Press, New York, 1981, pp. 119–49.

Anderson K.H., Butler J.S. and Sloan F.A., "Labour Market Segmentation: A Cluster Analysis of Job Groups and Barriers to Entry", *Southern Economic Journal*, 53, 1987, pp. 571–90.

Azariadis C., "Implicit Contracts and Underemployment Equilibria", *Journal of Political Economy*, 83, 1975, pp. 1183–202.

Baily M.N., "Wages and Employment Under Uncertain Demand", *Review of Economic Studies*, 41, 1974, pp. 37–50.

Becker G., "Investment in Human Capital: A Theoretical Analysis", *Journal of Political Economy*, 70, 1962, pp. 9–49.

Becker G., *Human Capital*, NBER, New York, 1964.

Boston T.D., "Segmented Labour Markets: New Evidence from a Study of Four Race-Gender Groups", *Industrial and Labour Relations Review*, 44(1), 1990, pp. 99–115.

Bulow J.I. and Summers L.H., "A Theory of Dual Labour Markets with Application to Industrial Policy, Discrimination, and Keynesian Unemployment", *Journal of Labor Economics*, 4(3), 1986, pp. 376–414.

Cain G.G., "The Challenge of Segmented Labor Market Theories to Orthodox Theory: A Survey", *Journal of Economic Literature*, 14(4), 1976, pp. 1215–57.

Cairnes J.E., *Some Leading Principles in Political Economy*, Macmillan, London, 1874.

Carnoy M. and Rumberger R., "Segmentation in the U.S. Labor Market: Its Effect on the Mobility and Earnings of Whites and Blacks", *Cambridge Journal of Economics*, 4, 1980, pp. 117–32.

Dickens W.T. and Lang K., "A Test of Dual Labor Market Theory", *American Economic Review*, 75(4), 1985, pp. 792–805.

Dickens W.T. and Lang K., "The Reemergence of Segmented Labor Market Theory", *American Economic Review Papers and Proceedings*, 78(2), 1988, pp. 129–34.

Dickens W.T. and Lang K., *Labor Market Segmentation Theory: Reconsidering the Evidence*, National Bureau of Economic Research, Working Paper 4087, 1992.

Doeringer P. and Piore M., *International Labour Markets and Manpower Analysis*, DC Heath, Lexington, Mass., 1971.

Dunlop J.T., "The Task of Contemporary Wage Theory", in Taylor W. and Pierson F.C., editors, *New Concepts in Wage Discrimination*, McGraw-Hill, New York, 1957, pp. 117–39.

Edwards R., "The Social Relations of Production in the Firm and Labour Market Structure", in Edwards R., Reich M. and Gordon D., editors, *Labour Market Segmentation*, DC Heath, Lexington, Mass., 1975, pp. 3–26.

Edwards R., Reich M. and Gordon D., editors, *Labour Market Segmentation*, DC Heath, Lexington, Mass., 1975.

Flatau P.R. and Lewis P.E.T., "Segmented Labour Markets in Australia", *Applied Economics*, 25, 1993, pp. 285–94.

Harrison B., *Education Training and the Urban Ghetto*, Johns Hopkins University Press, Baltimore, 1972.

Holmstrom B., "Moral Hazard and Observability", *Bell Journal of Economics*, 9, 1979, pp. 74–91.

Holmstrom B., "Moral Hazard in Teams", *Bell Journal of Economics*, 13, 1982, pp. 324–40.

IADB, *Good Jobs Wanted: Labor Markets in Latin America*, Inter-American Development Bank, Washington, 2003.

Jhabvala R., Sudarshan R. and Unni J., editors, *Informal Economy Centrestage: New Structures of Employment*, Sage Publications, London, 2003.

Kerr C., "The Balkanisation of Labour Markets", in Bakke E.W., Hauser P.M., Palmer G.L., Myers C.A., Yoder D. and Kerr C., editors, *Labour Mobility and Economic Opportunity*, MIT Technology Press, Cambridge, Mass., 1954, pp. 92–110.

Lazear E., "Why is there Mandatory Retirement?", *Journal of Political Economy*, 87, 1979, pp. 1261–84.

Lazear E. and Oyer P., "Personnel Economics", in Gibbons R. and Roberts J., editors, *Handbook of Organizational Economics*, Princeton University Press, forthcoming 2012.

Lazear E. and Rosen S., "Rank-Order Tournaments as Optimum Labor Contracts", *Journal of Political Economy*, 89, 1981, pp. 841–64.

Leontaridi M.R., "Segmented Labour Markets: Theory and Evidence", *Journal of Economic Surveys*, 12(1), 1998, pp. 63–101.

McNabb R., "Testing for Labour Market Segmentation in Britain", *Manchester School*, 55(3), 1987, pp. 257–73.

McNabb R. and Psacharopoulos G., "Further Evidence on the Relevance of the Dual Labour Market Theory for the UK", *Journal of Human Resources*, 16(3), 1981, pp. 442–8.

Mayhew K. and Rosewell B., "Labour Market Segmentation in Britain", *Oxford Bulletin of Economics and Statistics*, 41, 1979, pp. 155–71.

Mill J.S., *Principles of Political Economy*, Longmans, Green and Company, London, 1909.

Neumann S. and Ziderman A., "Testing the Dual Labour Market Hypothesis: Evidence from the Israel Labour Mobility Survey", *Journal of Human Resources*, 21(2), 1986, pp. 230–7.

Okun A.M., *Prices and Quantities: A Macroeconomic Analysis*, Blackwell, London, 1981.

Osberg P., Apostle R. and Clairmont D., "Segmented Labour Markets and the Estimation of Wage Functions", *Applied Economics*, 19(12), 1987, pp. 1603–24.

Oster G., "A Factor Analysis Test of the Theory of the Dual Economy", *Review of Economics and Statistics*, 61(1), 1979, pp. 33–9.

Osterman P., "An Empirical Study of Labor Market Segmentation", *Industrial and Labor Relations Review*, 28(4), 1975, pp. 508–23.

Pigou A.C., *Lapses from Full Employment*, Macmillan, London, 1945.

Piore M.J., "Notes for a Theory of Labour Market Stratification", in Edwards R., Reich M. and Gordon D., editors, *Labour Market Segmentation*, DC Heath, Lexington, Mass., 1975.

Psacharopoulos G., "Labour Market Duality and Income Distribution: The Case of the UK", in Krelle W. and Shorrocks A.F., editors, *Personal Income Distribution*, North-Holland, Amsterdam, 1978.

Rosen S., "Authority, Control and the Distribution of Earnings", *Bell Journal of Economics*, 13, 1982, pp. 311–23.

Rosen S., "The Theory of Equalizing Differences", in Ashenfelter O. and Layard R., editors, *Handbook of Labor Economics*, North-Holland, New York, 1986, pp. 641–92.

Ryan P., "Segmentation, Duality and the Internal Labour Market", in Wilkinson F., editor, *The Dynamics of Labour Market Segmentation*, Academic Press, London, 1981, pp. 3–20.

Schiller B., "Relative Earnings Mobility in the United States", *American Economic Review*, 67, 1977, pp. 926–41.

Shapiro C. and Stiglitz J.E., "Equilibrium Unemployment as a Worker Discipline Device", *American Economic Review*, 74(3), 1984, pp. 433–44.

Shavell S., "Risk Sharing and Incentives in the Principal and Agent Relationship", *Bell Journal of Economics*, 10, 1979, pp. 55–73.

Sloane P.J., Murphy P.D., Theodossiou I. and White M., "Labour Market Segmentation: A Local Labour Market Analysis Using Alternative Approaches", *Applied Economics*, 25, 1993, pp. 569–81.

Taubman P. and Wachter M., "Segmented Labor Markets", in Ashenfelter O. and Layard R., editors, *Handbook of Labor Economics*, North-Holland, New York, 1986, pp. 1183–217.

Thomson E., "Segmented Labour Markets: A Critical Survey of Econometric Studies", in Reich M., editor, *Segmented Labor Markets and Labor Mobility*, Edward Elgar Publishing, Cheltenham, 2008, Vol. II, chapter 12.

Thurow L.C., *Poverty and Discrimination*, The Brookings Institute, Washington, 1970.

Waldman M., "Job Assignments, Signalling and Efficiency", *Rand Journal of Economics*, 15, 1984, pp. 255–67.

Waldman M., "Theory and Evidence in Internal Labour Markets", in Gibbons R. and Roberts J., editors, *Handbook of Organizational Economics*, Princeton University Press, forthcoming 2012.

Further reading

Taubman and Wachter (1986) provides a detailed and authoritative discussion of segmented labour markets and is a good starting point to deepen understanding of the material covered in this chapter. Similarly, Cain (1976) also provides an excellent overview of segmented labour market theory and gives an outline of the historical development of the literature. He also places the segmented view of labour markets into context with the neo-classical approach. Meanwhile, Leontaridi (1998) provides a comprehensive review of the empirical evaluation of the segmented labour market hypothesis and Thomson (2008) gives a good insight into the strengths and weaknesses of the various approaches that have been adopted in the empirical literature.

Chapter 10

Wage incentives

Learning outcomes

At the end of this chapter, readers should be aware that:

- There are numerous types of incentive that may be utilised, depending on the nature of the work environment;
- Incentives will not be effective under all circumstances;
- Performance will vary over the course of the working day;
- The principal–agent problem is linked to problems of asymmetric information, adverse selection and moral hazard;
- Whether to use time rates or piece rates depends partly on the size of monitoring costs;
- The success of rank order tournaments depends on the strength of incentives to finish first or earn promotion;
- Profit-sharing schemes and labour-managed firms are based on group rather than individual incentives.

Introduction

In this chapter, we focus on methods of wage payment. A major concern of management is to discover and apply methods of wage and salary payment that will help optimise output per man-hour and at the same time be accepted as equitable by employees. In the recent financial crisis in 2008, this issue became one of considerable policy concern. In the sub-prime market in the US and Europe, mortgage salesmen had been incentivised to sell mortgages, regardless of the ability of the recipients to repay their loans. In the case of banks, bonuses were paid to staff on the investment side regardless of the degree of risk, and senior staff came to expect bonuses regardless of the financial position of the bank in which they were employed and despite the fact that some banks only remained solvent through government injections of funds – a classic **moral hazard** problem.

There are numerous methods of pay in existence including **time rates**, **piece rates** (or payment per unit produced), **payment by results** (PBR), which is a broader concept and could include quality dimensions, group- or plant-wide incentives and profit-sharing. Economists have also focused on tournament theory in the context in particular of top salaries and deferred compensation. What determines the choice among these alternatives is a focus of this chapter, though it should be recognised that for some firms choice may be limited by arrangements for collective bargaining (as discussed earlier in Chapter 8). National bargaining, for example, may inhibit the development of incentive pay schemes limited to the firm's own peculiar circumstances and this may be one reason why some companies opt for plant- or company-level bargaining.

In this chapter, we first consider the implications that follow from the fact that it may be difficult to apply incentives in certain service activities and in the public sector. We also consider the possibility that performance may be influenced by the time of day when work is undertaken, suggesting that employers should be aware in particular of fatigue if work spells are too long. There follows a more extensive discussion of the **principal–agent problem**, already examined in Chapter 5. In particular, managing risk is an important aspect of the principal–agent problem. The decision on whether to pay workers a fixed wage per unit of time or on the basis of PBR can be seen as a particular aspect of the principal–agent problem. Likewise, promotion or deferred payments (as discussed elsewhere in the book) is an alternative to payment by results. This leads on naturally to the question of executive pay and the application of **tournament theory**. The chapter concludes with a consideration of the related concepts of **profit-sharing** and the **labour-managed firm**, elements of which may be combined with the types of incentives outlined above.

10.1 Sector differences

In certain sectors, the measurement of productivity is difficult. This is true of some services and much of the public sector, so that the use of incentives is more problematical. Much of government output is not marketable in the sense that it is supplied free. This is particularly the case with collective services, such as defence or public administration, and even in the case of services supplied to individuals, such as health or education, no charge may be made so that there is no market transaction. Because of these problems, wide use has been made of the convention that output equals inputs, so that changes in the number employed are taken as indicators of changes in output for purposes of national income accounting. In the UK, following the Atkinson Report of 2005, the Office of National Statistics has introduced measures of output for part of the public sector where it is possible to identify output, although difficulties in capturing quality changes remain. For example, if the output of schools is measured by the number of pupils taught, an increase in the number of teachers for a given number of pupils might be taken to indicate a reduction in productivity, but the very purpose of increasing the number of teachers may be to raise the quality of tuition. Thus, a more appropriate measure may be exam performance. This, however, needs to take into account the social background of the pupils.

Productivity growth is, in fact, a complex phenomenon. It could be the consequence of technological progress, increases in the stock of physical and human capital, better management of labour and other resources or economics of scale as output expands. While, for purposes of measurement, it might be appropriate to sub-divide the economy into sectors, it is not appropriate to assume that sectors are independent of one another. Manufacturers depend on transport; government-provided services are dependent on taxation to which all sectors contribute and so on. That measured productivity advances more in some sectors than others is not necessarily an indication that they have in some sense performed "better", since the causes of productivity growth impact unevenly on the different sectors. Taking such a view of economic progress suggests that workers who happen to be in a sector of rapid growth of measured productivity may have no greater claim than others to growth in their real wages. This is not just a matter of equity. Efficiency demands that there should be a going rate of wages across all sectors, so that marginal products are equalised. Assume there are two sectors – a progressive sector A and a slow-growth sector B (Figure 10.1). We measure employment left to right for A and right to left for B. Now let technical progress raise productivity as reflected in the marginal productivity curves in A from MP_A to MP'_A, so that equilibrium shifts from E to E'. This requires that some labour shifts from B to A and we end up with wages higher in both sectors at W'. Thus, employees in sector B gain from productivity growth in sector A.

Now assume instead that pay is linked to sectoral performance (Figure 10.2), so that wages rise in A to reflect the productivity gain there, but are unchanged in B.

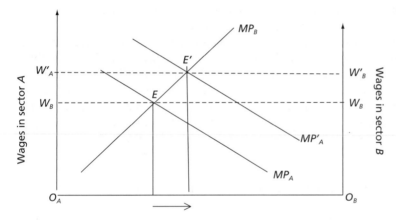

Figure 10.1 Progressive versus slow growth sectors.

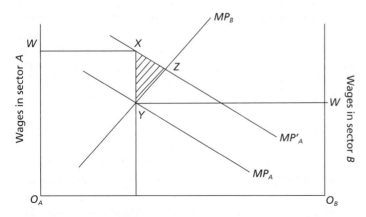

Figure 10.2 Distortionary output loss.

As increased wages have absorbed the productivity gain in A, there is no incentive for the employer in A to attract workers from B. As the marginal products are now different in the two sectors, there will be a distortionary output loss equal to the shaded area XYZ, as a movement from X to Y would produce more output along MP_A and the movement from Y to Z would produce more output along MP_B. This is not an optimal solution. A going rate of wages is necessary to promote both efficiency and equity, and this requires a movement of labour from low- to high-productivity sectors. This also supports the view that public- and private-sector pay should be kept broadly in line, emphasising the notion of sector inter-dependence.

Suppose sector B is the public sector, this still leaves the problem of how to encourage workers in that sector to work to their maximum capabilities. As Dixit (2002) observes, a special feature of public-sector bodies is the multiplicity of tasks, stakeholders and interests that makes the use of traditional incentives inappropriate. Even if some activities can be identified where incentives can be applied, this has dangers as individuals may focus on such activities to the detriment of others (see, for example, Fehr and Schmidt 2004). This may well attract workers into public bodies who are most averse to exerting effort, even if some employees are dedicated public servants. Delfgaauw and Dur (2008), for example, report surveys in the Netherlands and the US, which are consistent with those most averse to exerting effort moving into the public sector and those least averse moving into the private sector where they can gain more from incentive payments.

There are also issues relating to pay within the public sector with the suggestion that there should be spatial pay differences to reflect differences in the cost of living and local amenities (see Elliott et al. 2007). However, an alternative view is that one may want to relocate public-sector workers to relatively depressed regions where costs of providing services are lower and that national pay scales may help to persuade workers to move in the knowledge that real rates of pay will be higher in depressed regions and tend to offset any perceived loss of amenities.

10.2 The supply of effort – time of day effects

Law of diminishing marginal utility

As extra units of a commodity are consumed by an individual, the satisfaction gained from each unit declines.

Daily work curves

These measure fluctuations in output over the course of the working day and capture the effects of settling in and fatigue.

The supply of effort may vary either because of settling-in or fatigue effects (involuntary effort) or because workers choose to limit their output (voluntary effort). Focusing initially on the first of these, the classic theory was developed by Jevons in 1871, based on the notion that the individual optimising employee would choose wherever possible that level of hours that yielded him the greatest level of satisfaction. Resting the argument on two major propositions – the **law of diminishing marginal utility** and the increasing tediousness of work – Jevons demonstrated that in equilibrium the employee would work up to the point at which the marginal disutility of work equalled the marginal utility of wage income. The marginal disutility curve is drawn on the assumption that the early hours of work involve negative amounts of satisfaction consequent upon the upheaval of getting to work and settling into a rhythm, while the later hours involve an increasing extent of fatigue. Given the shape of the two curves in Figure 10.3 there will result an optimum length of work-week for an employee at A where marginal utility (AB) equals marginal disutility (AC).[1]

Daily work curves do seem to support the notion that significant changes take place during the course of the day in various indicators of performance such as

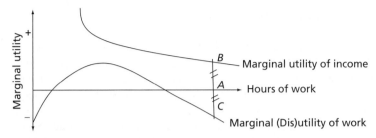

Figure 10.3 The law of diminishing utility of work.

output, spoiled work and accidents. All these variables show a deterioration towards the end of a continuous work spell which is symptomatic of fatigue.[2] Indeed, it may be that a substantial amount of **X-inefficiency**[3] is explicable in these terms and results from a sub-optimal arrangement of working hours.

Building on the above observations, Barzel (1973) constructed a value of the daily product (VDP) curve, which takes the shape given in Figure 10.4. An equilibrium position is derived at the point of tangency between the VDP curve and the individual employee's indifference curve (*U*). *OC* hours will enable the individual to reach the highest possible indifference curve consistent with his or her productive capacity, the non-linear VDP curve being the counterpart of the budget constraint in the conventional analysis. Since a long-run perfectly competitive equilibrium position is assumed to exist, the employee will receive the full value of his or her daily production (*BC*) such that the employer earns normal profits.[4]

One implication that Barzel draws from his analysis is that, as long as tastes differ, profit maximisation will ensure that there is non-uniformity of hours across industry. This would seem to depend crucially, however, on precisely how tastes differ and upon the distribution of those with differing tastes among firms and industries, as well as upon hourly output varying to a significant extent with the number of hours worked. Another implication is that the observed hourly wage should differ among those working different hours. For example, the implicit higher average hourly productivity for at least some part-time workers should lead to a higher hourly wage for this group, but this may be offset if there is a strong preference among a substantial number of workers for part-time over full-time work.

X-inefficiency

This describes a situation in which management fails to minimise the costs of production and/or maximise output from a given set of inputs due to the absence of competitive pressures.

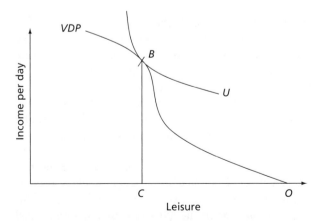

Figure 10.4 Value of the daily product curve.

10.3 The principal–agent problem

While the literature on the involuntary supply of effort has been sparse, that on the voluntary supply or its withholding has recently become abundant. A seminal paper by Alchian and Demsetz (1972) emphasised that one method of reducing shirking was for someone to specialise as a monitor to check the input performance of team working and act as a residual claimant with respect to profits, and this approach to the explanation of firm formation has been broadened out to incorporate related aspects of principal–agent analysis, efficiency wages and implicit contracts.

The initial contribution to the principal–agent problem, already introduced in Chapter 5, was made by Spence and Zeckhauser (1971). The basic idea is that the principal (e.g. the employer) delegates to the agent (e.g. the employee) a degree of responsibility for the selection and implementation of an action in a situation of **asymmetric information**. That is, the principal is assumed to possess less information than the agent concerning the latter's fulfilment of tasks delegated by the former. Thus, the agent has scope for the pursuit of his or her own interests undetected by the principal. Alchian and Demsetz emphasised that, while the outcome of the performance of an individual working on his or her own could be detected, where teamwork was crucial it would not be possible to isolate the contribution of an individual team member.[5] This would give rise to problems of moral hazard ex post – or the possibility that, in the absence of possibilities of effective monitoring or under uncertainty, the agents would pursue their own interests that were not consistent with the main objectives of the principal. For example, suppose an employer insures against being sued for negligence in the case of industrial accidents, but insurance is not experience rated in the sense that premiums are based on the accident rate for the whole industry rather than the accident rate in the firm concerned. Then there is little direct incentive to spend money on safety devices. This is essentially an ex ante **adverse selection** problem in which the agent is privy to information that he or she may refuse to share with the principal. For example, the agent may have detailed information on how a task can be performed most efficiently and realise that higher productivity is attainable with increased effort, but he or she has a strong incentive to suppress this information and economise on effort. This will be particularly so where more detailed knowledge for the principal is likely to raise the standards set for performing particular tasks and can thus explain the phenomenon of worker restriction of output.

It has been suggested, in line with the above (Ricketts 1987), that the monitor performs two conceptually distinct roles. First, it is necessary to overcome the problem of moral hazard and, to achieve this, some form of incentive such as piece-rate payment is required. Second, it is necessary to overcome the problem of adverse selection where labour is heterogeneous with respect to abilities.[6] This may be achieved by various screening devices or by monitoring performance through close supervision. In fact, the problem of motivating the worker may be tackled by a range of options, including direct supervision, incentive payments, promotion (or what is referred to in the literature as rank order tournaments) and deferred contingent payment, and it is necessary to examine under which circumstances each is likely to be used. First, however, it should be noted that it will rarely if ever be optimal to eliminate all X-inefficiency. A profit-maximising firm will devote sufficient resources to **monitoring** to ensure that the marginal costs of monitoring equal the marginal returns to monitoring effort. Second, we must consider attitudes

Asymmetric information models

In these models, it is assumed that some individuals or groups possess information that is not available to others.

Adverse selection

Examples are where those most at risk are more likely to purchase insurance or where those who are less productive choose to join a group incentive scheme.

Monitoring

Any mechanism for checking up on the performance of workers, usually involving the hiring of supervisors.

towards risks. If we assume that firms are risk neutral, but workers risk averse, a system of payment by results would introduce unwanted variability into workers' earnings. Under these circumstances, employers may effectively offer insurance to workers so that the effects of economic fluctuations are limited. Thus, many authors such as Baily (1974) have argued that there exists an **implicit contract** between employer and employee to insure the workforce against such fluctuations, and such implicit contracts can explain the relative rigidity of wage rates over the business cycle.[7] Taking the argument a stage further, Putterman and Skillman (1988) show that the incentive effect of increased monitoring depends critically on the type of incentive system, the risk preferences of the monitored workers and the information content of increased monitoring. Monitoring may only provide a noisy signal of effort (E) Assume that Θ represents monitoring effort and E is a random variable with distribution $F(E, \Theta)$. There are two possibilities as outlined in Figures 10.5(a) and 10.5(b). First, monitoring may have a first-order effect if it shifts the distribution of E to the right as in Figure 10.5(a). Second, monitoring may have second-order effects if it reduces the dispersion of $F(E, \Theta)$ as in Figure 10.5(b). In Figure 10.5(a), the whole of the distribution shifts to the right, so that monitoring increases equally the performance of all workers, though it is possible that there are differential effects depending on the relative performance of workers. Thus, in Figure 10.5(b), monitoring reduces the proportion of very low and very high performers, perhaps because it leads to a greater standardisation of what is expected.

It appears that workers may respond positively to increased monitoring, provided that their relative risk aversion is not too great and their absolute risk aversion does not decline too rapidly with income. This analysis casts doubt on the Alchian and Demsetz hypothesis that greater monitoring and the linking of payment to effort will increase both effort and the utility of the workforce under teamwork. (See also Gibbons 1987.) Further, Alchian and Demsetz suggest that the relationship between observability and profitability should be positive, but Bulow and Summers (1986) and Esfahani and Salehi-Isfahani (1989) derive conditions under which an economy is split into a formal sector where productivity is high and observability low and an informal sector in which productivity is low and observability high. The result for the formal sector arises because of the larger size of establishments, the complexity of tasks and the structured management hierarchy in this sector. Finally, Drago and Perlman (1989) argue that supervision may undermine trust, and that a degree of autonomy can, under certain circumstances, promote effort. Clearly, these are empirical issues that need further investigation.

Implicit contracts

A response to the fact that most workers are risk averse and often involving the minimisation of the variability of earnings and employment.

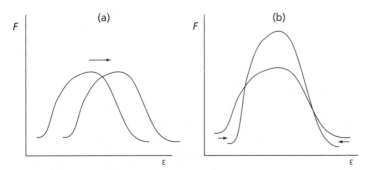

Figure 10.5 The effect of monitoring.

10.4 Time rates versus piece rates

A fundamental choice for the employer then is whether to reward workers according to their inputs (e.g. time payments) or outputs (e.g. piece-work). Pencavel (1977) interprets piece-work as "an on-the-job screening device to economise on supervisory personnel in situations in which the work performance of each employee is costly to detect and hence where the employee has occasion to shirk". Assuming employers are risk neutral and employees risk averse, Stiglitz (1975) derives the result that piece rates will be used more intensively where the risk is smaller, the degree of risk aversion lower and the supply elasticity of effort greater. As Bishop (1987) notes, there are three potential benefits for the employer or monitor of adjusting pay to reflect productivity. First, under certain circumstances, it can serve as an incentive to greater effort. Second, it can tend to attract to the firm the more able and productive individuals. Third, it may reduce the probability of losing the best employees to other firms and increase the probability that the least productive will leave. Sorting will in part be determined by whether information is symmetric or asymmetric (Lazear 1986). In the former case, let us assume that employers and employees are equally ignorant of potential output q, but both are equally aware of its distribution, then, under piece-work, payment w is given by

$$w = Rq - m \tag{10.1}$$

where
R = piece-rate share accruing to the worker
m = per worker monitoring costs

In such circumstances, the benefits of a piece rate will be greater, the greater the heterogeneity of the workforce in terms of productivity, since the potentially most productive workers will be encouraged to produce more.

In the asymmetric information version, it is assumed that employees are more fully informed about their output potential than are their employers. With positive monitoring costs, m, some workers with low output potential will always choose employment at a fixed time rate, since they can only earn $q - m$ at a piece-rate firm, whereas in a time-rate firm the wage will be determined by the performance of the average worker. An obvious implication is that time-rate firms will have a lower-quality labour force than piece-rate firms. In capital-intensive firms, it will be particularly important to ensure that only high-quality labour is recruited. Ignoring monitoring costs, this requires that a two-part piece-rate system rather than $w = Rq$ is employed, i.e.

$$w = a + bq \tag{10.2}$$

so that, if output falls below a certain standard, the employee's contract can be terminated. Thus, in Figure 10.6, suppose $W1$ represents the wage. Then, with the schedule given by $W(q) = q - r$, if a worker produces less than $q1$, he or she should be dismissed. Assume a technology in which each worker uses a machine to produce output at a rental cost r, so that the net output of a worker with ability q is $q - r$. Then efficiency requires that only workers whose net output $q - r$ exceeds the reservation wage w are employed (Figure 10.6).

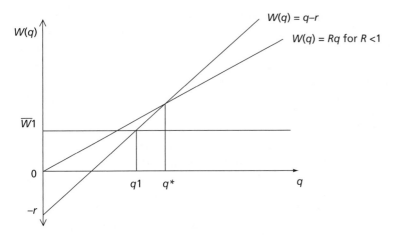

Figure 10.6 A piece rate with a fixed component.

If $R < 1$, the more productive workers with q greater than q^* will always prefer employment in a firm that pays $W(q) = q - r$ and only workers with $q < q^*$ will choose employment in a firm that pays Rq with $R < 1$. A piece rate with a fixed component, a, is only partially related to performance. Thus, as capital intensity increases and r rises, payment by input will rise relative to payment by output.

There are also disadvantages attached to piece rates, which may reduce their incidence. Even when work study is used, there may be errors in setting times for particular tasks. This will be particularly problematical where there are frequent changes to the productive process. Output may also be influenced by factors which are outside the workers' control and this may give rise to disputes. It is sometimes alleged that quality will suffer when piece rates are employed. Thus, Baker (1992) cites the case of R&D scientists. The firm cannot observe effort, and the true value of what a scientist produces is not known and cannot be contracted on. Suppose the firm introduces a scheme based on the number of patents awarded, taking into account the average effort required to produce a patent. Then scientists will use their superior knowledge to work too hard on easy inventions and too little on difficult ones. However, it is possible to take such factors into account when payment is based on sales revenue rather than output. Supervision will differ in the two cases. Under time rates (and also under measured day work), it is the pace of work which is under supervisory attention, while, under piece rates, it is the quality of work and care of machinery which is critical.

There are considerable variations in the incidence of piece rates across industries, work groups and nations. Differences between the US and UK are considerable. For the US, Pencavel (1977) reports that the percentage of production workers in manufacturing subject to incentive pay fell from 27 per cent in 1958 to less than 18 per cent by the late 1970s. Bishop (1987), drawing from US Bureau of Labor Statistics area wage surveys conducted in 1958 and 1970, reports that in only 14 per cent of establishments were plant workers subject to individual or group incentives and in no cases were office workers so covered. For Britain, McCormick (1977) reports that the percentage of male workers subject to payment by results in all industries rose from 18 per cent in 1938 to 41 per cent in 1974 and, though this increase was not matched for women (for whom the relevant figures were 46 per cent and 34 per cent respectively), he finds this result surprising in view of numerous criticisms made of

PBR and forecasts by some of death by technological execution as increased mechanisation reduces the link between individual worker effort and output. Elliott and Murphy (1986) report results from the 1980 Workplace Industrial Relations Survey, which indicate that for all industries and services in only 28.7 per cent of establishments are manual workers paid by results and in only 13.7 per cent is this the case for non-manual workers. Using the 1990 WERS, Heywood *et al.* (1997) report that 21.8 per cent of manual workers are employed on individual payment by results, while the figure for any group of workers is 31.8 per cent. These figures are not directly comparable to those reported above. Such international differences in the prevalence of payment by results are worthy of further investigation.

There have been a number of empirical investigations designed to explain the incidence of incentive pay. Several early US studies confirm that there is a negative relationship between capital intensity and incentive pay and a positive one between the latter variable and establishment size. For Britain, Elliott and Murphy (1986) find that the probability of an establishment using payment by results is significantly associated positively to size of establishment, whether UK owned (manufacturing only), the proportion of females employed and union density, and negatively with public sector, shift-working and proportion part-time. Heywood *et al.* (1997), using a later British Workplace Employment Relations Survey (WERS), find also that the age of the workforce exerts a strong influence on the probability of payment by results as does the proportion of short-tenure workers, who are less likely to be motivated by deferred payment. The elasticity of payment by results with respect to establishment size is large, –0.27 in non-union establishments. Unions are found – in contrast to the earlier findings of Elliott and Murphy – to be averse to PBR, perhaps because time rates promote solidarity, important for union cohesiveness. PBR also yields large savings on supervision costs, by enabling the ratio of supervisors to employees to be reduced. PBR also seems easier to introduce where there is a more favourable industrial-relations climate. A number of studies have attempted to investigate the relationship between productivity and earnings. Thus, in the above study, both productivity and financial performance were found to be related positively to the presence of PBR. Earlier US studies have also found positive effects on performance, Pencavel (1977) finds, using a sample of 183 male punch-press operators in 12 establishments in Chicago and 120 female operative in 8 establishments, *ceteris paribus*, that those on incentive pay earn 7 per cent more than those on time rates, confirming that it is possible to raise performance by such means.[8] Similarly, Singh and Gerber (1989), using data on 237 sewing-machine operatives in an apparel assembly plant in Mexico, find that workers behave rationally in adjusting their production in line with monetary incentives. In this case, production bonuses were geared to the attainment of output levels set at thresholds of 70, 80 and 90 per cent of the standard. Rational behaviour suggests workers will achieve production levels just above and not below these standards and this is what the investigators find. Bishop (1987) examines longitudinal data on wage rates/turnover and reported productivity of new hires for the same job in 659 different firms, using a 1982 US National Center for Research in Vocational Education Employer Survey. He finds that actual productivity has little effect on the starting wage rates after a year or so at the firm, with an elasticity of wage rates with respect to productivity of 0.19. Further, smaller and non-union establishments are found to be more likely to base wage increases on a worker's productivity. This is taken to imply that productivity is more difficult to measure in large establishments, while unions reduce the ability of management to adjust pay in this way. See also case studies 10.1 and 10.2 of individual companies in the US.

More recently, an experimental approach has been adopted to test the effect of incentives on performance. This approach is particularly useful where there is reason to believe that there may be an endogeneity problem insofar as the incentive system represents a choice made by the firm and such a choice could be influenced by unobservable factors that also influence worker productivity. One example of such an approach is Shearer (2004) who examines tree planting in a British Columbian firm. Normally, these workers are paid according to the number of trees planted per day, but they may be paid time rates where ground conditions are difficult. This enables Shearer to compare the performance of the same workers, holding such conditions constant, under each form of pay. He finds that productivity is 20 per cent higher when workers are paid under piece rates. In another experimental study in a German university (Pokorny 2008), subjects were given IQ and counting tests under varying incentives. In this case, low incentives improved performance, but higher incentives did not. It is suggested that this unexpected result occurred because agents are guided by a certain reference income, which they regard as equitable. While incentives lead to increased performance as long as income is below reference income, beyond this point agents fail to increase their efforts further. Thus, incentives need to be considered according to the environment in which they take place. Examples of individual schemes are provided in Case Studies 10.1 and 10.2.

Case Study 10.1

The incentive effects of piece rates

The Safelite Glass Corporation is the largest installer of automobile glass (windscreens) in the US. In the mid-1990s, the new management decided to introduce a piece-rate scheme (in place of time rates) under which installers were paid for the number of screens they installed, so that output could easily be measured as units-per-worker per day. As the change to piece rates was gradual, it was possible to compare the performance of workers under the old and the new systems.

Lazear (2000) examined data on 3,000 workers in the company over a 19-month period. The company offered a guarantee at approximately the former wage. Thus, it is not obvious that this piece-rate system will improve performance, as the minimum acceptable level of output could exceed the level chosen under the piece-rate scheme. The actual scheme took the form illustrated in Figure 1. Workers receive a wage equal to W for output (p) between p_0 and p^*. Beyond p^*, additional output leads to higher earnings. As long as a worker produces $p > p^*$, his or her compensation is given by the schedule $bp - L$, while workers who continually produce below the acceptable level of output (i.e. $p < p^*$) are eventually likely to have their employment terminated.

Low-ability workers have steep indifference curves because additional effort must be compensated by large increases in income. This is illustrated by the solid indifference curve IC_1 through A. The dotted indifference curve IC_2 through A reflects the preferences of a higher-ability worker, since it takes less income to induce an extra unit of effort. An even more able worker will choose B on indifference curve IC_3. There will also be a selection effect as some low-performance workers may leave as a consequence of the new scheme and some high-performance individuals will choose to be employed in the company.

Lazear shows that the introduction of the new scheme had four distinct effects:

1   The switch to piece rates led to a 44 per cent increase in output-per-worker.
2   Half of the gain resulted from the average worker producing more because of the incentive effect and the other half from the hiring of more-able workers and a reduction in the quit rate among high-output workers.
3   Both the company and the employees gained from the change. A given worker received a 10 per cent increase in pay as a result of improved performance and the company retained about half the value of the productivity improvement. Quality measured in terms of broken wind-screens actually improved as the installer responsible was required to replace the windscreen in his own time and pay the company for the replacement glass.
4   The variance in output went up as more-ambitious workers produced more.

Thus, it seems that workers do respond to incentives in line with economists' predictions.

E.P. Lazear, "Performance Pay and Productivity, *American Economic Review*, 90(5), 2000, 1346–61.

Case Study 10.2

The introduction of a firm-wide incentive in a large airline

It has long been held that firm-wide incentives, especially in large firms, are unlikely to be successful because of free riding, since employees are often unable to observe one another's efforts and are at the same time less willing to incur the costs of monitoring and imposing sanctions on their colleagues.

In the early 1990s, Continental Airlines (CA) performed badly and was facing serious financial problems. Its relative performance in arrival of planes on time was the worst among 10 major airlines in the US. In 1995, following the arrival of new senior management, CA introduced a firm-wide incentive scheme providing monthly bonuses of $65 to all 35,000 employees if CA's on-time record ranked among the top five in the industry, later modified to the top three, with a $100 bonus for a top-rated performance. The scheme proved to be successful with rankings in the top half of the ratings in 9 out of 11 months (the exceptions being affected by a pilots' strike). Regression analysis showed that over time the improvement was significantly greater in non-outsourced relative to outsourced airports (where employees were not subject to the scheme). The success of the scheme led to lower labour turnover and absence, so that the scheme was self-funding.

The authors attribute the surprising success of such a scheme to a number of factors. First, on-time arrival can be accurately measured and easily compared to that of competitors; it is directly affected by the actions of aircrew and airport employees; failure can lead to other problems such as delayed baggage and dissatisfied customers. Second, though the company's employees are dispersed among different terminals and airport locations, the organisation of workers into autonomous work groups can overcome such problems. Thus, ramp and gate employees work alongside one another in activities such as pushing out or waving in aircraft, loading and unloading baggage and greeting and boarding passengers. Poor performance by one employee can negate good performance by the rest of the group and result in mutual monitoring such that poor performers can be ostracised or reported to management.

It appears that, given appropriate settings, firm-wide incentives are not doomed to failure, even in large enterprises.

M. Knez and D. Simister, "Firm-wide Incentives and Mutual Monitoring at Continental Airlines", *Journal of Labor Economics*, 19(4), 2001, 743–72.

10.5 Promotion, deferred payments and tournament theory

Alternatives to payment by results are promotion and deferred payments. Malcomson (1984) contends that contracts can still be made enforceable in the presence of asymmetric information, provided that it is specified that a certain proportion of workers will be paid more than the rest (i.e. be promoted). He notes certain stylised facts of employment that are consistent with this proposition. Thus, organisational pay structures tend to be hierarchical, with a tendency for the number of employees to reduce with the level of pay. A high proportion of those in higher-paid jobs have been promoted from lower-paid jobs within the same organisation (one aspect of the **internal labour market**). Wages rise more in line with seniority and experience than with productivity. The variance of earnings rises with experience. Finally, wage rates attach to jobs rather than to the workers who fill them.

Tournament theory, taken literally, implies that Chief Executive Officer (CEO) salaries are predetermined. They do not depend on the ability of the incumbent. Most of the promotion activity in a typical firm is internal, being restricted to incumbents at the level below that of the job which is vacant. A worker is promoted not simply because he or she is good, but because he or she is better than anyone else at his or her current level. It is relative rather than absolute performance that matters. The level of effort that an individual puts in to achieve promotion is held to be dependent on the size of the potential increase in salary that a promotion entails, that is the spread between the top and next highest salary. The key point of tournament theory is that the larger the spread, the greater the incentive to be promoted. This implies that the salary of the CEO acts not so much as a motivation for the CEO him- or herself, but as a motivation for those aspiring to the post. A final point is that there is a limit to the size of the spread that is warranted, because the optimal amount of effort is limited by the fact that at some point the output produced by the extra effort will not be covered by the additional salary required to induce such effort. (See also Drago and Heywood 1989.)

Murphy (1999) notes that CEO median cash compensation nearly doubled in real terms between 1970 and 1996 in the US and median total realised compensation nearly quadrupled. The bull market of the 1990s created windfalls for CEOs, whose pay was increasingly tied to company stock price performance. Yet he laments, "in spite of the exploding inter-disciplinary literature, executive compensation has received relatively scant attention from labour economists". One

Internal labour market

A market in which promotion from within is the norm and wages rise in line with seniority and experience rather than with productivity.

exception is a study by Main *et al.* (1993), who examine a sample of 200 US corporations over the period 1980–4. They recognise that, in situations where there is high team inter-dependence, wide variations in executive team salaries are more likely to result in disruptive inter-agent rivalry than where work is structured in such a way that such inter-dependence is avoided. Nonetheless, they find that greater variance in top-level compensation is associated with greater team performance, so that overall the evidence for the operation of tournaments is positive. In a study of the pay of 2,600 executives in 210 Danish firms, Eriksson (1999) also finds that most of the predictions of tournament theory find support in the data with wider pay dispersion enhancing firm performance. The ratio of pay increases as one moves up the corporate ladder, because the value of winning is not only the winner's prize at a particular level, but also the value of being able to compete for larger prizes at higher levels in the organisation. As a consequence, there is a convex relationship between pay and organisation level. There have also been a number of studies of professional sports such as golf where the gap in prize money between the winner and the runner-up tends to be wider in major tournaments. This is seen to result in improved performance (i.e. lower mean scores – see Ehrenberg and Bognanno 1990(a), 1990(b)). One might expect golfers to exert maximum effort in all tournaments, but, in fact, some golfers achieve better average scores on the same course when the difference between the winner's prize and the prize for coming second is greater. A case in which perverse incentives can actually lead to a reduction in performance is found in the case of professional basketball (see Case Study 10.3).

Case Study 10.3

Tournament (dis)incentives in professional basketball

In the US sports majors (American Rules football, baseball, basketball and ice hockey), a player draft system operates under which teams bid for the services of the most promising young players in the college system in reverse order of their finish in the previous season's league competition. Taylor and Trogdon (2002) examine three National Basketball Association (NBA) seasons in which the draft rules were changed to determine whether team performance responds to changes in the rules for determining draft choices. In the 1983/4 season, draft order was determined strictly by inverse rank, so providing an incentive to lose once teams had failed to qualify for the play-offs. In the 1984/5 season, non-play-off teams were given equal probabilities of obtaining the top draft choices, thus removing any incentive to lose. In 1989/90, the draft rules changed again to give teams with worse regular season records a greater probability of obtaining higher draft choices, thus restoring the incentive to lose. They find that, controlling for venue and team quality, non-play-off teams were approximately 2.5 times more likely to lose than play-off teams in 1983/4. In 1984/5, this difference disappeared and in 1984/5 reappeared (2.2 times more likely). These results suggest that NBA teams respond to tournament incentives in a predictable, but potentially undesirable way.

B.A. Taylor and J.G. Trogdon, "Losing to Win! Tournament Incentives in the National Basketball Association", *Journal of Labor Economics*, 20(1), 2002, 23–41.

As we saw in Chapter 1 in relation to retirement, it may be optimal to construct age–earnings profiles that pay workers less than their MVP when young and more than their MVP when older. As Lazear (1981) notes, this means that wages will increase with experience even if productivity does not; that it may be necessary to impose hours restrictions to avoid workers offering too few hours early in their working lives and too many thereafter; that it may be optimal to engage some workers on temporary contracts; and that the self-employed and piece-rate workers will have flatter and more variable wage rates over the working lifetime than will time-rate workers. Using 1978 Current Population Survey data, Lazear and Moore (1984) find that self-employed workers do, in fact, have flatter age-earnings profiles than wage and salary earners, though it should be pointed out that the equations for the self-employed are not well determined. Arguing that the extent to which firms are able to monitor effort will be in part determined by the technology of production. Hutchens (1987), using data from the National Longitudinal Survey and the Dictionary of Occupational Titles, tested whether jobs that involved repetitive tasks tended to have fewer pensions, less mandatory retirements, shorter job tenure and lower wages for older workers. This is, indeed, found to be the case in line with Lazear's theory, though, as Hutchens acknowledges, this is also consistent with other theories such as dual labour market theory. These studies have also been challenged by Abraham and Farber (1987), who suggest that an alternative interpretation of the cross-section relationship between earnings and seniority is not that implicit contracts apply, but that more productive workers, with better jobs and closer worker–employer matches, tend to stay longer on the job. In other words, there may be a problem of omitted variable bias in earlier work. By controlling explicitly for completed job duration, they correct for this bias using the Panel Study of Income Dynamics. Contrary to conventional wisdom and their own prior expectations, the average return to seniority in excess of the average return to labour market experience is small (0.5 per cent per annum for the white-collar staff and 0.25 per cent per annum for blue-collar staff). They allow that for some groups implicit contracts may be important, and, given their finding that workers can move throughout their careers on longer-duration jobs, acknowledge that the results are consistent with efficiency wage models. Arvan (1989) has suggested a rationale for the Abraham and Farber results. If firms are able to pre-commit the payment of rent for only a short period, then it is more likely that rent will be more evenly distributed over the duration of employment and with it the level of monitoring. The rational worker will discount future income and this provides the firm with the incentive to provide some rent during the current contractual horizon. Indeed, the fundamental question is: why do contracts have fixed expiry dates? Cantor (1989) suggests that the reason is that a known date of expiry, by exposing the worker to the disciplines of the market, can induce additional effort and, as contract duration increases, the incentive to increase effort is diminished. Hence, actual contract length must trade off the marginal benefits of reduced shirking against the marginal costs of re-contracting.

Clearly, the relative weighting given to close supervision, incentive payments, promotional opportunities and deferred payment is one of the most important decisions facing any organisation. It is partly dependent on the characteristics of the worker, but also partly on the nature of the unit of employment. In an extensive survey, Prendergast (1999) concludes that it does appear that agents respond to incentives. The evidence suggests, however, that **free riding** is likely to occur

Free riding

The tendency to shirk or take it easy when success is dependent on the performance of a team rather than an individual.

323

where incentives are based on teams. Agents are also capable of acting in ways that are beneficial to them, but at a cost to overall efficiency. Contracts can have significant selection effects.

10.6 Profit-sharing

According to the 2004 British Workplace Employment Relations Survey (WERS), 30 per cent of workplaces have profit-related pay, but this rises to 36 per cent when attention is limited to the trading sector. In an influential book, *The Share Economy: Conquering Stagflation*, Martin Weitzman (1984) argues that profit-sharing may improve the functioning of the labour market in three ways:

- by encouraging employees to increase effort;
- by reducing labour costs in the recession as profits decline, thereby reducing unemployment;
- through encouraging full employment by driving a wedge between the marginal and average costs of labour, so that a profit-sharing economy will always display an excess demand for labour.

In a profit-sharing economy, each firm i will pay its workforce according to the schedule

$$W(L_i) = \alpha + \lambda \left[\frac{R_i(L_i) - \alpha L_i}{L_i} \right]$$ (10.3)

That is, the total payment to labour consists of a fixed amount and a share of the average profits earned by the firm. This implies that it is not possible to identify the precise contribution of each worker.

In equation 10.3, $R_i(L_i)$ equals total revenue as a function of labour; α equals the base wage; $\lambda > 0$ represents the profit-sharing coefficient and α and λ are fixed exogenously.

Net profits are given by

$$\Pi L_i \equiv (1 - \lambda)[R_i(Li) - \alpha L_i]$$ (10.4)

and, if labour is in unlimited supply, the firm will continue to hire workers up to the point where

$$\frac{dR_i}{dL_i} = \alpha$$ (10.5)

In the wage economy, $W > \alpha$, so the implied level of employment would be lower than in the profit-sharing economy. In Figure 10.7, with a conventional downward-sloping demand curve for labour, MP_L, employment in the profit-sharing firm is at $ON2$ and in the non-profit-sharing firm at $ON1$. This is because average wage cost, AWC, is defined by the wage W and marginal wage cost MWC by α.

It should be noted, however, that Weitzman's claims for the attractiveness of the share economy rest on this notion of an equilibrium in which there is continual excess demand for labour. Competition among firms to hire limited quantities of

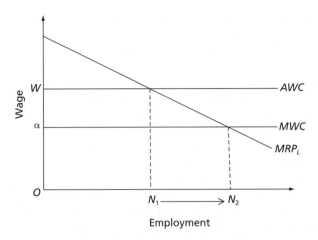

Figure 10.7 Profit-sharing and employment.

labour might gradually force up the wage level, so that the familiar wage system reappears. Workers will also be exposed to significant income risk and risk-averse workers might prefer a diversified portfolio. Existing employees may also oppose the hiring of additional workers as any expansion of the workforce will drive down that part of their own remuneration, which is represented by their profit share.

There have been a number of attempts to test whether profit-sharing has some of the positive effects claimed for it by Weitzman (though not for employment). Blanchflower and Oswald (1988) test whether the presence of profit-sharing improves reported financial performance and increases employment growth, but find no evidence of any relationship for the UK in either case. In contrast, Cable and Wilson (1990) find for 52 engineering companies that profit-sharing is associated with between 3 and 8 per cent higher productivity, higher basic earnings and substantially higher rates of return on capital. Wadhwani and Wall (1990) studied 101 British firms over the period 1972–82 and find a small, but barely significant effect on employment. Further, profit-sharing bonuses seem to be add-on payments, conflicting with Weitzman's key assumption and implying that profit-sharing could be inflationary. Finally, McNabb and Whitfield (1998) show that the presence of financial participation schemes at the workplace and the use of schemes enhancing downward personal communication between management and employees are both strongly and positively associated with financial performance. They also find evidence of strong interaction effects, which suggest that financial participation should not be analysed independently of other types of employee-participation scheme. The effectiveness of such schemes may depend critically on the way in which they are implemented.

10.7 The labour-managed firm

An extreme version of profit-sharing is the labour-managed firm in which it is the employees who make the key decisions. The seminal paper is by Ward (1958), but the most developed theoretical approach is contained in Vanek (1970), which draws from the Yugoslavian experience following the Second World War. Related examples in the UK are producer co-operatives in the footwear industry, the John Lewis

Partnership in retail distribution and partnerships among professionals such as doctors, lawyers and accountants. The theory represents another example of the way in which predictions about firm behaviour depend upon the assumptions made about firm objectives.

Maximisation of
income per
worker

The assumed
maximand in the
case of the labour-
managed firm,
which replaces the
assumption of
profit maximisation
in the case of the
entrepreneurial
firm.

The **maximisation of income per worker** is the objective function in the labour-managed firm rather than profit maximisation. Suppose net income could be increased by 10 per cent if the workforce were doubled. This would be opposed by existing employees as the effect would reduce income per worker by some 45 per cent. Therefore, the labour-managed firm will increase employment whenever the net contribution to total income by the last person employed exceeds income per head currently earned and decrease employment in the opposite case. Abstracting from differences in incentives and risks, it can be shown that both labour-managed and entrepreneurial (i.e. profit-maximising) firms will result in the same Pareto optimal situation in the long run if perfect competition prevails (Meade 1972). In the entrepreneurial firm, MVP_L or $\left(\dfrac{P_x\delta_x}{dL}\right) = W$ and MVP_K or $\left(\dfrac{P_x\delta_x}{dK}\right) = iP_K$, while,

in the labour-managed firm, $\dfrac{P_x\delta_x}{\delta L} = \dfrac{PxX - iPK}{L}$, which says that the wage is the

surplus arising from the difference between the income obtained from the sale of the product and the cost of capital as shown in Figure 10.8. For labour-managed firms, the Average Revenue Product (ARP) curve, on the assumption of price-taking behaviour, takes the conventional inverted-U shape, while the cost curve C is a rectangular hyperbola, declining from left to right as the fixed costs of capital are spread over more units of output. The difference between the two represents the surplus to be shared among the employees and has a positive range between a and b. To the left of a, average cost C is greater than ARP and similarly to the right of b. The difference between average revenue and average cost is maximised at employment level OL, as indicated by the highest point on the profit curve, and at this level of employment $W = MRP$ just as in the entrepreneurial firm.

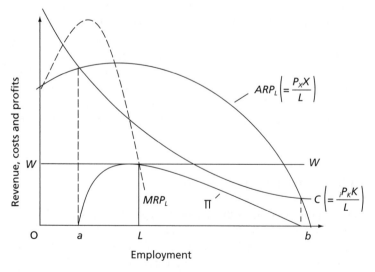

Figure 10.8 The maximisation of income per worker.

Figure 10.8 implies that in equilibrium the rental on capital and income per worker will be equalised throughout the labour-managed economy and will correspond to the normal rate of profit and the equilibrium wage of the perfectly competitive neo-classical economy. Both systems will result in *OL* employment. While the process is different, the final outcome is the same.

Differences arise, however, when we allow for differences in incentives, differences in risk, modify the assumption of free and costly entry of firms and allow for monopolistic conditions.

While entrepreneurial firms have the problem of motivating workers, labour-managed firms may have an advantage here. Further, the most efficient size for a co-operative is likely to be smaller than in the case of the entrepreneurial firm, since any reduction in the number of workers increases the percentage of the surplus going to the individual. However, individuals who own their own firm have to bear the risks as well as undertaking labour, and the risks are not spread over a number of firms. If their firm goes bankrupt, they lose their savings as well as their jobs. For these reasons, labour-managed firms are likely to be found in less risky sectors that are relatively labour intensive, so that the income per worker does not contribute a small difference between two large quantities. Labour-managed firms may also under-invest for similar reasons (Podivinsky and Stewart 2007). There is also a problem of short-run adjustment. In a profit-maximising system, an increase in demand will lead to a shift of resources to more highly valued uses, but in the labour-managed system, output will, paradoxically, be reduced, since MVP_L will be raised less than average earnings and remaining employees will gain more by dismissing workers. In that case, the product supply curve will be backward bending and this will be highly perverse and inefficient. This problem can only be overcome by the free entry of new firms, requiring unemployed workers getting together with employees in other industries who are earning less, which would be a lengthy and demanding process. Further, under any given monopolistic conditions in the product market, the labour-managed firm will produce less output than the profit-maximising firm (Figure 10.9). For simplicity, we give the example of constant costs over most of the range of output.

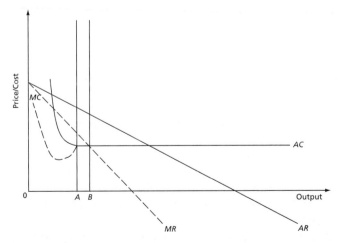

Figure 10.9 Monopoly power and the labour-managed firm.

The profit-maximising firm will equate *MC* and *MR*, operating at *B*, while the labour-managed firm (LMF) will maximise the difference between *AR* and *AC* by operating at *A*. This seems to be disadvantageous as price is higher and output lower, but, if more firms enter, there will be more competing firms and the economy will be more competitive (note the extra firms will make the demand curve more elastic). However, the profit-maximising economy is more likely to exploit any existing economies of scale.

Most empirical studies have faced the problem of the simultaneous presence of several types of incentives such as profit-sharing, active involvement in decision-making and share-ownership. For example, in Germany, where there is labour representation on the boards of large companies, Cable and Fitzroy (1980) derived quantitative indices for 42 firms, but their model included incentive pay, profit-sharing and worker capital. Participation in decision-making was highly significant but the incentive variables were not. Jones and Svejnar (1985) examined producer co-operatives in Italy and found that participation (the ratio of number of co-operative members to total employees), profit-sharing and individual ownership of assets all significantly influenced productivity. Defourney *et al.* (1985) examined 550 French producer co-operatives and found that the degree of participation increased output by between 2.5 and 5 per cent. Estrin *et al.* (1987) found positive effects for producer co-operatives in a number of Western Economies in relation to profit-sharing, share-ownership and participation in decision-making by workers. Bhargarva (1994) used panel data on 114 UK profit-sharing companies over the period 1979–89 and found that profit-sharing had a positive effect on the financial performance of the companies concerned. Thus, the combination of different types of incentive does seem capable of improving performance in different countries, though these do not exactly match labour-managed firms as defined in the literature.

It is doubtful if labour-managed firms can be efficient over all sectors of the economy. The three main problems are achieving conditions for the foundation of new firms; the conflict between efficiency and equality in the hiring of new workers; and finding effective mechanisms for overcoming the problem of risky ventures. Profit-sharing may, however, be a reasonable compromise between the two extremes of capitalists hiring workers at fixed rates of pay and workers hiring capital.

Summary

- Daily work curves suggest that significant changes take place during the course of the day in relation to various performance indications such as output, defective work and accidents.
- A principal–agent problem is likely to arise where there is asymmetric information, such that the agent (employee) has scope for the pursuit of his or her own interests undetected by the principal (employer), giving rise to problems of adverse selection and moral hazard. It is generally assumed that the employee is more risk averse than the employer.
- The need for monitoring can be reduced by using piece-work which may also have the effect of attracting and retaining more-able workers. But piece-work is

not appropriate in all situations and its incidence varies across types of firm, industries and countries.

- Promotion and deferred payments are alternative ways of motivating workers to increase their efficiency. Executive compensation may be widened in order to induce those below to seek promotion and there is evidence in support of this tournament theory and its effect on performance.
- Profit-sharing is another way in which employees are encouraged to improve performance and may have beneficial effects in terms of the stability of the economy over the business cycle.
- The labour-managed firm is an extreme version of profit-sharing with the maximisation of income per worker replacing the profit-maximisation assumption. While in the long run this might lead to a Pareto optimal outcome in terms of resource utilisation, there are problem in relation to short-term adjustment, risk and investment and restriction of output under monopoly conditions. This means that such a system may not be appropriate under circumstances that are found in many areas of the economy.

Questions

1. Explain what is meant by the principal–agent problem. Why is it important in determining the appropriateness or otherwise of particular types of incentive payment?
2. What circumstances are likely to make the use of payment by results appropriate or inappropriate?
3. Explain the concept of tournament theory and give examples where it might lead to improvements or reductions in efficiency.
4. Can profit-sharing eliminate the need for other forms of incentive?
5. Explain the concept of the labour-managed firm. What makes it unlikely to be a common form of enterprise?
6. Should bankers' bonuses be outlawed?

Notes

1. Jevons' theory implicitly assumes that the marginal utility of leisure is zero or subsumed in the marginal disutility of work. It seems preferable to use a utility function incorporating the marginal utility of income, the marginal utility of leisure and the marginal disutility of work, since an alteration in any one of these will alter the values of the other two.

2. For evidence of this, see Sargent Florence 1949. Unfortunately, the data are limited to the experience of certain US factories in the inter-war period and we do not appear to possess much post-war material on this important question.

3. H. Leibenstein coined this phrase to describe a situation in which managements failed to minimise the costs of producing a given output or to maximise the output from a given set of inputs due to a lack of competitive pressures. It

should be mentioned that this idea is not universally well regarded among economists.

4   It should be noted that Barzel's analysis presupposes that the employee receives the full value of his or her marginal product *for each hour worked*, which would seem to occur only under a proportional system of payment by results. Where time rates predominate, the wage line would be a straight line as in the conventional analysis. Further underlying the *VDP* curve is "the notion that the individual paces himself optimally". In practice, both *PBR* and supervision may fail to achieve this, as outlined below. Many studies, both in the UK and US, have found that workers tend to restrict output under incentive payment systems (widely referred to as "gold-bricking") with the result that, in such cases, performance over the working day may be far more even than warming-up and fatigue effects would lead us to expect.

5   Alchian and Demsetz define team production as a situation in which the product is not a sum of separable outputs of each co-operating resource. Thus, assume team production of Z involves two inputs X_i and X_j with $\alpha^2 Z/\alpha X_i \alpha X_j \neq 0$. The production function is *not* separable into two functions each involving only inputs X_i or only inputs X_j. If it is separable, this is not what is meant by team production. Hence, with team production, we have the problem of being unable to identify individual contributions to output.

6   Worker heterogeneity does appear to be substantial. In one study of Naval Reserve recruitment officers, Kostiuk and Follman (1989) estimated a population variance of 0.18 around a mean of one.

7   This may also explain the predominance of regressive over progressive piece-rate systems when the increasing marginal disutility of effort combined with the diminishing marginal utility of income suggests that progressive systems are more appropriate as a motivator.

8   Piece-workers tend to work shorter hours, however, than time-rate workers. McCormick (1977) points out that this substitution of effort for hours may explain the appearance of the backward-bending supply curve of labour.

References

Abraham K.G. and Farber H.S., "Job Duration, Seniority and Earnings", *American Economic Review*, 77(3), June 1987, pp. 278–97.

Alchian A.A. and Demsetz H., "Production, Information Costs, and Economic Organisation", *American Economic Review*, 62, 1972, pp. 777–95.

Arvan L., "Endogenous Monitoring Intensity, the Period of Contractual Pre-commitment, and the Slope of the Wage-Earnings Profile", *Economic Letters*, 29, 1989, pp. 173–7.

Atkinson A., *Atkinson Review: Final Report: Measurement of Government Output and Productivity for the National Accounts*, Palgrave Macmillan, Basingstoke, UK, 2005.

Baily M.N., "Wages and Employment under Uncertain Demand", *Review of Economic Studies*, 41, 1974, pp. 37–50.

Baker G.P., "Incentive Contracts and Performance Measurement", *Journal of Political Economy*, 100(3), 1992, pp. 598–614.

Barzel Y., "The Determination of Daily Hours and Wages", *Quarterly Journal of Economics*, LXXXVII(2), May 1973, pp. 221–37.

Bhargarva S., "Profit Sharing and the Financial Performance of Companies: Evidence from UK Panel Data", *Economic Journal*, 104, 1994, pp. 1044–56.

Bishop J., "The Recognition and Reward of Employee Performance", *Journal of Labor Economics*, 5(4), part 2, October 1987, pp. 536–56.

Blanchflower D. and Oswald A., "Profit-related Pay: Prose Rediscovered?", *Economic Journal*, 98, 1988, pp. 720–73.

Bulow J.I. and Summers L.H., "A Theory of Dual Labour Markets, with Application to Industrial Policy, Discrimination and Keynesian Unemployment", *Journal of Labor Economics*, 1(3), 1986, pp. 376–414.

Cable J.R. and Fitzroy F.R., "Productive Efficiency, Incentives and Employee Participation", *Kyklos*, 33(1), 1980, pp. 100–21.

Cable J.R. and Wilson N., "Profit-sharing and Productivity: Some Further Evidence", *Economic Journal*, 100, 1990, pp. 550–6.

Cantor R., "Work Effort and Contract Length", *Economica*, 55, 1989, pp. 343–53.

Defourney J., Estrin S. and Jones D.C., "The Effects of Worker Participation on Enterprise Performance: Evidence from French Co-operatives", *International Journal of Industrial Organisation*, 3(2), 1985, pp. 197–217.

Delfgaauw J. and Dur R., "Incentives and Workers' Motivation in the Public Sector", *Economic Journal*, 118(533), 2008, pp. 171–91.

Dixit A., "Incentives and Organisation in the Public Sector: An Interpretative Review", *Journal of Human Resources*, 37(4), 2002, pp. 696–727.

Drago R. and Heywood J.S., "Tournaments, Piece-Rates, and the Shape of the Payoff Function", *Journal of Political Economy*, 97(4), 1989, pp. 992–8.

Drago R. and Perlman R., "Supervision and High Wages as Competing Incentives: A Basis for Labour Segmentation Theory", in Drago and Perlman, editors, *Micro-Economic Issues in Labour Economics: New Approaches*, Harvester-Wheatsheaf, Herts, 1989.

Ehrenberg R.G. and Bognanno M.L., "Do Tournaments Have Incentive Effects?", *Journal of Political Economy*, 98(6), 1990a, pp. 1307–24.

Ehrenberg R.G. and Bognanno M.L., "The Incentive Effects of Tournaments Revisited: Evidence from the European PGA Tour", *Industrial and Labor Relations Review*, 43, 1990b, pp. 74–8.

Elliott R. and Murphy P.D., "The Choice between Time and Incentive Payment Systems: An Empirical Analysis", *Journal of Economic Studies*, 13(3), 1986, pp. 38–50.

Elliott R., Mavromaras K. and Meurs D., "Public Sector Pay Structures and Regional Competitiveness: Editors' Introduction", *Manchester School*, 75(4), 2007, pp. 373–5.

Eriksson T., "Executive Compensation and Tournaments Theory: Empirical Tests on Danish Data", *Journal of Labor Economics*, 17(2), 1999, pp. 262–80.

Esfahani H.S. and Salehi-Isfahani D., "Effort Observability and Worker Productivity: Towards an Explanation of Economic Dualism", *Economic Journal*, 99(397), September 1989, pp. 818–36.

Estrin S., Jones D.C. and Svejnar J., "The Productivity Effects of Worker Participation: Producer Co-operatives in Western Economies", *Journal of Comparative Economics*, 11, 1987, pp. 40–61.

Fehr E. and Schmidt K.M., "Fairness and Incentives in a Multi-Task Principal–Agent Model", *Scandinavian Journal of Economics*, 106(3), 2004, pp. 453–74.

Gibbons R., "Piece-Rate Incentive Schemes", *Journal of Labor Economics*, 5(4), part 1, October 1987, pp. 413–29.

Heywood J.S., Siebert W.S. and Wei X., "Payment by Results Systems: British Evidence", *British Journal of Industrial Relations*, 35(1), 1997, pp. 1–22.

Hutchens R.M., "A Test of Lazear's Theory of Delayed Payment Contracts", *Journal of Labor Economics*, 5(4), part 2, October 1987, pp S153–S170.

Jevons W.S., *The Theory of Political Economy*, 1871 (5th edition, A.M. Kelly, New York, 1965).

Jones D.C. and Svejnar J., "Participation, Profit Sharing, Worker Ownership and Efficiency in Italian Producer Co-operatives", *Economica*, 52, 1985, pp. 449–65.

Knez M. and Simister D., "Firm-Wide Incentives and Mutual Monitoring at Continental Airlines", *Journal of Labour Economics*, 19(4), 2001, pp. 743–72.

Kostiuk P.F. and Follman D.I., "Learning Curves, Personal Characteristics and Job Performance", *Journal of Labor Economics*, 7(4), April 1989, pp. 129–46.

Lazear E.P., "Agency Earnings Profiles, Productivity and Hours Restrictions", *American Economic Review*, 71(4), September 1981, pp. 606–20.

Lazear E.P., "Salaries and Piece Rates", *Journal of Business*, 59, July 1986, pp. 405–31.

Lazear E.P., "Performance and Productivity", *American Economic Review*, 90(5), 2000, pp. 1346–61.

Lazear E.P. and Moore R.L., "Incentives, Productivity and Labour Contracts", *Quarterly Journal of Economics*, 99, May 1984, pp. 275–95, reprinted in Akerlof G.A. and Yellen J.L., editors, *Efficiency Wage Models of the Labour Market*, Cambridge University Press, Cambridge, 1986.

McCormick B.J., "Methods of Wage Payment, Wages Structures and the Influence of Factor and Product Markets", *British Journal of Industrial Relations*, XV(2), July 1977, pp. 246–64.

McNabb R. and Whitfield K., "The Impact of Financial Participation and Employee Involvement on Financial Performance", *Scottish Journal of Political Economy*, 45(2), 1998, pp. 171–87.

Main B.G.M., O'Reilly C.A. and Wade J., "Top Executive Pay: Tournament or Teamwork?", *Journal of Labor Economics*, 11(4), 1993, pp. 608–28.

Malcomson J.M., "Work Incentives, Hierarchy and Internal Labour Markets", *Journal of Political Economy*, June 1984, pp. 486–507, reprinted in Akerlof G.A. and Yellen J.L., editors, *Efficiency Wage Models of the Labour Market*, Cambridge University Press, Cambridge, 1986.

Meade E.J., "The Theory of Labour Managed Firms and Profit Sharing", *Economic Journal*, 82, 1972, pp. 402–8.

Murphy K.J., "Executive Compensation", in Ashenfelter O. and Card D., editors, *Handbook of Labor Economics*, 3(2), Elsevier, 1999, pp. 2485–563.

Pencavel J.H., "Work Effort, On-the-Job Screening, and Alternative Methods of Remuneration", in Ehrenberg R.G., editor, *Research in Labor Economics*, 1, 1977, pp. 225–58.

Podivinsky J.M. and Stewart G., "Why is Labour-Managed Firm Entry So Rare? An Analysis of UK Manufacturing Data", *Journal of Economic Behavior and Organization*, 63, 2007, pp. 177–92.

Pokorny K., "Pay – But do not Pay too Much; An Experimental Study on the Impact of Incentives", *Journal of Economic Behaviour*, 66, 2008, 251–64.

Prendergast C., "The Provision of Incentives in Firms", *Journal of Economic Literature*, 37(1), 1999, pp. 7–63.

Putterman L. and Skillman G., Jr, "The Incentive Effects of Monitoring under Alternative Compensation Schemes", *International Journal of Industrial Organisation*, 6(1), March 1988, pp. 109–19.

Ricketts M., *The Economics of Business Enterprise: New Approaches to the Firm*, Wheatsheaf Books, Brighton, 1987.

Sargent Florence P., *Labour*, Hutchinson, London, 1949.

Shearer B., "Piece Rates, Fixed Wages and Incentives; Evidence from a Field Experiment", *Review of Economic Studies*, 71(4), 2004, pp. 513–34.

Singh H. and Gerber J., "On-the-Job Leisure-Income Trade-offs: A Test of Rational Behaviour", *Economics Letters*, 29(1), 1989, pp. 91–4.

Spence A.M. and Zeckhauser R., "Insurance, Information and Individual Action", *American Economic Review*, 61, 1971, pp. 380–7.

Stiglitz J.E., "Incentives, Risk and Information: Notes Towards a Theory of Hierarchy", *Bell Journal of Economics*, 6, 1975, pp. 552–79.

Taylor B.A. and Trogdon J.G., "Losing to Win: Tournament Incentives in the National Basketball Association", *Journal of Labor Economics*, 20(11), 2002, pp. 23–41.

Vanek J., *The General Theory of Labour Managed Market Economics*, Cornell University Press, Ithaca, New York, 1970.

Wadhwani S. and Wall M., "The Effects of Profit Sharing on Employment, Wages, Stock Returns and Productivity", *Economic Journal*, 100, 1990, pp. 1–17.

Ward B., "The Firm in Illyria: Market Syndicalism", *American Economic Review*, 48, 1958, pp. 566–89.

Weitzman M.L., *The Share Economy: Conquering Stagflation*, Harvard University Press, Cambridge, Mass., 1984.

Further reading

E.P. Lazear, *Personnel Economics for Managers*, John Wiley, 1998, is a relatively non-technical exposition of motivating workers to be more productive. His *Personnel Economics*, MIT Press, 1996, is a more technical exposition of such issues.

Canice Prendergast, "The Provision of Incentives in Firms", *Journal of Economic Literature*, 37(1), 1999, 7–63, is a comprehensive analysis of the provision of incentives contracts and how these induce effort among the workforce.

J.M. Malcomson, "Individual Employment Contracts", in *Handbook of Labor Economics*, 3, part 2, 1999, 2291–372, reviews recent developments and emphasises issues that arise from the problems of enforcing contracts in practice and from renegotiation by mutual agreement.

Chapter 11

Labour market policy

Learning outcomes

At the end of this chapter, readers should understand:

- That the justification for labour market regulation is based on the concept of market failure, the main forms of which are asymmetric information, externalities and monopoly/monopsony power;
- The distinction between active and passive labour market policies;
- The difference between the Phillips Curve, the Wage Curve and the Beveridge Curve;
- The case for and against minimum wages, employment protection, wage-related unemployment benefits and equal opportunities policies;
- Policies for dealing with the demographic challenge;
- That labour market policies may have unintended consequences.

Introduction

In this chapter, we consider several forms of intervention in the labour market including minimum-wage legislation, active and passive labour market policies and ways of tackling the demographic challenge. One of the main aims of this chapter is to show that many policies may conflict with one another and have unforeseen consequences.

We start, however, by asking the question: why intervene in the labour market rather than allowing market forces to predominate? The answer to this question rests on the presence of asymmetric information, externalities and the presence of monopoly/monopsonistic power in the labour market. One particular obstacle which prevents the market adjusting itself is the presence of downward wage rigidity.

Phillips Curve

The relationship between the rate of change of money wages and the level of unemployment.

Wage Curve

The relationship between the real wage rate and the local unemployment rate.

Active labour market policies

Policies that attempt to encourage those who are unemployed or inactive to become employed and that include incentives for training, job subsidies and public employment services.

Passive labour market policies

Policies that attempt to cushion individuals against adverse labour market outcomes, such as employment protection schemes and unemployment benefits.

Beveridge Curve

The relationship between the number of unemployed workers and the number of job vacancies.

The achievement of full employment lies at the heart of government policy, but this may conflict with another important objective, that is, the control of inflation. The **Phillips Curve**, named after its originator in the late 1950s, Bill Phillips, made this conflict explicit, but subsequently came under attack from those who believe that there is no long-run trade-off between inflation and unemployment. Rather, governments should attempt to keep the economy at that level of employment which is non-inflationary (the non-accelerating inflation rate of unemployment – NAIRU – sometimes referred to as the natural rate of unemployment).Others, following Blanchflower and Oswald in the 1990s, have argued that the level rather than the rate of change of wages, as encapsulated in the concept of the **Wage Curve**, is the key variable in understanding the relationship between wages and employment.

Next, we turn to the problem of low pay, which may be measured in absolute or relative terms, but whatever measure is used there are both equity and efficiency considerations. Key questions are whether or not some workers become trapped in low-paid jobs and whether or not outcomes can be influenced by particular institutional arrangements. Minimum-wage legislation has been introduced in many countries to protect the very low paid and this has proved to be a very controversial aspect of policy. Some economists, notably Stigler (1946), reject the usefulness of minimum wages, while others, such as Card and Krueger (1995) are more favourable on the grounds that the empirical evidence does not support the claim that raising the minimum wage must cause job losses.

Broadly, we may split labour market policies into two categories: **active labour market policies** (ALMP) and **passive labour market policies** (PLMP). The main elements of the former are training provision, job subsidies, public employment services and activation policies that attempt to encourage those who are either unemployed or inactive to enter the labour market. These will have the effect of shifting the **Beveridge Curve**, which measures the relationship between vacancies and unemployment, to the left, thereby increasing the ability of the economy to operate at high levels of employment. PLMP include employment protection policies and unemployment benefits. In many countries, however, in-work benefits have become the favoured approach and these could in principle lessen the need for minimum-wage legislation.

Particular groups in the workforce may need special consideration. Examples are younger workers, who are particularly vulnerable to adverse economic conditions, as they are more likely to be in precarious jobs or making their way in the labour market, and older workers who are prone to lose their jobs in times of economic crisis. Increasing longevity, combined with lower birth rates, particularly in Europe, increase both the dependency ratio and the pressure to extend the age of retirement.

Finally, the role of equal opportunities policies has been greatly extended to embrace gender, race, religion, age, disability and sexual orientation. The extent to which differences in employment outcomes between minority groups and the majority population represent discrimination is, however, contentious. To what extent, for example, does gender segregation result from employer discrimination as opposed to different preferences on the part of male and female workers?

The chapter concludes that labour market policies may well have unintended consequences.

11.1 Why intervene in the labour market?

The justification for labour market regulation of one form or another rests on the existence of **market failure**, the main forms of which are problems of asymmetric information, externalities and the existence of monopoly/monopsony power. These are considered in detail in Addison *et al.* (1997).

First, they consider the case of the introduction of a mandate, such as the right to a period of paid maternity leave (Figure 11.1). Prior to the introduction of the mandate, equilibrium is at E_1 with L_1 workers employed at a wage W_1. The mandate will increase employers' costs, so that the demand curve shifts down from D_1D_1 to D_2D_2, while the supply curve shifts to the right from S_1S_1 to S_2S_2 by the amount that the workers value the benefit provided by the mandate. If the workers value the mandate more than it costs firms to introduce it, the downward shift in the supply curve will exceed that of the demand curve and the new equilibrium will be at E_2 with employment higher at L_2, the pecuniary wage lower at W_2 but the full wage (including the workers' valuation of the mandate) higher at W_2'.

As Figure 11.1 illustrates, if workers value the benefits more than it costs the firm and wages are flexible, there will be a Pareto improvement with higher employment, higher GDP and a larger sum of producer and consumer surpluses. The initial sum of surpluses is triangle $D_1E_1W_1$, while the new one is $D_2E_2W_2$. If, however, wages are inflexible, equilibrium will occur at E_3 with employment at L_3 and only those who retain their jobs benefit. This emphasises the importance of retaining elements of flexibility in the labour market. As Addison *et al.* (1997) note, the question must be asked as to why the parties themselves would not negotiate such a Pareto optimal arrangement from which they could both benefit. The answer must lie in some obstacle to negotiation, such as imperfect information.

It should be observed that there is much evidence of **downward wage rigidity**. A recent feature on the phenomenon in the *Economic Journal* (2007) examined evidence in three countries (Germany, Italy and the UK). In Germany, 30 to 70 per cent of wage settlements were subject to real wage rigidity and between 13 and 20

Market failure

Outcomes that do not maximise market efficiency as a result of market imperfections such as asymmetric information or negative externalities.

Downward wage rigidity

The failure of wages to fall when the demand for labour declines or to fall less than implied by the decline in demand for labour services.

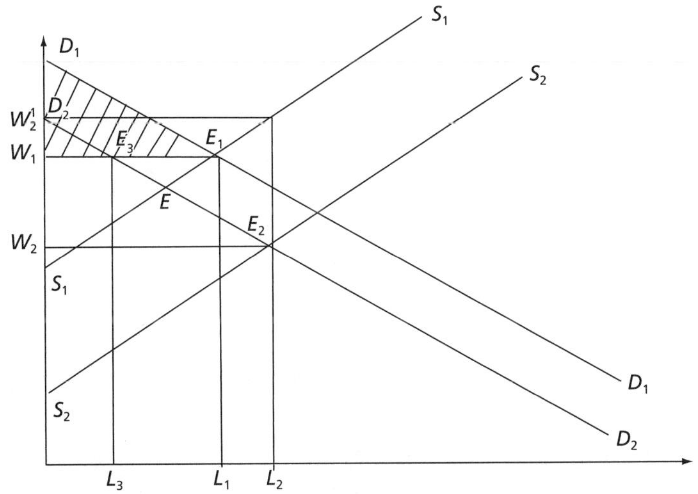

Figure 11.1 The effects of mandates.

per cent to nominal rigidity. In Italy, the corresponding figures were between 45 and 65 per cent and 22 and 24 per cent respectively, while, in the UK, they were 41 per cent and 14 per cent respectively. However, real wage rigidity appears to be becoming less important over time in each of the countries. Further, low inflation appears to decrease real wage rigidity, but to increase nominal wage rigidity. Finally, there is evidence in each case that rigidities are associated with unfavourable labour market outcomes, including higher unemployment.

11.2 General employment policies

Governments are generally committed to policies of full employment, but recognise that these can easily lead to overfull employment with the danger of inflation. In Britain, after the Second World War, William Beveridge defined full employment to mean that 3 per cent of the working population would remain unemployed, in recognition of the fact that zero unemployment is an unfeasible goal because of the presence of frictional and structural unemployment. **Frictional unemployment** arises because of time lags in the functioning of labour markets. This may involve time spent in searching for a new job. **Structural unemployment** arises from changes in demand or technology that lead to an over-supply of labour with particular skills or in particular locations and that is not the result of deficiency in demand. Rather, it requires retraining and/or relocation.

The problem facing governments is encapsulated in the concept of the Phillips Curve, which suggests that there is a trade-off between full employment and price stability. In a celebrated 1958 paper, Phillips hypothesises that, when demand for labour is high and there are very few unemployed workers, employers will tend to bid up wages in an attempt to attract sufficient workers. Since, in turn, workers will be reluctant to accept less than the prevailing wage (downward wage rigidity), when employment decreases, the relationship between unemployment (U) and the rate of change of wages (dW) is expected to be highly non-linear, as in Figure 11.2.

Frictional unemployment

The minimum level of employment at full employment, arising from lack of instantaneous job change through search delays or seasonal unemployment.

Structural unemployment

Unemployment arising from changes in demand or technology, which lead to an over-supply of labour with particular skills or within particular locations.

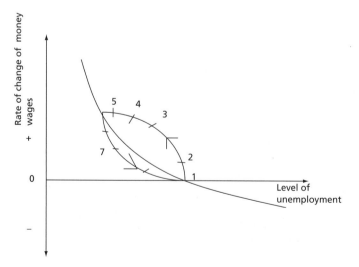

Figure 11.2 The Phillips Curve.

PC represents an example of the sort of Phillips Curve found for each trade cycle and fitted to observations on *dW* and *U* over a period of 100 years (1861–1957), which is found, in Phillips' words, to be remarkably stable. In fact, what Phillips discovered was not the curve normally portrayed in the literature, but a series of loops each describing a trade cycle. These show a tendency for dW to be high when *U* is low and to be low or negative when *U* is high. Further, there is a tendency for *dW* at any given *U* to be above the average for that level of *U* when *U* is decreasing during the upswing of a trade cycle and to be below average for that level of U_N when *U* is increasing during the downswing of a trade cycle. Thus, the loops capture the effect of *dU* on wages. Note that price inflation will be influenced by the relationship between wage growth and productivity growth.

$$dp_t = dW_t - dq_t \qquad (11.1)$$

where
dp_t = the rate of price inflation and
dq_t = the growth rate of productivity.

Following this approach, Cahuc and Zylberberg (2004) express the Phillips Curve as

$$d(W_t - p_t) = \lambda_0 - \lambda_1(dp_t - dp_{t-1}) - \lambda_2 U_t + \lambda_3 dq_t \qquad (11.2)$$

Thus, the left-hand side of the equation measures real wage growth. The parameter λ_1 captures the effect of price inflation in eroding the real wage. The influence of the unemployment rate on wage changes increases with λ_2 and the parameter λ_3 represents the degree to which real wages are indexed to productivity gains.

Phillips' 1958 paper generated a large literature attempting to replicate his results across a range of countries and over different time periods. In a critique of this literature, Seater and Santomero (1978) cited a total of no less than 228 papers. However, in the late 1960s and the 1970s, the relationship appeared to weaken or even break down and thereafter to shift upwards. This had been anticipated in a 1968 paper by Milton Friedman, who introduced expectations into the model and suggested that, in the long run, if the economy moved to the left of the **natural or non-accelerating inflation rate of unemployment** (NAIRU), inflation would accelerate as workers demanded higher wages in compensation to protect the value of the real wage. This would result in the Phillips Curve shifting upwards so that, in the long run, there is no trade-off. This is illustrated in Figure 11.3.

Let us suppose that the government attempts to reduce unemployment below the natural rate (U_N) to, say, U_X. Given productivity growth at, say, 2 per cent (its long-run trend), this will cause inflation. Given PC_1 wage growth will increase to 4 per cent through competitive bidding for labour. Expectations will adjust and the Phillips Curve will shift upwards to PC_2. Wage growth will now increase to 6 per cent and the Phillips Curve will shift upwards again to PC_3. Hence, the long-run Phillips Curve is vertical at the natural rate of unemployment and there is no scope for government to manipulate aggregate demand in order to reduce unemployment below its natural level. Only if expectations do not fully adjust, as might happen, for instance, if wage negotiations take place only once a year, will the Phillips Curve be downward sloping.

Natural or non-accelerating inflation rate of unemployment (NAIRU)

The level of unemployment that prevails when all markets in the economy are in equilibrium. Any attempt to hold the unemployment rate below the natural rate will result in accelerating inflation.

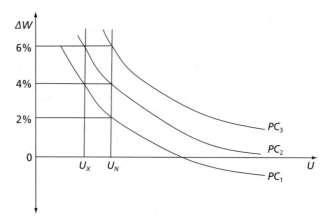

Figure 11.3 The expectations Augmented Phillips Curve.

A further attack on the Phillips Curve came with the emergence of the concept of the wage curve in the 1990s. Blanchflower and Oswald (1994) noted that the conventional wisdom of the time was that regions with high unemployment would have higher wages to compensate for adverse working conditions. This was based on the situation in developing economies where workers tended to migrate from rural areas to cities, despite the high unemployment experienced there (see Harris and Todaro 1970; Hall, 1970). Yet, Blackaby and Manning (1990) had found earlier that unemployment had negative effects on wages across UK regions. Likewise, Blanchflower and Oswald, using data for 12 countries, found that workers employed in areas of high unemployment earned less than identical workers in areas with low unemployment. The estimated employment elasticity of pay was –0.1 over most of these counties. They called this relationship the Wage Curve as in Figure 11.4. They are explicit in stating that the Wage Curve (WC in the diagram) is not a Phillips Curve.

First, the Phillips Curve is put forward as a disequilibrium *adjustment* mechanism, whereas the Wage Curve is an equilibrium locus which does not attempt to describe temporary or transitory phenomena. Second, the Phillips Curve relates *changes* in pay to the unemployment rate, while the Wage Curve links the *level* of pay to the unemployment rate. Third, the Phillips Curve is traditionally estimated

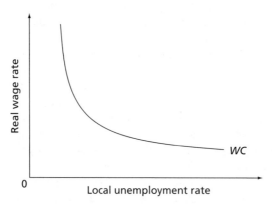

Figure 11.4 The Wage Curve.

using macroeconomic data, whereas the Wage Curve is generally estimated using microeconomic data. Cahuc and Zylberberg (2004) show, however, that the two concepts are related.

Let b_1 be the log of the real value of the reservation wage. Then,

$$w_t - p_t = \lambda_0 + b_1 \tag{11.3}$$

The reservation wage depends on the prospect of wage gains from job loss. This will be a function of unemployment benefits and the current level of productivity. Noting that the probability of exiting from unemployment decreases with the current unemployment rate, they obtain an equation that is identical to a Phillips Curve, but only when λ_3, the parameter on productivity growth is zero.[1]

11.3 The problem of low pay

Low pay has become a policy issue in a number of countries, especially those in which there has been a widening in the earnings distribution. Although trends in the overall dispersion of earnings measured by the ratio of the 90/10 percentile did not exhibit a generalised increase until the 1990s, prior to this and subsequently, the US and the UK, in particular, displayed a pronounced increase in earnings inequality and, to a lesser extent, so did Australia, New Zealand, Italy, Sweden and Finland.

Economic theory does not provide any clear guidance on how **low pay** should be defined, but either absolute or relative measures may be used, the former being more appropriate if the major concern is with poverty and the latter if it is with distributional or equity concerns. Using a measure such as the lowest decile, quintile or third decile has the effect of accounting for a fixed percentage of all workers. The alternative of defining low pay as a percentage (say, two-thirds) of the median allows for variations in the proportion of low-paid workers over time and is, therefore, more suitable for answering the question of whether the problem of low pay is becoming less or more widespread.

Generally speaking, reasons for studying low pay fall into equity or efficiency considerations. The former holds that there should be a fair reward for labour as embodied in the general principle of **equal pay for work of equal value**. Under this approach, some individuals who earn more than the mean may be regarded as low paid. On the other hand, some low-paid workers who have low levels of productivity or who prefer low-paid work because it is less exacting or more suited to their abilities may not be low paid in the equity sense. The efficiency argument may be based on the fact that pay is too low to maintain a reasonable standard of living, so that the State has to intervene to eliminate family poverty.

Alternatively, it may be argued that firms which pay below the norm for their industry are engaging in unfair competition. Some forms of efficiency wage argument also suggest that raising the pay of low-paid workers may raise productivity.

For policy purposes, it is important to consider the ability of individual workers to increase their earnings capabilities through time. To the extent that low pay is merely a transient phenomenon in which young workers acquire the necessary skills to enhance their lifetime earnings, low pay is not a matter for particular policy concern. To the extent, however, that certain workers become trapped in low-paid jobs, as suggested by the **dual labour market hypothesis**, in that case, a number of

Low pay

This can be defined in absolute or relative terms. It is often measured as a rate of pay below 60 per cent of median pay.

Equal pay for work of equal value

As applied to men and women, each gender should receive the same rate of pay when the work they do is equivalent in terms of value as determined by job evaluation or some other method of assessment.

Dual labour market hypothesis

The belief that the economy consists of "good" jobs and "bad" jobs with limited mobility between them.

Scarring

The idea that being
in an inferior
position in the
labour market or
being unemployed
results in an
unfavourable
carryover in terms of
future job prospects.

**State
dependence**

A causal link exists
between previous
labour market
experience and
future labour
market outcomes
independent of
personal
characteristics.

**Elasticity of
substitution**

A summary measure
of the ease of
substitution
between one factor
of production and
another, frequently
capital and labour,
as indicated by the
shape of an
isoquant, with a
value of zero
representing no
possibilities of
substitution and
infinity perfect
substitution.

**Skill-biased
technological
change**

The view that
technological
change leads to a
change in the
structure of
demand in favour
of more highly
skilled (educated)
workers, leading, in
turn, to an increase
in the skill wage
premium.

policy concerns are raised. One of these is the possibility that individual workers are in low-paid jobs with a high probability of exit from the labour market (i.e. a low-pay, no-pay cycle). Another is that workers' prospects of moving up the earnings ladder may worsen as the duration of a low-paid employment spell lengthens, which is sometimes referred to as the **scarring effect** of low pay. Low-pay persistence could be a consequence of the personal characteristics of those in this state (i.e. unobserved individual heterogeneity) or due to a causal link between previous labour market experience and low-wage employment (**state dependence**).

There are two problems to overcome in attempting to establish the degree of permanency of low pay. First, since the low paid are more likely to experience unemployment than the higher paid, a potentially misleading picture is obtained if attention is restricted to those in employment when modelling transitions between low pay and higher pay. Second, conditioning on being low paid at time $t - 1$ to model the probability of a transition out of low pay at time t may result in selection bias if the initial condition (being low paid at $t - 1$) is not exogenous. Using BHPS data and attempting to deal with both these problems, Stewart and Swaffield (1999) find evidence of considerable persistence in low pay.

Explanations of why certain individuals should be low paid centre on the question of skill or rather the absence of it. Katz and Murphy (1992) use a simple supply and demand model for relative skills in order to explain why the earnings of the more skilled should be rising relative to those of the less skilled.

Assume output Y is produced using skilled labour N_s and unskilled labour N_u in period t, that parameters a and b represent skilled and unskilled augmenting technological change, that α is the skilled labour share of employment and β the unskilled share, and that ρ is the parameter determining the elasticity of substitution between skilled and unskilled labour, where $\sigma = 1(1 - \rho)$. Then

$$Y_t = \left[\alpha_r (a_t N_s)_t^\rho + (1 - \alpha_t)(b N_u)_t^\rho \right]^{\frac{1}{\rho}} \tag{11.4}$$

From this is derived a relative wage equation on the assumption that the two types of labour are paid according to their marginal products

$$\ln\left(\frac{W_s}{W_u}\right)_t = \left(\frac{1}{\sigma}\right)\left[D_t - \ln\left(\frac{N_s}{N_u}\right)_t \right] \tag{11.5}$$

where

$$D_t = \sigma\left[\ln\left(\frac{\alpha_t}{1-\alpha_t}\right) + \rho \ln\left(\frac{a}{b}\right) \right]_t$$

The impact of changes in relative skill supplies on relative wages is positively related to the value of the **elasticity of substitution**, σ. Applying this model to the US, Katz and Murphy (1992) find that relative demand was shifting faster than the relative supply of skilled workers and this is why the skilled wage differential rose. This links in with the notion of **skill-biased technological change** (SBTC), whereby new technology favours those skilled workers who possess the necessary skills to operate it. Studies by Autor *et al.* (1998), Berman *et al.* (1998) for the US, and Machin (1996, 2004) and Machin and Van Reenen (1998) for the UK all find evidence in support of the SBTC hypothesis. Autor *et al.* (2003) suggest that computers raise the demand for jobs in which non-routine tasks are required of more-educated skilled employees, but reduce demand for routine tasks undertaken by middle-educated workers (which is referred to as **hollowing out**). Such polarisation is identified by Goos and Manning (2007), who find evidence not only of hollowing out, but also of an increase in the number of low-skilled, non-routine service-sector jobs.

Institutional arrangements may influence the degree of wage inequality. Lucifora (2000) notes that legislation on wages may reduce wage dispersion by skill and by gender; pay standardisation policies, by reducing management discretion may compress within-firm wage dispersion; industry-wide collective bargaining and the mandatory extension of collective-bargaining agreements to uncovered workers may reduce cross-firm wage dispersion; and more centralised bargaining may have the same effect. Those countries experiencing the largest increases in wage inequality tend to have the most de-regulated and centralised labour markets. Where unionisation is generally low, there tends to be a larger pool of low-paid workers. Lucifora estimates that such institutional features can explain about 60 per cent of differences in the extent of low pay across advanced economies. The most obvious response of governments to the issue of low pay is, however, minimum-wage legislation and to this we now turn.

Hollowing out

A situation in which many intermediate-level jobs, which can readily be automated, are lost, so that employment there shrinks.

11.4 Minimum-wage legislation

In 1998, 17 of the 29 members of the OECD had some form of minimum wage and, subsequently, Australia, Ireland and the UK have introduced minima. However, they vary substantially in their bite relative to the average wage, ranging from 20 per cent in the Czech Republic to 60 per cent in France. In most countries, the real value of the MW trended downwards in the 1980s, possibly in response to large increases in unemployment.

In a classic paper, Stigler (1946) considers the impact of a NMW under four heads: the allocation of resources, aggregate employment, family income and the problem of poverty.

In terms of the allocation of resources, Stigler examines first the competitive case. Here an effective MW must have one of two effects. Workers whose services were worth less than the MW will be discharged or the productivity of low-efficiency workers will have to increase to offset their higher costs. The former result will be greater the more the MVP falls short of the MW, the more elastic the demand for the product and the greater the elasticity of substitution. The latter result could occur through greater effort on the part of the worker or by the use of different production technologies by the employer. In a competitive industry, Stigler feels neither of these is likely to be significant.[2] In the monopsonistic case, he recognises the possibility that employment might increase, but the MW would have to be carefully chosen and its optimal level would vary across occupations, firms and over time. He suggests "a uniform NMW infrequently changed, is wholly unsuited to these diversities of conditions".

In terms of aggregate employment, Stigler feels there is a presumption that the net effects of a MW will be adverse. In contrast, Keynes argues a change in money wages is capable of altering the level of real income and employment as well as money income and the price level, although he feels that, in practice, a rise in wages would be slightly unfavourable to employment. The three possibilities – the classical view,

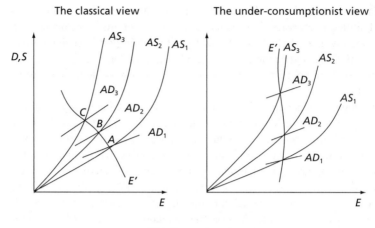

The classical view

The under-consumptionist view

The Keynesian view

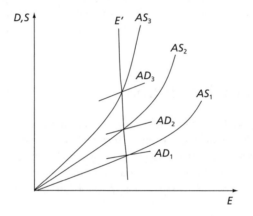

Figure 11.5 The classical view, the under-consumptionist view and the intermediate Keynesian view.

the under-consumptionist view and the intermediate Keynesian view – are illustrated in Figure 11.5.

AS (aggregate supply) represents the amount of money employers must expect to receive from the sale of output produced by that number of workers to make it just worthwhile to employ them (i.e. total cost). *AD* (aggregate demand) represents the total amount employers really do expect to receive from the sales of goods produced for each level of employment. Competition will move employment to the point where *AD* intersects *AS*. As the minimum wage shifts up both *AS* and *AD*, *E'* traces out the equilibrium points. Much will depend on the marginal propensities to consume and invest of capitalists and workers. Let m = marginal propensity to consume of workers and n their marginal propensity to invest, while m' and n' = the marginal propensities to consume and invest of capitalists. Further, assume $m > m'$ but $n' > n$ and that k = the fraction of the wage increase paid out of profits and $1 - k$ the fraction passed on to product prices. For employment to increase, we require

$$(m+n)-k(m'+n')>1-k. \tag{11.6}$$

Stigler argues that an effective MW is neither an efficient nor an equitable device for changing the distribution of personal income on four grounds. First, hourly wages are effective only for those who receive them. Second, hourly earnings and annual earnings are not closely related. Third, family earnings are the sum of the earnings of all workers in the family. Fourth, wages are by no means the only component of family income. He concludes,

> the connection between hourly wages and the standard of living of the family is thus remote and fuzzy. Unless the minimum wage varies with the amount of employment, number of earners, non-wage income, family size, and many other factors, it will be an inept device for combating poverty even for those who succeed in retaining employment. And if the minimum wage varies with all of these factors it will be an insane device.

He recommends the introduction of a **negative income tax** as a more equitable and efficient means of dealing with the problem of poverty.

It is clear that the impact of minimum wages on employment is ambiguous from a theoretical perspective and is an empirical issue. Up to the 1990s, there was a consensus that increases in the federal minimum in the US had a small but statistically significant effect on the employment of teenagers but not on other demographic groups (see Brown *et al.* 1982). The OECD, on the basis of a number of pooled time series regressions over the period 1975–96, which control for various cyclical and institutional factors, finds that a 10 per cent rise in the minimum wage would, *ceteris paribus*, lead to a fall in teenage employment of between 2 and 4 per cent (OECD 1998). However, this consensus was broken in the 1990s following the work of two Princeton economists, Card and Krueger, whose results were summarised in an influential book, *Myth and Measurement: The New Economics of the Minimum Wage* (1995). They observed that, during the late 1980s, a number of US States had raised their minimum wage rates, allowing for the comparison of labour markets outcomes for "treatment" and "control" groups using a difference in differences approach.

Puzzled by the seeming failure of a negative employment effect to emerge following the MW hike, they carried out a number of carefully designed studies. First, they categorised States on the basis of the fraction of teenage workers paid about the minimum prior to the increase, but found no meaningful difference in employment growth between high-wage and low-wage States. Second, they carried out a telephone survey of a sample of fast-food restaurants in New Jersey, where the MW was raised, and comparable restaurants in Pennsylvania, where it was not. The survey was carried out a month before the MW hike and repeated eight months afterwards, with checks on those restaurants that had failed to respond or closed down. The average starting wage in the New Jersey establishments rose by 10 per cent after the rise in the minimum, but employment increased there relative to Pennsylvania by about 11 per cent. They document several anomalous findings in relation to the standard theory. First, there is substantial wage dispersion for seemingly identical workers doing the same jobs that cannot easily be explained in terms of the standard model. Second, a sizeable spike in the wage distribution occurs at the minimum wage, which suggests that individuals of different ability earn the same wage and this occurs even for firms that are exempt from minimum-wage legislation. **Spillover effects**, whereby workers just above the minimum receive pay

Negative income tax

Rather than tax liabilities varying positively with income, benefits vary inversely with income according to a negative tax rate schedule, thus benefiting the low paid.

Spillover effects

In the case of minimum wages, a tendency for an increase in the size of the minimum to spread to other workers who are paid above the minimum in order to protect previous wage differentials.

increases, are also at variance with the standard model. They suggest that these results are, however, consistent with recent developments in economic theory and point to the dynamic monopsony model along the lines of Manning's model discussed in Chapter 5. What has been referred to as the new economics of the minimum wage has, however, sparked off considerable debate and led to further attempts to test the effects of minimum wages. The introduction of a national minimum wage in Britain in 1999 offered a unique opportunity to analyse its impact (see, for instance, the collection of papers in the *Economic Journal*, 2004). The effects appear to have been particularly benign. Thus, Stewart (2004), using a difference in differences estimation, finds no significant employment effects for any of the upratings for any demographic group. Machin and Wilson (2004) find that there was some employment reduction in a very low-paid sector – care homes – but even here where the wage effects were sizeable there appeared to be no effect on home closure. Arulampalam *et al.* (2004) could detect no adverse effects on training provision. Indeed, the probability of training incidence and the intensity of training increased by 8–10 percentage points for affected workers. Such benign effects were no doubt assisted by the buoyancy of the British labour market over this period.

A number of authors, however, have found evidence in favour of the traditional model. Thus, Aaronson *et al.* (2008) find that restaurant prices in the US unambiguously rise after minimum-wage increases are enacted and further that these price increases are larger for establishments that are more likely to pay the minimum wage. Further, they show that output price increases and employment are unambiguously negatively related in response to an exogenous change in wage rates. In addition, output and labour input are positively related. Hence, we can infer that, in a competitive market, which they feel represents the real situation in this particular sector, both output and labour input must have fallen (whether in terms of number of employees, hours or a combination of the two). Another explanation is provided by Portugal and Cardoso (2006) for Portugal, where the minimum wage was increased sharply for teenagers in the mid-1980s. Using a matched employer–employee panel data-set, they distinguish between worker accessions and worker separations. The main effect on teenagers of a rising minimum wage was a reduction of separations from employers, which compensated for a reduction in accessions to new and continuing firms. Thus, the effect of the minimum wage was to reduce the high job turnover that is characteristic of young workers. Perhaps, as Kennan (1995) suggested, Card and Krueger's lasting contribution may be to show that we lack knowledge of the precise effect of a minimum-wage increase and this owes more to a lack of sophisticated data than to the need to use more sophisticated models.

As Card and Krueger note,

> at some time during their lives most individuals are paid the minimum wage. [Indeed] more than 80 percent of all workers have worked for the minimum wage at some time during their careers. On any given day, however, only about 5 percent of US workers earn the minimum wage.

However, what is particularly important to policy makers is how long individuals remain on the minimum wage or in low pay. For the US, Smith and Vavrichek (1992) reported that over 60 per cent of workers in receipt of the minimum wage were earning more than the minimum one year later. More recently, Even and

Macpherson (2003) compared minimum-wage workers with a comparison group earning above the minimum, using panel data drawn from the Current Population Survey over the period 1979–99. Their evidence over the period 1979–99 suggests that minimum-wage jobs tend to be entry-level jobs and that they are also of short duration for a large majority of workers. Likewise, Jones *et al.* (2005) used the longitudinal element of the UK Labour Force Survey over the period 1999–2003 to model transitions between different labour market states using a **multinomial logit** approach. It appears that, for many minimum-wage workers in the UK also, payment at the minimum wage is of relatively short duration and a substantial number move into higher-paid jobs. The expected duration on the minimum wage was approximately 18 months.

Multinomial logit model

An econometric model that compares two or more response categories with a baseline category (i.e. what are the odds that a member of a particular group falls into one of the response categories as opposed to the baseline?).

11.5 Active labour market policies

Labour market policies cover a variety of interventions that are generally targeted at particular groups, as opposed to general employment policies such as measures designed to lower labour costs through non-targeted reductions in labour taxes or social security contributions. A distinction is generally made between active labour market policies (ALMPs) and passive labour market policies (PLMPs). The former focus on improving, say, the income prospects of unemployed persons by making it easier for them to enter the labour market, while the latter may simply provide income support for the unemployed without improving their chances of entering the labour market. Calmfors (1995) suggests that there are four basic functions of ALMPs, namely:

- to raise both output and welfare by getting more of the unemployed into work either directly or by investing in their human capital;
- to maintain the size of the effective labour force through competition for available jobs;
- to assist with the relocation of labour among different sub-markets;
- to alleviate the moral hazard problem arising from generous unemployment benefit systems.

The EU (2006) suggests that the objective of ALMPs is not only to improve employment outcomes, raise activity rates and decrease benefit dependency rates, but also to improve both the quality and productivity of jobs and strengthen social cohesion. In pursuit of these objectives, there are four main elements of ALMPs, namely: training, subsidised employment, the provision of public employment services (PES) and activation policies (including benefit sanctions, mandatory participation in training and workfare). These can be measured in terms either of the share of the workforce participating in such schemes or in terms of expenditure as a proportion of GDP. In European member states, average spending on ALMPs including PES totalled just over 2 per cent of GDP per annum during the period 1985–2004. There is, however, a wide variation across countries, ranging from less than 0.5 per cent in the Baltic countries, the Czech Republic and Slovenia to 4.4 per cent in Denmark in 2004.

It is generally assumed in line with Figure 11.1 that the matching process takes place in the presence of both externalities and transactions costs. To the degree that public intervention can reduce both of these, the matching process can be improved, thereby shifting the Beveridge Curve (see below) to the left, corresponding to a decline in structural unemployment. In the absence of ALMPs, unemployed individuals would tend to allocate insufficient resources to job-search activities, while firms would find it more costly to fill vacancies, so that fewer jobs would consequently be on offer. According to economic theory, the market for placement services should either be regulated or publicly provided as a monopoly. This is because of the fixed costs of setting up such a service. Otherwise unfettered competition would lead to inefficient provision (i.e. either under- or over-provision). In the case of labour market retraining, both workers and employers are likely to under-invest in general retraining because of lack of complete contract availability, friction in the matching process, monopsonistic power among employers or imperfections in credit markets. However, in this case, the empirical evidence suggests that public intervention is inefficient. While both theory and empirical evidence suggest that employment subsidies targeted at particular groups can raise net employment in the economy, they may be expensive as they are likely to put upward pressure on wages, as they encourage competitive bidding for the now cheaper labour.

A main objective of active manpower policies is to reduce the degree of frictional and structural unemployment in an economy. This is best illustrated by the Beveridge Curve (Figure 11.6), which relates unemployment to unfilled vacancies. It is assumed that there is labour market equilibrium when the number of unemployed (U) equals the number of unfilled vacancies (V). Then $U > V$ is a measure of excess supply (or demand deficiency) and $V > U$ is a measure of excess demand. This may occur not only at the level of the economy but also at the level of the region, industry, occupation or individual firm. If an economy is suffering from structural unemployment as a consequence of a recession, the Beveridge Curve may shift outwards. In contrast, policies that are successful in retraining employed workers to provide them with skills currently on demand may shift the Beveridge Curve leftwards.

In the steady state, the Beveridge Curve is based on the existence of a matching function $M = em(dU, V)$, where M is the number of hires from the stock of unemployed, U is unemployment, V is vacancies, e is a measure of matching efficiency and d represents the search efficiency of the unemployed. Assume S is the separation rate out of unemployment, then SN represents the flow into unemployment

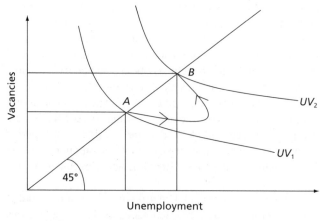

Figure 11.6 The Beveridge Curve.

and, in the steady state, $SN = M$, hence, $S = em\left(d\,\dfrac{U'}{N}\dfrac{V}{N}\right)$, which is the implicit

Beveridge Curve. In Figure 11.6, the loop AB represents the dynamic Beveridge Curve. As the economy moves into recession, unemployment will increase and one moves to the right along UV_1. However, if structural unemployment rises because new jobs are different from the ones lost in the recession, the economy may end up at B, where $U = V$ at a higher level (the Beveridge Curve has shifted to the right). The dynamic Beveridge Curve, therefore, takes the form of anti-clockwise loops.

A detailed examination of the Beveridge Curve in a number of European countries is contained in Padoa Schioppa (1991). She suggests that the optimal rate of unemployment is obtained when the U/V ratio coincides across all markets, or the non-accelerating inflation rate of unemployment (NAIRU) is at a minimum compatible with price stability. In this case, unemployment rates would be identical in every micro market. However, Jackman et al. (1991), in the same volume, suggest that the UV criterion has no theoretical basis, while Abraham (1991) argues that $U = V$ is not necessarily optimal as this is a function of the marginal social costs associated with either U or V.

It appears that the Beveridge Curve shifted to the right in many countries from the early 1960s to the mid-1980s, indicating that the equilibrium unemployment rate increased. After the mid-1980s, the situation stabilised in some countries, while, in others, such as Denmark, the Netherlands and the UK, it shifted leftwards. Nickell et al. (2003) estimated an aggregate Beveridge Curve for 15 OECD countries and found that the level of owner-occupied residential housing shifted the Beveridge Curve to the right by making workers less mobile. Likewise, so did the duration of unemployment benefits by contributing to lower search effort on the part of the unemployed (though this may also have improved the quality of matches in the long run). Nickell et al. (2005) found that, over the period 1960–90, both employment protection and employment taxes raised the level of unemployment, with the latter being modified in economies with co-ordinated wage bargaining. The impact of employment protection was mainly through increasing unemployment persistence. Other factors were the level and duration of unemployment benefits and changes in the behaviour of labour market institutions.

Ochsen (2009) estimates a Beveridge Curve for each of nine countries, eight of them European, over the period 1960–99. He finds that mismatch is not in general lower in those countries considered to have more flexible labour markets, though mismatch has decreased in some countries in which the labour market has become more flexible. Kluve et al. (2005) attempted to ascertain the effectiveness of ALMPs in raising employment prospects in Europe through a meta-analysis of over 100 evaluations. Training was found to have a modest impact on employment, with significantly better outcomes resulting from employment incentives and public employment service initiatives. Programmes involving direct job creation in the public sector fared even worse than training programmes, and youth programmes were particularly ineffective. However, such macroeconomic programme evaluations are far from straightforward and need to take into account the indirect effects of policies. Calmfors (1994) lists these as:

- **displacement** (subsidised activities may simply displace other activities in the economy);

Displacement effects

The negative effects of partial subsidisation on non-subsidised parts of the economy, leading to a reduction in the scale of such activities.

- **deadweight** (the same outcome may have occurred even in the absence of the programme);
- **creaming** (only the most employable of the unemployed may benefit from the programme);
- **substitution** (subsidised individuals may displace non-subsidised individuals);
- taxation (there may be distortions linked to the financing of the measures).

Such factors may explain why conflicting results have been found in some studies.

11.6 Passive labour market policies

The two main prongs of passive labour market policies are employment protection legislation (EPL) and unemployment benefits (UBs). As Boeri and Van Ours (2008) note, there are three key differences between them. First, EPL only protects those in employment and acts as a deterrent to employers enforcing lay-offs, while UBs provide protection to those without a job. Second, EPL does not impose any direct tax burden on workers, while UBs are effectively financed by a payroll tax levied on those in employment. Third, under EPL, the employer who enforces the lay-offs has to provide replacement income for those laid off, while UBs are essentially a risk-sharing device financed by both parties. However, such differences may be diminished by appropriate adjustments to the design of policies such as **experience rating**, which means that employers with a higher propensity to enforce lay-offs face higher payroll taxes.

11.6.1 Employment protection legislation (EPL)

EPL consists of a set of mandatory restrictions on the ability of employers to hire and fire labour with the purpose of increasing job security. It is possible to obtain an overall indicator by considering the rigidity of firing regulations for individual workers in the case of both those on permanent contracts and those on temporary contracts, as well as the rigidity of firing regulations in relation to collective dismissals. In addition, one must consider the proportion of the workforce subject to such regulations. Thus, while the US and the UK are generally regarded as having a high degree of labour flexibility and France, Portugal and Spain the least, taking into account coverage, Southern European countries seem to be much less strict as a large share of employment is in temporary work with a sizeable informal sector.

According to Autor *et al.* (2007), theory makes a clear prediction about the impact of EPL on productivity. Firms' adjustment costs will rise, so that firms will find it optimal not to hire some workers whose short-term marginal product exceeds their market wage and also to retain some workers whose wages exceed their marginal products. Such distortions in production choices will reduce worker flows and encourage firms to substitute capital for labour, as well as reducing productivity. Job turnover is likely, however, to become less countercyclical.

In the absence of universal EPL, we must consider the possibility of substitution of temporary for permanent jobs. In those countries where permanent workers have high levels of EP, temporary contracts (TCs) can provide a means for increasing labour market flexibility, as firms can adjust their labour forces by increasing the proportion of temporary workers. As Kahn (2007) notes, TCs tend to be low paid, offer less training opportunities and provide lower job satisfaction, so that they tend to reduce the welfare of the average worker. The young, women and immigrants are disproportionately offered TCs. In countries subject to high levels of EPL, such as Spain and France, there has been a dramatic growth in **temporary jobs** (reaching 32.9 per cent of workers in Spain and 17.2 per cent in France in 1998), whereas, in countries such as Britain with low EPL, the figure for TC has remained stable and low (at 7.1 per cent). Partial reforms such as encouraging fixed-term contracts instead of reducing EPL, as in France, may have perverse effects with higher turnover on fixed-term contracts leading to higher unemployment (Blanchard and Landier 2002). This leads to the conclusion that the expansion of temporary jobs as a means of increasing labour market flexibility may turn out to be undesirable.

One approach that might be considered a halfway house and has been termed **"flexicurity"** within the European Union is based on the objective of improving the balance between flexibility and security in the labour market. This has been used principally in Denmark and the Netherlands and is based on three elements: relatively loose legislation for employment protection; a generous social safety net for the unemployed; and high levels of spending on ALMPs. On average in Denmark, close to one-quarter of all workers have at least one unemployment spell each year, but the transition rate into employment is relatively high. Where this is not the case, individuals are referred to a comprehensive set of ALMPs in order to upgrade their skills or help them to adapt to economic change.

11.6.2 Unemployment benefits

Unemployment benefits, first introduced in the UK in 1911, are designed to protect individuals against uninsurable labour market risk. Generally, transfers are proportional to the previous wage, though there may be a flat rate component payable to those below a defined poverty threshold. In the UK, the net replacement ratio is 63 per cent for those on two-thirds of average earnings, 45 per cent for those on average earnings and 31 per cent for those on one and a half times average earnings. In many countries, the **net replacement ratio** is much lower than this.

Boeri and Van Ours (2008) suggest that, in imperfect labour markets, which can give rise to unemployment, unemployment benefits may have three distinct effects. First, they may increase the reservation wage of the unemployed, thereby reducing search intensity as the opportunity cost of having a job falls, and increasing the duration of unemployment spells (which they refer to as the job-search effect). Second, they will improve the fall-back option of those in employment, thus putting a higher floor on wage outcomes (the wage effect). Third, they will induce more people to enter the labour market (the entitlement effect).

As with employment services, unemployment insurance is generally publicly provided because of moral hazard and adverse selection issues. The former arises because workers will be less inclined to avoid unemployment and seek a new job if they are insured against the negative consequences of such action. The latter arises because of individual heterogeneity, which increases the probability of job loss for certain individuals over others. In such circumstances, a private agency would cherry pick and raise the cost of insurance to those with a high risk of job loss to unacceptable levels. Universal public provision can avoid this problem, but not that of moral hazard.

For this reason, there has been increasing reliance on in-work benefits in countries such as the US, UK, Canada and New Zealand through tax credits and work-conditioned transfers as a means of providing cash assistance to low-income

Temporary jobs

Employment in which there is no guarantee of the continuance of employment beyond a specified period.

Flexicurity

A term describing the attempt to achieve an optimal balance or compromise between labour market flexibility from the employer's perspective and job security from the employee's perspective.

Net replacement ratio

The ratio of net income received from benefits when unemployed to that when in employment.

Earnings Income
Tax Credit

A policy in the US
of in-work benefits
with subsidy rates,
maximum benefits
and taper rates
depending on the
number and ages of
children in the
family.

Working Families
Tax Credit

UK policy of in-
work benefits for
adults who work at
least 16 hours a
week.

families with children. Since the income supplement is conditional on work, this avoids adverse incentives for labour force participation. There are two major types of scheme. First, traditional welfare programmes on to which work requirements have been grafted. Second, refundable tax credit programmes administered through the tax system, such as the US **Earnings Income Tax Credit** (EITC) or the UK **Working Families Tax Credit** (WFTC) systems. In the former case, there are subsidy rates, maximum benefits and taper rates dependent on the number and age of children in the family. In the latter case, benefits are only provided to those adults who work at least 16 hours per week. Brewer *et al.* (2009) examine the operation of WFTC in the UK and finds that there are positive effects on employment, with lone-parent employment rates being raised by 4 to 5 percentage points through effects both on job retention and job entry. Hours of work also rise on average as some increase their hours to become eligible for the programme. While this suggests that the programme has largely been effective, there have also been some unintended consequences such as an increased propensity to marital breakdown as married women now have better outside options.

11.7 The demographic challenge

As we saw in Chapter 1, many countries are faced with ageing workforces. The proportion of the population in different age segments such as youths, prime-age employees and older workers can have important consequences for the labour market. Thus, Fertig and Schmidt (2003) suggest that it is appropriate to treat each birth cohort as a different factor of production, as workers of different ages are imperfect substitutes in production. Then, changes in the relative cohort size of any age group will result in a shift in relative labour supply and a downward shift in wages when cohort size increases. To the extent that relative wages fail to adjust, unemployment may result for larger cohort groups. The youth population is particularly vulnerable if economic conditions are adverse. At the beginning of their careers, young people tend to be highly mobile. The transition from school to work may not be straightforward, involving sequences of temporary jobs, unemployment spells and periods of training. Gregg (2001) finds evidence of unemployment scarring for young adults. Using the British National Child Development Survey, he finds the cumulated experience of unemployment from ages 16 to 23 is correlated with that from ages 18 up to 33. Low educational attainment, unmeasured ability, financial deprivation and behavioural problems all raise an individual's susceptibility to unemployment. However, while there is strong evidence of structural dependence induced by unemployment experience, there is evidence of only minor persistence in the case of women. It for such reasons as these that governments introduce youth training programmes. Thus, in Britain, a series of measures were introduced beginning with the Youth Opportunity Programme (YOP) in 1978, which was based on the principle that those who left school and were unable to get a job should have the opportunity of training or participating in a government-funded programme. By 1981, a third of school-leavers were entering YOP. In 1983, a successor, the Youth Training Scheme (YTS), was introduced in an attempt to raise the quality of training and further adjustments were made with the introduction of Youth Training (YT) in 1989. Doubts about the effectiveness of such schemes, however, remain.

According to Eurostat's baseline population projections, the median age within the EU will increase from 39 in 2004 to 49 in 2030, the EU being the only major region in the world where the total population is expected to decline over this period. As a consequence, the effective old-age dependency ratio (that is, the ratio of people aged 65 and over compared to the number of employed persons aged 16–64) is even higher than the demographic dependency ratio and is expected to rise from 0.37 to 0.70 in the EU25 by 2050 (EC 2007).

There are a number of possibilities for meeting potential shortages of labour in the workforce including:

i   discouraging early retirement;
ii   raising the legal retirement age;
iii encouraging people to have more children;
iv   encouraging immigration of workers from outside the EU;
v   encouraging part-time workers to change to full-time work;
vi   increasing working hours;
vii encouraging more non-working women to enter the labour force.

According to the 2008 EU Demographic Report, in 2007, 50 per cent of men and 40 per cent of women were still in employment at the age of 60, and, although these figures represent an increase of 10 percentage points compared to the year 2000, they are low. Further, rates of continuation in the labour force beyond retirement age are also low. Thus, the employment rate of 65–74 year olds in the EU, was only 5.6 per cent in 2003 compared to 18.5 per cent in the US. The report suggests that part-time work can be an effective mechanism for achieving a gradual transition from work to retirement, but, in fact, within the EC, only about 11 per cent of men aged 55–64 work part-time, compared to 38 per cent of women. In contrast, after the age of 65, part-time work is very common for those still in the labour force with 47 per cent of men and 61 per cent of women aged 65 and over working part-time in 2007. While the report holds that the potential for increasing employment through labour force participation remains strong, within a decade or so, the decline in working-age population is likely to be so marked that increasing reliance will have to be placed on increases in productivity derived from increases in human and physical capital, together with increases in innovation. An alternative is to encourage immigration. The expansion of the EU has led to substantial immigration into countries such as the UK and Ireland, thereby adding to the supply of labour, reducing inflationary pressure in the labour market and reducing the average age of the workforce. In the UK, immigrants represent no less than 12 per cent of the workforce. However, it has to be recognised that immigration flows may change the skill composition of the labour force, requiring short-run changes in wages and employment for different levels of skills or perhaps long-run changes in the economy's output mix. Immigrants may lack the experience of indigenous older workers who have left the labour force. They also tend to be concentrated in large urban areas such as, in the UK, London and the South-East. Many will lack English-language skills. Therefore, on its own, immigration cannot be a complete solution to an ageing workforce.

If the State is to influence the length of time people are in the workforce, it is necessary to understand, when given a choice, why workers retire when they do. Although some workers may retire because of mandatory retirement rules or because of health problems, a substantial number do so for economic reasons. Life-cycle models of the retirement behaviour of older workers suggest that the employment decision in a given period will depend on demographic characteristics, the wage offers of employers, the net worth of the individual and potential pension and social security benefits. The monetary gain from continuing in work can be defined in terms of discounted net present values. When retirement is postponed, benefits will tend to be higher, but obtainable over fewer years. The choice of retirement age will be determined by a comparison between this inter-temporal budget constraint and an inter-temporal utility function, with the goal being to maximise utility subject to the inter-temporal budget constraint. The **optimal retirement age** is then the age at which the marginal utility of income from an extra year's work equals the marginal utility from an extra year of leisure. But these values will themselves be determined by changes in the relative productivity of older workers compared to younger workers and the extent to which they face employment rigidities as a consequence of technological change.

As we have seen in Chapter 1, Lazear (1979) notes that employers may attempt to adjust the age-earning profile in such a way that it induces a greater input of effort from the worker by initially paying a wage less than the value of the marginal product, but eventually one that is higher than this value in order to develop a long-term attachment to the firm. Hutchens (1986) develops this idea by trying to answer the question: why do firms employ older workers, but not hire them? He offers two explanations: first, as Lazear implies, employers may back-load compensation in order to induce more long-run commitment from their workers. The nature of such an internal labour market suggests that hiring will be limited to younger workers. Second, jobs with substantial general training would be more attractive to younger workers because they can recoup the investment over a greater proportion of their working lives. Jobs involving substantial specific training will, in contrast, impose substantial costs on the employer and make it optimal to hire younger workers, thereby extending job tenure from which the investment can be recouped. Hutchens (1988) finds, for the US, that the ratio of all hires aged over 55 to the fraction of employees aged over 55 is less than one and negatively related to tenure, pension provision and the presence of mandatory overtime. Daniel and Heywood (2007) also find strong evidence for the deferred compensation and internal labour market hypotheses in the case of Britain, with an expected hiring ratio of older workers to their share in the working population of 0.6.

There are two ways in which technological change can affect retirement decisions. First, technological change will have a direct effect on the amount of on-the-job training that is required. Second, it will indirectly lead to depreciation in the stock of human capital, which tends to lead to earlier retirement. Unexpected increases in technological change may induce older workers not to retrain and earlier retirement will occur as the market wage rate for such workers falls below the value of leisure (Bartel and Sicherman 1993).

Recently, attention has focused on the polarisation of work or the hollowing-out phenomenon. Goos and Manning (2007) argue that skill-biased technological change has increased the demand for educated workers, but the widening income distribution has increased the demand for services by the relatively rich, so that jobs in both the upper and lower parts of the earnings distribution have grown in advanced countries, while routine tasks in the middle of the distribution have been mechanised, so that employment has declined here (the hollowing-out phenomenon). This may have adverse consequences for older workers who have less education, but more experience, leading them to be disproportionately employed in the middle-level jobs (see Case Study 11.1).

Optimal retirement age

The age at which the marginal utility of income from an extra year's work equals the marginal utility of an extra year of leisure.

11.8 Equality of opportunities policies

These have been given considerable prominence through the activities of the European Union, particularly in relation to gender equality. As early as 1957, Article 119 of the Treaty of Rome contained a provision imposing equal pay for men and women, and the principle of gender equality has greatly evolved since then, including a ban on all direct discrimination, the introduction of the concept of **indirect discrimination** and the reversal of the burden of proof. Since 1999, there has been action to ban discrimination on the grounds of racial or ethnic origin or belief, disability, age or sexual orientation. Individual countries are obliged to put in place legislation to provide the necessary protection to prevent discrimination against the above groups. The UK is a good example of how the application of the law in this area is far from straightforward. The Equal Pay Act 1976, as originally formulated, specified a requirement for equal pay for the same or broadly similar work where common terms and conditions of employment apply, or to cases where work is rated as equivalent under a job evaluation scheme.

Indirect discrimination

The imposition of a rule that, while not directly discriminatory, has the effect of disproportionately affecting a particular group in an adverse manner and cannot be justified in terms of the performance of the job.

Case Study 11.1

Are certain jobs getting old?

Autor and Dorn (2009) observe that job polarisation applies to the US as well as Europe. They attempt to answer the question of where workers in routine jobs end up. Their approach is relatively straightforward. As workers gain more work experience, they will increase the amount of specific human capital they possess, which implies that the costs of occupational mobility will be higher for older than younger workers. When an occupation declines, therefore, older workers have an incentive not to enter it. Firms will have similar incentives not to hire young workers into declining occupations. As a result, occupations will "get old" as their employment declines and middle-skill jobs fall into this category.

They estimate a simple regression of the form

$$\Delta Y_j = \alpha + \beta_1 \Delta E + \varepsilon_j$$

where Y_j is the mean age of workers in occupation j, E is the share of the occupation in total employment in a given year and Δ is the change over the period 1980–2005. Occupations that contracted by one percentage point as a share of aggregate employment gained in age by an additional 0.78 years relative to the mean. Using DOT data, the authors construct an index of routine task intensity and this turns out to be highly significant as a predictor of changes in occupational age structure. Finally, they hypothesise that local labour markets specialised in routine task-intensive occupations at the start of the period analysed should have experienced a faster contraction of middle-skill jobs over the subsequent 25 years and this turns out to be the case. The decline in routine employment is higher for non-college workers, but older workers are more likely to end up in low-skill non-routine occupations.

D. Autor and D. Dorn, "The Job is 'Getting Old': Measuring Changes in Job Opportunities using Occupational Age Structure", *American Economic Review, Papers and Proceedings*, 99(2), May 2009, pp. 45–51.

Therefore, to the extent that women are employed by different employers to men – for example, disproportionately in small establishments which tend to pay less – any resulting differences in earnings are not subject to amendment via legislation. However, the scope was broadened somewhat by the Equal Pay (Amendment) Regulations 1983, which extend the comparison to work of equal value, but differences in employment distribution remain an important source of differences in male and female rates of pay. Economists estimate discrimination on the basis that equally productive workers should receive the same rate of pay and that seems consistent with the notion of equal pay for work of equal value. But we should not assume that the economists' and lawyers' definitions of discrimination are necessarily identical. To the economist, discrimination is a demand-based phenomenon and the willingness of women to offer themselves for employment at a lower rate of pay than men would not normally be regarded as a manifestation of discrimination. Yet, the law may prevent the employer from offering a lower rate of pay where men are employed on comparable work, despite any market-forces argument. The concept of indirect discrimination also means that, in economic models, we must pay regard to the possibility that variables that are significant in explaining pay differences between men and women may not be strictly required for the satisfactory performance of a job and may, therefore, be held to constitute indirect discrimination.

The policy debate seems to have shifted from inequality of opportunity to inequality of outcomes. Thus, the UK government is concerned with the fact that a gender pay gap is still evident and proposes compulsory pay audits by employers. The EU in a *Roadmap for Equality between Women and Men 2006–2010* (2006) asserts that the persistence of the pay gap "results from direct discrimination against women and structural inequalities such as segregation in sectors, occupations and work patterns, access to education and training, biased evaluation and pay systems, and stereotypes". There is no consideration of the possibility that gender segregation may be a consequence of genuine occupational choice (different tastes for particular types of work on the part of men and women). There may also be constraints on the job-search behaviour of married women which are more severe than those relating to married men, as illustrated by differences in journey to work patterns. There may also be different preferences or constraints with respect to hours of work. Thus, Bryan (2006), using WERS (1998) data, finds large differences in the hours of women in the same workplaces, and in comparable jobs, according to whether or not they have young children. There is also some evidence that workers sort themselves into establishments working longer or shorter hours according to their individual preferences.

It is well known that, on average, males are more risk-taking than women (Scotchmer 2005). Thus, Ekelund *et al.* (2005) examine the effect of risk aversion on an individual's probability of being self-employed, by using psychometric data from a large population-based cohort of Finns in 1996. The fact that men are less risk averse than women makes them significantly more likely to become self-employed than women. By definition, these decisions cannot be influenced by employer practices. Using US data, DeLeire and Levy (2004) test the proposition that individuals with strong aversion to risk will choose safer jobs. Further, they suggest that workers who are raising children will be less willing to trade on-the-job safety for wages, since their children depend on them, and this should be even more marked in the case of single parents. Because married men with children are not in the role of primary caregiver, but married women with children are, the latter will be more risk averse than the former. Using a **conditional logit model**, they find that occupational choices are consistent with these propositions. In addition, there is an independent gender effect with the most safety-orientated men having the same level of aversion to risk as the least safety-orientated women. In total, these differences in risk aversion are estimated to explain no less than one-quarter of the extent of occupational segregation by gender in the US. A similar study conducted for the UK by Grazier and Sloane (2008) finds similar, though smaller effects. This is consistent with the fact that there is a lower accident risk across occupations in the UK relative to the US.

> **Conditional logit model**
>
> An extension of the multinomial logit model, in which explanatory variables may include attributes of the choice alternatives as well as the characteristics of the individuals making the choices.

11.9 Conclusions

Labour market policies may have unintended consequences and success may depend on achieving an appropriate blend of policies. As Cahuc and Zylberberg (2004) have suggested, the role of passive policies is not to create too many disincentives to gaining employment, and even active policies can be counterproductive. Thus, increasing employment by subsidising some jobs may occur at the expense of those jobs that remain unsubsidised. Imposing equal pay may reduce the ability of individuals to optimise their employment arrangements if preferences for pay and non-pay aspects of employment vary across individuals and groups. Minimum-pay legislation, if fixed too high, may generate youth unemployment. There remain important differences among economies in the extent to which flexibility is allowed to prevail over legal intervention. Thus, in Anglo-Saxon countries such as the US and the UK, there remains a high degree of flexibility, with relative low job security and low taxation. In France and Germany, there is intermediate to low flexibility, intermediate to high security and intermediate to high taxation; and, in the Nordic System and the Netherlands, there is high security, intermediate to high flexibility and intermediate to high taxation.

Summary

- The case for intervention in the labour market rests on the presence of market failure arising from the fact that labour markets are imperfect. Increasing labour market flexibility reduces the need for intervention, but wage rigidity increases it.
- The Phillips Curve suggests that there may be a trade-off between full employment and price stability, but, if expectations fully adjust, there is no such trade-off in the long run. Rather, it is necessary for governments to maintain employment and unemployment at levels where there is no tendency for inflation to increase (the non-accelerating inflation rate of unemployment, NAIRU). The Wage Curve also suggests that higher unemployment leads to lower wages and less inflation.
- The analysis of low pay involves both equity and efficiency considerations. Major concerns are whether there is a low-pay no-pay cycle, whether there is a scarring effect and whether there is low-pay persistence. The incidence of low pay may also be affected by the polarisation of the labour market.
- Minimum-wage legislation focuses on the very low paid. In a classic paper, Stigler examines the effects of a minimum wage on the allocation of resources,

aggregate employment, family income and poverty, and concluded that a minimum wage was neither an efficient nor an equitable policy. More recently, Card and Krueger carried out a number of studies, notably in fast-food restaurants in the US, and a number of studies were also carried out in Britain following the introduction of a national minimum wage in 1999. In each case, no adverse consequences were detectable.

- Active labour market policies (ALMPs) attempt to get more people into work through subsidies, retraining and improved public employment services. They are aimed at particular groups and are designed to minimise the conflict between full employment and price stability by shifting the Beveridge Curve to the left. In practice, the curve appears to have shifted to the right in some countries, and evidence does not support the view that ALMPs, particularly of the job-creation variety, have generally been successful.

- Passive labour market policies have two main prongs – employment protection legislation (EPL) and unemployment insurance (UI).

- EPL will increase employers' adjustment costs and tend to lead to the substitution of temporary for permanent jobs. UI effects depend on the replacement ratio and will tend to increase the size of the reservation wage with consequent moral hazard effects. An alternative approach is to use in-work benefits.

- Young workers are particularly vulnerable to adverse economic conditions and scarring effects from unemployment. Government-sponsored training programmes tend to be ineffective.

- Increasing the employment of older workers is a priority as the population ages. The optimal retirement age will be influenced by various economic factors including pay back-loading and the hollowing-out phenomenon.

- Equality of opportunity policies will not necessarily be efficient if different groups have different preferences for various types of work.

- To conclude, labour market policies may have unintended consequences.

Questions

1   Consider the arguments in favour of intervention in the labour market. What are the pitfalls?
2   Under what conditions, if any, is minimum-wage legislation likely to be successful?
3   Compare and contrast active and passive labour market policies as mechanisms for improving the operation of the labour market.
4   What are the similarities and differences between the Phillips Curve and the Wage Curve?
5   How useful is the Beveridge Curve in understanding the operation of the labour market?
6   What is the demographic challenge and how may the effects be minimised?

Notes

1 If $\Delta pt = \Delta pt - 1$, we obtain from the above equation

$$U_t = \frac{\lambda_0 - (1 - \lambda_3)\Delta qt}{\lambda_2}$$

Cahuc and Zylberberg suggest that, if nominal wages are not perfectly indexed to productivity gains $(0 \leq \lambda_3 < 1)$, a slowing of productivity growth will lead to a rise in the NAIRU. Thus, the NAIRU becomes a critical factor in the control of inflation.

2 Stigler neglects the possibility that employers may substitute workers for hours. Strobl and Walsh (2008) show that, if one assumes that the scale of production has no impact on hours per worker in a competitive market, then the change in the number of workers and hours per worker resulting from a MW are inversely related. Total hours worked could rise if there are small fixed costs to hiring workers. Thus, the effect on employment is ambiguous even in the competitive case. See also Stewart and Swaffield (2008).

References

Aaronson D., French E. and McDonald J., "The Minimum Wage, Restaurant Prices and Labour Market Structure", *Journal of Human Resources*, 43(3), Seminar, 2008, pp. 688–720.

Abraham K., "Mismatch and Labour Mobility: Some Final Remarks", in Padoa Schioppa F., editor, *Mismatch and Labour Mobility*, Cambridge University Press, 1991, pp. 483–8.

Addison J.T., Barrett C.R. and Siebert W.S., "The Economics of Labour Market Regulation", in Addison J.T. and Siebert W.S., editors, *Labour Markets in Europe*, The Dryden Press, London, 1997, pp. 62–104.

Arulampalam W., Booth A.L. and Bryan M.L., "Training and the New Minimum Wage", *Economic Journal*, 114 (494), March 2004, pp. C87–C94.

Autor D. and Dorn D., "This Job is 'Getting Old': Measuring Changes in Job Opportunities Using Occupational Age Structure", *American Economic Review, Papers and Proceedings*, 99(2), May 2009, pp. 45–51.

Autor D.H., Katz L.F. and Kruger A.B., "Computing Inequality: Have Computers Changed the Labor Market", *Quarterly Journal of Economics*, 113(4), November 1998, pp. 1169–213.

Autor D.H., Levy F. and Murnane R.J., "The Skill Content of Recent Technological Change: An Empirical Explanation", *Quarterly Journal of Economics*, 118(4), November 2003, pp. 1279–333.

Autor D.H., Kerr W.D. and Kugler A.D., "Does Employment Protection Reduce Productivity? Evidence from UK States", *Economic Journal*, 117(521), June 2007, pp. F189–F217.

Bartel A. P. and Sicherman N., "Technological Change and Retirement Decisions of Older Workers", *Journal of Labor Economics*, 11, 1993, pp. 162–83.

Berman E., Bound J., and Machin S., "Implications of Skill-Biased Technological Change: International Evidence", *Quarterly Journal of Economics*, 113(4), 1998, pp. 1245–79.

Blackaby D. and Manning D., "Earnings, Unemployment, and the Regional Employment Structure in Britain", *Regional Studies*, 24(6), 1990, pp. 529–35.

Blanchard O. and Landier A., "The Perverse Effects of Partial Labour Market Reform: Fixed Term Contracts in France", *Economic Journal*, 112(480), 2002, pp. F214–F224.

Blanchflower D.G. and Oswald A.J., *The Wage Curve*, MIT Press, Cambridge, Mass., 1994.

Boeri T. and Van Ours J., *The Economics of Imperfect Labour Markets*, Princeton University Press, Princeton and Oxford, 2008.

Brewer M., Francescani M., Gregg P. and Grogger J., "Introduction In Work Benefit Reform in a Cross-National Perspective", *Economic Journal*, 119(535), February 2009, pp. F1–F14.

Brown C., Gilroy C. and Kohen A., "The Effect of the Minimum Wage on Employment and Unemployment", *Journal of Economic Literature*, 20, 1982, pp. 487–528.

Bryan M.L., "Analysing Working Time: Why Use Linked Employer–Employee Data?", Bryson A., Forth J. and Barber C., editors, *Making Linked Employer-Employee Data Relevant to Policy*, DTI Occasional Paper No. 4, Department of Trade and Industry, 2006.

Cahuc P. and Zylberberg A., *Labor Economics*, MIT Press, Cambridge, Mass., 2004.

Calmfors L., "Active Labour Market Policy and Unemployment: A Framework for Crucial Policy Design Features", *OECD Economic Studies*, No. 22, 1994.

Calmfors L., "What Can We Expect from Active Labour Market Policy?", *Konjunkturpolitik*, 43, 1995, pp. 11–30.

Card D. and Krueger A.B., *Myth and Measurement: The New Economics of the Minimum Wage*, Princeton University Press, Princeton, New Jersey, 1995.

Daniel K. and Heywood J.S., "The Determinants of Hiring Older Workers; UK Evidence", *Labour Economics*, 14, 2007, pp. 35–51.

DeLeire T. and Levy H., "Worker Sorting and Risk of Death on the Job", *Journal of Labor Economics*, 22(4), 2004, pp. 925–53.

Ekelund J., Johansson F., Jarvelin M.R. and Lichtermann D., "Self Employment and Risk Aversion: Evidence from Psychological Test Data", *Labour Economics*, 12(5), October 2005, pp. 649–59.

European Commission, *A Roadmap for Equality between Women and Men 2006–2010*, Luxembourg, April 2006.

European Commission, "Effective Active Labour Market Policies", *Employment in Europe 2006*, Luxembourg, October 2006, pp. 119–72.

European Commission, *Europe Demographic Future: Facts and Figures on Challenges and Opportunities*, Luxembourg, 2007.

Economic Journal, "Special Session on the UK Minimum Wage", *Economic Journal*, 114(494), March 2004, pp. C84–C116.

Economic Journal, "Feature: Wage Rigidity", *Economic Journal*, 117(524), November 2007, pp. F499–F569.

Even W.F. and Macpherson D.A., "The Wage and Employment Dynamics of Minimum Wage Workers", *Southern Economic Journal*, 69, 2003, pp. 676–90.

Fertig M. and Schmidt C.M., "Gerontology in Motion? European Cross Country Evidence on the Labour Market Consequences of Population Ageing", IZA Discussion Paper No. 956, Bonn, 2003.

Friedman M., "The Role of Monetary Policy", *American Economic Review*, 54, 1968, pp. 1–17.

Goos M. and Manning A., "Lousy and Lovely Jobs: The Rising Polarisation of Work in Britain", *Review of Economics and Statistics*, 89(1), February 2007, pp. 118–33.

Grazier S. and Sloane P.J., "Accident Risk, Gender, Family Status and Occupational Choice in the UK", *Labour Economics*, 15, 2008, pp. 938–57.

Gregg P., "The Impact of Youth Unemployment on Adult Unemployment in the NCDS", *Economic Journal*, 111(475), November 2001, pp F626–F653.

Hall R.E., "Why is the Unemployment Rate So High at Full Employment?", *Brookings Papers on Economic Activity*, 3, 1970, pp. 369–402.

Harris J.R. and Todaro M.P., "Migration, Unemployment and Development", *American Economic Review*, 60, 1970, pp. 126–42.

Hutchens R., "Delayed Payment Contracts and a Firm's Propensity to Hire Older Workers", *Journal of Labor Economics*, 14, 1986, pp. 439–57.

Hutchens R., "Do Job Opportunities Decline with Age?", *Industrial and Labor Relations Review*, 42, 1988, pp. 89–99.

Jackman R., Layard R. and Savouri S., "Mismatch: A Framework for Thought", in Padoa Schioppa, editor, *Mismatch and Labour Mobility*, Cambridge University Press, 1991, pp. 44–94.

Jones M.K., Jones R.J., Murphy P.D. and Sloane P.J., "The Dynamics of the National Minimum Wage: Transitions between Labour Market States", WELMERC Discussion Paper No. 2005–05, Swansea University, 2005.

Kahn L.M., "The Impact of Employment Protection Mandates on Demographic Temporary Employment Patterns: International Microeconomic Evidence", *Economic Journal*, 117(521), June 2007, pp. F333–F356.

Katz L.F. and Murphy K.M., "Changes in Relative Wages, 1963–1987; Supply and Demand Factors", *Quarterly Journal of Economics*, 107(1), February 1992, pp. 25–78.

Kennan J., "The Elusive Effects of Minimum Wages", *Journal of Economic Literature*, 33(4), 1995, pp. 1950–65.

Kluve J., Festig M., Jacobi L., Nima L. and Schaffner S., "Study on the Effectiveness of ALMPs", European Commission, 2005.

Lazear E.P., "Why is there Mandatory Retirement?", *Journal of Political Economy*, 87, 1979, pp. 1261–84.

Lucifora C., "Wage Inequalities and Low Pay", in Gregory M., Salverda W. and Bazen S., editors, *Labour Market Inequalities*, Oxford University Press, Oxford, 2000, pp. 9–34.

Machin S., "Wage Inequality in the UK", *Oxford Review of Economic Policy*, 12, 1996, pp. 47–64.

Machin S., "Skill-Biased Technological Change and Educational Outcomes", in Johnes G. and Johnes J. editors, *Industrial Handbook on the Economics of Education*, Edward Elgar, Cheltenham, 2004.

Machin S. and van Reenen J., "Technology and Changes in Skill Structure: Evidence from Seven OECD Countries", *Quarterly Journal of Economics*, 113(4), 1998, pp. 1215–44.

Machin S. and Wilson J., "Minimum Wages in a Low Wage Labour Market: Care Homes in the UK", *Economic Journal*, 114(494), 2004, pp. C102–C109.

Nickell S., Nunziata L., Ochel W. and Quintini G., "The Beveridge Curve, Unemployment and Wages in the OECD from the 1960s to the 1990s", in Aghion P.,

Frydman R., Stiglitz J. and Woodford M., editors, *Knowledge, Information and Expectations in Modern Macroeconomics*, Princeton University Press, New Jersey, 2003, pp. 394–431.

Nickell S., Nunziata L. and Ochel W., "Unemployment in the OECD since the 1960s: What Do We Know?", *Economic Journal*, 115(508), January 2005, pp. 1–27.

Ochsen C., "On the Measurement of Mismatch", *Applied Economics Letters*, 16, 2009, pp. 405–9.

OECD, "Making the Most of the Minimum: Statutory Minimum Wages, Employment and Poverty", *Employment Outlook*, Paris, 1998, pp. 31–77.

Padoa Schioppa F., editor, *Mismatch and Labour Mobility*, Cambridge University Press, Cambridge, 1991.

Phillips A.W., "The Relationship between Unemployment and the Rate of Change of Money Wage Rates in the United Kingdom; 1862–1957", *Economica*, 25, 1958, pp. 283–99.

Portugal P. and Cardoso A.R., "Disentangling the Minimum Wage Puzzle: An Analysis of Worker Accessions and Separations", *Journal of the European Economic Association*, 4(5), September 2006, pp. 988–1013.

Scotchmer S., "Affirmative Action in Hierarchies", NBER Working Paper 11213, Cambridge, Mass., March 2005.

Seater J.J. and Santomero A. M., "The Inflation–Unemployment Trade-Off; A Critique of the Literature", *Journal of Economic Literature*, 16, 1978, pp. 499–544.

Smith R.E. and Vavrichek B., "The Wage Mobility of Minimum Wage Workers", *Industrial and Labor Relations Review*, 46, 1992, pp. 82–8.

Stewart M.B., "The Employment Effects of the National Minimum Wage", *Economic Journal*, 114(494), March 2004, pp. C110–C116.

Stewart M.B. and Swaffield J., "Low Pay Dynamics and Transition Probabilities", *Economica*, 66, 1999, pp. 23–42.

Stewart M.B. and Swaffield J., "The Other Margin: Do Minimum Wages Cause Working Hours Adjustments for Low Wage Workers?", *Economica*, 75(297), February 2008, pp. 148–67.

Stigler G., "The Economics of Minimum Wage Legislation", *American Economic Review*, 36, 1946, pp. 358–65.

Strobl E. and Walsh F., "The Ambiguous Effect of Minimum Wages on Workers and Total Hours", IZA Discussion Paper No. 3643, Bonn, August 2008.

Further reading

T. Boeri and J. Van Ours, *The Economics of Imperfect Labour Markets*, Princeton University Press, Princeton, New Jersey, 2008, has a particularly good coverage of a wide range of policies including minimum wages, retirement programmes, employment protection legislation, unemployment benefits and active labour market policies.

M. Gregory, W. Salverda and S. Bazen, editors, *Labour Market Inequalities*, Oxford University Press, 2000, analyses problems and policies of low-wage employment in an international perspective with a positive slant in relation to various policy alternatives.

P. Garibaldi, *Personnel Economics in Imperfect Labour Markets*, Oxford University Press, 2006, contains chapters on employment protection legislation and temporary versus permanent jobs.

Index

References to figures are shown in *italics*. References to tables are shown in **bold**. References to notes consist of the page number followed by the letter 'n' followed by the number of the note, e.g. 24n7 refers to note no. 7 on page 24

Index

Hampton, M.B. 97, 98
Hanoch, G. 21–2
Harding, C. *249*
Harmon, C. 61
Harris, J.R. 340
Harris, R.I. 183
Harrison, A. 244
Harrison, B. 288
Harsanyi, J.C., Zeuthen–Harsanyi model 231–3, *232*, 234–5, 258
Hart, R.A. 136, 145, **145**, 227, 244
Hartog, J. 155
Harvard School, trade unions and efficiency 207
Harvard University,, Lawrence Summers 2005 lecture 168
Harwood, Peter 260n16, 262n29; *see also* Acas
Hashimoto, M. 79n8
Haskel, J. 146, 155, 208
Hatton, T.J. 110
Hay, B. 253, 261n27
Hayes, B. 240
Hazledine, T. 244
health factor (retirement) 22; *see also* fatigue effects; sleep and the supply of labour
Heath, Edward 227–8
Heckman, J.J. 24n6, 28, 34, 57, 62; Heckman correction 60, 205
Heller Clain, S. 49n9
Hersch, J. 60, 155
heteroskedasticity 76
Heywood, J.S. 97, 98, 165, 318, 321, 354
Hicks, Joe 227, 259n2
Hicks, John: Hicks model 233–4, *233*, 235–8, *237*, 258; "Hicks paradox" 224, 231, 258; income and substitution effects 31; Marshallian rules of derived demand 132
higher education, and earnings prospects (case study) 10–11
HILDA (Household Income and Labour Dynamics in Australia) Survey 132
hiring costs, and labour hoarding 140–6, *142*, *143*, **145**
Hirsch, B.T.: strike incidence models 259n9; strike propensity versus bargaining power 243; strikes and asymmetric information 240; strikes and the Hicks paradox 231, 235; strikes as accidents 237, 238; strikes literature overview 269; unions and productivity 207; unions and wage dispersion 206; unions behaviour models 184
Hoffman, S.D. 155, 156, 169
Hofler, R.A. 60
Holden, K. 212n2
hollowing-out phenomenon 343, 354
Holmstrom, B. 276

Holtman, A.G. 74
Honig, M. 21–2, 24n12
Hope–Goldthorpe occupational rating 304n10
horizontal mismatch 156
hours, patterns of: absenteeism 30, 36–7, 43–5, *44*, 277, 296; double-jobbing 38–9, 46–7, 49n11, 137; income preferrers versus leisure preferrers 36–9, *38*; labour supply of taxi-drivers (case study) 36, 37; under- and over-employed workers 40; shift-work 138–40; standard work-week 30, 33–4, 36, 39; uniform hours 36; work-sharing 49n11, 137–8; *see also* hours, supply of; overtime; part-time employment
hours, supply of: backward-bending supply of labour curve 31, *32*, 33, *33*; budget constraints 31, 33–4, *35*; gross wage elasticity 35–6; income and substitution effects 14, 16, 30–3, *32*, 39; individual's indifference map *31*; individual's labour supply curve models 48n1; neo-classical model of labour supply 30–1; non-linearities (in budget constraint) 33–4, *35*; sleep and the supply of labour (case study) 33, 34; theoretical issues 34–6; *see also* hours, patterns of
Household Income and Labour Dynamics in Australia (HILDA) Survey 132
housing market: and job change 90, 104; and migration 106
Hubler, O. 46
Hughes, B. 45–6
Hughes, G.J. 103, 106, 114n7, 115n13
human capital model: case study (signalling hypothesis) 67; concept and models (Mincer and Ben-Porath) 53–6, *56*; discrimination measurement 163–4; empirical analysis 56–63; human capital earnings function 56–7; and inter-sector mobility 272, 299; job-screening approach 54, 63–7; and labour market mismatches 156, 158; and migration 104; predetermined segmentation studies 284–8; summary and questions 77–8; truncation bias 287–8, *287*, 291, 304n10; *see also* neo-classical model; training
Hunter, R.S. 115n16
Hunt, J. 138
Hutchens, R. 165, 323, 354

idleness, optimal degree of 139
Idson, T.L. 74, 97–8
immigration/immigrant workers: and ageing workforce 353; and asymmetric information 92–5, *93*, *94*; benefits versus costs 90; discrimination issues 112, 159, 162; immigration policies 110, 112; impact on native labour market 109–10, *110*, 111; inflow data (OECD) **108**; literature on 120; performance in host country 107, 108, *109*; temporary contracts 351
implicit contracts 277, 279–80, 303n4, 314, 315, 323

370

Index

Patrinos, H. 86
Paull, G. 13
Paxson, C.H. 40, 46, 49n10
payment by results (PBR) 309, 310, 317–18, 330n4
Pearce, D.K. 244
Pearson, M. 23n2
Pedersen, P.J. 244
peer groups, and future earnings 62
Pelletier, J. 183
Pemberton, J. 133
Pencavel, J.: labour supply of men 13, 28; piece-work 316, 317, 318; strikes 244; unions 181–2; union wage mark-up 203, 215n23
pensions: based on highest pay 21; and job search 114n7; and life-cycle theory 19–20; and part-time employment 12; and retirement age 24n13; *see also* retirement
perfect competition models 90
Perlman, R. 315
Perry, S. 41, 43
Peters, M. *249*
Petri, P.A 24n13
Petrongolo, B. 100–1, 114n10
Petty, Sir William 54
Phelps, E.S. 166
Phillips, A.W. (Bill), Phillips Curve 336, 338–41, *338*, *340*, 357
Phipps, A.J. 244
piece-rate payments 309–10, 314, 316–21, *317*, 330n7
Pigou, A.C. 275
Piore, M. 275, 276–8, 285, 300–1
Pischke, J.S. 75, 81n17
Pissarides, C.A.: Diamond-Mortensen-Pissarides search and matching framework 91; education and earnings prospects 6; employment-to-employment job flows 91; *Equilibrium Unemployment Theory* 120; information-gathering and unemployment 103; on-the- job search 114n7, 115n10; matching function 100–1; reservation wage 102
poaching (of trained workers) 68, 70, 72, 75, 77
Podivinsky, J.M. 327
Pokorny, K. 319
Polachek, S.W. 55, 56
Poland: European migration 111; strikes 228, **229**
portfolio model 46
Portugal: employment protection legislation 350; minimum wage 346
Portugal, P. 346
positive-sum game 233
Posner, R.A. 253
Prais, S.J. 80n10
predetermined segmentation studies 284–8
Prendergast, C. 323–4, 333

pre-strike ballots 178, 183, 227, 243; *see also* British Airways
primary/secondary markets *see* dual and segmented labour markets
principal–agent problem/theory 122, 238, 254, 310, 314–15, *315*
private sector: rates of return to education 23n1; and training 80n16; union membership 183; unions and employer policy 183
probit 43, 46, 67, 97, 201, 202
production function *124*; *see also* Cobb–Douglas production function
productivity: measurement issues 310–12, *311*; and strikes 245–6; and trade unions 207–8; and training 75–6
profitability, and trade unions 208–9
profit maximisation 68, 187, 189, 278, 279, 313; *see also* maximisation of income per worker
profit-sharing 310, 324–5, *325*; *see also* labour-managed firm
promotion 321–4; *see also* tournament theory
promotion signalling 276
proportionality rule 125, *126*
Pruitt, D. 255
Psacharopoulos, G. 2–3, 86, 106, 285, 299, 304n10
PSID (Panel Study of Income Dynamics) 40, 41, 46, 49n10, 61, 65, 295, 323
public employment services (PES) 347, 349
public sector: rates of return to education 23n1; strikes 230; training 80n16; union membership 183, 212n2; union wage mark-up 203; wage incentives 310, 312
pull and push factors, and migration 104
Putterman, L. 315

Quality of Employment Survey 45
quasi-rents 183, 240
Quinn, J.F. 22

Rabinovitch, R. 240
race: and labour market segmentation 285–6, 287, 291–4, **293**, 300; and male labour force participation 18; and retirement age 24n11; and training 73
racial discrimination 158–60, 163, 166, 167, 355
radical theory of segmentation 278–9
reaction speed concept 154
Reagan, P. 60, 74
recession, employee/hours reductions 143–4, *143*
Reder, M.W. 186, 237–8, 244, 246
redundancy: and seniority 196–7; and strikes *230*; and voluntary turnover 91
Rees, A. 92, 96, 186, 198–200, *199*
Rees, D.I. 62
regression to the mean 8

Reilly, B. 204, 244
Reilly, J. 12–13
relative deprivation, and job satisfaction 96, 97
Renna, F. 49n11
reservation wages: and housing market 106; and job
    search 90, 99–100, 103, 114n10; and productivity
    316; and retirement age 20–1; and speculative
    migration 104; and unemployment 103, 351; and
    union wage mark-up 201–2; and the wage curve 341;
    and wage offers *99*, 101, 102–3
residual approach (discrimination measurement) 152,
    164–7
responsive firm model 12
retirement: and ageing workforce issue 353–4; age of
    18, 24n10, 137; complete retirement 22; early
    retirement 18–19, 21; extension of age of 336;
    factors for retirement decision 22; and labour force
    definition 11; literature on 28; mandatory retirement
    20–1, 276; optimal age of 19–20; partial retirement
    21–2, 24n12; pay back-loading and retirement *21*;
    see also activity rates; older people; pensions
Reynolds, M.O. 207
Riach, P. 167
Ricardo, David 275
Rich, J. 167
Ricketts, M. 314
Rickman, N. 254
right-to- manage model 187–9, *188*, 231
risk aversion: and gender occupational segregation
    356–7; and implicit contracts 279–80, 315; and
    litigation 253; and piece rates 316; and principal–
    agent theory 122; and profit-sharing 325; and self-
    employment 13; and union behaviour 192, 213n12
Robertson, D. 9, 62
Robinson, C. 205
Rodríguez-Álvarez, A. 261n25
Romania, self-employment rates 13
Rooth, D.O. 159
Rosen, S. 6, 274, 276
Rosewell, B. 300
ROSLA (raising of school leaving age) 66
Ross, A.M. 184–5, 238
Rostker, B. 46
Rottenberg, S. 24
Rubinfeld, D.L. 253
Rufolo, A.M. 168
Rumberger, R.W. 156, 300
Ryan, P. 272

Sá, F. 137
Safelite Glass Corporation, piece-rate case study 319–20
Saks, D.H. 115n11, 179, 212n4
Salehi-Isfahani, D. 315

Salop, J. 65, 79n6
Salop, S. 65, 79n6
Salverda, W. 362
sample selection bias 204
Sanfey, P.J. 214n14
Santomero, A.M. 339
Sapsford, D. 231, 233, 240, 260n12
Saraydar, E. 233
Sargent Florence, P. 329n2
Saridakis, G. 254, 256, 257, 269
Sattinger, M. 156–7, 169
scale effect (or output effect) 127, *127*, 129, 133
Scandinavia: double-jobbing 46; *see also* Nordic
    System; Sweden
scarring effect (of low pay) 342
SCELI (Social and Economic Life Initiative) 67, 157,
    204
Schiller, B. 300
Schmidt, C.M. 352
Schmidt, K.M. 312
Schriver, W. 234–5, 243
Schultz, G.P. 92
Scotchmer, S. 356
screening *see* job-screening approach
Seaman, Paul T. 66, 67
search theory 95, 103, 104; *see also* job search
Seater, J.J. 339
secondary/primary markets *see* dual and segmented
    labour markets
secret ballots 227; *see also* pre-strike ballots
security of employment *see* "flexicurity"; temporary
    contracts/jobs
Seeds, K. *249*
segmentation theory 35, 272, 274–5, 276, 300–1, 307;
    see also labour market structure; radical theory of
    segmentation
selection effects models 60
self-employment: and activity rates 11, 13; and age-
    earning profiles 323; and double-jobbing 46; and
    education 65; and gender 356; and partial retirement
    21–2
self-selection model 65
self-serving bias 254
seniority *see* job tenure
seniority rules, and training 74
sequential search strategy (job search) 101–2
service industries: customer discrimination 163; gross
    labour market flows 91; hollowing-out phenomenon
    343; involuntary part-time employment 49n9;
    minimum wage 345; optimal staffing model 12; pay
    levels (compared with manufacturing industries)
    62–3; shift-work 139; wage incentives 310
Sessions, J. 43, 87